FICINO IN SPAIN

Ficino in Spain

SUSAN BYRNE

UNIVERSITY OF TORONTO PRESS
Toronto Buffalo London

Toronto Buffalo London
www.utppublishing.com

ISBN 978-1-4426-5056-5

Library and Archives Canada Cataloguing in Publication

Byrne, Susan, author
Ficino in Spain / Susan Byrne.

(Toronto Iberic)
Includes bibliographical references and index.
ISBN 978-1-4426-5056-5 (bound)

1. Ficino, Marsilio, 1433–1499 – Influence. 2. Spanish literature – Classical period, 1500–1700 – History and criticism. 3. Hermetism in literature – History – 16th century. 4. Neoplatonism in literature – History – 16th century. 5. Renaissance – Spain. I. Title. II. Series: Toronto Iberic

B785.F434B97 2015 186′.4 C2015-900425-X

University of Toronto Press acknowledges the financial assistance to its publishing program of the Canada Council for the Arts and the Ontario Arts Council, an agency of the Government of Ontario.

University of Toronto Press acknowledges the financial support of the Government of Canada through the Canada Book Fund for its publishing activities.

for Ottavio Di Camillo,
a model of intellectual generosity, rigour, and enthusiasm

Contents

Acknowledgments

In 2006, I was a lone conference presenter whose scheduled table for the Renaissance Society of America's annual meeting had fallen apart. Fortunately for me, the RSA's Ficinistas took me in, listened to my presentation, and asked me the questions that led to this book. I thank the full group of RSA Ficino scholars and particularly the indefatigable Valery Rees. Many thanks also to Fátima Macho, for her kind invitation to present on this project in 2009 at Madrid's Círculo de Bellas Artes, when the Escuela de Filosofía Práctica de Madrid celebrated its own publication of volume one of Ficino's Letters in Spanish translation.

My first introduction to Ficino came from noted scholar of Spanish humanism Ottavio Di Camillo, whose courses at CUNY's Graduate Center I had the great fortune to take, whose own work has been of enormous benefit to me, and whose unbridled intellectual enthusiasm is exemplary. A tripod of support and encouragement to continue with this study has been that formed by Ottavio, Lía Schwartz, and the now much-missed Isaías Lerner. My debt to those three is incalculable.

Thanks to librarians Carmen and Mercedes at the Biblioteca Histórica Marqués de Valdecilla of the Universidad Complutense in Madrid, who were of enormous help during my visit, and to the same library's Paz Sánchez, an ideal librarian of *fondos antiguos*. For permission to reproduce the images included here, I thank the Biblioteca de la Universidad Complutense de Madrid, Seville's Biblioteca Capitular Columbina, the Real Biblioteca del Monasterio de El Escorial, the *gestión fotográfica* unit of Spain's Patrimonio Nacional in Madrid, and the Biblioteca General Histórica de la Universidad de Salamanca. From this last, special thanks to José María Sanz Hermida and Óscar Lilao for their thoughtfulness and consideration.

I am indebted to the anonymous readers for the University of Toronto Press, whose suggestions led to many improvements in the manuscript, as well as to UTP Senior Humanities editor Suzanne Rancourt, Associate Managing Editor

Barb Porter, and copy editor Miriam Skey. An earlier version of the material contained at pages 112–29 was first published in Spanish as "Cuestionamiento del hermetismo ficiniano en dos manuscritos del siglo XV: El Escorial y El Burgo de Osma," *Bulletin of Spanish Studies* LXXXIX: 2 (2012), 173–92. I thank the editors of the journal for having published my article, and for their permission to include the material here.

This study was carried out, in part, with the generous support of a grant from the Griswold Research Fund of Yale's Whitney Humanities Center, and a Faculty Research Grant from Yale's MacMillan Center for International and Area Studies. I am very grateful to both committees and their sponsors/underwriters. This book was published with the assistance of the Frederick W. Hilles Publication Fund of Yale University.

Note on Texts

Unless otherwise noted, all translations from the Spanish are my own. Translations from the Latin are from a number of sources, all indicated in my notes and list of works cited. I include quotations from the original language in notes or, when brief phrases, in the text itself. Given that not all of Ficino's writings nor those of the other authors whose works are studied here have been published in modern editions, some quotations in Latin adhere to modern orthographical norms while others do not. For the older Spanish texts I have regularized only minimally, adding accents and letters in brackets to facilitate understanding of the text, but leaving capitalization and variant spellings as found in those sources. Similarly, ex libris in my first chapter are presented as they are found in the volumes referenced. Thus, for example, some read Colegio while others Collegio, as Latin and Castilian spellings were still both in use. My index lists the modernized forms. The names of Spanish monarchs are given in their English forms, with the exception of Alfonso X, who is also quoted as an author and whose name, therefore, is given with Spanish spelling. Index listings for Plato's dialogues are under the Greek philosopher's name when not specifically identified as references to Ficino's commentaries on, or summaries of, those dialogues. In those latter instances, they are listed under Ficino.

Illustrations

FICINO IN SPAIN

Introduction: Ficino and the *pia philosophia* in Spain

A consistent presence in Spanish letters in the centuries following his death, Marsilio Ficino was decisively written out of that literary history at the end of the nineteenth century as those who began to fashion what would come to be the Spanish literary canon excised his voice in favour of a purist, all-Spanish approach. In what follows, I restore that voice and demonstrate the pervasiveness of the Italian philosopher's thought and writings in early modern Spain.

Ficino (1433–99) was a fifteenth-century Christian theologian and Neoplatonist philosopher.[1] Renaissance thinkers considered those two disciplines an intellectual continuum of speculative thought on man and God, with theology as the first philosophy. From the fourteenth to sixteenth centuries, philosophy would evolve as a secular discipline (Hankins 2007, 39), but only after attempts to fashion syncretic *via media* solutions fractured in the face of irreconcilable differences. A similar process was underway in Western thought on other disciplines, as late-medieval Church control over the parameters of intellectual endeavour was challenged and compromised. Syncretism and eclecticism are hallmarks of Renaissance thought, and Ficino's particular blend of philosophy and theology, the *prisca theologia* or *pia philosophia*,[2] with its goal of finding concord in the primordial source of both disciplines, was a key part of intellectual discourse in all of Renaissance Europe.

With the *pia philosophia*, Ficino revived a model with a long history. Similarities in Christian, Neoplatonist, and Hermetic writings evoke the historical context of the first to third centuries AD, when the new Christian religion used philosophical argumentation to justify and promote its beliefs while philosophers, in turn, appropriated elements of faith, magic, and superstition.[3] Texts that combine religious and philosophical speculation, such as Plotinus's *Enneads* and Hermes Trismegistus's *Corpus Hermeticum*, are products of the earlier era; both would become foundational texts of the later, Ficinian Neoplatonism of the fifteenth century. Michael Allen (1984, vii) splits the earlier Neoplatonism into two distinct periods: first, the Plotinian and then a second, later stage with Proclus and his disciple Dionysius the Areopagite. Ficino incorporated the texts of both periods, reading Plato through the lens of the Neoplatonists.[4]

In a broader sense, the disciplinary boundaries between philosophy, theology, science, magic, medicine and astrology – all topics on which Ficino wrote – were fluid in the fifteenth century but, by the end of the seventeenth, had begun to assume more distinguishable constraints.[5] Science would move to investigate the properties of nature without attempting to control them, magus-style, for particular human ends; that task would continue to be the purview of magic as it evolved into an esoteric, underground practice.[6] Astronomy turned to the physics of celestial movements without regard for horoscopes or planetary influences in a personal sense; astrology retained that focus.[7] Medicine became more physiologically precise and less reliant on the healing properties of prayer and meditation, although psychosomatic influences and results continue to fascinate and are still studied today.[8] Philosophy evolved into its Enlightenment guise of pure, rational intellectual endeavour, a pointedly secular search for reason and meaning, while theology circumscribed itself to God and revelation as seen through irrefutable faith and adherence to dogmatic belief.[9] Prior to the splits in disciplinary foci, Renaissance scholars studied these materials as a coordinated although fractious unit, disputing their parameters and properties but seeing them as fundamentally integral, conjoined parts of theoretical speculation on essence, existence, nature, and cosmos. The Renaissance has long been described as a time of "universal analogy" linked "with affiliated Neoplatonic and mythological visions of the cosmos which stressed the interrelationship of all branches of human knowledge" (Kurtz 1986, 197). Mazzeo explains: "the doctrines of the microcosm-macrocosm analogy, universal analogy, cosmic affinities and varying versions of the *coincidentia oppositorum* ... were fully revived and became the basis for a new theory of knowledge" which "helped make the *forma mentis* of Renaissance men richly metaphorical and symbolic (1954, 302–3). The following quote from sixteenth-century Spanish philosopher Sebastián Fox Morcillo (c. 1528–c. 1558) is illustrative:

> Observe here how all disciplines reciprocally yield to each other, that is, the more common to the less common ... so that the principles of the less common disciplines are the conclusions of the more common disciplines ... so Physics has certain principles that she can only prove with the help of Theology or Metaphysics ... and Medicine has principles that depend on Physics. In the same way, among all the rest of the sciences, some are born of others. (2010, 149)[10]

From the fifteenth through the seventeenth century, Marsilio Ficino was the fulcrum, the main filter through whom ancient Platonic and Neoplatonic thinkers and their writings on these interrelated concepts, arts, sciences, and disciplines became known to his early modern world.[11] Others translated, commented, or summarized one text or another, but Ficino's translations made the full works of Plato, the Neoplatonists, and the Hermetic authors available to the Western world in Latin for the first time. Those volumes with his commentaries as well as his own corpus of writings and letters had wide circulation.

Sixteenth- and seventeenth-century references to Marsilio Ficino by Spanish writers in dialogues, histories, laudatory verse, legal compilations, and miscellanea attest to an unfettered incorporation of his thought on a broad range of matters large and small. Spanish poet Francisco de Quevedo (1580–1645) criticized another writer for misquoting the Italian philosopher as two different people so as to be able to say he had referenced exactly twenty-three authorities. The other writer used commas to separate the first and last names, pluralizing both so that the citation reads "Marsilios, Ficinos" although the truth, says Quevedo, is "that this was just one author, named Marsilio Ficino" (Quevedo 1993, 481).[12] At that early date, you could not fool a learned man in Spain on Ficino's identity. Over the course of the following three centuries, Spanish intellectuals would continue to rely on the Italian philosopher as a trusted authority, albeit with various points of debate.

German bibliographer of philosophers Johann Heinrich Boecler (1611–72) linked Ficino to two specific universities on the Iberian Peninsula: Coimbra in Portugal, and Alcalá de Henares in Spain. His entry for Ficino reads:

> Marsilio Ficino. Works. He was the renewer of the platonic philosophy, in which he was very well versed, as is obvious from his commentaries. He had a distinguished natural ability, but was not truly learned; and he is [his works are] read with a grain of salt. As mentioned above, the universities of Coimbra and Alcalá de Henares. (Boecler 1715, 603)[13]

Boecler's comments confirm that Ficino's writings still garnered respect although they should be read *cum grano salis*, and the bibliographer implies that studies at the two named universities were modelled on the Italian philosopher's thought. Unfortunately, the "as mentioned above" (iam supra) reference is nowhere to be found in the 602 pages *supra* of Boecler's book, nor in the 300 pages *infra.*[14] Confirmation is found, however, a little over 200 years later in a study of Fox Morcillo's philosophy. Writing in 1903, Urbano González de la Calle notes the attraction that Renaissance Neoplatonism held for members of various religious orders in Spain. The historian asserts that some began to privilege Plato over Aristotle to a surprising degree and he singles out the Jesuits, describing them as "dissidents within scholasticism itself" and adding that the universities of

Coimbra and Alcalá de Henares responded to this trend and "enthusiastically" promoted those teachings (1903, 70–2).[15] González de la Calle also mentions a less noteworthy trend of such studies at Salamanca and Valencia, which he illustrates with the writings of Jesuits: Juan de Mariana (1536–1624), whose *De morte et immortalitate* is described as reminiscent of Plato's *Phaedo*, and Gabriel Vázquez (1549–1604) who attempted "to give reality to the Ideas, affirming that what is in divine understanding has a positive existence" (González de la Calle 1903, 71).[16] This link between Ficino and the Jesuits is noteworthy but not exclusive; members of other religious orders also incorporated the Italian philosopher's writings and translations (Byrne 2007 and *infra*).

Early in the eighteenth century, Spanish Benedictine monk Benito Jerónimo Feijoo (1676–1764) published a series of curious transitional works that are part Renaissance miscellanea, part Enlightenment encyclopedia, and part essayist's diatribe, texts he himself denominates "discourses" (discursos). Ángel-Raimundo Fernández González notes that in the eighteenth century approximately four hundred thousand copies of these works were in circulation; he calls Feijoo the cultural leader of the first generation of eighteenth-century Spain, and details the broad impact of the Benedictine monk's writings (Feijoo 1998, 11, 12, 41–5). For his part, Feijoo does not hesitate to recommend Ficino as a classical medical authority for a surgical procedure that takes skin from the arm to repair the nose, referencing the title used for the first book of Ficino's *De triplici vita*, or *Three Books on Life* in the 1529 Basel edition: *Studiosorum valetudine tuenda*.[17] The Spaniard also references Ficino's medical-astrological opinion regarding Saturn's noxious influence on men of letters, although he adds a doubtful modern note:

> Complaints about accumulation of humors in the head are so common today that one hears them coming from the mouths of laborers almost as much as from university professors. Everyone complains about rheumatism, not because there is more today but because there are more finicky wimps (*melindres*). Rheumatism is flowing more towards the mouth than the chest, and the clamor is greater than the illness. (Feijoo 1778, 7.14, 187)[18]

Feijoo also quotes Ficino's astrological writings on the seven-year stages in the life of man, with a positive note for the Italian having included the impact of intermediate quartiles in his analysis, but also a criticism – that he failed to take into account the concomitant influence of the nine-year solar cycle (1778, 11.8, 235). The Spanish writer describes Ficino as a "passionate partisan" (su apasionado sectario) of Plato, and criticizes French philosopher Malebranche for not saying anything new about the Ideas as he purports to do, but merely plagiarizing Ficino on Plato (1778, 13.21, 272). On the doubtful side, Feijoo includes Ficino as one of the daring, yet delirious authors who believed imagination, rather than "hellish spirits" (espíritus infernales) to be the operative principle in magic (Feijoo 1774, 8.8, 95).[19] In these texts, Feijoo evidences a mixed but overall respectful attitude towards the Italian philosopher, accepting his opinions on medicine, astrology, and Plato, while criticizing only his writings on magic. Feijoo's wide readership would have assured that Ficino's ideas continued to be promulgated.

Later in the eighteenth century, Juan Pablo Forner (1756–97) calls Leibniz "Platonic," and adds: just like Iamblichus and Ficino. More extensive commentary is found in the work of a contemporary of Forner, Spanish Jesuit Juan Andrés (1740–1817), exiled in Italy following the 1767 expulsion of the religious order from Spain. Andrés quotes Ficino to describe Plato as a "most wise" (sapientissimus) philosopher, "most eloquent" (eloquentissimus) orator, and "most prudent" (prudentissimus) jurisconsult (1997–2001, 1:59–60)[20] then, with the phrase that Spanish Renaissance writers of all disciplines used for their works, approvingly denominates the fifteenth century a time of "Good Letters" (buenas letras).[21] According to Andrés, thirteenth-to-fifteenth-century Italian writers from Dante, Petrarch, and Boccaccio to Poliziano, Pico, and Ficino were all "grammarians" (gramáticos) and/or "philologues" (filólogos) (3:483–6) for reasons both practical and historical: they needed grammar to understand rediscovered classical texts; grammar faculties at universities were the most popular and their professors, the most well-remunerated; scholars flocked to Italy to study grammar and philology; and they published "philosophical grammars, critical editions, elegant and faithful translations, erudite commentaries and philological observations" (3:485–6).[22] Andrés comments approvingly that the fifteenth-century Good Letters trend "contribute[d] to animating theological study more and more, bringing it to the luster and vigour with which it would flourish in the following centuries" (6:258).[23] This general reference to translations and commentaries that "animated" theological study is followed by specific reference to Ficino. Echoing Feijoo, Andrés is critical of the Italian philosopher on just one point – his work on the health of scholars, not identified by title but obviously the Third Book of *De triplici vita* which, the reader is told, offers "astrological sophistry ... without practical utility" (5:310).[24] To the contrary is Andrés's opinion of Ficino as a Platonist:

> There is no one, neither Latin nor Greek, to whom the Platonic doctrine owes as much as it does to Marsilio Ficino who, not satisfied with exegesis of only the works of the master, Plato, also translated and managed to clarify the doctrines of Plotinus and other celebrated Platonists. These studies, although at times focused on questions of lexical interpretation, never devolved into insubstantial and capricious subtleties as did those of the scholastics but were, rather, aimed at acquisition and understanding of the true wisdom of Plato and Aristotle. (5:435)[25]

That same contrast is highlighted again when Andrés names various scholars who, not trapped in "sterile scholastic" parameters, wrote fine works on moral questions; he includes Ficino among them (5:486).[26] Andrés deems scholasticism a negative, inhibiting influence on university theological studies during the Renaissance, but he notes that progress was made outside those centres of learning and, here again, Ficino is the positive exemplar: "Platonist Marsilio Ficino used his philosophy and eloquence to illustrate the Christian religion as well as the piety, faith, and divinity of Christian law with solid theological argumentation" (6:258).[27] In Andrés, we find the unapologetic Jesuit support for Ficino and Renaissance Neoplatonism later identified by González de la Calle as that of the intransigents, with the singular exception of his quibble regarding the Italian philosopher's "astrological sophistry" (astrológicas sofisterías) in *De vita* (5:310).

With that one caveat, Juan Andrés considered Ficino, clearly identified as both Platonist and Plotinian, to be an important and respected scholar whose fruitful, progressive methods contrasted with those of the "sterile" scholastics.[28] The Jesuit values the intellectual symbiosis of the *pia philosophia*, although he slightly redefines its aim: whereas Ficino sought concord in both disciplines, Andrés reads the goal of all Renaissance thinkers as a specific wish to enliven and strengthen theological study with philosophical argumentation. This is resonant of the first Christian Neoplatonism of the early Common Era, when Church Fathers borrowed from Platonic thought so as to compete with the already-established philosophical schools. It also echoes other Renaissance thinkers, such as Pico della Mirandola (1463–94), who saw philosophy in the service of religion. Pico hoped that "recovering the esoteric truths of other religious traditions would make the mysteries of Christianity more intelligible" (Hankins 2006, 14). Ficino, on the other hand, saw "the Platonic doctrine as an authority comparable to that of the divine law" (Burroughs 1948, 186), neither subordinate, separate from, nor a rival to Christianity but rather an equal partner, in "complementary roles" with the goal to "unite philosophy and revelation" (Allen 2002a, xv, xx).[29] To the contrary, Andrés's reading of the aims and results of Renaissance intellectuals confirms that by the late eighteenth century, philosophy was once again becoming, for religious thinkers, a subordinate handmaiden to theology. Nonetheless, this Jesuit still privileges the Platonic school of thought as a worthy partner and respects Ficino as one of its most distinguished statesmen.

As the eighteenth century came to a close in Europe, modern rationalist philosophical trends confronted religious resistance and, in Spain, complicating political factors would add a further dimension to the polemic, along with intellectual defensiveness in the face of Italian, French, English, and German claims that Spain was a backwards place where speculative and artistic progress had been restricted by Catholicism and, particularly, by the Inquisition.[30] Italian Girolamo

Tiraboschi (1731–94) blamed Spain for the decline of the Italian Renaissance,[31] and Spaniard Xavier Lampillas (1731–1810) retorted that without the Greeks and the Spaniards, there would never have been any Italian cultural developments of any sort, ever (Lampillas 1783, 1:85–9). Lampillas, like Andrés a Jesuit living in exile, claimed that Italian Renaissance literature was pleasant enough but frivolous, mere "beautiful letters" (bellas letras) that paled in comparison to the "serious and solid" (serias y sólidas) works of Spanish writers of the same time frame (1783, 1:19). Lampillas respects Plato and even privileges the reading of philosophy, specifically Platonic philosophy, over poetry, which he describes as a fine diversion but not a noble literary pursuit (1:34). While his contemporary Andrés uses the phrase "good letters" (buenas letras) to praise Renaissance thinkers, Lampillas complains that it has become fashionable to restrict a different but parallel phrase, "beautiful letters" (bellas letras), to those literary pursuits which, in his opinion, are inconsequential.[32]

Lampillas divorces creative literature (*bellas letras*) from serious intellectual pursuit (*buenas letras*) and he observes that an upsurge in attention to the former, which for him are insignificant, has led to an almost complete abandonment of Latin. In turn, he reasons, this explains the lack of prestige accorded Spanish writers who, as serious scholars, wrote in that *lingua franca* throughout the Middle Ages and the Renaissance. In the two perspectives of Andrés and Lampillas, we find not only the reflection of currents of thought from their own day, but also the basic parameters of later divisive lines: scholastic is either "sterile" or "solid," philosophy "rational" or "religious," writing "good" or "beautiful" letters, and Spain "in" or "out" of the Renaissance. For one hundred years, Spanish intellectuals would define themselves and be defined by others according to one of those perspectives and a related, collateral outcome of those determinations would be recognition or rejection of Ficino's legacy in Spain.

Mid-nineteenth century, Juan Valera (1824–1905) spoke out to defend freedom of the press and of all intellectual endeavours, including the teaching of philosophy in Spanish schools. He rejects calls for the exclusion of "German pantheists" who might, he admits, have "perverted university teachings" (Valera 1913, [1863], 267).[33] Nonetheless, Valera supports the continued teaching of all philosophies by arguing that many fervent Catholics, and even many "sainted Church Fathers" were Platonists, adducing as examples Augustine, Synesius, Dionysius Areopagite, Pico, and Ficino. He concludes: "if one could be Aristotelian, Platonist or Stoic and Christian at the same time, there is no need to renounce the faith so as to follow Kant, Hegel, Fichte, or Krause" (1913 [1863], 267–8).[34] Valera's contemporary, Emilio Castelar (1832–99), who would later become president of the First Spanish Republic, also commends Ficino. Castelar rejects nationalist limitations on intellectual capabilities, and insists that "if German science is incomprehensible to anyone not born in the North," then

> Southern science will be incomprehensible to you because your cradle was not rocked under the great trees of India, or because you have not walked the desert sands of Jerusalem, or heard waves crash upon Alexandrian marble ... or because you have not, as did Marsilio Ficino, listened to the souls of the Platonists as they wander the banks of the Arno in the gardens of Florence. (1861, Second letter, topic 14)[35]

Both of these mid-nineteenth-century references to Ficino are quite positive, indeed almost deferential, and both were made by powerful figures in Spanish society who were politically advocating change and modernization. Valera and Castelar were not always in agreement,[36] but neither found fault with Ficino who was, for both, simply and unproblematically Christian and Platonist.

Contemporaneous with Castelar and Valera who continued to praise Ficino, and one hundred years after the pitched battles between Italian Tiraboschi and Spaniard Lampillas, noted Swiss writer Jacob Burckhardt (1818–97) took the by-then century-old complaint of Tiraboschi a step further, to demonize Spain as the villain who killed the Italian Renaissance: "what became of Spain, after she had destroyed Italy, is known to every reader"; "the enslavement of Italy begun by the Spaniards"; the Aragonese government of Naples realized "a social transformation in obedience to Spanish ideas, of which the chief features were the contempt for work and the passion for titles" (1938, 31; 52; 188). Burckhardt specifically focuses on the 1527 Sack of Rome:

> The Catholic King and Emperor [Charles V] owed it to his luck and nothing else that Pope and cardinals were not murdered by his troops. Had this happened, no sophistry in the world could clear him of his share in the guilt. The massacre of countless people of less consequence, the plunder of the rest, and all the horrors of torture and traffic in human life, show clearly enough what was possible in the "Sacco di Roma"... (1938, 66)

The Swiss historian excludes Spain from any positive intellectual and artistic achievements during the Renaissance, tying the country to the Counter Reformation, the Inquisition, and most importantly, as in the last quotation above, to the Sack of Rome.[37] The reaction from Spanish intellectuals was what one would expect and its results, long-lasting.

Parallel with the mid-century calls for modernization from thinkers like Valera and Castelar, and coming on the heels of Burckhardt's insistence on Spain's "backwardness," Spanish neo-scholastic conservatives responded by recuperating and highlighting the voices of medieval and Golden Age Spanish writers as examples of cultural distinction. In the last quarter of the nineteenth century, Spain's self-styled first historian of philosophy, Marcelino Menéndez Pelayo (1856–1912), classified those early modern writers as either canonical or heterodox.[38] He defended the Spanish Inquisition by arguing that it had not banned many works, including specifically those of Ficino, ergo it had not stifled intellectual progress[39] but, he added, perhaps those works should have been prohibited: "If the Sainted Office of the Inquisition can be accused of anything, it would be in not having restricted the circulation of books that well-deserved its rigours" (1992, 2:437).[40] The ecclesiastical censor who approved the Spanish historian's *Historia de los heterodoxos españoles* praised its author's ability to expose and dispel from Catholic Spain the "dark clouds" of heretical thought which "flee as if castigated by the clear breeze and brilliant sun of orthodox doctrine, leaving no trace of their existence" (Menéndez Pelayo 1992, 1:xi).[41] That wishful revisionist thinking would have an impact on critical literature studies throughout the first half of the twentieth century: the heterodox would be erased from Spanish literary history, and Ficino along with it.[42]

Menéndez Pelayo's defence of the role of Spanish intellectuals in historical-philosophical developments was well-founded, and he did recognize the ubiquitousness of what he called a certain "Neoplatonic aesthetic" in Renaissance Spanish works. However, the Spanish historian substituted León Hebreo (c. 1460–1521), a Portuguese Jewish doctor exiled to Italy in 1492, for Ficino as the conduit through whom this "aesthetic" was introduced, and flatly denied that Ficino himself had played a noteworthy part in its transmission: "The history of the Platonic Academy can be reduced to the biography of Marsilio Ficino" (1974, 1:541).[43] Menéndez Pelayo also accepted the existence of a "popular Renaissance concept" regarding a "great physical and moral Cosmos created by Divine Love," but he denied Ficino's depiction (and book title) of this cosmos as a *Platonic Theology* to insist that Hebreo was more correct in modelling this hypothetical concept as *philographia*, that is, in literal translation from the Greek, a "Love of Good Letters." For Menéndez Pelayo, the fifteenth-century "Neoplatonic aesthetic" was a mere rhetorical "grab-bag of set expressions and commonplaces" until Hebreo clearly formulated its "organic principle" (1974, 1:541).[44] Thus reclassified as "Love of Good Letters," Renaissance Neoplatonism was effectively stripped of any depth of philosophical-theological content. The *pia philosophia* was now *philographia*, a mere aesthetic on love and writing.

Ironically, exiled Jew León Hebreo had re-biblicized and de-philosophized the *pia philosophia* in such a way that neo-scholastic Menéndez Pelayo found it acceptable. The late nineteenth-century historian insists that the "so-called Florentine Neoplatonism" should more properly and comprehensively be designated

"Italo-Hispanic Neoplatonism," with Hebreo as its first representative ever, and as its finest: "León Hebreo [was] the purest representative of Florentine Neoplatonism, which was renovated and enlivened by his infusion of a powerful Semitic-Spanish element that gives his doctrine an ontological transcendence never achieved by Bessarion or Marsilio Ficino" (1892, 102; 97–8).[45] The historian attempts to recuperate this Iberian voice, albeit one in exile when Hebreo wrote, even to the point of postulating that the exiled Portuguese Jew was the first thinker to have searched for concord between Plato, Aristotle, and religious thought, a supposition that negates not only the philosophical-theological synthesis of the first to third centuries, but also all thinkers throughout the Middle Ages and Renaissance who debated just those points.[46] The *zeitgeist* of the Spanish historian's era was made manifest in Pope Leo XIII's 1879 encyclical *Aeterni Patris*, which called for a return to scholastic philosophy; Menéndez Pelayo recommended caution but, nonetheless, seconded the motion (1992, 2:1408).[47] Ficino, whom we have seen recommended by Juan Andrés as a non-sterile, non-scholastic thinker, was on the wrong side at this historical moment.[48] Further, for centuries the Italian philosopher had been consistently labelled a Platonist, an adjective that had also fallen out of favour: "all the anti-scholastic insurrectionists ... are, to a greater or lesser degree, Platonists" (Menéndez Pelayo 1892, 31).[49]

Menéndez Pelayo recognized Ficino's important legacy of translations, but he accepted and quoted an Italian contemporary, Pasquale Villari (1826–1917), to judge Ficino "an erudite man who philosophized without much originality" (Menéndez Pelayo 1948, 54).[50] Villari's opinion epitomizes the general late nineteenth-century perspective on Ficino, whose translations continued to be recognized for their influence in the transmission of the authors of antiquity, but whose own thought and importance as an independent or systematic thinker had been downplayed (Kristeller 1964, viii–x). Menéndez Pelayo supported his negative judgment of Ficino with another Renaissance Spanish voice, that of Juan Luis Vives (1493–1540), who had described Ficino as a "would-be philosopher" (filosofastro) (Menéndez Pelayo 1892, 86).[51] The full and sharp attack is found in Vives's treatise on letter writing (*De conscribendis epistolis*): "The would-be philosopher, Marsilio Ficino, included himself in this company [epistolists], like a gull among swans, and composed letters on Platonic questions that are unattractive and tiresome in style" (Vives 1989, 137).[52] As Ficino's fortunes began to change in the rest of Europe and the Americas at the turn of the nineteenth to twentieth centuries, neo-scholastic intellectual tendencies would prevail in Spain, despite certain attenuated responses.

At the turn of the century, for example, González de la Calle notes differing opinions held by his contemporaries on the importance of Ficino's work, from "prodigious and even original philosophical culturist" to "erudite if not original thinker" and, he compellingly argues, "we are indebted to Ficino for more or less perfect Latin versions of Greek texts, including those of Plato, Plotinus, Porphyry, Iamblichus and Proclus" (1903, 48).[53] Notwithstanding such individual encomiums, in Spanish letters the pattern of privileging Hebreo while downplaying Ficino would hold for the following fifty years. Other national literatures reformulated their canons and rewrote their literary and artistic histories, highlighting works of the Renaissance, increasingly recognized as a key period in cultural developments. During that same time, however, Spain suffered the intense political struggle that would culminate in the Spanish Civil War (1936–9), followed by Francisco Franco's forty-five year dictatorship. A considerable part of that political battle concerned movements like socialism, communism, industrialism, workers' rights, and modernization in any form, however defined.[54] In Spain, particularly, it was also a continuation of the nineteenth-century disputes between conservatives and liberals that had even resulted, at one point, in the banishment of theology from Spanish universities. Throughout the nineteenth century and at the beginning of the next those who resisted modernization, that is those who in Spain would prevail at the end of the Spanish Civil War, used the adjective "Platonic" as a frightening epithet for any and all of the movements listed above. The excision of Ficino, identified for 400 years as a "good Platonist," from the history of Spanish intellectual developments was a logical consequence. Menéndez Pelayo's immense corpus of writings from that time frame is an invaluable contribution to our understanding of Spanish thought and letters; his opinions were (and many still are) taken as dogma by scholars.[55] However, on the particular point of the impact of Ficino on Spanish authors there would be, continue to be, and need to be rewrites.

Throughout the twentieth century, critical perspectives on Italian-Spanish relations during the Renaissance began to vary albeit with continued debate and doubts.[56] In 1938, Otis Green allowed that certain mystic poets "show acquaintance with the *Symposium* of Plato" and added in a note "perhaps through Ficino" (98 and n.32), but then also asserted that "Neo-Platonism bears to Spanish mysticism the relation not of cause but of effect" (98–9), a syllogism that fails on basic chronological criteria. Green also refuted assertions made in earlier studies regarding mysticism as a national character trait in Spaniards, only to say that the national character is ascetical, not mystical (93). Both opinions clearly demonstrate the impact of sociological and anthropological studies of the late nineteenth and early twentieth centuries, as well as the insistent nationalisms of the day. With time, scholars would again begin to propose details linking Ficino to Spanish letters. In 1942, Dámaso Alonso outlined the influence of Ficino's Italian Neoplatonism in Renaissance Spanish verse; in 1959, Avalle-Arce related Neoplatonism to the pastoral novel; in 1958, Alan S. Trueblood noted the resonance of Ficino's work in that of Spanish playwright Lope de Vega (1562–1635); and in 1956, Elias Rivers described the Neoplatonic verse of Spanish poet Francisco de Aldana (c. 1537–78) (131).[57] Nonetheless, doubts persisted: Green, for example, rejected River's conclusions and insisted that Aldana's works were not Neoplatonic but, rather, Christian and, following Menéndez Pelayo, found them indebted to Hebreo (1958, 117–35). As a whole, mid-twentieth-century scholars of Spanish literature failed to recognize that during the Renaissance, and in large part due to Ficino, Neoplatonic and Christian doctrines were seen as compatible partners rather than antithetical belief systems.

Studies on specific Spanish writers, on Italian-Spanish relations, and on humanism have for the most part dispelled the notion of Spain's isolation from Renaissance cultural and intellectual developments.[58] Nonetheless, in certain quarters one still finds the lasting resonance of Menéndez Pelayo's assumptions regarding Ficino. For example, in an exhaustive study of expressions of love in medieval and Renaissance Spanish works published in 1996, a monumental critical work rife with mention of Ficino's name as well as Platonist and Neoplatonist language on love as reflected in the works of Spanish writers, author Guillermo Serés also states inexplicably, "although it seems that all of this is irrelevant, since Ficino, apparently, did not have much direct influence on Spanish authors" (1996, 171).[59] The statement is even more surprising given that seven years earlier Serés had published a critical edition of *Examen de ingenios* by Juan Huarte de San Juan (1529–88) in which he carefully noted multiple references to Plato, identified the details of specific dialogues, and discussed Huarte's accord or dissension with particular Platonic opinions (Huarte 1989). Other contemporary critical studies attest to a marked change in perceptions on the resonance of Ficino's work, particularly in Spanish writers of the late sixteenth and early seventeenth centuries.[60] Lía Schwartz has stated unequivocally that we have "factual evidence that indicates that certain poets and humanists in the seventeenth century knew and read Ficino's works" (2005, 186).[61] In what follows, I will expand that evidentiary range to show that the fifteenth and sixteenth centuries are also replete with mentions of and debate on the Italian philosopher's thought and writings.

Some Spanish authors of the Renaissance were familiar enough with Ficino's work to at times refer to him simply as "Marsilio," a reference that has not always been recognized by later scholars.[62] Spaniards also quote with some frequency key authors translated by the Italian philosopher, particularly Hermes Trismegistus and Plato, both at times conflated by Renaissance (and later) writers with Ficino himself. It has been noted that quotes attributed to Plato by other European authors are often references to Ficino's commentaries on the Greek philosopher's works rather than to the dialogues themselves (Kristeller 1956, 1:160). The same holds true in Spanish libraries: volumes with the Italian philosopher's translations and commentaries contain significantly more marginal notations alongside Ficino's commentaries than accompany the text of the dialogues. Spanish authors quoting Hermes Trismegistus invariably do so from Ficino's translation or commentary. Scholars seeking Ficino's influence on Spanish authors recognized as Neoplatonist have at times denied direct contact with the Italian philosopher's writings despite multiple citations to Hermes Trismegistus. For example, Spanish writers Pedro Malón de Chaide (c. 1530–89) and Miguel Servet (1511–53) do not specifically quote Ficino despite literally "borrowing" large portions of text: scholars have recognized and noted the source as Ficino, but have missed that both Malón de Chaide and Servet do repeatedly name Hermes Trismegistus.[63]

To appreciate the full resonance of Ficino in Spanish letters, it is incumbent on us to also take into consideration the writings of authors he translated. That admittedly daunting task will here be offered with a focus on certain specifics: a study of extant volumes in Spain's libraries (chapter 1); direct references by Spanish authors to Ficino as an authority on various topics (chapter 2); manuscript holdings and citations to his alter-ego Hermes Trismegistus (chapter 3); the resonance of Hermetic-Neoplatonic imagery in Spanish letters (chapter 4); and the influence of Ficino's translation and commentary on Plato's dialogues *Phaedo* and *Republic* (chapters 5 and 6). Multiple copies of Ficino's translations, original works, and published letters are catologued in Spain's libraries, in both manuscript and published form. Glosses written in those volumes, as well as archival and epistolary commentary about the texts and their authors, demonstrate their wide acceptance at all levels of society. I begin with those library holdings.

1 Ficino in Spanish Libraries

Early in the twentieth century, as Ficino was being written out of Spanish literary history, those who catalogued Spain's library holdings also failed to find any of the Italian philosopher's works. García Romero's 1921 catalogue of incunabula in the library of the Real Academia de la Historia lists nothing by Ficino, or Plato, or Hermes Trismegistus. García Rico's 1920 catalogue of ancient and modern books in Spanish libraries registers no entries for Ficino or Hermes and for Plato lists only the *Opera omnia* in a late nineteenth-century publication. Gallardo's four-volume catalogue of "rare and curious books" (1888–9) lists nothing for Ficino or Hermes but for Plato there are two titles: *Diálogo del menosprecio de la muerte*, apparently Díaz de Toledo's 1440 Castilian translation of the *Phaedo*, and a work listed as *Apuntamientos para su vida* [de Platón] *(original del siglo XVI)* (1:X, 241). While this supposed lack of library holdings might serve to reinforce assertions like those of Menéndez Pelayo regarding the inconsequentiality of Ficino in Spanish letters, the cataloguers failed to register quite a number of volumes that are found today in those same libraries. For example, despite the lack of Ficino listings in the 1935 catalogue of incunabula in Spain's Biblioteca Nacional Española [BNE] (Vindel), there are ten pre-1500 Ficino works in the same catalogue today, plus another sixty-six works dating to the sixteenth and seventeenth centuries, as well as further listings for Iamblichus, the uniform title for a collection of Ficino's translations of that author together with a group of Neoplatonist writers. Specifics as to when those volumes were purchased for individual collections are not always available. Nonetheless, as will be seen in what follows, many bear the ex-libris of particular university libraries that do allow the volumes to be identified as part of those early collections, and as circulating in the sixteenth century. Others are listed in dated purchase orders, or exhibit signatures that allow for more chronological precision. In what follows, I review overall numbers of specific titles and offer details on select volumes.

Ficino's brief treatise on the plague, titled *Epidemiarum antidotus*, was frequently published in Latin in composite [combined-text] volumes, and there are four copies of the 1529 and 1532 Basel editions of *Epidemiarum antidotus* bound with *De triplici vita* held by Spanish libraries today. The treatise on the plague itself (without the *De vita*) was translated into Spanish and published three times in the sixteenth century: by Alonso García Matamoros in 1553, Francisco Curteti in 1564, and Mathias Mares in 1598, this last at the cost of royal scribe Martín Gómez, whose personal copy of the edition is today held by the BNE (R/26692). As for the *De vita*, there are six incunabula in stand-alone volumes held in Spanish libraries today, and twenty-seven more copies of various editions published throughout the sixteenth century. Contrary to what one might expect, the third book of *De vita* is found intact in these volumes; see *infra* for details on specific holdings.

Ficino's translation of Plato's *Opera omnia* had wide circulation in Spain. There are 127 copies of fifteenth- and sixteenth-century editions of the work held today in Spanish libraries:

Edition	Number of copies held in Spanish libraries
1484 Florence	2
1491 Venice	3
1517 Venice	4
1518 Paris	1
1522 Paris	7
1532 Basel	3
1533 Paris	3
1539 Basel	14
1546 Basel	6
1548 Lyon	20
1550 Lyon	1
1551 Basel	8
1557 [1556] Lyon	18
1561 Basel	8
1567 Lyon	7
1571 [1570] Venice	4
1581 Venice	3
1588 Lyon	10
1590 Lyon	2
1592 Geneva Stoer	2
1602 Frankfurt	4
Total	127

The early educational curriculum of Spain's King Phillip II included this translation, purchased for the future monarch in 1542 (Sánchez-Molero 1998, 639, n.1107); that copy is held today by the Escorial library.[1] The Public Library in Córdoba holds the 1518 edition, annotated throughout by its owner, one "Licenciado Ramírez" (Patrimonio, Córdoba, *Platonis Opera*, ms. 8/324, notes).[2] A copy of the 1539 Basel edition indicates that it was at one time in the library of "Obispo Sancho" (Patrimonio, Barcelona, Biblioteca Pública Episcopal, ms. XVI-391, notes),[3] and a copy of the 1548 Lyon edition threatens excommunication to anyone who dares hide the work (Patrimonio, Cádiz, Biblioteca Pública, ms. XVI-643, notes).[4] The 1550 five-volume Lyon edition is scattered among various libraries, with one or two volumes each held in Oviedo, Badajoz, Valencia, Lugo, and Zaragoza. In addition to the numbers listed in the chart on the previous page, there are also scattered copies of individual volumes from the 1781–7 Biponti edition. I offer this detailed listing to emphasize the ubiquitousness of these volumes in Spain: nearly every fifteenth- and sixteenth-century published edition of Ficino's translation of Plato's *Opera omnia* can be found in Spanish libraries, frequently in multiple copies. Given those extant copies, despite the major upheavals in Spanish libraries and their holdings between the sixteenth and the twentieth centuries, along with ex libris and dated signatures, glosses, and censors' marks, it is indisputable that Renaissance Spaniards studied these dialogues in Ficino's translations and with his commentaries.

Ficino's Latin renditions of Neoplatonist thinkers also circulated widely in Spain. Patrimonio lists twenty-one entries for the 1502–3 edition of his translation and commentary on Dionysius, although many indicate only partial holdings, or missing folios. One of the complete copies belonged to Hernando Colón [Columbus], son of Christopher Columbus (Biblioteca Capitular y Colombina, 6–6–39). There are five copies of the 1538 (1539) Venice edition of this work held by Spanish libraries today. Twenty-two different copies of Ficino's translation of Plotinus are in Spanish libraries, fifteen of them Basel editions of the sixteenth century: seven copies of the 1559 edition, four of the 1562 edition, and five of the 1580 edition. The Spanish library holdings of a later edition of the same work hint at another possible detail on the overwhelmingly negative perception of Ficino by the late nineteenth century neo-scholastic group: there are eight copies of the 1855 Paris edition of Ficino's translation of Plotinus, which would have been a fresh reminder of the Italian philosopher's ties to Plotinus and the latter's emanationist doctrine. For the neo-scholastics, Plotinus is linked negatively to theurgy, a "philosophical and erudite magic" concerned with good and bad demons, he was an "insidious" influence on Maimonides with respect to the latter's pantheism, atheism, and emanationist beliefs, and he was the downfall of Miguel Servet, whose great error was to accept Plotinus's doctrines on the One, Nous, and Universal Soul (Menéndez

Pelayo 1992, 1:387, 592, 1291–2). As the translator who ennabled the spread of these doctrines, Ficino would have similarly been looked on with suspicion.

On the question of the Italian philosopher himself as an independent thinker, two copies of the 1482 princeps edition of Ficino's own magnum opus, the *Platonic Theology*, are held by Spanish libraries today, as well as sixteen more copies of sixteenth-century editions of the work (Patrimonio). Ficino's *Opera omnia* was first published in 1561 (Allen and Hankins 2001, xvi), and Spanish libraries hold at least ten full copies of that edition of the two-volume work, as well as various partial holdings of one volume only. There are three full copies of the two-volume, 1576 edition of Ficino's own *Opera*, as well as two copies of volume 1 only, and four of volume 2 only. Seville's Public Library holds a copy of the 1641 edition of this work with the ex libris of the "Capuchinos de Sevilla," and a censor's mark fully clearing the work for circulation: "This book has nothing needing correction, according to the 1707 index. Fr[ay] Arcadio de Osuna" (Patrimonio, *Marsilii Ficino Florentini*, mss. A 175/104 and A 175/103, notes).[5] The Index date and note support Boecler's and Feijoo's analyses: in the early eighteenth century, Ficino was still considered fully orthodox, and his writings were studied with impunity in Spain.

The 1476 princeps edition of Ficino's *De christiana religione* is held by one Spanish library, and there are twenty-one copies of the following sixteenth- and early seventeenth-century editions:

Edition	Number of copies held in Spanish libraries
1500 Venice	1
1510 Paris	2
1518 Venice	4
1559 Paris	13
1617 Bremen	1

Of the four copies of the 1544 Florence edition of Ficino's commentary on Plato's *Symposium*, titled *Convite, sopra l'amore* in his own Italian translation, we know that one belonged at one time to the same scholar who downplayed Ficino's influence on Spanish Renaissance thought and letters, Marcelino Menéndez Pelayo (Patrimonio, Santander, ms. 10.022); there is also one copy of the 1594 Florence edition, and one copy of the 1544 Venice edition of another Italian translation of this work, by Hercole Barbarosa, both held today at the BNE.

Ficino began to collect his letters in the 1470s and they were first published in 1495 in one volume of 12 books (Kristeller 1975, 17–18). There are four copies of that 1495 Venice edition of the *Epistolae* in Spanish libraries today,[6] and three more of the 1497 Nuremberg edition, as well as one copy of the 1546 Venice, Italian translation of the first volume of the two-volume Italian translation by Figliucci of the *Epistolae*;[7] this last belonged, at one time, to Dámaso Alonso (Patrimonio, Madrid, RAE, ms. 5b BA-I-4–8–16, notes), one of the first Spanish scholars to accept the intellectual resonance of Ficinian Neoplatonism in Renaissance Spanish verse. There are also two more copies of the 1563 (1549) reprint of that same Italian translation of the first volume of the *Epistolae.*

These detailed numbers strongly suggest that Ficino's translations and writings were a considerable factor in the intellectual discourse of Renaissance Spain and as we will see below, they were. The electronic *Patrimonio colectivo* catalogue of Spain's libraries lists a total of ninety-two different titles under Ficino's name, in multiple copies that include fifteen incunabula, 261 copies of sixteenth-century publications, seven volumes of seventeenth-century publications, twenty-one volumes of an eighteenth-century multi-volume publication of *Platonis philosophi*, nine volumes published in the nineteenth century, and one dated to the twentieth century. There are four more copies of works lacking publication information but assumed to be either fifteenth or sixteenth century, and not all of Spain's libraries have yet been incorporated into Patrimonio's electronic catalogue. Further, these compiled listings under the Italian philosopher's name do not include other titles, for example the Iamblichus volumes with Ficino's translations and commentaries and, as of yet, Patrimonio does not incorporate certain important collections such as that of the Escorial library, which holds twenty-two volumes related to Ficino as author or translator. Spain's libraries also hold multiple copies of volumes that combine Ficino's own works, like the *De vita*, with his translations of and commentaries on the Neoplatonist authors. These volumes with their various ex libris and personal holdings information show that Ficino's work circulated widely among monasteries and university colleges in Spain both during and after the Renaissance. Catalogues of specific libraries offer further detail on who was reading or collecting volumes related to Ficino.

Biblioteca Capitular Colombina

The personal library of Hernando Colón, son of Christopher Columbus and his Spanish mistress Beatriz Enríquez de Arana,[8] includes Ficino's *De sole et lumine*, in a composite volume identified by Kristeller as the Adelphus edition with title *Margarita facetiarum* (1963–92, *Supplementum*, 1:67, i, 5). Another composite volume catalogued as Caesarius, 1529, lists *De sole* among its titles but on examination I found that the only two pages of Ficino's writings in the volume are not *De sole* but, rather, two different items: the first, titled "Quid sit philosophia, & item quid sapientia ..." is the first chapter of Ficino's translation of Albinus, absent its first and last sentences but otherwise intact. The second page identified with Ficino in the volume is titled "De tribus apud philosophos differendi generibus, ex praefatione Marsilii Ficini in librum de uoluptate," and is a variation on Ficino's letter to Antonio Canigiani, included as the preface to *De voluptate* in the published Iamblichus; some of the wording, however, differs from that published version (BCC sign. 4–6–1). Many volumes were registered in the Colón library with information on purchase place and price: a 1501 edition of the *De vita* "cost 68 maravedis in Seville" (BCC 13–1–4), and a 1502 edition of Dionysius's *Opera*, together with the *De mystica theologia* and *De divinis nominibus* was purchased for "58 craicer" in Nuremberg (BCC 6–6–26); this last handwritten notation of price specifies that it included a second volume with the Ficino commentary ("commento de marsilio"), although that volume is, today, missing. Two copies of a 1519 edition of Ficino's *Epistola veritatis: De institutione principis ad Cardinalem Riarivm* are held by the library, with one marked as having been purchased in Nuremberg for "6 fenning" in December 1520, and an additional note on the exchange rate: "one gold ducat was worth 344 fenning" at the time.[9] Colón purchased his 1481 edition of Ficino's *Consilio contra la peste* for "one quatrin" in Rome in December 1515 (BCC 4–1–17), a 1497 Iamblichus for "136 maravedis" in Seville (BCC 6–6–39), and a 1497 edition of Plotinus for "675 maravedis" in Seville.[10] This last volume includes, next to Ficino's letter to the reader, a handwritten note in Castilian asserting that Plotinus followed Plato so closely that they "seem to have spoken from the same mouth" (BCC 15–7–19) (figures 1 and 2).[11]

Colón's collection also includes a 1522 edition of Ficino's translation of Plato's *Opera* (BCC 15–7–10). In the library catalogue, but not specifically registered as having been a part of Colón's personal collection, are more Ficino-related volumes: one 1532 Basel edition of Plato's *Opera omnia*, and one 1548 edition of the same, with only the latter expurgated as per the 1612 and 1614 Indices of prohibited books. There are three emendations: one word of the title page is lined through, so that it reads "Omnia ~~Divini~~ Platonis"; "autor damnata" is written next to Simon Grynaeus's name on that same title page; and Grynaeus's general preface to the volume is lined through. The work belonged at one time to a Licenciado Don Antonio Pedro García, who signed the title page, although whether prior to or after the censor's marks is unclear. The library also holds a non-expurgated 1567 edition of the same work, Plato's *Opera omnia*, with no changes to title page, nor to Grynaeus's name and text: this volume belonged at one time to Don Eugenio Nicolás de Guzmán, who identifies himself on the title page as owner of the volume and Censor for the Inquisition. Nicolás de Guzmán's copy has multiple underlinings throughout, as well as marginal annotations in Spanish that debate details of the story of Solon in the *Timaeus*: questioned are Solon's

EXHORTATIO MARSILII FICINI FLORENTINI AD AVDITORES IN LECTIONEM PLOTINI ET SIMILITER AD LEGENTES

P RINCIPIO VOS OMNES ADMONEO / QVI diuinum auditum Plotinum huc acceditis: ut Platonem ipſum ſub Plotini perſona loquentem uos audituros exiſtimetis. Siue enim Plato quondam in Plotino reuixit: quod facile nobis Pythagorici dabũt: ſiue Demon idem Platonem quidem prius afflauit: Deinde uero Plotinum / quod Platonici nulli negabunt. Omnino aſpirator idem os Platonicum afflat atque Plotinicum. Sed in Platone quidem afflando ſpiritum effundit uberiorem. In Plotino autem flatum anguſtiorem: ac ne anguſtiorem dixerim / ſaltem non minus anguſtum / nonnunquam ferme profundiorem. Idem itaque numen per os utrunq; humano generi diuina fundit oracula. Vtrobiq; ſagaciſſimo quodam interprete digna: qui ibi quidem in euoluendis figmentorum incumbat inuolucris. Hic uero tum in exprimendis ſecretiſſimis ubiq; ſenſibus / tum in explanandis uerbis ꝗbreuiſſimis diligentius elaboret. Mementote praeterea uos haudquaquã uel ſenſu comite uel humana ratione duce: ſed mente quadam ſublimiore excelſam Plotini mentem penetraturos. Profecto (ut Platonice loquar) caeteros homines rationales animos appellamus: Plotinum uero non animum: ſed intellectum. Sic omnes eum philoſophi ſuo ſaeculo praeſertim Platonici nominabant. Atque utinam in myſteriis huius interpretandis adminiculum Porphyrii aut Euſtochii / aut Proculi / qui Plotini libros diſpoſuerunt / atque expoſuerunt / nobis adeſſet. Spero tamen id quod admodum fęlicius eſt / diuinum auxilium in traducẽdis explicandiſq; diuinis Plotini libris Marſilio Ficino non defuturum. Sed iam caeleſtibus hinc auſpiciis & nos ad tranſferendum primum Plotini librum: & argumento breuiter exponendum / reliquoſq; deinceps fęliciter accedamus. Et uos Platonem ipſum exclamare ſic erga Plotinum exiſtimetis. Hic eſt filius meus dilectus / in quo mihi undiq; placeo: ipſum audite.

quelplotinosſigiotantoapl ſparececdevlyabladopor / meſmalosa

A R G V M E N T V M MARSILII FICINI FLORENTINI IN PRIMVM LIBRVM PLOTINI PLATONICI.

Anima rationalis media eſt inter formas diuinas atque naturales neque ineſt corpori: ſed adeſt: & uitam ex ſe propagat / quae ineſt corpori: ex qua & corpore fit animal unum compoſitum. Capitulum primum.

P ER opportune primus hic omnium nobis occurrit liber. In quo nos ipſos uelut in ſpeculo contemplemur: ne tanquam nimium curioſi aliena prius ꝗ noſtra quaeramus. Docebit enim nos ideſt hominem uerum / atq; hoc ipſum quod ipſi

b ii

Figure 1. First folio with marginal note attributed to Christopher Columbus in 1497 edition of Ficino's translation of Plotinus, Biblioteca Capitular Columbina 15–7–19. Courtesy of the Biblioteca Capitular Columbina. Seville.

chronology, the truth of his having left Egypt as alleged in the history, and a clarification that the flood spoken of in the text is not the Universal Deluge (BCC 23–7–2).[12] The Nicolás de Guzmán who owned the volume at one time is in all likelihood Eugenio Nicolás de Guzmán y Márquez, the author of a text published

Figure 2. Last folio with library registration mark and purchase price in 1497 edition of Ficino's translation of Plotinus, Biblioteca Capitular Columbina 15–7–19. Courtesy of the Biblioteca Capitular Columbina. Seville.

in Madrid in 1719 and titled *Escudo atomístico en que se propugna la philosophia platónica de nuestro príncipe Maygnan*; in his dedication to Joaquín Ponce de León, Nicolás de Guzmán boasts of his descent from a number of illustrious families, including that of Colonna (1719, f. 2v). Miguel Mancheño y Olivares identifies Nicolás de

Guzmán as an illustrious citizen of Arcos de la Frontera, as a Doctor in theology as well as canon and civil law, and as a "corrector" (calificador) of texts for the Inquisition who died in 1750 (1892, 389).

One specific volume held in Colón's library deserves special mention, despite its lack of connection to Ficino; it is a two-volume Castilian translation of Plutarch's *Lives* (BCC 2–4–12 and 2–4–13). The title page indicates that the work was originally written in Greek, then translated into Latin by multiple authors. The volume is noteworthy for two reasons: first, handwritten annotations in Spanish in the margins are identified, albeit tentatively, as having been made by Christopher Columbus and second, although not linked to Ficino this translation demonstrates the clear interest that Greek authorities had for Spanish intellectuals and rulers of late fifteenth-century Spain: the volume was compiled by Alfonso de Palencia, Royal Chronicler for the Catholic Monarchs Ferdinand and Isabel.[13]

The Escorial

In addition to the personal holdings of King Phillip II, the Escorial library also has some unique Ficino writings in the collection of Spanish nobleman Diego Hurtado de Mendoza (1503–75). Hurtado de Mendoza studied in Granada, Salamanca, Rome, and Padua; he was an emissary of Emperor Charles V in England, Venice, and at the Council of Trent; he frequently visited Italy, and he left his extensive personal library holdings to Phillip II. What remains of that collection is now housed in the Escorial (Manuel Sánchez Mariana 1998, 37–8), and includes a manuscript with Ficino's translation of *Dante, de monarchia*, dated 21 March 1467, and signed with "di Ales. Guglielmi et degli amici suoi" (figure 3).[14]

While in Venice, Hurtado de Mendoza also acquired many Greek manuscripts from, among others, Cardinal Bessarion (Antonio 1999 1:300), a defender of Platonism and one of Ficino's many correspondents. Although some volumes of the Hurtado de Mendoza collection were destroyed in a 1671 fire, we know from an inventory list that those holdings included Ficino's *Epistolae*, the 1516 Venice edition of the Iamblichus compilation of Ficino's translations of Neoplatonic authors, and two volumes (the second and fifth) of the 1550 León edition of Ficino's five-volume *Platonis Opera omnia* (González Palencia and Mele 1941–3, 494, no. 44; 514–15, no. 146). The two volumes of Plato's *Opera*, the Iamblichus, and the manuscript translation of Dante survived the fire and remain housed in the Escorial library today.

Within the Escorial collection, volumes from King Phillip II's personal library are identified by a specific binding that allows for identification of Ficino-related volumes among the monarch's own books:[15] among them are a 1510 Paris *De christiana religione*; a 1516 Venice Iamblichus; a 1536 Cologne edition of *Dionysii*

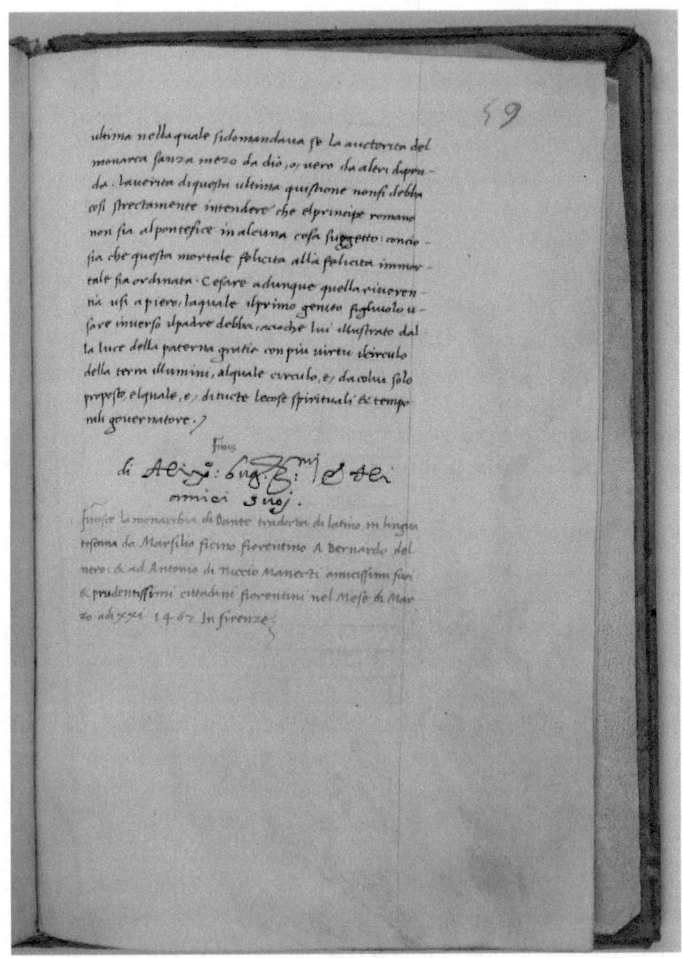

Figure 3. Autographed and dated last folio of Dante's *De Monarchia* in Ficino's Italian translation, with ex libris annotation of Diego Hurtado de Mendoza. El Escorial &-III-25. Courtesy of Real Biblioteca del Monasterio de El Escorial, San Lorenzo, Madrid, Spain. Copyright © Patrimonio Nacional.

Carthusiani; and a 1540 Basel edition of the works of Plotinus. Also held at the Escorial and in the library's binding but not that of Phillip II himself, are a manuscript of Ficino's *De voluptate*; a copy of the 1495 Venice edition of the Italian philosopher's *Epistolae*; the 1516 Basel *Athenagorae de resurrectione* in the *Aeneae*

[Aeneas of Gaza] *Platonici Christiani de immortalitate animae*; the 1525 Venice edition of Ficino's *Platonic Theology* bound with a 1537 edition of Pliny's *Natural History*; two copies of the 1536 Cologne *Dionysii Carthusiani*; one copy of the 1538 Venice *Dionysii Areopagitae*; one of the 1539 Basel edition of Plato's *Opera*; two copies of the 1549 Lyon edition of Iamblichus; a 1559 Paris edition of the *Platonic Theology*; the 1564 Zaragoza edition of the Curteti-sponsored Castilian translation of Ficino's work on the plague bound with two other works in Spanish on medicine; a 1567 Lyon edition of *De vita*; a 1580 Basel edition of Plotinus; a 1584 Venice edition of the *De vita* and the *De peste*, bound with other works on astrology, medicine, and mathematics; a 1590 bilingual Lyon *Tou theiou Platonos*; an undated Basel, Henric Petrina edition of Ficino's *Opera* (18-IV-1–2); and a composite volume that includes a number of works, along with chapter 25 (only) of Book 3 of the *De vita* (85-IV-24 [2°]). These volumes, not yet represented in the Patrimonio collective catalogue, provide solid evidence that Ficino's texts and translations circulated in the highest court circles.

Public and Personal Libraries

In other Spanish library holdings, we find more details on specific provenance and ownership: a *Corpus Hermeticum* with Ficino's *Argumentum* was owned by the Jesuits and sold to the Marucelliana Library in 1775 (Gentile and Gilly 1999, 49–50, ms. III). The library of one Diego López, medical doctor and surgeon to King Phillip II, included a book identified as "One Marsili Ficini" that, at his death in 1597, was priced for sale at "dos reales"; when attorney Gabriel de la Rey died in 1577, his list of goods included a "possible" "Ippolito de Marsili" (Prieto Bernabé 2004, 2: 247–53 and 2:260–9). Following the 1523 death of Don Rodrigo de Mendoza, marqués de Cenete, an inventory of his library includes: Ficino's *De triplici vita* (no. 31), the Italian philosopher's commentary on Aristotle's *De generatione et corruptione* (no. 85), another unidentified "Marcilii Ficinii" that Sánchez Cantón ventures to guess as the *Epistolae* (no. 115), the *Pimander* in Ficino's translation (no. 117), Plato's *Opera omnia*, not specified as to edition but in all likelihood that of Ficino's translation (no. 570), and Plotinus's *Enneads* identified as Ficino's translation with commentary (no. 571) (Sánchez Cantón 1942, 43–112). Another inventory of books to be sold, following the 1517 death of Don Pedro Fernández de Córdoba, marqués de Priego, includes an unidentified volume of Plato (*La definisión de Platón*), as well as "the Epistolary of Marsyli Ficini Florentine" (*las epístolas de Marsyli Ficini florentyno*) and a "Marsylio Florentine bound in black leather" (*Marsylio florentino enquadernado en cuero negro*) (Quintanilla Raso 1981, 357–68, nos. 5, 19, 97). Although unidentified as to title, this last was appraised on the 1518 list at 136 maravedis, close to the 170 maravedis for the *Epistolae*, although the list also includes more costly volumes, such as a large-sized Ptolemy (*un Tolomeo en marca mayor*) listed at 750 maravedis (no. 116), a nine-volume set of the works of Saint Augustine valued at 3,375 maravedis (no. 143), and two manuscript Bibles appraised at 18,250 maravedis (no. 268).[16] A 1559 inventory of the collection of Pedro Guerrero of Granada includes works by Plato (unspecified edition) as well as Ficino's own *Opera omnia* (Hernández González 1998, 427). A few of these listings of privately held libraries show, again, the simple reference to Ficino by first name only. In the sixth volume of his monumental *Iter italicum*, Kristeller lists a letter *Ad Marsilium* that is part of a collection of letters belonging to Spain's Álvaro Gómez de Castro (1515–80), held today at the BNE.[17] The public library of the city of Toledo holds a 1516 publication of Ficino's complete works, *Marsilii Ficini Opera* (ms. 1067), signed and dated 1629 by Don Fran[cis]co de Miranda y Paz, a chaplain in Toledo who wrote his own works on philosophy and theology (Madan 1905, 437–8), as well as a 1577 Iamblichus volume marked: "From the library of Saint Francis of Yepes" (*De la librería de S. Francisco de Yepes*) (ms. 16253), that is, the convent of discalced Franciscans in Toledo. As a testament to the orthodox status of Hermes Trismegistus and Hermetic works in general, another Toledo volume bearing the uniform title *Ptolomeus*, also signed by Miranda y Paz, is a 1519 Venice edition of astrological and Hermetic works, apparently not in Ficino translation, but with a handwritten and underlined note on the frontispiece assuring any possible reader: "this is not prohibited" (no está vedado) (Toledo, ms. 20745).

University of Salamanca

The University of Salamanca library today includes twenty-three different titles with Ficino as writer and/or translator, a number of them held in multiple copies. Vicente Bécares Botas has studied documentation relating to the purchase of books for the "new" University of Salamanca library founded in 1510, and offers wonderful detail on the specific purchases of 488 titles during the years 1531–3. This list includes Ficino's *De triplici vita* without indication of specific edition, although listed possibilities include 1501, 1529, or 1532 (A, no. 128),[18] the 1513 Venice Aldus edition of the *Platonis Opera omnia* (A, no. 134; B, no. 67), and the 1492 Florence edition of Ficino's translation of Plotinus (A, no. 135; B, no. 68). Bécares Botas notes a marked change in volume of acquisitions following the advent of the printing press, which brought a new "commercial offer" (oferta comercial) style to the buying and selling of publications (84), and he adds that documentation for the full decade 1530–40 indicates constant growth of this collection (88), which was only one of the libraries at Salamanca, as each residential Colegio had its own.

334

EX MICHAELE PSELLO DE DAEMONIBVS,

Interpres Marsilius Ficinus.

Figure 4. Censored page 334 of Psellus's *De daemonibus* in Ficino's translation of Iamblichus, *De mysteriis*.... Courtesy of Universidad de Salamanca (España). Biblioteca General Histórica. BG/ 17258.

Glosses and commentaries on specific volumes at Salamanca today reveal in more intimate detail the reception accorded Ficino's works. There is sporadic censorship of some of the authors translated: for example, in one copy of the combined Neoplatonist volume catalogued as Iamblichus, all pages corresponding to Michael Psellus's *De daemonibus* have been torn out, with the exception of the first and last, crossed out but left in the manuscript, apparently so as not to disturb the other treatises which begin and end on those same pages: Porpyry's *De divinis atque daemonibus* and Hermes Trismegistus's *Pimander* (see figures 4 and 5).

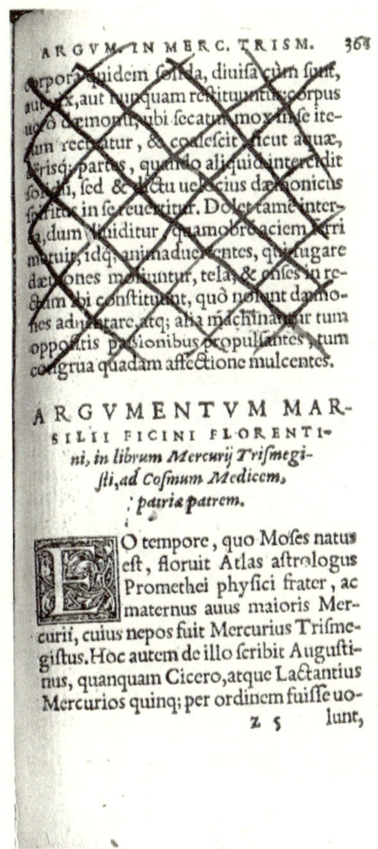
ARGVM. IN MERC. TRISM. 368

corpora quidem ſolida, diuiſa cùm ſunt, aut uix, aut nunquam reſtituuntur: corpus uerò dæmonum, ubi ſecatur, mox in ſe iterum recreatur, & coaleſcit ſicut aquæ, aeriſq; partes, quando aliquid intercidit ſolidi, ſed & dictu uelocius dæmonicus ſpiritus in ſe reuertitur. Dolet tamen interea, dum diuiditur, quamobrem aciem ferri metuit, idq; animaduertentes, qui fugare dæmones moliuntur, tela, & enſes in rectum ibi conſtituunt, quò nolunt dæmones aduentare, atq; alia machinantur tum oppoſitis paſſionibus propulſantes, tum congrua quadam affectione mulcentes.

ARGVMENTVM MARSILII FICINI FLORENTIni, *in librum Mercurij Triſmegiſti, ad Coſmum Medicem, patriæ patrem.*

EO tempore, quo Moſes natus eſt, floruit Atlas aſtrologus Promethei phyſici frater, ac maternus auus maioris Mercurii, cuius nepos fuit Mercurius Triſmegiſtus. Hoc autem de illo ſcribit Auguſtinus, quanquam Cicero, atque Lactantius Mercurios quinq; per ordinem fuiſſe uolunt,

z 5

Figure 5. Partially censored page 662 of Psellus's *De daemonibus* in Ficino's translation of Iamblichus, *De mysteriis…*, leaving *Pimander* uncensored. Courtesy of Universidad de Salamanca (España). Biblioteca General Histórica. BG/ 17258.

This volume is interesting for a number of reasons. It is a 1549 compilation of various writings on demons and magic, followed by the *Pimander*: the treatises listed are Iamblichus's *De mysterius Aegyptiorum, Chaldaeorum, Assyriorum*; Proclus's *In Platonicum Alcibiadem de Anima. atque Demone. Idem de Sacrificio & Magia*; Porphyry's *De divinis atque demonibus*; Psellus's *De Demonibus*; and Hermes Trismegistus's *Pimander* with *Asclepius*. The volume is prefaced with

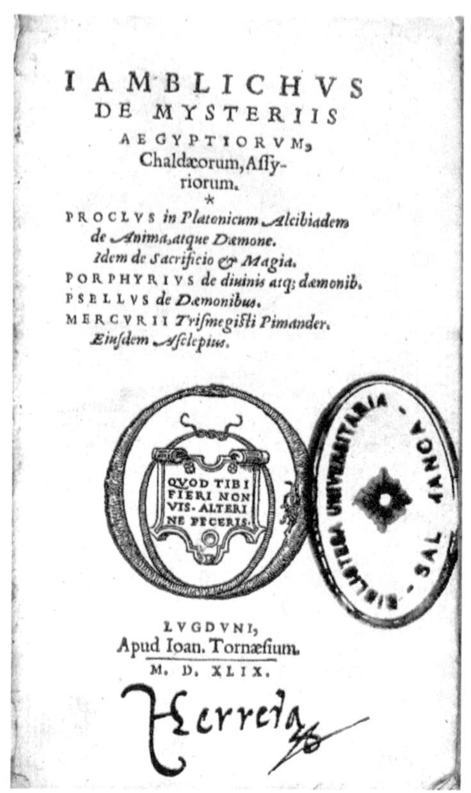

IAMBLICHVS
DE MYSTERIIS
AEGYPTIORVM,
Chaldæorum, Assy-
riorum.
*
PROCLVS in Platonicum Alcibiadem
de Anima, atque Dæmone.
Idem de Sacrificio & Magia.
PORPHYRIVS de diuinis atq; dæmonib.
PSELLVS de Dæmonibus.
MERCVRII Trismegisti Pimander.
Eiusdem Asclepius.

QVOD TIBI FIERI NON VIS. ALTERI NE FECERIS.

LVGDVNI,
Apud Ioan. Tornæsium.
M. D. XLIX.

Herrera

Figure 6. Title page with Herrera signature in Ficino's translation of Iamblichus, *De mysteriis...* Courtesy of Universidad de Salamanca (España). Biblioteca General Histórica. BG/ 17258.

a dedication letter from Ficino to Giovanni de' Medici, in which the Italian philosopher notes that only an ignorant person would believe that demons and magic are not Christian. The cover page bears an unidentified signature "Herrera" in what appears to be the same ink as that used to censor Psellus (figure 5), and the last page of the volume offers a note in Spanish by a different hand, which reads: "on the 23 of February, 1631 [1621?], I looked at the Baptism book and found that master Núñez had baptized me on November 5, 1609. Juan Pérez de Prado" (figures 6 and 7).[19]

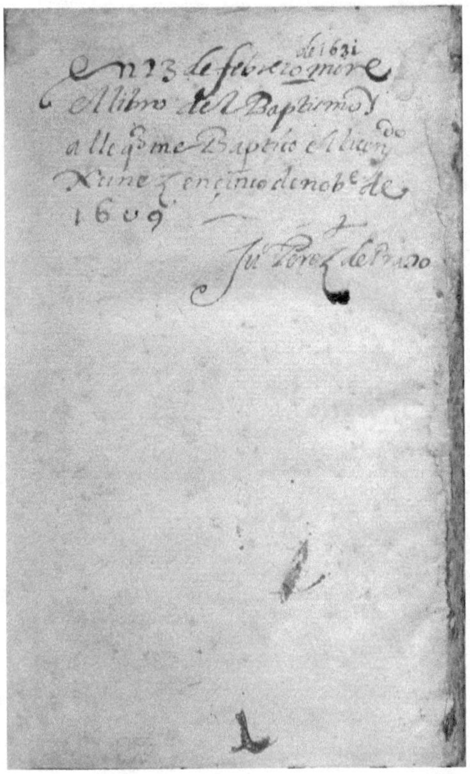

Figure 7. Handwritten note referencing baptism on flyleaf of Ficino's translation of Iamblichus, *De mysteriis*.... Courtesy of Universidad de Salamanca (España). Biblioteca General Histórica. BG/ 17258.

The handwritten note leaves no doubt that the volume still circulated openly among Catholic readers in the early seventeenth century. Per the Index, the offending text by Psellus had been expurgated but the rest of the volume is undisturbed. Other copies of the same Psellus text, in the same edition and held by the same library, as well as a copy held by the library in Toledo (ms. 16253) are not censored, which illustrates the difficulty faced by ecclesiastical censors, who had to find and expurgate volumes after they had been printed and distributed (Plata Parga 1997, 173). Another volume held by the University of Salamanca includes "autor damnatus" penned next to Simon Grynaeus's name (figure 8), although the

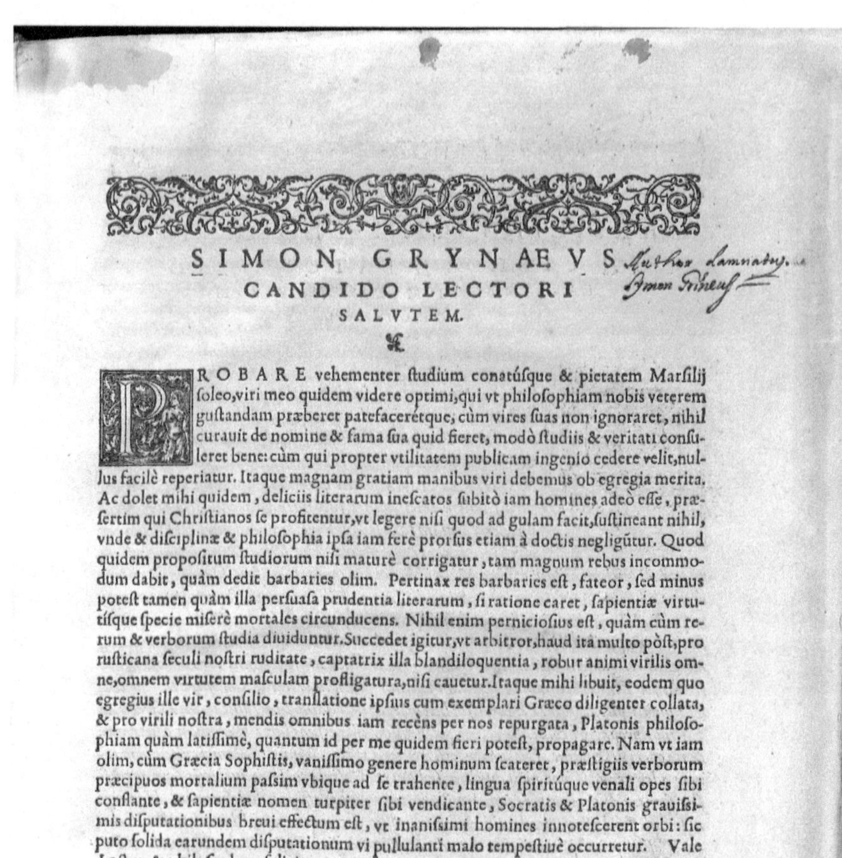

SIMON GRYNAEVS Author damnatus. Simon Grineus
CANDIDO LECTORI
SALVTEM.

PROBARE vehementer ſtudium conatúſque & pietatem Marſilij ſoleo, viri meo quidem videre optimi, qui vt philoſophiam nobis veterem guſtandam præberet patefaceretque, cùm vires ſuas non ignoraret, nihil curauit de nomine & fama ſua quid fieret, modò ſtudiis & veritati conſuleret bene: cùm qui propter vtilitatem publicam ingenio cedere velit, nullus facilè reperiatur. Itaque magnam gratiam manibus viri debemus ob egregia merita. Ac dolet mihi quidem, deliciis literarum ineſcatos ſubitò iam homines adeò eſſe, præſertim qui Chriſtianos ſe profitentur, vt legere niſi quod ad gulam facit, ſuſtineant nihil, vnde & diſciplinæ & philoſophia ipſa iam ferè prorſus etiam à doctis negligũtur. Quod quidem propoſitum ſtudiorum niſi maturè corrigatur, tam magnum rebus incommodum dabit, quàm dedit barbaries olim. Pertinax res barbaries eſt, fateor, ſed minus poteſt tamen quàm illa perſuaſa prudentia literarum, ſi ratione caret, ſapientiæ virtutíſque ſpecie miſerè mortales circunducens. Nihil enim pernicioſius eſt, quàm cùm rerum & verborum ſtudia diuiduntur. Succedet igitur, vt arbitror, haud ita multo pòſt, pro ruſticana ſeculi noſtri ruditate, captatrix illa blandiloquentia, robur animi virilis omne, omnem virtutem maſculam profligatura, niſi cauetur. Itaque mihi libuit, eodem quo egregius ille vir, conſilio, tranſlatione ipſius cum exemplari Græco diligenter collata, & pro virili noſtra, mendis omnibus iam recèns per nos repurgata, Platonis philoſophiam quàm latiſſimè, quantum id per me quidem fieri poteſt, propagare. Nam vt iam olim, cùm Græcia Sophiſtis, vaniſſimo genere hominum ſcateret, præſtigiis verborum præcipuos mortalium paſsim vbique ad ſe trahente, lingua ſpiritúque venali opes ſibi conflante, & ſapientiæ nomen turpiter ſibi vendicante, Socratis & Platonis grauiſsimis diſputationibus breui effectum eſt, vt inaniſsimi homines innoteſcerent orbi: ſic puto ſolida earundem diſputationum vi pullulanti malo tempeſtiuè occurretur. Vale Lector, & philoſophare feliciter.

* 2 MARS

Figure 8. Censorship note next to Simon Grynaeus's name and Dedicatoria al Lector on page 3 of Ficino's translation of Plato, *Diuini Platonis Opera omnia*. Courtesy of Universidad de Salamanca (España). Biblioteca General Histórica. BG/ 13798.

Grynaeus selection in the volume is otherwise undisturbed (BG/ 13798), and the remainder of the volume, unmarked.

Grynaeus's name figures on the Index as early as 1570, and continues to be listed in 1579 and 1583. He and Spaniard Juan Luis Vives were apparently good friends who corresponded by letter (Jiménez Delgado 1978, 605–8, letters 174, 175, and 607, n.1).

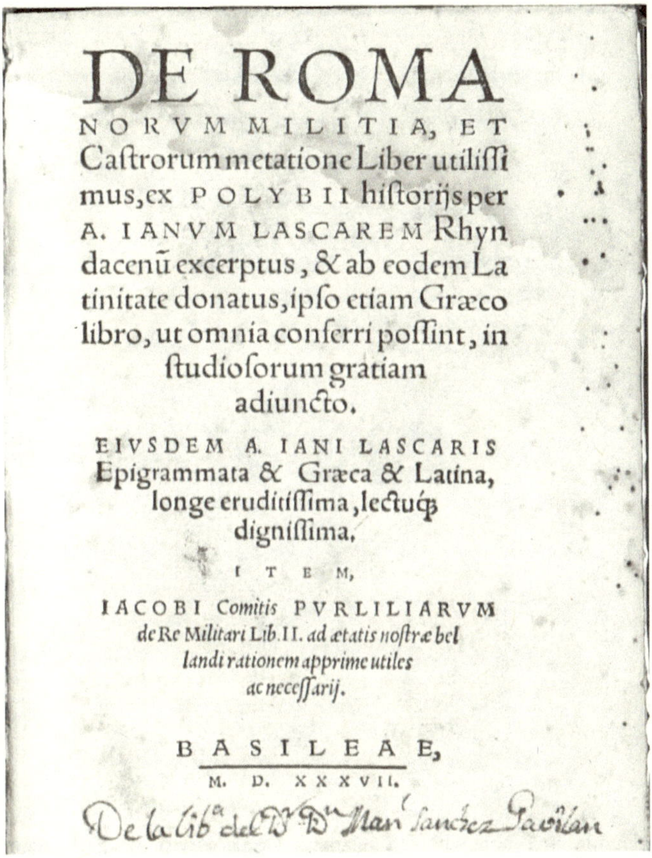

DE ROMA
NORVM MILITIA, ET
Castrorum metatione Liber utilissi
mus, ex POLYBII historijs per
A. IANVM LASCAREM Rhyn
dacenũ excerptus, & ab eodem La
tinitate donatus, ipso etiam Græco
libro, ut omnia conferri possint, in
studiosorum gratiam
adiuncto.

EIVSDEM A. IANI LASCARIS
Epigrammata & Græca & Latina,
longe eruditissima, lectuq;
dignissima.

ITEM,

IACOBI *Comitis* PVRLILIARVM
de Re Militari Lib. II. ad ætatis nostræ bel
landi rationem apprime utiles
ac necessarij.

BASILEAE,
M. D. XXXVII.

Figure 9. Title page with ex libris of Dr. Don Manuel Sánchez Gavilán in Polybius, *De Romanorum militia* (composite volume with Ficino's translation of Neoplatonists Albinus, Speusippus and Xenocrates). Courtesy of Universidad de Salamanca (España). Biblioteca General Histórica. BG/ 32463 (1).

As a counterpoint to the censorship of these particular translations, the University of Salamanca holdings also include another volume with a splendid laudatory note. In this composite volume, a Ficino translation of three Neoplatonists is bound together with a bilingual Greek-Latin edition of Polybius on Roman militia (BG/ 32463 (2)). The frontispiece indicates that the volume was owned at one time by Don Manuel Sánchez Gavilán (figure 9), who held the chair in Greek until his death in 1764, although there is no information on whether he, or someone

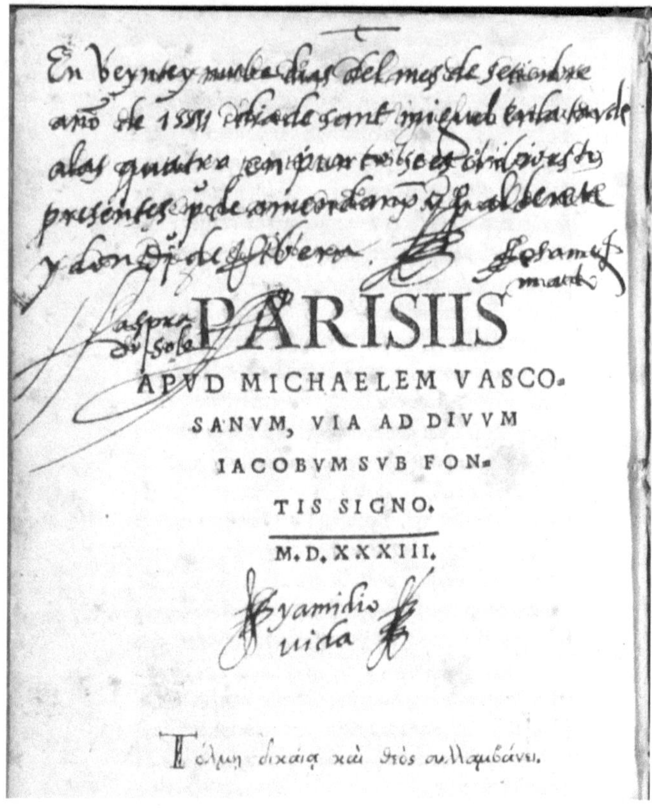
PARISIIS
APVD MICHAELEM VASCO-
SANVM, VIA AD DIVVM
IACOBVM SVB FON-
TIS SIGNO.
M.D.XXXIII.

Figure 10. Handwritten note with three signatures on colophon page of Ficino's translation of Neoplatonists Albinus, Speusippus and Xenocrates. Courtesy of Universidad de Salamanca (España). Biblioteca General Histórica. BG/ 32463 (2).

prior to him, had the texts bound together. The volume is catalogued under uniform title Albinus, but the first title in the bound volume is that of Polybius. The second treatise is Ficino's translation of three Neoplatonists: Albinus, Speusippus, and Xenocratis, published in Paris in 1533. The last page of this portion of the volume has printed publication detail, and also a handwritten note: "on the 29th day of September 1551, Saint Michael's day, in the afternoon at four o'clock on the dot, being present Pero de Mendoza, and myself, and don Juan de Ribera, [signed] Gaspra de Sole, we enjoyed it very much."[20] Under the printer's mark, the same hand of Gaspra de Sole, apparently, has also written "and he/she/it gave me life" (figure 10).[21]

Taken together, the University of Salamanca holdings show an evolution in reactions to Ficino's works, from early to late in the sixteenth century. Prior to the Counter Reformation and the published Indices of Prohibited Books, none of the translated authors presented a problem for a Christian readership and as late as 1551 they were "enjoyed very much" by groups of readers. After the first Index of 1559 one or two of the translated authors would be censored. Despite that, the remaining texts in a multi-author volume continued to be read and studied. Ficino's own writings were never on the Spanish Indices, nor is any criticism of him found in these volumes.

The composite bindings themselves can offer clues as to perception and reception of Ficino's writings during the Renaissance, although there are numerous difficulties in trying to draw any clear conclusions. The bindings are not always chronologically identifiable, and combined volumes at times resulted from simple pragmatic decisions such as similarity in the size of the printed treatises, or the aesthetics of uniformity of bindings in a personal collection. Nonetheless, some volumes do permit conjecture as to perceived affinity in the chosen texts: for example, one composite volume held by the University of Salamanca library includes the 1505 Paris publication of three Hermetic texts: Ficino's Latin *Pimander* translation, Apuleius's *Asclepius*, and Lazarelli's *Crater Hermetis*, bound together with three religious treatises, two by "Carmelite Brother Baptista" and a third by "Agostino Dati Senense." Carmelite Baptista can be identified as fifteenth-century poet Giovan Baptista Spagnoli, also called the Mantuan, who penned this text in 1463 and, in it, "praises the Cynics' disregard for riches as well as their rigor in criticizing evil doings" (Matton 1996, 251). Agostino Dati Senense was a "fifteenth-century Sienese chancellor" whose collected works were published in 1503 (Jackson 2006, 247). The last three texts of this composite volume, those by Baptista and Dati, are undated and not listed on the title page, which is that of the 1505 Paris edition of the first three texts (figure 11).

Baptista's first religious treatise, obviously not listed on the cover page in figure 11, follows directly after Lazarelli's *Crater Hermetis*, and its own printed title page reads: "Dialogue on the blessed life, by Carmelite theologian from Mantua Brother Baptista, just recently edited by the author and now seen [recognized] here with the opuscule on the same topic by Agostino Dati, a native of Siena, very correctly printed" (figure 12).[22]

Following that text in the volume are Baptista's second treatise titled "Three Golden Books on Patience, with Indices, and a Newly Examined Explanation of the Difficult Vocabulary on the Ascension,"[23] and Dati's *De vita beata*. Kristeller's *Iter italicum* notes a collection of 400 folios dating from 1466 to 1495 by what would seem to be the same Brother Baptista, held at Oxford's Bodlein library (Selden ms, various papers fifteenth to seventeenth centuries), that includes letters exchanged with Pico de la Mirandola (Kristeller 1989, 261–2). As indicated

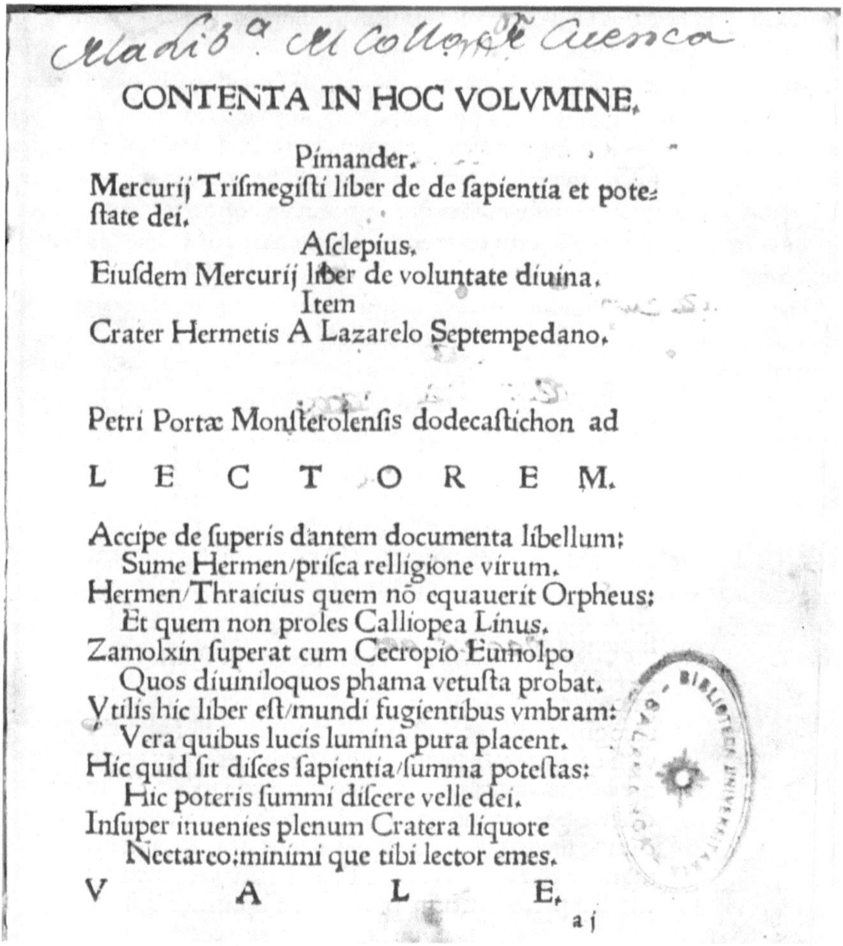

CONTENTA IN HOC VOLVMINE.

Pimander.
Mercurij Triſmegiſti liber de de ſapientia et pote=
ſtate dei.
Aſclepius.
Eiuſdem Mercurij liber de voluntate diuina.
Item
Crater Hermetis A Lazarelo Septempedano.

Petri Portæ Monſterolenſis dodecaſtichon ad
L E C T O R E M.

Accipe de ſuperis dantem documenta libellum:
Sume Hermen/priſca relligione virum.
Hermen/Thraicius quem nō equauerit Orpheus:
Et quem non proles Calliopea Linus.
Zamolxin ſuperat cum Cecropio Eumolpo
Quos diuiniloquos phama vetuſta probat.
Vtilis hic liber eſt/mundi fugientibus vmbram:
Vera quibus lucis lumina pura placent.
Hic quid ſit diſces ſapientia/ſumma poteſtas:
Hic poteris ſummi diſcere velle dei.
Inſuper inuenies plenum Cratera liquore
Nectareo:minimi que tibi lector emes.
V A L E.
a j

Figure 11. Handwritten ex libris of Salamanca's Collegio [Mayor] de Cuenca on volume of Hermetic treatises. Courtesy of Universidad de Salamanca (España). Biblioteca General Histórica. BG/53730 (1).

by a handwritten notation on the frontispiece of the University of Salamanca manuscript that combines these Hermetic, Baptista, and Dati texts, the volume was held by the Colegio de Cuenca, founded at Salamanca early in the sixteenth century. Here, the combination of these particular writings in one volume would seem to attest to a perceived affinity between Hermetic and Christian thought on the "blessed life" held by these Carmelites, quite a logical reading given Saint

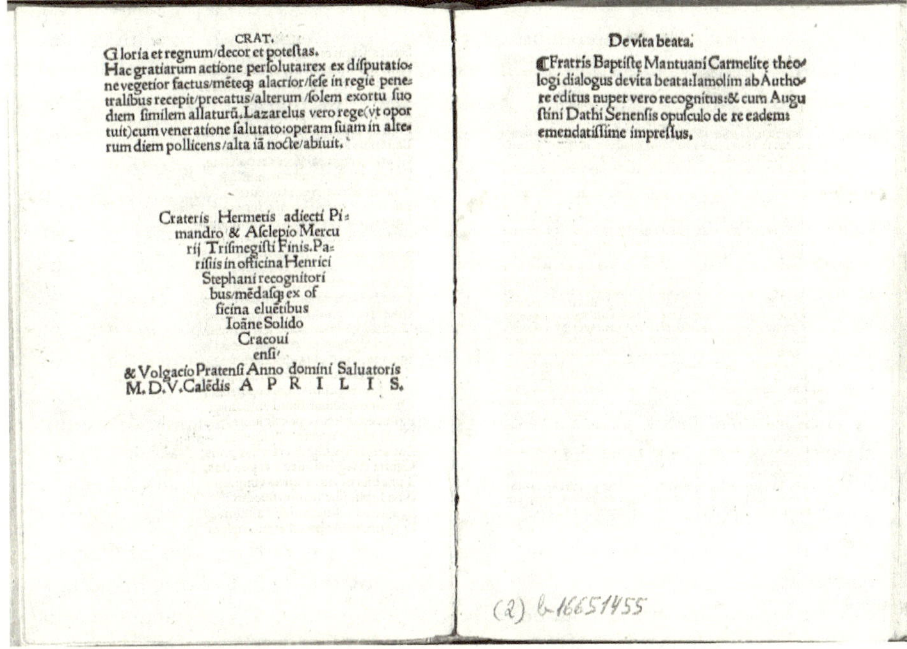

CRAT.

Gloria et regnum/decor et potestas.

Hac gratiarum actione persoluta:rex ex disputatione vegetior factus/mēteqꝫ alacrior/sese in regie penetralibus recepit/precatus/alterum /solem exortu suo diem similem allaturū.Lazarelus vero rege(vt oportuit)cum veneratione salutato:operam suam in alterum diem pollicens/alta iā nocte/abiuit.

Crateris Hermetis adiecti Pimandro & Asclepio Mercurij Trismegisti Finis.Parisiis in officina Henrici Stephani recognitoribus/mēdasqꝫ ex officina eluētibus Ioāne Solido Cracouiensi & Volgacio Pratensi Anno domini Saluatoris M.D.V.Calēdis APRILIS.

De vita beata.

Fratris Baptiste Mantuani Carmelite theologi dialogus de vita beata:Iamolim ab Authore editus nuper vero recognitus:& cum Augustini Dathi Senensis opusculo de re eadem:emendatissime impressus.

Figure 12. Last page of Lazarelli's *Crater Hermetis* with title page of works by Brother Baptista and Agostino Dati. Courtesy of Universidad de Salamanca (España). Biblioteca General Histórica. BG/53730 (1).

Augustine's description of Hermes Trismegistus as an ancient thinker wise enough to accept the idea of a single God and predict the downfall of his own pagan deities.[24] By the end of the sixteenth century, debates on Hermes and his work would begin to crop up: in Spain, Augustinians and Dominicans held opposing views on the Hermetic author (Bell 1925, 115–20), in France, Gilbert Genebrard began to question the writings, and in Italy there were epistolary debates regarding Hermes between Angelucci and Patrizi (Purnell 1978 and 2002). However, when Isaac Casaubon denounced Hermes as a fraud in the early seventeenth century, Catholic intellectuals responded by defending the Hermetic author against the attacks by Casaubon, a Protestant.[25]

Another composite volume (BG/40913) that belonged at one time to the Colegio mayor del arzobispo at Salamanca bears uniform title Hermes and contains the same 1505 Paris volume of three texts (*Pimander*, *Asclepius*, *Crater Hermetis*) bound with a treatise on letter writing by Heinrich Bebel, who lived from

1472 to 1518. This last, which is missing some final pages, has a publication date of 1513. While this combination of works could well have been a pragmatic decision for size or uniformity, intention may be read into it given that Hermes was also identified as the god of writing. Ficino, the translator of the first two texts, was closely identified with Hermes, and himself recognized for his fine epistolary skills. With his last name spelled with a cedilla, Fiçino is among those listed as good examples of letter writers in Latin in another Renaissance Spanish work, Antonio de Torquemada's *Manual de escribientes* (1970 [1552], 174). One more composite volume at Salamanca combines the 1540 publication of Ficino's Latin translation of Plotinus's *Enneads*, including Bessarion's defence of Plato, bound with Aristotle's *Metaphysics* and Theophrastus's *Metaphysics* (BG/ 38007). Here, the perceived affinity would be studies of cosmic structures and natures, i.e., early metaphysics.

The volumes listed above from the Colegios mayores at Salamanca cannot always be definitively traced for provenance. The colleges were founded in the fifteenth and sixteenth centuries but then, sometime in the seventeenth and eighteenth, their library holdings were newly bound, which led to the loss of some publication and provenance information. Also, a number of volumes held by the University of Salamanca today bear the ex libris of the Jesuit College, first established in Salamanca in 1548 but not officially founded until 1614. The documents (*cédulas*) on the expulsion of the Jesuits from Spain in 1767 include instructions to confiscate their library holdings and add them to the university library. The website of the library at the University of Salamanca notes that volumes marked "Old university library" can be reliably dated only as "prior to 1800." Notwithstanding those difficulties, the volumes listed above with handwritten dated commentaries, glosses, and ex libris do attest to an active and eclectic Hermetic-Neoplatonist group in the various colleges at the University of Salamanca during the sixteenth century. Those volumes of Ficino's writings and translations on theological and philosophical matters were an integral part of Renaissance university life at Salamanca.

Complutense – Biblioteca Histórica Marqués de Valdecilla

In 1499, Pope Alexander VI issued the bull that formally founded the University of Alcalá de Henares and in 1508 Archbishop of Toledo Cardinal Cisneros (1436–1517) opened the doors of what was then called the Complutense.[26] Reorganized and moved to Madrid in the early nineteenth century, the Complutense is now the University of Madrid; in 1977, university studies at Alcalá were re-established at what is once again called the Universidad de Alcalá de Henares, but no longer the Complutense, an identification now reserved for the university in

Madrid.[27] The Complutense library in Madrid inherited the holdings of Alcalá's Colegio Mayor San Ildefonso (founded by Cisneros at Alcalá in the late fifteenth century), the Colegio Imperial de los Jesuitas (founded in Madrid, 1609), the Real Colegio de Medicina y Cirugía de San Carlos (founded in Madrid, 1785), and a few other personal and institutional collections.[28] In the year 2000, all rare books and manuscripts of the various libraries within the university system were moved to the Biblioteca Histórica Marqués de Valdecilla, or Biblioteca Histórica de la Universidad Complutense de Madrid. The call numbers (*signaturas*) indicate the most immediate holdings history of a given volume from within the library system to the Biblioteca Histórica [Complutense BH in all subsequent references]: BH DER [Derecho] for Faculty of Law, BH FLL [Filosofía y Letras] for Philosophy and Letters, BH MED [Medicina] for the Medical School, BH FG [from the collection of Don Francisco Guerra], BH FOA [Fondo Antiguo] for Old Collection. Like the library at Salamanca, the Complutense was in its day, and still is, rich in Ficino holdings.

The Complutense BH holds two 1559 editions of Ficino's *De christiana religione* (BH DER 1531 (1), and BH FLL 9218). The latter is marked, in hand on the title page, as having belonged to the library of the Imperial College of the Company of Jesuits, and the former bears the ex libris of Alcalá's Colegio Mayor San Ildefonso, as well as a handwritten notation dated 1705 that confirms the volume was, on that date, in the library of the Company of Jesuits at Alcalá. This composite volume combines the 1559 *De religione*, which is the first text in the volume, with a later work dated to 1649 and titled *Life, Passion and Death of Christ by martyr Dionysius Areopagite.*[29] Handwritten on the last page of the combined volume, in what seems to be the same hand that penned the 1705 Company of Jesuits property information, is a critique of the Italian philosopher: "Ficino is not an author of solid merit: he accepted the dreams of predictive astrology, as did all those of his era: he wanted to make Plato, Plotinus, and others Christians."[30] The statement is signed with what appears to be a large letter 'B' (figure 13).

Judicial [predictive] astrology was one key point on which Spaniards would begin to reject Ficino's writings. The topic, contentious throughout the Renaissance, was quite polemical by the end of the sixteenth century and, writing in 1705, this librarian illustrates that point. He also, however, recognizes that Ficino was not alone in the belief; to the contrary, he identifies it as a common error of Ficino's day.

Another volume held by Complutense BH is a 1568 Florence edition of Ficino's *De religione* in "Lingua Toscana," with an introductory letter from Jacopo Giunti to Piero de' Medici (BH FLL 9263). In this copy chapter 4, which begins with Ficino's statement that all religions are good as they all praise God, is completely lined through: title and all, with the sole exception of the number 4 (figure 14).

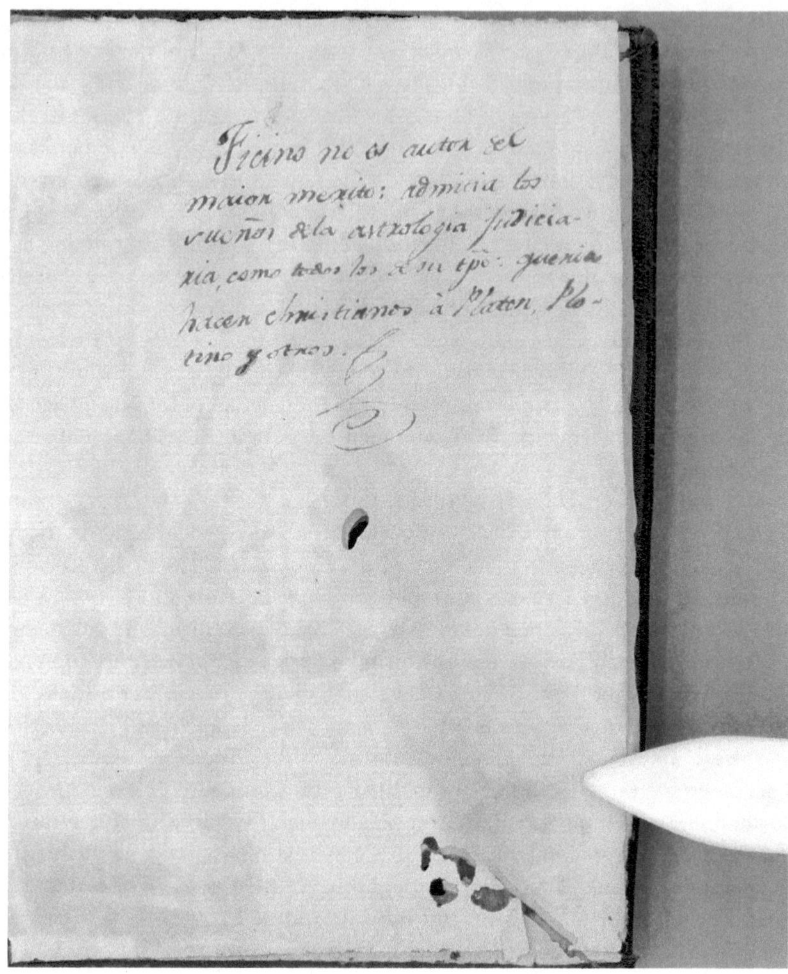
Ficino no es autor del
maior merito: admitia los
sueños dela astrologia judiciaria, como todos los de su tpo: queria
hacer christianos à Platon, Plotino y otros.

Figure 13. Critical commentary of Ficino on last page of composite volume. Courtesy of the Biblioteca de la Universidad Complutense de Madrid. BH FLL 9218.

Hankins (2008a) speaks of Ficino's rather unorthodox posture in asking that all religious creeds be accepted as valid. Other volumes of the same text (*De religione*) in Latin, held today in the same library, are not censored in any way. When this copy was altered is not clear but it was done, apparently, by someone acting

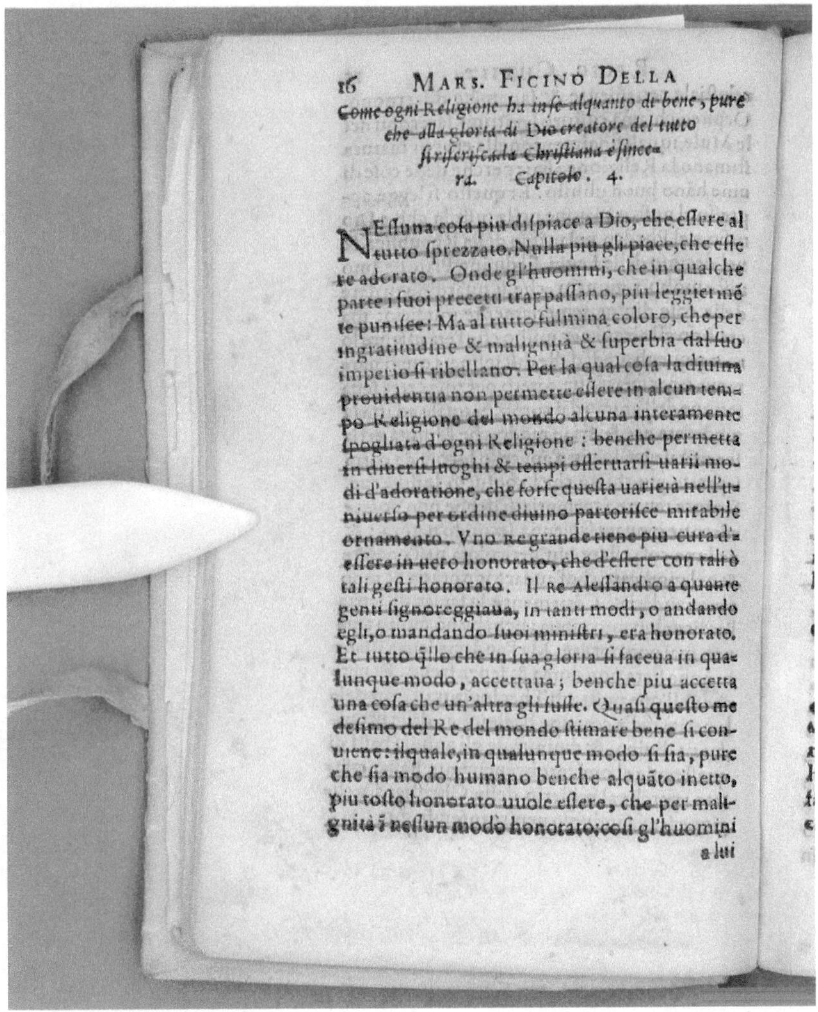
16 MARS. FICINO DELLA

Come ogni Religione ha in se alquanto di bene, pure che alla gloria di Dio creatore del tutto si riferisca, la Christiana è sincera. Capitolo. 4.

NEssuna cosa piu dispiace a Dio, che essere al tutto sprezzato. Nulla piu gli piace, che essere adorato. Onde gl'huomini, che in qualche parte i suoi precetti trappassano, piu leggiermẽte punisce: Ma al tutto fulmina coloro, che per ingratitudine & malignità & superbia dal suo imperio si ribellano. Per la qual cosa la diuina prouidentia non permette essere in alcun tempo Religione del mondo alcuna interamente spogliata d'ogni Religione: benche permetta in diuersi luoghi & tempi osseruarsi uarii modi d'adoratione, che forse questa uarietà nell'uniuerso per ordine diuino partorisce mirabile ornamento. Vno Re grande tiene piu cura d'essere in uero honorato, che d'essere con tali ò tali gesti honorato. Il Re Alessandro a quante genti signoreggiaua, in tanti modi, o andando egli, o mandando suoi ministri, era honorato. Et tutto q̃llo che in sua gloria si faceua in qualunque modo, accettaua; benche piu accetta una cosa che un'altra gli fusse. Quasi questo medesimo del Re del mondo stimare bene si conuiene: ilquale, in qualunque modo si sia, pure che sia modo humano benche alquãto inetto, piu tosto honorato uuole essere, che per malignità ĩ nessun modo honorato: cosi gl'huomini a lui

Figure 14. First page of chapter 4 of Ficino's *De christiana religione*, showing censorship. Courtesy of the Biblioteca de la Universidad Complutense de Madrid. BH FLL 9263.

independently, as the *De religione* was not on the Indices of prohibited works. Bound with this Italian *De christiana religione* is Ficino's *De vita* in Italian, with multiple marginal notes and underlinings throughout and, inside the back cover, a hand-penned schematic of angelic hierarchies (figure 15).

Figure 15. Schematic of angelic hierarchies on page 428 of Ficino's *De christiana religione*. Courtesy of the Biblioteca de la Universidad Complutense de Madrid. BH FLL 9263.

The writing, difficult to discern even in the original, reads:

1ª Hierarchia

orden	1. Seraphines ...		Por si mismo
Consideran	2. Cherubines ...	al Padre	Generavit
	3. Tronos ...		producavit

2ª Hierarchia

	1. Dominaciones ...		[illegible]
consideran	2. Virtudes ...	al Hijo	nascente
	3. Potestades ...		producente

3ª Hierarchia

	1. Principados ...		En si mismo
consideran	2. Arcángeles ...	al Spíritus	derivante
	3. Ángeles ...		procedente

The schematic is that of pseudo-Dionysius Areopagite who, in the *Celestial Hierarchy*, adapted the Neoplatonic order of beings to Christianity: "There were three hierarchies each containing three choirs: Seraphim, Cherubim, and Thrones; Dominions, Virtues, and Powers; Principalities, Archangels, and Angels" (Allen 1975, 219–20). On examination, I was unable to determine if the hierarchical chart of angels was penned by the same hand that lined through the chapter on the validity of all religions.

The Complutense BH also holds nine individual copies of Ficino's *De vita*, in the following editions: 1518 Venice, 1529 Basel [Io. Beb.], 1532 Basel, 1547 Paris (2 copies, different publishers), 1549 Basel, 1560 Lyon, 1567 Lyon, and the 1568 edition of the Italian translation mentioned above. A number of these volumes have underlinings and marginal notations calling attention to certain sections, in agreement or disagreement with a proposed remedy. None, however, are missing Book 3, nor are they marked with censors' prohibitions. As a matter of fact, the 1529 Basel edition at one point lost the printed pages for the last sections of Book 2 (pp. 97–120) and that section was replaced by handwritten pages. The volume's printed pages pick up again at p. 113 with the beginning of Book 3. This volume has been digitized and can be accessed through the library website. Some of these *De vita* volumes are signed with personal names: a copy of the 1529 Basel edition [BH MED 1234] is signed by one Doctor Oliva with the date 1592. A copy of the 1547 Paris Gaultherot edition [BH FG 900] bears the personal ex libris of Prof. Dr Césare Dubler, and also a handwritten notation identifying it as volume number 100 of the Collegio Ballearis Montis Sion Soc[iety] of Jesu[its]; this volume is particularly well-worn, and at one point its leather tie-straps were replaced. The last page has a handwritten prayer that begins "Lauda mater cortesia ..." (see figure 16). The volume came into the Complutense BH in 2006, from the library of Don Francisco Guerra.

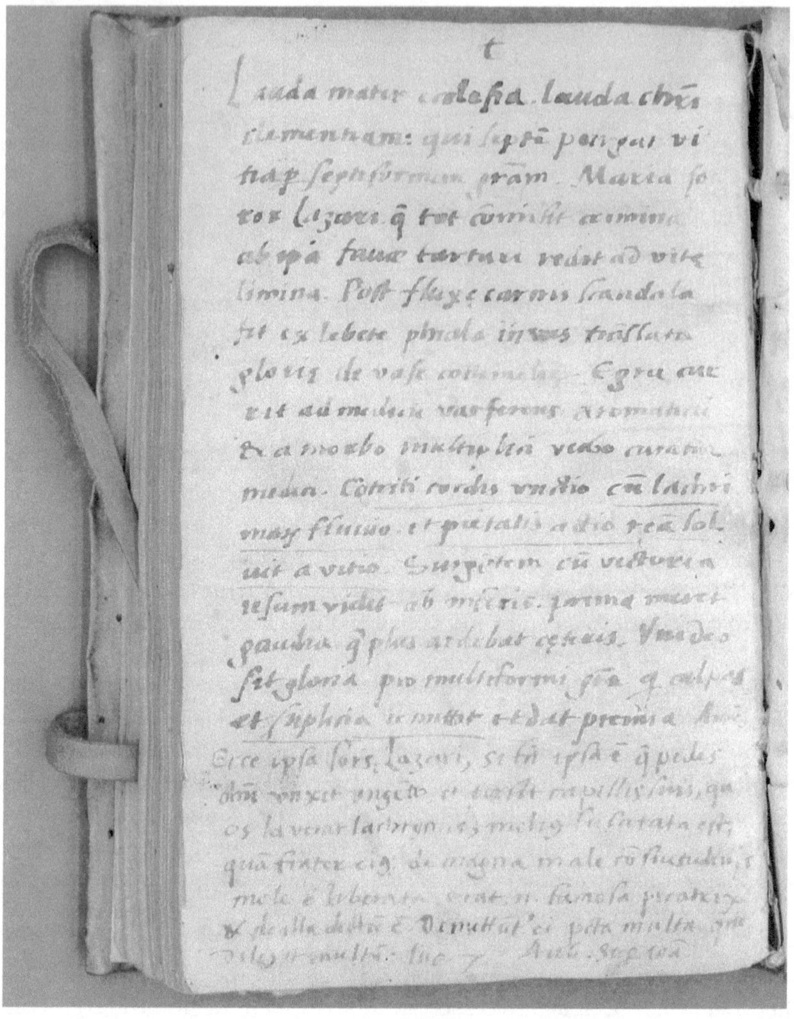

Figure 16. Handwritten prayer on last page of Ficino's *De triplici vita.* Courtesy of the Biblioteca de la Universidad Complutense de Madrid. BH FG 900.

The second 1547 Paris *De vita* (BH MED 386) in the library is the Guillard edition. Handwritten on its title page is "Collegio Theologo" and, in the same hand, the signature of D. Julián [Sánchez de] Villegas, as well as another ex libris: "I am from the Library of the College of the Conception at Alcalá."[31] Another

De vita copy (BH MED 385) is the 1549 Basel edition in a composite volume that combines the *De vita* with Ficino's treatise on the plague, titled *De peste*, and three additional works on diet and health by authors Pauli Aeginetae (seventh-century Greek physician), Gulielmo Insulano Menapio (sixteenth-century), and Ioanne Guinterio Antoniaceno (Johannes Guinterious of Andernach, sixteenth century). BH MED 1278 is a copy of the 1560 Lyon edition of *De vita*, with an owner's signature on the frontispiece, partially crossed out but legible as Licenciado Antonio Jacinto de Jaraba.[32] BH FG 906 was signed by one D[on] Estevan de Aguilar, and has marginal glosses and underlinings. Based on the marginal notations in these various volumes, the Spaniards who held them were very interested in the sections on theriac, the elusive catch-all antidote to poison. Two more volumes once held by the School of Medicine also show pragmatic debates on the plague: a 1518 copy of the Paris edition of Ficino's treatise *De epidemiae morbo* ... (BH MED 1827), as a stand-alone in Latin translation from the Italian, and a 1577 rebuttal (BH MED 2008) to the same Ficino treatise. The title of the latter claims to "rebut the opinion of Marsilio Ficino," as well as "the major part of all writings on the universal plague" (Dialoghi sopra le cause della peste vnivsale [*sic*] Di M. Alessandro Puccinelli Fisico Lucchese, Ne' quali con verissime ragioni, non solamente si reproua l'opinione de Marsilio Ficino, seguita dalla maggior parte delli Scrittor sopra la detta Peste vniversale; ma s'insegnano ancor le regole apparenenti alla preseruatione di essa).

The Complutense BH also holds a number of copies of the 1576 edition of Ficino's *Opera omnia*: one copy of volume 1 only, held in two different parts, BH FLL 17540 (part one of volume 1), and BH FLL 14917 (part two of volume 1), both bearing the ex libris of the Colegio Imperial de la Compañía de Jesuitas, but no other extraneous marks. BH DER 2166 is the Gnomology with which volume 1 of Ficino's *Opera* ends, followed by volume 2 of the same edition, identified as having belonged, in 1705, to the library of the Company of Jesuits at Alcalá. BH FLL 16837 is another copy of the Gnomology, followed by volume 2 of the full edition, although it ends abruptly on page 1536, absent the pages containing the treatises by Plotinus and Theophrastus, as well as the *Pimander* and *Asclepius*. This volume is also marked as having belonged to the Colegio Imperial de la Compañía de Jesuitas.

Volumes 1 and 2 of Ficino's collected letters are held in Figliucci's 1563 [1549] Italian translation: BH FLL 28325 (books 1–5 of the letters), and BH FLL 28326 (books 6–12). These volumes are also marked as having belonged to the Colegio Imperial de la Compañía de Jesuitas, and the first page of volume 1 has a handwritten ex libris of "Francisco de Monegro, chaplain of our monarchs" (*De Francisco de Monegro capellán delos reyes nuestros*), which allows for some precision in dating its reader-owner: Francisco de Monegro lived from 1531 to 1606, and was a chaplain in Toledo (Marías 1985, 117). The Complutense BH also holds two copies of Ficino's *Platonic Theology*, both in the deluxe 1559 edition (BH FLL 23578 and BH DER 1607). The first belonged to the Casa Profesa [religious house] of the Company of Jesuits at Madrid, and the second to the Company of Jesuits at Alcalá; this last volume evidences handwritten marginal notations and underlinings.

Ficino's translations are also well represented in the Complutense BH: one composite volume identified on its spine as Arnobius Commentary in Psalms includes, following commentaries on the Psalms by Arnobius and Erasmus, Ficino's translation of Dionysius's *Mystic Theology* (BH DER 972 (2)). The volume bears two ex libris from Colleges at Alcalá: Colegio Teólogo and Colegio de la Concepción. The first half of the volume was expurgated by one Francisco Gómez who offers details on the inside back cover:

> In the city of Santiago on the 9th of October of 1585 I, Doctor Francisco Gómez, Canon and Professor of Theology in the sacred Church and University of said city ~~corrected thi~~ [deletion in original] Commissioner and Qualifier of the Holy Office [of the Inquisition], corrected this book in conformance with the new catalogue [Index of Prohibited Books] of last year, 1584, and in truth to such I sign below
> D. gómez[33]

Francisco Gómez's emendations are fairly minor, as he simply pens "*author damnatus*" alongside any textual indication of Erasmus's name. The Arnobius/ Erasmus commentaries, published in 1522, are signed on the title page by the same Julián Sánchez de Villegas whose name is found on a number of the volumes identified as having belonged to the Colegio Teólogo at Alcalá. The second treatise bound in this volume is Erasmus's Commentary on Psalms, bearing a handwritten note, "this is expurgated 1640." This second round of emendations to the text, following those of Gómez in 1585, includes selective lining through of certain passages, and one paragraph-sized selection pasted over with a piece of blank paper. The final treatise in the volume, Ficino's *Praeclarum opusculum Dyonisij Areopagite de Mystica Theologia. et de diuinis nominibus Marsilio Ficino interprete impressioneque noua luculentum*, is the only Ficino text in the volume and it is not marked in any way, nor is its presence in the volume indicated in the catalogue listing. The 1585 signature with date verifies that the three works had been bound together prior to that time, and the lack of expurgations or markings on Ficino's treatise confirms that the Italian philosopher was still considered an orthodox thinker at the time of both rounds of censorship, 1585 and 1640.

A 1503 edition of the complete works of Dionysius (*Pseudo Dionisio Areopagita*) bears the ex libris of the Biblioteca Complutense, as well as a handwritten notation identifying it as belonging at one time to the Company of Jesuits at Alcalá. In this volume, there are minimal marginal indexing notations. The library also holds one copy of the 1577 Lyon Iamblichus (BH DER 1225), also with ex libris Biblioteca Complutense. A number of editions of Ficino's translation of the *Opera omnia* of Plato are held by the Complutense BH. The earliest is the 1532 Basel edition (BH FLL 15938), held at one point by the Colegio Teólogo at Alcalá, with a handwritten signature of the same Licenciado Julián Sánchez de Villegas mentioned above. This volume is heavily annotated with marginal notes and commentary in at least three different hands and, as is the norm in these volumes, the most heavily annotated sections are Ficino's commentaries [Argumenta].[34] In the 1539 Basel edition (BH FLL 15903), Simon Grynaeus has been censored:

> Simon Grynaeus Lutheranus, Aucthor Damnatus, hoc opus permissum
> Ex Commiss^{e}. Inquisitionij.
> Sr. Claudio Adolfo de Malboan,
> Socii Jesuiti

This volume bears another signature, by one D. Emilio [illegible last name] and, again, marginal notes and markings mostly alongside Ficino's commentaries. The library holds one copy each of Ficino's *Platonis Opera omnia* in the following editions: the 1557 Lyon edition (BH DER 2963), held at one point by the Colegio Teólogo at Alcalá and signed by Julián Sánchez de Villegas; the 1571 [1570] Venice edition (BH FLL 15944); the 1588 Lyon edition (BH FLL 26783), missing title page and preliminaries. The 1592 Stoer edition is represented with one partial copy of volume 1, which ends at page 864 (BH FLL 16100), and one partial copy of volume 3, missing pages 1171–97 (BH FLL 17259). A later, bilingual Greek-Latin edition of a selection of Plato's *Opera omnia* that used as its base text Ficino's Latin translations, published by Joannes Hayes at Cambridge in 1673, bears the ex libris of the Biblioteca Complutense and the signature of one William Milnore (BH DER 10695).

The Complutense BH catalogue also includes two incunabula of Ficino's translation of Plotinus's *Enneads*, both the deluxe 1492 Florence edition. BH INC FL-20 is identified on its frontispiece as the property of the library of the Casa Profesa of the Company of Jesuits at Madrid, and bears a few marginal indexing-type notations. BH INC I-256 is a second copy, with initial letters decorated very intricately at the start then more simply, with just preliminary colour tracings, throughout the volume. The title page confirms that the volume belonged to the library of "this Collegio mayor de Alcalá Soc[iety] of J[esuits]," and there are marginal notes contesting certain sections: for example, "Error" is written next to Ennead II, chapter 3.8, by a section on magic as a divine art conceded to man so as to allow him to overcome fate.[35] The Ficino commentaries are highlighted – "Arg[umentum] M[arsilii]" in the margins – to call attention to them. On the final leaf, where Ficino's 9 May 1492 letter to Piero de' Medici ends, there is another handwritten notation: "offered in memory of Pedro de Mota" (pertinet ad memoriam Petrum de Mota) (BH INC I-256), a figure I have not been able to identify.

The Complutense BH also holds a number of editions of Ficino's translation of the *Pimander*: one copy of the 1494 Paris Hopyl edition that bears two ex libris, Biblioteca Complutense [San] Ildefonsina, and Librería del Collegio maior, both at Alcalá. That same page holds what appears to be a censor's notation clearing the work in 1614, that says merely "seen 20 November 1614" (visto 20 Nbre 1614). There are two copies of the 1532 Basel edition, one with the marks of two colleges at Alcalá (Colegio Teólogo and Colegio de la Concepción), as well as the signature of Julián Sánchez de Villegas (BH DER 2455). This last is a one-volume edition of the *Pimander*, the *Asclepius*, the *Opuscula sanctissimis myteriis, ac uere coelestibus oraculis illustrissima*, the works of Iamblichus and Proclus, and *Quae omnia solerti cura repurgata, ac suo tandem candori restituta sunt.* Apart from the Sánchez de Villegas signature, the only other extraneous marking in the volume is a marginal line without commentary on pages 197–8 of the Iamblichus work, next to a section dealing with the differences between gods and daemons. The second copy of the same publication is marked as having belonged to the library of the Colegio Imperial of the Compañía de Jesuitas at Madrid, and has handwritten marginal indexing notes (BH FLL 6624). There is also one copy of the 1554 Paris, Turnèbe, bilingual Greek-Latin edition of the *Pimander*, missing the first half of the publication (the Greek text) (BH FLL 19709). The only ex libris in this volume, "Decanato de filosofía y letras, legado Camus," identifies it as having belonged to the private collection of a scholar of French origen, Alfredo Adolfo Camus (1797–1889), who was Professor of Greek and Latin Literature at the Complutense in Madrid beginning in 1848 (Romero Recio 2004, 31–2). Thus, this volume testifies to the continued existence of university faculty at the Complutense with an interest in Ficino's translations through the mid nineteenth century. There are also two different sixteenth-century French translations of the *Pimander*: one is a translation from the Greek by M. de Chastelnau, published in Paris in 1557 by d'Estiene Groulleau (BH MED 90). This volume, which includes not only the *Pimander* but also other Hermetic writings, came into the Complutense BH collection from the Real Colegio de San Carlos, which was founded in 1780. The second French translation, by Francois Monsieur de Foix, was published by S. Millanges in Bordeaux in 1579 and dedicated to the "Very exalted, very illustrious and very powerful princess, Marguerite of France, daughter and sister of very Christian Kings"[36] (Complutense BH DER 1847). In the dedication letter, Hermes is described as he whom the ancients called "thrice very-great" (trois fois tresgrand) and in the author's prologue, following Saint Augustine, he is identified as a pagan precursor to Christian philosophy (Foix 1579, f. 4r). This volume came into the current Complutense BH collection from the University Faculty of Law in 2000, and there are no earlier legible *ex-libris*. However, the dedication, penned and signed in 1578, the prologue, and the French title for this volume: *The Pimander of Hermes Trismegistus on Christian Philosophy, Knowledge of the Divine Word, and of the Excellence of God's Works*,[37] clearly illustrate how closely Hermes Trismegistus was identified with Christian philosophy, and the high regard in which he was held by Christian princes and kings at the end of the sixteenth century. The continued presence of the volumes in the later library collections demonstrates the persistence of Hermes's prestige. The *Pimander* is also included in the 1577 Iamblichus publication, and there are a number of alchemical works attributed to Hermes Trismegistus held by the library, in Latin and in French translation: the *Tabula smaragdina* is part of a 1545 edition titled *Alchemiae Gebri Arabi* (BH MED 126), and there is another 1541 edition of the same work (BH MED 2022); both the *Tabula smaragdina* and *Septem Tractatus* by Hermes are included in a 1566 Strasbourg publication titled *Ars Chemica* (BH MED 42); "De decubitu infirmorum" by Hermes is part of a volume by Thomas Boderio of the Rhotomagensis Dioecesis, published in Paris by Adoëni in 1555 and titled *De ratione & vsu dierum criticorum opus recens natum* (BH FLL 14839), in which Boderio claims to be publishing the unedited Hermetic work for the first time.

The markings and ex libris in these Ficino volumes held at the Complutense BH and at the University of Salamanca substantiate González de la Calle's statements regarding the Jesuits, whose library colleges at one time or another held quite a few of them. Pursuant to the 1599 Ratio Studiorum, which remained in effect for close to two hundred years, Plato was also read in the first and second curriculum levels at Jesuit schools, as part of the study of grammar and rhetoric (Bernad 1951, 5, 35, 39). The founder of the Jesuit order, Saint Ignatius of Loyola, himself studied at Alcalá de Henares. Even after the 1767 expulsion of the Order from Spain, these volumes continued to circulate having been, by the same order of expulsion, confiscated from the members of the Jesuit order as they went into exile, to be distributed for use in other libraries in Spain. They were not, however, prohibited. Beyond those library holdings, certain Ficinian ideas are prominently featured in writings by Spanish authors of the sixteenth and following centuries, as will be seen in what follows.

2 Ficino as Authority in Sixteenth-Century Spanish Letters

Spanish writers called Ficino "the great Marsilio Ficino" (el gran Marsilio Ficino) as early as 1508 (Ávila 2000, 353, v. 10416), and continued to praise him at the end of the same century: "great doctor and philosopher" (gran médico y filósofo) Marsilio Ficino in 1589 (Pineda 1963, 169:262)[1] and "prince of Platonic philosophers" (el príncipe de los filósofos platónicos) Marsilio Ficino in 1597 (Álvarez Miraval 1597, f. 155v). They described his "marvellous" commentaries on Plato (Arce de Otálora 1995 [1550]), referenced him as an excellent model for epistolary in Latin (Torquemada 1970 [1552]), disputed his medical remedies (Guevara 1994 [1529]), or praised them (Álvarez Miraval 1597), and questioned his mathematics (Núñez 1567). Most of these examples are expanded in dedicated sections below but two are not and so I include details on them here: on letter writing, Antonio de Torquemada offers Ficino as one of many "serious and esteemed authors" whose letters are full of doctrinal matters but also a delight to read (1970, 174),[2] and Álvarez Miraval references Ficino directly on the possibility of man sustaining himself on nothing but sun and air, a story attributed to Aristotle and told by Olimpiodorus "as related by Marsilio Ficino in his commentary on the *Phaedrus*" (1597, fol. 52v).[3] Álvarez Miraval also highlights Ficino's "very authoritative" commentaries (disertísimamente lo nota) regarding the use of Venereal acts to cure the Saturnian ills of melancholy (1597, fol. 109r).[4] This last reference is to Ficino's *De vita*, and the Spanish author specifies his source as Book 2, chapter 16, which is titled: "A Confirmation of the Aforesaid, and That We Should Avoid Both Continual Thinking and Sexual Intercourse" (Confirmatio superiorum; et quod devitare debemus assiduam cogitationem et coitum).

While explaining the meaning of the word 'theology,' Juan de Pineda (c. 1521–c. 1599) tells us that "Marsilio Ficino, speaking of a Platonic theology, says that poetry proceeds from neither art nor fortune but is, rather, a gift from God and the muses; that god being Apollo and the muses, the souls of the world spheres"

(Pineda 1963, 161:72).[5] Pineda accepts Ficino's combined Christian-Platonic doctrinal reading without criticism, and his dialogue's interlocutor continues to speak of poetry as philosophy: verse is an art that might at times deal in poetic fantasy but that, when directed to the "highest god" (sumo dios), "admits no fabulous, immoral turpitude" as "all the Doctors of the Church understand the divine mind [described by the pagan poets] to be the Son of God" (Pineda 1963, 161:73).[6] The tenets of the *pia philosophia*, with its concord between Christian and Platonic thought, are completely orthodox for this post-Tridentine, late sixteenth-century writer. The particular references to Ficino on topics we might today consider out of the mainstream are informative as to the unrestricted breadth and depth of Spanish authors' incorporation of the Italian philosopher's ideas. In what follows, the references are ordered by connection to specific texts or translations by Ficino although there are, at times, multiple intersections.

De triplici vita, Epistolae, *Platonic Theology*

The library holdings reviewed above show that Ficino's volume on the health of scholars, the esoteric *De triplici vita*,[7] had an immediate and long-lasting impact in Spain. Patrimonio lists six extant incunabula of this text, which "daringly combines philosophical, astrological, magical and psychiatric speculations" (Allen and Hankins 2001, xiv),[8] and was "attacked by various clerical enemies as a work of demonic magic and necromancy" (Boer 1980, xxi), but nonetheless published in 1489 after Ficino fended off the charges "successfully, if disingenuously, by asserting that he was presenting ancient views rather than his own" (Allen and Hankins 2001, xiv–xv). *De vita* "rightly announces itself as the first treatise on how to be an intellectual and still keep your health" and, in it, Ficino combines psychology, pharmacology, hygiene, astrology, philosophy, and occult speculation (Kaske and Clark 2002, 4). The volume is subdivided into three books: in the first, Ficino tells melancholic intellectuals how to have a healthy life and in the second, how to live a long life. Book 3 of the *De vita* is titled "On Obtaining Life from the Heavens" and ends with the Italian philosopher's apology for having repeated what might be taken as scandalous opinions that are, he insists, those of others rather than his own, followed by a Ficinian postscript on living a life free from care. Individual chapter titles in the three books sound like those found today in the Self-Help section of any bookstore: "The Nine Guides of Scholars," "Care for the Corporeal Spirit: Cultivate the Incorporeal," "The Medicine of the Magi for Old People," "On the Harmony of the World," and "On the Power of Words and Song for Capturing Celestial Benefits."[9]

It is interesting that despite the later disputes with Ficino's astrological beliefs, the volumes in the Complutense BH all include in uncensored condition Book 3, the most problematic treatise for Ficino, and the one for which he wrote an apology to protect himself against charges of heresy. Were one to accept the Burckhardtian version of Spain's backwardness and extreme adscription to the Inquisition, the expectation would be wholesale censorship of the astrological third book which not only deals with making one's life conform to the heavens, but also speaks of astrological-magical figures (talismans) fashioned so as to draw down the power of the stars. D.P. Walker noted the negative reaction of one late sixteenth-century Spanish author, Martín del Río, who criticized Ficino for not having censored some of these ideas in *De vita* (Walker 1975, 184–5), but in the copies held by the Complutense BH, this third book received scant attention and is barely annotated whereas much more frequent commentary is found alongside specific medical prescriptions in Book 2, indicating a more practical and less speculative approach to the volume.

On Magic Stones

In his *Silva de varia lección*, Pedro Mexía frequently relies on Ficino as an authority, and his twentieth-century editor Isaías Lerner notes the multiple references to precise places in Ficino's *De vita.* Here, on the marvellous properties of stones:

> It is due to man's curiosity that these [properties of stones] and other virtues of which we will speak in the next chapter have been discovered and observed; they are not called secret and occult because they are seen as untrue, given that most of them have been tested but, rather, because their primary cause is unknown ... Hermes and many other astrologers, and Marsilio Ficino agrees with them, attribute it all [the properties] to the stars and celestial figures; this is the most common opinion and we will follow it here. (Mexía 2003, book 1, chapter 39, 507–8)[10]

Mexía was named official chronicler to Charles V in 1547, and his *Silva* had wide circulation: first published in 1540, it was reprinted in more than 100 editions within 200 years (Lerner 2003, 12). Mexía's incorporation of information from Ficino's text led to wide circulation of those ideas in court, academic, and popular circles. For example, in a dialogue written in the first half of the sixteenth century by Spanish jurist Arce de Otálora (c. 1510–61), two characters who are law students at Salamanca frequently refer to the *Silva* as they discuss the magic properties of stones; one (named Pinciano) tells the other (Palatino) that he is following Pliny and Mexía (Arce de Otálora 1995, 1:298). The two characters use Mexía again when speaking of natural animosity or attraction between two persons, and when they decide to augment the topic with a discussion of natural affinities between persons and animals, they note that they will have to tell Mexía to add that to his *Silva* (Arce de Otálora 1995, 2:1012–23).

In his 1599 picaresque novel *Guzmán de Alfarache*, Mateo Alemán offers similar information on "occult properties" but expands the parallels from the animal kingdom to animosity between social classes:

> The peasantry always has a certain natural hate for the noble class, due to some occult property – much as does the lizard for the snake, the swan for the eagle, the rooster for the black partridge, the lobster for the octopus, the dolphin for the whale, oil for fish, the vine for cabbage, and others like this. Asked for a natural cause, we can only compare it to the magnet that attracts steel to itself, the heliotrope that follows the sun, the basilisk that kills by looking, swallowwort that helps sight. For due to celestial influence, some things naturally love each other, while others mutually hate: man has not yet found a reason for this. (2000, 1:251)[11]

This is a popularized version of how celestial influences determine certain actions and reactions on earth, that is, the focus of Book 3 of Ficino's *De vita*, although many of the particular comparisons and contrasts are also found in Pliny or Mexía, and Alemán does not directly reference Ficino. Other Spanish authors, however, do make their source clear: in 1589, Juan de Pineda relies on the Italian philosopher for the special properties of a different stone:

> Aelianus names many birds that know naturally and instinctually that evil eye exists, and they prevent against it by putting some tree branches in their nests ... although the eagles put the rock called eaglestone ... Marsilio Ficino, as a great doctor and philosopher, deals with these matters from their natural principles. (Pineda 1963, 169:262)[12]

Ficino speaks of the eaglestone [aetites] in *De vita*, where he says that it draws the power "to incite a quick and easy child-birth," as testified by "Rhazes, with Serapion confirming" (2002, 3.12, 301); Kaske and Clarke relate the information to the stone's legendary role in helping eagles bring forth their eggs (Ficino 2002, 440, n.8), a detail also found in Pliny's *Natural History*.[13] Ficino adds the astrological influence of Venus and the moon as reasons for the stone's efficacy, and returns to the idea in his apology to *De vita*: "snakes cure themselves with fennel; swallows cure their eyes with chelidonia; and eagles, when they have a hard time giving birth, have discovered by divine inspiration the eaglestone with which they successfully bring forth their eggs right away" (2002, Apology, 397).[14] Pineda, in the cited section of his work, is speaking of the soul's power to transcend corporeal evils brought on by enchantments; following the general reference to Ficino, he supports his argument with Saints Thomas and Paul, then returns to Ficino:

> I wish to perfect the above with what Marsilio says: that in youth, the blood is such that it generates clear, subtle, sweet, warm spirits but that, when one has come to old age those subtle parts of blood dissipate ... the spirits that emanate from such blood, taken in through the eyes, then exit the same way combined with the virtue of sight, and they poison those seen at close range. (Pineda 1963, 169:263)[15]

This reference to what "Marsilio says" is from Ficino's commentary on Plato's *Symposium*: "The blood in a young man is thin, clear, warm, and sweet, for [but] with increasing age, as the thinner parts are all spent, the blood becomes thicker and therefore darker" (Ficino 1944, 7.4).[16] Like Ficino in that place, and again referencing him as "Marsilio," Pineda relates the spirits to old men, menstruating women, and certain cases of youth of very "poor complexion" (tan mala complexión) (Pineda 1963, 169:263) all able to transmit these evil spirits to others through their eyes. Ficino offers similar opinions in *De vita* 3.16, speaking about "how quickly an inflamed eye afflicts whoever looks at it ... [and how] certain families ... when they were angry, killed people by looking at them and that certain women in Scythia did this habitually" (Ficino 2002, 3.16, 325).[17] An interesting distinction is that here, Pineda uses Ficino's *De amore*, or Commentary to the *Symposium*, only as reference for the concept of an evil eye. In his text, Ficino describes the "bewitchment" of love: "this vapor of blood, which is called spirit ... sends rays like itself through the eyes as though through glass windows"; that spirit enters through the eyes of another and "pierces the heart" (Ficino 1944, 7.4).[18] The Italian philosopher refers to Aristotle's comments on a menstruating woman looking at a mirror to explain the impact of the density of a surface: the mirror is hard, and so does not absorb the gaze but rather reflects drops of blood. However, adds Ficino in regard to the same power from one body to another, a boy can be bewitched by the "sight of a stinking old man or of a woman suffering her period" and "the sight of a youth bewitches an older person" but the humour of the old person is slow, and the spirits emanated cannot so bewitch the young (Ficino 1944, 7.4).[19] The two concepts, spirits that leave one body to enter another through the eyes, and the evil eye, from two different Ficino texts, are combined by Pineda so as to highlight the latter. More than just comment on Ficino's ideas, Pineda has processed the information and uses it independently. Kurtz has noted that "the sources Pineda adduces in his mythographic exegesis are as varied as the interpretations offered" (1986, 194), and the same can be said of his philosophical sources. For their part, Arce de Otálora's law students Pinciano and Palatino speak in a tone fully at odds with Ficino's seriousness of purpose and expression, although they also show respect for the Italian philosopher; for example, they take his advice on avoiding the evil eye of old women and sick persons, while accepting his explanation of how the subtle spirits of love penetrate through the eyes and reach the heart, in accordance with the specific complexion of the two parties (Arce de Otálora 1995, 2:1007).

In his 1605 popular picaresque novel *La pícara Justina*, Francisco López de Úbeda will repeat the eaglestone reference without attribution to Ficino and with a different tone and purpose:

> Seeing that you have a painted serpent, or dragon, the eagle's wings of my own daring wit fail me, and it seems that just as it is the wont of the dragon to soar up to the covered nest of the royal eagle where he places poison so as to take the life of its nestlings if, that is, the eagle has not made use of the precious eaglestone ... (López de Úbeda 1977, 1:122)[20]

López de Úbeda's reference makes clear that the information, from Pliny's *Natural History* and Ficino's *De vita*, at first incorporated into Spanish works in direct authorial references, had become by the early seventeenth century a part of popular folk-wisdom, an amusing bit to be included in a popular novel: eaglestone will ward off the evil eye, and evil acts. While López de Úbeda does not specify his source, he makes numerous references to Plato, as well as to the Neoplatonic figures of Asclepius as god of medicine and Mercury as god of the discrete and well-spoken, all used in his novel for witty analogy to the bleak situation of his down-at-the-heels protagonist. These specific adaptations for novelistic entertainment comport with what has been recognized as a key component of baroque style: ironic or burlesque commentary on the themes and figures of classical antiquity (Damiani 1980, 199). Ficino's translations made these writings the focus of scholarly commentary throughout the sixteenth century; by the early seventeenth, they had become a part of daily discourse and erudite entertainment for the Spanish reading public.

On Medicine

Ficino was well-respected as a medical authority by sixteenth-century Spanish authors: Mexía, for example, refers to *De vita*'s "wonderful prescriptions" on how to preserve memory.[21] In 1553, Alonso García Matamoros argues for improved medical treatises, and includes Ficino in a list of works that bear imitation in this regard (Green 1963, 2:230). In 1564, the city of Zaragoza suffers a plague, and bookseller Francisco Curteti translates and publishes at his own expense Ficino's *Consilio contra la pestilentia*, with the laudatory Spanish title *Book composed by the famous and exceptional philosopher and great doctor Marsilio Ficino, the Florentine.*[22] Curteti dedicates the entire volume, which privileges Ficino's text but also incorporates a few short treatises on the plague by other authors, to the "Jurados" or jury members, that is, the local medical board examiners, of Zaragoza.[23] The same Ficino text on the plague would be reprinted in Pamplona in 1598, by Mathias Mares at the behest of royal scribe Martín Gómez, with the same commendatory title.

Ficino's *De vita* was also read literally, as a medical text, by Spaniards who commented on specific prescriptions: in one copy held in the Complutense BH, a reader penned "non" in the margin by a particular stomach remedy at 1.11, the Latin "vide" (look) at 3.10 by a section on the power of Aries over the head and Taurus over the neck, and the Spanish "ojo" (look), without further comment, in the margin by Ficino's caveat regarding his own culpability in simply repeating what the ancients had said about the power of talismanic figures created by man to draw down the powers of the heavens, at 3.18 (BH MED 1233).[24] In the same library's 1532 copy of the work (BH MED 399), "Nota" is written four times in Book 3, once each in the margin by four different medical observations on the natural properties of specific substances: "licorice and rose-oil make colder things warm and hotter things cool" (3.6, 269); "By the same power cinquefoil resists poisons; one of its leaves drunk twice daily in wine cures the one-day fever" (3.12, 301–3); "as letters written with the fat of a goat on a stone, absolutely unseen, if the stone is submerged in vinegar, emerge and stick out as if they were sculptures" (3.18, 343); and

> just as the natural power and spirit, when it is strongest, not only immediately softens and dissolves the hardest food and soon renders harsh food sweet but also generates offspring outside of itself by the emission of the seminal spirit, so the vital and animal power, when it is most efficacious, not only acts powerfully on its own body when its spirit undergoes a very intense conception and agitation through song but soon also moves a neighboring body by emanation. (3.21, 359)[25]

The brief "look at this" notes call attention to these sections with no sign of approval or disapproval, although the mere fact of the "Nota" would seem to indicate the former. In the same copy (Complutense BH MED 399, Apologia), there is another marginal note next to a section about the power of love entering through the eyes (3.16), and two words in Ficino's Apologia are crossed out: "and images" (uel imagines), although the rest of the statement is left unmarked: "you too rise, O mighty Guicciardini, and reply to intellectual busybodies that Marsilio is not approving magic and images but recounting them in the course of an interpretation of Plotinus" (Ficino 2002, Apology, 397).[26] In a 1547 copy of the work (Complutense BH MED 386, Apologia), a number of passages are underlined, again without any sign of disapproval, with "Nota" penned in the margin by the section that reads: "while the Sun and Moon occupied the same degree in the second face of Leo; they reduced the bird to ashes and poured it into a lamp, whereupon the house seemed as a result to be full of serpents" (Ficino 2002, Apology, 399).[27]

The Spanish medical community was particularly interested in *De vita*'s sections on theriac, an antidote for multiple poisons first devised, according to tradition, by Mithridates, King of Pontus and Armenia minor in the first century BC. Legend has it that Mithridates's father was assasinated by poison and, to inure himself against the same fate, the son ingested small doses of poisons over time, eventually developing a multipronged antidote. Ficino comments on the powers and composition of theriac in the second book of *De vita*, and the multiple marginal notations in the Complutense BH's holdings attest to a heightened interest in this possibility among the Spanish medical community. Uses of theriac in sixteenth and seventeenth century Spain include the substance as a literal but also a moral antidote, that is, theriac protects against poison, against poisonous thoughts, and even against moral transgression: Antonio de Guevara (c. 1480–1545) notes that a good life functions as theriac to cure the ills of a Republic (1994, 1.35), and Baltasar Gracián (1601–58) offers the inverse perspective of "political theriac, as an antidote to prudence" (2001, f. 65v).[28]

A few Spaniards did dispute *De vita*'s prescriptions. Guevara derides all medical remedies from "the aphorisms of Hippocrates and Avicenna to the particular cases of Ficino, the compounds of Rhazes and the Canons of Herophilus" (Guevara 1950–2, 1:343).[29] The Spanish author's screed against the medical doctors of his day, however, neither privileges nor especially condemns Ficino, who is just one among all physicians vilified for malpractice and for failing to agree even among themselves (1950–2, 1:359). Bernardino Gómez Miedes (1515–89) disputes recommended cures for gout, with particular criticism for a practice that involves rubbing parts of the body with a marble or ebony comb. Gómez Miedes points out that although Galen, Ficino, and others recommend such bodily friction, they only mention it as a general good-health practice, and not for particular diseases like gout against which, in the Spanish physician's opinion, the remedy is ineffective (1589, f. 82r–v). Gómez Miedes is correct in his reading of *De vita*, in which Ficino recommends this type of massage but only as a daily practice for scholars:

> But before you get out of bed, first massage all your body for a while pleasantly with your palms, then massage your head with your nails, but a little more lightly. Let Hippocrates be your adviser in this matter. For he says that strong rubbing hardens

> the body; light, softens the body; much rubbing makes the body smaller, a moderate amount fills it out ... comb your head carefully and moderately with an ivory comb ... Then rub your neck with a rather rough cloth. (Ficino 2002, 1.8, 129–31)[30]

In contrast to Ficino, Gómez Miedes believes that the practice cannot be self-administered and so for "women, the elderly, and religious persons" it would be "dishonest" and "indecent" (1589, f. 83r).[31] As with Guevara's complaint about doctors in general, Gómez Miedes's dispute of this one specific remedy is not critical commentary of Ficino himself; the Italian philosopher is simply included as one of a number of recognized medical authorities on the practice, and in the fine company of Galen.

Other Spanish writers follow Ficino without hesitation or cavil. In his book on how to conserve one's health in body and soul, Álvarez Miraval sums up a section on contagion:

> We have learned the natural reason behind all that we have said on this from that great philosopher Marsilio Ficino in the third book, 23rd chapter, of his *De triplici vita*, where he says: "remember to strike up friendship with those persons who have heaven's blessings, whom you will know by their spiritual goods in fortune and body. For just as amber and musk emit and exude fragrance and odour, thus in no greater nor lesser way does good stick to one who communicates with the good." (1597, fol. 137r)[32]

Álvarez Miraval does not question the astrological or magical nature of the third book of *De vita*, nor the particulars of chapter 23, which includes advice on getting to know one's own "star" and "guardian daemon" through the "astrological art" as well as advising, as the Spaniard notes, to "go in the company of those to whom the celestial 'Graces' are propitious ... for just as odour from musk, so something good exhales from the good man to his neighbour and, once infused, often persists" (Ficino 2002, 3.23, 372–7).[33] The same author again references Ficino on the joining of soul to body: "Marsilio Ficino said that our mother, Nature, joined body and soul with such harmony and consonance that the body's movements penetrate easily and forcefully into the soul, as do those of the soul into the body" (Álvarez Miraval 1597, fol. 144r).[34] This reference is to *Platonic Theology* VI, in which Ficino argues that soul itself is substantial form and "not the body, but the body's inner bond or binding substance," and "a substantial form, simple, and indivisible, which through its power and natural art tempers the body's spirits, humors, and limbs" (2001–6, 6.8.3, 6.9.3).[35] Soul makes "bodies move in every direction"; soul and body together are a "complexion" (complexio) yet soul "is tied to no one quality and to no one movement of its own"; the emotions of the body "are motions of the rational soul" to which "the nature of the body is entirely subject"; and "with regard to our motions ... of those beginning from the body, some do not penetrate to the soul while others do penetrate" because "the body's passions can penetrate to the soul, not through the corporeal nature, but through the judgment of the soul itself" (Ficino 2001–6, 6.12.3; 7.7.2; 13.1.3; 13.1.5; 13.1.7).[36]

Following Ficino, Álvarez Miraval's medicine is both corporeal and incorporeal. Speaking on the therapeutic power of music, the Spaniard tells us that "Marsilio Ficino keenly noted, in the first book of his letters to Canigiani [Caluisiano] ... that music has a kind of hidden virtue or great efficacy to cure us of certain illnesses" (1597, fol. 162r).[37] While this specific point is also found in Plato's *Republic* and in Ficino's commentary to that dialogue, as well as in various other Ficino texts, Álvarez Miraval here confirms his knowledge of Ficino's *Epistolae*. Like Ficino, the Spaniard glosses over thorny aspects of astrological determinism by saying that he merely relies on the opinions of other very wise men, and he lists among them Saint Augustine, Pythagoras, and Ficino (1597, f. 347v). He also uses Ficino as an authority on prudence: "They say that prudence is perfected with time and long experience, along with observation of human events, as Marsilio Ficino writes" (1597, f. 224v).[38] Álvarez Miraval had apparently read a number of Ficino's writings and he uses the Italian philosopher not only for medical opinions but also as a model on how to placate contemporary authorities who might be troubled by certain ideas, noting that he merely repeats the observations of ancient wise men.

In his Spanish translation of Pliny's *Natural History*, first published in 1599, Jerónimo de Huerta (1573–1643) updates the text with references to more contemporary figures. In an edition printed in 1624 (vol. 1) and 1629 (vol. 2), printed marginal glosses add specific references to Plato in the *Timaeus*, Ficino in the *Platonic Theology*, Aristotle in *De caelo*, and Mela's *In principio historia orbis* [*De situ orbis*]. Ficino is referenced by full name in the Proemio, as one of a group of authors who denied the existence of multiple worlds (1624, 1:f. 3r),[39] then again by first name only as a medical authority to resolve the question of who might have been the inventor of medicine. Huerta reviews the opinions of Diodorus, Siculus, Macrobius, Pliny, Boccaccio, and Plutarch, to conclude that "beyond this wide diversity of opinions, the real truth is that it began with Adam, as noted by Marsilio and Origen" (Huerta 1624, 1:315).[40] Huerta's volume contains a marginal gloss indicating the precise place in Ficino's *Epistolae* and, in the referenced letter Ficino does review various opinions on the inventor of the medical arts, among them those who posit Adam and Apollo, although he does not specifically choose among them other than to say that the magic of soul's power over the body "appears to accord with the Hebrew and Christian view that through the initially healthy soul of Adam, the first father, all things were healthy" (Ficino 1975–<2012>, 3:24).[41]

Portuguese Hieronymite friar Héctor Pinto's (c. 1528–84) *Image of Christian Life* was first published in 1563, then printed in Castilian translation in 1571; all of the privileges to print, in all editions, comment specifically that the work has been found to be "Catholic" in all respects.[42] Pinto says that following Plato, he has structured his work in dialogue form, with full corroboration by divine authorities and approved, excellent authors: on his list is Marsilio Ficino (spelled Fiscino), along with a number of Ficino's translated Neoplatonist authors.[43] In a section on the necessary qualities of one who would govern, Pinto relates the story of Phidias the famous painter, who fixed the eye of his understanding on the perfect image of beauty so as to paint a work of extreme artifice: to this concept Pinto adds a defence of the Ideas along with Ficino's description of Plato as doctor of the soul:

> these figures traced in our conceit were called Ideas by the illustrious Plato ... who not only in Philosophy but also in eloquence eclipsed the memory of his predecessors, and taught men to flee from sensuality, such that the gentiles made an epitaph for him that said the god Apollo had two sons, Asclepius and Plato, Asclepius to cure bodies and Plato to cure souls (as related by Marsilio Ficino in Plato's life). (1595, 47r)[44]

In his Proem to *De vita*, which is a letter to Lorenzo de' Medici, Ficino identifies Galen as doctor of the body and Plato, doctor of the soul (2002, Proem, 103); in his summary of *Protagoras*, we read: "Phoebus begat two sons in particular ... Aesculapius to heal bodies, and Plato to heal souls" (2006, 65).[45] Apparently aware of possible concern over the Platonic Ideas, Pinto supports his argument with Saint Augustine, "who says that they exist, and that they have such force that no one will be wise who does not understand them" (1595, 47r).[46] Like Ficino, Pinto finds support for Platonic tenets in respected Church Fathers.

On Astrology

Writers of the late sixteenth century expressed many doubts about the value, efficacy, and legitimate nature of predictive astrology. Like Ficino, Álvarez Miraval recognizes medicine and astrology as two distinct yet related approaches to study of man and the world: he questions whether an illness is better cured by a medical doctor or an astrologer, then posits that reading portentious signs in nature so as to predict the future is parallel to studying a patient's symptoms in order to diagnose his illness. However, contrary to Ficino's general acceptance of the value of astrological cures and medicaments, Álvarez Miraval questions their use in the absence of independent proofs, on both physiological and moral grounds. For example, Ficino placed the mandrake root in the context of planetary linkages and astrological importance: "the force of Saturn, therefore, cautiously taken, will sometimes profit ... even those things which stupefy, as opium and mandrake" (Ficino 2002, 3.2, 253).[47] One hundred years later, Álvarez Miraval notes the root's literal effect on a human being, reviewing opinions from Demosthenes to Lucian, Pythagoras, Albertus Magnus, and Dioscorides, so as to warn against the mandrake's narcotic properties and compare it to worldly delights that intoxicate men into a "fantastic and profound dream" (phantástico y profundíssimo sueño) from which they should awaken so as to live sensibly, following the example of the sun whose movement through the day is consistent and well-planned (Álvarez Miraval 1597, f. 395r). The planets are still a touchpoint, but the mandrake is an opiate without connection to them. Rather than finding in the root's shape and properties an incentive to draw down the power of the heavens as Ficino advises in *De vita*, Álvarez Miraval connects the observed scientific effects of the root to a Christian moral message. Ficino is incorporated, but also adapted.

A ship's manifesto dated June 1600 for a vessel leaving Seville shows that Luis de Padilla sent, on the ship Trinidad bound for New Spain, one copy of *De vita* (no. 330), along with a two-volume set of Ficino's *Opera omnia* in Latin (no. 595), and other volumes of authors translated by Ficino (Plato, Iamblichus) (Leonard 1992, appendix, document 5).[48] I have not extended my hands-on bibliographical search for Ficino-related volumes to Ibero-American libraries, but currently available electronic catalogues do list fifteenth- and sixteenth-century publications of those volumes held today: for example, one 1576 Basel edition and one 1588 Lyon edition of Ficino's *Platonis Opera omnia* are held by the library of the Universidad Nacional Autónoma of Mexico; the former bears the ex libris of the Convento de Nuestra Señora de la Merced, first founded in the city of Mexico in the early seventeenth century and the latter, the ex libris of the Bibliotheca Turriana, the first public library of Mexico, originally attached to the Cathedral in Mexico City and offically established in 1788 with volumes from a number of private collections (Weigand and Davis 1994, 432). The same library (UNAM, Mexico) also holds one copy of the 1568 Florence edition of *De christiana religione*, and the Biblioteca Nacional de Perú holds one copy of the two-volume 1576 Basel edition of Ficino's *Platonis Opera omnia*. The electronic catalogue of the Fundação Biblioteca Nacional in Brazil includes one copy of the 1497 Nuremburg edition of Ficino's *Epistolae*, the 1550 Lyon *Platonis Opera omnia* in five volumes, and one 1581 Venice edition of the *Platonis Opera omnia*.

What is quite clear is that Ficino's volumes had an impact in the New World: Hermetic elements in the writings of Sor Juana Inés de la Cruz have been studied (Beaupied 1988). In the late seventeenth century, a well-regarded Mexican intellectual and Jesuit, University of Mexico professor Carlos de Sigüenza y Góngora (1645–1700), directly referenced Ficino on astrology:

> Without a doubt, this was why credit was given to the prophecies of Apollonius of Tyana, as Hiarchas recognized when he said: "No one should wonder, O Apollonius, that you have acquired the knowledge of divination, since you bear in your soul so much ether," as Marsilio Ficino states in *De Triplici Vita*. (Sigüenza y Góngora 1959, 171)[49]

The citation is to *De vita* 3.3, where Ficino speaks on the "spirit of the world" through which "the World Soul gives birth to the four elements," and notes that "Hiarchas the Indian testified that Apollonius of Tyana drank of this spirit in great abundance," followed by the quote as repeated above (Ficino 2002, 3.3, 257).[50] Sigüenza y Góngora's opening – "without a doubt" – is followed by the attribution to Ficino, but he adds a subsequent critical doubt on astrological prediction in general, based on the natural skills of the practitioner: "and this is the first principle that might falsify astrological prognostication, for even if this science were most perfect, if an organic proclivity for fantasy is lacking, prophecy will be futile" (Sigüenza y Góngora 1959, 171).[51] The problem with astrology, explains the Mexican professor, is that not everyone has the proper natural (and God-given) talent to practise it and he adds, quoting Ptolemy, that not even a good education can compensate for that: "The soul that is more apt for knowledge will attain a higher level of truth than that which has trained, albeit to a greater degree, in the science" (1959, 171).[52] Sigúenza y Góngora wrote his treatise in response to debates on the significance of a comet that appeared in 1680, responding with a "bibliographical arsenal" (arsenal bibliográfico) (Gaos 1959, v, xv) to those who claimed to be able to extrapolate the expectation of great evils from a comet's appearance. This arsenal included everyone from Aquinas and Cicero to Descartes and Ficino.

Shortly after this time, we find criticism of *De vita* in the writings of Benito Jerónimo Feijoo, who rebukes those who would accept astral influences, specifically in regard to talismans fashioned so as to attract and control celestial powers. Feijoo directly references and criticizes Ficino in the third book of *De vita*:

> 17. Those men who wish to make use, in the world, of the science that deals with astral influences point to a special type of secrets in the mysterious mixture of elemental and celestial things: this superstitious brainchild of the Platonic doctrine has made some men, who are in other respects very competent, delirious. This is how one should classify talk of planetary figures, the making of certain devices under determined [astrological] aspects, stamps bearing the images of constellations made in stone, metal, or other materials: Marsilio Ficino wrote many dreams about this in his book *De Vita caelitus comparanda*, following Psellus, Iamblichus, and other Pythagoreans. (Feijoo 1765, 2.5.17, 30)[53]

The criticism is of *De vita*'s third book. As I have noted, the copies held by the Complutense BH do not evidence much discussion of Book 3, although a gradual distancing from its talismanic counsel does become evident in the writings of later Spanish authors. Michael Allen points out that Ficino follows "Albert the Great and Aquinas ... [to] treat of the therapeutic powers of talismans and amulets when properly fashioned and inscribed, drawing upon scholastic notions of acquired form and the hylomorphic structuring of both corporeal and, *contra* Aquinas, of incorporeal entities" (Allen 2002a, xiv). By the late sixteenth century, some will be critical: Martín del Río (1551–1608) insists that talismans "have no natural power from figures, words, or planetary influences, and can produce effects only by demonic agency" although he does allow for an exception in the case of God granting "supernatural power" through "beneficence" or "grace" to Christian rites and liturgies (Walker 1975, 180–1).[54] On the other hand, del Río's contemporary Lope de Vega incorporates talismanic magic into his pastoral novel *La Arcadia* (de Armas 1983, 352–8). By the time Feijoo wrote, late seventeenth to early eighteenth century, these aspects of Ficino's work were being relegated to the category of "magic" or, as here, "dreams" deserving of scorn. Other shapes and figures, however, would continue to be considered special.

On the Figure of the Cross

In his *Silva*, Pedro Mexía writes: "And if we take a good look at this, they were right because, as Marsilio Ficino says about this in his *De triplici vita*, just looking at the cross as a shape, without any consideration other then its geometric shape, it is a perfect and excellent shape, given that it is equal in length and breadth" (2003, 1.3, 57).[55] Mexía supports the argument with the Egyptians (in general), followed by Rufino and Crinito,[56] then returns to Ficino, this time as "Marsilio, in the book cited above" (en el libro citado) [i.e., *De vita*] (2003, 1.3, 59).

Three quarters of a century later, in a work comparing Spanish and Latin orthography, Bartolomé Jiménez Patón (1569–1640) identifies the shape as that of the Greek letter 'thau' used to signal the foreheads of the penitent so as to protect them. He notes that the Egyptians also worship the sign, which is found on the chest of their god Serapis, that they perform cures on the basis of cross-shaped stars, and that "certain Arab doctors had this same faith, as Marsilio Ficino notes,"[57] supporting with further authorities Saints Augustine and Anthony, as well as the lay knights of the Order of Saint John (Jiménez Patón 1965, 63). Jiménez Patón's references and phrasing are found in the same book and chapter of Ficino's text, but are more explicit than the exact references used by Mexía, which demonstrates that this Spanish author also knew, independently of Mexía, Ficino's *De triplici vita*. By the early seventeenth century, Jiménez Patón was the "indisputable authority" (autoridad indiscutible) on all matters relating to the humanities in seventeen different towns of the zone of La Mancha and Jaén, and he was also a scribe for the Office of the Inquisition (Quilis and Rozas 1965, *lámina* 6, XLI). Jiménez Patón's friends, who included Lope de Vega and Francisco de Quevedo, frequently mentioned that his second surname, "Patón," was just one letter removed from "Platón" or Plato in Spanish (Quilis and Rozas 1965, XLII–XLIX). An introductory poem to the 1621 edition of another of the author's works highlights the same reference: "If from Patón to Platón/there is just one letter less" to explain: "because Patón, like Platón, teaches eloquence" although, the poetic voice insists, more eloquence with fewer letters (Martin 1987, 314, vv. 1–10).[58] Jiménez Patón also authored one of the approvals for publication of Thomas More's *Utopia*, in a 1637 Spanish translation (Quilis and Rozas 1965, LXIV). Like Mexía, his texts had wide circulation and through them, so did Ficino's name and ideas.

On Melancholy and Dogs

The importance of the melancholic humour in relation to creative intellect and/or pathological illness is a well-recognized factor in Renaissance writings (Klibansky 1979, Babb 1951). In *De vita*, Ficino writes the first medical guide for scholars, intellectuals, and artists ruled by Saturn and that planet's melancholic humour, alleging that given their work habits, these individuals need special care so as to live a long and productive life. Spaniards who followed Ficino in their "high estimation of the melancholy scholar" include both Huarte de San Juan and Miguel de Cervantes (1547–1616) (Soufas 1990, 21). Keitt links Huarte's arguments on prophecy and the "elevated soul" directly to Ficino's *Platonic Theology* (2013, 33–4), and Egido has noted that "in the age of Cervantes and Shakespeare, the *melancholic Spaniard* came to be as common a topic as the *splenetic Englishman*" (Egido 1994, 93).[59] Michael Allen has related Ficino's interest in the subject to Virgil's fourth eclogue, in which Tiphys is foretold to be the mysterious child through whom the new golden age will be reborn, and an echo of both Virgilian optimism and Ficinian melancholy is found in a dedicatory epigram to Miguel de Cervantes that is included in the author's *Viaje del Parnaso*. In this verse panegyric to Cervantes, Augustini de Casanate Rosas addresses the "proles Saturnia" or sons of Saturn, telling them to "shake their blue-tinged hide" and to "beat the four-stallion chariot of Tethys's sentient soul" in their pursuit of a new reasoned, intellectual verse.[60] They will be led to Delphi and Mount Parnassus by Miguel of Spain (Cervantes 1991, 57), that is, Cervantes is presented as Virgil's mysterious child, and his guide for the voyage to Parnassus will be Mercury.[61] The opening words of Ficino's *De vita* advise the same: "Anyone who enters upon that rough, arduous, and long journey which barely, at the last, by continual hardship leads through to the high temple of the nine Muses, seems to need exactly nine guides ... To begin with, in the heavens, Mercury either impels or exhorts us that we should undertake the journey in search of the Muses, since to Mercury is attributed the charge of every investigation" (Ficino 2002, 1.1, 109).[62] Egido has demonstrated the specific expression of melancholic memory in *Don Quijote* as evidence of Cervantes' rejection of the medieval rhetorical, mnemotechnical tradition in favour of memory as "mental force" (potencia anímica) for imagination and creation (Egido 1994). This is also Ficino's approach in *De vita*, in which the nine necessary guides for the journey to the Muses include three heavenly: Mercury, Phoebus, and Venus, as well as "three guides of this journey in the soul ... a fierce and firm will, sharpness of intelligence, and a tenacious memory," and three earthly: "a prudent father, a thoroughly accredited teacher, and a thoroughly experienced physician" (2002, 1.1, 109).[63] Black bile, the humoral cause of melancholy, "is congruent ... with Mercury and Saturn, of whom the second, the highest of planets, carries the investigator to the highest subjects ... especially when their soul ... is filled from above with divine influences and oracles, and it always invents new and unaccustomed things" (Ficino 2002, 1.6, 121–3).[64] The tenacious memory of melancholics is, for Ficino, accompanied by the "constant activity of their imagination" (imaginationis motus assiduus) (2002, 2.2, 169; ll. 17–18). Cervantes' model for Don Quijote shares those qualities of will, intelligence, and memory, along with an unmatched imagination. As for the author himself, in his *Viaje del Parnaso* he follows Ficino's advice in selecting Mercury as guide to the temple of the Muses.

A further, structural parallel to Ficino's *De vita* is found in Cervantes' *Coloquio de los perros*. Following his Apology to *De vita*, Ficino appends a letter written to "his most beloved brothers in the hunt for truth," with an analogy of men to hounds: "Aptly have I called men who philosophize 'hunters,' because they always labour, panting to encircle the truth. So are they aptly called hounds? 'Most aptly,' says Socrates in the *Republic*. For people who philosophize are either legitimate or illegitimate, and both are hounds" (Ficino 2002, Freedom from Care, 403).[65] Ficino asks his friends, "keen-nosed hounds of the Academy" to "go forth among wolves" and defend his book from attacks, adding that "among philosophers the hounds claim so much for themselves that not only have they infiltrated into any sect, but they have at some point made a sect of their own with their very name – 'Cynic'" (2002, Freedom from Care, 403).[66] Another Italian, Jacopo Mazzoni, also a contemporary of Cervantes and a friend of Torquato Tasso, similarly makes use of the canine analogy, calling Aristotle and Plato: "'two outstanding dogs'... exceptional barkers capable of laying open the truth with their sharp arguments and exposing the mysteries within" (Purnell 1971, 88).[67] Cervantes' *Coloquio de los perros*, in which two dog characters philosophize on life and society, is the final text of the author's *Novelas ejemplares* (Cervantes 1997a, 2:297–359). As did Ficino with his final letter to *De vita*, Cervantes places the story as the closing salvo for his collection of novels. The *Coloquio* has been read as a parody with variations of the picaresque genre (Sieber in Cervantes 1997a, 2:35–8; Riley 1997, 47–8), as a Menippean satire (Forcione 1984, 100), as a complex, profound "literary-novelesque revolution" (revolución literario-novelesca) (Rey Hazas 1983, 143), as an exploration of language, "grounded in desire, and ... therefore by its nature an instrument of deception" (El Saffar 1976, 88), and as "a complex game of mirrors, illusions, and philosophical as well as narrative refractions" (Clamurro 1997, 265). The novel can also be read in parallel to the canine analogies made by Ficino in his apology to *De vita*, and by Mazzoni in his comparison of the two Greek philosophers.

Cervantes' two dogs, Berganza and Cipión, muse on the meaning of life in a novel written in the form of a Platonic dialogue, with Cipión questioning Berganza on his experiences while both dogs extrapolate valuable lessons from the telling, particularly on the importance of language. Cervantes gives the dialogue a literary focus, as Cipión teaches Berganza how to tell a better story. The irony in the two discussants being four-legged animals instead of human beings calls into question human pride, and the exposition of the foibles of Berganza's various owners further blurs the supposed distinctions between rational men and irrational brutes. Cervantes differs from Ficino in that the two dogs state at the outset that reason distinguishes rational man from irrational beast (Cervantes 1997a, 2:299) whereas for Ficino, the distinguishing point is religion rather than reason (Hankins 2006, 148–9). The two authors agree, however, on other details. Ficino asks his friends to go forth "among wolves" (inter lupos), understood as men who might criticize the Italian philosopher (2002, Apology, 403, l. 14); Cervantes' characters literally state that certain men were themselves the wolves who attacked sheep they purportedly guarded (los pastores eran los lobos) (Cervantes 1997a, 2:311) as they note, throughout the novel, both the marvels and the dangers of speech. The principal focus for both authors is the importance of taking advantage of the time one has to live and speak well. One of Cervantes' dog-characters also echoes, albeit with a twist, Ficino's comment on the Cynics: "You call gossiping philosophy?... that will give us the name cynics, which means gossiping dogs" (Cervantes 1997a, 2:319).[68] The Spanish author's placement of the *Coloquio* as final salvo for his collection of novels can be seen as a parallel to Ficino's Apology although his characters are not so much friends of the author with a mission to protect him as alter egos bent on scornfully revealing deep truths about the human condition. Ficino's optimism is missing, having been replaced with Cervantine satire.

The *Platonic Theology* and the Commentaries on Plato's *Dialogues*

Certain specific references to Ficino's authority are brief and, as far as I have been able to determine, singular in Spanish letters, such as the following notice by Bartolomé de las Casas regarding sacrifices to Asclepius:

> Goats were sacrificed to Asclepius, the god of medicine because, as the natural philosophers say, the goat always has the fever that we call *calentura*. They also sacrificed roosters to him, to symbolize the vigilance a doctor should have ... this is referenced by Plato in book 29 of his dialogue *De animae inmortalitate*, at the end of that dialogue and, as Marsilio makes clear in his argument, Socrates understood the part about the rooster in an allegorical sense, because the rooster is messenger of the day and of the sun, that is, of the divine beneficence that cures all illnesses, called daughter of divine providence, and of the day to which is owed, as Socrates confesses, the light of the soul. (Casas, 1992, 2:1001)[69]

Referring to the Italian philosopher by first name only, Las Casas adds the qualification "allegorical" to what is, for the most part, a direct quote from Ficino's prefatory summary to the *Phaedo*: "To Aesculapius the physician, son of Apollo, the ancients used to sacrifice a cock, the herald of the day and the sun. In this way they were declaring that they owed daylight – the light of life – to that divine beneficence which heals all ills and which is called the daughter of divine providence" (Ficino 2006, 139).[70] In his own commentary on the *Phaedo*, published in 1556, Fox Morcillo repeats the same details, referencing only the general authority of the "Platonists" (2010, 200).[71] One other example of this type of stray, singular reference is the following counsel given by Pedro de Ribadeneira (1527–1611) in the last decade of the sixteenth century, on how to avoid heretics:

> Writing about Plato, Marsilio Ficino spoke seriously when he said that it is impious to have contact and communication with those who, for their sins, have been excommunicated and removed from sacred office; [this is] because, given that they are infected, one cannot help but be infected by them if in their presence. (Ribadeneira, 1788, 146)[72]

Ribadeneira's book is, as its full title makes clear, an anti-Machiavellian diatribe: *Treatise on Religion and the Virtues that a Christian Prince should have, and Against the Teachings of Nicholas Machiavelli and Contemporary Politicians*,[73] and below (chapter 6) I will further contextualize this writing in its reflection of the ideas in Plato's *Republic*. Most of those other writers, however, do not specifically mention Ficino in discussing the dialogue and its socio-political concepts, whereas Jesuit Ribadeneira unambiguously names Ficino as an authority on avoiding heretics like Machiavelli, who was, says the Jesuit: "impious, without God, and so his doctrine (like water from an infected well), is cloudy, poisonous, and able to infect those who drink from it" (1788, I).[74] Among the many authors cited by Ribadeneira (biblical, classical, saints, prophets, kings, philosophers, poets, popes, Church Fathers) figure a few translated by Ficino: Iamblichus, Hermes Trismegistus, and "the divine Plato" (el Divino Platón), as well as Ficino himself (Ribadeneira 1788, 10–11). Far from controversial, Ficino is proposed as a model of rectitude on this philosophical-political topic.

On Daemons and Genii

In his 1490 Latin-Castilian vocabulary, Alfonso de Palencia defines 'demon': "they say the Greeks used this word for those who were very learned and wise about things. So in Greek, a demon is a very wise man, and it is written with 'ae'" (Palencia 1967).[75] Writing contemporaneously with Palencia, Antonio de Nebrija notes the Greek spelling "daemon" but adds that written without the dipthong, as "demon," the word signifies "devil" (Nebrija 1951). At the beginning of the seventeenth century, Covarrubias offers the etymology of the Spanish *demonio* as from the Greek daemon, notes that "Plato calls the God-Governor of the universe the Great Daemon," and stresses that in Greek, "the word means spirit or angel, indifferently good or bad" but "in the Sacred Letters, demon is always taken for evil spirit or slanderous devil" (Covarrubias 1994).[76] Ficino frequently uses the version with dipthong in his writings as, for example, in his translation of the *Pimander*'s description of those souls fortunate enough to rise to the chorus of daemons where they will sing happily forever (Ficino 1554, X). In the *Platonic Theology*, Ficino specifies that the good daemons "are called genii [because] they are tireless leaders of our own ingeniousness; and they lead us not by force but by persuasion" whereas the "bad daemons" are our "adversaries" (2001–6, 18.10.3).[77] The genii and the daemons are linked as guides for men and, in his commentary on the *Republic*, Ficino describes them: "The airy daemons thus remain as the intermediate guides through the intermediate realms, the companions of divine reason leading human reason along this journey" into the world of men (2009a, 67).[78] Michael Allen explains Ficino's use of the Latin term *ingenium* and its cognates, along with the etymologically related *gignere* ("to beget or create") and *genius* as "the attendant daemon or spirit that in Latin folklore watches over our begetting and birth and thereafter over our physical fortune and our eventual death," also in relation to the use and understanding of *habitus* for "character" and/ or "condition" (Allen 1994, 88). These same semantic distinctions were debated by sixteenth-century Spaniards.

Bartolomé de las Casas explores the etymology of the word 'genio,' using the singular with the sense of "genie" or "spirit" as he lists authorities and opinions on the subject from Plutarch, Censorino, and Servius to Virgil on the good guardian angel who accompanies us from birth (1992, 2:822–3). Las Casas notes that in Plutarch's *Life of Brutus*, a daemon is man's evil angel (1992, 2:822), and he further specifies that from reading Pliny he knows that Genio is god of the forehead (1992, 2:866). In the last third of the sixteenth century, Juan de Pineda addresses the same concept:

> Marsilio Ficino says that the doctrines of both astrologers and Platonic philosophers specify that each man might have two guardian angels: one for his birth and begetting, and the other for his habits; the one belonging to procreation must be the genie (speaking of each one's own) that the gentiles say each man has when he is begotten, and even the Socratic Euricles, and not Euclides (as some mistakenly assert), said that two genii are provided, one good and the other bad, and Empedocles and Menandro concede the same, as well as Lucilius, attested by Censorino and Servius. (Pineda 1963, 163.20)[79]

Pineda's direct reference to Ficino, with the same list of supporting authorities incorporated by Las Casas, suggests that the latter was also using the Italian philosopher as a base text. In his *Letters*, Ficino makes frequent reference to man's guardian angel who, "a good daemon and a guiding spirit, is either present everywhere at all times, as Plotinus, Porphyry and Iamblichus believe, or, like a ray of the sun, is easily and swiftly present wherever it wishes to be" (Ficino 1975–<2012>, 8:3).[80] The Italian philosopher points out that Michael Psellus "reconciles the Platonists with the Christians in their understanding of daemons,"[81] and tells Piero de' Medici that "the ancients believe that dreams are sent by daemons" (Ficino 1975–<2012>, 8:12; 8:17).[82] In his summary of the *Apology* of Socrates, Ficino speaks at length of "the nature of Socrates's daemon":

> it is fiery, because it raised him aloft to the contemplation of the divine. It is also Saturnian, because every day it wondrously withdrew the focus of his mind away from the body ... the lofty daemon, as the interpreter and messenger of God, inspired Socrates. But can we give the name of 'daemon' to the actual intellect of Socrates? Certainly we can. For Timaeus says that God has granted us the highest part of the soul as a daemon. Again, in the *Symposium*, the longing of the mind to contemplate divine beauty is called a daemon. (Ficino 2006, 124)[83]

This is the daemon as genie or inspiring force of man's intellect and, so, of his artistic creations. At the start of the sixteenth century, Garcilaso de la Vega writes:

"The customary course of ingenuity,/ although lacking the genie to move it,/ runs a bit with its haste" (1966, Eclogue II, vv. 948–50), and Fernando de Herrera glosses the verses by explaining that 'ingenuity' is "that strength, natural power, and innate ease of perception we have," adding that 'genie' is "a specific virtue, or particular property, of each living thing. One who thought that Aristotle's agent of understanding was the same as the Platonic genie would not be far off" (Herrera 2001, 860–1).[84] At the beginning of the seventeenth century, Lope de Vega explains: "the genie is ... that inclination that guides us more to one thing than to another, and so, to defraud the genie is to deny nature something it desires" (2002, 235).[85] Lope adds that in ancient times, one's genie would be placed on the forehead, so that others would know "if we do a thing willingly, or not" (2002, 235),[86] thus combining Pliny's Genio as god of the forehead with Ficino's Platonic genie as creative talent, what we now might call "having a genius" for something.

By the end of the sixteenth century, along with ever more rigorous explorations of writing as a profession and of literary genres, perceptions of Plato as reflected in Spanish letters also change. Consistently considered either a philosopher or a poet, late medieval and Renaissance writers vacillated in their descriptions and, at times, used both qualifiers. At the end of the fourteenth century Pero López de Ayala (1332–1407) stated that Plato was a philosopher, but Ayala's contemporary Alfonso de Villasandino (c. 1340/50–1424) identified the Greek philosopher as a poet, in a group with Virgil, Dante, and Horace. In the first half of the fifteenth century, Plato was recognized as a poet by Juan Alfonso de Baena (c. 1365–1435?) in his *Cancionero*, by Alfonso Martínez de Toledo (1398–1468) in the *Corbacho*, and by Juan Rodríguez del Padrón (1390–1450) in *Siervo libre de amor*, but by the second half of the fifteenth century and throughout the sixteenth, Plato was described mainly as a philosopher who wrote skilfully, thus masking his lessons in creative metaphor and allegory. Ficino, for example, considered Platonic poetry the perfect means with which to communicate philosophy (Allen 2002a, xvii), as evident overall in Plato's *Phaedrus* which "establishes poetry as the philosophic mode par excellence and the poetical style as the authentically Platonic style" (Allen 2008b, xx).

With the greater attention to and debates over literary genres at the end of the sixteenth century, Plato was identified by Spanish writers as both a model of divine inspiration, and a philosopher. Two late sixteenth-century authors offer divergent opinions: for Juan de Pineda, Plato is a philosopher (*Catálogo de quasi setecientos autores*) but Alonso López Pinciano (c. 1547–1627?) says "poet": "Lucan in his Pharsalia was a historian and Plato, in his dialogues, a poet" (1998, 1:83).[87] Cervantes points out that Plato exiled poets from his republic (2005, 2. 38), but also that he called them "interpreters of the gods" (intérpretes de los dioses) (1997a, 2:58). *Don Quijote*'s author puts Plato in a group with Aristotle and "all the horde of philosophers" (toda la caterva de filósofos) (2005, 1, Prólogo), and in another work uses him for ironic commentary: "The truth of this question/ will come from the groundlings [spectators in the theater's pit]/for such is there created/[with] the genius of Plato" (1984, vv. 2219–22).[88] A change in readings of the words *genio* and *ingenio* runs parallel to these developments. Plato, once philosopher and poet, will still be recognized as an "ingenious intellect" by the discipline that reads him for philosophical meaning, which is itself beginning to secularize, but he will be adopted as the "genie, inspiring voice" for Spanish writers, who at the end of the sixteenth century were experimenting with the possibility and forms of a new genre, creative imaginative writing in prose. They followed Ficino's perspective on poetry as philosophy, although not necessarily in verse, to invent fictitious worlds and so comment on their own. In our readings of those texts, we at times tend to privilege the creative letters over the philosophical content they mask. Nonetheless, it is there. Renaissance Spanish authors were more inclined to synthesize interdisciplinary ideas and generic models into their hybrid texts. Rather than exclude what might to us seem doctrinal material, they experimented with its incorporation into various prose and verse models.

On the Ideas

On the Ideas, Plato states: "If mind and true opinion are two distinct classes, then I say that there certainly are these self-existent ideas unperceived by sense, and apprehended only by the mind" (*Timaeus*, no pag.).[89] In the *Phaedo*, Plato further explains "[249E4] As we said, every man's soul has intuited the things that truly are, otherwise she would not have come to dwell in this animate being. But it is not easy for everyone to remember the things up there from the things that are down here ... just a few men, in approaching the images of these [Ideas], see the class [or Idea] of that which is merely being imaged" (Plato 2008, 1:xxvii).[90] Werner Beierwaltes clarifies: "Plato's Ideas are conceptualized as existing reasons and origins that ground and determine each individual existent, themselves being unchanging existents and at the same time thinking structures of a timeless, absolute Mind, and thus the point of reference between this Mind and the thinking that is identified with being" (2003, 269).

Ficino discusses the concept at length, calling the Platonic Idea the "rational principle" of a "nature," and linking it to his Christian God as a supreme Idea: "Thus the one essence of God is the one Idea that plays the role of all the Ideas, and through this unique Idea God ponders all things" (2001–6, 8.1.6; 16.1.12).[91] In his *Timaeus* commentary, Ficino compares Plato's statements on "the Idea of the Good" (ideam appellat boni) in the *Republic* and the Idea of "good things" (uero bonorum) in his letters to conclude: "and so he calls it the Idea of the Good itself and of those good things that come forth from the Good" (2010, 17; 1576, 2:1442).[92] God "understands all things through the one Idea of being or the good," which becomes multiplied in subsequently lesser creatures, so that the "first angel" directly below God in the hierarchy of being receives "perhaps two Ideas, the one of substance, the other of accident" (Ficino 2001–6, 16.1.14).[93] The process continues down through the angelic realms to the human soul which, "when it first emanates from God but is not yet clothed with a body ... will receive as many Ideas as there are species of created things, one Idea of each species" (16.1.16).[94] The "divine ray" of God, when it has descended into a human being in this world, "overflows with Ideas" and "in this matter it sketches out the last, particular, and shadowy likenesses of the Ideas in the manner light paints the images of colours in a mirror, or rather light outlines the shadows of bodies on the earth" (16.3.1).[95] That divine ray is also the inspiration for artistic creation, as it fills the human soul with the capacity to create, in imitation of God and his creation of the world.[96] Spanish authors would explore these concepts in prose and verse.

In the last tercet of Garcilaso de la Vega's Sonnet XXI, written to praise one "Illustrious Marquis" (Clarísimo Marqués), we read:

> and, finally, from only you did nature form
> one rare Idea, not visible to the world,
> thus making thought equal to art. (1966, Sonnet XXI, vv. 12–14)[97]

The identity of the dedicatee is still debated (Herrera 2001, 411; Heiple 267–75), but in 1580, Herrera glossed these verses by saying: "Idea is the first form, figure, and representation of a thing, which is like its appearance in all things. The Platonists say that it exists in mind, and they call Idea the exemplary and intelligible form. Because Plato asserted certain universal species of all singular things, that he called Ideas" (Herrera 2001, 412–13).[98] Herrera discusses Aristotle's opinion that the Ideas were conceit and illusion, substance inseparable from matter, versus that of Socrates and Plato who insisted that the two were separated, to conclude with Saint Augustine, who identified the Ideas with "principle, immutable forms ... contained in the divine inteligence" (Herrera 2001, 413).[99] Ficino comments the tenth book of the *Republic* with: "the Idea of the Good produces Ideas, which are the particular forms of all things, distinct one from another by type, within the intelligible nature ... All intellects look up to this intelligible nature and from it they receive the enduring exemplars of Ideas" (Ficino 2009a, 48).[100] For Garcilaso, just as God creates by thought, so nature created the Marquis in the world of man, thus equalling art to divine thought. This is the same Neoplatonic sequence laid out by Ficino in his commentaries on the *Timaeus* and the *Republic* (2010, chapter 10; 2009a, 48–50).

Writing in the last decades of the sixteenth century, Juan de Pineda explains the Ideas by saying that they are stored in the son of God, called "mind and archive of the Ideas ... because he was engendered by divine understanding, he is the subject of wisdom, and the Ideas are the primordial reasons to which God looks so as to understand and create things" (Pineda 1963, 169:150).[101] Pineda notes the opinion of "the most famous Trismegistus ... [who] says that idea comes from *Idin*, which means 'to see,' because they are invisible spiritual forms and, so, in the opposite sense, are called that" but adds that he is not convinced by this etymological explanation (Pineda 1963, 161:111).[102] The reference is not to Ficino's translation of Trismegistus's *Pimander* but rather to the *Asclepius*, available in Latin from the fourth century on, in which Hermes counsels that what man sees in the cosmic sphere "is called in Greek *Haides*, from *ideîn*, 'to see,' because the essence of the sphere is in-visible – the forms are also called 'ideas' to the extent that they are visible" (Renau Nebot 1999, 449).[103] According to Pineda's contemporary Malón de Chaide, the Ideas exist: "Because God, who is capable of everything, seems to paint in himself the ideas, or examples, of all things ... and these species of all things conceived in the supreme mind were called Ideas by Plato" (1959, 3, 87).[104] Héctor Pinto also describes the Ideas as "figures traced in mind, according to the illustrious Plato" (1595, 3.4, 47).[105] Malón de Chaide directly echoes Ficino, who explains that the divine mind "conceives within itself manifold Ideas from the warmth of the single and supernal light and of the Idea of the One" (2010, 17)[106] and, as quoted above, "sketches out" or "paints" those images in man's mind (Ficino 2001–6, 16.3.1).

Sixteenth-century Spanish poet Francisco de Aldana also follows Ficino to describe God and his creation:

> and so every creature exists in theory
> and obedience to the supreme Creator,
> but God, who has the same world
> made in himself, himself being not made,
> when he made it, when he placed it
> outside of himself, with the Idea remaining in him,
> He finished it so perfectly that
> the world is the same now as it was then, (1985, L, vv. 454–61)[107]

This is another basic construct of Ficino's Christian-Platonic synthesis: God as repository of the Ideas, who creates their image outside of himself (Ficino 1944, 128). Lope de Vega's protagonist Dorotea claims that nature taught her to love someone "before he had being" (antes de ser) by showing him to her when he was still "in his idea" (cuando estaba en su idea) (1996, 207). From Garcilaso's "one rare Idea" (1966, Sonnet XXI, v. 13) and Herrera's commentary on that verse work, through Pineda, Malón de Chaide, Pinto, Aldana, and Lope, sixteenth-century Spanish and Portuguese authors celebrated and adapted the concept of the Ideas.

On Free Will

Robert Kane studies the history of philosophical thought on free will and determinism from the pre-Socratic Empedocles through a resurgence of interest in the topic that began in the 1970s and continues today, noting the importance of St Augustine's *De Libero Arbitrio Voluntatis*, and speaking to seventeenth-century interest in the topic in England (1996, 5–14). During the Renaissance, however, a period that is not a focus for Kane, first with Lorenzo Valla (c. 1406–57) and Erasmus (1467? –1536), then in debates between Spaniards Domingo Bañez (1528–1604) and Luis de Molina (1535–1600), the problem of reconciling God's foreknowledge with man's free will was a consistent topic of concern.[108] In 1569, Torquemada used Ficino's authority to insist that planetary influences and the sun's rays shower men with only the good, and that man himself is the cause of any evil that might exist in the world. Torquemada cites at length from Ficino on the effects of the planets, referring first to authors either translated or referenced by the Italian philosopher: Iamblichus, Plotinus, Averröes, and then, as quoted below, directly to Ficino and Plato, to refute the idea that the planets are entirely deterministic of man's fate and to uphold his own role in his destiny:

> And Marsilio Ficino, in his commentary on the sixth dialogue of [Plato's] *De legibus*, says: "One thing we must keep in mind: all the force and movement of the superior bodies that descends into us is always, due to its nature, the cause of our good and guides us to the good; and so, we do not have to deem that the sadness and miserliness of ill-adjusted men comes from Saturn, [nor] ferocity and daring from Mars, nor tricks and maliciousness from Mercury, nor lascivious loves from Venus ... those who are under the beneficence that tends to result from the sun's rays can, due to their own fault in not knowing how to take advantage of it, be damaged, and also those who are under the influence (*fuerza*) of the stars, by their own nature good, might at times due to a vicious habit fall into or have evil fall onto them, notwithstanding that the [stars' own] inclination would lead them to the contrary effect." Following these words and the authority of Marsilio, the determinations of astrologers, mathematicians, and doctors are not well-founded and their opinions, although taken as commonly held, are not so well established nor do they have such force that with these

> [other] evident reasons they might not be reproached. (Torquemada 1994 [1569], 781–2)[109]

Francisco de Aldana offers the same concept in verse form, with the poetic voice of God speaking to his Son as his intermediary (*medio mío*) to tell him that much as the sun is situated in the middle of the seven spheres (*siete cielos*) and moves through the twelve signs of the zodiac (*los doce si[g]nos*) thus giving light to the stars:

> so you, my intermediary, should grant to men,
> for use against the seven evil spirits,
> seven sacred gifts of our love,
> and the light of your twelve sainted men.
> In order that, reckoning fairly
> with the power of free will,
> and with merit in place,
> will be [man's] agreement or deflection, (Aldana 1985, XLIII, vv. 869–76)[110]

The stanza ends with the news that the archangel Gabriel has been sent to announce the Son's birth to the Virgin (vv. 877–80). In the same verse work, titled "Virgin Birth," Aldana includes Jupiter, Apollo, Venus, the prophet Elijah, and God speaking with his Son the Redeemer. Like Ficino and Torquemada, the Spanish poet insists on man's role in accepting or deflecting his destiny, in later verses emphasizing "predetermined order" (orden prevista) (v. 881) and "predestination that is written" (sea predestinado el que es escrito) (v. 886) but always, as quoted above, according man the power to agree with or reject that destiny. For his part, Ficino follows Ptolemy to also uphold free will over fortune and fate: "the wise man can repel the stars that threaten him and favor those that hold out promises" (2001–6, 9.4.14).[111] Aldana explores those same ideas in verse, with a lexicon resonant of Ficino's translations of both Plato and the *Pimander* (1554, XI: 5–6), as well as the Italian philosopher's own *Platonic Theology* (2001–6, 2.13.10–11; 9.4.13–14), offering detailed explorations of phrases such as: first cause, immortal cause, and eternal archetype (*causa primera, causa inmortal, arquetipo eterno*) (Aldana 1985, XLIII, vv. 481, 627, 855). For Ficino: "God alone exists through Himself such that He exists without any cause" (2001–6, 5.5.1) and for Aldana, God is "the universal Cause, sole and first/of all that lives, understands, exists, grows and feels" (1985, XLIII, vv. 753–4).[112] Comparable to what we have already seen on other topics, on the theme of free will Aldana follows

Plato as read by Ficino, using poetic imagery as the perfect medium to communicate philosophy.

On Atlantis

Regarding the existence of the fabled Atlantis, Ficino states in his summary of *Critias* that "whenever he [Plato] imagines something, his custom is to call it a fable; but here he does not hesitate to call it history," then adds that in the *Timaeus*, Plato calls the story of Atlantis "amazing but totally true" (Ficino 2006, 143).[113] On Ficino's authority, Bartolomé de las Casas accepts that history:

> I would have to call Plato's stories regarding the marvels of that island fable rather than history, were they not confirmed by Marsilio Ficino in his compendium on the *Timaeus*, and in his argument on Plato's next dialogue, called *Critia*, or *Atlantis*, in which he speaks of the antiquity of the world. Marsilio affirms this as true history, and not fable, and he proves it with the judgments of many who have studied Plato's works. (Casas 1986, 1:50)[114]

In his compendium on *Timaeus*, Ficino also calls the tale "indeed amazing, but totally true" (ualde mirabilis, sed omnino uerus) and supports it with multiple sources (2010, 5; 1576, 2:1439). As to the time frame for the existence of Atlantis, Las Casas again turns to "Marsilio," and Ficino's brief biographical sketch of Plato:

> From what has been said it is clear that in Plato's day – which was 423 years before the coming of our saviour Jesus Christ, thus a little less than 2000 years ago, as Marsilio notes at the beginning of the works of Plato, the ocean, from the Straits of Gibraltar or just about the mouth of the same, from whence Atlantis began, was non-navigable due to the existence of sunken islands, like those we now find in these Indies. (Casas 1986, 1:51)[115]

In 1567, Cervantes de Salazar accepts the same history, although with some hesitation, as he attempts to be more geographically precise:

> All those who write on Plato say that this history is certain and true to such an extent that the majority of them, especially Marsilio Ficino and Platina, do not even admit a possible allegorical reading although there are others who do so aver, as Marsilio himself notes in his *Annotations on the Timaeus*. So, accepting the supposition that this history is true, who could deny that this island of Atlantis began at the Straits of Gibraltar, or just a bit after Cadiz, then continued and extended through this great

gulf, from whence to the north and south, as well as the east and west, it had space to be perhaps larger than Asia and Africa? (1772, no pag.)[116]

A contemporary of Cervantes de Salazar, Pedro Sarmiento de Gamboa (1532–92), also assures his reader of this "marvellous history that is full of truth" told by "the divine Plato" (1572, 25).[117] At the end of the sixteenth century, however, one truculent dissenting voice is clearly heard as Antonio de Herrera y Tordesillas (1559–1625), Head Chronicler of the Indies, categorically pens in the margins of Cervantes de Salazar's original manuscript: "this is a fable" (es fábula) (BNE, MS 2011).

In a 1648 book on political jurisprudence in the New World, we find Ficino's definition of merchants as those "who must leave their houses and lands so as to, with their persons, belongings, and goods, walk and pass through those of others" (Solórzano Pereira 1776, 1:116).[118] The author states specifically that the definition is that of Marsilio Ficino, and he follows with further details from "the wise doctor Father Juan de Pineda" (el docto padre Juan de Pineda) (1776, 1:116). A footnote to the text of this edition indicates that the information comes from the second book of Ficino's *Letters*.[119] Solórzano Pereira disputes the name Indies for the New World, and also rejects "Americas" as "false or stolen" (falso o hurtado) (1:6). He notes that following Plato in the *Timaeus*, some want to call the New World the Atlantic Islands but he calls that idea "an incredible ... fantasy story" (increíble ... fabulosa narración) and a few pages later adds that it is "a dream, or fable" (sueño, o fábula) (1776, 1:6, 24).

Despite the debates and doubters, later writers continued to trust Ficino on this matter, affirming Atlantis as the source of those who populated the New World pre-Columbus, as here in 1680: "and Ficino at the start of the dialogue *Critias*, or *Atlantis*, of Plato" (Sigüenza y Góngora 2005, 18–19).[120] Sigüenza y Góngora allows that there has been discussion of the history, but advises the careful reader to accept it as proven "indubitably" (invíctamente), following the authority of Gómara, Agustín de Zárate, Gregorio García, Athanasius Kircher, and Marsilio Ficino.

On Mathematics

Thorndike reviews a number of texts published in the sixteenth century on mathematics, astrology, cabala, magic, and numerology, noting the attention paid to mystical number and word combinations (1929–58, 6:44). On Ficino in particular, Allen studies the resonance of the concepts of world "as cipher" and "man as mathematician" in relation to Pythagorean ideas reflected in Plato's writings, and points out that "although none of Plato's dialogues focus primarily on mathematics, several do contain significant *loci mathematici*" (1994, 3–4). Allen details in particular Ficino's fascination with a passage in the Republic concerning the "fatal" number that mandates change and, eventually, decline and death for all wordly entities (1994, 12–25). From his commentary on the *Timaeus*, which was Ficino's earliest on a Platonic dialogue, to his essay on the *Republic*'s "fatal" number, published in a 1496 collection, the Italian philosopher addressed questions on mathematics, and Allen notes that in that last essay, Ficino "was still uncharacteristically circumspect" as he described the "prodigious enigmas" of Plato's ideas in the problematic passage of the *Republic* (Allen 1994, 23). In his commentary on that dialogue, Ficino explains that even a "happy" state will "fall eventually ... on account of some general defect and cause" and he calls Aristotle's quibbles with this point laughable as "he should have been satisfied with a general cause" (2009a, 41).[121] The Italian philosopher ponders the enigma at length, invoking planetary revolutions, saying that "fate coincides with nature," noting that "the condition of mobile nature does not suffer it to remain for a long time in the same or in a similar disposition," and concluding that "the fatal order seems to determine that when the number 12 ... arrives at its solid [i.e., its cube] of 1728 ... thereafter gradually it declines by the fatal law to a worse condition" (Allen 1994, 174, 182, 209–10).[122] Without the number 12 but maintaining all the weight of celestial influences from stars and planets, the concept of the fatal number or day became a predilective image, in Spanish letters, for discussion of fate and fortune.

In his second Eclogue, Garcilaso de la Vega's shepherd Albanio speaks of his desperation when faced with the loss of his loved one, saying that he considered ending his life in a bitter way, even though such an end was not yet the one predicted for him by the fates (Garcilaso 1966, Eclogue II, vv. 662–7).[123] Herrera discusses the passage with reference to Aristotle's writing on the "fatal generation" (fatal generación) and "fatal death" (muerte fatal) as that ordained by nature; he reviews the opinions of classical authors (Virgil, Cicero), as well as contemporaries (Adrian Turnebus), and concludes: "in the *Phaedo*, the divine philosopher [i.e., Plato] reprehended those who seek a violent death" because one should wait for nature to take its course (Herrera 2001, 845–6).[124] In late sixteenth-century verse, we read of the will's struggle when faced with the "fatal decree/governed by the celestial machines/and to which the vigour of reason is subject" (Argensola 1951, 2:Rima 48, vv. 156–8).[125] Francisco de Aldana criticizes life at court, where tyrants pretend to understand that which they do not and where, nonetheless, they await the "grave punishment of the just heavens" for their "fatal hour" will arrive (Aldana 1985, XXXI, vv. 69–72).[126] Juan de la Cueva similarly asserts that one cannot "extend the thread so as to lengthen one's days" once "completed the fatal course [of time]" (Cueva 1917, 2:142).[127] Gómez Tejada describes Apollo's ire when faced with man's ignorance: "with lightning streaming from his eyes and body, he grabbed ahold of the earth and would have turned it all into ashes if the sciences themselves, on their knees on the ground, had not pleaded for mercy and advised him that Jupiter would be indignant with the world's destruction prior to its decreed fatal hour" (1636, f. 281r).[128] The fatal number that mandates decline in earthly matters became, for Spanish writers, poetic code for the fatal hour of destiny.

Speaking on a more pragmatic numeric level, in his 1567 publication on mathematics, Portuguese writer Pero Nunes [Pedro Núñez] (1502–78) criticizes Ficino for what he perceives to be an error: "And in this, as one can see in his commentary on Plato's *Timaeus*, Marsilio Ficino was fooled because he thought that these three numbers, 7, 5, and 3, conform in both arithmetical and geometrical proportions. The truth, however, is that they share arithmetical, but not geometrical, proportion" (Núñez 1567, 2, f. 72v).[129] In a later passage, still speaking of those geometrical proportions, Núñez notes that "the same Marsilio Ficino, realizing that when three numbers are proportional in a geometric proportion ... responded to this possible objection by saying that this was understood to be the case for the multiple and superparticular groups, but not in the superpartient group, and here he was gravely mistaken" (Núñez 1567, 2, f. 73r).[130] In the criticized passage of his *Timaeus* commentary, Ficino speaks of those numbers in regard to music and harmony. He excludes the superpartient proportion as "unsuitable for harmony" and a producer of dissonance because of its proportions, whereas the superparticulars "always refer to a part which is based on a single whole" (2010, 54–8).[131] Allen notes that "the figural and geometric importance" of "certain fundamental number series" in Pythagorean terms accepted by Ficino are today "largely unfamiliar to us," but were perceived by the Italian philosopher as part of the skills of a "geometer-magus" (Allen 1994, 58–63, 88–100). Apparently, Núñez neither followed nor accepted those arguments, nor does he even mention any concerns apart from the strictly arithmetical. *Autoridades*[132] states that the first usages of the terms "superparticular" and "superpartient" in Spanish are found in *Arithmética práctica y especulativa* by Juan Pérez de Moya (c. 1513–96?), published in 1562, although Pérez de Moya does not indicate his sources, and his text is more a practical than theoretical approach to arithmetical calculations.[133] Portuguese author Pedro Núñez is recognized as having made important contributions to the disciplines of mathematics, astronomy, and navigation, specifically in having "announced a new and accurate solution of the astronomical problem of minimum twilight and suggested an instrument for the measurement of angles" (Linehan 1911, no pag.). The title page of his book on algebra, arithmetic, and geometry identifies him as Head Cosmographer to the Portuguese king, as well as Professor Emeritus of the University of Coimbra. Núñez also spent six years at the University of Salamanca, and he published his *Libro de Álgebra en Aritmética y*

Geometría in Spanish, despite having written it thirty years earlier in Portuguese.[134] As we saw with Hector Pinto, Núñez's work demonstrates that Ficino's impact on the Iberian Peninsula was not restricted to questions of philosophy and theology but, rather, extended to a number of disciplinary fields.

On Beauty and Love

Ficino completed his Latin commentary on Plato's *Symposium* (*Convite*, *Banquet*) in 1469, and revised it himself in 1475; the treatise was published with the editio princeps of the *Platonis Opera omnia* in 1484 and with all subsequent editions. The Italian philosopher also translated the text into Italian, in a version first published as a stand-alone publication titled *De Amore* in 1544, then republished in twenty-three different editions between that date and 1602 (Villa Ardura 1994, xix). As has been noted, Ficino's commentary on the *Symposium* "was the seminal text of Renaissance love theory" (Allen 2002a, xiii).[135] Ficino's commentary on the *Phaedrus* dialogue was also published in Latin with the *Platonis Opera omnia* and, like *De Amore*, published in Italian translation in 1544 (Allen 2008b, xiii). Allen distinguishes the two commentaries in that the dominant theme of the *Symposium* is love and that of the *Phaedrus*, beauty (2008b, xv), following Ficino who differentiates the two dialogues in terms of cause and result: "The *Symposium* principally treats of love and of beauty as a consequence; but the *Phaedrus* talks about love for beauty's sake" (Ficino 2008, 2.1.2).[136]

In *De Amore*, Ficino inextricably links the two terms 'love' and 'beauty,' stating that "the definition of love among all philosophers" is "the desire for beauty," and love "regards the enjoyment of beauty as its end" (Ficino 1944, 1.4; 2.9).[137] That precise definition is repeated by Miguel de Cervantes in his 1585 pastoral novel, *La Galatea*,[138] in which characters Lenio and Tirsi debate the topic of love. Between them, the two characters repeat the definition three times, with slight variation: "Thus, as I have heard from my elders, *love is a desire for beauty*; and this definition, among many others, is given by those who have best understood this topic"; "all the happiness of the lover consists in *enjoyment of the desired beauty*"; love is "desire for beauty" (Cervantes 1999, 417, 419, 435, my emphasis).[139]

Scholars who have examined the philosophical questioning of love in *La Galatea*, including the statements above, have closely scrutinized a range of possible sources and influences for those definitions with one glaring exception: Ficino. In an article written in 1876, Salvador Sanpere y Miquel noted specific parallels between Cervantes' text and Plato's *Symposium*, showing that in certain instances Cervantes' characters echo the words of Plato's character Diotima. This reference to a direct influence was all but forgotten following Menéndez Pelayo's later assertion that only León Hebreo could be a possible source for Cervantes' text: "the sense of this debate [between Lenio and Tirsi] is entirely Platonic and derived from León Hebreo, even as to the words" (1974, 1:549).[140] Careful philological study of those same words, however, did not bear out the claim, so scholars continued to look for other parallel texts to signal as source material. Nonetheless, on the basis of a sly jest written by Cervantes regarding the capacity of León Hebreo's *Dialoghi d'amore* to "give one the full measure" (que os hincha las medidas) on the topic of love (Cervantes 2005, 1, Prologue, 12), most of those same scholars maintained the posture that Hebreo's text was influential for Cervantes while simultaneously noting the irony of the *Quijote* reference and incorporating doubts as to that perspective. In 1948, López Estrada added Bembo, Equicola, and Castiglione as possible sources for *La Galatea*'s discourses on love. In 1959, Stagg reviewed critical opinion from the 1876 article onward, and attempted to clarify specific editions of those other sources in Italian or Spanish as more recognizable in the text of *La Galatea*. In 1986, Barbara Mujica noted that the definition given by Tirsi and Lenio conformed to the general "Neoplatonic sense" of love (1986, 187), without further exploration. In 2010, Aurora Egido added another facet of influence for Cervantes in the form of Castiglione's writings on the topic of discretion.

All those other writers (Hebreo, Bembo, Equicola, Castiglione) however, postdate and follow Ficino,[141] and none of them offer the exact definition of love given by, as seen above, both Ficino and Cervantes. Over the past thirty years, scholars have begun to specifically incorporate some details from Ficino's writings into studies on *La Galatea*: in 1985, Edgar Paiewonsky-Conde offered parallels on the theme of love, procreation, and the *appetitus naturalis*; in 1992, Steven Hutchinson suggested Ficino as a source for the ideas on desire as movement (56); in 1995, Gabriella Rosucci reviewed the list of Italian Platonic and Neoplatonic writers of the Renaissance known generally in Spain, and included Ficino among them; in 2004, Bruno M. Damiani referenced Ficino's *Commentary on the Symposium* as underpinning for Cervantes' exploration of the love-death theme in *La Galatea* (432) and noted a question in Plato's *Phaedrus* regarding the ambiguity of love as positive or negative emotion for its resonance in a poem by Cervantes' character Artidoro (437).[142] In their introduction to a 1996 edition of *La Galatea*, Florencio Sevilla Arroyo and Antonio Rey Hazas mention Ficino as one in the line of classical bucolic and Neoplatonic writers whose texts had resonance in the Spanish pastoral: "Theocritus, Virgil, Sannazaro, Plato, Ficino, Bembo, Castiglione and León Hebreo" (Cervantes 1996, IX), and note both his *De Amore* as the source for Tirsi's verse regarding love as the "root from which is born/the lucky plant/ that lifts us to the heavens," and the *Phaedo* for the idea of knowledge as memory (Cervantes 1996, 271, n. 158; 275, n.167).[143]

Those referenced studies, however, do not note the textual parallels shown above for the definition of love. The most recent critical edition of *La Galatea* offers, for that definition of "love as desire for beauty" only that the theme is "of a general order and found in the most common, Platonically-inspired treatises on love, beginning with that of León Hebreo" (Cervantes 1999, 417, n. 99), while immediately adding that Cervantes' precise phrasings are not found in Hebreo, nor in Bembo, nor in the other writers mentioned. Some editors have begun to incorporate mention of Plato's *Symposium* into editions of *La Galatea*: Sevilla Arroyo and Rey Hazas note the dialogue for that topical definition of love in general, but specify only that "similar ideas" (ideas semejantes) are expressed by Castiglione and Hebreo (Cervantes 1996, 244, n. 60), without mention of Ficino's commentary with its precise phrasings. A similar pattern holds with studies of other Spanish authors: in 1983, Frederick de Armas argued convincingly that Lope de Vega's pastoral novel *La Arcadia* shows the influence of various Ficinian writings including the commentary on the *Symposium*; in 2006, nonetheless, referring to the same definition I have quoted above of love as "desire for beauty," and noting that Ficino uses it in the *Symposium* commentary, editors Antonio Carreño and Antonio Sánchez Jiménez point to Lope's use of the definition in his rhyme [35]/ Sonnet XXXI, and in his stage plays *Fuenteovejuna* and *Los locos de Valencia*, only to insist that despite his literal use of that "Platonic definition" Lope "is only responding to the models of Petrarchan letters so as to reject them" (Lope 2006, 173, n. [35], and 174, n. to v. 6).[144] Following de Armas, I would argue to the contrary: the examples clearly attest that many Spanish authors were intimately familiar with Ficino's *De Amore* (and other treatises) and that they incorporated his ideas into their own creative writings.

In the other texts adduced as sources for Cervantes in *La Galatea*, the definition given is "love is desire," but as we have seen, Cervantes specifies "desire for beauty" and adds the goal "the enjoyment of that beauty"; that is, Cervantes directly follows Ficino, in whose *De Amore* we read: "When we speak of Love, you should understand it to mean desire for beauty" and "Love considers its goal to be the enjoyment of the desired beauty"; "love is the desire of enjoying beauty" (Ficino 1944, 1.4 [two quotations], 2.9).[145] Of possible texts previously adduced as sources for Cervantes the closest on this point, although still not precise, is Castiglione's *Cortesano*, which advises that the Courtier "direct his desire towards beauty" (1561, 242r–v)[146] but does not so define love itself. Even more tellingly, according to Cervantes' character Lenio, Ficino is the philosopher who best understood and explained love (*ha llegado más al cabo*).[147] Beyond those definitions repeated by Lenio and Tirsi, the full dialogue section of Cervantes' text, which consists of Lenio's vituperation of love followed by Tirsi's defence of the same emotion, incorporates multiple points from Ficino's commentary.[148]

Lenio first offers the definition above and Tirsi, in his response, repeats it only to say that "it is the most general [definition] that one hears; nonetheless it is not so accepted that it cannot be contradicted," and he insists that love and desire are two "different things" or "different affects of the will" (435), adding that reason "moderates and restrains our disordered desires" (440).[149] In this, Tirsi echoes both *De Amore*, in which we read that "love and the desire for physical union are not only not identical impulses, but are proved to be opposite ones" (Ficino 1944, 1.4),[150] and Ficino's commentary on the *Phaedrus*, which teaches that love pertains to will (Ficino 2008, 3.14.1) but desire, "far deviant from reason" (a ratione longe deviam) is the disorderly horse that must be controlled by reason (Ficino 2008, 3.31.3). In both texts love is an "affect" [passion] instead of an "effect" [result of the exercise] of will. Tirsi also supports a division between love and desire by arguing that one does not desire that which is already possessed: "desire presupposes the lack of that which is desired" (Cervantes 1999, 444).[151] This is another direct echo of *De Amore*: "the desire of anyone is satisfied by the possession of that which he wants" and "who desires what he has?" (Ficino 1944, 5.3; 6.2).[152]

Further parallels include the division of beauty into corporeal versus incorporeal, and the perception of one or the other through bodily eyes versus those of the mind. Lenio explains:

> it must be conceded that, as is the beauty that is loved, such will be the love with which it is loved. Because beauty is of two types, corporeal and incorporeal ... incorporeal beauty is perceived with the clean and clear eyes of the mind, and corporeal beauty is seen through the body's eyes which, in comparison with the incorporeal [eyes], are cloudy and blind. (Cervantes 1999, 417–19)[153]

Ficino first describes the two loves as "two Venuses": "one is clearly that intelligence which we said was in the Angelic Mind; the other is the power of generation with which the World Soul is endowed. Each has as consort a similar Love. The first, by innate love is stimulated to know the beauty of God; the second, by its love, to procreate the same beauty in bodies" (1944, 2.7).[154] Then, as does Cervantes' Lenio, the Italian philosopher speaks about contemplation of such beauty:

> the [corporeal] eye alone enjoys the beauty of the body. Since love is nothing more than the desire of enjoying beauty, and beauty is perceived by the eyes alone, the lover of the body is content with sight alone ... [but] we comprehend that light (and beauty) of the soul with just the mind. Therefore, he who loves the beauty of the soul is content with mental perceptions alone. (Ficino 1944, 2.9)[155]

López Estrada and López García-Berdoy's notes to the parallel section of Cervantes' text indicate that the author follows although "at some distance" Hebreo's

Dialoghi d'amore (1999, 417, n. 100). To the contrary, what Cervantes does is follow very closely Ficino's text.

Both Ficino and Cervantes also posit love as the force that governs the arts and sciences: Lenio admits that corporeal beauty is a positive force when its focus is on "non-living bodies" (cuerpos muertos) such as "paintings, statues and buildings" and, as to the non-corporeal beauty of "the virtues and sciences of the soul," it is always to be read in positive terms: "it is inevitable that love of virtue is good, and neither more nor less can be be said for virtuous sciences and agreeable studies" (Cervantes 1999, 418).[156] Ficino states explicitly: "Love is the teacher and master of all the arts ... justly called Ruler of the Arts ... artists in each of the arts seek after and care for nothing but love" (1944, 3.3).[157] Following that, the Italian philosopher details how each art is governed by love, to conclude:

> Wherefore, all the parts of the world, because they are the works of one artist, the parts of one creation, like [akin to] each other in life and essence, are bound to each other by a certain mutual affection so that it may justly be said that *love is a perpetual knot and [bond] (binder) of the world*, the immovable support of its parts and the firm foundation of the whole creation. (1944, 3.3, my emphasis)[158]

In the *Platonic Theology*, Ficino's Latin for the soul's intermediary position in the cosmos is "nodusque et copula mundi," translated by Allen as "the knot and bond of the world" (2001–6, 3.2.6). The Italian philosopher uses similar wording with the addition of an adjective in his commentary on the *Symposium*: "nodus perpetuus, et copula mundi" (1944, 3.3),[159] that is, love as knot and bond is an eternal one. On this point, Cervantes again directly follows Ficino lexically to assert that love "joins two different souls in such an [in]dissoluble knot and bond that from the two, thoughts and works might become one" (1999, 445).[160] This particular textual parallel lends solid support to López Estrada's reading of Cervantes' use of "dissoluble" here to mean "indissoluble" or "dis-soluble" (1999), that is, not soluble. The contrast between the two authors' statements is that Ficino's knot of love binds the entire world, whereas Cervantes employs the image for two individual lovers, and thus personalizes that perpetual knot. In a later text, the 1632 *Dorotea*, Lope de Vega will follow Ficino in both letter and spirit of the statement to say: "Love is a perpetual knot and coupling of the world, the immovable support of its parts and the firm foundation of its *máquina*" (1996, V, III, 431).[161]

To begin his vituperation of love, Cervantes' Lenio invokes reason as his muse. Tirsi responds to praise the passion by first invoking love itself as his inspiration, then rebukes Lenio for having spoken only of the negative "effects" of love and desire, without having noted that "love and desire are different affects of will" (Cervantes 1999, 417, 434, 435).[162] This parallels the opening to Ficino's commentary on the *Phaedrus*, in which we read that "Lysias is justly rebuked for asking what kind of effect love has without first defining or distinguishing love itself" (2008, 2.1.2), as Socrates invokes the Muses to help him differentiate between base love: "a certain passion or lust that rebels against the reason" as a result of "our inborn appetite for pleasure," and "legitimate opinion that we gradually acquire through learning and that directs us towards what is honorable" (2008, 2.1.3).[163] Like Ficino, Cervantes clearly paints the distinction between affects [passions] and effects [results] of the exercise of will regarding love, as his characters, Lenio and Tirsi, echo Lysias and Socrates.

As Hutchinson suggested, Cervantes also follows Ficino to describe love as the first movement of soul, with beauty as the moving force. Tirsi speaks of that first impulse:

> It is true that love is the father of desire and, among other definitions given for it, this is one: love is that first movement we feel in our mind, due to appetite that moves us and attracts us to it by delighting and pleasing us; that pleasure produces a movement in the soul, a movement we call desire. In sum, desire is movement of the appetite towards that which is loved, and a wish to possess it, and its object is the good ... love is a species of desire that serves and admires the good that is called beauty. (Cervantes 1999, 435–6)[164]

Later in the text, Tirsi repeats: "And so this first movement (love or desire, whichever you wish to call it) cannot be born except from a good beginning ... the knowledge of beauty which, once recognized as such, is almost impossible not to love" (Cervantes 1999, 438).[165] That is: beauty (the good) stirs the mind to love (the first movement, i.e., desire) and that brings pleasure.

The fragment is similar to one in Equicola's text (Stagg 1959), but the source for both is Ficino, in whose *De Amore* we read: "to beauty, Love, as soon as it was born, drew the Mind, and led the Mind formerly un-beautiful to the same Mind made beautiful" (1944, 1.3).[166] This pattern of love stirring mind to desire through contemplation of beauty repeats in the world of man, where "Love begins in Beauty and ends in Pleasure" and "Love is necessarily Good, since from good, whence He is born, He returns to good again" (Ficino 1944, 2.2).[167] Cervantes' process has its parallel in Ficino's text: "When the beauty of a human body first meets our eyes, the mind, which is the first Venus in us, worships and adores the human beauty as an image of the divine beauty," and "a soul burns with glowing love when, having found some pleasing image of a beautiful thing, it is aroused by that foretaste to desire full possession of the beauty" (Ficino 1944, 2.7; 6.2).[168] Cervantes echoes Ficino in highlighting the sequence of visual perception of beauty, then natural reason as an innate and inductive guide to love which is, of necessity, the good. On the full process of cause and effect, we read in Ficino:

> beauty is a certain vital and spiritual charm first infused in the Angelic Mind by the illuminating light of God, thence in the souls of men, the shapes of bodies, and sounds; through reason, sight, and hearing, it moves our souls and delights them; in delighting them, it carries them away, and in so doing, inflames them with burning love. (1944, 5.6)[169]

For Cervantes, human beauty leads "our affects and inclinations" (1999, 440) after it, and beauty itself

> has such force to move our souls that she alone was sufficient so that ancient philosophers, still blind without the light of faith to guide them, but following natural reason and attracted by the beauty they contemplated in the star-filled skies, and in the workings and face of the Earth, wondering at such orderliness and beauty, went searching with their understanding, stopping to admire these secondary causes, until they came to the first cause of causes, and recognized that there was one sole beginning without beginning of all things. (Cervantes 1999, 438–9)[170]

And for Ficino:

> In all these cases, it is an internal perfection which produces the external. The former we call goodness, the latter beauty. For just this reason, we say that beauty is the flowering, so to speak, of goodness. By the allurements of this flower, as though by a kind of bait, the latent interior goodness attracts all who see it. But since the cognition of our minds has its origin in the senses, we would never know the goodness hidden away in the inner nature of things, nor desire it, unless we were led to it by its manifestations in exterior appearance. (Ficino 1944, 5.1, Jayne trans. with slight modification)[171]

These parallel passages demonstrate Cervantes' goal for *La Galatea*, as professed in his prologue to the "curious readers" (curiosos lectores): to mix philosophical with amorous reasoning and arguments (Cervantes 1999, 158).[172] In the infamous book-burning scene in the first part of *Don Quijote* (1, 6), one character (*el cura*) describes the pastorales as "books of understanding" (libros de entendimiento) with the sense of understanding as *intellectus*, or reasoning, one of the three faculties of the soul [the other two being memory and will]. Many modern editions of the *Quijote* make the mistake of changing this reference to "books of entertainment" (libros de entretenimiento) a rewrite that confounds the author's own reading of the philosophical nature of the pastorale as a genre. The clear statement in his prologue to *La Galatea*, which has been noted as the Spanish author's concept of "poetry as science" (poesía como ciencia) (Egido 1994, 51),[173] is also reflected in specific lexical choices of the same passage in Cervantes' pastoral, such as the "workings and face of the Earth" (máquina y redondez del mundo), "beginning without beginning" (principio sin principio), and first and secondary causes. Those phrasings suggest Cervantes' familiarity with another translation by Ficino, the *Pimander*, in which a guide appears to the narrative voice to reveal the "beginning without beginning" of the cosmos, as well as all first and secondary causes, so as to instruct him on the mysteries of God and the universe. Like his contemporaries, Cervantes was acquainted with a number of Ficino's writings and translations, and his own creative works incorporate both the imagery and the ideas of those texts. His "poetry as science" (Egido 1994, 51) is an inventive literary elaboration of Ficino's "poetry as the philosophic mode par excellence" (Allen 2008b, xx) and in later writings, he will further refine this approach.

Speaking of *La Galatea*, Rosucci notes that it is common in Renaissance religious treatises to offer a dual division, in "*amor frui v. uti*" but that Cervantes' division in three is distinct (Rosucci 1995, 215). Sevilla Arroyo and Rey Hazas point to the Spanish author's tripartite division as an introduction of "interesting novelties" (interesantes novedades) into "Neoplatonic proposals" (planteamientos neoplatónicos) with reference to Herrera on Garcilaso and León Hebreo (Cervantes 1996, 262, n. 128). In this division too, however, the Spanish author follows Ficino to distinguish three types of love: for Cervantes, the passion can be "chaste, useful, or pleasure-giving" or, as he states in another place with a one-word alteration: "chaste, advantageous, or pleasure-giving" (1999, 436–7).[174] For Ficino in the *Phaedrus* commentary, love is "intemperate, temperate, and divine" (incontinens, continens, divinus) (2008, 3.13.1), and in *De Amore*, man will be disposed to one of three types of love: "contemplative, practical, or voluptuous" (1944, 6.8).[175] In the latter text, Ficino explains these three loves: "the love of the contemplative man is called divine; that of the practical man human; and that of the voluptuous man, animal" (1944, 6.8).[176] For Cervantes, the three types are similarly defined: chaste love (*amor honesto*) is "clean, simple, pure and divine," useful love is "natural and should not be condemned," and pleasure-giving love is "even more natural than useful love" (1999, 437).[177] The Spanish author does not, however, follow Ficino to deride the latter as an "animal" love; rather, he recognizes its "even more natural" character.

For both Ficino and Cervantes, man is a compound being, nature's perfect combination of the four elements which, once known, must be loved. In Cervantes, we read: "the composition of man is so ordered, so perfect and so beautiful, that he came to be called a microcosm (*mundo abreviado*)" and "Nature's beauty is scattered throughout her but in the figure and composition of man, this beauty is condensed and sealed; due to this, once that beauty in him is known, it is loved (Cervantes 1999, 439–40).[178] Ficino describes in detail the necessary proportion, arrangement, and adornment of the body in order for it to be called beautiful, and specifies that in man is found

> a temperate combination of the four elements, such that the [human] body is most like heaven, whose substance is temperate, and does not deviate by any excess of humours, with the soul's form. For thus the heavenly glow will easily light up in a body much like heaven, and that perfect Form of man which the soul possesses will be reflected in [the] quiet and compliant matter. (1944, 5.6, Jayne trans. with slight modification)[179]

In Cervantes' verse for character Tirsi, we find an echo in this description of love as a:

> mirror in which Nature is seen to be
> liberal, putting perfect generosity
> in appropriate measure;
> a spirit of fire
> that lights up him who is most blind,
> and is the only remedy for hate and fear; (Cervantes 1999, 450, vv. 62–7)[180]

In both authors, love and beauty reflect in the most optimistic terms a natural affinity and harmonic balance between man, heavens, and nature. Both Cervantes and Ficino also agree that love is the source of all virtues, although each posits a different need for those virtues. In Cervantes, the four prime virtues: temperance, fortitude, justice, and prudence, are listed as nature's means of moderating natural love's excesses (1999, 441). In Ficino, the same four virtues (*prudentia, fortitudine, justitia, temperantia*) are necessary to lead man to divine bliss (1944, 4.5; 1576, 2:1332). The abstract nature of the discussion by Ficino is in many subtle ways altered by Cervantes, who echoes the Italian philosopher's ideas but whose focus is more human than divine. The Spanish author's novelistic realism in *Don Quijote* has been widely recognized,[181] but it is also a prominent feature of his pastoral, in an embryonic stage and couched in more ethereal, poetic (and Platonic) language.

Just as love moderates, in *La Galatea* it also equalizes and calms: "making the small like to the sublime," love "moderates differing conditions" with the result that lovers "forget past discomfort and disagreeableness ... the frightening dreams, the uncertain sleep, the watchful nights and restless days, all become complete tranquillity and happiness" (Cervantes 1999, 446),[182] another passage noted by Stagg for its parallels to Equicola's text (1959, 267–8). In the same passage, love is defined as a happy medium between extremes, an idea also expressed by the character Diotima in the *Symposium*: love is "an intermediate state, between wisdom and ignorance"; it is not a god, but "a great spirit ... midway between what is divine and what is human ... He acts as an interpreter and means of communication between gods and men"; and "We would classify wisdom as very beautiful, and Eros is love of what is beautiful, so it necessarily follows that Eros is a lover of wisdom (lovers of wisdom being the intermediate class between the wise and the foolish)" (Plato 1989, 202a; 202d–e; 204b).[183] Diotima's counsel has a parallel in these words of Tirsi: "the gifts of love, if used in moderation, are worthy of perpetual praise, as the middle courses are praised in all things, just as the extremes are vituperated" (Cervantes 1999, 442),[184] a counsel the character repeats in verse: "in sum, love is life, glory, pleasure/ a fertile and happy calmness" (Cervantes 1999, 451, vv. 82–3).[185] Cervantes does eliminate any mention of Ficino's image of daemons, or mediating spirits, to explain this idea of means versus extremes (1944, 6.2–3). For the Spanish author, it is "love's grace" (la gracia suya) or "love's gifts" (los dones de amor) that temper differences and extremes (Cervantes 1999, 446).

Tirsi describes the human soul "in perpetual movement with desire, unable to stop except in God, as in its own centre" and the character adds that, knowing this tendency and wishing to keep the soul from pursuit of vain and temporal things, God placed reason over the soul's three faculties, so as to guide it but still allow it the exercise of free will (Cervantes 1999, 440).[186] These ideas are found in Ficino's *Phaedrus* commentary: "soul is the principle of motion ... [and] this motion is universal, complete, circular, and sempiternal"; soul holds three powers: life, understanding, desire; and "soul makes progress in its life and learning together, and exercises its free will to improve itself" (Ficino 2008, 2.5.1; 2.5.2; 2.5.3).[187] Further comments by Tirsi regarding the soul and its centre also echo the Italian philosopher's *De Amore*, in which a "single circle, from God to the world and from the world to God, is identified by three names": beauty, love, and pleasure, further explained by Ficino with Plotinian imagery of God as a centre surrounded by four more circles: "Mind, Soul, Nature, and Matter" (1944, 2.2; 2.3).[188] In verse, Tirsi describes the same circular and consistent motion, with love's power to raise to the heavens (*subir al cielo*) both its own light (*valor*) and his own, he calls it the root from which grows a plant that brightens the world, inspires love in the heavens, and lifts man to that place, then he emphasizes that love is:

A natural instinct that moves us
to lift our thoughts high, so very high

that human sight can scarcely reach;
it is a ladder on which he who dares may climb
to the sweet regions of the saintly heavens. (Cervantes 1999, 450, vv. 43–7)[189]

Both authors explore the intricate circular workings of that perpetual knot and bond we saw them reference earlier. In the same passage of *De Amore* quoted above, speaking of the World Soul, Ficino adds that "Soul is moved *through* and *in* itself: 'Through itself,' I say, because it is itself the source of motion; and 'in itself' also because the operation of reason and the senses resides in the very essence of the Soul" (1944, 2.3).[190] Later sections of *De Amore* relate the same properties and yearnings to the human soul which, as we have seen, perceives human beauty as an image of the divine; it also "carries out man's most important function, intelligence," and "is attracted, by a certain natural instinct, towards its parent, God" from whom it receives the second light of "divine providence [which] decreed that the soul should be mistress of itself," that is, able to exercise free will (1944, 4.3; 4.4).[191] In Cervantes' text, there is a subtle distinction drawn in each character's commentary on free will: Lenio negates the power of the will when faced with corporeal beauty and love, whereas Tirsi admits only that such beauty "calls and draws the will to love it" without "denying it the freedom of free will" to resist (Cervantes 1999, 420; 440).[192] For his part, Ficino insists that both love and free will are "free": "everything obeys Love but He Himself, no one"; "love is free and rises of its own accord in free will, which not even God, who decreed that it should be free in the very beginning, controls" (1944, 5.8).[193] As noted by Sears Jayne, Ficino follows the Neoplatonists to insist on man's free will (Jayne in Ficino 1944, 158, n. 14) and on this point, through Tirsi, Cervantes fully agrees with the Italian philosopher.

The negative effects of love, according to Cervantes' Lenio, are: "sighs, tears, complaints and vexations ... excessive desire, too much joy, great fear of future misery, great pain with present calamities ... like unfavourable winds that perturb the tranquility of the soul" (Cervantes 1999, 419–20).[194] The character further describes love's effects as "supernatural" because the lover is "in the same instant fearful yet confident, burning when far from his loved one then frozen when closer to her, mute when garrulous yet garrulous when mute" (Cervantes 1999, 426).[195] Those effects echo this description of the lover from Ficino's *De Amore*: "lovers both worship and fear the sight of the beloved ... those snared by love alternately lament and rejoice in their love ... they are alternately hot and cold, like those suffering from undulant fever ... alternately timid and bold" (1944, 2.6).[196] At other points in his text, however, Cervantes includes a Ficinian idea only to negate it. For example, Ficino says that following Orpheus, Hesiod, and Hermes Trismegistus, "love is the oldest and wisest of the gods, and perfect in himself" although he also explains that "our theologians" call these gods "angels" or "divine beauty" (1944, 1.2–3).[197] In *La Galatea,* Lenio admits that the ancients called love a god, but insists that he was an "imagined god" (dios imaginado) (Cervantes 1999, 427).

Certain topics found in Ficino's text are not present in *La Galatea*: the origin of love as the first god to emerge from primordial chaos; the World Soul; the Angelic Mind that contains the primordial Ideas; the full Plotinian concentric design; and, as I noted above, the daemons. That is, the boldest of "pagan" philosophical concepts, those that would not lend realistic credence to a literary text even if they might contribute some entertainment value. Given contemporary censorship they might also, it should be noted, have prevented its publication. Cervantes considers, experiments with, and uses Ficino's ideas on love; on the other hand, he freely rejects or challenges certain tenets of the Italian philosopher's texts. Characteristically, Cervantes also adds to the debates on love the problem of jealousy: for Ficino, there is no envy in the "divine chorus" of love (Ideo liuor ... abest a diuino choro) (1944, 4.6, 1576, 2:1334). On this point, perhaps Cervantes does follow Hebreo, for whom the lover is also, of necessity, "vexed with jealousy" (Hebreo 2002, 1, 80).[198] Another possible model, of course, would be Dante.

I would like to add two further details in support of my conclusion that Cervantes was familiar with Ficino's writings on love: the first is the name of a character in *La Galatea* and the second becomes evident in various Cervantine comments on reciprocal love. In the prologue to his pastoral, Cervantes tells the reader that his sheperds are "disguised" (disfrazados) and scholars have identified a number of the characters as friends and acquaintances of the author. I would add to that list Cervantes' shepherd Marsilio, specifically described as a melancholic, "desperate" (desesperado) and "doleful" (lastimado) (Cervantes 1999, 337; 595). This would seem to be a deliberate reference to Ficino who, born under Saturn, so identified himself throughout his life. It is well known that during the Renaissance, melancholy was perceived to be a negative but also a positive characteristic; in the latter sense, it was taken as both a stimulus to creativity and the sign of an apt intelligence. Villa Ardura notes that Aristotle was the first to speak of the connection between the melancholic temperament and an aptitude for arts and sciences (1994, XXXIII) and, in the introductory study to his Spanish translation of Ficino's *De Amore,* outlines in detail the resonance and importance of the concept for the Italian philosopher. In *De Amore,* Ficino avers that once in love, the melancholic will most likely never free himself of the passion ("Melancholici ... sed capit, nunquam postrea liberantur") (Ficini 1576, 2:1360). This is Cervantes' Marsilio, first presented to the reader during the wedding celebration of Daranio and Silveria; the bridal couple offers a *convite* also described as a "generous banquet" (el generoso banquete) (1999, 344), that is, the two most common titles for the Platonic dialogue commented by Ficino in *De Amore*. Cervantes' Marsilio describes himself as dead in life; he refers to his "inexorable star" (mi inexorable estrella), his "will" (mi voluntad), and the pain of his soul covered with "mortal, corporeal veil" (mortal, corpóreo velo) – all vocabulary and imagery easily associated with, or found in, Ficino's texts (Cervantes 1999, 350, vv. 142, 143, 153). Marsilio speaks of his anxieties and of his "insane illness," describes his love as a "universal woman of beauty," and insists that: "From the cradle I have been unlucky" (Cervantes 1999, 351, vv. 182; 355, v. 295; 358, v. 372).[199] At the close of this wedding scene, during which Marsilio and three other shepherds have represented a pastoral eclogue, the others in attendance judge which is the saddest of their laments. Another character, Damón, insists that it cannot be Marsilio because he who loves cannot expect to be loved in return: "Thus, she is not obligated, as I have already said, to love me the way I am obligated to adore her" (Cervantes 1999, 370).[200] To the contrary for Ficino, he who is loved must love in return: "Therefore, anyone who is loved ought in very justice to love in return, and he who does not love his lover must bear the charge of homicide, nay, rather the triple charge of thief, homicide, and desecrator" (Ficino 1944, 2.8).[201] For Ficino love itself, as we read above, is free but the loved one, once s/he is loved, may not reject the lover.

Cervantes rebuffs this dogmatic opinion in multiple instances in both the *La Galatea* and in *Don Quijote*, with characters who specifically dispute this mandate for reciprocal love. In *La Galatea*, Gelasia rejects her lover and declares: "I was born free, and I ground myself in freedom" (1999, 615, v. 14)[202] and in *Don Quijote*, Marcela admits both that her beauty attracts and that her own God-given natural understanding tells her that everything beautiful is to be loved, but she rejects the idea that being loved demands loving in return. Marcela refuses to accept blame for the death of Grisóstomo, a shepherd who died due to his unrequited love for her. Don Quijote agrees with Marcela, and refutes the conclusions of Grisóstomo's friends who insist, as does Ficino, on the reciprocal debt of Marcela to have loved their deceased friend (2005, I, 14).

Ficino's *De Amore* can also offer a plausible reading for Grisóstomo's unexplained death. Cervantes offers no direct evidence for the manner of the character's death, but his "Desperate Song" poem has been read as a possible indicator of suicide.[203] In *De Amore*, however, we read that a "simple love" exists when the loved one does not return the lover's passion, and "in this case the lover is completely dead, for he neither lives in himself, as we have already sufficiently proved, nor does he live in his loved one, since he is rejected by him. Where, then does he live?" (Ficino 1944, 2.8).[204] Ficino offers various possibilities only to reject them all and conclude: "Therefore, the unrequited lover lives nowhere; he is completely dead. Moreover, he never comes back to life unless indignation revives him" (1944, 2.8).[205] In the light of this passage, Cervantes' Grisóstomo was simply not indignant enough to continue living.

In sum, it is not at all surprising that the disputes on love by Cervantes' characters clearly reflect the most well-known treatise of his day on the subject, Ficino's philosophical *De Amore*. Indeed, the only surprise is that the parallels I highlight above have not been studied previously in relationship to that text. In other Spanish writers of the time, we find direct attributions to the Italian philosopher's treatise. Juan de Arce de Otálora, for example, praises Ficino's description of love:

> Its causes and natural effects are marvellously described by Marsilio Ficino in his commentaries on Plato's *De Amore*, where he [Ficino] shows it to be the natural grief of lovers, derived from the blood which, made more subtle in courage and spirit, flows out from the eyes and penetrates through them to the heart, where the blood of the lovers is found mixed together, causing grief and anxiety mixed with delight, more or less, according to the cause and nature. (1995, 1:447)[206]

Rather than a direct quote, Arce de Otálora's passage is a paraphrase of ideas found in *De Amore*. Also following Ficino, Portuguese writer Hector Pinto distinguishes between "saintly" and "dishonest" love:

> We read about the ancient history of this sacred love in the dialogues of Trismegistus, the *Theology* of Hesiod, the *Book of Nature* of Parmenides, and the commentary of Marsilio Ficino to Plato's *Banquet* dialogue. In this last, he [Ficino] shows that illicit, dishonest love is not love, because love loves beauty, which is virtue and decorum, and [illicit love] loves ugliness, which is dishonesty and vice. (Pinto 1595, 3.22, f. 266v)[207]

Pinto's reference is to the following section in *De Amore*: "A mad lasciviousness drags a man down to intemperance and disharmony, and hence seems to attract him to ugliness, whereas love attracts to beauty. Ugliness and beauty are opposites" (Ficino 1944, 1.4).[208]

For Juan de Pineda, love is transformative. Character Panfilo speaks of unrequited love and Filaletes responds:

> You will be comforted by the good Platonist Marsilio Ficino, in his *Letters* and on Plato's *Banquet*, where he proselitizes the idea of a love so free and precious, in his estimate, that it neither wishes to, nor can be sold, exchanged, or bartered for anything other than itself. Do you follow this reasoning, sirs? (Pineda 1963, 169:74)[209]

This idea that love is only paid with love is a concept also expressed by Tirsi in *La Galatea*: "love has no other payment or satisfaction except for love itself, and he himself is his own and truthful payment" (Cervantes 1999, 444).[210] In his *Letters*, Ficino writes to Bembo: "Other things are usually acquired at the cost of something else. But since love is born of its own free will, it is therefore free and is never bought or sold at any price but itself" (Ficino 1975–<2012>, 1:145).[211] In Pineda's dialogue, one of speaker Panfilo's interlocutors fails to understand the lesson offered, which brings the sharp retort: "Marsilio spoke wonderfully for all who have, at a minimum, ears" along with further explanation: "No one loves without giving himself to the loved one, and no one gives himself who does not also give all that he has, and all he does not have to his lover; and so Marsilio was right when he said that one does not give except for himself, which is to say that he does not love except for the one who might love him" (Pineda 1963, 169:74).[212] In Ficino: "He who loves, dies; for his consciousness, oblivious of himself, is devoted exclusively to the loved one" and "a man who does not even have possession of himself will that much less take possession of someone else" (Ficino 1944, 2.8).[213] Pineda's reading, however, obviates the unrequited love possibility that Ficino does mention and that, as we have seen above, Cervantes would later reject.

Also writing in the late sixteenth-century, Álvarez Miraval recommends following Ficino on love for medical reasons:

> And if we ask the reason and cause for this truth, the prince of Platonic philosophers, Marsilio Ficino, says it wisely and keenly in his commentary on Plato's *Banquet*, in chapter 8, and also in the first book of his [Ficino's] *Letters*, where he says that love is so free and precious that it will not sell itself for any price nor exchange other than itself. (Álvarez Miraval 1597, 155v–6r)[214]

The first reference is to the same places quoted above, in Ficino's *De Amore* (Ficino 1944, 2.8), and in his *Letters* (Ficino 1975–<2012>, 1:145).[215]

There is one mid-sixteenth century writer who prefers Hebreo to Ficino, as would Menéndez Pelayo three centuries later, but he is an Italian, not a Spanish author. In Tullia D'Aragona's *Dialogue on the Infinity of Love*, two characters named Varchi and Tullia compare León Hebreo and Marsilio Ficino on love.[216] When Varchi opts for "Filone" [León] as the best writer on love, Tullia asks if he has not also considered Plato and Ficino's *Convivium*, and Varchi replies that he thinks both are marvellous, but that he finds Hebreo more pleasing, "perhaps because I do not understand the others" (credo perché non intendo gli altri) (D'Aragona 1997, 92; 1912, 224). The two characters continue to discuss the merits of various writings on love, complain that most (including Plato and Hebreo) are not "peripatetic in character" (non erano peripatetiche) and Varchi elaborates that he prefers those who write on love not theoretically "but as they themselves have experienced it" (ma como lo hanno avuto) (D'Aragona 1997, 92; 1912, 224). This would explain Varchi's preference for Hebreo over Ficino, as the latter is recognizedly more theoretical: "For Ficino and his followers, knowledge comes not from experience but from within the soul, where all universal forms are buried" (Russell 1997, 31). Varchi wants the story of a love experience, not theory on love as "the universal force binding the world and the divinity together," that is, as Ficino explored it (Russell 1997, 27). The Spaniards, as we have seen, had no problem understanding and discussing Ficino's theoretical version, in their own dialogues and novelistic treatments. Cervantes even illustrated that theory in the form of practical love experiences.

Lope de Vega will follow Cervantes' lead in a 1632 dramatic work in prose. Two characters (Don Bela and Laurencio) discuss Plato's ideas on beauty as, they note, explained by Ficino:

> DON BELA: Tell me, Laurencio: Was Plato wise?
>
> LAURENCIO: They call him divine.
>
> DON BELA: Well, he said that all the good was beautiful. So we have to conclude that all that is beautiful is also good, and that what is good is worthy of being loved; no one can be reprehended for loving what is good.
>
> LAURENCIO: Unsupported exagerations! It seems to me, sir, that this little bit that we have studied does us both much damage. But look, God save you, at how Marsilio Ficino spoke about the ancients painting the god Pan as half man and half beast.
>
> DON BELA: What was the reason for this?
>
> LAURENCIO: Given that he was the son of Mercury, they wished to show both manners of speaking represented in the two forms: when speaking the truth, he is man; but when falsehoods, beast. (Lope de Vega 1996, III, II, 251–2)[217]

Don Bela offers an unsupported reverse syllogism (if all good is beautiful, then all beautiful is good), and Laurencio uses it to reflect on the concept of a little knowledge being a dangerous thing. At a later point in the same work, other characters discuss Ficino's explanation of poetic fury as found in both *De Amore* (Ficino 1944, 7.13) and the *Phaedo* commentary (Ficino 2008, 2.4). Lope's characters begin with a list of admired poets of their day, including two who merit the classification "divine" (Francisco de Figueroa and Fernando de Herrera), then describe one contemporary (Bautista de Vivar) as an improvisor with an "admirable impetus from the muses, and that poetic fury that Marsilio Ficino, in his Plato, divides into four parts ... The first is the poetic, the second the mysterious, the third the prophetic, and the fourth the amorous" (Lope de Vega 1996, IV, II, 349).[218] In a subsequent dialogue, Love is identified as the inventor of music, "because harmony is concert, concert is concord of high and low notes, and concord was instituted by love; from that reciprocal benevolence it follows that music's effect is to delight. Marsilio Ficino called this amorous union his minstrel" (Lope de Vega 1996, V, III, 423).[219] As Trueblood (1958) noted, this is a reference to *De Amore*, in which we read that love is the teacher and ruler of the arts, who makes "high and low voices, naturally different, blend together better," and so leads one to harmony (Ficino 1944, 3.3).[220] In a later passage of Lope's text, another direct citation to Marsilio Ficino is followed by references to melancholic men and astrological imagery; in this section, as Blecua has made clear, Lope follows Ficino's *De Amore* "step by step" (Blecua in Lope de Vega 1996, V, III, 425, n. 65).[221]

For the most part, but with some divergence as seen above, Spanish writers accepted, explored, and debated the various concepts in Ficino's commentary on the *Symposium*. With one particular notion however, they took exception: the idea of Platonic love.

Platonic Love

Ficino coined the phrase "Socratic love" [Platonic love] in his preliminary argument to the translation of Plato's *Phaedrus* to speak of a love between two persons that was friendly, charitable, and intellectual, but specifically not carnal. This concept would have a particular resonance in Spanish letters.[222] In one of his *Novelas ejemplares*, Cervantes paints the character of an "illustrious scullery maid": she is a woman whose beauty captivates men with a "clean love" that is "not vulgar," and one character exclaims: "Oh, Platonic love! Oh illustrious scullery maid! Oh happy these times of ours, where we see that beauty enamours without malice, honesty enflames without burning, charm gives pleasure without inciting, and the lowliness of a humble status obliges and forces that a man be raised on the wheel they call Fortune!" (Cervantes 1997a, 2:165).[223] In comparison with the quotations in the previous section regarding beauty that enamours, these passages from the *Novelas ejemplares* offer a more jaundiced view on love, in a collection of stories published more than twenty-five years after *La Galatea*.

In the 1605 *Quijote*, Cervantes' protagonist knight errant insists: "Dulcinea does not know how to write or read, and in all of her life has never seen my handwriting nor had a letter from me, because my love and hers have always been 'Platonic,' without going any further than an honest look" (Cervantes 2005, I, 25).[224] Here, 'Platonic' is not only chaste in thought but also a lack of written communiques – the assumption is that any letter from one lover to another implies erotic corruption. 'Platonic' can be poetic only in so far as it is not admitted to in script. In the 1615 *Quijote*, Sancho Panza speaks about "the honesty and continence of those very Platonic loves between yourself [Don Quijote] and my lady Doña Dulcinea del Toboso" and, in a later section of the novel, the protagonist himself excuses his professional need to be in love while again insisting on its abstemiousness: "I am in love, but only because it is incumbent on knights errant that they be so, and in so being, I am not a licentious lover but, rather, one of the continent Platonic types" (Cervantes 2005, II, 3; II, 32).[225] These are references to the three types of love named by Ficino in his *Phaedrus* chapter summaries: "intemperate, temperate, and divine" in English translation or "incontinens, continens, divinus" in Ficino's Latin (Ficino 2008, 3.13), which is closer to Cervantes' ironic "continent Platonic types." In *De Amore*, as we saw previously, these three types of love are named as ways of life: voluptuous, active, or contemplative (Ficino 1944, 6.8; 1576, 2:1345–6). In his own life, Don Quijote eschews the voluptuous and practises an active yet *continens* love for Dulcinea who, even more ironically given the statement about no further than "an honest look" (un honesto mirar) (Cervantes 2005, I, 25), he has never laid eyes on.

It is in Cervantes' *La Galatea* that we find the earliest caustic commentary on the concept of Platonic love in Spanish letters. In the same debate studied above for its definitions and philosophy of love, Tirsi emphasizes that the desire to propagate is as natural as it is good (Cervantes 1999, 439–41), just as Ficino does in *De Amore*, approving of natural love or the "functions of generation and coition" when performed "within the bounds prescribed by natural law and civil laws drawn up by men of wisdom" (1944, 2.7).[226] In Cervantes' novel, however, after speaking in analogous terms about nature and the "blessed yoke of matrimony, under which most of the pleasures and contentments of natural love are licit and proper to a man and a woman," Tirsi concludes: "if we didn't have it [natural love], both we and the world would end" (Cervantes 1999, 440–1).[227] Later, he repeats the argument: "the generations of both rational and brute animals would cease to exist if love did not continue and lacking on earth, the planet would become deserted and empty" (Cervantes 1999, 442–3).[228] This is the earliest example I have found of criticism of Ficino's concept of Platonic love. In subsequent Spanish letters, ridiculing the idea would become a commonplace.

At the end of the sixteenth century and throughout the seventeenth, Platonic love would still be praised by some: "It is Platonic doctrine that the harmony and universal order of the world form an amorous conceit with Love's own harmony and fabric" (Quevedo 1999, I, 510, poem 332).[229] However, other writers would roundly reject the concept on practical grounds, as an impossible love predictive only of the end of the human race: "I always thought that Platonic love was a chimaera and contrary to nature, because [with only it] the world would end" (Lope de Vega 1996, II, V, 199).[230] Lope uses the phrase "Platonic love" to say that his desire is anything but that: "a desire is born that throws to the ground/ that sought by Platonic love" (Lope de Vega 1993, Rima CV, vv. 7–8),[231] and carefully distinguishes between it and "vulgar love" (amor vulgar), defining the former as that of he who "loves the virtues of the soul" (1973, 423).[232] Another contemporary, Diego Duque de Estrada (1589–c. 1637), states in his (semi-fictionalized) autobiography that having known his fiancée since childhood incited in him not "dishonest desires but, rather, a certain Platonic love" although he also notes a change: "the communication of love's matters brought me to the desire of effects from affects" (1982, 99).[233] As we saw above in Ficino's and Cervantes' texts, the word play with affects-effects had also become common in Spanish discussions on love. Bartolomé Leonardo de Argensola, writing from 1592 to 1631, insults a woman who prides herself for her declared "elevated metaphysics" (metaphissica eleuada) of wishing to unite two souls in Platonic love by saying that she must have failed to understand the subtleties of the Greek phrase, as more than one lover has known her. Whereas this woman, named Gala, might say that her desire is only to unite their souls in an uplifting, metaphysical way, he believes that Apulieus is more pleasing to her in corporeal form (when he brays like a donkey) than incorporeal (when he is eating roses) (Argensola 1951, 2:X).[234] Without directly mocking the concept, and like Cervantes, Bartolomé de Argensola does ironically question it.

In a novel by Tirso de Molina published in 1635, character El conde ridicules the idea of Platonic love, insisting that beauty is composed of two parts, the corporeal and the incorporeal – which only together form a complete person. Love

> is the power of procreation and has as its object a person – if it does not desire more than one of these parts [of beauty], it will be a Platonic, mutilated love. Nature introduced love in mortals so as to perpetuate its species in individuals, and if everyone agreed with you, sterilizing their propagations, she would in short order give up her fecundity; you would not have had life, nor would the world have enjoyed more than the first two individuals from whom we are all descended. (Molina 1979, 228)[235]

Here, Platonic love is mutilated, sterile, and predictive of the end of the species. Two verse works from the middle of the seventeenth century elaborate this same concept. In 1647, a Platonic love is a fire that does not touch, a theoretician's love that pays only in preambles, lightning instead of thunder (María de Zayas).[236] In a similar vein in 1665, the poetic voice of Alberto Diez de Foncalda laments having "turned into a frigid icicle": her lover's "scholastic master" might say that a "gaggle of Platonic rogues" recommends swallowing the "pretty pill" of love, and writing some "diabolical verse" that the poetic voice will then "avenge with distich rhyme" (Diez de Foncalda 1861, 2:535).[237] Here, play on poetic theory is combined with the ridicule of Platonic love.

By the early eighteenth century, in a neoclassical poetic manifesto, "Platonic love" has been redeemed: Ignacio de Luzán will echo Cervantes as he describes two types of lyric poets: the lascivious and those who write of love. The former speak of "manifestly dishonest" matters whereas the latter follow the concepts and ideas of Platonic philosophy, writing about their passions honestly and without obscenity (1956, 1:93).[238] In the nineteenth century, theorists will use "Platonic" to describe the "vague, monotonous love without character" of the pastoral, or the "delicateness and perfume" of Spain's finest Golden Age poets, who might have offered "artificiality and falseness" in subject matter but who, nonetheless, exhibit "such beauty of diction, such poetic colours, that they leave the reader astounded enough to overlook their intrinsic defects" (Milá y Fontonals 1888, 430).[239] Platonic love has gone from purity of intention to ridiculous, impractical ideal, and then to weak, vague, and delicate expression without action. Anything erotic is non-Platonic. The discussion by and evolution of this concept in the works of Spanish authors, in response to Ficino's coining of the phrase in the *Phaedrus*, apparently began with Miguel de Cervantes' early challenge to the idea in *La Galatea.*

On Law

A number of Spanish writers rely on Ficino for the history of law and lawgivers, most often quoting directly from his summary of Plato's dialogue *Minos, concerning Law*, which reads:

> The origin of law ... all the kinds of law emanate, although in different ways, from the Creator of the universe. For this reason all the illustrious lawgivers have ascribed the discovery of laws to God, but through different names and means: Zoroaster, lawgiver to the Bactrians and Persians, acknowledged Horomasis; Trismegistus, lawgiver to the Egyptians, acknowledged Hermes; Moses, lawgiver to the Hebrews, most justly referred to Jupiter; Charondas, lawgiver to the Carthaginians, acknowledged Saturn; Lycurgus, lawgiver to the Spartans, Apollo; Draco and Solon, lawgivers to the Athenians, Minerva; Pompilius, lawgiver to the Romans, Aegeria; Mahommed, lawgiver to the Arabs, Gabriel; Zamolxis, lawgiver to the Scythians, Vesta; our Plato, lawgiver to the Magnesians and the Siculians, acknowledged Jupiter and Apollo. (Ficino 2006, 22)[240]

In a work first published in 1538, Hugo de Celso studies the particular history of Spain's laws and begins with a direct reference to Ficino on the origins of law:

> mortal man received his laws from Moses, who received them from God. According to Marsilio Ficino, the philosopher Plato, in his book 7 of *De legibus*, attributed the principle and beginning of the laws to God ... he [Ficino] says this in another

> place, too, although not as clearly, when he states that Prometheus, understood to be human wisdom, received the laws that Mercury gave him, that is, the angel that Jupiter (who they thought was God), had given him. (Celso 2000, f. 4v)[241]

In addition to the direct attribution to Ficino's commentary on the *Laws*, the information Celso notes as from "another place" comes from the Italian philosopher's summary of *Protagoras*, in which Prometheus is "ruler of the rational soul," and "Jupiter, through the agency of Mercury, the messenger who interprets the divine will, writes [in our minds] (on our hearts) the laws of civic knowledge, that is to say, the decrees of his will that relate to the welfare of society and of mankind"; "Jupiter established through Mercury the law by which all are happy to partake of civic life" (Ficino 2006, 68, 69, 70).[242] Celso's disclaimer on "not as clearly" would seem to be a reference to the same place in *Protagoras*, where Ficino also tells us that Prometheus "represents the highest level of daemons" (qui daemonum sublimium ordinem significat) (2006, 68; 1576, 2:1298). Non-problematic for Ficino, that concept would be contentious fifty years later, and we see Celso equivocate to describe it, simply, as "not so clearly" explained.

Spanish jurist Juan de Arce de Otálora, who served as prosecutor in the Chancellería de Granada and judge in both Granada and Valladolid, was known principally for his writings on law pertaining to Spanish nobility, texts that were published in his lifetime (Ocasar Ariza 1995, xiii, xii). In a different type of work, the aforementioned dialogue between two vacationing University of Salamanca law students not published in printed form until 1995 and titled *Coloquios de Palatino y Pinciano*, Arce de Otálora aims to reflect student life at Salamanca. The dialogue's interlocutors Pinciano and Palatino discuss love, the magic properties of stones, and the evil eye, as we have seen, but they also converse on religion, rhetorical tropes, and other matters. One principal focus for the two is the merits of their respective fields as students, civil and canon law, and on this topic, they repeat the history of details given by Ficino in the *Minos* summary: Pinciano offers the information on Zoroaster, Trismegistus, Charondas, and the rest of the named lawgivers in Ficino's summary, while insisting that all those figures simply "put order to" (ordenaron) laws that originated from "the one true God" (el Dios verdadero) (Arce de Otálora 1995, 1:253–4). Palatino the canonist takes the role of either critic or naive voice in most sections of the dialogue and here, to Pinciano's list and explanation, Palatino responds by saying the stories about those other figures are "fables and imaginings," only to have Pinciano retort that there must have been laws "that governed the republic" in civil societies because "according to Plato ... law is the soul of a republic" (Arce de Otálora 1995, 1:254–5).[243] In both the *Republic* (book 4) and the *Laws* (book 1), Plato describes the tripartite nature of soul as reason, wrath, and appetite, represented in a society in the three figures of ruler, soldier and craftsman, with justice as the harmony of all three. In his commentary on the *Laws*, Ficino notes that in a state in which judges have too much freedom to overstep the law, "the state, lacking justice as its soul, will die" (Ficino 2009a, 153).[244] Arce follows Ficino to read 'justice' as law, ergo as the soul of the republic.

Arce de Otálora's dialogue is chock-full of references to a whole host of authorities: Isaiah, Saint Paul, Aristophanes, Cicero, Horace, Boethius, Ovid, Erasmus; for this humanist jurist, the Philosopher by antonomasia is Aristotle but Plato is "the most divine" (el más divino) of all ancient philosophers (1995, 1:468). Both Plato and Socrates are trusted figures on a number of matters although not fully credible when it comes to a few of the former's "fables," for example the Ideas, or Theuth as inventor of all arts and sciences (1995, 1:197–8). On the other hand, for Pinciano, Plato was correct in saying that "the city where there are many officials is a fortunate one, because there will be few vagabonds" (1995, 1:226),[245] and both Plato and the Visigoths agreed that if a patient dies due to negligence on the part of his doctor, that medical practitioner should be stoned to death (1995, 1:280). Regarding Plato's story, in the *Phaedrus*, of the cicadas whose only sustenance is song and music, for Ficino it must be treated as an allegory (Ficino 2008, 3.35.1–2), whereas for Palatino those stories are "old wive's tales" (cuentos de viejas) although other similar cases are possible "miracles" (milagros) (1995, 1:290). In a later section of the text and again on the topic of the cicadas, Palatino complains that Plato has offered "rumours and fables" but Pinciano replies: "Fables are part of philosophy, and he who wishes to have the whole must also accept each part" (1995, 1:433).[246] No matter the explanation: fable, allegory, or miracle, Pinciano and Ficino show a willingness to, in Coleridge's words, "suspend disbelief" although their focus is philosophy rather than fiction.

Arce de Otálora's characters take trusted philosophical *dicta*, such as the influence of the four humours on a man's disposition, only to add ironically that "from those fours dispositions [choleric, sanguine, phlegmatic, melancholic], are derived four more, which are: crazy and foolish and stupid and wise" (1995, 1:64).[247] The debate on the various permutations on insanity is lengthy, but one early conclusion is that no one can be wise "if they do not have a little bit of crazy in them" (1995, 1:65).[248] Authorities are not only challenged but also frequently pilloried in this text. Ficino's seriousness is replaced with sceptical ridicule, often tinged with a juridical tone, as fits the two law student interlocutors. Plato's *Euthydemus* on the views of the sophists is described as "the litigious dialogue" (el diálogo litigioso) (1995, 1:364), a description taken from Ficino's subtitle for the work: *Euthydemus, vel litigiosus* (Ficino 1576).[249] Palatino and Pinciano would like to have many books from other disciplines in their own personal library, "especially those on Christian and moral philosophy" because they give "much pleasure and consolation to the soul" whereas legal tomes from their own profession "are against both soul and body, making us martyrs without any small moment for recreation" (1995, 1:578–9).[250] Pinciano praises as particularly noteworthy the libraries of Ptolemy, Alexander, King Alonso of Aragón and Sicily, and Hernando Colón in Seville (1995, 1:579). Those who presume themselves erudite doctors dressed in their caps and gowns are compared to Aesop's ass who, dressed up as a lion so as to gain the respect of the other animals, revealed his true identity when he had to bray; the learned doctors will also, one day, give themselves away by braying according to their true nature and they, like the ass, will be eaten by wolves and lions (1995, 2:666). Despite Arce's generally jocular tone, Ficino is, throughout his text, a credible and respected authority.

Hector Pinto also offers the same basic history of the law found in Ficino's *Minos* commentary, although he adds further detail. Following on the blanket statement that all laws emanate, in the first instance, from God, Pinto avers:

> The legislator of the Egyptians, Osiris, attributed the laws to Mercury (whom they took to be God); the Carthaginian Charondas attributed his laws to Saturn; Zoroaster the jurisconsult of the Persians and Bactrians attributed his to Horomasis; Athenian Solon attributed his to Minerva, and the Scythian Zamolgis said they were from the goddess Vesta, the Cretan Mino said Jupiter, the Lacedemonian Lycurgus said Apollo, Roman Numa Pompilius said Aegeria, and the Arab Mohammed said the angel Saint Gabriel, sent by order of God, a falsehood with which they have fooled a large part of the world. Anyone who wishes to see this in detail, read Ficino on Plato, and Georgio Veneto in the second [part] of his *Harmony of the World.* (1595, f. 261r)[251]

A comparison of Ficino's version with this passage from Pinto highlights two noteworthy changes introduced by the Portuguese author: the apparently specific omission of Moses as lawgiver to the Hebrews, and the addition of the disparaging commentary on Muslim law. Both are clearly illustrative of the particular social climate on the Iberian Peninsula. Pinto also replaces Trismegistus with Osiris as lawgiver to the Egyptians, and uses Mercury [Latin name] instead of Hermes [Greek name] as the source of those laws. These changes are made by Pinto in the Portuguese edition, then copied by the anonymous Spanish translator (Pinto 1952, 3:220–1).

The three jurists above – Celso, Arce de Otálora, and Pinto – all wrote during the first half of the sixteenth century. Writing in the second half of that same century, Juan de Pineda also references Ficino as authority on the origin of law. Pineda's full discussion on civil law spans twelve chapters and includes a host of authorities, as well as multiple nations and their lawgivers, beginning with Plato, "who says that God is the author of the laws" (Pineda 1963, 163:300).[252] That blanket statement, while obliquely suggested in the quotation above from Ficino's commentary on *Minos* (2006, 22), is explicit in his commentaries on the *Republic*: "God, the author of all laws" (2009a, 4), and on the *Laws*: "Plato shows that God is the founder of all laws" (2009a, 98).[253] Other particular points of interest in Pineda's sections on law include "the conclusions of philosophers are moral laws ... [and] philosophy is a defensive barricade and cave for the law, as a mother is for her daughters," along with an insistence that the law stems from the republic itself, or from its ruler with the consent of the public, for having promised himself to the republic (Pineda 1963, 163:300).[254] Ficino is specifically referenced, albeit wrongly: "In his preface to the works of Plato, Marsilio Ficino says that Aristonymus and Phormio, both disciples of Plato, were sent by him to give laws, Aristonymus to Arcadia and Phormio to the Trojans," and that "his [Plato's] Marsilio" says that Plato also gave laws to the inhabitants of Zaragoza (Pineda 1963, 163:318–19).[255] Aristonymus is mentioned in the *Republic* (1, 328B) but neither of the two figures referenced by Pineda in this section is found in Ficino's prologue to the *Opera omnia*. Both Aristonymus and Phormio, however, are found in Plutarch's "Against Colotes: The Disciple and Favorite of Epicurus," in which one reads that Plato sent the former to Arcadia and the latter to the Eleans "to set in order their commonweal" (1874, 382). While correctly pointing out that Ficino is a source and authority on as well as a follower of Plato, Pineda conflates information from various sources to additionally, if mistakenly, also credit the Italian philosopher for details from Plutarch.

In a 1595 manual for Spanish magistrates (*Política para corregidores*), author Jerónimo Castillo de Bobadilla (c. 1546–1605) cites Plato, without mentioning Ficino, for the same details on lawgivers. The magistrate first notes that in his *Laws*, Plato says that a governor must judge by law rather than whim (*albedrío*) and then, without specific reference to the Italian philosopher, offers the full list from Ficino's summary of *Minos* including Draco, Solon, Licurgus, Trismegistus, Zoroaster, Pompilius, Mahommed, Moses, Plato, and Minos. Castillo de Bobadilla adds a few more names from other sources: Seleucus, Protagoras, and Philolaus, to end with King Alfonso X and his predecessors who gave laws to "our Spain" (nuestra España) (1616, 2:10).

In 1612, Francisco Bermúdez de Pedraza (1585–1655) published a pedagogical instruction manual for students of law (*Arte legal para estudiar la jurisprudencia*). Like his predecessors, he repeats Ficino's specifics on the history of law, saying first that all gentiles attributed the invention of the laws to their own god whom they called Jupiter, Apollo, or Minerva:

> And Marsilio Ficino explains. Apollo signifies power, Jupiter clemency, Minerva wisdom; because of these attributes they pretended that Minos, legislator of Crete,

> received the laws from Jupiter; Lycurgus, legislator of the Lacedemonians, got them from Apollo; Solon, legislator of the Athenians, received them from Minerva, thereby giving to understand that the legislator must be powerful, as well as a wise and clement sovereign. (1992, 25)[256]

This particular reference is to the first book of Ficino's commentary on the *Laws*: "These three also follow in the footsteps of the authors of laws – Minos, Lycurgus, and Solon – who refer laws to three divinities: Jupiter, Apollo, and Minerva. And this is quite right, for the Sun, which is the Lord of the Planets, holds power, while Jupiter is filled with mercy, and Minerva with wisdom. These three embrace the whole nature and perfection of law" (2009a, 76).[257] Bermúdez de Pedraza's "they pretended" (fingieron) is a change to Ficino's version ("this is quite right"), in which the three lawgivers are accepted without question. When the Spaniard was writing in 1612 the word *fingir* still had two meanings: "from the Latin verb fingo, gis.xi.ctum, to shape, to give shape to ... to form, i.e., to make with one's understanding, or with one's hands" but more common in Spanish is its use as "to pretend" (Covarrubias).[258] Jurist Bermúdez de Pedraza's next sentence clarifies his meaning as to the latter: "And reducing what the blind gentiles said to Catholic truth, I say this means from God, who is Three in persons, and author of the laws, with his three gifts: power to the Father, wisdom to the Son, and clemency to the Holy Spirit" (1992, 25).[259] The Spanish jurist's commentary accepts Ficino's reading of the mythopoetic explanation of planetary attributes (wisdom, clemency, and power) but rejects (*fingieron*) the interaction of those planets themselves as gods with the groups who attributed to each the giving of their laws. Further, while classifying the opinion as one of "blind gentiles" (versus Ficino's "three divinities"), Bermúdez de Pedraza adapts the format to his Christian Trinity.

The Spanish jurist then proceeds, however, to outline the special properties of the number three ("la excelencia de este número ternario") along with its perfect multiplication of three times three for nine ("tres veces repetido el número de tres hazen nueue"), supporting the assertion with proof of the divisions of the various legal tomes of Justinian (1992, 25). Here, with adaptation in the form of those Justinian proofs, he again follows Ficino from the same passage of his commentary on *Laws*: "the number three is within the beginning, the middle, and the end of all things and of all actions" and "nine indicates here the threefold use of power, the threefold nature of wisdom, and the triple nature of mercy ... and three times three clearly produces the number nine" (Ficino 2009a, 77).[260] Bermúdez de Pedraza then adds another direct reference to the Italian philosopher:

> And what Plato said, that Minos, he who gave laws to the Cretans, spent nine years in a cave so as to learn them, which signifies, Marsilio says, the nine hierarchies of the

> angels; through those hierarchies, God communicates the laws that must be promulgated to men. This is not a fable, the sacred letters tell us the same thing. (Bermúdez de Pedraza 1992, 25)[261]

Here, the Spanish author insists on the truth of the history that, as he sees it, conforms to biblical sources. This assurance could also be from Ficino who notes, in the very same passage of his commentary on *Laws*: "And of course you are not unaware that this number nine in relation to angels is used not only by Christians but by Platonists, too, especially Proclus and Syrianus, as we clearly show in the *Theology*" (Ficino 2009a, 77).[262] A marginal printed note in the 1612 edition of Bermúdez de Pedraza's text indicates *Protagoras* as the source of this information but that sourcing itself is also from the same passage in Ficino's *Laws* commentary where, with the references above to the lawgivers and perfect numbers, we also find the specific note:

> Plato, in *Minos* as well as in this present dialogue, often refers to a nine-year period as being necessary for inwardly receiving the laws from Jupiter and conveying them to men; he may be pointing to the nine orders of angelic minds, through which, as if through interpreters, the very reason for the establishment of law may be passed on to men. In *Protagoras* he subsumes all these orders, which are the interpreters of the laws, under the single name of Hermes. (Ficino 2009a, 77)[263]

Bermúdez de Pedraza makes no mention of Hermes, but he does note that God communicates his laws and divine will to princes (*príncipes*) by means of their "custodian angels" (Angeles Custodios) (1992, 25). More than half a century earlier Arce de Otálora's civil-law character Pinciano, who also adapted the tripartite division of power, wisdom, and clemency to the Christian Trinity, had made a similar although slightly distinct reference, saying that Minos "spent nine years in a cave, three years at a time, to learn the laws that he later promulgated" (1995, 1:254).[264] In his *Laws* commentary, Ficino relates the story of Plato as the Athenian stranger, with Megillus the Spartan and Clinias the Cretan, en route to the "sacred cave of Jupiter for consulation on this matter" of laws; Plato intercepts and helps the others. In *Minos*, Plato relates that every ninth year, Minos visited with Zeus for counsel. The adaptation to nine years spent in a cave is apparently from Strabo (Antoine Banier 1740, 485), the Greek geographer and historian who died in the first century AD.

Bermúdez de Pedraza also tells his reader that Prometheus "signifies human providence" (significa la humana prouidencia) (1992, 24), and the printed textual note to the 1612 text indicates Plato's *Protogoras* as the source. In that dialogue, Prometheus must provision man with a means to protect himself after

Epimetheus has squandered all other protections (hoofs, hides, etc.), that is, Prometheus provisions man with the protections of wisdom and fire, but he is not specifically called "human providence" although his name in Greek does signify forethought. Ficino, however, makes that clear statement in a number of places: in his commentary to *Protagoras*: "to imitate ... the providence of Prometheus rather than the haste of Epimetheus" (2006, 73); in his discussion of Plato's "Second Letter ... to Dionysius, Tyrant of Syracuse": "Jupiter is power, while Prometheus is providence" (2006, 152), and in the *Platonic Theology*: "from Prometheus, from the providence, in other words, that is particular and created" (2001–6, 14.9.3).[265] As did Arce de Otálora, Bermúdez de Pedraza specifies that "law is the soul of the Republic" (la ley es el alma de la República), then adds that the human body cannot survive without its soul, nor the Republic without its laws (1992, 27).

In sum, for theoretical, philosophical, moral, and practical Spanish jurists, Plato as read through Ficino, with or without specific mention of the Italian philosopher, is the authority on law and its history. Law students and scholars in Spain, throughout the sixteenth and into the seventeenth centuries, followed Ficino to understand the principles of their discipline. At times, as we have seen, they adapted the Italian philosopher's texts to conform to their own evolving opinions and mores; nonetheless, Ficino formed a solid basis from which they continually drew.

Praise of Ficino

Francisco de Ávila's *La vida y la muerte o Vergel de discretos* was first published in 1508. In a recent edition of the work, Cátedra describes it generally as classical spiritual literature and, specifically, as a treatise in which "etymological, poetic, rhetorical, and spiritual extravagance" is presented as the norm (Cátedra in Ávila 2000, 9).[266] Following on various preliminary texts – Dedication letter in prose, Dedication letter in verse, Presentations, Exhortation to the reader, and Prologue – Ávila includes a debate with Death, a sermon filled with theological arguments, long lists in verse form of deceased notables, and a meditation on the "vile human condition and the inevitability of death itself" (2000, 12).[267] The Spaniard dedicates his work to Cardinal Cisneros, founder of the Universidad at Alcalá de Henares. With literary resonance of the medieval "dances of Death," Ávila offers a number of stanzas in which Death lists notable deceased persons who despite their various talents could not escape the inevitable, then proceeds to menace some of the living. The particular section that includes Ficino's name, subtitled "Artists of the liberal arts" (Artists de las artes liberales), is a varied list of known "philosophers, astrologers, medical doctors, orators, logicians, musicians, poets, and other artists, along with other singular men": Socrates, Plato, Aristotle, Solon, Virgil, Horace, Homer, Quintilian, Pythagoras, Dionysius, Euclid, Aristophanes, and many more (Ávila 2000, 127).[268] Parmenides is identified as the inventor of logic (vv. 10414–15), Homer's verse is the "most esteemed" (vv. 10375–6), Dante and Petrarch are highly praised (vv. 10487–504), and Ficino is called simply "the great Marsilio Ficino" (el gran Marsilio Ficino) (v. 10416).

In 1568, Spaniard Benito Arias Montano (1527–98) was sent to Antwerp to work on the Polyglot Bible. There he met Flemish engraver Philips Galle (1537–1612), and in 1572 they joined to produce *Virorum Doctorum de disciplinis benemerentium effigies XLIIII*, a work that combines Galle's talents as engraver with Montano's as writer. According to Gómez Canseco and Navarro Antolín, the editors of a recent edition, the text is intended as "a panegyric of Christian humanism" in its combination of "astronomers ... doctors ... geographers ... printers ... humanists ... [and] poets"; it celebrates "tolerance" in its inclusion of various figures, notwithstanding their differences and despite any classification as heretic, Lutheran, or Christian; all are identified as having "contributed to the progress of knowledge," and are celebrated for their "dedication to the *studia humanitatis*, through which they combine to form a type of antidote against fanaticism" (Gómez Canseco and Navarro Antolín 2005, 20, 11).[269] The frontispiece of the volume as published in 1572 includes Neoplatonic iconography with two figures holding a placard that reads "To wisdom, cultivator of men" (Sapientiae, hominum cultrici) (2005, 115). The second project of Montano and Galle, published one year later, is titled *Humani generis amatori Deo liberalisimo sac. divinarum nuptiarum conventa et acta*, and the editors of *Virorum Doctorum* ... describe this second collaboration as illustrative of "the use of Neoplatonic symbolism to treat the mystical union between the soul and God."[270] Both works were successful enough to be republished a number of times in the sixteenth and seventeenth centuries (Gómez Canseco and Navarro Antolín 2005, 80–102). In *Virorum Doctorum* ... Montano's four-verse poem for Ficino's engraved portrait reads:

> What great things might I say of you, Ficino, that you
> yourself would not surpass by leaps and bounds?
> If I were to search, Ficino, for the truest disciple of ancient wisdom,
> who truer than you could I possibly find?"
>
> (Arias Montano and Galle 2005, 206–7)[271]

This praise panegyric confirms the high regard in which Ficino was held by Spanish intellectuals of the sixteenth century. When it comes to the Italian philosopher, Montano can only resort to praise with the rhetorical flourishes of mystic ineffability.

The sections above demonstrate the ubiquitousness of Ficino as a respected authority in Golden Age Spanish letters. His influence, however, extends beyond these literal quotations of and dialogues with his writings. Two key authors translated by Ficino, both integral parts of his *pia philosophia*, were Hermes Trismegistus and Plato. In an earlier study (Byrne 2007), I highlighted the resonance of the Hermetic work known mainly in the sixteenth century for the name of its protagonist, *Pimander*, in the verse works of Francisco de Aldana, Fray Luis de León, and San Juan de la Cruz. Attributed to Hermes Trismegistus, today considered an apocryphal figure, the Hermetic treatises or *Corpus Hermeticum* and their author are also consistently referenced throughout the sixteenth century, as will be seen in the following chapter.

3 Ficino as Hermes Trismegistus: The *Corpus Hermeticum* or *Pimander*

The writings referred to as Hermetica are generally subdivided into either philosophical or technical, with the latter category encompassing magical, alchemical, and astrological writings.[1] During the Renaissance, most were attributed to one author named Hermes (AKA Mercurius, AKA Tat/ Theut/ Theuth) Trismegistus. Neoplatonist Iamblichus put the total number of Hermetic writings at 20,000 (as listed by Seleucus) or at 36,555 (as listed by Manetho), although "the numbers of actual survivals ... are less imposing, something more than two dozen known titles" (Copenhaver 2002, xvi). Early in the seventeenth century, Isaac Casaubon would use the exaggerated numbers to debunk Hermes's authority, jesting that "if he had written all the works attributed to him, he would be the author of 25,000 volumes" (1655, 69).[2] Hermes's *bona fides*, however, had solid classical references. In the fourth century, Lactantius cited the Hermetic author on multiple points and Saint Augustine accepted Hermes as a contemporary of Moses, calling him a wise gentile for his prediction that the idols of his own Egyptian society would fall to a greater god (1969, XVIII, xxxix). In the tenth century Byzantine *Suda*, Hermes is described as "an Egyptian wise man who flourished before Pharaoh's time. He was called Trismegistus on account of his praise of the trinity, saying that there is one divine nature in the trinity" (Copenhaver 2002, xli). In the twelfth century, Gratian stated that Mercurius Trismegistus was the first to hand down written laws to the Egyptians (1486, Distinctio VII, 1),[3] and a thirteenth-century canon of Toledo, Gonzalo Palomeque, owned a composite volume that included a work by "T[r]imegistro" (Round 1993, 43). In the late thirteenth-century *General estoria* King Alfonso X, known as Alfonso el Sabio (the Wise), "calls Mercury god of the trivium," and links the name Trismegistus to those three arts; Faulhaber notes that this identification was a commonplace by the end of the twelfth century (Faulhaber 1969, 109–11). Alfonso X accepted all Hermes's cognomens: "On the philosopher Tat, whose name was Hermes, and he was son of the other Hermes

Trimegistus, and he was Mercury"; "he was an accomplished master in the three arts of the trivium" (Alfonso X, 2001, I:48).[4] Hermes is also referenced in the thirteenth-century *Bocados de Oro*, as well as a few fourteenth-century works; that is, he remained a respected authority in Spanish letters throughout the Middle Ages.

The two main philosophical works of Hermetica, now both dated to the early Christian Era, are the fourth-century *Asclepius* which continued to be known during the Middle Ages, and the first to third century *Corpus Hermeticum*, lost to the West then rediscovered mid-fifteenth century. As a testament to the esteem in which Hermes was held, Marsilio Ficino delayed his translation of Plato's *Opera omnia* in 1462, at the direct request of his patron Cosimo de' Medici, so as to concentrate on the recently discovered manuscript by the more important author Hermes Trismegistus. Although Ficino did at times adjust the names and ranks of the six *prisci theologi* of his *pia philosophia*, Hermes was frequently second (and at one point first) in this line of revered ancient gentile authors, all considered precursors in one way or another to Christian doctrine: Zoroaster, Hermes Trimegistus, Orpheus, Aglaophemus, Pythagoras, and Plato.[5] Today, Hermes Trismegistus is recognized as the apocryphal name of a writer of the first centuries of the Common Era with, as noted above, its own synthesis of religion and philosophy. Following on Ficino's Latin translation of the *Corpus Hermeticum*, first published in 1471, this collection of fourteen philosophical treatises would come to be commonly known and referenced as the *Pimander*, for the name of the spiritual guide who comes to Hermes in the first treatise when the latter is in a somnambulant state.[6] Although certain alchemical and mythological writings attributed to Hermes Trismegistus were prohibited by the 1559 Spanish Indices, the *Pimander* was never included on that list. Three manuscripts titled *Corpus Hermeticum*, held in three different Spanish libraries, offer perspective on the late fifteenth-century Spanish reception given to the writings of Hermes.

The BNE Manuscript

Contrastive to the general tendency for catalogue identifications, Madrid's BNE holds a notebook of mixed technical and literary Hermetica that was, for some time, classified under the general title *Corpus Hermeticum* which is usually reserved, as noted above, for the philosophical Hermetica (BNE ms. 7443). That general title has recently been changed to *Tratados y apuntes sobre alquimia y materias similares (Treatises and notes on alchemy and similar subjects)*. The notebook's contents illustrate the sixteenth century's multifaceted perspective on and interest in Hermetic topics, with a range of particularly eclectic entries: letters, magic spells, recipes, potions, *romancero* versions of mythological tales, and even accounting notations.[7]

Alongside straightforward ledger entries such as "Margarita Villar paid me the money and took her clothes," we read a Latin inscription about Sumanus, the Roman god of the nocturnal heavens and night lightning, which identifies him as the god of blood, water, and air; information about the "fifth essence"; and a recipe from someone named Perilla for "how to make coral from the horns of a billy goat."[8] A letter dated 18 September 1552 from Luis Centrelles in Valencia to Doctor Manreza in Murcia concerns a visit to letter writer Centrelles from someone named Balthasar de Zamora, supposedly a very good friend of Manreza. Centrelles complains that Zamora questioned him on "occult philosophy" (oculta philosophia) which, he insists, is neither his focus nor the term used where he lives, although he does know about philosophy and "prime metalurgical matter" (primera materia methalurgica). Recognizing Zamora as a truth seeker: "I saw him as a man who wished to find the road to the truth" (BNE ms. 7443, f. 3r),[9] Centrelles taught his visitor about Aristotle, Arnaldo de Vila [Villanova?],[10] Raimundo Llull, Saint Thomas of Aquinas on being and essence, and Mercurius philosopher: the letter outlines the lessons given, with explanations and citations to the same sources, in a text that switches easily from Spanish to Latin and back.[11] There are subsequent marginal glosses by another, anonymous hand who disputes Centrelles's words: a section of the letter dealing with Aristotle and prime matter is glossed with "this guy is lying" (miente este). The same anonymous hand also comments on other sections in the manuscript unrelated to Centrelles's letter, for example, a disputed magic recipe: "this man did not understand the philosophers, nor do they say anything like what he says" (BNE ms. 7443, f. 11v).[12]

Other writings in this BNE manuscript include excerpts from the *Tabula smaragdina* as interpreted by Hermes Trismegistus, Roger Bacon on alchemy, Raimond Llull on the philosopher's stone, a recipe for silver, a tractate on man as microcosm, "alphabets" or translation guides for alchemy, as well as for the Chaldean and Persian languages, and two different verse versions of the *romancero* verse work that relates a romantic encounter between the son of Mercury and a goddess of beauty named Salmacis.[13] This poetic character Mercury is identified as Hermes Trismegistus, the putative author of the *Corpus Hermeticum*; that is, here the Hermetic author is conflated with the mythological figure. The poem tells the story of Salmacis falling in love with Troco, son of Mercury and his sister Venus, with details that conform, but only in part, to genealogies of the gods as related by Cicero, Ovid, and Boccaccio. In those earlier versions, the offspring of the Hermes-Venus relationship is sometimes named Hermaphrodite, for his fusion of the genders of his two parents Hermes and Aphrodite (the Greek Venus). In the BNE manuscript version he is Troco, an exclusively male figure at the beginning of the poem, although the story ends with the image of Troco and Salmacis apparently hugging and kissing, while the reader is told that he is resisting her advances. The amorous intention of Salmacis and rejection by Troco lead to their fusion into one androgynous being. That is, in this version, Troco is not a hermaphrodite due to his parents' incestuous relationship but, rather, because he rejected a goddess of beauty.

In sum, the BNE manuscript paints an eclectic version of Hermes Trismegistus as magician, mythological figure and, to a certain extent, poet. It offers a glimpse of the alchemical-astrological Hermetic writings but is quite unlike the philosophical Hermetica. In addition to this manuscript, the BNE holds four different incunabula of the Ficino *Pimander* translation: one copy of the 1494 Paris Higman-Hopyl edition, and three copies of the 1491 Venice edition. Of these latter, one is the personally glossed copy of Queen Isabel's confessor, Fray Ambrosio de Montesinos (Béhar 2010, 471), which lets us know that the Hermetic work was being read in the court of the Catholic Monarchs Ferdinand and Isabel. The chaplain of a key supporter of the same royal couple, Pedro Núñez de Toledo, made a copy of the only known fifteenth-century Spanish translation of the *Pimander*, from the original of that Castilian translation sent from Rome to the Spanish poet Gómez Manrique, legal magistrate of Toledo.

Pimander Manuscripts: Escorial and El Burgo de Osma[14]

The *Pimander*, the most widely circulated Hermetic philosophical text of the Renaissance, is structured as a dialogue between spiritual guide Pimander and protagonist/narrative voice Hermes Trismegistus. Pimander is the representative of Mind (Mens/Nous), the primordial god who created the cosmos by means of an essential intellectual act. Curry points out this key distinction in the act of the Christian versus Neoplatonic God: the latter creates due to its essence while the former does so by an act of will (Curry 1933, 407). Ficino, however, combines the two: "Mark the words of Plato when he says that God does not merely understand, but wills also, for he means that God conceives by understanding within Himself and, through willing, makes outside Himself" (2009a, 49).[15] After Pimander appears to and instructs Hermes, the latter then writes the *Pimander* as an account of his meditative, visionary journey to wisdom.[16] Included also in the *Pimander* are the subsequent lessons of Hermes as instructor-guide for his own son, Tat, and for Asclepius.

The *Pimander* was written between the first and third centuries AD, that is, during an earlier era of religious and philosophical blending that gave fruit to similar syncretic mixes, like Plotinus's *Enneads*. In the century and a half after its Latin translation by Ficino, the *Pimander* was enormously popular, and would eventually be published in more than two dozen different editions before the end of the sixteenth century (Salaman, van Oyen, and Wharton, 1999). Hermeticism is part of the original Neoplatonic synthesis, a key element of the second, Ficinian Neoplatonism, and a persistent even if frequently secretive strain of thought throughout history. Like Ficino, Spain's mystic poets effortlessly mixed Christianity and Hermeticism (Byrne 2007); at the end of the sixteenth century, Justus Lipsius appropriated elements of the Hermetic texts for his Neostoic physics (Byrne 2005); Stoops (2011) finds resonance of Hermetic thought in Cervantes' *Novelas ejemplares*; philosophical Hermeticism resurfaced with the nineteenth-century's theosophical movements, and we hear its echo in Hispanic modernist poetry as, for example, with Rubén Darío's "fairy-spirit friend" (Hada amiga) (Darío 1995, "Autumnal") who pulls back the veils of wisdom and beauty on the universe; it is resonant again in late twentieth century-California New Age philosophies. The basic idea of the *Pimander* is a direct understanding between mortal man and a primordial god identified as the creator of the universe. Narrator Hermes begins the first treatise with a description of himself in a somnambulant state interrupted by the sudden appearance of the spirit-guide Pimander, who announces that he is the representative, voice, and son of the supreme primordial divinity. Pimander instructs Hermes to follow him so as to learn about his own capacity for immortality. Theologians and philosophers of the Renaissance accepted both the method and goal of Hermeticism: use the mind to understand the cosmos, and purge yourself of corporeal matters so as to become more like, closer to, or even one with, the divinity itself. Christians and Neoplatonists alike, who as we have seen were not always two distinct species during the Renaissance, embraced this Hermetic treatise.

In 1485, Diego Guillén de Ávila rendered Ficino's 1463 Latin translation of the *Pimander* into the Castilian vernacular.[17] Guillén de Ávila sent his translation to the legal magistrate (*corregidor*) of the city of Toledo, Spanish poet Gómez Manrique (c. 1412–90), with a letter dated 1487. When Gómez Manrique died three years later the work was not in his library but one year after that Juan de Segura, chaplain to Pedro Núñez de Toledo, made a copy of the same manuscript and incorporated the details on its origin, including the dedication letters from Ficino to Cosimo de' Medici, and from Guillén de Ávila to Gómez Manrique. In his own *explicit* dated 1491, Juan de Segura specifies that he has copied the "original" Guillén de Ávila manuscript translation.

The manuscript is contained in a composite volume in the Escorial library that combines one printed text titled *Letters of Rabbi Samuel* (*Epístolas del rabí Samuel*) with the Castilian *Pimander* in Juan de Segura's manuscript copy (see figure 17). The volume is covered with the specific grill-marked binding of the library, and the work is listed in Gracián's 1576 inventory of works donated to the Escorial by Spain's King Phillip II. According to the list, the volume arrived with the two texts already bound together.[18] This composite volume raises tantalizing

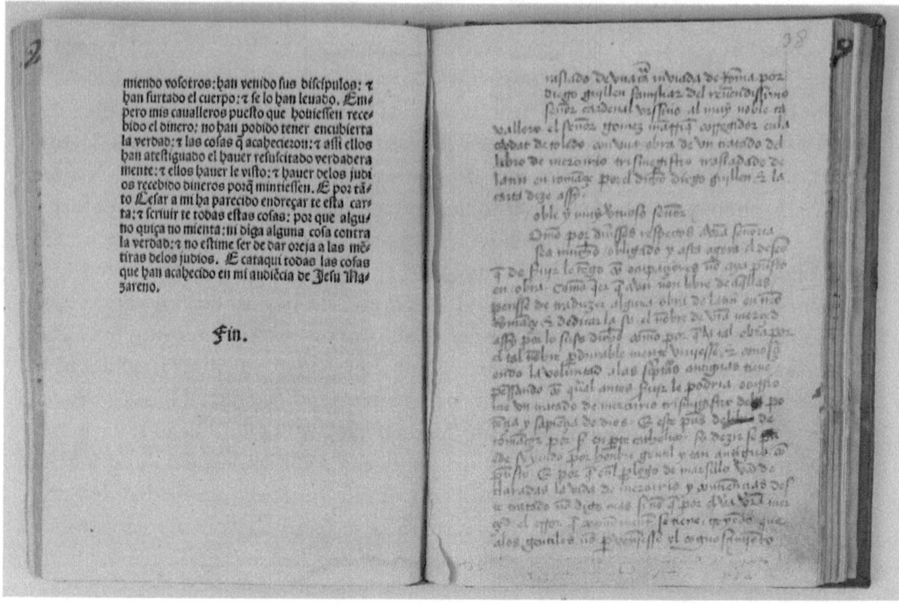

miendo vosotros: han venido sus discipulos: ⁊
han furtado el cuerpo: ⁊ se lo han leuado. Empero mis caualleros puesto que houiessen recebido el dinero; no han podido tener encubierta
la verdad: ⁊ las cosas q̃ acahecieron: ⁊ assi ellos
han atestiguado el hauer resuscitado verdadera
mente: ⁊ ellos hauer le visto: ⁊ hauer delos judi
os recebido dineros porq̃ mintiessen. E por tã-
to Cesar a mi ha parecido endreçar te esta carta: ⁊ scriuir te todas estas cosas: por que alguno quiça no mienta: ni diga alguna cosa contra
la verdad: ⁊ no estime ser de dar oreja a las mẽ-
tiras delos judios. E cataqui todas las cosas
que han acahecido en mi audiẽcia de Jesu Na-
zareno.

Fin.

Figure 17. Last page of Rabbi Samuel's printed treatise and first page of *Pimander* manuscript in Castilian translation from Ficino's Latin. El Escorial b.IV.29. Courtesy of Real Biblioteca del Monasterio de El Escorial, San Lorenzo, Madrid, Spain. Copyright © Patrimonio Nacional.

questions, addressed below, as to the early reception given the *Pimander* and Hermetic thought in Spain, both in subtle changes made by Guillén de Ávila as he translated the *Pimander* text, and in its combination of works.[19]

Studies of the volumes and collection of Phillip II offer no specific detail as to how these two works came into his library, nor as to why they were bound together. Neither is found on the lists of works purchased by Phillip II himself, nor on those purchased for the future monarch by his teachers and professors, although there are various enigmas in this documentation, which at times reads simply, "and another book," without further detail. An on-site search of the Escorial catalogue today turns up twenty-two works linked to Ficino's name as translator or author, and a number of those volumes are bound in the Escorial's distinctive grill binding.[20]

The lack of detail on the acquisition of the *Pimander* manuscript and the rabbi's epistle allows for various conjectures. The monarch might have inherited the works, and we do know that Queen Isabel was a friend of Pedro Núñez de

Toledo, whose chaplain Juan de Segura copied the manuscript in 1491. Arguing in favour of this supposition is the fact, as noted above, that one fifteenth-century copy of the *Pimander* held today by the BNE was the personal volume of Isabel's confessor. When Pedro Núñez de Toledo's father died, then Princess Isabel visited the family and stayed for fifteen days to console the widow. Letters from the Catholic Monarchs to Pedro Núñez de Toledo mention their mutual friendship.[21] Weighing against this conjecture is the fact that neither of the two works is mentioned in the inventories of Queen Isabel's library although these lists also contain enigmatic entries such as "another book ... but we do not know what it is" (Ruiz García 2004, 327, no. 11).[22] Another possibility is that the manuscript and/or the epistle were among the books that Phillip II purchased from a Núñez de Toledo in 1572 (Gonzalo Sánchez-Molero 1998, 42), although those volumes are not listed individually in the purchase documentation, which references only the patronym, not exclusive to that one family. As we have seen, Phillip II's librarian Benito Arias Montano praises Ficino in his 1572 *effigies* publication, and at his death Montano left his own manuscript collection to the Escorial, although these two volumes are not found in that inventory, either.[23] The only available concrete detail is that Gracián's list of books donated by Phillip II to the Escorial prior to 1576 includes this composite volume.

The first point of interest regarding the volume is the reason for the combination of these two works, which differ in various basic aspects: printed text (Rabbi Samuel) versus manuscript (*Pimander*); accepted dating (during the fifteenth and sixteenth centuries) as tenth to fourteenth century for Rabbi Samuel versus sometime around Moses for the *Pimander*; Jewish versus Egyptian author. What the works do clearly have in common is that both supposed authors questioned their own religious beliefs on points that favour Christian dogma.

Other manuscript copies of the rabbi's epistle, in Latin and in Catalán, have been studied.[24] The author has been identified as Rabbi Samuel Jehudi, "hailing from the Kingdom of Morocco ... sometime around the year 1068 AD" (Rodríguez de Castro 1781–6, 1:7),[25] and as "the famous Jew from Fez, who converted to our sainted faith in Toledo around the year 1087" but then "back in Morocco after his conversion, waged the famous dispute with the erudite Moor Albucaleb, whose written history in Arabic was conserved in a copy in the Escorial at the time of Nicolás Antonio ... but which must have been destroyed in the 1671 fire, as it is no longer to be found" (Lorenz Villanueva 1804, 2:141).[26] Villanueva notes that in 1418, Álvaro de Villaescusa translated the letter into Spanish, and that in 1511 the work was published in Valladolid. Ramón Hernández offers bibliography and information about the text and its author, saying that there are "many manuscripts" in both Latin and the vulgar tongues, but he seems unaware of this Spanish printed edition, which does not figure on his lists. Hernández does point out that one of the oldest existing codices of the work is another, Latin mansucript found in the Escorial.[27] A different manuscript in the BNE indicates that Pope Sixtus IV sent a copy of the work in Spanish to "Prince of Castile, son of King Ferdinand" together with other "devout works" prior to the end of the fifteenth century.[28] On its spine, this volume is identified as *Devocionario del R.D. Fernando*, which confirms that the rabbi's work, like the *Pimander*, was known in the circle of the Catholic Monarchs. The most recent studies of the rabbi's letter link it to the Dominican Order,[29] date it to the fourteenth century, and debate whether or not Rabbi Samuel ever truly existed, or whether he was invented by the writer who identifies himself only as "translator" of the rabbi's epistle, and offers his name as Alfonso Buenhombre.[30]

The Escorial's printed edition of the rabbi's letter is not dated, nor does it bear any publication information. Rabbi Samuel writes to Rabbi Isaac to confess his doubts about the Jewish rejection of Christ as son of God. The Spanish translator hides himself behind a literal translation of the supposed Latin translator's name Alphonsus Bonihominis, calling himself Alphonse Goodman (Alfonso Buenhombre) while translating all the details of Bonihominis, telling us that the letter was originally written "in Morisco" in the year 1000, and that he found and translated it into Latin in 1339. According to Bonihominis, Rabbi Samuel wrote in *morisco* – the language of Spain's Christianized Moors – so as to hide his doubts from the Christians, few of whom understand that tongue (Escorial ms. b.IV.29, f. 2v). Apparently, Bonihominis was one of those few, and he assures the named recipient of his own translation of the letter, one "Fray Hugo," that he has faithfully translated Samuel's letter, even leaving the biblical citations as found there, instead of substituting with text from the Saint Jerome version, that is, the Vulgate Bible (Escorial ms. b.IV.29, f. 2v).

In his epistle, Samuel uses Old Testament prophecy to adduce that the Jews should accept Christ as the Saviour. Nineteen of his twenty-seven chapters begin with an expression of fear – I am afraid that, I am scared that, I have qualms that, I fear much that, Sir I find myself afraid, I am frightened, I am terrified, it alarms me that – and each one refers to the fear of suffering eternal exile for not having accepted Christ as Saviour. The letter is, fairly obviously, preparation for a scholastic debate, and Bonihominis does explicitly so state: "I wish to advise all lay persons who might not be theologians, that they read this letter so as not to fear debate, even in public, with the Jews ... For if the other tries some apparent sophist's reasoning, and the lay person does not know how to respond, this could lead to scandal in the hearts of the listeners ..." (Escorial ms. b.IV.29, f. 3r).[31] Rabbi Samuel provides the Old Testament prophetic testimonies supporting Christ as Saviour, notes that both Moors and Christians understood the importance of the Messiah although the Jews did not, then negates the importance of Muhammad and the Koran while defending the Evangelists. The rabbi's epistle is followed by a short letter purportedly from Pontius Pilate to Emperor Tiberius Caesar, written to announce Christ's death. Pilate lists the various miracles performed by Christ and witnessed by multitudes, states that most Jews thought him to be the Saviour although certain envious others lied, and ends with the accusation that the latter, claiming the miracles were enchantments contrary to Jewish law, tortured and killed Christ. Pilate offers his guards as witness to the resurrection of "Jesú Nazareño."

With no clear reason for the combination of these two works in this volume, one aspect that deserves mention is the similarity of the rabbi's epistle to chapter 27 of Ficino's own *De christiana religione*.[32] In that chapter, just as Bonihominis in the rabbi's epistle, Ficino enumerates Old Testament prophetic testimonies supporting Christ as Saviour, then alleges that the Jews have two volumes that state the same, one in Hebrew and the other in Chaldean script. The combination of the epistle with Ficino's *Pimander* translation is noteworthy, although both the form and the exact content of the epistle differ from those of the Hermetic treatise.[33] The two works do, however, share their respective author's identification as pagan (Hermes) or heretic (Rabbi Samuel) prophet of Christianity, and both were popular texts among Christians.[34]

The second half of this Escorial composite volume is the *Pimander* translation. Manuscript scribe Juan de Segura includes Guillén de Ávila's letter to Gómez Manrique, which reads:

> Noble and virtuous sir,
> In recognition of my multiple obligations to your grace, and wishing to repay them in some way, I have decided to translate a Latin text into our Romance tongue, and to dedicate it to your grace, due to the foregoing and also so that the work, with your name, might live on. Knowing your affinity for ancient writings, and pondering which might most please you, I decided on a treatise by Mercurius Trismigistus [*sic*] titled *Of the potency and wisdom of God.* I took the liberty of translating it into Romance due to its being, in part, a Catholic work – if of course one can say such a thing of a work composed so long ago by a gentile. Since one can read of Mercurius's life and the contents of the treatise in Marsilio's prologue, I won't elaborate further except to say that, in this tractate, Your Grace shall see the error in that commonly held belief that the gentiles did not come into the knowledge of one God, maker and ruler of all things.
>
> May your noble grace and all around you prosper. From Rome, the fifth of April 1487, with the utmost respect,
>
> Diego Guillén[35]

Worthy of note is the reference to Marsilio, without need of last name, which allows us to speculate that both letter writer and recipient were on familiar terms with Ficino and his work. Even more noteworthy is the "Catholic" reference, and the use of Mercurius (Hermes) as an example of a gentile who believed in one, as opposed to many, gods. This confirms the continued acceptance of Saint Augustine's opinion, and is also reflected in the treatise itself.

Letter writer Diego Guillén de Ávila is, as he says, a member of the inner circle (*familiar*) of Cardinal Orsini. The Spaniard lived most of his life in Rome,[36] but at some point returned to Spain, and was named Canon of Palencia (Antonio 1999, 297). Guillén de Ávila is the author of a work titled *Panegírico a la reina Isabel*, published in Valladolid in 1509, as well as another *Panegírico* dedicated to a recently deceased patron, Archbishop of Toledo Alfonso de Carrillo (1410–82). In the latter text, Guillén de Ávila evokes Dante as his guide through hell in search of the whereabouts of Carrillo, who is eventually found in the Elysian Fields. Guillén de Ávila also translated the *Histories* of Sextus Julius Frontinus, as well as those of Herodian.[37] Víctor Infantes describes Guillén de Ávila as a member of a "notable group of writers who haven't received much attention from the critics," says he apparently had a relationship "probably on a personal level and in Rome," with one of Spain's early playwrights, Torres Naharro (c. 1485–1530), and notes a general Platonic influence in his writings (Infantes 1989, 76, 79). Through Diego Guillén de Ávila's father, Pedro Guillén de Segovia (1413–74), come the ties to the literary circle of Archbishop Alonso de Carrillo (Perea Rodríguez 2007, 92–3).

Letter recipient Gómez Manrique was a member of one of Spain's most illustrious noble families, with relatives that included daughters of kings and the first marquis of Santillana.[38] He spent much of his youth in the court, took part in the battles of the Reconquest, was named legal magistrate (*corregidor*) of Salamanca in 1454, of Burgos in 1465, and of Toledo in 1476. Gómez Manrique died on 20 November 1490, three years after the date on the letter with the manuscript sent by Diego Guillén from Rome. His books were inventoried on his death, but the *Pimander* manuscript does not figure among those listed (Round 1978–9, 34, and n. 59). Throughout his life, Gómez Manrique kept company with kings and nobles, and he was one of those instrumental in bringing about the marriage of the Catholic Monarchs, Ferdinand and Isabel. In short, Ficino's *Pimander* translation came in at the highest levels of Spanish court (and Church) society, and among some of its most Catholic representatives.

Juan de Segura's 1491 copy of the Guillén de Ávila translation begins with the manuscript's identification and provenance. The first paragraph identifies the "copy of a letter" sent with the "book by Mercurius Trismegistus":

> Copy of a letter sent from Rome by Diego Guillén, familiar of the most reverend Cardinal Orsini to the most noble knight Sir Gómez Manrique, corregidor in the city of

> Toledo, with a written treatise of the book by Mercurius Trismegistus translated from Latin into Romance by the same Diego Guillén, and the letter reads as follows ...[39]

Following is the letter from Diego Guillén de Ávila to Gómez Manrique, as cited *supra*, and then Ficino's dedication to Cosimo de' Medici:

> The written tractate begins in this manner. Argument of Marssillio Ficuro [*sic*] Florentine in the book of Mercurius Trismegistus translated from Latin into Romance by Diego Guillén familiar of the Most Reverend Cardinal Ursino. In the time when Moses was born flourished the winged astrologer, brother of metaphysician Prometheus and maternal grandfather of the first Mercurius, whose nephew was Mercurius Trismegistus.[40]

Following Ficino's letter to Cosimo, the treatise is again identified and the translators, again named:

> Here begins the book of Mercurius Trismegistus on the Power and Wisdom of God, translated from the Greek into the Latin by Florentine Marsillio [*sic*] Ficino and sent to Cosimo de' Medici, then from Latin translated into Castilian Romance by Diego Guillén and sent to the magnificent and noble gentleman Sir Gómez Manrique.[41]

The last paragraph of the manuscript recaps with a dated colophon from copyist Juan de Segura:

> Here ends the book of Mercurius Trismegistus, translated from Greek into Latin by Florentine Marsillo Fricino [*sic*], in the month of April of the year 1463, and from Latin translated into Castilian Romance by Diego Guillén, a personal friend of the most reverend Cardinal Ursino, in the month of February of the year 1485; from which first translated copy I, Juan de Segura chaplain to Sir Pero Núñez of Toledo, have made this second copy in the month of November of the year 1491.[42]

In this second letter, Ficino is named as translator three times, but his name is properly spelled only once, with two different misspellings as Ficuro, then Fricino, which allows us to conclude that Juan de Segura did not have the same familiarity with the Italian philosopher as did Diego Guillén de Ávila. Throughout the sixteenth century, the *Pimander* itself will also be referenced with variant spellings *Pymander*, *Poemander*, and *Pimmadro*.

We have only very sketchy information as to who this last letter writer and copyist might be: two Juan de Seguras are listed in the parochial archives of Saint Leocadia in Toledo, father and son bearing the same name, listed as members of the brotherhood (*cofradía*) of Santa María la Blanca, a synagogue converted to a church in the early fifteenth century; the information is found in a ledger dated 23 June 1493.[43] Juan de Segura of Toledo is referenced in certain legal documents from the beginning of the sixteenth century, which tell us that on 2 June 1514, silversmith Gutierre de Vargas asked Toledo's legal magistrate for permission to "open a shop" in the "alleyway named for Juan de Segura"' (Porras Arboledas 2004, 70).[44] Of the three patronymic names connected with one University of Salamanca holding referenced above (figure 5): Herrera, Núñez, and Pérez de Prado, the first two are also linked in a legal document dated 27 November 1493: "Alfonso de Herrera brings the case to the city council that Canon Pedro Núñez wants to reopen a process regarding water services that since time immemorial have been provided to certain homes that he had purchased in the Caleros neighbourhood" (Porras Arboledas 2004, 61).[45] This letter writer, acting on behalf of Herrera and Núñez, is Juan de Segura, who identifies himself as chaplain to Pedro Núñez of Toledo. To date, that is the only information available on Juan de Segura.

In order to compare Guillén de Ávila's Spanish manuscript version with Ficino's Latin, I have collated four editions on the points studied: Ficino's Latin text as published in 1554; Guillén de Ávila's 1485 Spanish translation of Ficino's Latin (dated as per Juan de Segura's colophon, *supra*); a 1995 Spanish translation of the Greek made by Renau Nebot; and the 2002 Copenhaver English edition. Together, they allow for comparison of changes made by Ficino from the Greek to his Latin, and by Guillén de Ávila from Latin to Spanish. I will refer to these four editions as Ficino, Guillén de Ávila, Renau Nebot, and Copenhaver. Any translations from Guillén de Ávila's Spanish into English are my own.[46] The editions differ in the specific tractates included, but all contain the first fourteen which are the only ones known to Ficino and, so, the only ones translated by Guillén de Ávila. I will also refer to a separate fifteenth-century Latin manuscript of Ficino's text of the *Pimander* conserved in the cathedral library at El Burgo de Osma, Spain. Ficino is clearly noted as the translator, and his dedication letter to Cosimo de' Medici is included with the manuscript but his commentaries to the fourteen treatises are omitted. It seems that the idea was to re-gloss the text, and to that end a full half of the column space on each page, as well as broad margins at top and bottom, were left blank for notes. Three different, anonymous hands comment on the text in various sections, offering interesting contemporary counterpoint to Guillén de Ávila's translation.[47] This manuscript will be identified bibliographically as El Burgo de Osma.

At the start of the first tractate, having shown Hermes the divine, blinding, ineffable light at the centre of the cosmos, Pimander explains: "I am that light, your god, older than the humid nature that emerged from the shadow. Seed of mind, light-filled word, and son of god" (Guillén de Ávila, I, 6).[48] The parallels with Christian thought are obvious in Pimander's identification of himself as god, word and son of god. In the Hermetic text, there is also a third creator described as a mind of fire and spirit. Ficino calls this third creator a "spiritus tenuis, intellectualis" and the anonymous hands of El Burgo de Osma do not comment on the passage. For Renau Nebot this third creator is "un aliento vital, sutil e inteligente" and for Copenhaver, it is "a fine, intelligent spirit." A breath or spirit for all the others, Guillén de Ávila will fully conflate this third creator with the third figure of his Christian Trinity, calling it literally the "Holy Ghost" (spíritu sancto) (Guillén de Ávila, III, 1). The Spaniard not only accepts, but furthers, the *pia philosophia* parallel of the Hermetic trio to his Christian Trinity.

The question of man's immortality is uniformly accepted in all four editions.[49] Pimander relates the story of the first man to be created who, having seen his own beauty reflected in nature's waters, descended through the seven planetary spheres to unite with them. The result – part Narcissus, part Christ – was the combination of mortal and immortal, human and divine:

> And following on this, taking on the form of a similar existence in existence itself as in the water, he loved her [nature] and took her to himself. In effect, he realized his will and engendered the form that lacks reason. Nature embraced that which was brought to her in the sphere (*rueda*). She joined and mixed completely with him and for this reason, only man of all earthly living things is known to be of a dual nature, mortal of course for his body but also immortal due to that same essential (*substancial*) man. He is certainly immortal ... (Guillén de Ávila I, 14–15)[50]

In the "realized his will" phrasing, we see Guillén de Ávila offer a Christian version of God's manner of creation by an act of will, versus the Neoplatonic concept of creation due to essential nature (Curry 1933, 407). In this place in the Hermetic text, however, the act is that of the Son of God, not the Father. Guillén de Ávila does not comment on the "demiurge" aspect of this "second Creator," a key point in the *Pimander*, and one Ficino does take pains to explain in various writings.[51]

According to the Hermetic text, at some future moment man's material, mortal body will separate from his immortal soul. Hermes asks Pimander: "What will happen after the ascension?" and Pimander responds:

> Undoubtedly first in the resolution, the material body will dissolve itself into another, and that sensate form that it previously had *will hide itself in time to come*. Lazy habits and customs will be conceded to, and left with, the devil. The five senses, having turned into spiritual souls, will return to their sources so as to be reborn when they *will be once again* in their acts. The forces of the ineffable and concupiscient will devolve into unreasoning nature, and the soul will then harmoniously blend into the higher places ... (Guillén de Ávila, I, 24–5, my emphasis)[52]

Guillén de Ávila makes clear that the sensate form will hide itself *in time to come*, and the corporeal senses *will be* again. That is, the body will be resuscitated. Apparently, this particular point is not in the Greek text, as neither Renau Nebot nor Copenhaver include it. Respectively, they tell us that the "figura que tienes se vuelve invisible" (Renau Nebot) or that it "vanishes" (Copenhaver) and the senses "retornan a sus fuentes" (Renau Nebot) or "rise up and flow back to their sources" (Copenhaver) (I, 24–5). Neither speaks of those corporeal senses existing again in future time. Ficino introduced corporeal resurrection into this section of the *Pimander*[53] and he also assures us in his *Platonic Theology* that the same body man once had in life will be that resuscitated for the afterlife (Ficino 2001–6, 18.9.15). Although debated by Christian theologians throughout the Middle Ages, this dogma was mandated as a belief by various Church councils, and here Ficino conforms the Hermetic text to his church's ideals. On this point, Guillén de Ávila translates without change or commentary, but one of the anonymous hands at El Burgo de Osma surprisingly and sharply glosses the passage in the margin, saying: "The body will not be resurrected" (Non resurrectios corporem). In these two late fifteenth-century manuscripts, we hear the debate still being waged despite dogmatic Church declarations. It is notable that, in rejecting this doctrinal stance, the anonymous hand is denying a long list of ecclesiastical *dicta* that mandated this specific belief; two significant examples are the Lateran Council of 1215 and the Lyon Council of 1274.[54] Close to one hundred years later, post-Council of Trent and its publications again mandating the belief,[55] we read a more vivid version of the "yes, it will be resurrected" perspective in the verse of the late sixteenth-century Spanish poet Francisco de Aldana. Aldana describes Judgment Day in all its literally hair-raising detail, with rotted, old mortal eyes and ears seeking their particular bodies, fleshless skeletons and whitened bones running to join up again. His verse version of the general resurrection also follows Ficino in combining biblical resurrection of the earthly body: "The ashes are transformed into flesh" (En carne se transforma la ceniza) (Aldana 1985, XXVIII, v. 121) with a Neoplatonic-Hermetic return to an aethereal material that existed prior to time:

> the accidental, parvenu form
> seeks a different material, a different element
> without disturbing place, time, or fortune,
> or, in the movement of things, any thing. (Aldana 1985, XXVIII, vv. 125–8)[56]

Aldana's accidental form seeks another material or element with which to cloak itself, one that does not involve consideration of place, time, fortune, or movement. That makes it one that does not conform to the Christian dogma of souls and bodies of men created in time (Allen 2008a, 41). The Spanish poet furthers the ideology of the *pia philosophia* with language and ideas that make it more Neoplatonic and less Christian, although other aspects of the same verse work, studied in more detail below, do fully emphasize the literal recomposition and reconfiguration of body parts.

Unlike Guillén de Ávila's conformity with man's immortality and corporeal resurrection, on the Hermetic idea of an immortal cosmos he will emend the text minimally yet significantly. In the eighth tractate of the *Pimander*, Ficino's text reads: "Imprimens qualitatem materiae existenti immortali"; in Renau Nebot's Spanish: "Envolvió entonces al cuerpo entero con la inmortalidad"; and in Copenhaver's English: "The matter that he invested with this spherical quality is immortal, and its materiality is eternal" (VIII, 3). All three state clearly that the cosmos is immortal, and the anonymous hands at El Burgo de Osma do not comment on this section. Renau Nebot offers the history of this philosophical debate about the eternity of the cosmos, including a distinction between the terms 'eternity' and 'immortal' (1999, VIII, 3, n. 92). In his *Platonic Theology,* Ficino speaks of two worlds: the first, spiritual world has always been and will exist eternally, but the second, which is corporeal, gained eternity in the moment of its creation by God. The latter passed from non-being to being, and the authority who best explains this detail, according to Ficino, is Hermes Trismegistus (2001–6, 18.2.10–14). Guillén de Ávila, however, modifies the *Pimander* passage with the adverb "almost": "with all the forms completed, the father seeded qualities into the sphere as one would in a field. By seeding these qualities, he wished to adorn that which came after, *almost* nurturing each and every body with immortality" (Guillén de Ávila, VIII, 3, my emphasis).[57] That additional adverb irrevocably changes the proposal and meaning of the passage, and the translator here makes the Hermetic message conform to his reading of Christian doctrine.[58] He has no qualms about altering the text, which tells us two things: he wants to accept it and he feels a sense of autonomy with respect to its doctrinal stances, ergo he adapts it to make it work. This parallels Ficino's own "experimental, exploratory attitude to Christian doctrines" (Hankins 2005, 5), and is reflective of the intellectual dogmatic independence and desire for syncretism at the basis of the *pia philosophia.*

In another passage, Guillén de Ávila again alters the text with the same adverb "almost." Here, the passage speaks to man's perception of god in the cosmos. In Ficino's Latin, we read: "atque adeo se notum praestat, vt non intelligere modo, sed manibus etiam ipsis, vt ita dixerim, liceat attrectare." With the verb "licet, licere" that is, to be licit,[59] in a subjunctive form, the phrasing reads in translation: "so to speak, it may be licit to touch him (god) with one's own hands" (V, 2). Each of the translations I have compared offers a slightly varied wording for this passage.

For Renau Nebot, that which is touched is "your own thought" (tu mismo pensar) and god is only seen, or contemplated. For Copenhaver, the phrase becomes a direct question: "Can you see understanding and hold it in your hands?" Ficino uses the subjunctive, as we've seen, and Guillén de Ávila tempers the textual enthusiasm with another "almost": "and in such a way he [God] manifests himself that not only can we understand him but also, in a manner of speaking, it is *almost* licit to touch him with our hands" (Guillén de Ávila, V, 2). The translator here could have followed Ficino with a subjunctive, "may be licit," and the introductory phrase "so to speak," but he decided to attenuate even further by adding the adverb: "almost licit." With that addition, he questions the physicality, or materiality, of god in the cosmos, again conforming the Hermetic message to his own reading of the doctrinal point. In the same section of the El Burgo de Osma manuscript, one of the anonymous glossers draws a little hand in the margin pointing to this phrasing and says simply "Non." Both of these negations of the idea of a tactile god in the universe evade the "pantheist" label that, 400 years later, Menéndez Pelayo would apply to many writers of this time frame. However, if we think about the mystical union of, for example, San Juan de la Cruz (1562–91) with his god in various moments of rapture: "I flew so high, so high/ that I reached the hunted one" (Juan de la Cruz 2000, "Tras de un amoroso lance," vv. 3–4)[60] or "He who is suffering from love/ having been touched by the divine being" and "Will, having been/ touched by divinity" (2000, "Por toda la hermosura," vv. 21–2, 37–8)[61] – the idea of "touching" god, that Guillén de Ávila had to qualify with his "almost," has lost its danger for the saint, whose verses are interpreted by most critics to mean being touched by divine grace. The fusion of Platonic cognition and divine grace was one of Ficino's goals with the *pia philosophia*, and in another verse line of San Juan de la Cruz, we read that goal realized: "There he gave me his breast, there he taught me a delightful science" (2000, "Cántico," stanza 27).[62] Scholars have attempted to excuse or explain away San Juan de la Cruz's "dangerous" brush with pantheism (Sanson 1962, 191), but that qualifier only highlights a critical failure to appreciate the Christian-Neoplatonist syncretism in the saint's writings. San Juan de la Cruz did fuse divine grace and Platonic cognition, realizing in verse the theoretical aim of Ficino's *pia philosophia.*

In another passage, the *Pimander*'s author speaks about the various lives and transmigrations of an individual soul passing from one form to another as it perfects itself (X, 7–8). Ficino, Renau Nebot, and Copenhaver do not differ notably in their translations of this passage although in his commentary on the tractate, Ficino does dispute the idea of a soul transmigrating "backwards" in a hierarchical sense, from rational to non-rational form. The Italian philosopher calls this possibility an allegorical fiction (*fictionis allegoriam*) and argues that divine law prohibits such a "nefarious error" (lex enim divina violationem tam nefariam prohibit) (Ficino 1554, X, commentary). This topic had long been contentious and was accepted by some but disputed by others, with Plotinus as one of those in favour (Renau Nebot 1999, 164–5, n. 116). Ficino accepts Plotinus in most things, but not for this possibility of an inverse metempsychosis, man to animal.[63] Lawrence Fine comments that, among the Jews of the Iberian Peninsula during the thirteenth and fourteenth centuries, such transmigrations became a significant point of debate, with Spanish cabalist Nahmanides (Rabbi Moses Ben Nahman, who lived from 1194 to 1270) stating that Job had to suffer in this lifetime due to sins in a previous incarnation (Fine 2003, 304–5). Ogren notes that "a heated debate of unprecedented nature erupted concerning the doctrine in the Jewish community of Candia on the island of Crete" sometime in the second half of the fifteenth century (2004, 80). Ficino reads Platonic writings on the subject as fiction or allegory, arguing for the immortality of the soul, and noting that the souls of animals die with their bodies but that men's souls "are consecrated to the endless life of the mind ..." (vitae mentis perpetuae dedicatas) as he explains Platonic writings on the transmigration of souls and the soul's circuit as allegorical poetic interpretation (2001–6, 16.7.10; 17.4). At the end of the fifteenth century and throughout the sixteenth, the topic was discussed by Italian cabalists (Ogren 2009), and Bertholet (1909) offers examples in literature from Homer to Dante to Ibsen. Schwartz notes its resonance in satiric dialogue, particularly the anonymous sixteenth-century Spanish *Diálogo de las transformaciones de Pitágoras*, with animals who narrate their "successive metamorphoses, from human being to animal" in a dialogue named for the person to whom the doctrine was attributed (1990, 268). One more addition to that list is Pineda, who uses the term *palingenesia* but calls the idea "a big lie, condemned as heresy" (Pineda 1963, 162:340).[64] Ficino attributed that same term *palingenesis* to Zoroaster, while noting that "Mercurius has much to say about it with his son Tat" (Ficino 2001–6, 17.3.5).[65] Ficino strongly rejects the possibility of an "inverse" metempsychosis from mortal man to animal but, in the passage quoted below, we see that Guillén de Ávila accepts not only this inverse transmigration, but also the Platonist-Averroist idea of a World Soul:

> From one World Soul all souls flow out gathering around and then being distributed throughout the world. And certainly of these souls, there are many that change for the better and happier, but then there are some that change for the worse ... fallen into the human body, a soul that perseveres in evil will not in any way enjoy immortality but, rather, with the field turned upside down (*rrebuelto el campo*) it will fall down into that of the serpentine animals. (Guillén de Ávila, X, 7–8)[66]

Here, Guillén de Ávila accepts all transmigrations, even from human to the lowliest, earthly, serpent form.[67] The anonymous hands of the El Burgo de Osma manuscript do not comment on the passage. It is interesting to note that Bartolomé de las Casas also speaks briefly on this idea of an immortal soul: "It was a very celebrated opinion among the ancient philosophers, who believed in the immortality of the soul [and] that, after this life, those who had lived virtuously would have their place readied in certain fertile countryside" (1986, 1.20.59; 3:454).[68] Although Las Casas does not mention the inverse, human-to-animal transmigration, Guillén de Ávila's "rrebuelto el campo" seems to proceed from the same general idea: the Elysian Fields are for the virtuous and then other fields, "topsy-turvy" (rrebueltos), for sinners. Guillén de Ávila's heterodoxy as to this point highlights the fluidity of his own Christianity. Like Ficino and the anonymous hands at El Burgo de Osma, the Spaniard selectively questions the text he translates, and makes it conform to his own reading of the dogmatic ideals. He participates in the modelling of the *pia philosophia.*

In another section of the same treatise, we read a contradictory version of the same theme. Here, the evil soul will be reborn but only into another human form "because certainly the human soul will not choose another type of body, nor is it licit for the rational soul to fit into the body of an animal lacking in reason" (Guillén de Ávila, X, 19).[69] All versions studied here read similarly as to this metempsychosis for the impious, with restrictions to movement into another human form. The treatise continues with the destiny of a soul that is "pious, blessed, and divine" and which, once freed of the "jail of the body," will become "mind or god" (X, 19).[70] The only commentary on this destiny for the pious comes from one of the anonymous hands at El Burgo de Osma, who glosses in the margin: "this is not pious" (non de pietate). Like Guillén de Ávila, this commentator accepted the various transmigrations, even from human to serpent; however, the idea of man becoming god, admitted without question by translator Guillén de Ávila, is unacceptable for this anonymous glosser at El Burgo de Osma. The Spanish translator had, in previous sections, changed that which he deemed necessary or inconvenient; here, his conformity with this passage again highlights his eclectic approach and free hand with the text. In the verse of poets of the later sixteenth century, we read about various transmigrations: Fray Luis de León hopes that his soul will be converted into "resplendent light" (en luz resplandeciente convertido) (1995, X, v. 10), and the soul of Francisco de Aldana will be "transformed into its first cause" (en su primera causa transformada) (Aldana 1985, LXV, v. 81). These are poetic versions of the Hermetic mind-light and god-cause. The only Spanish work I am aware of in which man actually becomes god is a short theatre piece written in 1518 by Juan Luis Vives. Vives's protagonist, mortal man, puts on various masks in front of an audience of Greek gods. His final act is to assume the mask of the supreme god Jupiter which, although shocking to the assemblage in general, pleases Jupiter himself. Vives, however, presents only an audience of pagan gods, and his protagonist does not don the mask of the writer's own Christian divinity.[71]

Notwithstanding his conformity with the various reincarnations mentioned, Guillén de Ávila introduces another specific lexical alteration to the text regarding those progressive transmigrations. The Hermetic metempsychosis describes the route of the soul through various forms: first existing as a serpent it then becomes in sequence: creature of water, creature of land, and creature of air, respectively, to eventually take the form of a human being. Finally, it becomes a daemon and joins the chorus of the gods: "from there men cross over into the immortal souls of daemons, and then they revolve happily in the chorus of the gods" (Ficino 1554, X, 7).[72] In this and subsequent treatises, Guillén de Ávila accepts without commentary or change all transmigrations but he does substitute, in the final instance, "angels" for "daemons."

> Because some serpent souls transmigrate into those of water animals. And the souls of water creatures into those of land. Those of the land animals transform themselves into those who fly. Creatures of the air transform or transmutate into men and from there, some turn into angels. Finally they revolve happily in the chorus of the gods and in that place some move around while others are still [fixed], and this is the greatest glory of the soul. (Guillén de Ávila, X)[73]

One of the anonymous hands of the El Burgo de Osma manuscript repeatedly discusses the use of the word "daemon" in the *Pimander*. In one passage, we read that various intentions are born of mind, good ones due to divine seeds but evil ones through a harvest of seeds from daemons (IX.3). The section is marked with a marginal line, and the anonymous hand pens: "Demons and their works are not of the mind" (El Burgo de Osma, IX, 3).[74] To the contrary in tractate XII,13, where the text speaks of the "good daemon" and its relation to the "blessed god," the commentator adds the marginal indication "good demon" (Demon bonus) without further dispute. In both of these places in the text, Guillén de Ávila substitutes "angel" for "daemon."

More than fifty years later, Arce de Otálora describes compatible natures mutually attracted to each other due to the force of their horoscopes, and notes that the Platonists use the name demon for these seductive, innate angels or genii (1995, 2:1013). In the *Platonic Theology*, Ficino also identifies these platonic genii as the good daemons (2001–6, 18.10.3) and, as we saw above, late fifteenth-century Spanish writers Palencia and Nebrija discussed the spelling and meaning of the word. Given those definitions, we can deduce that in late fifteenth-century Spain the word spelled with dipthong 'ae' signified a wise man. In the *Pimander*, Ficino employs the word with dipthong in his Latin, which leads to the conclusion that

Guillén de Ávila intentionally altered the text to "angels" because despite those contemporary definitions of Palencia and Nebrija, the word had already begun to have the reduced significance it would take on by the seventeenth and eighteenth centuries. In the late sixteenth century, Pineda alleges that Cicero and Plato called Hermes Trismegistus "Theuth" because this was the name of a *demonio* meaning a wise man, as also used for Aristotle (Pineda 1963, 163:308). In 1636, Gómez Tejada de los Reyes will repeat this story about Aristotle being called *demonio* to mean a wise man, explaining: "because he argued so very wisely on those things under the moon, where demons inhabit," and adding a comparison: as Plato is properly called "Divine" for his teachings, so Aristotle might be called "Divine in a hidden way" (1636, fol. 172 r).[75] I showed earlier how the daemon-genii reference developed in Spanish letters. As to "daemon" separately, by 1732 *Autoridades* will offer only one meaning, spelled *demonio*, from the Latin *daemon*, "the same thing as devil."[76] The definition that survived in the move from Latin to Castilian is that of the sacred letters and Guillén de Ávila's substitutions show us that, already in 1485, the word had begun to lose its positive meaning.

In this Spanish translator's changes to the *Pimander*, and in his consensus to portions we might expect him to dispute, we find indications of an early reaction to, and reception of, Ficino's *pia philosophia*. With minimal touches such as adjectival qualification so that an intelligent spirit can become the "Holy Ghost," a flexible concept of daemon versus angel, and a few subtle uses of "almost," the translator resolves key dogmatic points of difference with Christian doctrine. Guillén de Ávila's Christianity is as fluid and open as Ficino's and his language is just as flexible and forgiving of the Hermetic author's text. Most noteworthy is that he wants to accept, and has accepted, the Hermetic work with those minimal yet relevant alterations. As we read in the accompanying letter sent to Gómez Manrique with the work, the translator decided to "put into romance" (romancear) this text "because it is, in part, a Catholic work."

From Gómez Manrique, to Pedro Núñez de Toledo, to Phillip II's library: this particular manuscript probably did not have many readers, and I have not found any indication of a printed edition in Castilian from the time. However, the printed Latin text did circulate extensively, and a number of fifteenth- and sixteenth-century editions are found in Spain's libraries. One more point on author Hermes Trismegistus deserves mention. One late eighteenth-century study of rabbinical Spanish authors that I consulted for information on Rabbi Samuel's letter points out that a jurist by the name of Immanuel Aboab, who died in Amsterdam in 1625, used the honorific Trismegistus for Spain's León Hebreo, who fled to Italy at the time of the 1492 expulsion (Rodríguez de Castro 1781–6, 1:371–3) and who, 400 years later, Menéndez Pelayo would insist on substituting for Ficino and his Neoplatonism as the source of mystical love imagery in sixteenth-century Spanish writers. The two texts of Phillip II's library do end up having this one additional point in common: the name of the pagan in the composite volume, Trismegistus, would be adapted to identify León Hebreo, who fled the Iberian Peninsula rather than convert from Judaism to Christianity.

Hermes Trismegistus as Named Authority

Throughout the sixteenth century the *Pimander*, the *Asclepius*, and author Hermes Trismegistus were consistently referenced and quoted by Spanish writers from Miguel de Servet and Juan Luis Vives to Fray Luis de León and Lope de Vega, by historians, theologians, doctors, lawyers, and poets. Apart from the manuscripts studied above, the earliest mention I have seen of the author comes in a letter written in 1488 to royal councillor (and bishop of Ávila) Hernando de Talavera, in which Pedro Mártir de Anglería speaks of the popularity of Hermes Trismegistus at the University of Salamanca: "It is impressive to hear the immense cohort, in their distinct groups, of those who scrutinize, analyse, and investigate divine secrets; some resolve the enigmas of Podalirius with the arcane knowledge of Trismegistus, while others unravel the knots of the Laws" (Mártir de Anglería 1953, no. 60, 15 October 1488).[77] Podalirius was the son of Asclepius, Greek god of the medical arts, a secondary interlocutor in the *Pimander* and author of another philosophical Hermetic treatise that bears his own name as its title.[78] Letter writer Mártir de Anglería, Italian by birth, was *preceptor* in charge of the education of Spain's Prince Juan, son of the Catholic Monarchs Ferdinand and Isabel, and he would later become royal historian for Charles V (Madrigal in Guevara 1994, 2, 6). In his 1490 *Vocabulario universal*, Alonso de Palencia identifies the figure Mercurius as the "grandson of Atlas," as does Ficino in his dedication of the translated *Pimander* to Cosimo de' Medici, and as "hijo de su hija Maia," a reference found in Augustine (Allen 1998, 30, n. 51). Palencia reads the honorific Trismegistus as "virtue in many arts, three-times great" and also notes that "Mercurius is known as the interpreter of the gods" (Palencia 1967).[79] Later Spanish writers would be equally respectful.

Juan Luis Vives might have called Ficino a *filosofastro* but he also opined that Hermes [Theuth] was, in all likelihood, the biblical Abraham: "I think that Theut [*sic*], with greater verisimilitude, is Abraham who, having gone from Chaldea to Egypt, taught writing and mathematics to the Egyptians" (1947, 1:567).[80] Vives also approvingly quotes "Mercurio Trismegisto" on the well-known description of man as a "great miracle" (gran milagro) although he does add: "if he [Mercurio] really did exist" (si él fue en realidad) (1947, 2:1234). As we saw above, Vives's contemporary Pedro Mexía includes Hermes with Ficino on useful knowledge of the "occult properties" of certain stones. In 1546, Francisco Cervantes de

Salazar glosses the character name Mercurio as "not only the god of language and messenger to the gods, but also the patron of fraudulent contracts" (Cervantes de Salazar 1772, 5:30).[81] In the annotated text, Mercurio and Isis are at first the parents of Fraud but, in a later section, Mercurio assumes his role as messenger of the gods to remind another allegorical figure, Labricio (Labour), that he is a mortal man and that human language is incapable of understanding the secrets of the heavens (Strosetzki 1997, 14–15).[82] Hector Pinto explains the connection of Trismegistus to the Christian God, who is "fountain of life, admirable splendour ... the only one who can say, as he did to Moses: 'I am who I am' ... It seems that the ancient Trismegistus must have read this, because in the fourth dialogue of his *Pimander* he says that God is unity, and he who engenders all number, without being engendered from it ..." (1595, f. 266r).[83] Pinto also notes that when they speak of the body as an impediment to contemplation, the Platonists are imitators of ancient Egyptian Trismegistus.[84]

In Italian historian Paolo Giovio's *Elogia of illustrious men, virtuous in war*, first published in Florence in 1551, and then in Granada in Spanish translation in 1568, Hermes's honorific Trismegistus, from the Greek for "three times great," is adapted for Spain's King Charles V: "May God protect you, Magnanimous Charles V, Augustus, Emperor three times Great" (1568, f. 206r), and the antonomasia is repeated in verse, following on that prose description:

To whom nature gave
The cognomen Great
Three times for more greatness
Emperor Charles V. (Giovio 1568, f. 209v)[85]

This adaptation of the honorific indicates just how familiar the Hermetic author's name had become by the middle of the sixteenth century. Trismegistus was a recognizable literary trope whose name and words had been and would continue to be easily incorporated into Spanish letters.[86]

In his 1568 *De re metallica*, Bernardo Pérez de Vargas combines Avicenna, Albertus Magnus, Rasis, Plato, Hermes, and others as authorities for the basic properties and compositions of metals, and identifies Hermes Trismegistus as "father of philosophers" (padre de los Philosophos) (1568 18v). In his 1585 *Philosophia secreta*, Juan Pérez de Moya calls Hermes variably Mercurio, Hermes, or Apollo, and paints him as the representative of the soul's capacity to reason, as well as "knowledge of divine will" (1995, 2.23, 283, 278–85).[87] Pérez de Moya also uses the descriptor "runner" (trotero) for Hermes, recognizing him as messenger of the gods, the bearer of news and of wisdom, and even the first to say that the world was created by God (1995, 281, 283).[88] In 1490, Alfonso de Palencia had used the word "middle-man" (medianero) for this facet of the figure. Among other accomplishments, Mercurius was considered the inventor of both the syringe and the lyre, and he was also known as the "father of eloquence" (padre de la eloquencia) (Pérez de Moya 1995, 285). Pérez de Moya references Cicero on the five men of ancient times named Mercurio, relies on Theodosius to identify Hermes as fourth in this line, and explicates the honorific Trismegistus to mean he was "so excellent that there could be none better" (Pérez de Moya 1995, 280).[89]

In Juan de Pineda's 1589 *Diálogos de la agricultura cristiana*, we read that Trismegistus, "my intimate friend" (mi familiar) of Pineda, is an author who writes on "exalted matters of God and religion" (cosas subidísimas de Dios y de religión) in *Asclepius* (Pineda 1963, 161:39). Pineda reviews details of Mercurio's life and deeds as found in Saints Augustine and Isidore, as well as Horace, Lactantius, Eusebius, and Cicero, notes that the latter identified Mercurio's father as "the third Jupiter," and offers two possibilities for the triple honorific: Hermes was great "in three things: the priesthood, philosophy, and theology" or, if one follows Suidas, he is so-named because he "confessed the Trinity" (Pineda 1963, 163:308).[90] Pineda quotes Trismegistus from the *Pimander*, with full attribution, as to the latter's opinion on the scourge of ignorance (1963, 162:147), and cites from multiple sources to unravel the "complicated genealogy" (su enrevesada geneología) of Hermes Trismegistus, as well as his role as lawgiver to the Egyptians (1963, 163:307). In another work titled *Monarchia ecclesiástica*, Pineda conflates biblical and pagan sources to re-narrate Creation as per both Moses and Trismegistus:

> When the Archetype, Ideal and Eternal world gave birth to its self-portrait, which it had always guarded as conceived eternally within itself, and which we call the created, temporal world (and in saying world we also say beautiful, neat, adorned, and very well-ordered and graceful), it did no more than wish that it would effectively be born, as it had always maintained it [that self-portrait] within itself as an Ideal concept: and Trimaximus, commonly called Trismegistus, priest and prophet of the Egyptians, spoke about this with his profound knowledge. This is what Moses says in the first words of the Sacred Book, that in the beginning, God created heaven and earth. (Pineda 1620, f. 1r)[91]

Allen (1987) has studied Ficino's interpretation of the Platonic Demiurge of the *Timaeus* in its relation to the Christian God as Creator in Genesis. In that commentary, Ficino describes a threefold cause of the world as "the efficient cause, which is the divine mind; the model cause, or the series of Ideas conceived by the divine mind; and the final cause, which is the Good" (Ficino 2010, 10).[92] Pineda does not employ that precise terminology, nor does he use the term "demiurge"; nonetheless, he does offer a tripartite adjectival combination, "Archetype, Ideal, and Eternal world," that proposes a single intellectual entity serving as a model creator. In the *Platonic Theology*, Ficino uses "architect" for this image: "the architect of the world, insofar as he is intellectual, acts through [his] intellectual nature," and "The world machine had always been inscribed beforehand in the architect of the world, and the moment of its inchoation was signified in the architect's will" (Ficino 2001–6, 2.11.6; 18.1.8).[93] In his summaries of the *Republic*, Ficino links the visible sun to the Son of God, the latter as "the invisible archetype" (inuisibilem & archetypum) (Ficino 2009a, 29; 1576, 2:1408). In a later passage of his text, Pineda again references "famous theologian" Trismegistus, who "proclaimed that man is a mortal god, and a great miracle, and also an animal who deserves to be honoured and even adored" (Pineda 1620, 1.5.2, f. 14r).[94]

The 1575 censor's approval for the *Monarchia ecclesiástica* assures the reader that Pineda has skilfully combined biblical and pagan chronologies.[95] The text is a full revision of world history from a late sixteenth-century Spanish Christian perspective, and Pineda simply writes Hermes Trismegistus and other ancient sources into the biblical story. On the role of Mercurio as inventor of writing, for example, Pineda reviews numerous philosophical and historical sources on the subject, including Lactantius, Saint Augustine, Xenophon, Tacitus, Diodorus, and others, to conclude that he will agree with Joseph and say that Adam created writing (1620, 1.13.4, ff. 35v–6r). Yet another contemporary, Jerónimo Castillo de Bobadilla, although denying Hermes's law-giver role as poetic "fable" (*fábula*) (1616, 1.1.3),[96] like Pineda interprets the thrice-great of Trismegistus to mean "great philosopher, great priest, and great king, all in one" (Castillo de Bobadilla 1616, 1.9.28).[97] Fray Luis de León relies on Hermes for the date of the end of the world (1891–5, 3:474–5). For Lope de Vega, Hermes is an authority on questions of love (*infra*, letter to Don Francisco López de Aguilar). For medical writer Álvarez Miraval, due to his "multifaceted knowledge and much erudition" (su varia sciencia y mucha erudición) Hermes Trismegistus is an authority on the importance of first-born progeny, who alone have and reflect the vital life energy of their parents (1597, f. 194r).

Counter Reformation thinkers defended Hermes when (Protestant) Isaac Casaubon's early seventeenth-century philological study questioned the veracity of textual attributions to the Hermetic author (Copenhaver, personal communication). One 1630 edition of the *Pimander* held today by the University of Salamanca bears on its frontispiece an emblem that combines the Christian cross with IHS lettering and the shroud of Turin surrounded by angels, all under the title *Divinvs Pimander Hermetis Mercvrii Trismegisti* (BG/ 6222) (figure 18).[98] The second page of the same volume offers another very Christian illustration for the text (figure 19).

A cover list of the philosophical holdings catalogue of the Complutense historical library prepared in 1770 shows that even at that late date,

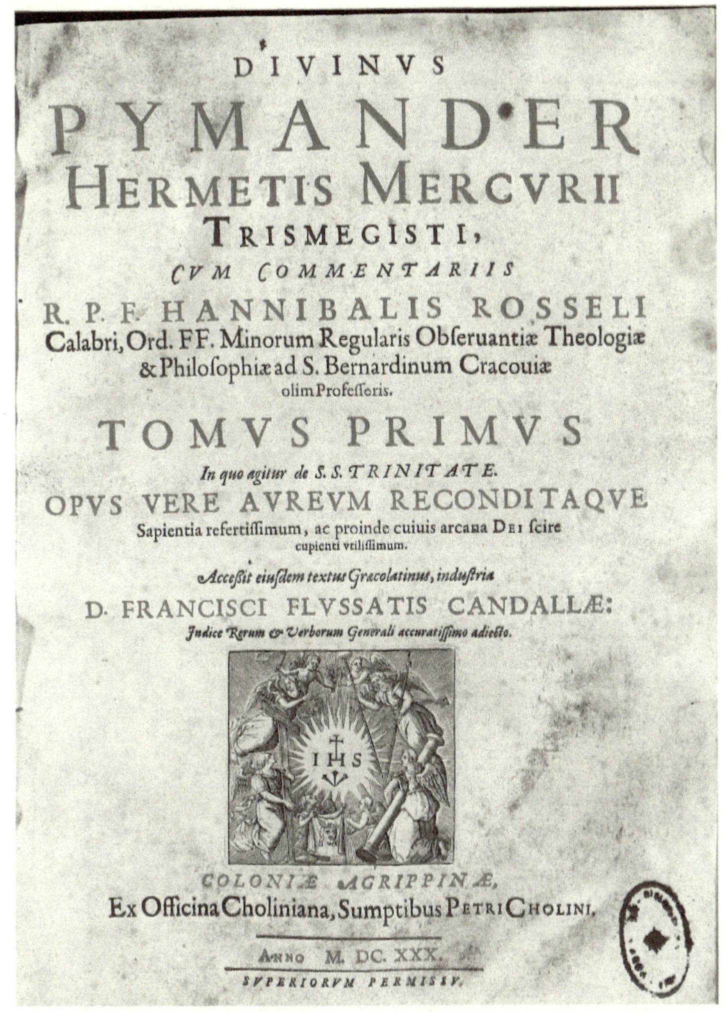
DIVINVS
PYMANDER
HERMETIS MERCVRII
TRISMEGISTI,
CVM COMMENTARIIS
R. P. F. HANNIBALIS ROSSELI
Calabri, Ord. FF. Minorum Regularis Obseruantiæ Theologiæ
& Philosophiæ ad S. Bernardinum Cracouiæ
olim Professoris.
TOMVS PRIMVS
In quo agitur de S. S. TRINITATE.
OPVS VERE AVREVM RECONDITAQVE
Sapientia refertissimum, ac proinde cuiuis arcana DEI scire
cupienti vtilissimum.
Accessit eiusdem textus Græcolatinus, industria
D. FRANCISCI FLVSSATIS CANDALLÆ:
Indice Rerum & Verborum Generali accuratissimo adiecto.
COLONIÆ AGRIPPINÆ,
Ex Officina Choliniana, Sumptibus PETRI CHOLINI.
ANNO M. DC. XXX.
SVPERIORVM PERMISSV.

Figure 18. Title page of 1630 *Pimander* edition with Christian iconography. Courtesy of Universidad de Salamanca (España). Biblioteca General Histórica. BG/ 6222.

Spaniards still considered Mercurius Trismegistus the first of all ancient Greek philosophers, prior to Pythagoras (figure 20). This follows Ficino who, in his introductory Argumentum to the *Pimander* translation, called Hermes "the first among philosophers" (Hic inter philosophos primus) (Ficino 1576, 2:1836). In 1859, the Biblioteca de Autores Españoles

REVERENDISSIMO PATRI, PATRI FRATRI FRANCISCO GONZAGÆ, TOTIVS ORDINIS S. FRANCISCI FRATRVM MINORVM MINISTRO GENERALI:

Frater Hannibal Rosseli Calaber, eiusdem Ordinis de Obseruantia Cracouiæ ad Sanctum Bernardinum Philosophiæ & Theologiæ Professor,

Patri nostro Obseruandissimo, subiectionem, &c.

VM ex tuis literis intellexerim Reuerendiss. & in Christo Iesu amantissime Pater, paruum meæ obedientiæ obsequium, cæteraq; mea studia, quæ tibi viro prudentissimo, & grauissimo, in studiis promouendis, apud almam prouinciam Poloniæ præstiti, grata tibi esse, vehementer gauisus sum: animosque addidit, vt indies maiori curæ mihi esset, religiosam pietatem vestram, animumque vere Christianum, solicitudinem non vulgarem circa omnes, præcipue circa studia nostræ sacræ religionis promouenda, omnibus meis studiis atque officiis prosequi: tametsi ita à te, morum honestate, generis nobilitate, vitæ integritate, regularis disciplinæ obseruantia, doctrinæ denique grauitate amplificata sit, vt nihil addi posse videatur. Hæc mihi magis magisque cogitanti, in mentem venit, nullum gratius obsequium à me tibi Pater Reuerendiss. offerri posse, quam ex multis nostris labotibus, aliquem fructum, nempe, Primum librum Pymandri Mercurii Trismegisti, quem ipse in Prouincia Sancti Francisci, in ciuitate Tudertina, in monte sancto Anno 1571. commentatus sum, non sine multis curis animi & corporis; vt sub felici Reuerendiss. paternitatis vestræ auspicio sit excussus. Ne autem alicui mirum videri possit, quod quasi præposterum in edendis nostris Commentariis ordinem seruauerimus, cum prius liber quartus in lucem prodierit; facile nos excusatos habebit, si & rem ita postulasse, & mandatum Illustriss. & Reuerendiss. Domini Archiepiscopi Gnesnensis, cuius liberalitate & impensis etiam impressus est, accessisse intellexerit. In lucem autem venit, in primis quidem gratia Domini nostri Iesu Christi, deinde per pios labores, & sanctam solicitudinem Reuerendi Patris F. Erasmi Pencicii, Ministri Prouinciæ Polonæ: qui feruentissimum animum habens, circa pia opera, & studia, gratum quoque se putans facere Reuerendiss. paternitati vestræ, ita omnem operam nauauit, apud pios & egregios viros, præsertim vero apud venerabile Capitulum Ecclesiæ Cathedralis Crac. cuius liberalitate, liber iste in lucem facilius prodiit, atque excussus est. Ipsi ergo Reuerendo Patri Erasmo, pro suis sanctis laboribus; viris autem illis, quorum eleemosynis liber venit in lucem, immortales gratias ago, suppliciter orans, vt ille, cuius amore hæc fecerunt, sit illorum merces & premium. Quamobrem impense & ex animo vestram Reuerendiss. Paternitatem rogo, vt huiusmodi munus oblatum boni consulas, grato animo suscipias, ac Paterna dilectione prosequaris. Habes enim Mercurium Trismegistum Regem antiquissimum, Regem sapientissimum, de omni scientiæ laude bene meritum, de nostra sacra religione Christiana egregie disserentem, suis indumentis regalibus ornatum. Læto ergo animo, colendissime semper Pater, suscipe Mercurium: non enim tædium aut molestiam aliquam habet conuersatio illius; sed lætitiam & gaudium. Id vt facias, ita rogo, vt maiori studio, magisque ex animo rogare non possim. Quod si feceris (vti spero) sanctæ obedientiæ labores, ærumnas, perplexitates, omniaque incommoda feliciter mihi cessisse putabo. Vale. Datum Cracouiæ ex ædibus nostri Cœnobij ad S. Bernardinum. Anno 1585. 3. Non. Ianuarij.

✱ 2 CATA-

Figure 19. Second page Dedicatoria of 1630 *Pimander* edition with Christian iconography. Universidad de Salamanca (España). Biblioteca General Histórica. BG/ 6222.

published the *Obras* of seventeenth-century author Francisco de Quevedo and, in the second volume, editor Aureliano Fernández-Guerra y Orbe glossed Quevedo's reference to "the author of the Pimander" in *Perinola* by saying: "The author of the *Pimander* is Mercurius Trismegistus, one of the greatest

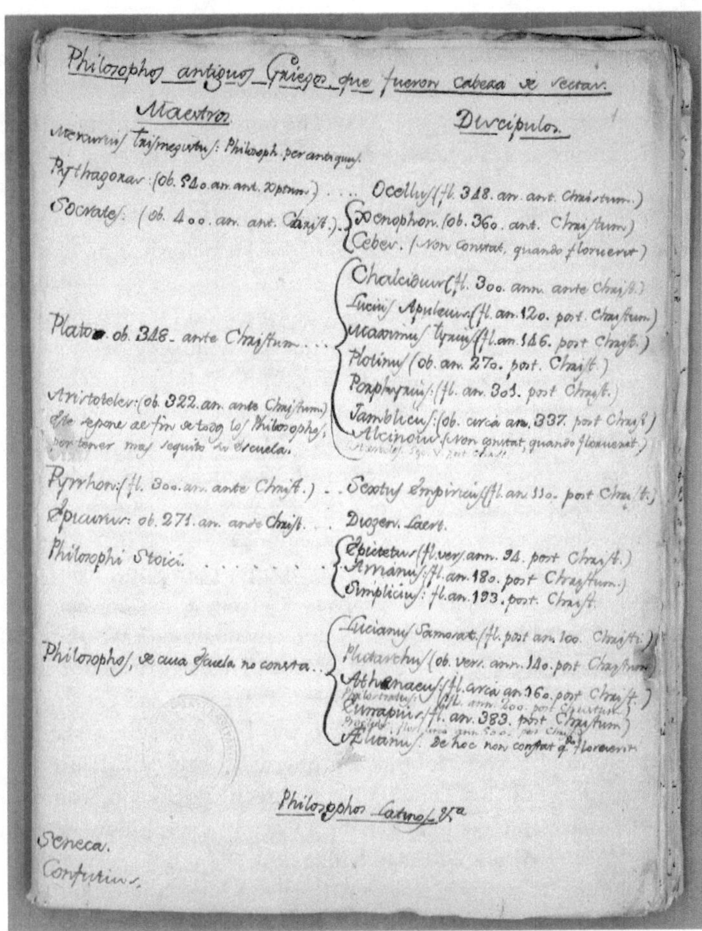

Philosophos antiguos Griegos que fueron cabeza de sectas.

Maestros — Discipulos.

Mercurius Trismegistus: Philosoph. perantiquus.

Pythagoras: (ob. 540. an. ant. Xptum.) . . . Ocellus (fl. 348. an. ant. Christum.)

Socrates: (ob. 400. an. ant. Christ.) . . Xenophon. (ob. 360. ant. Christum.) / Cebes. (non constat, quando floruerit)

Plato. ob. 348. ante Christum . . . Chalcidius (fl. 300. ann. ante Christ.) / Lucius Apuleius (fl. an. 120. post. Christum) / Maximus Tyrius (fl. an. 146. post Christ.) / Plotinus (ob. an. 270. post. Christ.) / Porphyrius: (fl. an. 301. post Christ.) / Jamblicus: (ob. circa an. 337. post Christ.) / Alcinous (non constat, quando floruerit)

Aristoteles: (ob. 322. an. ante Christum) Este se pone al fin de todos los Philosophos, por tener mas sequito su escuela.

Pyrrhon: (fl. 300. an. ante Christ.) . . Sextus Empiricus (fl. an. 130. post Christ.)

Epicurus: ob. 271. an. ante Christ. . . Diogen. Laert.

Philosophi Stoici. . . . . Epictetus (fl. vers. ann. 94. post Christ.) / Arrianus: fl. an. 180. post Christum.) / Simplicius: fl. an. 193. post. Christ.

Philosophos, de cuia escuela no consta . . Lucianus Samosat. (fl. post an. 100. Christi.) / Plutarchus (ob. vers. ann. 140. post Christum) / Athenaeus (fl. circa an. 160. post Christ.) / Eunapius (fl. an. 383. post Christum) / Aelianus: de hoc non constat q.do floruerit

Philosophos Latinos &c.a

Seneca.

Confucius.

Figure 20. Catalogue list of philosophers whose works were held by the Complutense library in 1770. Courtesy of the Biblioteca de la Universidad Complutense de Madrid. BH MSS 589.

theologians of ancient pagan times" (Fernández-Guerra y Orbe in Quevedo 1859, 466).[99] For Spanish intellectuals, Hermes Trismegistus remained a trusted and respected authority through the middle of the nineteenth century.

A number of twentieth-century critical studies denied Ficino's influence in Spanish letters due to the lack of specific textual references to the Italian philosopher. However, as noted above, there are a good number of actual citations of Ficino, Ficinus, or simply "Marsilio" without patronym. In addition, many

Spanish writers who do not name Ficino himself frequently do cite Hermes Trismegistus, who became something of an alter-ego to Ficino. A 1924 catalogue of the Escorial library in Spain includes Ficino in its index only to say "See Mercurius Trismegistus" (Zarco Cuevas 1924, 3:255). The number and variety of references to Hermes Trismegistus in Renaissance Spanish letters is daunting. Following are a few examples.

Fernán Pérez de Oliva (c. 1492–1530) refers to Trismegistus's comment on man as miracle in his *Diálogo de la dignidad del hombre*, published in 1546 in Alcalá de Henares (Pérez de Oliva 1995, 138).[100] Alejo de Venegas (c. 1498–1562) condemns any men who have not found the one true God by studying nature, lays out all the arguments of those who have deduced one first cause, "an immutable cause that moves without being moved," and supports his statements with Aristotle, "especially in the *Metaphysics*," the "ancient philosopher named Timeo about whom Plato wrote the dialogue of that name," Cicero who got his information from Plato's *Timaeus*, and "a most ancient philosopher called Trismegistus in a dialogue called *Pimander* and in another titled *Asclepius*" (Venegas 1983, 2.3, ff. 35–6).[101] In his role as censor for the Inquisition in Toledo (Eisenberg in Venegas 1983, 10), Venegas approved for publication a translation from the Italian by Alonso de Lobera, His Majesty's Chaplain (*Capellán de su Magestad*), only after saying that he believes his own corrections and emendations have purged the text of some Italian Platonizing tendencies.[102] Hermes Trismegistus is not excised but, rather, accepted and kept in the fine company of Aristotle and Cicero.

Studies on Miguel Servet (1511–53), who was burned at the stake by Calvin, allege that he no doubt read Plotinus, Porphyry, Proclus, and Plato in Ficino's translations but question his failure to cite directly to Ficino, comparing the absence of the Italian philosopher's name to Servet's scrupulous references to other sources (Ángel Alcalá 2003, and Manzoni 1974, 88). Servet does, however, frequently cite Hermes Trismegistus, calling him "the father of ancient philosophy" (veteris philosophiae pater) and one who "speaks with the spirit of truth" (de spiritu vero loquens) (1790, 132–3) in book four of his *Christianismi Restitutio*, the same text that Calvin burned with its author. Juan de Pineda exalts Hermes as "the greatest of the Egyptian theologians," and lists him as "Trismegistus Mercurius, pagan theologian" among his "almost seven hundred" referenced authorities (1963, 162:356; 161:14). Similarly, Malón de Chaide says that he follows the famous writers Hermes Trismegistus, Orpheus, Plato, Plotinus, and the great Dionysius Areopagite on the subject of love and beauty (1959, 130:83), and he quotes from the *Pimander*: "Hermes Trismegistus, speaking with his son Asclepius, says "*Magnum, o Asclepi, miraculum est homo*" (1959, 104:101).[103] In 1621, Jiménez Patón (1569–1640) republishes, with a new title, a work that first appeared in 1604 as *Spanish Eloquence in Art*; in 1621, the new title is *Mercurius Trimegistus, sive de triplici eloquentia sacra, española, romana,* which echoes one of Ficino's translations, *Mercurii Trismegisti Poemander, seu de potestate ac sapientia divina* and the Italian philosopher's *De triplici vita.* In his introductory text to the volume, Jiménez Patón specifies that the "triple" of his own volume's title is a reference to the "thrice-great" Hermes Trismegistus,[104] and all the professors in Jiménez Patón's geographical region of La Mancha and province of Jaén signed documents promising to teach rhetoric from no other book except this one (Jiménez Patón 1965, LI). In response to questions that Dominican friar Esteban de Arroyo raised as to his title and his reliance on the figure of Hermes, Patón appends a 21-page defence of the figure to his 1621 *Mercurii Trismegisti* volume. Ficino is one of many authorities used in this defence in support of not only Hermes but also Socrates and Plato, along with Saints Augustine and Thomas. Another Spanish author, Hieronymo de Saona, uses both Mercurius and Hermes interchangeably, telling his readers that Mercurius "vividly described the Trinity [as God, Mind or Wisdom, and Soul] in a sphere, or circle, with a compass" then quoting Hermes: "wisdom, nonetheless, is not to be found in any specific place since, as Hermes says, it cannot be comprehended" (Saona 1598, 23).[105] Medical doctor Álvarez Miraval also refers to "the great philosopher Hermes Trismegistus, who said that man is a marvellous miracle made in the image and likeness of God," and further references the figure on various points, including this definition of fate: "Hermes Trismegistus and Apuleius define fate by saying that it is a certain inflection or inclination in secondary causes, that proceeds from the primary cause" (1597, ff. 8v, 327v).[106]

In two dialogues whose publication dates are separated by nearly a century, we see the figure of Mercury move from arbiter of Christian ethics and wisdom to poetic theorist. In his *Diálogo de Mercurio y Carón* (1528), Alfonso de Valdés (c. 1490–1532) paints Mercury as the voice of Christian ideals, who searches in vain to find them in the terrestrial world: "I could not find in all the world anything but vanity, evil, affliction and insanity"; "having learned about the signs by which Jesus Christ wanted his people to be known among all others, I circled the globe without being able to find any groups that had such characteristics" (1993, 80, 81).[107] An acquantance tells him that if he wants to find Christians, he should look for people who live contrary to Christian doctrine (81), and when Carón asks if Christ would be pleased that those persons call themselves Christians, Mercury responds: "If he does or not, I cannot say. But for my part, I can promise you that I would be insulted if they called themselves Mercurians" (88).[108] Throughout the text, Mercury is represented as someone who not only understands Christian doctrine but also employs it to excoriate bishops, cardinals, and friars for not having practised what they preached. He frequently quotes from the Bible and, when he and Carón are faced with a theologian who prides himself on having read Aristotle, Duns Scotus, Thomas of Aquinas, and Nicholas of Lyra, the response is that he should have concentrated on the sacred texts themselves, as well as Saints Augustine and Ambrosio, that is, two Fathers of the Church who incorporated Neoplatonist thought into Christian dogma. Able to cross from the land of the living to the shores of the river Styx, Mercury keeps Carón updated on historical developments that will fill his boat with passengers for Hades, and advises him on the true identities of those who present themselves for passage. He is pre-emptive psychopomp more than friendly guide for the souls of the dead. Valdés's Mercury resembles the figure of the *Pimander*'s Hermes but only to a certain extent in his presentation of unfiltered truths; he is more satirical critic than source of revelation.

Close to one hundred years later, in his *Viaje del Parnaso*, Miguel de Cervantes will use the figure of Mercury to narrate a journey to the mountain of the nine classical Muses. The Cervantine poetic voice is guided by a Mercury who, more than Hermes, resembles the Greek god of the same name:

> In whose clothing and severe gesture
> I saw vividly the figure of Mercury,
> messenger of the imaginary gods.
> In his gallant poise and composure,
> on his winged feet, and with his caduceus,
> symbol of prudence and judiciousness,
> I say I saw the same paranymph,
> who carried fictional messages
> to the land of the exalted Coliseum. (1991, I, vv. 184–92)[109]

The poet-voyager prostrates himself at the beautiful winged feet of Mercury, only to be admonished by the "garrulous god" (dios parlero), who calls Cervantes "Adam of the poets" (Adán de los poetas) praises him as a valiant soldier and talented writer with Cyllenic (i.e., Mercury-like) spirit, then invites him to share the comfort of his luxurious vessel for the trip (1991, I, vv. 193–240). These two representations evidence the persistence yet also the evolution of the Hermes-Mercury figure and of his ideas in Spanish letters.

Cervantes' complex portrayal of mythological figures in the *Viaje* has been studied as a critique of humanist pedantery (Benedetto Croce), as a battle between light and shadow (Gustavo Correa), as part of an ancient literary tradition of burlesque gods (Rodríguez Marín), and as self-promotion (Gitlitz, Rivers, Gaos) (Rivers 1993).[110] Rivers notes Lucian's dialogues as a source for both Valdés's and Cervantes' texts (Cervantes 1991, 14). Taking that point of comparison, Valdés portrays Mercury as a serious and respected pagan who understood Christian morals, that is, as akin to the ancient figure recognized by Augustine, a gentile who predicted the coming of Christianity. His Lucianesque satire criticizes the corrupt morals of so-called Christians. Cervantes, in contrast, paints the imagery of paranymph Mercury with a doubtful, perspectivist remove – "imaginary gods" with "fictional messages" – and lightly ridicules him as the "garrulous god," but also selects him as the only appropriate guide for the voyage to Parnassus. The classical Mercury, god of writing and poets, interpreter and messenger of the gods, father of eloquence, is the Spanish author's respected but also chatty companion who, in turn, respects the author. Cervantes' satirical criticism is literary rather than ethical, as he and Mercury journey on a ship entirely fabricated of verse (glosses, romances, sonnets, tercets, etc.). As Correa has noted, for Cervantes the real divinity is Poetry herself, described as omniscient and universal: "she knows all, and arranges all" (todo lo sabe, todo lo dispone) (Cervantes 1991, IV, v. 142), in line with both the divine fury of Platonic tradition and the Aristotelian theory on the universal truth of verse (Correa 1960, 117–18). Pimander guided Hermes to Mind (Nous) and the origin of cosmic creation, but Cervantes' guide exposes Apollo's difficulties in controlling poets and their verse. Mercury leads the author to "true Poetry" (Poesía verdadera) (Cervantes 1991, IV, v. 160), she who holds the keys to all secrets and sciences (vv. 184–5), who resides with moral and divine philosophy (v. 191), and who is the measure (*la cifra*) of all good in the universe (vv. 209–10). Here, cosmic design is literally in the hands of Poetry, the goddess of verse.

Notwithstanding their differences in tone and focus, Cervantes' text does offer a tenuous echo of Hermetic-Neoplatonic imagery. Hermes Trismegistus describes his first vision of Mind (Nous): "everything became light ... darkness arose separately and descended ... Then the darkness changed into a ... watery nature ... agitated and smoking like a fire ... Earth and water ... mixed with one another" (Copenhaver 2002, I, 4–5),[111] and Cervantes portrays the invasion of Parnassus by a pestilence of bad poets: "I saw night and day combined in one" and "I saw all the elements in tumult;/earth, water, air and even fire" (Cervantes 1991, II, vv. 331, 334–5).[112] The result in each case is patently distinct: through the vision, Hermes understands Mind (Nous) and its cosmic creation, but Cervantes sees the clouds open to rain down bad poets in such abundance that they threaten to capsize Apollo's ship of verse. In similarly iconoclastic fashion, the Spanish author's presentation of man's mix of mortal and immortal natures is anthropomorphized as his mount: at the start of his journey, the poetic voice describes himself setting out on foot yet "mounted on the haunch of Destiny" which "at times tends to fly through the air/as lightly as an eagle or an arrow,/but can occasionally move with feet of lead" (Cervantes 1991, I, vv. 58, 67–9).[113] As I read that, Destiny is man's dual nature, soul and body with as Cervantes says, "[the faculty of] will in the saddle" (la Elección puesta en la silla) (1991, I, 59). The poetic voice emphazises that even if it might seem a "marvellous mount" (cavalgadura maravilla) it is the one used throughout the world and no "mortal traveller can refuse it" (ni mortal caminante lo reúsa) (I, vv. 59, 61, 66). This Cervantine adaptation of the Ficinian-Phaedran charioteer will always fly lightly, we are told, when carrying a poet, as the latter travel without encumbrance of suitcase or riches (I, vv. 70–4).[114]

Michael Allen has pointed out that Ficino laboured "under the Virgilian goad of Mercury ... For the promise of the sandalled psychopomp is that he can lead us across the threshold of the mind's darkness and the reason's death into the life of eternal Truth; lead us, in Plato's great metaphor, from the shadows of opinion's cave out into the brilliance of the intelligible sun" (1998, xiv). In his study of Cervantes' *Viaje* as ironic parody of Dante's *Comedia*, Maurino notes that "Mercurio is the poet's guide much as Virgil is for Dante; and finally, he brings Cervantes to salvation through Apollo, as Virgil guides Dante to the *summum bonum* through Beatrice" (1956, 8).[115] Cervantes' Mercury is filtered through multiple sources, and the Spanish author paints his winged guide with more modern irony than Dantean hope, Hermetic enthusiasm, or Ficinian optimism. Nonetheless, Mercury is the guide who reveals "real Poetry" (la Poesía verdadera) dressed in all her divine splendour (con vestidura rozagante) (Cervantes 1991, IV, vv. 160, 163). In addition to that privileging of Poetry as supreme divinity, and along with the modified traces of Hermetic and Platonic imagery quoted above, Cervantes also introduces one additional and very noteworthy change in his relationship with his guide.

The Spanish author alters the direction of the flow of knowledge. Mercury shows Cervantes the work of Apollo, that is, he lights his mind by showing him the ship of verse and inviting him to share the journey with him. It is Cervantes' task, however, to select from Mercury's list of Spanish poets those who might be more worthy of praise. That is, the criteria of knowledge and selective judgment will flow in the opposite direction, from human to god. In due course, Mercury will offer Cervantes' opinion to Apollo, and the best of the poets designated and approved by the Spanish author will be marked with a white cross and directed to Parnassus to join in a Crusade of poetry and rescue the art, considered to be "in dire straits" (en duro estrecho) (Cervantes 1991, I, v. 315). Cervantes' multiple models in the *Viaje del Parnaso*, from Menippean and Lucianesque satire to Dante, Seneca, and Erasmus, as well as Spanish and Italian *cantos* and *viajes*, have been studied;[116] the *Pimander* is one more text to add to that list, in the same sense of playfulness or a "burlesque mythology" (la mitología burlesca) (Rivers in Cervantes 1991, 13) that coats with ironic commentary a serious substrata. Both Cervantes' messenger of the gods and his Apollo, model poet and ostensible leader of the chorus of Muses, learn from the modern writer. The Spanish author's

Mercury is not Hermes; rather, the author himself usurps the role of psychopomp to guide the two gods through the earthly poetic realm. It is Cervantes who reveals poetic truth.

Notwithstanding that one Golden Age revision of roles, the Ficinian version of Hermes as *magus* and spiritual guide to the secrets of the cosmos remains pervasive even today in Spanish letters. In a volume published in 2007, *Simbolismo y hermetismo: Aproximación a la modernidad estética*, editors Luis Beltrán Almería and Luis Rodríguez García offer a group of studies on the modernist Hermetic aesthetic in late nineteenth- through twentieth-century literature. As Beltrán Almería notes: "Hermeticism is, in first instance, *a radical aesthetic didactic*" but "modern Hermeticism is, more than anything else, an aesthetic" (2007, 98, 100).[117] Early adaptations of Hermetic imagery in Spanish letters, illustrative of that move from didactic to aesthetic practice, are the focus of my next chapter.

4 Persistence and Adaptation of Hermetic-Neoplatonic Imagery

The use of Hermetic imagery and ideas in sixteenth-century Spanish writings extends beyond the specific references noted above. Following are further examples to illustrate the resonance of that thought, at times without specific mention of Ficino or Hermes Trismegistus, at times with it, and in certain surprising contexts.

Sun

As noted above, the Hermetic-Neoplatonic world view is structured with a specific father-son relationship: God (the father) is variably called Jupiter, Mens, or Nous, and his son/ sun is Apollo.[1] For Renaissance intellectuals seeking concordance between ancient philosophy and contemporary theological dictates, the parallel to the Christian God the Father and Christ his son was logical, with a simple explanation of semantic distinctions but substantive compatibility, the same argument used by those of the *comparatio* tradition in seeking to reconcile the teachings of Aristotle and Plato (Purnell 1971). In the *Pimander*, man's share of the intelligence and light of Sun, the second god, empowers him to strive towards that of the first god, Nous or Mind. Creation of the demiurge Sun was the first act of the first creator: "Mens, Mind, who was hermaphrodite, life and light in one, engendered with his word another creative Mind, he who is the god of fire and vital breath" (Renau Nebot 1999, I, 9).[2] The Latin text of Ficino's translation reads similarly but elaborates on the concept of androgyne: this god Mens was "full of the fecundity of both genders" (1554, I, 9),[3] that is, life and light are those genders. Dodd specifies that the author of the first tractate of the *Pimander* "clearly regards the identification of the supreme Being with the union of Life and Light as a cardinal point of revelation" and this is, for Dodd, an Iranian idea with parallels to Egyptian, but not Hebrew beliefs, given that the latter do not identify but, rather, only associate the supreme Being with light and life (133).[4]

In Ficino's chapter summaries of *Phaedrus*, the sun mediates between the upper and lower worlds: "In the heavens [the planets] Jupiter and the Sun are totally in accord in their hidden power: the Sun is the principal minister of Jupiter the craftsman, and his illuminating power accompanies Jupiter's crafting power" (2008, 3.13.3).[5] As regards the impact on man: "the Sun's power incites via Mercury to the Muses [that is, to poetry], and via Venus to love" (2008, 3.14.1).[6] The Hermetic *Asclepius* also highlights this mediating act of the sun: "The craftsman (I mean the sun) binds heaven to earth, sending essence below and raising matter above, attracting everything toward the sun and around it, offering everything from himself to everything, as he gives freely of the ungrudging light" (Copenhaver 2002, XVI, 5).[7] For the Hermetists, the sun sees and knows the thinking essence of God-Mind-Nous whereas man has to conjecture as to that essence through the solar planet as an intermediary light. In the *Platonic Theology*, Ficino employs a sun-God analogy to explain how a "prime agent acts through being": the sun's being, or essence, is light and "with utmost ease [sun] lights up an infinite number of things in a way in a single act, and in illuminating generates them" as "God through His being, which is an utterly simple universal centre whence everything else is spun out like lines, with the utmost ease and command makes whatever depends on Him tremble" (Ficino 2001–6, 2.8.2).[8] In the same text, the Italian philosopher also uses the sun, Mercury, and the moon to represent the relationship between God (sun), angel (Mercury), and soul (moon) (3.1.16), and describes the Apollo-God figure as an "invisible Sun": "Thus the nine Muses along with the nine Bacchuses together celebrate their ecstatic rites around the single figure of Apollo, that is, around the splendor of the invisible Sun" (4.1.28); he also emphasizes that men's minds are heated and illuminated by the "divine Sun" (Ficino 2001–6, 18.8.26).[9] In his *De sole* and *De lumine*, Ficino fully explores solar attributes, powers, movements, and acts as described by theologians, philosophers, physicists, and astrologers who linked the sun to their gods: Arabs, Egyptians, and Chaldeans, Dionysius the Areopagite, Iamblichus, Proclus, Macrobius, Plato, Plotinus, Moses, and Orpheus; the latter calls the sun god Apollo and describes him as "the eternal all-seeing eye" (Ficino 1493, VI).[10] In his commentary on the *Republic*, "light is threefold ... the divine light is called the Sun of the other two Suns; the intellectual light is called the angelic Sun, the Sun of the universal Sun; and lastly, the visible light is the Sun in the heavens and its effulgence" (Ficino 2009a, 33).[11] In one letter to Filippo Carducci, Ficino calls his Christian God "the true Phoebus" (Rees 2002, 345, n. 20) and in another, from Ficino and Cavalcanti to Lotterio Neroni, the sun is compared to God while the two letter writers recommend that "by looking up at the celestial Sun ... we may decry in it, as in a mirror, that super-celestial One who has set His tabernacle in the Sun" (1975–<2012>, 5:47).[12] A number of these images of the sun are also found in the works of sixteenth-century Spanish writers.

In a letter in verse to Don Bernardino de Mendoza, Francisco de Aldana writes that nature, acting with mystery and providence, placed Jove (the sun) between Saturn and Mars so as to endow Mendoza with an ideal character: like the sun, Mendoza is "easy-going, pure, friendly and kind" (fácil, puro, amable y blando) (v. 22), which tempers "the blind fury" (la ciega furia) (v. 24) of Mars and "the cold inaction" (la pereza helada) (v. 26) of Saturn. The poet offers two analogies, one to the sun placed in middle of the planets as "eternal eye of both worlds" (de entrambos mundos ojo eterno) (v. 28) and a second to the heart located in the middle of man's body:

> and so he placed in the middle of the chest
> that vital body, whose figure
> imitates that of the Egyptian pyramids,
> and by name is called the heart, (Aldana 1985, XLVI, vv. 30–3)[13]

Aldana's editor Lara Garrido cites Fernando de Herrera, who in turn cites Avicenna and Galen, so as to explain similar allusions in Garcilaso de la Vega.[14] As regards Aldana's verse, however, the references fall short. Avicenna calls the heart "the first root of all virtues" and Galen "puts in it all the force of the vital spirits" (Lara Garrido 1985, 348, n. 30–44).[15] In earlier verses of the same poem, Aldana stressed Mendoza's "virtue" and in later verses, he specifies the "thousand vital spirits" in the heart that "minister the air of life to the lungs" (Aldana 1985, XLVI, vv. 12, 41, 43).[16] That imagery, as Lara Garrido notes, echoes Galen's phrasing. However, neither the description of the sun as "eternal eye between two worlds" nor the heart-to-pyramid analogy are found in the works referenced by Lara Garrido and Herrera. The first can be traced to Ficino's *Liber de sole*: "the eternal all-seeing eye" (1493, VI), with an accompanying reference to the sun as heart of the sky: "Ancient physicists called the Sun the heart of the sky" whose function, according to "most Platonists" who "placed the soul of the world in the Sun," is to fill that entire solar sphere with rays emitted through the fiery globe just as a heart pours its spirit into all things. The sun apportions "life, feeling and movement throughout the universe" (1493, VI).[17] The third image unexplained by the named references, the heart-to-pyramid analogy, is a detail found in the *Pimander*,[18] when Hermes Trismegistus questions his son Tat as to the necessity of an artisan, or God, to fashion the wonders of the cosmos, asking: "Who made the heart in the form of a pyramid?" (Copenhaver 2002, V, 6).[19] Thus, Aldana's syncretic verse combines the imagery (sun-heart-pyramid) of both Ficino's *De sole* and his *Pimander* translation.

In the same poem, Aldana asserts that "Lie" has disguised itself as "Truth" and so convinced mortal man to "run wherever the bestial impulse/ calls him, that one [beast] for whom it is said/ that reason is lost where force presents itself" (Aldana 1985, XLVI, vv. 113–15).[20] Those who find the strength to resist "look for the summit closest to the sky" (v. 27), and "here they wish to spend the brief hours/ of their soul's temporal exile" (vv. 133–4).[21] Once raised to heaven's heights, they become "almost like separate intelligences" (casi inteligencias separadas) (v. 135), find their "Maker" (Hacedor) (v. 138), and "leave the cold and shadowy cave/ so as to take in, with open breast/ the new rays of the man of Delius [Apollo]" (Aldana 1985, XLVI, vv. 141–3).[22] The Spanish poet follows this clear reference to man's isolation in the Platonic cave with the story of Socrates standing motionless to watch the sun in its course for a full day then remaining, unmoving, on foot overnight so as to hail its arrival again at dawn:

and thus, as they say about Socrates
that he spent a full day contemplating
the great path of the one who lights the world,
and that, without moving in the least all night long,
he again saluted Phoebus the following day. (Aldana 1985, XLVI, vv. 144–8)[23]

Ficino relates the same story of Socrates's vigil in *De sole* with its means: contemplation of the visible sun, and its goal: to thus transcend to the invisible, first intellect,[24] making it clear that for Plato the visible, corporeal sun leads to the divine, incorporeal intellect.[25] The Italian philosopher also points out that Moses identified light, albeit not that of the sun, as God's first creation,[26] and adds that the difference between visible and invisible illuminations relates directly to their corporeal versus incorporeal natures.[27] In Ficino's *De lumine* we read that God's invisible and infinite light is the truth of truths that causes all things,[28] and chapter 6 of that work is titled "On what principles we ascend from the visible to the invisible light."[29] These Ficinian images are incorporated by Aldana, whose "separate intelligences" (inteligencias separadas), once out of the cave:

look at the morning eye of the sky,
and the light, pure in itself how in itself
it sparkles with quickened turn,
but not to stop there, for no body
is the proportional object of soul

but, rather, to rise up from that visible Sun
to the invisible Sun, soul's author (Aldana 1985, XLVI, vv. 149–55)[30]

The final verse of Aldana's stanza, with the image of that invisible Sun as author of the soul, is a particular phrasing that echoes Ficino in *De sole*: "Is not the author of life Christ, that Sun who breathes in the middle of the heavens like a poet ..." (Ficino 1493, X).[31] Aldana's "separate intelligences" (inteligencias separadas) are those freed souls who have reached the heights where the corporeal does not interfere with the soul's true pursuit, and where those of "pure intellect" without the encumbrance of the body can see the intelligible light of the divinity. The Spanish poet's "light, pure in itself how in inself/ it sparkles with quickened turn" echoes Ficino's: "the light of the divine intelligence springs from there, bending back on itself" (Ficino 1493, X).[32] The poetic voice ends with the same means and goal for his "separated intelligences" as those proposed for Socrates by Ficino: contemplation of the visible sun so as to gain the light of the invisible, divine sun.

Like Ficino and Aldana, Fray Luis de León also links the sun to his God. Describing himself as a depressed sinner, the Augustinian laments the resultant painful isolation from the capital letter, divine Sun: "and so I was left without the light of the divine Sun" (León 1995, Atribuido III, v. 87).[33] A different verse work in which Fray Luis adapts an Horacian ode is described by Juan Francisco Alcina as "a transposition of pagan characters and myths into their Christian equivalents" with "a certain inclination to rationalize the Christian religion and add to it a certain lay quality, although this might be unconscious on the part of the Augustinian" (León 1995, 163–4).[34] Rather than an unconscious attempt at secular-religious syncretism, I believe the work should be read, unapologetically and along with Spanish mysticism in general, as a further development of Ficino's *pia philosophia*. One specific image in Fray Luis's poem, not linked to the Horacian ode, leaves little doubt:

equal to the Eternal Father,
equal to him who was born and lived on Earth,
he who makes hell tremble,
he whom the sun adores,
in whom all being lives and is made better.
(León 1995, XIX, vv. 26–30, my emphasis)[35]

The image has its source in the *Pimander*, where we also read that the sun, eternal governor of destiny, needs a figure to adore and fear:

> And what can be said of the sun, of that most powerful of the celestial gods to whom all the rest give way as king and sovereign, of a star of such dimensions, greater than the earth and seas, who shoulders on himself the lesser stars in their orbits. Whom can the sun revere, my son? Whom can he fear? (Renau Nebot 1999, V, 3)[36]

The Hermetic author resolves that "there is someone, Tat, who is maker and master of all this. Without someone to make them, neither place nor number nor measure could have been maintained" (Copenhaver 2002, V, 4), then expresses a wish for his son:

> Would that you could grow wings and fly up into the air, lifted between earth and heaven so as to see the solid earth, the fluid sea, the streaming rivers, the pliant air, the piercing fire, the coursing stars, and heaven speeding on its axis about the same points. (Copenhaver 2002, V, 5)[37]

Hermes tells Tat that this perspective on the "order of the cosmos," which is also "the cosmos of order," would allow him to understand "the invisible god, who crafted them all by his own will" (Copenhaver 2002, V, 5; 7).[38] This section of the *Pimander* parallels quite closely the expressed desire of the Augustinian's poetic voice in another work:

> When will it be that I might,
> freed from this prison fly up to the sky,
> Felipe, and in the sphere,
> that flees the furthest from the ground
> contemplate pure truth without pain? (León 1995, X, vv. 1–5)[39]

Fray Luis continues with a series of images in verse that echo those of the Hermetist in the chapter quoted above (Copenhaver 2002, V, 5), as both authors posit and describe contemplation from a celestial standpoint. Below in pairs, each Hermetic prose quote is followed by Fray Luis's verse from the same poem X:

– "see the solid earth" (Hermes); "I will see how/ the sovereign hand planted the foundation" (León, vv. 11–12);[40]

– "the fluid sea" (Hermes); "the boundaries and signs,/ with which to the swollen sea .../ why ebb and flow/ the waters of the ocean;/ (León, vv. 18–19, 24–5);[41]

– "the streaming rivers" (Hermes); "who nurtures and supplies the rivers/ with perpetual currents" (León, vv. 27–8);[42]

– "the pliant air" (Hermes); "of the frozen cold/ and of summer I will see the causes, / the sovereign waters/ of the airs, who sustains them" (León, vv. 29–32);[43]

– "the piercing fire" (Hermes); "of lightning its forge" (León, v. 33);[44]

– "the orbit of the stars and heavens" (Hermes);

And there raised up,
I will see the celestial movements,
both the contrary pull,
and the natural ones;
the causes of fate, its signals.
Who governs the stars,
I will see, and who lights them with beautiful
and brilliant sparks; (León 1995, X, vv. 51–8)[45]

Fray Luis will see the *primum mobile* and its contrary pull exerted against nature's planetary orbits, the reasons for fate, destiny, and the ordered motion and lighting of the stars. For what I translate as "the contrary pull" the poet uses *arrebatado*, a verb taken to mean a movement that drags something else against its will, for the contrary pull on nature by the higher heavens. In *De sole*, Ficino calls this a reverse movement (*retro mouentur*), a going back versus a moving forward (*regrediunt ... progrediuntur*).[46] The *Pimander*'s author uses the terms "resistance," "opposite mode," and "beating back" to describe this motion, which is "not conjoint but opposed, for the spheres are not moved in the same way; they move contrary to one another, and the contrariety keeps the motion balanced through opposition. Resistance is the stilling of motion" (Copenhaver 2002, II, 6–7).[47] Fray Luis follows his "contrary pull," "causes of fate," and sparks of light with a return to the sun:

I will see this eternal fire,
fountain of life and light, where it stays
and why in winter
it comes so hastily;
who detains it during those long nights. (León 1995, X, vv. 61–5)[48]

Eternal fire, font of life and light, and its movements; all are images that, again, resonate with Ficino's *De sole*: "producer of both life and heat, it moves, invigorates and regenerates all, it warms and comforts: and all that might be hidden, its arrival makes manifest: it rises and sets again completing the four seasons of the year: and those intemperate regions far removed from the Sun, are likewise lacking in life" (Ficino 1493, V).[49] Another parallel to Ficino's work on the sun is found in Fray Luis's Poem XIX, in the stanza that follows the verse quoted above, "he whom the sun adores" (a quien el sol adora) (v. 29). Fray Luis invokes the mother of Light:

> Then the womb in full,
> the Mother of this Light will be praised in song,
> clearest of Lanterns,
> in this turbulent sea
> faithful advocate of humankind. (León 1995, XIX, vv. 31–5)[50]

The descriptors – lantern in the turbulent sea, faithful advocate of humankind – are also explored by Ficino in *De sole*, in which we read that Minerva's Sun/ Son is fruit of the divine intelligence, and that all justice reigns and is directed from the middle of the Sun's throne, through her from whom He is born:

> No one lifted my veil. That fruit I brought forth, the Sun, was born. Whereby appears the best fruit, the Sun of Minerva, that is, the birth of divine intelligence. Ancient theologians, and Proclus was witness to the same, said that all justice reigns and is centred in the Sun's throne, from which all proceeds and is directed. (Ficino 1493, VI)[51]

In fourteenth-century Spanish works of the *marianismo* movement, the Virgin is frequently represented as an advocate for justice for humankind, but Neoplatonist solar and light imagery is not a part of that tradition. For Ficino, the image is justified by ancient theologians who called Apollo the "judge."[52] With his capital letter "Luz-Lucero," Fray Luis makes that same connection of the Virgin to Christ and the sun. The Augustinian poet broadens thematic *marianismo* advocacy to include Neoplatonist Sun/ Son divine light.

As to the effects of contact with the light of that divine intelligence, both the Hermetist and Fray Luis offer the same analogy, that of a blinding ray of the sun's light, although they differ in that the Hermetist recommends that he who is capable admit the intellectual splendour that can grant immortality:

> The vision of the good is not like the ray of the sun which, because it is fiery, dazzles the eyes with light and makes them shut. On the contrary, it illuminates to the extent that one capable of receiving the influence of intellectual splendour can receive it. It probes more sharply, but it does no harm, and it is full of all immortality. (Copenhaver 2002, X, 4)[53]

Fray Luis is more circumspect, and in *De los nombres de Cristo* he counsels that one should admire the brilliance of this divine light around us in all creation, while warning that its own vivid understanding will blind us:

> And just as with the sun, that simultaneously we see yet we cannot look at (we see it because we look at its light in all things that we see; we cannot see it because, if we rest our eyes on it, it dazzles them), so with God we can say that he is clear and dark, hidden yet also manifest. For we do not see him in himself, and if we raise our understanding to look at him, he blinds us; while we do see him in all things that he does, because through them his light shines. (León 2008, III, 357)[54]

In this distinction in expectations, we see a movement away from Ficino's syncretic optimism. For the Augustinian, writing a full century later, man's limits are more restricted, and the blinding dazzle of the visible sun acts not as an enticement but, rather, as a warning against any effort to ascend to the ultimate splendour, which will only blind us. Man is once again, as he was for Plato himself, back in the cave of shadowy images, incapable of the splendour of the Ideas.

In Ficino's *De sole*, we also read that Heraclitus called the sun a fountain of celestial light (*Heraclitus luminis coelestis fontem*) (Ficino 1493, VI), just as it would be for San Juan de la Cruz, who celebrated in verse that same celestial fountain from which comes all origin without origin and all light, even at night:

> Its clarity is never darkened
> and I know that all light comes from there
> even at night. (Juan de la Cruz 2000, "Fonte," copla 5)[55]

In *De sole*, Ficino describes the magnitude of the sun's light and power with mathematical analogies, adding that the sun is the *ab initio* creator (and cause) of all out of the void (1493, XI).[56] This same imagery is also employed by Aldana:

> I say that the point without beginning
> the infinite line that turns on itself,
> the ray of its glorifying light,
> that ray that in its light includes itself
> ...
> whose power was such *ab initio*, (Aldana 1985, XLIII, vv. 929–32, 941)[57]

The infinite line, the point without beginning, the ray that in its light includes or syncopates all, has been so *ab initio*. Aldana continues with a dialogue between father and son in which the son-character is named Sun and, like Christ, promises to die in order to restore life to mortal man:

> «... Substantial nature, live image
> I am of your exact being, similar and sure;
> ...
> after unfriendly death I will achieve, Father,
> revival in life, my protection,
> since my death will give death to death
> and man will find at last grace with which to work».
> This he seemed to say and this before that,
> and even before showing its light to the human world
> the sun had showed and placed
> before its Sun the superwordly Sun.
> Oh Sun, oh Sun, oh Sun who has composed
> the emptiness, giving all being without conceit,
> thanks with loud voice is given and proffered
> to you by even the silence which lacks voice!
>
> (Aldana 1985, XLIII, vv. 945–6, 957–68)[58]

In *De sole*, Ficino similarly explains that the sun dies each day and is resurrected,[59] and that it generates all life beyond itself and out of itself.[60] The Italian philosopher began that work with reference to the sun as a creator comparable to God,[61] followed by Pythagoras's precept about the divine mysteries that cannot be spoken of without divine light,[62] an image also found in the *Pimander* (Byrne 2007, 240–3). Again echoing Ficino, Aldana repeatedly links Sun and Christ:

> Already rising through the air is the sacrosant
> immortal body of our divine Sun, (XLI, vv. 41–2);
> Who could but the Sun, first cause (XLIII, v. 481);
> from the new ray that the supreme Sun
> brought out, to give happiness, to give light and sight, (XLIII, vv. 490–1)[63]

In another chapter of *De sole*, we read that sunlight stimulates the muses. Wherever there are solar daemons, "the ancients called them Muses presiding over all sciences, most especially of poetry, music, medicine, purification, oracles, and prophecy" (Ficino 1493, XII).[64] Aldana also follows Ficino on this point. At the start of a 1210-verse poem that relates the story of Phaethon trying to manage his father Apollo's chariot,[65] Aldana invokes the god of the sun with multiple names: Apollo, Phoebus, and Sun, asking each to favour his muse:

Immortal high god, sacred Apollo,
new and precious light that to mortals
has always granted light, life and growth,
...
choose golden god, receive Apollo,
do not fail to choose, do not forget Phoebus
...
Reason it is, Sun, since you so form yourself
that in all the rest you might form yourself
to thus live conformed in reciprocal love
as each one seeks its likeness.
Look at my sun, oh Sun! and you will see if only
here, as you there, she might be alone
...
and I will dare to swear an oath
about my sun (oh Sun, who also swears
by your own deity!) that surely you think
those to be your rays and, so believing,
you will accept that she [his muse] is the Sun although she
will swear on herself that the Sun is surely you,

(Aldana 1985, VIII, vv. 1–3; 20–1; 27–32; 34–9)[66]

This heartfelt poetic apostrophe to the Sun as god and muse, an echo of Ficino in *De Sole*, is perversely reflected in a very different, prose invocation to the same by Miguel de Cervantes. Writing in the second part of *Don Quijote*, more than thirty years after the man he himself called "the celebrated Aldana" (el celebrado Aldana) (Cervantes 1996, 373) had penned the verse quoted above, and just one year after Isaac Casaubon had published a scathing critique of the Hermetic treatises and of all who gave them credence, Cervantes' invocation highlights the persistence of the Ficinian sun images in Spanish letters. It also, however, clearly illustrates the move of Hermeticism from didactic practice to poetic aesthetic:

Oh perpetual discoverer of the antipodes, torch of the world, eye of the sky, sweet melter of ice, Timbrio here, Phoebus there, here the puller, there the physician, father of Poetry, inventor of Music, you who always come out and, although it might so seem, never set! To you I say, oh sun, with whose help man engenders man! to you I say please favour me, and illuminate the dark recesses of my mind, so that it might proceed to narrate the details of the great Sancho Panza's governance; for without you, I feel weak, languid, and confused. (Cervantes 2005, II, 45)[67]

Cervantes runs through the full gamut of Neoplatonic images of the sun: "discoverer of the antipodes, torch of the world, eye of the sky," only to follow with the quotidian "sweet melter of ice." He offers two common epithets for Apollo, syncretizing both the Aristotelian Timbrio and the Platonic Phoebus only to add in a patently belittling tone: "here the puller, there the physician." The respectful "father of Poetry, inventor of Music," is followed with the taunting riddle about he who comes out but never sets. Cervantes' next invocation again takes us to the same creative and inspirational images of the sun that we read in Ficino and in the poetic works, but with another ironic twist: "Oh sun, with whose help man engenders man! Of you I beg that you favour me, and illuminate the dark recesses of my mind." The abstract and glorifying tones of Ficino's *De sole* and *De lumine*, in which the sun inspires procreation on the part of all beings[68] due to its generation of light and colour in their eyes are, in Cervantes' work, reduced to the physical fact followed by emphasis on the negative, pre-inspired state, the "dark recesses of my mind." To end his mock invocations, Cervantes reveals that this help is needed in order for his narrator to be able to tell the reader about comic figure Sancho Panza's transformed role as governor. The final line plaintively complains that without the sun, the narrative voice feels weak, languid, and confused. For Hermetists and Neoplatonists, light inspires movement, that is, procreation. Here again, we see Cervantes wrenching images out of Ficino's philosophically ideal realm to place them squarely in the context of human poetic creation.

Cervantes' invocation is an ironic inverse of the positive Hermetic and Neoplatonic perspectives with their respectful, hopeful pleas for the Sun's intellectual light. Cervantes, like Ficino, was a syncretist. However, the Italian philosopher wove from ancient sources an exalted, hopeful picture of man as an intellectual and spiritual being capable of transcendence. In contrast, the Spanish novelist incorporates the very same imagery for use by a derisive narrative voice, with resultant ridicule of the muse and of the expressed goals. Further, Sancho Panza's transcendence/ transformation will be narrated by this "weak, languid, and confused" voice that has consistently been presented as a mistrusted observer of the minutiae of mundane reality. The muse is invoked to help this feeble, untrustworthy voice feel strong, rather than to provide a final transcendent impulse to the "great miracle" that is man. Divine philosophy and optimistic splendour have become, for Cervantes in 1615, comic poetic tropes. This Cervantine manipulation and adaptation of the Hermetic-Neoplatonic solar images is well-suited to another recognized role for the sun which, as Ficino notes, "transforms and metamorphoses things in a continuing spiral" (Ficino 1554, XVI, 9).[69] In the mid-sixteenth century, Spanish mystic poets like San Juan de la Cruz and Francisco de Aldana incorporated and celebrated those images, yet writers like Fray Luis de León began to temper their exhuberance. As Cervantes gave them a thoroughly prosaic twist Lope de Vega, as will be seen in the following section, fought to defend their integrity as ideals.

Fire

For Hermes Trismegistus in the *Pimander*, fire is immolation and the end of mortal life. It is described as "immersing oneself" (Copenhaver 2002, IV, 6) in the mind at the centre of the universe after purging all earthly concerns. Ficino glosses the passage to say that the act is an immersion in the "divine crater" and to add previsional details: "one must hate his own body, love only God and, indifferent to all mortal things, sacrifice himself to, share in, and meditate on the divinity, until such point as one burns with love" (Ficino 1554, commentary, 30).[70] That journey and immersion are described in verse by Aldana and Fray Luis de León, the first with fear as the poetic voice approaches the unknown:

> But, woe is me! I head into the depths,
> where neither shores nor banks are seen,
> and if I do not turn back, I will sink and drown.
>
> (Aldana 1985, LXV, vv. 277–9)[71]

Fray Luis de León offers the perspective from within the crater:

> Here soul navigates
> in a sea of sweetness and finally
> immerses itself in it,
> neither hearing nor feeling
> any exterior, passing accident. (León, III, vv. 31–5)[72]

But it is San Juan de la Cruz who, like Hermes, versifies the fiery yet sweet immolation of self:

> Oh living flame of love,
> that delicately wounds
> my soul in its most profound centre
> be no longer cautious,
> finish if you will;
> break the veil of this sweet encounter. (Juan de la Cruz 2000, Llama, vv. 1–6)[73]

Fire is also, in the *Pimander*, the creative force: "Mind, which is the most penetrating of all the divine thoughts, has for its body fire, the most penetrating of all the elements" (Copenhaver 2002, X, 18).[74] Man's internal spark of mind, wishing to imitate its maker by creating in turn, is incapable of divine designs due to being encased in a corporeal shroud: "Since it is stripped of fire, the mind in humans is powerless to craft divine things because it is human in its habitation" (Copenhaver 2002, X, 18).[75] Once released from that oppresive cloak, this soul-mind will again be able to create but, until then, it can only realize that power through human arts and sciences (Byrne 2005; 2007, 126–39).

Beyond that image of fiery immolation, Spanish writers also incorporated a Neoplatonic three-part division for fire. Fray Luis de León speaks of the "similarities, consonance, conformity, and unity" seen throughout the world by the "Platonic school" (escuela platónica), and offers the example of fire:

> In this world fire is an element; in the celestial [world] exists the fire of the sun; and in the angelic [world], the fire of the seraphim; but each [works] in its own way: the fire here burns, that in the heavens gives life, and that of the seraphim loves. Doubtless, one cannot negate a force, a virtue, a hidden link, that weaves, knots, and embraces all the grandeur and variety of this world. (León 1885, 4, 233)[76]

Those same three fires are Lope de Vega's focus in a sonnet first included in a 1613 dramatic work titled *La dama boba*.[77] In his own gloss of the sonnet's meaning, Lope will also remit directly to Platonic and Hermetic works. The sonnet reads:

> My love resists the elemental nature
> and aspires to heavenly virtue
> it sees itself in the Angelic minds
> where is found the idea of heat.
> No longer as element does fire dress the soul,
> marvelling at its flight to the sun,
> as it withdraws from lower worlds,
> to that of resplendent cherubim.
> Nature's fire cannot scorch me
> the life-giving heavenly virtue
> envies the sight of me risen to the supreme
> Here where angelic fire is recovered
> How could mortal power touch me?
> For eternal and end imply contradiction. (Lope de Vega 1989, 1:401, vv. 1–14)[78]

In a letter written in 1624 to Don Francisco López de Aguilar, Lope notes that his sonnet has spawned a great variety of opinions by ignoramuses who distort its meaning, and so he will offer a verse-by-verse commentary for his friend. First he states that the main theme of the sonnet is modelled on Pico's *Heptaplus*:

> The sonnet is based on three fires, which correspond to three worlds. Heat is, in us, a basic principle of nature: its celestial nature is a warming virtue, and its angelic nature is the very idea of heat. Fire is an element in us, the sun in the sky, and seraphic intelligence, but they differ in that the element burns, the celestial gives life, and the supercelestial loves. That is how Pico discusses it, divinely and subtly, in his *Heptaplus*.[79]

For the third verse of the sonnet, *it sees itself in the Angelic minds*, Lope relies on authorities including Saints Augustine and Bernard, as well as Roman poet Martial, John Chrysostom, and the book of Matthew,[80] then he adds:

> Marsilio Ficino says that the light of the divine mind doesn't enter into the soul unless the latter, like the moon to the sun, turns to it, and that this doesn't happen until the soul leaves off the deceptions of the senses, and the clouds of the *phantasia*, and rids itself of that fog and shadow, as Theophylactus called ignorance, condensing itself into the very deepest recesses of that same mind: and Mercurius in the *Pimander* introduces divine mind which says: "Comprehend me, and I will show you" and he says that, finally, when divine mind showed him, he saw in his own mind the true light, with innumerable rays in an unending chain, and a fire surrounded by great power.[81]

The reference is from the *Pimander* which reads, in Ficino's Latin: "Tua me mente complectere, & ego te in cunctis quae optas, erudiam" (Ficino 1554, 1) directly reflected in Lope's Spanish: "Comprehéndeme tú, que yo te enseñaré" (Lope 1989, 1:404). In addition to Ficino and Mercurius as like-minded philosophers, Lope's gloss of "the soul ... turns to it [divine mind]" also echoes Ficino's commentary to Book XI of the *Pimander*: "incline your mind to the thought of the mind" so as to know and understand the cause of all (Ficino 1554, commentary, 77).[82] Lope also separates the senses from *phantasia*, as two distinct categories to be abandoned, just as Ficino does in his *Platonic Theology* (Allen 1989, 124, 198; Kristeller 1964, 235–6).

Lope explains the following verse of his poem: "Where is found the idea of heat," with reference to Saint Dionysius, Theophilus Folengo, Andreas de Acitores, and Isaías, then he concludes: "And so Trismegistus in that most ancient of theologies called God the God of fire, Majesty and Spirit" (Lope de Vega 1989, 1:404).[83] For the verse "withdrawing from lower worlds," Lope again glosses with reference to Ficino: "this seems very clear for ours and for the heavenly, until moving on to the Angelic. Marsilio distinguishes between these two worlds, splitting divine Wisdom into two acts: one that is found in the nature of God himself and another that includes external things. The first is that which conceived the first, eternal world: the second, that which nurtures the second, temporal one" (Lope de Vega 1989, 1:406).[84] This is, as we saw above in relation to the architect/archetype imagery, from Ficino's *Platonic Theology*: "The world machine had always been inscribed beforehand in the architect of the world, and the moment of its inchoation was signified in the architect's will ... God had perfected the substantial world wholly in himself from eternity" (Ficino 2001–6, 18.1.8).[85] Ficino also, in the same text and on the topic of where to find wisdom, describes God's nature as operating on two axes: "He is present in the very heart of all things. He does not toil away in many [actions]; rather, through his own being, which is the universal axis, he rotates the axes which follow upon it: essence, life, mind, soul, nature, matter" (Ficino 2001–6, 2.13.4).[86]

Lope's two worlds are also found in the *Pimander*, in which the first act of creation by Mind is to create a second craftsman who is "the god of fire and vital breath" and who, in turn, creates the seven spheres of the perceptible world: "The mind who is god, being androgyne and existing as life and light, by speaking gave birth to a second mind, a craftsman, who, as god of fire and spirit, crafted seven governors; they encompass the sensible world in circles, and their government is called fate" (Copenhaver 2002, I, 8).[87] Lope's "temporal world" is that governed by fate or, as we saw above with Cervantes, the one in which man rides Destiny. From this same Hermetic fragment, but writing close to a full century prior to Lope, Garcilaso de la Vega had extracted the image of the androgyne for a lover's reference to "this half a part" (esta media parte) (Eclogue II, v. 969), which was then explained by Fernando de Herrera as an allusion to the "Platonic fable" (fábula platónica) (Herrera 2001, 863). Herrera did not attempt to clarify the reference, expecting that his readers were familiar with the idea of an original, hermaphrodite precursor to man's current engendered state of being, and with its classification as a fable.[88]

The final direct reference to Ficino in Lope's letter comes with his explanation of the verse, "to that of resplendent cherubim," for which Lope quotes the Italian philosopher directly:

> "Not by any imagining or perception of man's intelligence but rather through contact with intellect's true substance and superior virtue, in which it not only sees but also tastes and touches, how sweet is the Lord." And thus says Marsilio Finicio [*sic*][89] about the Platonist Plotinus in the second book of the first Ennead. (Lope de Vega 1989, 1:406)[90]

Lope's text reads "contractum" in the 1771–90 edition, and also in Blecua's 1969 edition, but Ficino's original is "contactum"; Lope also uses the accusative "intellectum" rather than Ficino's ablative "intellectu." I translate with an eye to Ficino's original text, and the internal logic of the passage.[91] Either Lope or, as I suspect, a later transcriber of the letter, has misspelled Ficino's name (but only here, spelling it correctly in the previous passage quoted above), substituted 'contactum' with 'contractum' and made other minimal emendations to Lope's quoted extract from the Italian philosopher's text. With the exception of 'contactum,' none of the others substantially alter the meaning of the passage. Hankins has studied Ficino's conception of *reminiscentia* and notes that it "is not just an unlimited place in the mind lit by the divine light" but, rather, "a broadening out of the *acies mentis*, consciousness, to embrace all of reality from a higher metaphysical plane" (2005, 19). In the last verses of his sonnet, Lope directly references Ficino's commentary on Plotinus to indicate a similar philosophy on the transcendent effect of love: his poetic voice speaks from that higher metaphysical plane, where "mortal power" cannot touch him and "angelic fire is recovered" (Lope 1989, 1:401, vv. 13, 12).

The sonnet in full can be read as a verse exploration of the *Pimander*'s description of the soul's release at the moment of corporeal death when thought, man's inherited divine spark, has been released from the terrestrial body and resumes its original body of fire: "the mind, since it is divine by nature, becomes purified of its garments and takes on a fiery body ... Then, when the mind has got free of the earthy body, it immediately puts on its own tunic, a tunic of fire, in which it could not stay when in the earthy body" (Copenhaver 2002, X, 16–18).[92] At that moment, as Lope tells us, "elemental fire cannot burn me" because the poetic voice has once again been clothed in the "angelic fire" and, as Lope adds in his gloss, at that moment the surrounding cloak of fire "will metamorphose from human to divine" (Lope de Vega 1989, 1:407).[93] The sonnet's gloss-letter ends with a complaint against those calling themselves poets who merely mask in circumlocution and ambage what should be perfectly clear: as he sees it, they "*usurp the name Poet without knowing anything of the science*" (Lope de Vega 1989, 1:409, emphasis in orig.).[94]

The fire of love is, of course, a poetic image of long-standing, but aethereal escape from the body as it is consumed by these flames of love, with an enveloping body of fire clothing the soul after mortal death, is specific to the *Pimander*. Lope confirms his source with direct attribution here, and further references Hermes in other texts. In a novel that has been described as the only pastoral written "*a lo divino*" (Carreño in Lope de Vega 2010, 11) Hermes is, for Lope, "the great theologian Mercurius Trismegistus" who "spoke so highly of the divinity" (Lope de Vega

2010, 466, 400).[95] In another letter, to an unnamed "Your Excellence" (vuestra excelencia), Lope again quotes Hermes Trismegistus to state that, as the ancients all said, the basis of the poetic art is philosophy: "Don't be surprised, sir, if here I speak at length, given that speech is such a dignified topic: Mercurius Trismegistus in the *Pimander* says: 'God gave speech and mind only to man, two things that are judged to be as important as immortality'" (Lope de Vega 1989, 4:467).[96] Lope's unattenuated respect for both Hermes and Ficino is obvious in these writings.

Taken together and writing contemporaneously, Lope and Cervantes offer a wonderfully dual perspective on the continued influence of Ficino's Hermetic and Neoplatonic imagery in Spanish letters. Lope fully incorporates and embraces the Italian philosopher's ideals while Cervantes appropriates yet radically adapts the same concepts with modern independence. The latter's secular, irreverent use of the imagery contrasts in large measure with Lope's unquestioning explanations. Both, nonetheless, illustrate the pervasiveness of Ficino's legacy in early modern Spanish writers. They are Beltrán Almería's two faces of Hermeticism, traditional didactic practice and modern aesthetic, coexisting at the beginning of the seventeenth century. As will be seen in the following section a third voice, once again that of poet Francisco de Aldana, offers his own perspective on a traditional, if polemic, point of dogmatic theology.

Resurrection

The manuscript copy of Ficino's Latin translation of the *Pimander* held by the Cathedral at El Burgo de Osma, Spain,[97] mentioned above for certain marginal glosses, includes three specific commentaries relating to bodily death and resurrection. The *Pimander*'s author speaks of corporeal death as the moment when the body's senses will rise up and flow back to their particular sources, becoming separate parts and mingling with the cosmic energies:

> To this Poimandres said: "First, in releasing the material body you give the body itself over to alteration, and the form that you used to have vanishes. To the demon you give over your temperament, now inactive. The body's senses rise up and flow back to their particular sources, becoming separate parts and mingling again with the energies." (Copenhaver 2002, I, 24)[98]

In the Burgo de Osma manuscript, next to the last phrase of the quotation, ending with the word "surrecturi," one commentator debates in the margin: "The body is not resurrected" (Non resurrectio corporem). This anonymous hand has no problem with the text's following description of the afterlife, during which the resurrected souls are said to sing sweet hymns to God, and he pens in the margin:

"the glorious life of the blessed heavens" (gloriosa celestis vita beatis). Later in the manuscript, the text again speaks about death and the soul's release from the body:

> Some hold, therefore, that the soul is blood, mistaking its nature and not seeing that the spirit must first be withdrawn into the soul and then, when the blood thickens and the veins and arteries are emptied, this destroys the living thing; and this is the death of the body. (Copenhaver 2002, X, 13)[99]

The manuscript commentator adds in the margin: "Death unbinds (or dissolves) the body" (Mors. resolutio corporal).[100] Taken together, the three comments show that the anonymous hand's only point of debate is the physical resurrection of the actual body, with which he clearly disagrees.

Michael Allen points out that the question of the immortality of the soul was only made dogma by the Fifth Lateran Council in 1513, and that resurrection of the body, "another of Christianity's cardinal dogmas and certainly one that dominated the intellectual and theological horizons of the Middle Ages and the Renaissance," was a focus for Ficino in his *Platonic Theology* (Allen 2008a, 26).[101] In my estimation, the most telling counterpart to the Burgo de Osma manuscript commentator's antidogmatic declaration disputing corporeal resurrection is a verse work by Francisco de Aldana who, as we have already seen, frequently makes use of Ficinian imagery. In his "Eight-verse Stanzas on Judgment Day" (Octavas sobre el juicio final), Aldana offers a poetic gloss on statements made by Ficino in his *Platonic Theology* to describe the moment when disjointed, rotting body parts search for and reunite with their former souls, as marble tombs crack open to allow the eyes and ears of the "rotted old mortal flesh" to seek out their former soul inhabitants.

The poem consists of twenty stanzas of eight hendecasyllable verses each. The full work can be read as an ekphrastic exercise, as the poetic voice describes throughout what he *sees* at the moment of Judgment, and Aldana's editor Lara Garrido believes, quite rightly in my view, that the writing of the poem could have been influenced by Michaelangelo's Sistine Chapel fresco on the same theme, painted from 1533 to 1541. In turn, Shrimplin-Evangelidis (1990) has noted Michaelangelo's probable debt to Ficino's Neoplatonist writings, as well as to sixteenth-century heliocentric iconography and symbolism linking Christ, Apollo, and the Sun.

The first stanza of Aldana's poem describes a ring of golden light, a theatre, and a throne; the second, the movements of "a thousand winged spirits" (mil espíritus alados) (v. 10), and a "great ring of golden angels,/ archangels and others ..." (el gran cerco de ángeles dorados,/ de arcángeles y de otros) (vv. 14–15), all laughing as they circle around the divinity; in the third stanza, the clouds are described as hyacinths, emeralds, and diamonds wandering as nimbi, "sparkling splendours/ in the form of pacific lovers" (resplandores centellean/ y en forma de pacíficos amantes) (vv. 20–1) joining and circling in the heavens; in the fourth, the poetic voice *sees* (*veo*) the cessation of movement on the part of the sun, moon, stars, sea, and wind, with the light of the two principal planetary bodies now a "degraded, cloudy, bloodied colour" (denegrido colour turbio y sangriento) (v. 28), and the world is all in silence awaiting "the news of an ancient, bestial cry" (nueva de llanto desusada y fiera) (v. 32). In the fifth stanza, the poetic voice *sees* both "the great ancient mother,/ Nature, all confounded" (la gran madre antigua veo,/ Naturaleza, estar toda turbada) (vv. 33–4) and "Time without change or encirclings;/ full of itself, bearing the sickle,/ almost invisible, reduced to an echo,/ atop a fallen, dried trunk" (Aldana 1985, XXVIII, vv. 37–40).[102] The sixth stanza details Fame's broken wings and man's "decrepit mortal glory" (mortal caduca gloria) (v. 42); the seventh, the elements praying, land trembling, waters crying, air sighing, and "fire almost burning itself up" (casi a sí mismo arder se muestra el fuego) (v. 54), to end with an apostrophe to God: "Do you perish, or does your creation?" (¿Pereces, o perece tu hechura?) (v. 56). In the eighth stanza, the poet first describes the divinity as "only and immensely act" (acto inmenso y solo) (v. 57), "all and every part" (el todo y parte) (v. 60), untouched by the idea of want, then ends with another rhetorical question: "But, where can I hide, or how,/ from you, great God, who is all in all?" (Mas, ¿dó podré guardarme o de qué modo/ de ti, gran Dios, que todo eres en todo?) (Aldana 1985, XXVIII, vv. 63–4). Then the poetic voice turns to the procession of the living, raising their eyes in faces that already seem dead, seeking pity and forgiveness (stanza nine), in a large procession heading to the valley of Joshaphat (stanza 10).

Stanzas 11 through 19 describe in gory detail the reuniting of dead bodies with their former souls. In the last two verses of the eleventh, the dead rise from the profound depths to the world of the living. The twelfth through sixteenth read as follows:

> Oh, how much marble do I see from sepulchres
> rising up under the burden of its own weight
> how many on earth, oh God, how many fissures
> from whence are risen so many heads!
> Oh, what a range of mendings!
> One stirs, another begins to incarnate,
> one is missing an eye, and one an ear
> rotted and old, from mortal flesh,
>
> One flees from himself, another touches himself,
> joining movement to demand, yet
> another tries with tremulous, crazed voice
> to speak with a sound that fails to issue;

this one moves his tongue and another, his mouth,
they fear to draw their own breath,
and, as this one reforms and sets himself,
this other still leaps with his shroud.
From that one's veins, dried and blighted
comes the hot humour of pure blood,
another asks of death the stolen
relics of his human dress;
fleshless skulls seek their skin,
not feeling nature's horror,
whitened bones run to join up
and shelter under new cover.
Down to the last follicle, each one links
up to the same singular being he had when alive
with burning fervour each conjoins
to the body where had been his soul;
all the vile matter of the mortal veil
hidden away in that same matter,
rises and flees from the twisted forms,
to settle back into its first place.
Ash is transformed into flesh
and exhalation becomes water and wind,
as a useless, false creation
crashes down on its own foundation;
the accidental, foreign form
seeks another substance, another element
so as not to disturb place, time, fate,
or any thing in this transitioning. (Aldana 1985, XXVIII, vv. 89–128)[103]

The last four stanzas describe, respectively, "legions of the lost,/ as countless thousands of demons/ emerge from the abyss" (vv. 134–6), the "terrible, deafening buzz" as "hell opens its cavernous centre" (vv. 138–9), "apparitions ... shadows and horrors,/ masks, phantasms and visages" who are "forming new conditions [existences] here and there" (vv. 145–6, 150), closing with the sound of a heavenly trumpet then silence as all await the "sentence of the Word" (v. 158).[104]

Contrary to the manuscript glosser and his "Non resurrectio corporem" the poet's description leaves no doubt as to a belief in bodily resurrection; not only will it happen, but the details are painstakenly celebrated. The biblical reference to the moment is found at 1 Corinthians 15, where Paul also speaks of the corporeal resurrection, but the only image from that text with resonance in Aldana's work is that of reaping the seeds one has sown, which Aldana versifies as:

each now comes with his handful
of seeds, losing no grain or speck,
and I, too, oh terrible, sacred God,
in my hands carry a similar yield. (Aldana 1985, XXVIII, vv. 69–72)[105]

Like Aldana, Ficino also describes the moment when men's souls return to their earthly bodies, with God ruling over the process, although with less intimate detail:

> And in the *Statesman* Plato writes that after the present, fatal course of the world, the souls of men, with God commanding and reviving them, will receive the bodies they have lost in this fatal course, with the result that, just as human bodies once upon a time had succumbed to fate on earth, so under the rule of divine providence they will rise from the earth and live again. (2001–6, 18.9.4)[106]

Aldana's God is, throughout the poem, omnipresent and dominant, mainly addressed in fearful or praise-filled epithets: "Oh, sovereign God!" (¡Oh soberano Dios!) (v. 13); "Marvellous God!" (¡Maravilloso Dios!) (v. 25); "But, where might I hide or how, from you, great God, who is all and is in all" (Mas, ¿dó podré guardarme o de qué modo/ de ti, gran Dios, que todo eres en todo?) (vv. 63–4), and ending with: "But, oh great God, judge, propitious is this [...]" (Mas ¡oh gran Dios!, jüez, propitius esto) (v. 160).[107]

A more philosophical yet less poetic description of the End of Days is Ficino's, in his *Platonic Theology*:

> Therefore the highest and ultimate end of the universe ... will not be motion but rest. For rest is more perfect than motion and individual things are moved for the sake of rest ... At length when the sky's course (wherein all things are begotten) is completed, nothing is to be generated further; but men's individual bodies, for whose sake all things were first generated, will rise again from the earth at God's command. (Ficino 2001–6, 18.9.4)[108]

This is the moment as described by Aldana, who also specifies the frightening sight of a motionless "Time without change or encirclings" (v. 37), "the sun and moon unmoving" (v. 26), and tells us that "the sea has stopped flowing, the wind rests,/ all is silent, as if to await/ the news of an ancient, bestial cry" (vv. 30–2).[109]

In a later section of the *Platonic Theology*, Ficino calls the moment of bodily resurrection a "second creation" (recreatio) and again posits the cessation of time: "God will perform [the second creation] after the world's motion ceases" to add that from then on, "the body will remain forever conjoined to the soul" (Ficino 2001–6, 18.9.12).[110] We hear the echo in Aldana's verse, as

Down to the last follicle, each one links
up to the same singular being he had when alive
with burning fervour each conjoins himself
to the body in which had lived his soul. (Aldana 1985, XXVIII, vv. 113–16)[111]

Aldana describes the "confused day, both longed for and/ feared by the soul" (vv. 151–2),[112] and Ficino's proofs for bodily resurrection include that same longing, as "it is contrary to the order of the universe and of its own nature alike that the soul remain apart from the body" (2001–6, 18.9.6), and "souls separated from bodies will always be inclined naturally towards bodies" (18.9.7), for

> the soul separated from the body, insofar as it is soul, is imperfect, just as the part is customarily imperfect when outside the whole for the constituting of which it has been appointed. Therefore its natural appetite will never be at rest. No soul will ever be blessed unless, having recovered its body, it is led back (or hopes to be led back) to the whole. (2001–6, 18.9.8)[113]

Aldana tells us that flesh, ear, eye, skin, skull, bones, all down to the last follicle, will be seen reforming and resetting as bodies rejoin souls. Ficino's images are less detailed but quite resonant: "the bodies that have been dissolved into the elements, [God will] reassemble them again from the elements that remain ... the same body will be rewoven because the same form will exist as before, that is, the soul" (2001–6, 18.9.10).[114] Aldana's description of "all the vile matter of the mortal veil/ hidden away in that same matter" (vv. 117–18),[115] reflects and expands on the Italian philosopher's argument regarding that reweaving since the "same form will exist as before, that is, the soul" and "the same prime everlasting matter that is one and subject to all things will exist" (Ficino 2001–6, 18.9.10).[116]

On arguing for the immortality of rational soul in book seven of the *Platonic Theology*, Ficino states: "Let us accept then that soul is form alone; and I do not mean by this accidental but substantial form" (2001–6, 6.7.2).[117] In his verses on Judgment Day, Aldana recognizes the same difference: "the accidental, foreign form/ seeks another substance, another element" (vv. 125–6).[118] In sum, Aldana's poetic gloss on the religious-philosophical question incorporates both Ficino's and Hermes's arguments for bodily resurrection. The poet's detailed ekphrastic exercise evidences his knowledge of those texts, and attests to their continued influence on Spanish letters. Unlike the anonymous hand that glossed "non resurrectios corporem" on the *Pimander* manuscript at El Burgo de Osma, Aldana's poetic gloss on this point of dogma easily combines Hermetic authority with Ficino's Christian-Neoplatonic theology.

5 Ficino as Plato

The scattershot knowledge of Plato and Platonic philosophy in Spain during the Middle Ages and up to the beginning of the Renaissance has been studied and we know that, as in the rest of Europe, the *Timaeus* was available but other dialogues were mentioned only through reference to ancient and classical authorities such as Seneca, Virgil, Cicero, Saints Paul and Augustine.[1] In the first part of King Alfonso X's *General estoria*, Plato is "the philosopher, from Athens" but, in the *Libro de buen amor*, Juan Ruiz identifies him as, simply, an astrologer.[2] By the end of the fourteenth century, Plato will be called either philosopher or poet and when it is the latter, he is grouped with Virgil, Dante, and Horace (Villasandino 1993, 107).[3] During the first half of the fifteenth century, humanist scholars began to make available the translations from Greek into Latin that would enable fuller intellectual engagement with Plato's works. Leonardo Bruni translated Plato's *Phaedo* (1400–5)[4] and Enrique de Villena, Virgil's *Aeneid* (1427–8), which Villena glossed with specific mentions of various Platonic dialogues, among them the *Republic*, the *Timaeus*, the *Phaedo*, and the *Phaedrus*. The noted Church Council that took place in, successively, Basel (1431), Ferrara (1438), and Florence (1445),[5] with the goal of reconciling the Orthodox Greek with the Apostolic Roman Church, and the subsequent 1453 fall of Constantinople to the Turks, were events for a time considered the main stimulus to renewed interest in the study of Greek language and letters in western Europe but those dates fail to explain the earlier developments. Monfasani points to Manuel Chrysoloras as "the Greek who started the Hellenization of the Italian Renaissance" with his move to Florence in 1397 (2004, 9). Gil Fernández notes the paucity of detail on formal university study of Greek in Spain prior to 1495 (2009, 41–2), but Di Camillo (1976 and 2010) has detailed early fifteenth-century exchanges between Spanish and Italian humanists, in some cases regarding specific Latin translations from the Greek, as well as the importance of "the role that Spanish prelates and ambassadors played in the various Church Councils convened between 1414 and 1449" (2010, 21).

According to the Corpus Diacrónico del Español (CORDE), which offers a fairly comprehensive catalogue of Spanish language use, Alonso Fernández de Madrigal's repeated references to a Platonic aphorism on friendship ("the Platonic saying" [*el dicho platónico*]) in a treatise written between 1440 and 1455 is the first appearance of the adjective 'Platonic' in Spanish letters. Those uses conform to the norms of medieval wisdom literature, with exemplary adages by various named authorities used to inspire certain conduct. Pero Díaz de Toledo's 1458 use of 'Platonic' in his *Diálogo y razonamiento en la muerte del Marqués de Santillana*, the second such appearance of the adjective in Spanish letters, is a bit different: Virgil "showed himself to be Platonic" (se mostró ser platónico) when he spoke of successive reincarnations, in the words of the Spanish translator: "of the souls ... that are to dress themselves in bodies through a succession of times" (Díaz de Toledo 1892, 276).[6] Díaz de Toledo compares Christian and Platonic perceptions on life after death, affirming Christian belief that at death, the soul will separate from the body but only until Judgment Day, when it will reunite with that same body it once inhabited on earth, and the Spaniard notes that Virgil's ideas on successive reincarnations are "more curious than true" (Díaz de Toledo 1892, 276).[7] Here, in 1450, the Platonic concept of transmigration of souls is noted and rejected as distinctly at odds with Christian dogma. Ten years prior to making that statement, however, Díaz de Toledo had produced the "first complete version in any European vernacular of a dialogue by Plato" (Round 1993, ix)[8] with his 1440 Castilian translation of the *Phaedo*. In that work, the same author praised Plato for having affirmed and proven the immortality of the soul.[9] Approximately one hundred years later, in his own commentary on the same Platonic dialogue, Sebastián Fox Morcillo will assure his reader that Platonic and Christian ideas on the immortality of the soul are identical, and he will even allow for metempsychosis into animal form as punishment for human evildoers. By the end of the sixteenth century, addressing Albertus Magnus's doubt on the soul's immortality, Spaniard Álvarez Miraval will write:

> But what apparently undermines this doubt is what the ancient Trismegistus affirms, and the divine enchanters, saying that the spirits we call angels or demons and the naked souls who have lost their earthly bodies all move from one place to another. This truth we ourselves have also seen realized in magic practices. Believing in and hoping for this immortality of soul, many philosophers and ancient Romans were comforted and took with great spiritual restraint the deaths of their family members and friends. (Álvarez Miraval 1597, ff. 377v–8r)[10]

This radical change in perception must be attributed in large part to Ficino's writings and translations, which had made Plato available, orthodox, and a frequent topic of discussion. The editors of a recent volume on the Italian philosopher specify that he translated the dialogues "in a way that especially emphasised their relevance for contemporary readers. This meant finding an approach that did not compromise his or their Christian outlook" (Clucas, Forshaw, and Rees 2011, 1). As Hankins notes: "Ficino's broad position provides a built-in defence against criticism [of Plato]" by first providing order to the dialogues, and then offering allegorical, moral, selective and, at times, inventive readings of problematic sections (1990, 350, 350–9). From the last decade of the fifteenth century, we have the following description of Plato from Spaniard Alfonso de Palencia:

> Plato was the most eloquent and most praised of all philosophers, because to his teachings on Socratic discipline he added a form of contemplation that among the ancients was attributed to Pythagoras the Samnite; and so they say he [Plato] made philosophy perfect. He said that God is without time, and unchangeable and the healer and the arbiter, affirming that God is judge: because of this, he was privileged over all the other gentile philosophers who had diverse opinions on the divinity. Platonists took their name from the philosopher Plato and they are, in general, called Academics but, due to certain diversity [of opinions] they were somewhat divided [among themselves]. It is affirmed that Plato was so-named due to the breadth of his chest. (Palencia 1967)[11]

That last detail on the attribution of name to breadth of chest is found in various ancient sources, but the specific phrasing used by Palencia would suggest Seneca as the most likely.[12] The other details in the description are found in Ficino's *Platonis Opera omnia.* The combination of Socrates, Pythagoras, and contemplation that find their perfect balance in Plato, for example, is from Ficino's commentary to the *Laws*: "We have found, however, that the wisdom of Pythagoras puts greater emphasis on contemplation, while that of Socrates stresses action and that of Plato gives equal weight to both contemplation and action" (Ficino 2009a, 73).[13] For this biography and, as referenced above, various other details included in his *Vocabulary*, we can surmise that Palencia read Ficino on Plato.[14] This, in turn, again places Ficino squarely in the court of the Catholic Monarchs.

The first edition of Ficino's translated *Platonis Opera omnia* was published in 1484, and it incorporates the only Ficino commentaries on the dialogues finished at that time, those on the *Symposium* and the *Timaeus*, along with some *argumenta* and summaries. Later editions, beginning with that of 1491, incorporate all Ficino's commentaries, chapter summaries, and *argumenta.* As we have seen, the volumes had wide circulation in Spain, attested to by the number of extant copies in Spanish libraries today with ex libris and glosses that allow for dating their readership. There are also signatures: "licenciado Dn. Antonio Pedro García" in Seville (Biblioteca Columbina, ms. 23–4–5, *Opera* ed. 1548), "licenciado Juan Sánchez de Villegas" at the Theological School of the University at Alcalá de Henares (Complutense BH FLL 15938, *Opera* ed. 1532), and one: "I belong to Don Eugenio Nicolás de Guzmán, Censor appointed by the Inquisition, parish priest with original benefice of the High Church of the Brotherhood of Saint Mary of the city Arcos de la Frontera" (Bib. Columbina, ms. 23–7–2, *Opera* ed. 1567).[15] In addition to the dates given above (chapter 1) for the circulation of a number of the *Platonis Opera omnia* volumes, for these three signatures I can add that the volume signed by Don Antonio Pedro García was in circulation in Spain at least as early as 1612, as attested by the dated censor's signature of one J. de Vargas.[16] For the second signature, María Luisa López Vidriero (1987) studies a Complutense manuscript dated 1651 that lists a number of volumes censored by Juan Sánchez de Villegas in the library by that date and, for the third, Nicolás de Guzmán died in 1750 (Mancheño y Olivares 1892, 389).

Spanish writers followed the Italian philosopher in considering Plato not only orthodox but also divine.[17] Ficino justifies the adjective in his *Life of Plato*: "From all this it is understood that although the Greeks considered Aristotle a very wise man, they called Plato divine. Clearly, the life and science of Aristotle was mainly human and natural; whereas Plato joined knowledge and life with the divine" (Ficino 1557, 2: no pag.).[18]

Mentions of Platonic dialogues, as well as attributions to the "divine Plato" are frequent in the writings of sixteenth-century Spanish authors. Alonso de Fuentes references "the divine Plato" on music (1547, f. 169v)[19] and Pedro de Luján, "the divine Plato" on friendship (1990, 139).[20] Sebastián de Horozco advises that "the divine Plato says, in his *Republic*, that those who speak with princes owe them [the courtesy] of saying what they have to say in few words" (1994, II, 344, proverb 282),[21] and Francisco Cervantes de Salazar speaks of the "confused information that the divine Plato had about this New World" (1971, chapter 2).[22] Antonio de Guevara relates a tale told in the *Attic Nights* but adapts it by adding the adjective: "Aulo Gelio ... says that among the disciples of the divine Plato was one named Demosthenes" (1994, 160).[23] Hieronymo de Saona postulates that "Plato earned the name 'divine' because, although a gentile, he said one thousand divine things about God" (1598, 43).[24] Juan Huarte de San Juan finds the epithet justified on the basis of the Greek philosopher's opinion regarding the "incorporeal, spiritual, and incorruptible" nature of man's immortal soul as well as its rewards or punishments in the afterlife (1989, 376–7).[25] I quoted above a section of Juan de Pineda's *Monarchia ecclesiástica*, with its incorporation of Hermes Trismegistus into the biblical account of Genesis. Pineda also includes "the divine Plato" in that narration, as do those who wrote dedicatory verse to the 1620 publication. Fray Juan de Mesa, for example, describes man's natural thirst for knowledge, and says that Plato "learned so much,/ that he deserved fame as divine," adding that "Dionysius placed the divine Plato, triumphant, in Zaragoça" (Pineda 1620, Dedication "Vn alto rostro").[26] This last reference could be to Plato having visited and spoken of divine matters in Syracuse, noted by Ficino in his discussion of Plato's seventh letter (Ficino 2008, 166–70). Alternatively, in the Italian philosopher's *Life of Plato*, which figures as preliminary material to the *Opera omnia*, Plato expels tyrants from and gives laws to Syracuse (*Syracusanis vero expulso tyranno leges dedit*) (Ficino 1576, 2:no pag.). In Pineda's text, however, the place name given is Zaragoça, as quoted above, and possibly related to late medieval sources that reference members of the Spanish house of Zaragoza (a name itself derived from Caesar Augustus of Roman times) having moved in the thirteenth century to properties near Syracuse, Sicily. Syracuse would continue to be called, in Spanish sources, the "Zaragoza of Sicily" (Zaragoça de Sicilia) (Panzano Ibañez de Aoiz 1705, 84).

In his *Monarchia ecclesiástica*, Pineda argues for a "very theologized philosophy" (Philosophía tan Theologizada), although he also notes the need for caution in the use of ancient sources. According to Pineda, Plato was wrong when he said that the world would never end, because in Apocalypse we read that time will end and that, when it does, so will the temporal world (1620, f. 2r). Despite that, as we saw above, Pineda also begins his treatise with reference to the "Archetype, Ideal and Eternal world" (f. 1r) that gives birth to the temporal; the later statement about the end of the created, temporal world on the basis of the biblical source would not, of necessity, obviate the continued existence of that "Archetype, Ideal and Eternal world." Again, Pineda follows Ficino, who so states in the *Platonic Theology*: "Certainly, that spiritual world, the model of this [corporeal] world and the first work of God, has the same [eternal] life as the architect" (Ficino 2001–6, 18.1.10).[27] Following that same Ficinian model, Pineda's careful choices include conflation of Platonic Ideas with Christian doctrine, and the use of Plato and Trismegistus as coprotagonists with God and Moses in the creation of the world. Pineda dedicates his volume to Jesus Christ whom he calls, in Platonic fashion, the *Summo Bien* (1620, f. 2r). The identification is neither rare nor surprising in sixteenth-century Spanish letters although as a whole in this text, Pineda does offer an extremely daring and thorough combination of Christian, Platonic, and Hermetic doctrine. This Spaniard not only accepts Ficino's concept of a *pia philosophia*, he also attempts to develop it further. The first part of Pineda's *Monarchia ecclesiástica* was published in 1576. Later editions, beginning with that of 1588, totaled thirty books in five volumes, and were reprinted in 1594, 1606, and 1620.

In 1597, with specific citations of a number of Platonic dialogues Álvarez Miraval references "the divine Plato" on a wide range of topics: the *Timaeus* for the excellence of land (fol. 55v); *Laws* for the benefits of the hunt as exercise (fol. 104v); the fourth book of the *Republic* to note that music is universally good for all illnesses (fol. 163r); *Alcibiades* and *Laws* to call wise and good men fortunate, and to commend them as natural rulers (f. 257r; fol. 260r–v; f. 290r); the *Republic* about freedom as the most powerful and excellent good (f. 263v); *Timaeus, Menexenus, Republic*, and *Laws* regarding the impact of his environment on a man's health (f. 310v); *Laws* about following without complaint one's "luck" (suerte) in governing or being governed (f. 383v). Álvarez Miraval also specifies how "the divine Plato": divides time into past, present, and future in the *Parmenides* (f. 253v); recognizes four classes of nobility (f. 301v); defends himself by saying he bested the will of the stars through knowledge (f. 333r); was "divine" more for his wisdom than for his birthplace (f. 350v); and asserted, as had many philosophers, that man must not fear death (ff. 433v–4r) but that he should cure himself of ills that are born of bad habits (ff. 453r–v). Plato is a consistent and preferred source of information for Álvarez Miraval in his treatise on medicine; here, I have repeated only the references that specifically call him the "divine" Plato.

Also writing at the end of the sixteenth century, Gutiérrez de los Ríos remarks on what "the divine Plato" says about the liberal arts (1600, 138, 191),[28] and a dedicatory sonnet to a 1598 publication titled *Geometric Discoveries* (Descubrimientos geométricos) praises the book's author, Juan Alfonso de Molina Cano, for having triumphed in all ways over "the divine Plato and Ptolemy, Euclid and many more writers" (1999, "El comissario Francisco de Molina a su hermano").[29] Spanish magistrate Jerónimo Castillo de Bobadilla tells his reader that "the divine Plato" (el divino Platón) determined that men who govern should be educated or at least literate (*letrados*) (1616, 1.9.28). Plato's divine wisdom became a standard reference and, even as late as 1651, in Baltasar Gracián's novel *Criticón*, the character Critilo says: "I would listen for a while to Socrates and then to the divine Plato" (2009, I, 4, 109).[30] As a counterpoint to these multiple laudatory references, as we saw above, only one copy of the first volume of Ficino's *Platonis Opera omnia* in a Spanish library is emended with a line drawn through the epithet "divine," although the date of that emendation is not indicated, and nothing further by or about Plato is affected in the volume.[31]

In the middle of the sixteenth century, Spaniard Sebastián Fox Morcillo published his own commentaries on three Platonic dialogues: *Timaeus*, *Phaedo*, and the *Republic*. Fox says that Plato is not widely read but should be and in his prefatory letter to the first published commentary, he identifies Plato as one of the "divine philosophers" (diuini philosophi) (1556c, f. 2v). Extended discussion of Platonic ideas is found in Fox's 1556 *Commentary on the Phaedo*, a gloss that is 25 per cent longer than the text itself, and is interspersed into the dialogue, which itself is divided into four parts: exordio, introduction, proofs, and epilogue. With the exception of the exordio, each of those four parts is further subdivided, with particular commentary following each subsection. The Spaniard uses Ficino's translation of the dialogue as his base text without so stating, then within the commentary references the Italian philosopher once openly to dispute the translation of a particular Greek term, and a second time with a veiled insult. Whether or not Fox Morcillo was aware of Díaz de Toledo's 1440 Castilian translation of the dialogue is unclear but unlikely, as he neither refers to nor makes use of it. While I cannot pretend to address in analytical terms the type of philosophical question Fox poses in his commentary, as it is not within my range of expertise, there are a few points on which the Spanish writer engages with Ficino's opinions, and those are outlined below.

The subtitle of Ficino's *Platonic Theology: On the Immortality of the Soul*, "comes from the identical titles of a treatise of Plotinus, the *Enneads* 4.7, and of an early work of Augustine" (Allen and Hankins 2001, xiii). The same subtitle is found in several Greek manuscripts: it is the "alternative title" used by Plutarch, it is how the Plotinian work was known to Macrobius, Lactantius, and St Augustine (Round 1993, 1, n.3), and in 1440, following Bruni's Latin, Díaz de Toledo also used it for his translation of the *Phaedo*. Fox Morcillo, in 1556, follows this by-then common practice, calling his work *Commentary on the dialogue Phaedo or The Immortality of the Soul*. Like Ficino, Fox wishes to advance and prove the immortality of the soul, which the Spaniard identifies as the most basic fundamental tenet of Christianity. Writing after the 1513 papal bull *Apostolici regiminis* that decreed as dogma the individual soul's immortality, after further negations of immortality by secular Aristotelians like Pomponazzi, and after Martin Luther, who criticized the Lateran Council for making "philosophical theory" on the soul's immortality "an article of faith" (Constant 2002, 370), Fox is unremitting and creative on this point. Early Christians, he says, defending the primitive Church against an impious citizenry, used this dialogue of Plato to justify that they were not inventing new doctrine, but rather continuing the ancient philosopher's themes. That is to say, the primary basic assumption of Ficino's *pia philosophia*, an unbroken line of thinkers leading to Christianity, is taken as a given, and offered as positive support for belief in the soul's immortality. According to Fox, Eusebius, Tertulian, Origen, Lactantius, and many other writers used this dialogue by Plato to defend "the doctrines of our religion" (2010, 21).[32] Platonists and Peripatetics used it to stand against Stoics and Epicureans (who, respectively, negated immortality and providence) (2010, 21). Like Ficino, Fox sees concord in Plato and Aristotle: it is not Neoplatonists versus scholastics as it will be later for critics who read the sixteenth century in the light of the Counter Reformation but, rather, those two groups on the side of the Christians.

Although Fox does not merely repeat or copy from Ficino's work, a number of dicussions from the *Platonic Theology* are incorporated into his text. His approach in general is described by González de la Calle as "philosophical independence" combined with a "firm belief in revealed dogma" so that his independence "does not extend to extremes that were not common in his era" (González de la Calle 1903, 94, 122).[33] We see this combination clearly in his approach to the question of the immortality of the soul. Fox first cites a multitude of ancient sources very specifically by book and chapter to an admirably pedantic degree, then builds on those opinions from authority with his own innovative arguments. For example, he explains the thinking of Plato, Aristotle, Plotinus, Aquinas, Cicero, and Lactantius on the immortality of the soul, offers his own reading of the arguments of Saint Thomas of Aquinas which "clearly, in my opinion, defend and almost demonstrate the soul's immortality" (2010, 75),[34] then declares his intent to augment the voices of those authorities with his own arguments (*Addam his ego aliam*) (Fox 1556a, 51). Fox explains why soul cannot perish completely, running through points that parallel to a certain extent those of Ficino in the *Platonic Theology*, tellingly those contained in a chapter that has also been linked to the works of Aquinas.[35] Ficino argues why soul "in itself has no potentiality to not exist" (Ficino 2001–6, 5.12, subtitle):[36] soul is and exists, therefore it cannot perish completely unless reduced to nothing; soul's essence does not so permit; soul is act, motion, etc. (5.12). The Italian philosopher concludes that soul, as essence and of its essence, cannot be changed (2001–6, 5.12).

Fox, however, purports to follow the logical development of such a possible change (Fox 2010, 78). If soul changes, he asks, what would be then born of it? He first reasons that a corporeal cannot be born of an incorporeal, ergo another incorporeal would be born. Given that, he conjectures, what could this new incorporeal be like? Fox posits three general alternatives: the same as before, or better, or worse, and then one by one considers each of the three. The last option, 'worse,' is rejected outright with the argument that soul's essence cannot be destroyed even if, in some manner, a condition of it has been.[37] The first option, "same as before," leads Fox to conclude that if it is the same, then soul will still be immortal, ergo there is no problem to resolve. The third possibility leads to a very interesting conclusion: if the new incorporeal is "better" than the original, then it will be even more pure, ergo even more immortal [!].[38] This highly pragmatic yet existentially questionable option of "even more immortal" is neither explained nor pursued further. This one example shows Fox attempting to move beyond Ficino's conclusion (soul, as essence and of its essence, cannot be changed (2001–6, 5.12)), but the resulting hypothesis and probe is more dogmatically driven than philosophically argued. The conclusion is simple linear optimism.

The one direct reference to Ficino by Fox comes in the form of criticism of a particular translation from the Greek. The disputed term relates to the difference between *suntrefetai* – to grow by composition of substances – versus *suntribetai* – to rub together and, so, to crush – a distinction between developing versus perishing as the result of contact. The question under discussion is the relationship of heat and cold to growth, a point discussed at length by Ficino in the *Platonic Theology*, with details that Fox also incorporates, but with attribution only to ancient sources: analogy of heat as life to a living being, the breaking down of foodstuffs, etc. (Ficino 2001–6, 5.14.3; 7.8.1; 10.4.2). Instead of referencing Ficino, who explains fully the actual process of heat-to-growth, Fox merely says that how it happens is an even more difficult question than whether it happens, and he recommends book four of Aristotle's *Meteorology* for a reader who wishes to explore the point further. With this simple reference to its complexity, Fox elides the difficult point that Ficino had specifically addressed at length. Given the pertinent nature of the material discussed, and the detailed treatment of it found in the *Platonic Theology*, one has to ask why Fox Morcillo, who conscientiously references a multitude of sources, would omit Ficino. Given that his arguments parallel those of the Italian philosopher, with whom he has specific points of disagreement, and that he uses Ficino's *Phaedo* translation as his base text, his failure to even mention the Italian philosopher is surprising. One simple explanation might be Fox's own definition of "argument from authority" as one "formulated on the basis of testimony from the tradition of an ancient opinion" (2010, 79).[39] Ficino would not have been considered "ancient opinion" in the early sixteenth century. At the start of the seventeenth, in *La Dorotea*, Lope de Vega will offer an ironic comparison of reliance on ancient versus modern authorities, contrasting the standard preference for an older authority to that for women, always preferred when young (Lope de Vega 1996, IV, III, 361).[40] More revealing and probable a reason for Fox's rejection of Ficino as authority, however, can be found in another passage of his commentary on the *Phaedo*, with the Spaniard's oblique reference to another charged point of dispute.

The subject is the relationship of body to soul, and the destiny of the latter after death. In the dialogue, Socrates points out that if in a pure state when it separates from the body, the soul will "emigrate to a place pure like itself" where it "will live in the company of the gods" (Fox 2010, 99).[41] If, however, it is not in that pure state because it has been "seduced by the passions and pleasures of the body," the soul will be dragged into a visible place where it will remain fearful of the invisible, spin around funeral monuments and sepulchres, and live in the company of shadowy phantasms or animated simulachra (Fox 2010, 99–100).[42] These are the souls who lived for the body and, as Socrates states, they are like asses and similar animals; they put injustice, tyranny, robbery, and pillage before all else, and they "become a part of the lineage of wolves, falcons, and hawks," that is, those souls literally become animals (Fox 2010, 100).[43] In his Commentary on this section, Fox identifies the place of the non-pure souls after death as Tartarus (2010, 106), and then addresses what he calls the difficult question of metempsychosis of souls from human to animal form.[44]

Fox notes that Plato supports the idea both in the *Phaedo* and in the *Timaeus*, admits that it has caused much debate as some read it literally while others only wish to concede the acquisition of qualities but not the form of an animal, and then the Spaniard asserts that the opinion was, without a doubt, first found in Pythagoras. Fox tells his reader that Plotinus, "a serious author of great authority among the Platonists,"[45] affirms the opinion of human-to-animal metempsychosis as punishment for evildoers, but that others including Cronus, Theodorus, and many more Fox says he will not name so as to not "be tedious" also hold the same opinion.[46] Fox does, however, go on to name Lactantius Firmianus, Plutarch, Apuleius, and Porphyry, as well as Saints Justin, Augustine, and Basil, as those who accept Plato literally on this point. The passage ends with an oblique reference to Ficino: "so as to those who wish to say that Plato is speaking allegorically here – they only twist his words and they are far from his real opinion, having failed to sufficiently comprehend his thought" (Fox 2010, 107).[47] The target of that critique is Ficino who, in his commentary on the *Pimander*, describes human-to-animal metempsychosis as "an allegorical fiction" (fictionis allegoriam) prohibited by divine law (Ficino 1554, commentary, 64); in his summary of the *Phaedo*, Ficino says it is a Pythagorean idea and, contrary to how Fox reads it, Ficino assures us that Plotinus "denies that the soul becomes a beast but says that it assumes, undergoes, or passes into the nature of a beast" (Ficino 2006, 134);[48] in his commentary on the *Republic*, the Italian philosopher calls metempsychosis "a laughable tale ... the whole account needs to be expounded allegorically" (2009a, 68).[49] In the *Platonic Theology*, Ficino vacilates on the question: "doubtless a number of his [Plato's] words are poetical rather than philosophical," and Plato "did not affirm these particular Pythagorean views at all" although "perhaps for the sake of discussion he did affirm them" (2001–6, 17.3.2; 17.4.5; 17.4.14).[50] Ficino offers various examples of Plato distancing himself from the concept and concludes that the Greek philosopher referred only to beastly habits, not bodies (17.4.7–9). Fox's critique of the allegorical reading on metempsychosis suggests that he has read various works by the Italian philosopher, as the details of his rebuttal relate to Ficino's opinion in his own *Phaedo* and *Pimander* commentaries, as well as in the *Platonic Theology*.[51] The critique, however, is weakened by Fox's own allegorical readings of the *Phaedo*, as discussed below.

Fox's symbolic interpretations of Plato include a reading of the Elysian Fields to mean the biblical Paradise (Fox 2010, 179–83): "many illustrious men, and even some saints" have offered support for the idea, and "Personally, I do not disagree with what these authors say, having found that in Plato's writings there are clear vestiges of Genesis, even if they are wrapped up in fables and false opinions, as happens in just about all writing that the Greeks or Egyptians took from the Hebrews" (Fox 2010, 179).[52] Faced with what he himself calls "the allegories that Platonists tend to offer" regarding the twelve celestial zones of the zodiac, Fox completely evades the question:

> We will overlook the allegories that the Platonists tend to offer when commenting on these passages about this celestial land that they divide into twelve regions, that is, the twelve signs of the zodiac; and we will also omit other similar things, since they matter little in understanding Plato; besides, they are obviously things extraneous to a philosopher, who should try to reach the truth of things and not just appearances, as do others. (2010, 183)[53]

In his own *Phaedo* commentary, Ficino is slightly more expansive on the twelve regions, noting as does Fox that they correspond to the signs of the zodiac but adding that they are "ruled by the souls of the twelve spheres, and the twelfth is the sphere of the world" (Ficino 2006, 138).[54] Fox completely elides this point on the souls of the spheres, and by the end of the sixteenth century, Martín del Río will categorically deny "that the heavens are animated, and that occult qualities are astrologically caused, thus removing the bases for both demonic and natural, or spiritual, planetary magic" although he will allow for "natural science, including 'good' astrology" within narrow limits (Walker 1975, 178–9). The vehemence of these debates is illustrative of the polemical vacillations in dogmatic stances of the sixteenth century, and specifically the ongoing evolution of attitudes regarding astrology as a science. Their resonance in creative letters is perhaps best exemplified in Calderón de la Barca's early seventeenth century *La vida es sueño*, in which astrologer-king Basilio defies the predictions of the stars in a putative attempt to alter their prognostication of doom for his kingdom and himself. Basilio denies his son the hereditary right to reign by exiling him to a dark, cave-like tower, but through these supposedly preventive acts brings about the very events he hoped to avoid.[55]

As to the Elysian Fields, Ficino speaks of the similarity between Moses's earthly paradise and life on earth but does not mention the fields themselves and, according to the Italian, after death "perfectly purified" (perfecte purgatae) souls will "soar aloft to the super-celestial realm" (in locum supercoelestem euolant) (Ficino 2006, 138, 139; 1576, 2:1394). Like Ficino, Fox also relies on Moses's authority to say that Paradise is in our world, but adds that this place should be understood as "that celestial region, under which is our own land, [and it] is the happiest of all and more excellent than this our own; but that one is as the poets paint the Elysian Fields" (2010, 182).[56] For the Spaniard, after death honest and pure souls are "raised to the Elysian Fields, to a superior place where they become gods, as Plato says in the *Republic*, and they unite with the celestial star that is most like them, as he also says in the *Timaeus*" (2010, 188).[57] Fox describes as enigma and fable the poetic allegories used to explain these points; nonetheless, he insists that "all these teachings are in accordance with our religion" and that "the great power of truth is impressive; even peoples who did not know the true religion have believed that to pious men will come rewards and, contrarily, to the evil will come torments" (2010, 189, 191).[58] Like Ficino, Fox found the similarities in beliefs to be telling, and indicative of Platonic thought as a precursor to Christian belief.

On the final doctrinal point in the dialogue, the sacrifice of a rooster to Aesculapius, Fox directly echoes Ficino to explain the tradition of the ancients sacrificing a cock to the son of Apollo given that daylight is the "light of life" (uitae lumen) (Ficino 1576, 2:1395) or, as Fox states it, the "harbinger of day and night" (deie ac noctis nun(c)[t]ium) (Fox, 1556a, 158), accompanied by reference to the freed soul en route to heaven uttering a cry to Phoebus along with confirmation of Beneficence as the daughter of Providence. Fox adds one more note: "there are those who criticize Socrates for this sort of superstition" but then he offers a legal defence: "what cannot be doubted is that he did it to show his innocence in the matter for which he was being reproached" (2010, 199, 200).[59]

Scholars have observed that Ficino had to shield his writings from charges of heretical opinion, even to the point of adding a disclaimer at the end of the eighteenth and last book of the *Platonic Theology*: "In all I discuss, either here or elsewhere, I wish to maintain only what meets with the approval of the Church" (Ficino 2001–6, 18, postscript).[60] Metempsychosis, for example, was one highly charged point of debate, which begs the question of why Fox was not only more open than Ficino in his acceptance of this particular passage but also quite insistent on a literal meaning for the text. One very plausible answer: Ficino had already made Plato an accepted source. We can also read Fox's lack of caution as an indicator that, in Spain, this point was still being discussed openly in the middle of the sixteenth century.[61] Apparently, Ficino had made not only Plato but also Plotinus such orthodox sources that they could be read without allegorical dress, even by the Spaniard Fox Morcillo who, 350 years later, would be described by neo-Catholic Menéndez Pelayo as a "pure" Platonist who rejected the syncretic tendencies of the Alexandrian school, and never fell into the abyss of gnosis, theosophy, cabala, theurgy, or pantheistic mysticism (Menéndez Pelayo 1892, 159–60). In Fox's *Phaedo* commentary, to the contrary, after Plato and Aristotle, the next most frequently cited authority by Fox is Plotinus and not just generally, but with all specifics, book and chapter, of the *Enneads*: *Quid homo*, *De beatitudine*,

De daemone propio, *De triplici ascensu*, *De descenso animorum*, *De caelo*, etc. Fox accepts the definition of a "true philosopher" given by Plotinus in *De beatitudine*, as he who practises a life spent in "contemplation and separation from the body" (Fox 2010, 57).[62] Against Menéndez Pelayo, this might be read as aiming for gnostic, pantheistic ecstasy, but I believe that Fox is more fittingly described by Urbano González de la Calle: "His works respond more to a sense of erudite Neoplatonism than to that of the first Academy" (1903, 9).[63] Unable to assure his reader of a specific university for Fox's early education, the historian asserts that it was, in all likelihood, the Complutense (1903, 19–20), that is, the university identified with Ficino-like studies.[64]

Fox also offers an innovative reading of the *Phaedo*'s treatment of the daemons: the Spaniard distinguishes the good from the bad daemons not only because the latter are evildoers, per se, but also at times because they are inept at their assigned tasks (2010, 39).[65] When rational soul controls bodily passions it is called a "good daemon" (bonus daemon) (Fox 1556a, 19), like those genii that Ficino identifies as non-problematic (Ficino 2001–6, 18.10.3). Fox explains the genii (daemons) at length, describing the five types as per their specific tasks outlined by Plato in the *Timaeus*, and noting that for both Plato and Plotinus, the latter in *De daemone propio*, the "intimate, or personal 'genio' is really indistinguishable from the soul, and is so-called when its reason rules over the body" (2010, 39).[66] The daemon is the "luminous force of the soul" (praeclaram eiusdem animi uim) (1556a, 19) for all Platonists who write of it, although Fox notes to close discussion, without further comment, that both Lactantius Firmianus and Saint Augustine believed that the daemons were evil, adulterated spirits (2010, 39–40). That is, the Spaniard explores ancient opinion but ends with the dogmatic doubters, not explicitly adapting their stance but leaving it as the final word on the matter. In this, he is apparently closer to the beliefs of Guillén de Ávila who, as we saw above, substituted "angel" for all mentions of "daemon" in his *Pimander* translation.

On the theme of rewards and punishments after death, Fox recommends that Plato's doctrine on the existence of Tartarus be accepted as reasonable, although he does believe it might be "convenient" (conveniente) to further corroborate with testimonies from the Bible and from experience (González de la Calle 1903, 132). However, Fox does make one slight change in his commentary: Plato asserts that the worst, incurable souls are condemned to Tartarus from whence they will never leave. Fox repeats that these souls are banished to Tartarus "perpetually" (in Tartaro perpetuo sunt) but the Spaniard then puts a limit on that time frame: "ten thousand years" (decem annorum millia), after which they are once again delivered into bodies (Fox 1556a, 149). In Plato's *Phaedrus*, this is the time frame given for the soul of each person to be "brought around to the same place from which she started" after multiple reincarnations (Ficino 2008, 1.25.13).[67] Regarding the slightly less evil souls, Fox asserts that having repented their sins there should be a limit on punishment. Following Plato, the Spaniard states that those less-evil souls will go through a specific cycle: first Tartarus as punishment, then Cocito to be re-examined, and finally to Lake Aquerusia for further purification as necessary.[68] As Fox explains it, repentance allows for limits on time served.

A different rereading by Fox reveals that one particular feature of the *Phaedo* was, in Spain, more problematic than it had been for Ficino. Fox addresses at length what he calls the "type" of suicide recommended by Socrates, and vehemently denies a literal reading of the term. The Spaniard asserts that the *Phaedo* dialogue on the soul's immortality can make one confront death with a "fine and strong spirit" (alacri, & deliberato animo appeterent) (1556a, 4), but insists that as for those who condemn and reproach the *Phaedo* for having inspired certain men to commit suicide (for example, Cato, Cleombrotus), the fault is with the men and not with Plato's dialogue. Studies of the evolution of thought on suicide note early Greek and Roman attitudes both for and against the practice, then the development of Christian prohibitions, notably by Augustine in the fourth century and Thomas Aquinas in the thirteenth (Barry 1995, 450–80). Important to the time frame when Ficino was writing is that Renaissance thinkers, including many Christians, were once again openly considering the possibility without necessarily condemning it. Renaissance philosophers "turned the light of critical reason to Christian teachings on suicide," reviving and reconsidering ancient views of the practice, and in his *Oration on the Dignity of Man* Ficino's contemporary, Pico de la Mirandola, even "made suicide a mark of human dignity" (Barry 1995, 482). Religious leaders "continued to oppose suicide" but civic laws against it relaxed (483). Those debates persisted and at the end of the sixteenth century, Castillo de Bobadilla's manual for Spanish magistrates would even allow suicide in certain instances such as, for example, the need for a magistrate to protect the town he guards.[69]

In that spirit, Ficino is not very concerned with the *Phaedo*'s suicide message. Although in his summary of the *Phaedo* the Italian philosopher repeats Socrates's admonishment that "men are under the careful protection of God and have no right to leave it unless God so wills," he also quotes the dialogue to add that since "all the study of a philosopher is nothing but detachment from the body," one "should certainly not fear the detachment from the body which occurs at death but should look forward to it with supreme hope and joy" (2006, 131).[70] In his *Platonic Theology*, Ficino directly poses the question of how a rational soul can ever "kill its own body, whether ... by design or out of wrath or fear or grief," to answer that man "though he is an animal with more discretion, often kills himself, predicting, I suppose, that he will outlive the body and that, rather than destroying himself, he is discharging himself of the body's burden" (2001–6, 9.3.8).[71] Ficino's perspective, like that of Socrates, is that the soul does not have its origin in the body and acts freely in its own best interest; therefore, ridding itself of the body is not problematic.

Fox Morcillo, however, insists throughout his *Phaedo* commentary that when Plato speaks of death by suicide, those passages must be read in a very restricted manner as a simple recommendation for transcendent philosophical contemplation, and nothing further. Socrates asks: "would it not be irrational for such a man [a true philosopher] to fear death?" but Fox re-reads for: "despite saying that the philosopher should 'claim' (reivindicar) death, Socrates believes that no one may commit suicide" (2010, 50, 52).[72] The Spaniard offers an innovative alternative reading: "Socrates says that, evidently, no one is permitted to commit suicide, but that it is useful to practise a sort of contemplative suicide"[73] and tells the reader that Socrates uses "a certain prosopopoeia [personification]" to pretend that he is speaking with the Athenian judges, and to defend his desire for only this "philosophical death" (mortem philosophicam) (1556a, 34, 35). Fox supports his reasoning with Macrobius in *Scipion's Dream*, who describes the "dual nature" of the soul's death (duplex mortis genus) (1556a, 33): a natural death, when the soul abandons the animated form of a sentient being, and a second death that can be attained while "the animal still lives" but the soul "frees itself from the body, in a certain sense, through contemplation" (2010, 54).[74] The Spaniard insists that only this last is Plato's focus in the *Phaedo*: a meditation through which the soul separates from the body by fleeing its enticements so that as the passions become calmed, the body dies a philosophical death. That is, the dialogue's actual message of a real, punitive, legally induced suicide faced with fortitude is dismissed, even excised from the range of possible readings. On this point, Fox Morcillo reads the dialogue allegorically to say that with the right kind of philosophy, the soul can separate from the body by fleeing its enticements and calming the passions so as to die, even if only in a metaphorical sense, through contemplative ecstasy and transcendence of the body, thus attaining true, divine science (2010, 56–63). In another passage of his commentary, Fox accepts Plato's description of the soul as comprised of "harmonious numbers," and he notes that Plotinus went even further to "say that souls are separated from bodies and raised in contemplation of divine things by music's harmony" (2010, 40).[75] As he explains these arguments, the Spaniard does not flatly deny the possibility of transcendence through contemplation, although he does express conflicting views on it by stating, for example, that this contemplative philosophy "cannot be sufficiently attained in this corporeal life" (2010, 61),[76] but then also allowing that the soul might separate from the body through dreams and contemplation (2010, 104). For Ficino, neither suicide nor transcendence were prohibited topics. In contrast, Fox is forced to accept transcendence despite misgivings about its feasibility, as for him it is the only valid Christian reading of the *Phaedo*'s discussion on suicide.

To the contrary, within a few decades a very real, unapologetic transcendence and ecstatic unity very much in conformance with Ficino's thinking would be expressed in verse by Spanish mystic San Juan de la Cruz:

> And if you wish to hear of it
> this utmost science consists
> in a stirring sensation
> of divine essence,
> a result of his clemency
> that leaves one not understanding
> yet transcending all science. (Juan de la Cruz 2000, "Entéme," stanza 8)[77]

In his explication of another poem, "Noche," San Juan expresses a goal of "detachment of spirit," with the soul purged of its "desires [appetites] and imperfections" thus raised to divine contemplation and for the poetic voice the act is experience, not merely hope (Juan de la Cruz 1953, Prólogo 8; Book 1.1.1).[78]

As I briefly commented above, fusion of Platonic cognition and divine grace was one of Ficino's goals with the *pia philosophia* (Lauster 2002, 60). In the *Platonic Theology* he writes: "uplifted on Platonic wings and with God as our guide, we may fly unhindered to our ethereal abode" where divine light "is suddenly set ablaze in us from on high, in a perfect conjoining to our life" (Ficino 2001–6, 1.1.1; 14.10.12).[79] Ficino explains that the quickest route to this perfection is not through knowledge but, rather, love: "because the power of knowledge consists more in distinction, the power of love, in union" (14.10.12).[80] In San Juan de la Cruz's verse, that expressed hope is realized through a mystic flight ennabled by love:

> I soared so high, so high
> that I overtook my prey
> ...
> in flight I fell short
> but the love was so inspired
> that I overtook my prey.
> ...
> because the lance was made of love
> I leapt blindly into the dark
> and I flew so high, so high,
> that I overtook my prey.
> (Juan de la Cruz 2000, "Tras de un amoroso lance," vv. 3–4; 10–12; 17–20)[81]

The image of a hunt for prey (*caça*) also has its parallel in Ficino's *Platonic Theology*, where the Italian philosopher specifies that our soul "chases after" (aucupatur) God (2001–6, 14.5.1–2), and in the *Pimander*, where Ficino tells us that man, from his place in the centre of the cosmos, "hunts God himself" (venatur ipsum deum) (1554, commentary, 21).

In another verse work, the saint explains the results of that search:

> There he gave me his breast,
> there he taught me a very sweet science,
> and I gave him in turn
> myself, leaving nothing;
> there I promised to be his wife. (Juan de la Cruz 2000, "Cántico," stanza 27)[82]

God's "giving his breast" is divine grace and the learned *ciencia muy sabrosa* is cognition, with the result that wife-as-soul is conjoined with the divinity. In Plato's terms, once out of the cave we will remember and see again the real Ideas; Ficino reads this as being conjoined to God after our intellect is suddenly touched and set ablaze by the divine light; San Juan glosses his own verse by saying this is "science and intelligence in love" and "science through love" (Juan de la Cruz 2002, "Cántico," 18.3).[83] In another verse work, the moment is expressed as "lover with loved one,/ loved one transformed into lover" and possessed of that "sweet science" (Juan de la Cruz 2000, "Noche," stanza 5).[84] San Juan further glosses the "Cántico" verses by describing the moment as that in which the soul's will and intellect – which are, of course, the two wings of Ficino's gloss on the Platonic flight (2001–6, 14.3.7) – are rendered inactive and the soul, losing even its "first movements" (primeros movimientos) is made "divine, godlike" (divina, endiosada) (Juan de la Cruz 2002, "Cántico," 18.5).

San Juan explicates in prose another verse of the *Cántico*, "and then I knew nothing," by saying that the soul has achieved "knowledge of the highest God" which, in comparison, makes worldly science seem "pure ignorance" to the happy soul that finds itself joined to the divinity, "detached from and having conquered" all mortal concerns.[85] This moment results from drinking of the lover:

> In the interior cellars
> I drank of my Lover, and on leaving
> all throughout that field,
> I knew nothing,
> and the gain I had sought was lost. (Juan de la Cruz 2000, "Cántico," stanza 26)[86]

Ficino attributes the same drinking image to Zoroaster, quoting from the *Chaldean Oracles*: "the human soul contracts God into itself when, retaining nothing mortal, it becomes utterly inebriated on the draughts divine" (2001–6, 13.4.12).[87] In his Commentary on the Epistle to the Romans, Ficino describes this moment of "cognition of God (is) [as] a kind of deification" (Lauster 2002, 50). San Juan also explains that the knowledge gained with this drink leads to "deification" (endiosamiento) that leaves man aware of nothing mortal (Juan de la Cruz 2002, "Cántico," 17.11). The saint is consistent in his use of this imagery:

I was so taken with this drink
so absorbed and detached
that my [mortal] sense was left
barren of all feeling
and my spirit gifted
with an understanding that could not understand
transcending all science. (Juan de la Cruz 2000, "Entréme," stanza 3)[88]

San Juan's science is true, perfect, and divine. For Ficino, similarly, after long contemplation the theologian's mind "begins to know superhumanly to the extent that it is no longer unaware that it is itself contemplating God through God and in God" and "purged souls, who have loved the divine beauty preeminently, eventually immerse themselves utterly in the very sea of the divine beauty, and not only quaff down there the draughts divine but also pour these draughts out of themselves now into other souls" (2001–6, 12.3.4; 18.8.8).[89] The Italian philosopher is quite poetic in his own description of the moment when a human soul, focused on God, is "set ablaze, rarefied, lifted up, borne thither in the aetherial and airy body like tow wafted through the flame" (2001–6, 13.4.16).[90] We hear the echo in San Juan's verse:

On a dark night
with anxiety inflamed by love
oh blessed fortune!
I left but none took note
as my house was already calmed. (Juan de la Cruz 2000, "Noche," stanza 1)[91]

The corporeal house of the passions has been calmed. San Juan explains the image of night: "as the philosophers say, the soul, once God has infused it into the body, is as a clean and smooth slate, in which nothing is painted ... like ... in a dark cell" in which it only sees through the windows (*ventanas*) of that jail (Juan de la Cruz 1954,

"Subida," 27).[92] Ficino is one of those philosophers, and he uses the same imagery: "Hence that mystery" (Hinc illud Platonis nostri mysterium) of the soul in the body gazing "through the windows and phantasmal images of the senses" (sensuum fenestras atque phantasmata) (2001–6, vol. 6: Appendix, no. 34). Ficino's flame and lifting up of the aetherial body are further echoed in another of the saint's verse works:

> Oh flame of living love,
> that tenderly wounds
> my soul in its most profound centre!
> hesitate no more,
> finish if you will;
> break the veil of this sweet encounter. (Juan de la Cruz 2000, "Llama," vv. 1–6)[93]

The flame wounds so as to break the veil that holds body and soul together. In his *Phaedo* commentary, Ficino points out that the soul carries with it "a kind of veil that is made of air or of the spirits and vapours of its own body ... a veil new-woven from the circumambient air" (2006, 134).[94] Only following dissolution of that veil and subsequent purification is mind "set aflame" (accendatur) (Ficino 2001–6, 18.11.7). As noted above in the discussion of Lope de Vega's letter and its three fires, we also find in the *Pimander* similar imagery of the soul as intellect that, once freed from its corporeal body will be clothed in the "fiery tunic" (igneum videlicet corpus) (1554, 60) that is its original and proper body; in that transcendent moment, "thought, having purified itself of that [corporeal] clothing, acquires a body of fire" (Ficino 1554, X, 18).[95] San Juan's "break the veil of this sweet encounter" is a plea for dissolution of the veil so that the soul can be reclad with its fiery body or the "flame of living love" which is, we are told in the *Cántico*, a "flame that consumes yet does not harm" (2000, "Cántico," stanza 39).[96] The final moment of that experience of transcendent science:

> Of peace and piety
> was the perfect science,
> in profound solitude
> the path straight and known
> it was such a secret thing
> that I was left stammering,
> transcending all science. (Juan de la Cruz 2000, "Entréme," stanza 2)[97]

The Ficinian semantic and syntactic precursor is found in his Latin translation of the *Pimander*. Faced with the brilliance of Mind at the centre of the cosmos, the narrative voice exclaims: "thus I understood the words of Pimander and the discourse was such that it left me stammering" (me quedé balbuciendo) – in Ficino's Latin, "me stupore attonitum" (Ficino 1554, 3). Ficino's commentary to a later passage adds that the experience reveals "the proportion that escapes all proportion" and leaves one "comprehending the incomprehensible" (Ficino 1554, 77).[98] San Juan's variants include: "his knowledge will so increase/ that he will be left not knowing"; "he who knows this/ is left forever not knowing"; "this unknowing knowing"; "an understanding without understanding"; and

If you wish to hear it
the highest science consists
in an elevated sense
of divine essence
it is an act of his clemency
to leave one not knowing
yet transcending all knowledge. (Juan de la Cruz 2000, "Entréme," stanza 8)[99]

This is, once again, the combination of divine grace (*clemencia*) and Platonic cognition or, in the saint's words, the "highest science" (summa sciencia) that leaves one "not knowing/ yet transcending all knowledge."

San Juan de la Cruz's verse works are the poiesis of the *pia philosophia*, an ecstatic and creative expression of the same philosophy argued by Ficino and debated by Fox Morcillo. The soul, seeking science, calms the passions and ascends, leaving the corporeal body and all its concerns far behind. After all, it is immortal and does not need them. We tend to read religious and theological overtones into Spanish writings of the time frame, but we are not always correct in our understanding of what constituted religious thought in that era. Ficino's *pia philosophia* was part of the collective and quite orthodox imaginary of Renaissance Spain, as well as a common source for the esoteric symbolism of Spanish mysticism.[100] Both Fox and San Juan de la Cruz further develop Ficino's *pia philosophia* through their very distinct reflections on the multiple points of agreement found in Platonic and Christian doctrines. Other Spanish writers would follow suit, with or without specific reference to Ficino. 'Platonic' was popular throughout the sixteenth century, and multiple uses of the adjective are catalogued in works on philosophy, poetry, love, and even a manual for magistrates.

Philosophical and Poetic Readings of 'Platonic'

Early sixteenth-century uses of the adjective include disinterested descriptions of writers as Platonists: "Platonist Apuleius" (Apuleyo platónico) (Fernández de Madrigal, 1507, 255); "Platonist Xenocrates" (Xenócrates platónico) (Toro 1999

[1548], f. 61r); but also explicit parallels to canonical Church figures: Pedro Mexía notes that Saint Thomas of Aquinas adopted the opinion of the Platonists on man's "spirit" and "heat" being the reasons he walks upright (Mexía 2003, 1.16, 136–9).[101] A 1554 analogy offers that, just as Platonists are so-named because they follow Plato's doctrine, so men who follow Christ call themselves Christians (Meneses 1567, f. 71v).[102] In the mid-sixteenth century, the adjective is read as a positive epithet in a work translated from Italian to Castilian: "Plotinus, who was an excellent Platonist, after having very effectively practiced this astrological art, finally found it to be full of vanity and showmanship, and rejected it" (*Reprobación* ...1546, f. 19v).[103] While criticizing the art of [predictive or judicial] astrology, this anonymous author praises "excellent Platonist" Plotinus. In his commentaries on Garcilaso de la Vega's poetry, Fernando de Herrera draws analogies from Platonic to Christian thought on the importance of the sense of sight in matters of love and knowledge: "the Platonists call it *viso,* and the theologians, intellectual and intuitive knowledge" (Herrera 2001, 320).[104] Two late sixteenth-century theoretical works by Juan de Pineda and Alonso López Pinciano, the first with a theological-philosophical focus and the second more poetic, offer a clear perspective of the era's thinking on 'Platonic.'

Pineda frequently employs the adjective in a factual and non-judgmental way, as he explicates Christian doctrine while citing from a list of "almost seven hundred" (quasi setecientos) ancient authorities, including a number identified as "Platónicos."[105] He compares the opinions of ancient philosophers and Christian theologians on various Platonic beliefs and practices. For example, regarding "that famous World Soul" (aquella famosa alma del mundo) and the souls of the planets in their "celestial animation" (cielos animados) we read that everyone from Plato to Saint Thomas is in agreement.[106] Pineda's characters Pánfilo, Filaletes, and Policronio explain that Platonists celebrate music and proclaim it the underlying component part of souls,[107] and they note that the "great Platonic philosopher" Lucius Apuleius probably never dreamed that his writings would come to be so well "Christianized" (acristianadas) (Pineda 1963, 163.275).[108] In a chapter titled "Love is Transformative," Filaletes praises "the good platonist" (el buen platónico) Marsilio Ficino for his *Letters* and his *Commentary on the Banquet*, where Ficino describes love as free and precious, to be neither sold, exchanged, nor bartered for anything other than itself, that is, a reciprocal love. A failure to understand that doctrine by Policronio brings a sharp retort from Filaletes who insists: "the good Marsilio spoke marvellously for anyone who has, at a minimum, ears" (Pineda 1963, 169:74).[109] Pineda's characters are in dialogue with the ancient authorities, but also with Ficino, intimately, as "the good Marsilio" (el buen Marsilio) (1963, 169.74). They marvel at the almost Christian tenets expressed by various Platonists and Neoplatonists, buttressing their defence with the words of

Saint Augustine, among others.[110] Links between theology, philosophy, and poetry bring more reliance on Ficino along with Orpheus on the relationship between God, Apollo, and the Muses. Pineda describes the allegories of Platonic doctrine as the nectar and ambrosia of God, and as pleasures accorded those adept in divine contemplation (Pineda 1963, 163:77–84; 161:271–3). Pineda assures his reader that not only Plato but also Orpheus, Trismegistus, Proclus, and Plutarch, among many other Platonists, agree with Christians on the existence of hell and on its location under the earth, although he also notes that the school of another Platonist, Macrobius, while conceding the existence of hell, seems to believe that it is this life on earth, as the true habitat of man is a celestial one.[111] Plato understood the "Sainted Trinity" (La Santísima Trinidad conoscida de Platón) and the Greek philosopher advised man to flee this world by making himself like God, as Plotinus has written (Pineda 1963, 169.151; 163.90).

Pineda's characters marvel at the theological language of the Platonists, among whom they highlight three in particular: first, Macrobius who "located the ideas of the virtues in the divine mind" and "said there was a Son of God ... called with suitable language mind and storehouse of the ideas"; second, the "most famous theologian [Hermes] Trismegistus" who called the son of God, "precisely Word of God, by whom the Father created the world"; and third, "Diogenes Laertius, a pagan just like Trismegistus" who, nonetheless, called the son of God "Word [of God]" (Pineda 1963, 169.151).[112] The referenced works are those translated and elucidated by Ficino one hundred years earlier, incorporated into this work titled *Diálogos familiares* ... and directed by its author to "those persons who are not knowledgeable about scientific letters" and rhetorical niceties (Pineda 1963, 161:5).[113] Pineda's interlocutors speak pointedly on matters both weighty and not, and the author takes pains to explain that the *familiares* in his title means that the characters are good friends having a normal conversation one might hear any day of the week, without "the details of ceremonial complement" (Pineda 1963, 161:5).[114] Neoplatonist doctrine and its close association with Christian perspective are considered everyday food for thought for this group of intimate friends; Platonic is, as it was for Ficino, inspirational and orthodox, a way of life in conformance with Christian doctrine.

Pineda's contemporary Alonso López Pinciano tells us that 'Platonic' is specifically rhetorical. In his dialogue on poetic theory, titled *Philosophía antigua poética*, characters Hugo, Fadrique and Pinciano discuss Plato's expulsion of poets from the *Republic*. Knowing as they do that poetry is "useful" (útil) they question its outright rejection (1998, 1:100). Fadrique explains that Plato's *Republic* is imagined on the order of a celestial republic, a place whose inhabitants are so noble that poets are not needed to unsettle men's souls with lies that purportedly calm them, amuse them, or induce them to virtue (1998, 1:101).[115] He buttresses his argument with the authority of Saint Paul who, the reader is told, also said that if men were virtuous, fables would not be needed to convince them of doctrine (1998, 1:101). Hugo argues that Saint Paul reprehended only "vain" (vanas) fables, not "solid, doctrinal" ones (sólidas y que llevan doctrina), but Fadrique responds with a more restricted reading that has Plato as well as Saints Paul and Augustine reprehending all fables because they hoped for perfection in man, so that he would "taste virtue without the sauce of fables" (1998, 1:101).[116] Pinciano requests further confirmation of this idea by another ancient author, and Hugo specifies that it should be someone who called himself a Platonist and who understood Plato's "intention" (ánimo) (1998, 1:102). López Pinciano uses Aristotle's distinction between history (what was) and poetry (what might have been) to conjecture that since Plato's dialogues and colloquia did not, in all probability, happen exactly as they are written, they, too, should be considered poetry (1998, 1:113–14). When Pinciano complains that those writings are not in poetic form, Hugo rejoins that content, not form, differentiates history from poetry, then adds that Aristotle taught theory whereas Plato practised the craft, to conclude that Aristotle's writings teach whereas those of Plato give pleasure (1998, 1:114–15). Here, 'Platonic' is pleasurable prose, poetic because it is not, in all likelihood, historically accurate. López Pinciano does not specifically reference Ficino himself, but he does confirm that he is using Ficino's translations of the dialogues by making allusions such as "in the *Phaedo* or *On beauty*" (en el Phedón o De pulchro) (1:124) and "*Cratylus* or *On the Good Reason for Names*" (Cratilo o De la Buena Razón de los nombres) (1:236), that is, he employs Ficino's subtitles for the dialogues.

In these two late sixteenth-century dialogues we find a supportive theological-philosophical exploration and continuation of Ficino's *pia philosophia* with its Christian-Platonist concord (Pineda), and a search for agreement between Plato and Aristotle on matters of poetic theory (López Pinciano). Both authors appropriate the form of a Platonic dialogue for their writing. For late sixteenth-century Spaniards, Platonic was Christian, popular, poetic, and philosophical. As we will see in what follows, the adjective was also read in political and economic terms.

6 Persistence of Political-Economic Platonism

The Republic and Laws

From the thirteenth century on, the writings of Aristotle and Cicero on the question of a republic and its governance were known to the West, but Alison Brown describes those treatises with their "preference for the rule of law and pluralism" as "increasingly outmoded" in fifteenth-century Florence, in which there was a move towards sovereign rule with executive power held by a group of professional elite (Brown 1986, 387). Brown notes parallels in France and England, but the political situation she describes for those countries is also quite relevant to fifteenth-century Spain: "Spain was by any account one of the first quasi-rationalized political entities in Europe" where inherited privileges "were in turn administered by an intricate network of government functionaries" (Cascardi 2012, 5). Santos Herrán and Santos López explain the various responsibliites and manoeuvrings of those functionaries (2008, XVI–XLI), and Richard Kagan (2009) offers full detail on how the crown's chroniclers wrote, and so created, the history of that developing Spanish state.

By the end of the fifteenth century, the various reigns and holdings of what we today call Spain had been consolidated under the Catholic Monarchs Ferdinand and Isabel. Over the next century, the centralized bureaucracy would further develop and strengthen as the Spanish crown attempted to regularize legal and administrative processes in the various regions of the Peninsula while also gaining and maintaining control over holdings in the New World. Along with references to burgeoning bureaucratic concerns, one frequently finds in treatises of the period both philosophical and political discussions on types of republic, the good of the republic, and the ideal qualities of a ruler. Spanish explorations in the New World inspired debate among Salamancan scholars on the concept of "an international community of sovereign states," an important "idea in the evolution of Spanish political thought from Vitoria to Suárez (1548–1617) [that] is difficult to overestimate," and that included discussion of Plato (Fernández-Santamaría 1977, 113, 88).[1] There are many fine studies of these developments in historical-political thought in sixteenth-century Spain,[2] and it is not my intent to address here the full range of ideas on government expressed in these volumes. Rather, I will look at the *Republic's* controversial ideas on equity, distributive justice, and, as Hankins aptly phrases it, "marital and material communism" (1990, 1.352–3).[3] My intent is to outline the resonance of the "divine Plato" as well as Ficino's translations of and commentaries on the *Republic* and the *Laws* dialogues in certain Spanish authors who take a stand on these express principles: communal holdings, and the concept of good laws as a means to achieve equity and balance in a state.

In 1402, Plato's *Republic* was translated into Latin by Manuel Chrysoloras and Uberto Decembrio; between 1437 and 1441 the son of the latter, Pier Candido Decembrio, offered an improved translation (Boter 1989, 261).[4] In 1440, Italian Antonio Cassarino dedicated his own translation of the *Republic* to Alphonse V "the Magnanimous" of Aragon and Naples (Round 1993, 70), a monarch later described as one with gifts of "uncommon prudence and letters" (rara prudencia y letras) who ordered "translation of Greek works into Latin, [and who] managed to revive and enrich those letters that had been buried [in time]" (Giovio 1568, ff. 73v, 74r).[5] Following on those early translations, specific mentions of Plato's *Republic* began to appear in Spanish letters: in his 1427–8 translation and gloss of the *Aeneid*, Enrique de Villena notes that "Plato said in the book *On the Republic* that public matters would be blessed when rulers of republics were wise" (Villena 1989, Prohemio, 45, n. 35),[6] a clear reference to Plato's recommendation for the philosopher-king. In his *Suma de la política*, written between 1454 and 1457, Sánchez de Arévalo repeatedly refers to the *Republic*, like Villena as to its perfection although not in rulers but rather inhabitants: "So, according to what Plato says in his book *De republica*, the city cannot be perfect unless its inhabitants are" (1944, 40).[7] This opinion is also found in book 4 of the *Laws* where, as Ficino would later gloss it, the "form [of government] can never be beautiful unless the souls of the citizens are beautiful" (2009a, 91).[8] Sánchez de Arévalo also references the *Republic* on celestial bodies (44), business (53), and the need for "honest and restful pleasures" or entertainments as "purging or medicine for the human body" (1944, 56–7).[9] Also writing in the middle of the fifteenth century was Íñigo López de Mendoza, who notes that Plato carried heavenly laws down to place them in the human mind (1982, xcic, 90),[10] and Fray Íñigo de Mendoza who tells us that, for the Greek philosopher, "fortunate is the region/ governed by magicians" (1968, copla 202).[11] In 1497, Luis de Lucena points out that Plato divided his *Republic* into two groups: "laws and men of arms" (Lucena 1954, 89).[12] The details from these fifteenth-century works attest to incrementally greater knowledge of the dialogue and to its resonance in two specific realms: court and war, that is, the operational setting of a monarch; both the *Republic* and the *Laws* would figure prominently in Spanish political treatises of the following century.[13] As Hankins makes clear, there were both previous and subsequent translations of Plato's dialogues but "it was Ficino's version, built upon the foundations of humanist tradition, informed by the philosophical intelligence of Western scholasticism and ancient Neoplatonism, and perfected by the philological learning of the sixteenth century, that presented Plato to the world" (Hankins 1984, 198). Given the familiarity with Ficino and his writings already noted above, as well as the quantity of volumes of Plato's *Opera omnia* in Ficino's translation extant in Spanish libraries, my quite valid assumption in what follows is that reference to the dialogues, where not indicated, is to those volumes.

Valery Rees observes that "Ficino is not commonly regarded as a political philosopher, yet woven into his copious correspondence and philosophical works are many recurrent strands of political counsel," and she connects Ficino's ideas on the "principle of unity" in cosmological, theological, and philosophical terms to his political thought as expressed in letters and commentaries (Rees 2002, 339, 345–7). Ian Mason clarifies that "central to Plato's view of civil society is *arete*, justice or righteousness"; however, he notes, this is not justice as we might conceive of it today, that is, as a right dispensed by a state or by a court but rather:

> Plato's view, endorsed by Ficino, is very different. For them justice is a state of the soul over which every man and woman has personal command. It is an orderly state of the inner being which is cultivated by good practice of other virtues: wisdom, temperance and courage, which combined in one person produce that state of being that is called just. (Mason in Ficino 2009a, ix)

Mason also connects the idea to basic concepts of English common law: "the free and lawful man ... [was] presumed to know the law because the law was nothing else but reason, and reasonable conduct was sufficient to keep the individual within the law" (Mason in Ficino 2009a, x). Hankins reviews Ficino's use of earlier translations for his own, and finds that with the *Republic*, "his [Ficino's] version is for the most part entirely fresh" and "represents a clear advance in philosophical understanding over the earlier versions" (1990, 2:471–2) as it is more faithful to the original and communicates "Plato's sense with clarity and accuracy" (1984, 190–2).

Ficino's commentaries on Plato's *Republic* and *Laws* are extensive, chapter by chapter analyses of the Greek philosopher's arguments, and his briefer summary of the *Statesman* also addresses societies and their governance. In this last, the images used for a king are shepherd, ship's helmsman, judge, model of virtue, one who desires peace above all, doctor to the populace but also fellow-citizen and, "in the manner of the Egyptians, as a priest, a high priest of the sacred mysteries" (Ficino 2006, 59–64, 62).[14] In the *Republic* commentary, Ficino describes the ruler of a state as he who "contemplates the divine and thus provides for the human" (2009a, 32).[15] In his commentary on the *Laws*, the Italian philosopher offers the analogy of a lawgiver as a farmer who should "cultivate the whole State with the utmost care, like a field ... selecting and sowing seeds ... rooting out ... weeds and thorns as soon as they appear" (2009a, 79).[16] Ficino's reader is told that a monarchy is the best type of government and a tyranny, the worst; aristocrats are praised but oligarchs denounced; democracy according to law is well-regarded, and the principle duty of a ruler is analogous to a musician's harmonies: "to bring into harmony the hearts and minds of all the people, through the most judicious blending of courage with temperance" (2006, 62).[17] A good republic is a place in which man lives in peace and justice with a certain economic parity if not exact equality, and rulers described with the images found in Ficino's commentaries, with the exception perhaps of the analogy to a priest of the Egyptian mysteries, are not rare in European letters of the sixteenth century. Debates on institutional (both government and Church) ideals and abuses are common in this period of socio-political change, and many writers proposed both civic and creative solutions. Well-known examples are Thomas More's *Utopia*, Machiavelli's *Il príncipe*, Campanella's *La città del Sole*, and Erasmus's *Enchiridion Militis*; the debts of those authors to Ficino have been studied.[18] The political, economic, and social forces behind these various volumes is a complex weave of elements specific to each environment and author, and I do not wish to suggest that they can all be simply classified as derived from any one given text. Nonetheless, Ficino's translation of Plato's *Republic* and *Laws* dialogues, as well as his commentaries on them, engendered debate on the points to be studied here. Law as reasonable conduct had particular resonance in sixteenth-century Spain, given the Spanish legal system's processual and substantive upheaval,[19] and Francisco Rico finds Plato's concept of man and city linked under the sway of justice, as expressed in the *Republic*, a common theme in sixteenth-century Spanish political treatises (Rico 1970, 107–17). The backdrop against which Ficino wrote, described as one of "factional politics, local wars, plague, death and poverty, corruption in public life, a looming Turkish threat and other ills" (Rees 2002, 357), has its match in sixteenth-century Spain, and Ficino's political-philosophical counsel was put to good use by Spanish writers.

One key facet of Ficino's innovation in his commentaries on the *Republic* and the *Laws* is his argument that Plato, recognizing the difficulty in the first dialogue's prohibitions on private property, allows for an easier "ascent" on "gentler slopes" to that ideal state in the *Laws* (2009a, 74).[20] In the latter dialogue, good laws achieve what man alone will not, that is, a certain equitable balance in treatment and holdings: "in that state in which property is held by individuals many laws are necessary to deal with a variety of disagreements, lawsuits, and offences" (Ficino 2009a, 74).[21] Ficino attributes the *Republic*'s views on communal holdings to Socrates and the Pythagoreans, and the "gentler slopes" approach of the *Laws* to Plato. Hankins finds in this separation of Socrates from Plato Ficino's "awareness of what modern scholars call the 'Socratic problem'" (1990, 1:321), that is, the need to distance oneself from certain polemical statements and behaviours attributed to Socrates. Spanish writers follow Ficino on that point as well as others.

A polemical figure in his time, Antonio de Guevara replaced Pedro Mártir de Anglería as royal chronicler to Charles V in 1526; his *Libro Aúreo de Marco Aurelio* was published in 1528 without the author's permission. One year later, Guevara published his *Relox de príncipes*, described by Madrigal as a combination of three literary models: mirror of princes, biography, and doctrinal treatise, but also a work in which Guevara "continually tries to surprise the reader ... by painting capricious character descriptions, enumerating outrageous laws, and mixing fable with history" (Madrigal in Guevara 1994, 4–16, 19, 25).

In the *Relox*, Guevara is consistent in his references to the *Republic* and the *Laws*, as well as in his reliance on the "divine Plato" as authority for a number of opinions: the dangers of evil men who bear defensive and offensive arms (I, 38); the path of philosophers who study as youth, travel as men, and retire when old (I, 40); the wisdom in women not having friends independent from their husbands (II, 8); discussion of ancient societies governed by good laws (II, 32); and the need for fair judges (III, 9).[22] These references to the "divine Plato" are often followed by an approving statement that validates whichever opinion is being discussed although, as Madrigal notes throughout his edition of the *Relox*, Guevara frequently mangles and mixes his sources: "the result is a merry-go-round in which Charlemagne is a dwarf, Aristotle speaks like Pope Innocent III, and Plato mimics the common sayings of popular folklore" (Madrigal in Guevara 1994, 22–3).[23] Rather than humanist *controversia* argument for and against one specific point, a model used by Cicero and adapted by Renaissance humanists like Erasmus (Cascardi 2012, 82–4), Guevara's work is more representative of the "mixed genre, capable of inclusion of both doctrinal and fictitious elements" that is characteristic of classical and humanist dialogues (Wyss Morigi 2006, 17).[24] The sheer quantity of Guevara's re-readings and misattributions suggests intentional subversion of all authoritative voices or, at the least, a wilful intent to conform them to Guevara's own message, whether serious or in jest, for a Christian prince.[25] The Spaniard does not hesitate to attribute to Plato statements that directly contradict the Greek philosopher's actual opinions, such as his supposed advocacy of the benefits to a child of being reared by its own mother (Guevara 1994, II, 18). As

Madrigal notes, in the *Republic* Plato argues to the contrary, that is, that child-rearing be a common endeavour. At times, however, Guevara posits what seem to be intentionally pragmatic and logical solutions, such as a reasonable utopia that combines communal property along with the pleasure of private holdings under the recommendation, following Plato in the *Laws* and Ficino in his commentary, that an individual should not hold more goods than those necessary to survive, thus "avoiding covetousness" (Rallo Gruss 1979, 125–7, 126).[26] As does Ficino, Guevara includes notice of the Garamans as a people who shared all property and houses (Ficino 2009a, 22; Guevara 1994, I, 32), but the Spaniard also elaborates an extended reproach by the senior Garaman representative of Alexander the Great for his covetousness (I, 33–4), a harangue that ends with a list of the few but good laws of the Garamans including, contradictorily, those on communal property (I, 34).

Another example of this Spanish author's model of a seed of Platonic truth mixed with free elaboration is an opinion attributed to the Greek philosopher on the inappropriateness of an undisciplined man as ruler of a republic: Guevara insists that in the *Laws*, Plato recommends that such a man should either be exiled or "tied up like a crazy man" (Guevara 1994, Prologue, 133–4).[27] While not found in the dialogue itself, this statement can be read as an interpretation of Socrates's *dicta*, as reported in Ficino's commentary on the *Republic*, that "the full truth should not be revealed to a madman, or weapons returned to him" and that "evil men are not to be admitted to the magistracy" (Ficino 2009a, 5, 6)[28] or, perhaps, as an exaggerated version of Ficino's commentary on the *Laws*, in which we read that Plato "forbids the power of magistracy to be granted to any man who, through lack of restraint, is unable to govern himself," and that "men of depraved nature are not masters of themselves" (2009a, 89, 125).[29] In another passage, Guevara notes that for Plato, "there is no better sign that a republic will be lost than when many heads try to govern it" (1994, Prologue, 174).[30] This could be a reference to book three of the *Laws*, in which the danger of democracy degenerating into mob rule is addressed, or it might remit to Ficino's summary of the *Statesman*, in which the Italian philosopher expresses the need for "a single king ... as judge of all the others" (2006, 61).[31] In a later section of his text, contrarily, Guevara laments the sorry state of man on earth under a single ruler as a fall from Paradise, and he blames Adam who "refused to obey a command ... for refusing to obey one ruler then, we are now slaves of many" (I, 28).[32]

Guevara follows Ficino in his treatment of the "Socratic problem," attributing the *Republic*'s ideas on communal holdings to Socrates rather than Plato, and thus forgiving the "divine Plato" on this point as it regards material goods.[33] On the concept of marital communism, however, the Spaniard goes a bit further to deride the concept with tongue-in-cheek use of the same epithet for the Greek philosopher: "The divine Plato, in the books of his *Republic*, advised and counselled that all things should be held in common, not only animals and properties but also that women should be held in common ... Plato is called divine due to many good things that he said, but with this very profane advice he might better be called human" (1994, II, 3).[34] With that one ironic exception, and despite the quite possibly deliberate misreadings, Guevara shows a consistent respect for the "divine Plato" throughout the *Relox*. In sum, on the three points of my focus here the Spaniard recommends limitations on private property as well as good laws to assure equity, but he rejects marital communism. Guevara directly echoes Ficino in his consistent use of the epithet "divine" for the Greek philosopher, even adding it to quotes from other authorities when it is not found in the original source, and the Spaniard further follows the Italian philosopher's lead to address the Socratic problem by distancing Plato from Socrates on polemical points.

Spanish jurist Arce de Otálora has been referenced above for his praise of Ficino in both direct quotations and comments on a number of topics ranging from demons to magic to love to laws. As for the *Republic*, the jurist follows Guevara to criticize the dialogue's prescription for shared women: "the greatest abomination that was said to be Plato's [was] his law regarding women as common property" (Arce de Otálora 1995, 1:478),[35] although he simultaneously praises the Greek philosopher as the "most divine" of ancient thinkers: "Even [of] that same Plato, who was the most divine of them all, Saint Chrysostom says in the fourth homily of the Acts of the Apostles that he promulgated some execrable laws, such as women and children being common property, and virgin maidens fighting naked in public" (1:468).[36] Given that the spectacle of naked, wrestling virgins is not addressed by Ficino in his commentary, Arce de Otálora has apparently read the full dialogue itself, in which Plato argues for a community of wives and children among the guardians of a republic, and for "women exercising unclad in the palestra together with the men" (Plato 1969, 449c–50c; 452a–b). Despite that disagreement, Arce uses Plato's *dictum* prohibiting private property as positive analogy to the happiness of a married couple when all property between them is held in common (Arce de Otálora 1995, 1:523),[37] and he repeats the Greek philosopher's advice on music to calm the passions of the soul (1:429), the need to exercise both body and soul (1:386), and the exile of poets (1:455–7). He also approvingly takes from Plato's *Laws* the dispensation for older men to get drunk at parties so that they might sing happily, repeating this advice in two separate sections (1:428; 2:1067), although he omits the reason, as explained by Ficino in his commentary: so that the older men would "sing to the ears of the younger men and at the same time, as we might say, enchant their souls" (Ficino 2009a, 85).[38] As we saw above with Alfonso de Palencia, some but not all of Arce's details on Plato can be found in Diogenes Laertius's *Life of*

Plato; in the case of Arce, one noteworthy exception is the reference to Plato's death on his eighty-first birthday (2:1008). Among ancient and classical sources, only Seneca includes that story (Swift Riginos 1976, 26), and Arce does directly reference Seneca on other matters. A chronologically closer source for the detail, however, would have been Ficino's *Life of Plato* in the *Platonis Opera omnia*, and as we have seen in prior sections herein, Arce was quite familiar with Ficino's writings. Further and as noted above for Guevara, for Arce, too, Plato is "the most divine" of all ancient philosophers (el más divino dellos) (1995, 1:468). Arce uses Plato as an example for how to persuade mortal man to love first the gods and then the laws, followed by Cicero to support the role of law in assuring equity (1:255). In his overall approach to the three points of my focus here, Arce follows Guevara to criticize Plato on marital communism, but to praise him on equity and the need for laws.

The third of Fox Morcillo's treatises on the Platonic dialogues, following his *Timaeus* and *Phaedo* interpretations, was a commentary on the *Republic*. For this dialogue Fox uses Ficino's Latin, with full attribution, as his base text, and he again disputes the Italian philosopher's allegorical readings (1556b, 4v–5r).[39] Truman finds in Fox's *Republic* commentary "frequent reference to, and a discriminating acceptance of, the views of Plato" and he highlights a number of places in which Fox repeats or seems to share opinions expressed in the *Republic* and the *Laws* dialogues (Truman 1999, 42). However, Truman also notes that rather than an idealistic discussion of the ruler's religion and virtues, Fox prefers one "of a rather different kind concerning the practical needs facing the ruler and the tasks of government generally" with a specific attempt to put pragmatics over "imagination" or "some imaginary king such as never existed" (Truman 1999, 30–1; 40). While this might remind one of *The Prince*'s pragmatic approach to governance, and its criticism of ideal or imagined state models, we know that Fox refutes at least one Machiavellian idea, that "a lie might be licit in affairs of state" (González de la Calle 1903, 205).[40] In a political sense Fox's pragmatic ideals, "dictates of reason combined with Christian maxims" (González de la Calle 1903, 204),[41] would seem to be more resonant of Ficino, who also sought "a more profound integration of the active and contemplative life whereby the latter could give health and wisdom to the former" (Hankins 1990, 1:296). As Ficino himself describes it in his commentary on the *Republic*: "the wisdom of Pythagoras puts greater emphasis on contemplation, while that of Socrates stresses action and that of Plato gives equal weight to both contemplation and action" with the result that "the contemplative discipline of Pythagoras and the moral discipline of Socrates both seem somewhat remote from the common customs of men. But the teaching of Plato, which is both speculative and moral, seems to provide a universal marriage of the divine with the human" (2009a, 73).[42] This Ficinian recommendation for contemplation and action is slightly modified by Fox, however, who instead of their "universal marriage" favours the latter over the former.[43]

In his own brief summary of the *Republic*, Fox concludes that Plato's marital and material communism cannot truly exist in practice, and the Spaniard proposes instead that the Greek philosopher merely describes this as an "optimal" state.[44] That is, Fox follows Ficino in this opinion, although he is slightly less credulous as to the ideal republic's potential to actually exist. Fox does not, however, go so far as to ridicule the idea, as had Guevara and Arce de Otálora. On the subject of laws to assure equity, Fox is in complete agreement with Ficino's conclusions. In his commentary on the *Republic*, Ficino speaks of distributive justice: "A society can hold together only to the extent that some just distribution is maintained" (2009a, 7),[45] and in his own text titled *De regni et regnibus*, Fox expresses the same opinion, speaking "in the first place about justice as a virtue that, based on the well-being of all, consists in giving to each one his due" (González de la Calle 1903, 207), and elaborating on the idea of justice as "either common or special. Common justice is legal if it has as its end the observance of the law, and equitative if it refers to an adequate moderation of such observance. Special justice is called distributive when it consists in giving to each one his due, and commutative when it proportions the same to each lawful being through an exchange of services or things in general" (González de la Calle 1903, 207).[46] Fox defines equity: "Equity consists of a certain moderation or explication of law that, if not found in the literal text, can be understood and defined by the overarching legal reasoning" (208–9),[47] and he notes that through use of distributive justice, a monarch can punish or reward, whereas commutative justice refers only to personal dealings between persons, that is, contracts (210–11). Spanish law on economic dealings is a paramount concern by the first half of the sixteenth century: the *Leyes de Toro*, a legal compilation first conceived and prepared during the Cortes held in 1505, is heavily weighted towards such concerns and would become the favourite legal consultative source of many jurists by the middle of the century (Byrne 2012a, 46–51). In Spanish legal writings, justice as a social concept or as an ideal of governance would begin to incorporate economic and contractual principles, that is, commutative over distributive norms although Fox, writing at mid-century, expresses his belief in equity. His four-part division of justice can be summed up as: 1) common justice is strict obeisance to the letter of the law; 2) distributive justice consists of slight modification of legal norms (this might be read as adherence to the spirit of the law); 3) equity is giving to each his due; and 4) commutative justice refers to exchange of property between individuals. Neither Plato nor Ficino describe such divisions, although Aristotle does split justice into distributive and corrective (Strijdom 2007, 40).[48] Today's common division of justice into legal, distributive, social, and commutative is similar to Fox's schematic, and it is interesting to note that the earliest Spanish dictionaries define 'justice' as did Ficino, that is, as a virtue synonymous with 'equity' (Nebrija 1495 and 1516). Although Covarrubias does not include the word in his 1611 *Tesoro*, in the same year Rosal offers for "just thing" (justa cosa) and "from there, justice" (y de allí, Justicia) a three-part definition: "law, justice, reason" (Derecho, justicia y razón) (*Nuevo tesoro lexicográfico*). By 1734, *Autoridades* will define 'justice' in the first instance as a "virtue" (virtud), with a second meaning of "attribute of God" (atributo de Dios) and a third as "reason or equity" (razón o equidad). Equity maintains its place in that definition today.[49]

The three writers quoted above – Guevara, Arce de Otálora, and Fox Morcillo – are representative of Spanish political thought on these concepts during the first half of the sixteenth century. By the end of that same century, opinion would shift heavily in favour of private property. The Bank of Spain identifies Jerónimo Castillo de Bobadilla's *Policies for Magistrates, and Landowners, in Times of Peace and War, and for Prelates in Spiritual Matters as well as Temporal Matters among Lay Persons* ... (1597), as the first treatise on the topic written and published in Spanish. Castillo de Bobadilla does not try to reconcile Plato and Aristotle on the concept of an ideal republic but, rather, rejects the former in favour of the latter, on the specific basis of Plato's rejection of private property.[50] The magistrate's volumes were widely circulated, and reprinted for use as the standard how-to manual for magistrates over the following two hundred years.[51] Everything from ancient philosophy to the Bible has a place in this manual, which begins with a comparison of the ideal republics of the two Greek philosophers.[52]

In his dedication letter to King Phillip II, Castillo de Bobadilla states: "Among all sciences and human actions, none requires so many [constituent] parts as that of the governance of a Republic, and so Plato and others called it the art of arts"; the magistrate then compares himself to Plato: "and so I took notes for my own instruction, much as the account that Plato, fearing for his own memory, made in his books on the Republic, to serve as directions for others who might be interested" (1616, "Al muy alto y muy poderoso príncipe").[53] While governance described as the "art of arts" is consistent with statements made in the *Republic*, the magistrate's reading of Plato "fearing for his memory" is directly contradicted in the dialogues themselves, and in the well-known passages of Plato's seventh letter: "And this is the reason why every serious man in dealing with really serious subjects carefully avoids writing, lest thereby he may possibly cast them as a prey to the envy and stupidity of the public" (Plato 1966, 344c). In the comparison of written versus spoken transmission of knowledge, the latter prevails for Plato.[54] Ficino tells us that Socrates "laughs at the study of writing in the person, that is, who trusts that through letters he can reveal indubitable truth to posterity. In the manner of the Pythagoreans, he affirms that the contemplation and transmission of truth occurs in rational souls rather than in books" (Ficino 2008, 2.3.3).[55] Like his predecessor Guevara, Castillo de Bobadilla takes a very free hand in adapting opinions from authority. His re-reading of the importance of writing for Plato, while directly contradicted by the Greek philosopher's own statements on the practice, is nonetheless illustrative of the historical situation of the Spain of his day, with its ever-expanding record-keeping bureaucracy, of which the magistrate and others like him were a very integral part.[56]

Castillo de Bobadilla addresses his reader directly to state that his intent "(discreet reader) has been to aid the curious in the good governance of their republics" (1616, "Al letor"),[57] and he criticizes, but also makes good use of, Plato: "Plato (although with a different meaning) said that our knowledge is the memory of past events, as he believed that souls move from one body to another and thus inform the new body by reminiscence: and in his sense of it, this belief was a notorious error, but in ours it is quite fitting" because "as the well-written past has become forgotten, the intelligence of the present is becoming ill: and we need an invention that, with reminiscence, will remember it [that well-written past]" (Castillo de Bobadilla 1616, Proemio, 2).[58] Thus the concept of transmigration of souls is neatly reduced to traditional legal memory. The magistrate promises not to deal with

> absolute novelties ... but, rather, to bring out into the open, and to the marketplace (as Pythagoras called the world), advice found in [the writings of] ancient wise men, and in the findings of legislators: so that those who govern republics, whether by science or by reminiscence (or however they order it to be) might, with caution, put [those tenets] into action. (Castillo de Bobadilla 1616, Proemio, 3–4)[59]

The magistrate's interpretation of the Platonic concept of metempsychosis as a pragmatic need to remember history and enforce law illustrates a particularly acute political agility. Ficino had Christianized the problematic concept of *reminiscentia* by transferring it "from a temporal to an ontological scale. The mind in recollecting does not return to things it knew in a past life, but ascends the hierarchy of being to enjoy a higher kind of knowledge" (Hankins 1984, 185). For his part, Castillo de Bobadilla reduces the existential philosophical debate on recall through transmigration of souls to the very practical purpose of law enforcement in the ideal republic.

The magistrate argues for laws over ideals, asserting the impossibility of achieving the latter. As had Ficino in his commentary on the *Laws*, Castillo de Bobadilla argues that legal means are necessary because where there is private property, there will be complaints and lawsuits. However, his reading of man's nature is diametrically opposed to that of the Italian philosopher: for the magistrate, man is avaricious and ambitious by nature ergo, absent the need to protect what is his own, he will never live in peace: "with things held in common ... who could prevent the great questions and fights that have existed since ancient times over how to appropriate goods? I have never seen agreement except where all things are held privately, because each man will defend his own" (1616, 1.1.19).[60] Whereas Plato argued for and Ficino defended the ideal of communal holdings in order that all members of a society would see each child and every piece of property as their own, Castillo de Bobadilla inverts the argument to say that without particular private holdings, no man will defend any thing or person.

As had Fox Morcillo, the magistrate addresses equity, types of justice, and the distribution of goods. The first chapter of the first book of the manual is titled "Which is the better republic, that instituted by Plato or that ordered by Aristotle" (Castillo de Bobadilla 1616, 1.1)[61] and it begins with Aristotle's division of justice into two parts: the first is "legitimate, or common" (legítima [o común]) and the second, "particular" (la particular) (1616, 1.1). The reader is told that Aristotle founded his republic on the legitimate-common type, which also "encompasses" the second, whereas Plato founded his ideal republic on just the second, "particular" justice which is also known, Castillo de Bobadilla tells us, as "equity, according to which man, as a rational being, uses his reason to apportion to others the same as he desires for himself" (1616, 1.1–2).[62] Following that statement, Castillo de Bobadilla asserts that laws were necessary for the founding of all biblical cities because men "naturally want more for themselves than for others" (Castillo de Bobadilla 1616, 1.1.5),[63] then the magistrate justifies private property by moving from biblical examples to Aristotle:

> From all this it becomes clear how ancient the order and policies of Aristotle are: it is called Aristotle's Republic not because he invented it, but because he spoke and wrote about it so wonderfully. From this, too, it becomes obvious that from the very beginning of the world there has always been private property and division of goods. (Castillo de Bobadilla 1616, 1.1.9)[64]

There is further reference to the Bible: "Jabet, son of Lamech, branded cattle with his own mark so as to distinguish and recognize them; so even then there was mine, yours, and ownership of things" (1.1.10),[65] followed by the conclusion that Aristotle, in his version of an ideal republic, was in conformity with the Bible in allowing for private property.

Having justified Aristotle as biblically consistent, Castillo de Bobadilla turns to consider Plato's ideas: "Plato wanted ... that men would not have private property, neither mine nor yours but, rather, that all things be held in common, as was the opinion of Socrates and other philosophers ... and the Philosopher affirms that men would live very peacefully in this world if two words were to be erased: that is, *mine* and *yours*" (1616, 1.1.16, emphasis in original).[66] As had Fox, the magistrate follows Ficino to attribute the basic idea to Socrates although he also indicates Plato's willing acceptance of it. Castillo de Bobadilla's own opinion is that communal property is impossible because "men are absolutists by nature" and, turning the principle of uninterested Christian generosity on its head, he says that if men are expected to help the poor and needy, there will have to be a reward for so doing: "no one would do it, lacking the interest of a reward" (Castillo de Bobadilla 1616, 1.1.17 and 20).[67] The magistrate dismisses marital communism as a principal failing of Plato's republic, which "does not have the required foundational basis: in great measure because if women were to be held in common, as he says, men's reason would resist, as would the reason of natural and divine law, and even the instinct of certain beasts" (Castillo de Bobadilla 1616, 1.1.24).[68] The magistrate eventually concludes that even Plato finally realized the "inconveniences and errors" of his plan for communal holdings, and "tacitly renounced his first Republic so as to give way to the second one" (1.1.25).[69] This last is apparently a reference to the *Laws* dialogue which, as we have seen, Ficino also glosses by reference to its "gentler slopes" approach: "the ten books of the *Republic* smack more of Pythagoras and Socrates, while the *Laws* now under review are deemed to be Platonic ... he [Plato] will not compel men against their will to have all things in common among themselves, but he will allow individual men, according to the custom, to have their own property" (Ficino 2009a, 73–4).[70] For Castillo de Bobadilla, private property is a necessity and equity is synonymous with particular justice, which is read as either communal property or proportional fairness. The magistrate will later return to the idea of equity to re-interpret it as nearly complete judicial freedom, extending to and encompassing the term "reason of state."

Not found in Ficino's commentaries on the dialogues regarding states and their rulers is any concept allowing that "reason of state" might justify ignoble behaviour. Ficino's reading of Plato emphasizes the betterment of self with a focus on the life of the immortal soul after earthly existence. The ideal ruler is a philosopher whose wisdom naturally leads him to act for the good of the populace. In Ficino's *Life of Plato* we read: "Either the philosophers govern, or the rulers study philosophy," and "States will be most blessed if either philosophers rule or at least, by some divine destiny, those who govern study philosophy" (1975–<2012>, 3:35, 43),[71] advice the Italian philosopher repeats in his commentary on the *Republic*: "only after the philosopher has contemplated God, who rules the heavens, will he, and he alone, be able to rule the earth in god-like fashion" (2009a, 31).[72] Antonio de Guevara would argue for the same: "according to Plato, in those days and in those kingdoms, either philosophers ruled or those who ruled philosophized" (Guevara 1994, I, 21, p. 366).[73] Ficino follows Plato in his belief that justice, whether attained in this life or the next, is preeminent; ideals and morals dominate over pragmatic concerns. The ideal republic is "a discussion about justice rather than about a Republic, teaching thereby, as I judge, that every situation and every action, both public and private, should be related not to abundance, not to power, and not to victory, but to justice herself" (Ficino 2009a, 3).[74] Reason of state, a phrase attributed in the first instance to Machiavelli,[75] was an argument for the inverse, that is, for the perceived needs of the state to triumph over and, if necessary, obviate such ideals of governance.

By the end of the sixteenth century, Church opposition to Machiavelli's *The Prince* was firm, and the book was prohibited by the Spanish as well as the Roman Indices.[76] Nonetheless, Spanish politicians who sought to manage and control their early modern state continued to find his methods effective and to a certain extent indispensable.[77] Helena Puigdomenech Forcada describes the "profound and long-lasting presence of Machiavelli's works" in Spain during the sixteenth and seventeenth centuries, with details about library holdings, translations, and circles of influence (1988, 10).[78] As to the apparent dearth of translations, and specifically the lack of any Castilian printed edition of *The Prince*, Puigdomenech denies that this might be due to a rejection of the doctrines or to Church prohibitions, noting quite rightly that Spaniards would have been capable of reading Machiavelli in Italian.[79]

In 1603, Spanish historian Antonio de Herrera y Tordesillas translated Giovanni Botero's *Reason of State* and offered this standard definition of the concept: "Reason of state is the notice of those means convenient for the foundation, conservation, and enrichment of a seignorality" (1599, f. 1).[80] Just two years prior to the publication of Castillo de Bobadilla's manual for magistrates, Jesuit Pedro de Ribadeneira had published a treatise on the virtues of a Christian prince, subtitled "Against the teachings of Nicholas Machiavelli and contemporary politicians" (1788).[81] Ribadeneira calls Machiavelli the "Minister of Satan," describes his doctrine as "perverse and diabolic" (1788, III),[82] and denounces all philosophers and historians who advocate similar ideas. Diego Saavedra Fajardo would proclaim in 1640 that "reason of State has been transformed into an art of trickery or of avoiding deception" (1999, 547).[83] In Spain, Machiavellian thought would be reformulated and the idea of a Christian Prince put forth as a counter to *The Prince*'s political expediency, yet Spanish rulers continued to take advantage of the same concepts regarding states' concerns by incorporating them under cover of traditional moral virtues added to translations of Tacitus.[84] Even Ribadeneira, who includes Tacitus among those criticized as impious and evil, "on a number of occasions offers his [Tacitus's] opinion as proof of truths obtained by natural reason, in concordance with Christian faith" (Maravall 1997, 380).[85] In addition and more to the point here, after excoriating all those he identifies as enemies of Christianity, Ribadeneira praises Hermes [Mercurio] Trismegistus, quotes him on religion and virtue, refers his reader to the words of "the divine Plato" on religion and piety, and highlights the "grave words of Marsilio Ficino" in his commentary on the *Laws*, regarding Plato's condemnation of contact with the impious (1788, 146).[86] As a counterpoint to the political expendiency of Machiavelli, Botero, and others, this Christian writer turned back to Plato, Hermes, and Ficino as models to be respected and emulated.

Castillo de Bobadilla wrote during this same late sixteenth-century moment in which the "reason of state" concept was hotly debated yet still without specific limits and just a bit ambiguous. In one chapter of his manual, the magistrate speaks to the place of the concept "reason of state" in legal decisions:

> And be careful not to stray from justice so as to follow the reason of government and state, because this is quite dangerous, and particularly in cases in which there is a danger of prejudice to a third party; many precautions are necessary so that free will in cases of state and government does not degrade and pervert (*tuerçe*) justice, nor that which is convenient. (Castillo de Bobadilla 1616, 2.2.82)[87]

Reading between the magistrate's lines, one may judge according to reason of state when there is no prejudice to another, while taking the necessary precautions to assure that this juridical "free will" perverts neither justice nor "what is convenient." Following on the above, Castillo de Bobadilla continues:

> Frankly, reason of governance, and of state, does not tend to nor should it prevail except in cases where reason of justice is lacking. And on this point, Cornelius Tacitus says that Ticiano and Proculus, bested by reasons [logic], took advantage of reason of state: and in another writing, speaking about Nero who wished to destroy Vestino, he says that, unable to find any crime on his part, nor any accuser – he couldn't justify a charge by legal means, so he made use of reason of state. (Castillo de Bobadilla 1616, 2.10.17)[88]

The magistrate's words belie his supposed intent: reason of state may be substituted for justice in cases of necessity, determined at times quite arbitrarily. If the law is not in your favour, use reason of state. If you cannot find a crime, or even an accuser, use reason of state. When all else fails in an attempt to destroy an enemy, resort to reason of state. Following that, the magistrate reveals a problem in the legal system of his day: "The lower court judges, many of them with little Christian kindness and most out of ignorance (because they do not even master grammar), stop judging by the laws and, more often than not, judge according to their own opinion and will" (Castillo de Bobadilla 1616, 2.10.18).[89] Although he might seem critical of the practice for that brief moment, he immediately notes that it is not all bad, given that "the world is in such a state that, in just about nothing can one do good for someone else, nor offer a friendly act, nor grace, with the sole exception of matters of justice, and using one's will in them" (Castillo de Bobadilla 1616, 2.10.18).[90] Then the magistrate offers another general rule:

> In sum, on this matter of judging by will, one rule can be given to the magistrate and it is that in those cases not determined by laws, canons, or doctrine, he may proceed to sentence by his will, well-informed and circumspect, with orderly consideration of the manner and parameters of legal judgments, and according to process, and with equity and rights, and with the opinions of wise men, and not on just his cerebellum and whim. (Castillo de Bobadilla 1616, 2.10.27)[91]

Here, equity is judicial favour. In a subsequent section of his manual, after counselling that candidates for judgeship should be aware of allowable limits on punishments, that is, those ordered by law and permitted by common opinion of jurists, Castilo de Bobadilla adds: "but according to another common opinion, one cannot give a strict ruling or doctrine on this, and so it must be left to the free will of the judge" (Castillo de Bobadilla 1616, 5.3.10).[92] These blanket statements invert the philosophical ideals. Compare, for example, Ficino's gloss on the *Laws*: men should approach the laws "with the intention of diligently observing them in their decisions and faithfully keeping them in their actions"; "the laws should particularly consider as their end in the state that to which they direct all things as if to a standard"; and "the lawgiver, seeking the happiness of all, will make his prime objective the cultivation of prudence in the minds of the citizens" as well as "ensure that wealth is distributed evenly, as far as is possible, so that no men are very rich while others are in need" (2009a, 75, 78, 88–9, 105).[93] That version of the ideal Platonic republic is rejected by Castillo de Bobadilla, and the concept of equity is reduced to judicial freedom and favouritism.

In what can be read as a response to this type of willingness to adopt a nefarious approach to ideal republics and reason of state, Spain's creative authors began to satirize the concept. Bartolomé Leonardo de Argensola, in his *Dédalo*, "criticizes royal justice and particularly reason of state, for which character Dédalo was jailed prior to his sentence having been read" (Schwartz 2013, 32).[94] Miguel de Cervantes is similarly caustic in his presentation of the ills of the republic, and the moral of his protagonist Don Quijote has been described as "the idea of justice ... as the basis and essential content of Christian political society" (Maravall 2005, 242).[95] Maravall found in Cervantes' works a general resistance to and critique of the politics of the new modern state (2005, 197–266), but both Cascardi and Walter Ghia have signalled parallel passages in the *The Prince* and in Cervantes' *Quijote* on new governors (Cascardi 2012, 17; Ghia 2013, 69–70), and Ghia has, as well, convincingly shown Cervantes' adaptation of Machiavellian bellic principles to the field of combat in love in *Quijote*, II, 21 (86–7). For his part, Cascardi sees the *Quijote* and its "new generic prism" (33) in direct relation to a full range of political treatises including both Machiavelli's *Prince* and Plato's *Republic* (3–19), and he points out that "nearly all of Don Quijote's extended speeches in Part I ... provide a framing for political questions that aspire to some level of insight" and "suggest themselves as alternative versions of what political theorizing might be" (Cascardi 2012, 53, 55). In any case, as to Plato's *Republic* and *Laws* with their focus on justice, it is clear that through Don Quijote, Cervantes takes a stand on the issue.[96]

Whereas magistrate Castillo de Bobadilla calls the arbitrary decision of a judge "reason of state" it is, for Don Quijote, "the lace [arbitrary] law" (*ley del encaje*), that "tends to be found frequently among those ignorant men who presume themselves quick-witted" (Cervantes 2005, II, 42),[97] and it was not a problem when "justice was in its proper state, when those seeking favours and self-interest did not yet dare to perturb or offend it" (2005, I, 11).[98] In the 1605 First Part of *Don Quijote*, the author tells us that his protagonist's goal is to serve "his republic" (su república) by undoing "all sorts of wrongs" (todo género de agravio), thereby putting into action his idea of justice, not exactly on the basis of his "reminiscence" of traditional legal norms as counselled by Castillo de Bobadilla but, in parallel fashion, on the basis of his recall of the readings of old books of knight errantry (Cervantes 2005, I, 1). In the first chapter of the 1615 Second Part of the *Quijote*, a key discourse directly addresses the politics of reason of state. The priest and the barber have refrained from visiting Don Quijote for a while so as to "not remind him, or bring to his mind, things from the past" (Cervantes 2005, II, 1).[99] They do finally decide to pay him a friendly call, and Cervantes' narrator tells us that once in the protagonist's house:

> in the course of their discourse [the three great friends] began to deal with what is called reason of state and methods of governance, fixing this abuse and condemning that one, reforming one custom and sending another into exile, each of the three becoming a new legislator, a modern Lycurgus or a brand new Solon: and they renovated the republic in such a way that it seemed as if they had put it into a smithy's furnace, and taken out another, different than the one they had put in. (Cervantes 2005, II, 1)[100]

Scholars have noted that the conversation seems "serious" without specifying much more. Cascardi calls this possibly the "most intriguing of all" discussions of politics in the *Quijote* but adds that "the reader never knows exactly what is said" (2012, 49). In the light of Ficino's reading of Plato's concept of justice and the subsequent permutations and perversions found in political writers, Cervantes' statements in this opening chapter for the 1615 Second Part of his novel gain particular resonance.

As the three "great friends" speak of using reason of state to reform customs and address abuses, Cervantes offers two examples of legislators worthy of imitation, Solon and Lycurgus. Those are two of the three mentioned by Plato at the beginning of the *Laws*, along with Minos, for whom another dialogue, *In Minoem, uel de lege*, is named. Ficino identifies the three as "the best three founders of Greek laws" linked closely to Jupiter, Apollo, and Minerva as representatives of power, mercy, and wisdom (2009a, 74, 76).[101] The two named by Cervantes were known for their legal reforms and the mention of Solon is specifically noteworthy for two reasons: 1) a legend that he pretended insanity so as to carry out a particular feat in the service of his republic, and 2) his reforms of the laws on debt. These two elements of his story link him not only to character Don Quijote (feigned insanity in the service of the republic), but also to author Cervantes, whose life-long legal issues with debt are well-known. Castillo de Bobadilla offers further information:

> Among the laws of Solon there was one stating that honours and moral esteem should be bestowed not on the basis of riches or power but, rather, only on the basis of age; that is, not to young men even if they might appear to be wise; and before Solon, Lycurgus composed the Senate of old men only, opining that honours and esteem were due only to those whom age had adorned with virtue. (Castillo de Bobadilla 1616, 1.7.3)[102]

The magistrate further supports the proposal with Plato who, "in his *Republic*, said that judges should be mature, and not young" (1616, 1.7.3).[103] In his commentary on the same dialogue, Ficino describes the selection of "a good and sensible old man with experience of many types of people, both good and evil" (2009a, 15).[104] Cervantes' reason of state, apparently, has everything to do with the honour due to the elderly, represented in person by the three great friends who discuss these matters in the knight's home, with the daring feats of the knight himself pretending (or not) to be crazy, and by his author Cervantes who, when the Second Part of the novel in which the conversation takes place was published, was approximately sixty-eight years old. Another wry commentary on reason of state is found in Cervantes' *Coloquio de los perros*: "This glorious life and calm was taken away from me by a woman who, apparently, in that place is called reason of state, and in order to comply with her, one must fail to comply with many other reasons" (1997a, 2:317).[105] The dog character Berganza is speaking of his exile from the life of a student: the Jesuit teachers evicted him from the classroom because students enjoyed playing with him during recess. Here, reason of state is any unreasonable step taken by an authority although, as some have read it, Cervantes is perhaps specifically insinuating its use by the religious Order (Maurice Molho 1970, 30–9).

On the *Republic's* ideal of communal property, Cervantes' Don Quijote is clearly in favour: "Blessed age and blessed centuries were those called by the ancients "golden"… because those who lived then took no heed of the two words *yours* and *mine*. All things, in that sainted age, were held in common" (Cervantes 2005, I, 11, emphasis in original).[106] Cascardi notes that this speech on the Golden Age is "not so much political as prepolitical ... a vision of the world from outside the historical conditions that make politics necessary" (2012, 55), and he suggests possible parallels to Plato's dialogues, although that connection is not his focus.[107] Nonetheless, his description of the problem of connecting theory to practice as "one of the animating aspirations of politics" and as a feat realized by Cervantes in his novel if only in "the discourse of fiction" (Cascardi 2012, 99–100) resonates clearly with Ficino's philosophical goal of mixing contemplation and action. While, as Cascardi notes, the dialogues themselves might not present theory in a modern sense, Ficino's commentaries on those dialogues do theorize on the ramifications of Plato's ideals in a practical sphere, and the Italian philosopher's political statements add further contextualization to Don Quijote's own mix of contemplation and action in just those terms. If I may rephrase Cascardi in regards to my focus here, the speech is not so much political as philosophical, specifically Platonic and ideal, in reaction to contemporary political writers who denounced and ridiculed the concept of communal property or, minimally, of equity among men. Cervantes uses the same imagery and precise phrasing as anti-Platonic magistrate Castillo de Bobadilla to compare the most minimal of descriptive detail, such as the acorns eaten by Sancho Panza and Don Quijote with the shepherds during the knight's discourse. Those nuts are a common part of classical references to an idyllic Golden Age but the magistrate highlights them with a sharply different tone so as to ridicule that supposed Golden Age when men "lived like beasts, sustaining themselves on acorns" (1616, 1.1.3).[108] For his part, Cervantes describes the idyllic scene as just that: a better age when laws were not needed. Cervantes enacts his political theory in his literary myth, expressing the ideals in pragmatic and active theatrical form rather than in deliberative or contemplative prosaic terms.[109] The symbolic yet at least fictionally real acorns trigger a moment to explore life in the myth in all its ideal ramifications, and to thus dispute implicitly its supposed impossibility. Cervantes praises the moral kindness suggested by the myth to sharply contrast it with "these detestable centuries of ours, when no one is safe" (2005, I, 11).[110] He harkens back to Ficino's readings of the *Republic* and the *Laws* dialogues, and his character's actions and words incorporate and comment on those same ideals.

Cervantes also argues for equity and distributive justice through his protagonist who wants to "put distributive justice into action, give to each that which is his due, and understand and be sure that good laws are followed" (Cervantes 2005, I, 37).[111] Here, distributive justice is equity, in contrast to Fox Morcillo for whom, as we have seen, the two terms are distinguishable.[112] Don Quijote argues for a return to that "sainted" Golden Age when "arbitrary law had not yet found its place in a judge's understanding, because at that time there was nothing to judge, nor one who might be judged" (Cervantes 2005, I, 11).[113] For Cervantes equity is, as it was for Ficino, justice in a peaceful and fair society. As Ficino reads the *Laws*, Plato decrees "most wisely that no one is permitted to enlarge his property beyond a fixed modest limit, lest some have too much, while others have too little and many be obliged to be beggars in the arms of their mother-land, a condition he considers to be quite wretched" (Ficino 2009a, 74).[114] This type of equity is quite distinct from that described by magistrate Castillo de Bobadilla, for whom equity is a point to be considered by the judge so as to render decisions on the basis of reason of state and arbitrary will. For Cervantes equity is, as it was for Ficino, the assurance that each receives his due.

Equity is a common theme in the works of Don Quijote's creator: in *La gitanilla*, we read that a sum of money is distributed with "equity and justice" (equidad y justicia) (Cervantes 1997a, 1:105); in the *Persiles*, that "discrete judges castigate but do not take vengeance for crimes; prudent and pious ones mix equity with justice and, somewhere between rigour and clemency, offer the light of their good understanding" (Cervantes 2003, 538);[115] in the advice Don Quijote gives to governor Sancho Panza: "When equity may and should be operative, don't let all the rigour of the law fall on the delinquent, because the fame of a rigorous judge is not any better than that of a compassionate one" (Cervantes 2005, II, 42).[116] In yet another reading of the concept, the protagonist suggests that his chronicler might have left out certain details of the First Part of his history: "for equity ... because those actions that neither change nor alter the truth of the history do not have to be written, if they will result in contempt for the history's protagonist" (Cervantes 2005, II, 3).[117] That is, Cervantes' characters employ equity literally as a recommendation for equal treatment and for judicial mercy, but the author also appropriates the term as a foundational piece of his narrative poetics. Platonic, Ficinian equity is extended to refer to fair and just authorial treatment of characters in a fictional creation.

Cervantes accords similar treatment to the concept of "prejudice to a third party." As we have seen, magistrate Castillo de Bobadilla allows for the use of judicial "reason of state" with one caveat, forbidding its use "in cases when there is a danger of prejudice to a third party" (Castillo de Bobadilla 1616, 2.2.82).[118] Cervantes also explores this related concept, commenting on it in relation to unchained ambition in both the *Persiles* and the *Coloquio de los perros*: "I do not deny that it is a worthy virtue that each should seek to better themself, but it has to be without prejudice to a third party" (Cervantes 2003, 308); "It is ambition, but a generous ambition, that of he who seeks to better his standing without prejudice to a third party" (Cervantes 1997a, 2:314).[119] The last quote comes from Berganza, who is speaking of merchants and their ambitions for their progeny. His interlocutor Cipión responds, doubtfully: "In few, or even no instances is ambition met without damage to a third party" (Cervantes 1997a, 2:314).[120] The Jesuits, teachers of the merchant's sons in the exemplary novel, themselves used the concept as dispensation to ignore rules: one 1581 privilege of the Order says that confessors "may remit or relax any oaths whatever, without prejudice to a third party," a loophole that Steinmetz described as "a salvo so vague that it stood for nothing" (Steinmetz 1848, 2:65).[121] But it does stand for something: Ficino's ideal of unity and justice as individual principle writ large incorporates the Christian maxim of doing no harm to others. All actions will, eventually, impact on third parties. As he had done with "equity," Cervantes adapts the concept of prejudice to a third party as part of his literary poetics: it is dispensation for the pastoral novels in the *Quijote*: "books of understanding without any prejudice to third parties" (Cervantes 2005, I, 6),[122] as well as justification of the writer's discretion, as we read above: the author should not include details that "will result in contempt for the history's protagonist" (Cervantes 2005, II, 3).[123] Rejecting his contemporaries' negative, positivist legal interpretations, Cervantes appropriates these concepts as fundamental pieces of his own poetics, a creative reason of state that comports with the Platonic ideal of justice as harmony, and equity as fairness for all.

Arguing from a moral and civic perspective, as does Plato in the *Republic*,[124] Cervantes' political voice is obvious above all in his characters' discussions of and search for justice. The creative author offers multiple commentaries that parallel those of Plato in that dialogue – on censorship, on good theatre, and on illicit games, although they have not been commonly studied with that focus.[125] In many works by Cervantes the reader finds a call for well-ordered or well-run republics, for the need to elect officials in a republic and find arms to defend it, warnings about the damage caused to a republic by untruthful letters, private property, and gambling, defence of the rights of all members of a society and of individual freedoms, precepts for the proper behaviour of governors and governments, and even a description of justice as the realization of the divine will.[126] In Cervantes' ideal if fictional republic, the good guy wins and in this, Cervantes follows not only Ficino but also Ignatius de Loyola who, according to his first biographer, founded the Jesuit Order to reflect both Aquinas's maxims on poverty and Plato's ideal republic.[127]

Writing in 1631, Juan Eusebio Nieremberg tells us that Aquinas allowed the contemplative religious to "only hold riches in common," while permitting those who mixed contemplation with spiritual action to "live by the charity of others" (fol. 30v).[128] Nieremberg outlines how Saint Ignatius founded the Jesuit Order to conform with Aquinas's precepts, but also explains "how Plato's Republic was the shadow [i.e., foreshadowing] of the Jesuit Order":

> Let's speak of philosophy now, and we will see how what Socrates and Plato judged to be an impossible idea, that is, a well-ordered Republic, was put into place by Saint Ignatius when he removed what some had criticized as imperfections in the Republic of those philosophers. Marsilio Ficino called Socrates's Republic an invention, or a charitable creation, a name that well suits the Company of Jesuits ... the same Ficino saw that Socrates's doctrine would not suit a secular republic; and he said that it described more how a religion should be than a reign, or a seignorial state. (Nieremberg 1631, f. 38v)[129]

For Nieremberg, the four cardinal points of such a republic, according to "noted Platonist" (insigne Platónico) Marsilio Ficino are 1) charity with no private property, 2) obedience and truth in dealing with superiors, 3) the virtue of its youth and the care taken in raising them well, and 4) the virtue and practices of its superiors (Nieremberg 1631, 39r): "On these four rocks, says Ficino, that wise philosopher founded all the apparatus of his Republic" (39r).[130] The Jesuit Order, says Nieremberg, observes all four principles. The biographer expands on the points one by one, describing how the Jesuits comply with Plato's ideas as expressed in the *Republic* and also in the *Symposium* where, as Nieremberg notes, Socrates says: "If there were a Republic in which all loved each other, it would be so strong that it would prevail even if it were comprised of only a few men against all the rest of the world" (Nieremberg 1631, fol. 40r).[131] The Jesuits alone, assures Nieremberg, adhere to that precept. According to Plato's *Republic* and *Laws*: "Let obedience be the mark of a republic's sons" (fol. 40v); "on Socrates's third precept, the obligation taken on by the Jesuit Order, to form its youth, is not found in any other major [religious] community" (fol. 42r); and "the fourth founding block of Socrates's Republic," which orders that superiors have twice the responsibility of the others, is also a basis for the Jesuits, "because as Plato says in his book, just as an animal cannot lead and guide another without man's help, so men cannot be governed nor led by another man without God's help" (Nieremberg 1631, fol. 43r).[132] As he expands on the four points, with one exception Nieremberg identifies the specific writings in which each is found: charity and communion of goods (*Republic* book 5); obedience (*Republic* book 1; *Laws* book 7); regulations for superiors and magistrates (*Republic* book 5; *Statesman*). The only source not specified by the biographer is that for the training of youth, which is *Republic* book 5. As evidenced in Nieremberg's treatise, as well as by the number of volumes in Spanish libraries today bearing ex libris of the first Jesuit colleges at Spanish universities, the Company followed Ficino in their acceptance and incorporation of Platonic thought. Most noteworthy is the detail about the Jesuit Order being intentionally modelled on, as well as the realization of, Plato's ideal republic, a claim that is easily supported by other parallels. For example, Ignatius de Loyola's emphasis on contemplation as a founding principle for the Jesuits is matched by Ficino's summary of the first book of the *Republic*: "contemplation is the beginning and end of action" (Ficino 2009a, 3).[133] Kristeller notes that for Ficino "the special act of prayer is related in substance to inner conversion toward God; and so the contemplative experience appears as the concrete foundation of every religious phenomenon" (1964, 316). The belief and process were identical for Loyola, for whom meditation and contemplation were key to inner conversion (O'Malley 1993, 24–5); Jesuit action has, as Ficino recommended, its beginning and end in contemplation.

In a different treatise published in the same year as Nieremberg's (1631), Juan de Mariana addresses a perceived need for reform in the Jesuit order by referencing Ficino's reading of Plato's *Laws*. Ficino offers that three factors – freedom, prudence, and a good disposition in governance – "are united with greater ease in that state which holds the mid-point between the power of one and the power of the people, so that it does not subordinate itself totally to the will of a single ruler or to the power of a few men ... [but] has both a royal element and a democratic element" (2009a, 90).[134] Mariana describes this same combination of monarchy and democracy as the optimum form of government for the religious order that he believed to be, as he wrote, beset by the problem of too many trying to exercise control at once, even to the point of bringing lawsuits against each other (1631, 10–17). Mariana likens the upheavals (*revueltos*) to what Ficino says regarding political structures: "There are heated disputes among philosophers over which government is better, that by one or that by many ... They conclude that monarchy is better, as long as the one accepts the help of the many, which grants it an advantage," as governance by one provides the necessary force, while that by many offers greater prudence and less passion (1631, 39).[135] One key point addressed by Mariana is a lack of conformity in teaching materials: although the Jesuits' *Ratio Studiorum* indicates that theology should be taught according to Aquinas's maxims, in practice, says Mariana, everyone teaches what they will (1631, 25). He calls on his fellow Jesuits to guard "distributive justice" and argues that "in the end, it is necessary so that the harmony so praised by Plato might conserve this community" (1631, 45, 47).[136] Mariana's statements confirm Nieremberg's description of the Jesuit Order's self-image as the realization of Plato's ideal republic. Further, it is obvious that the Jesuits, educators of first instance already in the late sixteenth century, were committed to and propagandists for Ficino's thought.

References to Platonic republics will become common in Spanish political writings. By the early eighteenth century, the descriptor takes on the guise of a socio-political program, as Benito Jerónimo Feijoo proposes what he says might be considered a Platonic idea: that workers be excused from the evils of war and not have to serve in militias, nor suffer hostile acts against themselves and their homes. As Feijoo sees it, this would keep war from disturbing "agrarian culture" (la cultura de los campos) (2003, Discurso XIII, para. 1, numbers 1–2). In 1750, Campomanes defends the ideals of a Platonic republic, saying that both human frailty and failures in education have had negative social repercussions. Employment is granted to the well-connected but denied to the meritorious, and this author vehemently disagrees that attempting to displace this old boy's network is to "try to establish a Platonic republic" (Campomanes 1984, 41).[137]

By 1811–13, the political winds have shifted. Fray Francisco Alvarado proposes that all who favour schemes of redistribution of wealth might happily be banished to Siberia with, of course, the express permission of the Russian emperor. Once there, they could recreate from scratch the human species, beginning with a return to life as savages, then social pacts and the establishment of a republic *plusquam platónica* (Alvarado 1824, 286); that is, he says, they can settle for equality such as that found among ruinous cattle. Alvarado notes that this is how some French thinkers would have it, with a group uniting not to pray the rosary but to philosophize and work, sweating as they compose encyclopedias or read aloud to each other from the works of Rousseau and Diderot (Alvarado 1824, 286–7). In 1830, Gallardo mocks the idea of a utopia: "And this is, truthfully, a part of that elegant utopia with which some Platonic politicians believe they can reduce to one single family household the entirety of the human race, making it subject to one law and one language (*et legis, et labii unius*)" (Gallardo 1928, 1:47).[138] Gallardo implicates not just the political, but even the poetic ruin caused by Platonic concepts, lamenting that sixteenth-century Fernando de Herrera "was addlepated by Petrarch's Platonic poetry, the ruin of so many fine and talented Spaniards!" (Gallardo, 1928, 1:261).[139]

During the late nineteenth century, this perspective became common. Joaquín Costa writes on the history of ideas regarding agrarian collectivism in Spain, and quotes from yet another eighteenth-century voice, Rafael de Floranes, who had praised the spirit of shared labour with which an entire community survived the vicissitudes of climatological adversities and poor harvests. Costa points out that Floranes had wishfully opined: "What a pleasure it would have been to have lived in those days" (1983, 1:237), and he rejects the "false politicians who have us fooled into fearing that if there were no private property, nor coveting of each other's wealth, men would not have reason to apply themselves to working," but he also notes that the collective ideal, "whose most exalted representation is to be found in the classic *Republic* of Plato" never found wide favour among Spaniards, although he does note particular historical instances of such political will and actualization in the service of the poor and the sick (1983, 1:295–6). At the turn of the nineteenth to twentieth centuries, 'Platonic' had also become the all-embracing accepted term for political discontents. The phrase "Platonic republic" was used to decry contemporary movements like communism and socialism. The later bogeyman phrase of "communist state" did not yet have resonance but, from the late eighteenth-century revolutions onward, "Platonic republic" served this same purpose. In Spanish letters, the adjective 'Platonic' had evolved from simple onomastic descriptor of a philosophical school to founding principle of a religious order, fictional preceptive ideals, positive agrarian policy, and finally, negative destructive collectivism to be understood as predictor of the end of human dignity and liberty.

Similar usages of 'Platonic' with positive and negative political slants are also found in coetaneous writings in the United States. On the positive side, the review of an 1853 commencement speech delivered at Yale University describes "the Platonic ideas of society as the natural condition of man ..." (Evarts 1853). Within twenty years, however, a negative reading of the phrase would be predominent. One 1871 article describes a declaration issued by Paris communists that calls for a number of social changes: the overthrow of government and establishment of new "Industrial Societies, to which every citizen must belong or lose his civil rights"; common decisions on wages and the rearing of children; and "marriage, of course, in this so-organized society, this Platonic Republic, is to be free and the man or woman can remarry as often as they like" ("The New Socialist Republic in Paris," 1871). The ideas are described as those of "fanatics," "ruffians," and "*canaille*." Seven years later, a brief piece describes "the Platonic scheme for the reorganization of the world":

> To say that there is a connection between Plato and the pot-house communism of Chicago and New York may seem a grotesque fancy, but it is certain that our Schwabs' minds, could their operations be exhibited, would in social speculation betray a much closer resemblance to the Platonist mental operations than to those of most of their living fellow-creatures ... they dream of a world in which there shall be no more property ... ("Socialism," 1878)[140]

A book review of W.H. Mallock's *New Republic* ... states that the overriding theme of Maddock's book is "the consideration of an ideal form of society and government in England after the fashion of the Platonic Symposium" ("Mallock's

New Republic," 1878). On both sides of the Atlantic, 'Platonic' is now read as it was by Spanish magistrate Castillo de Bobadilla in 1597, that is, as a political configuration dangerously contrary to private property. This trajectory in use of the phrase exemplifies Leo Spitzer's concept of "historical semantics" (1967) or Mazzeo's regarding the history of ideas as, rather, "the life of ideas" (1972, 393). Over the course of three centuries, the idea of a Platonic republic regularly cycled through positive and negative phases in its interpretation. At the end of the nineteenth century, once again read in its anti–free market iteration, it excluded idealistic readings of a time of plenty and sharing among men. During the same time period, dogmatic declarations regarding Spain's literary past made by scholars like Menéndez Pelayo would similarly exclude ideas that did not conform to conservative political or philosophical-theological principles, along with writers like Ficino who espoused them.

Conclusion

The foregoing study makes clear that Ficino's writings and translations had a solid and pervasive impact on Spanish letters. From specific mentions of his name to glossed volumes of his works in Spanish libraries, in both direct adaptations and subtle commentaries, Ficino was a considerable factor beginning in the fifteenth century, throughout the sixteenth and seventeenth, and well into the nineteenth. Hankins has warned that "the influence of a philosopher cannot always ... be measured by the number of extant manuscripts and printed editions" but must be "combined with an adequate doctrinal knowledge which exhibits the actual impact of a philosopher's doctrines upon the thought of a given figure or group of figures" (1984, 3). In Spanish letters we find just such knowledge, impact, and incorporation of Ficino's translations of ancient figures, and of his own thought. Spanish intellectuals accepted many of the Italian philospher's ideas yet debated others. They adapted his Hermetic and Neoplatonic imagery for their own creative works. The authors studied above constitute a broad swathe of Spanish thought and letters. Many of their writings had, and in some instances continue to have, extensive circulation. Both collectively and individually, their respectful yet at times quite innovative incorporation of Ficinian themes and images deepens our understanding of intellectual life in Renaissance Spain, and of the creativity that it engendered.

The sixteenth century is particularly rich in adaptations, interpretations, debates on, and consideration of the Italian philosopher's writings. The seventeenth opens with Juan de Pineda's world-history version of the *pia philosophia* incorporating Hermes Trismegistus and Plato, Gutiérrez de los Ríos's expression of all arts as philosophy, Nieremberg's history of Ignatius de Loyola with his founding of the Jesuit Order on the model of Plato's ideal republic, and Miguel de Cervantes' fictionalized treatment and preceptive adaptation of the same Platonic dialogue's concepts of justice and equity. Spanish writers from Garcilaso de la Vega and Bartolomé de las Casas to Cervantes and Lope de Vega addressed specific points made by Ficino, and customized his philosophy to express their own creative ideas. Sixteenth-century Spanish mysticism is awash in Hermetic imagery, and historical treatises include Atlantis in discussion of the New World because Spanish authors trusted Ficino's word on the matter. Luc Brisson has pointed out that thanks to "historians, philosophers and theologians" myth was "'saved' by allegory, which made it possible to associate the most scandalous of narratives and bizarre details to deep truths" (2004, 1). On Ficino's role in this process, Brisson adds that in the "Platonic Academy of Florence, the quest for a deep meaning hidden under the superficial meaning came close to being an orthodoxy" (2004, 158). Spanish thinkers both exploited and debated the literal and allegorical Ficinian readings of ancient sources to continue that search for deeper meaning, using the Italian philosopher's works as a starting point. Contrary to a traditional critical perspective that imagines the Spanish Renaissance solely as a moment of Counter Reformation and Inquisition, careful consideration and incorporation of those ancient sources translated by Ficino brought no resultant charges of heresy. For Spaniards, Ficino, Plato, and Hermes Trismegistus were completely orthodox and would remain so for centuries.[1] For a number of reasons, this facet of Renaissance developments has not been universally recognized.

Early in the twentieth century, Julián Juderías coined the term "Black Legend" to refer generally to anti-Spanish sentiment, and we know that resentment of Aragonese political occupation of Naples and Sicily can be traced back to thirteenth-century Italy (Arnoldsson 1960; García Cárcel 1998, 30; Kamen 2008, xiii). The long-standing competitive relationship between Spain and Italy is evidenced in a number of Renaissance Spanish texts: in 1498, Italy was alleged to be the source of the heretical "enlightened ones" (alumbrados) by "Ferdinand the Catholic's amusing physician Doctor Francisco de Villalobos" who said: "those cursed *aluminados* came from Italy" (Márquez 1972, 71–2).[2] Spanish humanists celebrated the reign of the Catholic Monarchs as the rebirth of ancient Rome (Biersack 2009, 37). Throughout the sixteenth century, Spaniards debated and tried to refute the negative portrayal of their soldiers in Italian histories (Byrne 2012a, 108–14). In 1566, Jerónimo de Arbalanche wrote an inventive history of the Spanish kingdoms that includes an "alternative national myth" regarding a babe suckled by an animal, a deer for the Spanish child instead of the wolf of the Italians Romulus and Remus, as a new account to "compete[s] with classical Roman mythology, advancing the objectives of the Spanish empire and overcoming the traditional complex about Italian cultural superiority" (Irigoyen-García 2013, 87). Sometime around 1650, Spanish poet Luis de Góngora was criticized for "things Italian" in his works, a critique that even extended to the poet's use of formal aspects such as Italian verse metre (R. John McCaw, personal communication). At the end of the seventeenth century, national literary bibliographies such as that readied by Nicolás Antonio in 1672 began to be compiled. Throughout the eighteenth century the merits of national literatures were hotly debated and by the end of the nineteenth, the prevailing trend in most European scholarly studies was to highlight the accomplishments of one's own compatriots with an exclusionary eye towards those of others.

The eighteenth century brought ever increasing specialization in scholarly materials and as disciplines developed into distinct entities, "letters" themselves became selective and nationalistic. The multidisciplinary "good letters" of the Renaissance would lose prestige following French coinage of the term "belles lettres" in the middle of the seventeenth century. In the eighteenth, Spanish writers would alternately censure or defend the writings of their compatriots, and both postures only served to marginalize those writers as world figures. In his 1737 neoclassical poetic manifesto, Ignacio Luzán criticizes Spanish Golden Age authors for having ignored Aristotle's rules, and for having written in innovative ways without the polish that study of classical forms might have provided (Luzán 1956, 1:32–5). Luzán claims that unlike the French and Italians, Spaniards did not write preceptive treatises, and he attributes this to a lack of care for classical form. Apparently, Luzán was unaware of or not convinced by treatises like López Pinciano's *Philosophía antigua poética*, Pineda's *Diálogos familiares*, or the multiple preceptive commentaries by Spanish authors found in prologues to their works and incorporated into the text of their writings. By the end of the eighteenth century, reacting to a specific criticism from Tiraboschi regarding the lack of belles lettres produced in Spain, Xavier Lampillas would defend Spanish Renaissance writers by privileging their "serious, solid and sacred" letters (buenas letras) over the "frivolous" belles lettres of other nations (1783, 19). One hundred years later, Jakob Burckhardt endorsed and ratified that perspective by simply excluding Spain from Renaissance artistic and intellectual developments. It is through that lens that Renaissance Spain continues to be seen by some, but it is a very incomplete picture. The persistent idea that Ficino was not a factor in Spanish thought and letters is, frankly, an obsolete anachronism.

Following on two hundred years of polemic regarding Spain's role in the Renaissance, Ficino's impact on Spanish letters was denied by Spaniards themselves as part of an attempt to recuperate the voices of Spanish thinkers in that key historical time frame.[3] Christopher Celenza has noted that "nineteenth-century nationalist assumptions shaped the study of the fifteenth-century Italian Renaissance" for much of the twentieth century (Celenza in Celenza and Gouwens 2006, Preface).[4] Similar arguments have been made regarding French and English letters (Bullen 1994), as well as for study of the Renaissance in Spain. Di Camillo points out that the nineteenth-century Romantic aesthetic sought to exclude all tendencies not perceived as indigenous from the national canon: "All artistic expressions associated with the restoration of classical learning or with any form of erudition, from the fifteenth century on, were unconditionally branded as foreign, imitative and servile art" (1995, 353–4). Juan Carlos Elorza Guinea describes the nineteenth century as "a crucial moment when national stereotypes were constructed (2000, 13).[5] Richard Kagan details how that same century's events and writings about Spain by North Americans created and cemented the image of the people and country common in the United States throughout much of the twentieth century, that is, Spaniards as "fanatical Catholics" in a country ruled by priests, but with a romanticized "love for liberty" (2000, 420–1).[6] As testament to the pervasive effect of such representations, one article referenced by Kagan was published in Boston in 1973 (Kagan 2000, 420). In a collection of essays that focus on the nineteenth century's creation and re-elaboration of myths regarding Spain's sixteenth century and its monarchs Charles V and Phillip II, García Cárcel speaks of the "enormous influence of positivist historiography at the end of the nineteenth and beginning of the twentieth centuries" (2000, 370),[7] and the same writer has also highlighted Menéndez Pelayo's role as "defender of the Spanish cause" (1998, 15).[8] Against this backdrop of historical rewrites, European Renaissance norms that included multifaceted and multidisciplinary exchanges were not only downplayed but denied. Twentieth-century political events in Spain helped foster and preserve the undeserved caricatures of a picturesque Spanish backwardness that never existed but that had been formed over time in response to various factors: Italian resentment of Aragonese holdings in Italy, fear of Spanish military power during the sixteenth century, anger at the 1527 Sack of Rome, competition over New World riches, and Enlightenment rivalries regarding the relative merits of national literatures.

The "profound and enduring impact on Renaissance thought and culture" made by Marsilio Ficino, as well as his "abiding influence on the next two European centuries" (Allen 1989, 1, 83) includes Spanish letters, and not only those of the first decades of the seventeenth century, in which scholars have already noted direct references to Ficino. I have shown that by the late fifteenth century Ficino's translations and writings were already circulating in Spain. The court of the Catholic Monarchs Ferdinand and Isabel welcomed not only Christopher Columbus, but also the writings of Marsilio Ficino, Hermes Trismegistus, Plato, and the Neoplatonists. At Isabel's behest, Alfonso de Palencia compiled his bilingual Latin-Castilian dictionary with information on Hermes, Plato, Pythagoras, the daemons, and other topics incorporated from Ficino's writings. During the last decades of the fifteenth century, scholars and students at the University of Salamanca were already debating the merits of Trismegistus and Podalirius. The University at Alcalá de Henares, founded as a locus for humanist study in Spain, would become known as a fertile field of Ficinian studies over the course of the next few centuries.[9] The earliest surviving, 1523 catalogue of library holdings at

Alcalá includes listings for *Platonis* in Greek and *Platonicorum* identified as "*Liber a Marsilio traductus*," as well as "various editions of Plato's *Opera omnia*" (Urriza 1941, 438, nos. 164–5; 64). Many specific collections of the early colleges at Alcalá, as I have shown above, also contained Ficino's volumes of translations and writings. As the annotations in those volumes and subsequent references to them by Spanish authors make clear, they had a broad readership.

Following the Catholic Monarchs, Charles V's chroniclers Pedro Mexía and Antonio de Guevara made direct reference to Ficino and his writings, as did those who explored the New World and debated its place in history. Charles V was awarded the honorific Trismegistus. Phillip II read the Italian philosopher's translations as part of his formative curriculum, and among his personal library holdings is found the only surviving fifteenth-century Castilian translation of the *Pimander* in manuscript. In all likelihood, this was an inherited volume from Queen Isabel, whose personal confessor Cisneros owned a copy of the work in Latin. Spanish historical, political, theological, philosophical, medical, legal, and creative writers explored Ficino's concepts in their own treatises, in prose and verse, some of them fully adopting and furthering the aims of the *pia philosophia.*

The Jesuits, educators of the first instance not only in Spain but throughout Europe and the Americas, founded their order to reflect Plato's ideal republic, praised Ficino himself, and stocked their library shelves with his translations and writings. Madrid's Colegio Imperial of the Jesuits was known as the school "in which all of Madrid's nobility was educated" during the early modern period in Spain (Martin 1987, 13). Through the common Jesuit curriculum that included the dialogues in the early levels of study, Madrid's nobility was introduced to Plato through Ficino. The long-standing respect for Hermes Trismegistus, still described as the first of ancient philosophers in 1770, and as a "great theologian" in 1859 is also, in all likelihood, a factor in the spiritist movement of the mid-nineteenth century, recognized by Ricardo Gullón as an underlying element in Spanish modernism (Gullón 1979).

Ficino's intellectual, philosophical, and literary impact on Spanish authors was immediate, deep, and long-lasting. As Walter Ghia has said: "The history of ideas in that era ... is neither Italian nor Spanish nor French but, rather, European on its way to becoming Western" (Ghia 2013, 78).[10] The Renaissance itself has come to be better understood in the light of Ficino's writings, but the Spanish contribution to that explosive artistic and intellectual stimulus has, previously, neither been fully recognized nor appreciated. With the foregoing study, that oversight has been rectified, although I have probably only scratched the surface. Ficinian Hermeticism and Neoplatonism are key factors for an understanding of the Renaissance in Spain, particularly for the first half of the sixteenth century. Even further, and again contrary to common critical belief, those philosophical currents did not disappear in Spain as the Counter Reformation took hold.

Rather, they were adapted by Spanish writers who interpreted them differently than we do. Christian and Neoplatonic tenets were perceived by Renaissance Spaniards, as they had been by Ficino, as orthodox and intriguing partners. The Italo-Hispanic Neoplatonism proposed by Marcelino Menéndez Pelayo is, in fact, a lot closer to the truth of the matter, even if not precisely as imagined by the Spanish historian.

Notes

Introduction

1 For bibliographical information, see Kristeller 1964, 3–29; Allen 1984, 1–47; Garfagnini 1986; Rees 2002, xiii–xxii; and Clucas, Forshaw, and Rees 2011, 1–9.

2 For an explanation of Ficino's *pia philosophia* and its relation to earlier eclectic, syncretic traditions, see Purnell 1986, Hankins 1984, and Allen 1998. On the concept of a *prisca theologia*, see Walker 1953, 1954, 1972, and Charles Trinkaus 1970, vol. 2, pt. 4, sec. 15. Shumaker asserts that "the Renaissance thirst for synthesis, for syncretism, was unquenchable" (1972, 205), and Hankins describes Ficino's view of Platonism as "part of God's providential design for the human race, a *philosophia perennis*, springing intertwined with Christianity from the same soil of religious experience" (1990, 1:285).

3 See Dodd 1964 [1935], Walker 1972, Blázquez, Martínez-Pinto, and Montero 1993, Fortín 1996, Hadot 2002, and Brisson 2004. These are of necessity broad references, as each author approaches the question differently but addresses in general the cross-fertilization of religious and philosophical thought in a book-length study.

4 John Dillon offers specifics on Ficino's "delicate juggling act" (2011, 24) with those Neoplatonic sources by highlighting both the Italian philosopher's inspiration in their ideas and his caution with their terminology. James Hankins, in turn, elaborates Ficino's debts to the later, medieval methods of Aquinas, Augustine, and scholastic systems of religious thought as well as his innovations, noting that the Italian philosopher does not follow those medieval theologians in elaborating "a structure of belief articulated by a chain of logical demonstrations" but, rather, offers a "holistic metaphysical architecture" in which "harmoniously each element fits into the whole," a "neo-Augustinian approach that would favor meaning and coherence over demonstrability" (2008a, 111–12; 114).

5 Today, historians of science are reappraising the transmission and classification of scientific knowledge from early modern times through the so-called but now

questioned scientific revolution of the seventeenth century. One volume that offers a number of fresh perspectives, along with a solid bibliography of this trend, is that edited by Josep Simon and Néstor Herran (2008).

6 For eighteenth-century developments in the division of the historiographies of science and philosophy, see Celenza 2013. A collection of studies edited by Clucas (2006) looks at the science-magic mix in sixteenth-century England, with a specific focus on John Dee. Elaine Leong and Alisha Rankin's edited volume on the history of medicine in context (2011) offers a number of studies on developments in science and medicine from 1500–1800, beginning with the sixteenth-century rage for publishing "secrets" or recipes for all types of ills. See also Shumaker 1972, Boas 1962, Thorndike 1929–58, White 1896, and Draper 1874.

7 Newman and Grafton (2001) review the status of alchemy and astrology in the early modern period. Thorndike lists various works from the ninth, tenth, and eleventh centuries that combine "astrology and divination" with "ecclesiastical calendars" (1929–58, 1:676). For the concept of astrology during the time period, see Garin 1983 [1976]. By the end of the sixteenth century predictive, judicial astrology became quite controversial: well-known commentaries in Renaissance Spanish letters include Calderón de la Barca's *La vida es sueño*, scattered narrative quips in the works of Miguel de Cervantes, Juan de Pineda's insistence on the distinctions between predictive astrology and "demonstrative astronomy" (Pineda 1963, 161:159), and the advice of Saavedra Fajardo (1584–1648) to his student prince on the dangers in "creer que todo se obra por las causas segundas: con que niegan a la Providencia divina" (1958, 1:156). See also Sagrario López Poza's 1999 edition of Saavedra Fajardo's text, with full introduction and study, and Emil 1953.

8 See Lachman 1972, Reiser 1975, Bakal 1979, and Levenson 1994.

9 The *Stanford Encyclopedia of Philosophy* lists Johann Jacob Brucker (1696–1770) as the first to move philosophical concerns to a "critical, rationalistic enterprise" (SEP online, "Ficino," "Legacy"). Christopher Celenza notes Brucker's history of philosophy as the turning point, when "natural philosophy (what became natural science) separated itself from philosophy ... a gradual turning away from the notion of philosophy as a style of life ... philosophy ... concerned itself ever more with epistemology," and reviews Brucker's comments on Ficino in regards to this development (2013, 368–9). See also Kristeller 1978 on philosophy and medicine in the Middle Ages and Renaissance.

10 Juan Cruz Cruz offers a Spanish translation of Fox Morcillo's original Latin commentary (Fox Morcillo 2010). In my text, I offer my own English translation of Cruz Cruz's Spanish with page reference to that edition, then include Fox's original Latin in note: "Hic animaduerte, disciplinas omnes sibi esse mutuo subiectas, communiores uidelicet minus communioribus ... ita ut minus communium principia conclusiones communiorum sint: ueluti Physica principia quaedam habet, quae ipsa

probare non potest, nisi Theologiae, seu metaphysicae adiumento. Medicina etiam habet sua, quae ex Physica pendent: atque, eodem modo artium reliquarum aliae ex alijs nascuntur" (Fox 1556a, 116).

11 "The age of Ficino is crucial, and Ficino is a pivotal figure" (Celenza 2004, 100).

12 "citando con sus comas en medio: 'Ficinos, Marsilios'; y ello de verdad fue un mismo autor que se llamó Marsilio Ficino" (Quevedo 1993, 481). On Ficino in the works of Quevedo, see Schwartz 1995.

13 "Marsilii Ficini Opera. Is instaurator fuit Philosophiae Platonicae, in qua etiam fuit probe versatus, ut ex notis eius apparet. Ingenium eius insigne est; eruditio vero non respondet; adeoque cum grano salis legendus est. *Collegium Conimbricense*, & *Collegium Complutense* iam supra nominata sunt" (Boecler 1715, 603). German Johann Heinrich Boecler lived from 1611 to 1672, but this work was published posthumously, in 1715. I thank Valery Rees for her assistance with this translation. It is interesting to compare Boecler's opinion with that of Brucker, published in 1740, who praises Ficino's own erudition but also thought he had been "captivated by the trifles of later Platonists" (cited by Celenza 2013, 367).

14 There are very few similar place references in Boecler's work: one to Aristotle in the "Academia Parisiensi" (1715, 591), a few to libraries where a particular manuscript is located, and maybe a dozen to professors in specific universities, including a Claudium Richardum in Madrid in the year 1645. I have been unable to find any clear information on Richardum.

15 "dissidentes dentro de la misma escolástica" (1903, 71). Another historian, Aguado Bleye, differentiates two basic types of university in Renaissance Spain: "Salamanca, que encarna la tradición; y Alcalá, el espíritu del Renacimiento" (cited by Jiménez Delgado 1978, 245, n.1). See also Bataillon 1950, who describes the University at Alcalá de Henares as a bastion of Christian humanism.

16 "dar realidad a las ideas, affirmando que lo que está en el entendimiento divino tiene positiva existencia" (González de la Calle 1903, 71).

17 The surgical practice mentioned by Feijoo, however, is not to be found in that place. The 1529 Basel edition offers titles that differ from those of the princeps edition of 1489, and some editions of Feijoo's work mis-transcribe the title as *De studio forum*. The 1529 Basel edition of Ficino's *De vita* was published by Andreas Leenius, who claims on the title page that he has "freed" the work from errors, although today's editors claim that Leenius "corrupted rather than corrected" the text and chapter titles (Kaske and Clark 2002, 9).

18 "las quexas de fluxiones de la cabeza hoy son tan universales, que tanto casi suenan ya en las bocas de los Gañanes, como en las de los Cathedráticos. Todos se quexan de reumas: no porque haya más reumas en este siglo que en los antecedentes, sino porque hay más melindres. Más fluyen a la boca que al pecho: porque más es el clamor que el daño" (Feijoo 1778, 7.14, 187). Each anthology of Feijoo's *Teatro*

crítico presents selected discourses, but not the same writings. Given that, I cite book, chapter, and page (each where relevant to the specific publication) of various eighteenth-century editions, many of which are available in digitized format. All are listed in my bibliography.

19 "carece de toda verisimilitud, ni aun merece el nombre de opinión, sino de delirio, el de otros autores temerarios, que estienden la fuerza de la imaginación a cuerpos estraños, y distantes, en tal grado que a ella, y no a la asistencia de los espíritus infernales, atribuyen los mayores portentos de la magia ... De este sentir fueron Algazel, Alchindo, y Avicena ... los siguieron ... Marsilino [*sic*] Ficino, Pomponacio, y Paracelso" (Feijoo 1774, carta 8.8, 95).

20 "El divino Platón, no satisfecho con ocupar un puesto tan distinguido en la Elocuencia, en la Filosofía y las Matemáticas, quiso también ser respetado de los jurisperitos. Por lo cual Marsilio Ficino dice de él: *Quemadmodum philosophorum omnium sapientissimus, & eloquentissimus oraturum, ita jurisconsultorum omnium prudentissimus.* En efecto, sus diez libros *De Republica* y los doce *De Legibus* se pueden considerar como el código platoniano y como un tratado filosófico del espíritu de las leyes" (1:59–60, italics in original). A note in the cited edition offers details on the source: "in *Arg. ad Dial XI de Leg.*" Andrés's very early comparative literature treatise titled *Origen, progresos y estado actual de toda la literatura*, first published in Italian in 1782, and then in Spanish between 1784 and 1793, has been reissued in a six-volume publication (1997–2001).

21 See Byrne 2012a, 144–5.

22 The following quotation from Andrés incorporates my paraphrase as well as the direct quotation: "El siglo XV fijó en Italia y esparció por toda Europa el amor a las Buenas Letras, y el siglo XV puede llamarse por antonomasia el siglo de los gramáticos ... Las escuelas más frecuentadas y pagadas con mayores estipendios eran las de Gramática ... El entendimiento humano, acostumbrado por mucho tiempo a la inercia e inacción, no podía pensar por sí mismo, ni dar un paso en las ciencias sin el auxilio y como llevado de la mano por los escritores antiguos. Y ¿cómo podía lograrse el auxilio de éstos sin conocerlos y entenderlos? ... y ¿cómo conocerlos y entenderlos sin el socorro de la Gramática ... Las gramáticas filosóficas, las ediciones críticas, las traducciones elegantes y fieles, los eruditos comentos, las observaciones filológicas empezadas en aquel siglo han seguido, aunque en menor número, ocupando a los doctos filólogos del siglo pasado y del presente" (Andrés 1997–2001, 3:485–6).

23 "contribuir a animar cada vez más los estudios teológicos y llevarlos al lustre y vigor con que florecieron en los [siglos] siguientes" (Andrés 1997–2001, 6:258).

24 "con astrológicas sofisterías y sin utilidad práctica" (Andrés 1997–2001, 5:310).

25 "me atreveré a asegurar que no hay ninguno, ni latino ni griego, a quien deba tanto la doctrina platónica como a Marsilio Ficino, quien, no contento con la ilustración

de las obras del maestro Platón, tradujo también y procuró aclarar la doctrina de Plotino y de los más célebres platónicos. Estos estudios, aunque a veces versaban sobre cuestiones de palabras, no terminaban como los escolásticos en caprichos y en sutilezas insubsistentes, sino que se dirigían a adquirir la verdadera inteligencia de Platón y de Aristóteles" (Andrés 1997–2001, 5:435).

26 Andrés notes Petrarch as the first: "¿Cuántas alabanzas, pues, no merece el Petrarca, que en medio de la escolástica esterilidad supo producir frutos de sana Moral ... que sirvieron de estímulo a los posteriores filósofos para tratar argumentos morales sin las espinas escolásticas ... Así Leonardo Aretino ... así Filelfo ... así Ángelo Policiano ... y Marsilio Ficino y los platónicos introdujeron con el entusiasmo de su maestro ideas de Moral poco familiares a los escolásticos peripatéticos" (Andrés 1997–2001, 5:486).

27 "El platónico Marsilio Ficino aplicó su filosofía y elocuencia a ilustrar la religión cristiana y la piedad, la fe, la divinidad de la ley cristiana y otros teológicos y sólidos argumentos" (Andrés 1997–2001, 6:258).

28 Hankins notes Ficino's own "self-definition as a Platonist ... in contradistinction to what he saw as the failure of scholastic method and Aristotelian philosophy to achieve the true goals of moral and religious education" (1990, 272). See also Edward Mahoney 2006.

29 D.P. Walker points out that "the main motive of platonizing theologians, from Ficino to Cudworth, was to integrate Platonism and Neoplatonism into Christianity, so that their own religious and philosophical beliefs might coincide" (1972, 2).

30 For the continuation of these pitched battles in Spain between secularizing trends and Church resistance during the next century, see Valis 2010, 1–56. For the nineteenth century's nationalist perspective and rewriting of the history of sixteenth-century Spain and its monarchs Charles V and Phillip II, see Martínez Millán and Reyero 2000.

31 See Di Camillo 1995, 356, n. 7.

32 Oxford (1955) dates the first use of the French phrase "belles lettres" in English letters to 1710, with Jonathan Swift in the Tatler. There were numerous French treatises composed during the seventeenth and eighteeenth centuries regarding the concept. A 2006 book of compiled conference proceedings titled *Bonnes Lettres, Belles Lettres* looks at the question in French letters (see Poulouin and Arnould).

33 "Que yo estoy condenado, o poco me falta, porque he defendido las escuelas panteístas de Alemania en su relación con la enseñanza universitaria viciada y pervertida por ellas" (Valera 1913 [1863], 267).

34 "hasta muchos Santos Padres de la Iglesia, han sido platónicos, como San Agustín, Sinesio, San Dionisio Areopagita, Marcilio Fiscino [*sic*] y Pico de la Mirandola ... Ahora bien: si se podía ser aristotélico, platónico y estoico, sin dejar de ser cristiano y hasta siendo sacerdote, ¿por qué, sin renegar de la santa religión de Jesucristo, no se ha de seguir a Kant, a Hegel, a Fichte o Krause?" (Valera 1913 [1863], 267–8).

35 I include here the full quotation, which is beautiful: "Si por no haber nacido en Alemania no podemos comprender la ciencia del Norte, V. no puede comprender la ciencia del Mediodía porque no se ha mecido su cuna bajo las ramas de los grandes árboles de la India; porque no ha pisado V. las arenas del desierto que rodean a Jerusalén; porque no ha oído el rumor de las ondas que besan las sandalias de mármol de Alejandría; porque no ha respirado el aire que baja del Hibla y del Himeto a acariciar a Grecia; porque no tiene ni un átomo de la tierra sagrada del Panteón y del Foro en su cuerpo, ni una gota de sangre latina en sus venas; porque no ha podido sentarse en la Sorbona a escuchar la voz de Abelardo y Santo Tomás; porque no ha oído como Marsilio Ficino el lamento de las almas de los platónicos, que vagaban por las orillas del Arno en los jardines de Florencia; porque no entiende las palabras perfumadas de mirto y de azahar que se exhalaban de los filigranados muros de las escuelas de Córdoba y Sevilla; porque no alcanza cómo todas nuestras ideas filosóficas se trasformaron en una revolucion y se resumieron en derechos, agitando el mundo, porque, hijo del Norte, descendiente de aquellas tribus que profanaron nuestros templos y destruyeron nuestras estátuas, y sepultaron en lodo y sangre a la reina de las naciones, lo único que de la vida histórica tiene en sí, es algun átomo de la gleba de los castillos feudales, algunas partículas del hierro de Arminio, de Alarico o de Atila. ¿Le parece a V. lógico que, por no ser indio, no pueda comprender a Capila, y por no ser griego a Platón, y por no ser africano a San Agustín, y por no ser francés a Descartes, y por no ser español a Luis Vives, y por no ser italiano a Vico?" (Castelar 1861, Second Letter, topic 14).

36 In Spain's nineteenth-century political-religious debates, both Valera and Castelar were "liberal Catholics," although "Valera inclined toward the *moderados*, and Castelar was a progressive democrat" (Valis 2010, 39).

37 For studies of this event and its resonance, see Van Dyke 1897, Guicciardini 1993, Gouwens 1998, García Cárcel 1998, and Kamen 2008. Most important for his focus on "not only the objective facts, the undoctored incidents that actually occurred, but also the subjective conception of the nature of these facts" as important in interpretations of the Renaissance, see Ferguson (2006 [1948], xiii).

38 Here and throughout, I use the writer's name in conformance with most modern citations, which have dropped the 'y' of Menéndez y Pelayo. In his excellent biography of the Spanish thinker, Serrano Vélez explains that Menéndez Pelayo adapted the 'y' to join his two patronyms when he was at the University of Barcelona, in all likelihood following Catalan custom (2012, 48).

39 Marta Campomar studies Menéndez Pelayo and the neo-Catholic movement of the late nineteenth century, with its debates on the role of religion in art and intellectual endeavour, and on "Protestant liberalism" versus "Catholic obscurantism" which had excluded Spain from modern Europe "because of her excessive and intolerant religiosity" (Campomar 1987, 174). Serrano Vélez describes numerous figures from

these movements as regards Menéndez Pelayo's relationships with them, finding in the Spanish historian a progressive distancing from some of the ideas and calling him more eclectic than most (2012, 53–97). Valis (2010) analyses the resonance of those pitched debates on late nineteenth- and early twentieth-century literature.

40 "¿No nos autoriza todo esto para decir que es una calumnia y una falsedad indigna lo de haber cerrado las puertas a las ideas filosóficas que nacían en Europa, cuando si de algo puede acusarse al Santo Oficio es de descuido en no haber atajado la circulación de libros que bien merecían sus rigores?" (Menéndez Pelayo 1992, 2:437). The Spanish historian does not mention the third book of Ficino's *De vita*, which did appear on the 1580 Italian Index (Kraye 2002, 378, n.6), because he is only defending the Spanish Index, which did not ban any of Ficino's volumes. In a 1994 study on Garcilaso de la Vega, without providing a source for the information, Heiple states that Ficino's *Platonic Theology* was condemned (Heiple 1994, 236), but the Indices of prohibited works contain neither that work by Ficino, nor the Italian philosopher's name. For Menéndez Pelayo's own later opinion of his *Heterodoxos*, see Serrano Vélez 2012, 92–3 and 163–6.

41 "como las nubes tormentosas y pasajeras del estío, que huyen azotadas por las brisas y flechadas por los rayos de un sol brillante, sin dejar rastro de su paso" (Menéndez Pelayo 1992, 1:xi). For details on editorial negotiations regarding the first publication (1880, three volumes), the second edition (1912, first volume only), and critical reception of the work, see Serrano Vélez 2012, 171–8.

42 For the impact of Menéndez Pelayo on subsequent literary studies, see Lasso de la Vega 1956.

43 "La historia de la Academia Platónica se reduce a la biografía de Marsilio Ficino" (Menéndez Pelayo 1974, 1:541).

44 "la popularidad y la importancia histórica de la doctrina son innegables"; "gran Cosmos físico y moral, creado por el Amor Divino"; "un florilegio de frases hechas y de lugares comunes"; "el principio orgánico de esta Philographía o *Teología Platónica* (como la llama Marsilio Ficino), sólo León Hebreo la formuló con claridad" (Menéndez Pelayo 1974, 1:541).

45 "El primer representante de esta tendencia armónica dentro del neoplatonismo que comúnmente se llama florentino, y con más propiedad y vocablo más comprensivo debería llamarse *neoplatonismo italo-hispano*, fue un médico, judío español de los que arrojó a Italia el edicto de los Reyes Católicos en 1492 ... León Hebreo"; "León Hebreo, representante el más puro del neoplatonismo florentino, renovado y vivificado por la infusión de un elemento semítico-español muy poderoso, que da a su doctrina una trascendencia ontológica, no lograda jamás por Bessarion ni por Marsilio Ficino" (Menéndez Pelayo 1892, 102, 97–8).

46 For the intermingling of religions and their philosophies from the fourth century BC through the fourth century AD, see Blásquez 1993, esp. pp. 395–616; for the

mix of Judaic, Hermetic, and Christian elements during the first centuries AD, see Dodd 1964 [1935]; for the history of the *comparatio* tradition and its resonance in the Renaissance, see Purnell 1971 and Hankins 2006; for the *comparatio* tradition at the University of Salamanca in the sixteenth century and its importance in later creative letters, see Cuevas 1982, 8.

47 This movement had begun 150 years earlier, with another encyclical calling for a return to the teachings of Thomas Aquinas (Sarrailh 1930, 204). Alvaro Huerga (1979) reviews the debates and history.

48 Menéndez Pelayo also underlines the importance of Juan Andrés as the inventor of literary history, and Lampillas as a defender of Spanish art against Tiraboschi (Menéndez Pelayo 1992, 2:613–15).

49 "todos los insurrectos de la escolástica ... son en mayor o menor grado platónicos" (Menéndez Pelayo 1892, 31).

50 "un erudito que filosofa sin mucha originalidad" (Menéndez Pelayo 1948, 54, quoting Villari).

51 "nuestro Vives relegó desdeñosamente a Marsilio Ficino al grupo de los filosofastros" (Menéndez Pelayo 1892, 86, and n.1).

52 "Admiscuit se his philosophaster Marsilius Ficinus, ut oloribus gavia, atque epistolas composuit ut de Platonicis quaestionibus disputaret, dictione invenusta et molesta" (Vives 1989, 136). Here, I use Fantazzi's English translation (Vives 1989).

53 "Estiman algunos prodigiosa su cultura filosófica y hasta originales las conclusiones que adopta; le juzgan otros como un erudito desprovisto de toda originalidad; pero sin tomar parte en la discusión, nos interesa hacer constar que somos deudores a Ficino de versiones latinas más o menos perfectas, de textos griegos; entre estos se encuentran las obras de Platón, Plotino, Porfirio, Jámblico y Proclo" (González de la Calle 1903, 48).

54 Menéndez Pelayo was in full agreement with Pope Pius IX's *Quanta Cura* or *Syllabus of Errors*, which condemned "the most obvious and capital modern errors" (Menéndez Pelayo 1992, 2:1205), that is, "liberalism, pantheism, indifferentism, socialism and secularism" (Valis 2010, 24).

55 See Rudolph Schevill on the founding of the Society Menéndez Pelayo, and on the "unparalleled learning" and "epoch-making publications" of Don Marcelino (1919, 308, 309).

56 There is a parallel in critical developments on the impact of Erasmus in Spain. See Wiffen 1865 on Juan de Valdés and Erasmus, and Bataillon 1950 on Erasmus in Spain. In a note to the *Diálogo de Mercurio y Carón* by Alfonso de Valdés, Ricapito offers further sources and details on sixteenth-century positive and negative reactions to the Dutch thinker (1993, 77, n.25).

57 Aldana has been described as the poet who "opened the door for our [Spanish] mystics" (Cernuda 1971, 52–3).

58 See Rivers 1956, Trueblood 1958, D. Alonso 1958, Gil Fernández 1966, Manzoni 1974, Di Camillo 1976, Garin 1981, de Armas 1981, 1992, Parker 1985, Yndurâin 1994, Gómez Moreno 1994, Aladro Font 1998, Schwartz 2005, Alcina Rovira 2007, Byrne 2005, 2007, and García 2010. In a recent doctoral dissertation, Ginés Torres Salinas (2013) studies Ficino's light imagery in Spanish Renaissance verse. The influence extends beyond the written art: a recent edition of the first volume of Ficino's letters translated into Spanish includes a prologue detailing Neoplatonic elements in Spanish plateresque art and architecture (Ordieres Díez in Ficino 2009b, 19–32).

59 "Aunque parezca que todo esto no hace al caso, ya que Ficino, directamente, no parece que influyó demasiado en los autores españoles" (Serés 1996, 171).

60 See Heiple 1994 and Wescott 1995 on Garcilaso; Noreña 1998 and Egido 2007 on Juan Luis Vives. Westcott offers further references.

61 "contamos con datos que indican que algunos poetas y humanistas del siglo XVII conocían y seguían leyendo la obra de este inventor del amor neoplatónico" (Schwartz 2005, 186).

62 A thirteenth- to fourteenth-century Italian philosopher and writer named Marsilio of Padua was also at times referred to by his first name only, which could have caused confusion. Herein, citations to 'Marsilio' alone, when read to mean Ficino, are those accompanied by the Italian philosopher's writings, or reference to them.

63 On Miguel Servet, see Alcalá 2003 and Manzoni 1974; on Malón de Chaide, see Carozza 1964 and Vinci 1961.

1. Ficino in Spanish Libraries

1 Phillip II did not make annotations in his own books, and the notations in hand in his copy are attributed to "frailes jerónimos de El Escorial" (García Rico 1920, 74).

2 Here and following, Patrimonio is used for Spain's *Catálogo Colectivo del Patrimonio Bibliográfico Español.* The catalogue contains many, but not yet all, of Spain's library holdings.

3 Patrimonio lists fifteen copies, but one each in the Complutense are volume 1 and then 2 of what would seem to be one full copy, and another indicates that it begins on page 559, so I list this as one copy. The Patrimonio list does not include those volumes held by the Escorial library, which I have added here, one each of editions dated 1539 and 1590.

4 "S. Franc[is]co de Cádiz contraqu[ie]n lo oculte [h]ay excomunión" (Patrimonio, Cádiz, Biblioteca Pública, ms. XVI-643, notes).

5 "No tiene este libro que corregir, según el expurgatorio del año 1707. Fr. Arcadio de Osuna" (Patrimonio, *Marsilii Ficino Florentini*, mss. A 175/104 and A 175/103, notes).

6 Three are listed in Patrimonio, one more in Gregorio Andrés 1964, 51, no. 946.

7 The first volume of Figliucci's two-volume translation of the letters includes books 1 through 5 of Ficino's twelve-volume epistolary.

8 For a study of Colón's library, see Wagner (1992, 475–92).

9 "y el ducado de oro vale 344 fenning" (BCC, 8–2–36, last folio).

10 In 1475, the value of one real was fixed at 34 maravedís (Rees, personal communication).

11 "que plotino sig[u]ió tanto a pl[atón] que parece aver hablado por la misma boca" (BCC, 15–7–19 f. 1).

12 "Solon ubo en tiempo de Creso y Cyn ansí mucho antes que este suceso"; "No va de Egypto"; "Este no es el Diluvio Universal" (BCC 23-7-2, 475).

13 In 2008, Spain's Biblioteca Nacional hosted an exhibition, then subsequently published a catalogue of images and articles that includes details on the teaching of Greek in Spanish universities as well as notice of Greek manuscripts and printed books held today in Spanish libraries (Biblioteca Nacional de España 2008). See also Di Camillo 1976, and Monfasani 1984, 101–8.

14 This manuscript is listed in Kristeller's *Supplementum Ficinianum* (1937).

15 See José Luis Gonzalo Sánchez-Molero 1998. For the Escorial's architecture in relation to hermetic works, ideas, and texts, see René Taylor 1992.

16 Quintanilla Raso notes the presence of Ficino in the library of one Bishop Juan Bernal Díaz de Luco, as studied by Tomás Marín. I have not been able to consult Marín's volume, which is held in one copy at the Universidad de Deusto, although María Isabel Hernández González's summary transcription of the list (1998, 422–3, no. 52) does not include Ficino's name. Hernández González, who reprints catalogue information from earlier studies of a number of personal libraries, also lists Plato without further specification for the following: a 1533 list of the Biblioteca del Cabildo de Salamanca (cat. no. 19, pp. 395–6); a 1550 list of the collection of Fernando de Aragón, Duke of Calabria (cat. no. 45, pp. 414–16); a 1552 inventory of the holdings of Alonso de Escobar of Seville (cat. no.47, pp. 417–18); and a 1558 list of the collection of Constantino Ponce de la Fuente (cat. no. 58, pp. 426–7).

17 Published in seven volumes, between 1963 and 1997, the *Iter italicum* is an essential reference for Renaissance scholars. Kristeller includes the referenced letter in volume 4, listing number 8624. Álvaro Gómez de Castro had ties to Fray Luis de León, whose work I have studied for its incorporation of Hermetic thought (Byrne 2007).

18 Bécares Botas has compared the list to the holdings in the library today, so as to deduce the probable editions referenced in the documentation (1998, 89). The lists are separated into "A" and "B" on the basis of the specific notarial documents: ordering, receipts, and signed deliveries.

19 "en 23 de febrero de 1631 [1621?] miré el libro del Baptismo y [h]allé que me baptizó el licenciado Núñez en cinco de nobe [noviembre] de 1609. Juan Pérez de Prado" (Salamanca, Biblioteca General Histórica, BG/ 17258). I have translated "licenciado" as "master" given that the act referred to is not that of an attorney, which would be a more common translation of the word.

20 "en beynte y nueve días del mes de setiembre año de 1551 día de sant miguel en la tarde a las quatro en punto estando presentes Pero de Mendoza y yo el señor y don Juan de Ribera, Gaspra de Sole, gosamos mucho" (Salamanca, Biblioteca General Histórica, BG/ 32463[2]). Gaspra is, in all likelihood, Gaspar, although the signature clearly reads 'pra.' Beltrán de Heredia lists course maticulations at the University of Salamanca for the relevant years, and two of the names are identifiable: "Don Juan de Ribera, bachiller artista" for the years 1551–2 and 1553–4; in 1554–5 and 1556–7, both "Don Juan de Ribera, bachiller artista, bachiller teólogo" and "Don Pedro Hurtado de Mendoza, canonista" are on the lists (1972, 35–6 and 40).

21 "y a mi dio vida" (Salamanca, Biblioteca General Histórica, BG/ 32463[2]).

22 "Fratris Baptiste, Mantuani Carmelite theologi dialogus de vita beata: Iam olim ab Authore editus nuper vero recognitus: & cum Augustini Dathi Senensis opusculo de re eadem: emendatissime impressus" (Salamanca, Biblioteca General Histórica, BG/ 53730[1]). My thanks to Isaías Lerner for his Spanish translation of this title, from which I offer the English above.

23 "Reverendi Fratris Baptistae Mantuani Carmelite de patientia aurei libri tres cum indicibus. Et vocabulorum difficiliorum explanatione ab Ascensio recens recognita" (Salamanca, Biblioteca General Histórica, BG/ 53730[1[).

24 See Hankins 1984, 4–5 for a discussion of the importance of the Church Fathers in the transmission of Platonic thought; Yates 1991 for the Hermetic tradition in Giordano Bruno; Quispel 1999 for Hermes in earlier philosophical thought, and in Ficino; Byrne 2007, 42–3 for Hermes and the Augustinians at the University of Salamanca in the sixteenth century.

25 I thank Brian Copenhaver for this information on the early seventeenth-century Catholic response to Casaubon's work.

26 Francisco Jiménez de Cisneros was Queen Isabel's confessor; he promoted the Complutense Polyglot Bible, was named Regent of Castile in 1504 and of Spain in 1516. In 1507 he was named cardinal and Grand Inquisitor of Spain. For his biography, see Rodríguez-Moñino Soriano 1978. An early work, more panegyric than biography, attests to the high regard in which Cisneros was held, with stories regarding his miracles and virtues; in one entry, witnesses testify to the cardinal's revelation from God predicting the Spanish victory at Oran (Quintanilla y Mendoza 1653, 225). Jiménez Moreno (1996) offers a collection of articles that provide historical, political, philosophical, scientific, and literary contextualization for the university's founding and its importance.

27 In 1998, UNESCO declared the university at Alcalá a World Heritage Site.

28 The Complutense BH has made many of its volumes available electronically. See their catalogue: http://cisne.sim.ucm.es/.

29 The full title reads: *Vita, Passio, Sepultvra Christi martyris Ariopagitae Dionysii sociorumque eius: Corporum eorundem Inuentio ac Translatio, per pium regem Dagobertum. Quibus iuncta est*

Dominicae precationis quaedam breuis explanatio, ad iuuenes Dionysiani monasterii Coenobitas, Ioanne Docaeo, eidem praefecto, authore (Complutense BH FLL 9218).

30 “Ficino no es autor del maior mérito: admitía los sueños dela astrología judiciaria, como todos los de su época: quería hacer christianos a Platón, Plotino y otros” (Complutense BH DER 1531 [1]).

31 “Soy de la Librería del Colegio de la Concepción de Alcalá” (Complutense BH MED 386).

32 I thank Mercedes of the Complutense BH, who helped in identifying this name.

33 “En la ciudad de Santiago a 9 de octubre de 1585 años yo el doctor Francisco Gómez Canónigo y Cathedrático de Theología en la sancta iglesia y universidad de la dicha ciudad ~~corregí est~~ comisario y qualificador del sancto oficio corregí este libro conforme al catálogo nuebo del año pasado de 84. y por verdad la firme D. gómez” (Complutense BH DER 972[2]). There is little information available on Francisco Gómez: one letter in a collection of diplomatic exchanges relates that Prince Carlos (firstborn son of King Phillip II) offered a letter of support for “Dr. Francisco Gómez, catedrático de prima de Teología y penitenciario de Santiago” in a dispute argued in the Papal Curia in Rome (Serrano 1914, 2:83–4, n.2). According to Iglesias Ortega, Francisco Gómez Cuesta was confessor (*penitenciario*) for two terms, from 1564 to 1573, and was then named canon/ theologian (*lectoral*) of Holy Scripture from 1573–97 (2010, 375, n. 1204).

34 See Kristeller 1956–96, 1:160.

35 The section of text reads: “Unde aperte patet, magicam hominibus arte divinitus esse concessam, ut aliquo modo fatum repellerent. Haec Porphyrius. Posse vero per magiam valetudinem animi corporisque curari, et immortalitatem denique comparari, in Charmide Plato significat, temperantia, praesertim per virtutem sapientiae comparata” (from Plotinus 1492, *Ennead* II, chapter 3.8).

36 “Tres-haute, tres-illustre, & tres-puissante Princesse, Marguerite de France, fille et soeur de des Rois tres-Chrestiens” (Complutense BH DER 1847).

37 *Le Pimandre de Mercure Trismegiste de la philosophie chrestienne, cognoissance du verbe diuin, & de l’excellence des oeuures de Dieu.*

2. Ficino as Authority in Sixteenth-Century Spanish Letters

1 In his introduction to Juan de Pineda’s work, Meseguer Fernández dates its composition between 1578 and 1580 (Pineda 1963, XXXVIII) on the basis of internal references, but the publication date is 1589. For this work, I cite volume and page number of the BAE edition or, in the case of Meseguer Fernández’s introduction, page number alone from volume 161.

2 “muchos autores ha auido graues y estimados que han querido mostrarlo, que pretendían de su dotrina por cartas, tratando diuersas materias tan artifiçiosa y

compendiosamente que no deleytan menos al que las lee que otro qualquiera género graçioso de escritura ... Entre los latinos: Séneca, Hierónimo, Çipriano, Agustino, Anbrosio, Símaco, Sidonio, Fran[cis]co Petrarca, Leonardo, Aretino, los dos Filelfos, Eneas Silvio, Fabelico, Angelo Poliçiano, Ermolao, Bárbaro, Marsilio Fiçino" (Torquemada 1970, 174). Torquemada's manuscript is dated by internal reference to 1552, and was first published in 1574 (12).

3 "Y Olimpiodoro cuenta vna historia de Aristóteles el qual dezía que auia visto vn hombre que con solo el ayre y el Sol se mantenía, como lo cuenta Marsilio Fiscino, en el argumento del *Phedro* de Platón" (Álvarez Miraval 1597, fol. 52v). There is scant biographical information on Álvarez Miraval, who was active from 1597 to 1601.

4 "Aunque es verdad que en quanto toca a la melancholía no conuienen los Astrólogos con los médicos, porque dizen que la Venus y Saturno son enemigos, y assí si procurassemos remediar a algún melanchólico con los actos venéreos, dizen que será en balde y que antes se offendería, porque son remedios muy distantes, y que mucho mejor se haría esto por ciertos remedios de Phaebo y Iúpiter que son medios entre Saturno y Venus como disertíssimamente lo nota Marsilio Ficino en el libro de vita longa, en el capítulo diez y seys" (Álvarez Miraval 1597, f. 109r).

5 "Una teología platónica trata Marsilio Ficino, diciendo que la poesía ni viene por arte ni por fortuna, sino por don de Dios y de las musas; y que aquel dios es Apolo y las musas las almas de las esferas del mundo" (Pineda 1963, 161:72).

6 "Para concluir con esta doctrina poética digo, con Macrobio, que cuando los poetas hablan de sus muchos dioses sacan sus fundamentos de los manantiales de la filosofía; mas que cuando se elevan a hablar del sumo dios, que llaman Tagatón o de la mente divina, ningún resabio fabuloso admiten, y todos los doctores cristianos entienden por aquella mente divina al Hijo de Dios" (Pineda 1963, 161:73).

7 Most commonly abbreviated as *De vita*, as it will be referenced here.

8 One of the *De vita* volumes is held by the BNE, among its ten incunabula related to Ficino; the others are held by various libraries.

9 "Novum studiosorum duces, Corporeum quidem spiritum cura; incorporeum vero cole, Magorum medicina pro senibus, De concordia mundi, De virtute verborum atque cantus ad beneficium coeleste captandum." The chapter titles are translations from the bilingual Latin-English Kaske and Clarke edition. In what follows, all quotes from *De vita* are taken from this edition, listed as Ficino 2002 in my bibliography. For the English translation, I cite book, chapter, and page number, and for the Latin, book, chapter, and lines; in both cases, the text is that of Kaske and Clarke's bilingual edition. The list of chapter headings is on pp. 92–9.

10 "Estas y otras virtudes de que en el siguiente capítulo diremos, la curiosidad de los hombres las ha conoscido y visto; y no se llaman secretas y ocultas porque no se tengan por ciertas, y las más dellas se han experimentado, sino porque no se sabe la causa de donde las vengan ... Hermes y otros muchos astrólogos, con los cuales se

conforma Marsilio Ficino, todo lo atribuyen a las estrellas e figuras celestiales; la cual es más común opinión y a ella seguiremos agora" (Mexía 2003, 1.39.507–8). Lerner notes that the reference is to Book 3, chapter 12 of Ficino's *De vita* (Lerner 2003, 507–8, n.34).

11 "La gente villana siempre tiene a la noble – por propiedad oculta – un odio natural, como el lagarto a la culebra, el cisne al águila, el gallo al francolín, el lagostín al pulpo, el delfín a la ballena, el aceite a la pez, la vid a la berza, y otros deste modo. Que si preguntáis deseando saber qué sea la causa natural, no se sabe otra más de que la piedra imán atrae a sí el acero, el heliotropio sigue al sol, el basilisco mata mirando, la celidonea favorece a la vista. Que así como unas cosas entre sí se aman, se aborrecen otras, por influjo celeste: que los hombres no han alcanzado hasta hoy razón que lo sea para ello" (Alemán 2000, 1:251).

12 "Eliano nombra muchas aves que con instincto natural saben haber mal de ojo, y que se proveen contra él poniendo en sus nidos algunos ramos de árboles ... aunque las águilas la piedra etites ponen ... Marsilio Ficino, como gran médico y filósofo, trata la materia por sus principios naturales" (Pineda 1963, 169:262). Pineda's editor identifies the reference as from "Aelianus, li. 1 *Histo. Animal.*, 36." Claudius Aelianus (175–235 AD) was the author of *De natura animalium*, but the reference is actually to chapter 35 of book 1, titled *De Fascinatione*, here in Conrad Gessner's sixteenth-century Latin translation: "Fascinantium et praestigiatorum oculos, etiam rationis expertes bestiae natura quadam arcana et mirabili cavent. Nam palumbi, ut audio, fascinationis amuletum laurinos ramulos tenues avellunt, deinde in nidos imponunt ... aquilae gentili suo lapide aetite" (Aelian 1744, 38).

13 In Ficino's Latin: "Lapis aetites vel aquilinus habet a Lucina, id est Venere atque Luna, ut admotus vulvae partum mox et facillime citet. Quod Rasis confirmante Serapione frequenter se dicit expertum" (2002, 3.12, ll. 57–9). In Pliny, the detail is found in book 10, chapter 3: "Eagles have in their nest a stone named aetites, which some call gagates; of extensive use as a medicine, and suffering no injury from fire. Now this stone is also pregnant; for if it is shaken, another is heard to rattle within, as if it were in its womb" (1847–9, 2:191).

14 "Sic instinctu coelesti divinitus instigante, serpentes quidem marathro, hirundines autem chelidonia oculis medicantur; aquilae vexatae partu aetitem lapidem divinitus invenerunt, quo feliciter ova statim eniterentur" (Ficino 2002, Apologia, ll. 48–50).

15 "Y quiérolo limar con lo de Marsilio diciendo que en los mancebos está la sangre tal que engendra spíritus subtiles y claros, dulces y calientes, mas llegándose a la vejez desvanécense consumidas las partes subtiles de la sangre ... Cual es la sangre tales spíritus envía, los cuales, dando en los ojos, salen por ellos con la virtud visiva, y emponzoñan a los que de cerca ven" (Pineda 1963, 169:263).

16 "Sanguis in adolescentia subtilis est, clarus, calidus atque dulcis. Procedente enim aetate subtilioribus partibus resolutis, sit crassior; propterea sit & obscurior" (Ficino 1576,

2:1357). The English translations of Ficino's *De amore* are from the first Sears Jayne edition, see Ficino 1944 in my bibliography. I cite book and chapter of that edition. Although Jayne updated his translation in 1985, I prefer the basic text of the earlier edition, although I do make minimal adjustments (indicated with brackets for insertions and parentheses for deletions). In notes, I include Ficino's Latin text from the Biblioteca Histórica Complutense online copy of the 1576 *Opera*, citing volume and page number.

17 "Mitto quam cito rubens oculus inficiat intuentem ... et familiae quaedam ... iratae intuitu homines interemisse feruntur, et feminae quaedam in Scythia idem facere consuevisse" (Ficino 2002, 3.16, ll. 58–62).

18 "Quemadmodum uero spirituum uapor huiusmodi creatur ex sanguine: ita & ipse similes sibi radios per oculos quasi uitreas fenestras emittit"; "Hinc uirulentus aculeus transuerberat oculos ... cor uulnerat" (Ficino 1576, 2:1357, 1358).

19 "Aspectus adolescentis fascinat seniorem. Quoniam uero senioris humor frigidus est atque tardissimus, uix dorsum cordis attingit in puero: & ineptus ad transitum, cor nisi propter infantiam sit mollissimum, parum admodum commouet" (Ficino 1576, 2:1358).

20 "En ver que tenéis culebrilla o dragón pintado se me caen las alas de águila, tan propias de mi arriscado ingenio, y me parece que, así como es propiedad del dragón subirse al encumbrado nido de la real águila, donde, con el veneno que allí pone, quitara la vida a sus polluelos, si el águila no se valiera de la preciosa piedra etites, llamada comúnmente piedra del águila, que es única para malos partos, para ser gratos y amorosos, y tiene otras excelentes propiedades" (López de Úbeda 1977, 1:122).

21 In Ficino's text, those prescriptions are found in Book 3, chapter 8, page 579. In Mexía: "Y Marsilio Ficino, en el libro que hizo *De triplici vita*, da grandes receptas y avisos para curar y conservar la memoria" (2003, 3.8, 579).

22 *Libro compuesto por el famoso y singular philosopho y gran médico Marcilio* [sic] *Ficino florentino* (see Ficino 1564).

23 The text is available on-line, through the Goldsmiths'-Kress Library of Economic Literature, but only with a participating library subscription (Gale document number U100020474). This electronic edition offers 196 page images: Curteti's translation of Ficino's work is contained at images 1–107, and the authors of the other tractates are "Dino del Garbo" (images 108–27), "maestro Velasco de Tarenta" (images 128–66), "Manardo doctísimo médico en sus epístolas" (images 167–90), and "Antíphona devotísima de beato Sebastiano martyre contra pestem" (images 190–1). Following are "Tablas" (Indices) of the chapters of each tractate (images 192–6).

24 This 1518 edition held by the Complutense BH does not follow the same chapter numbering as the Kaske and Clarke edition I use for comparison: this first notation is found in chapter 9 of Book 3 in that 1518 edition, which is chapter 10 in the Kaske and Clarke translation. The marked Latin text begins with: "Proinde

necessarium est meminisse Arietem praeesse capiti atque faciei" and continues through "Huius enim ordinis memor cavebis membrum" (Ficino 2002, 3.10, ll. 43–9) in Kaske and Clarke.

25 "glycyrrhiza et oleum rosaceum frigidiora calefacit, calidiora refrigerat" (Ficino 2002, 3.6, ll. 76); "pentaphyllon resistit venenis; eiusque folium bis quotidie unum vino bibitum curat ephimeram" (3.12, ll. 66–7); "Atque litterae hirci adipe inscriptae lapidi, prorsus occultae, si lapis submergatur aceto, prodeunt et quasi sculptae eminentes extant" (3.19, ll. 172–4); "Sicut enim virtus ac spiritus naturalis ubi potentissimus est, mollit statim liquefacitque alimenta durissima atque ex austeris mox dulcia reddit, generat quoque extra se seminalis spiritus productione propaginem, sic vitalis animalisque virtus ubi efficacissima fuerit, ibi intentissima quadam sui spiritus per cantum tum conceptione agitationeque in corpus proprium potenter agit, tum effusione movet subinde propinquum" (3.21, ll. 92–8).

26 "Surge post haec et tu, Guicciardine vehemens, atque curiosis ingeniis respondeto magiam vel imagines non probari quidem a Marsilio, sed narrari, Plotinum ipsum interpretante" (Ficino 2002, Apologia, ll. 55–7).

27 "dum Sol et Luna secundam Leonis faciem occuparent, eundemque gradum ibi tenerent, generabant avem merulae similem serpentina cauda, eamque redactam in cinerem infundebant lampadi, unde domus statim plena serpentibus videbatur" (Ficino 2002, Apologia, ll. 82–5).

28 "no es en la otra cosa la buena vida sino una muy fina triaca para curar su república" (Guevara 1994, 1.35); "triaca política, por contraveneno de prudencia" (Gracián 2001, 65v). See also Donald Beecher in Allen and Rees 2002a, 243–56.

29 "Agora digo que reñego de los consejos del conciliador de los amphorismos de Ypocras, de los fines de Avicenas, de los casos de Ficino, de los compuestos de Rasis y aun de los cánones de Erophilo" (Guevara 1950–2, 1.344).

30 "Sed antequam e lecto surgas, perfrica parumper suaviterque palmis corpus totum primo, deinde caput unguibus, sed id paulo levius. Hac in re te Hippocrates admoneat. Nam frictione, inquit, si vehemens sit, durari corpus; si levis, molliri; si multa, minui; si modica, impleri... eburneo pectine diligenter et moderate pectes... tum cervicem panno asperiori perfrica" (Ficino 2002, 1.8, ll. 3–13).

31 "por no ser muy honesto a las personas, a causa que no se pueden estregar a solas, sino en baño desnudos, lo que a mugeres, viejos y religiosos sería indecente" (Gómez Miedes 1589, f. 83r).

32 "De todo lo que auemos dicho nos enseñó la razón natural aquel grande Philosopho Marsilio Fiscino en el libro tercero que escriuió de Triplici vita, en el capítulo veinte y tres, adonde dize estas palabras, acuérdate de trauar amistad con aquellos que tengan gracias del cielo: lo qual podrás conocer de los bienes del ánimo de la fortuna y del cuerpo: porque de la manera que echa y ex[h]ala de sí fragrancia y olor

el ámbar, y almizcle, assí ni más ni menos del bueno se le pega algo de bien al que lo comunica" (1597, fol. 137r). Álvarez Miraval spells Ficino's name as Fiscino, as do certain other Spanish authors of his day. I translate with spelling "Ficino" but leave the original phrasing in each Spanish-language text in my notes.

33 In Ficino's text, the passage reads: "Memento rursus familiaritatem eorum inire, quibus Gratiae coelestes afflant. Quod ex bonis animi, corporis, fortunae perpendes; sicut enim odor ex musco, sic ex bono nonnihil exhalat in proximum, ac saepe perseverat infusum" (Ficino 2002, 3.23, ll. 96–9).

34 "dize Marsilio Fiscino que la naturaleza nuestra madre juntó con tal consonancia y harmonia el cuerpo y el alma, que los mouimientos del cuerpo penetran con gran facilidad y, con grandíssima vehemencia al alma, y los de el alma al mismo cuerpo" (Álvarez Miraval 1597, fol. 144r).

35 "Igitur anima neque est corpus, sed copula corporis intima vel substantia copulatrix"; "forma quaedam substantialis, simplex, indivisibilis, quae virtute et arte naturali spiritus, humores membraque temperat" (Ficino 2001–6, 6.8.3; 6.9.3).

36 "Agitat corpus in omnem partem"; "Anima nulli qualitati, nulli proprio motui est astricta"; "Sunt autem hi motus ipsius animi ... Unde sequitur naturam corporis animae motibus penitus subiici"; "Certerum de nostris motibus hoc est diligenter animadvertendum, quod aliqui incipientes a corpore non penetrant ad animam, alii penetrant"; "Ex quibus apparet non per corporalem naturam, sed per animae ipsius iudicium passiones corporis posse in animam penetrare" (Ficino 2001–6, 6.12.3; 7.7.2; 13.1.3; 13.1.5; 13.1.7).

37 "notó agudamente Marsilio Fiscino, en el libro primero de las epístolas a Caluisiano, dando en esto a entender que la música tiene alguna virtud occulta o alguna efficacia grande para remediarnos de argunas [*sic*] enfermedades" (1597, fol. 162r). The reference is, in all likelihood, to Letter 1:92, Ficino to Antonio Canigiani, *On Music*. See Ficino, *Letters*, 1:143–4, and also Lackner (2002, 30, n.48).

38 "Dizen también que a la prudencia la perficiona [*sic*] el tiempo y la larga experiencia juntamente con la obseruación de los humanos acaezimientos como lo escriue Marsilio Fiscino" (Álvarez Miraval 1597, f. 244v).

39 "Otros dixeron auer muchos mundos: lo qual reprouaron Platón, Marsilio Ficino, Aristóteles, y Pomponio Mela, y prouaron ser solo vno" (Huerta 1624, 1:f. 3r). I cite from a two-volume edition printed in 1624 (volume I) and 1629 (volume 2). Volume 1 has folio numbers for the preliminaries, then page numbers for the text.

40 "Pero dexando tanta diuersidad de opiniones, la más verdadera es, auer tenido principio desde Adán, como lo traen Marsilio, y Orígenes Adamantino" (1624, 1:315).

41 "Magica haec opinio videtur cum illa hebreorum christianorumque sententia consentire: Adae primi parentis animo prius quidem sano sana fuisse omnia" (1495, CVIr). All twelve books of Ficino's letters were first published in print in 1495, although they also circulated in manuscript prior to that. For the *Letters*, I cite volume and

page number of the English translation by members of the Language Department of the School of Economic Science, London, currently comprising nine of the twelve books. For the Latin text, which I include in notes, I use the 1495 edition with reference to folio number.

42 I cite from a 1595 copy made available electronically by the Biblioteca Nacional de España, their catalogue number U/4597, under name with Portuguese spelling Heitor Pinto.

43 "auctoridades de las diuinas letras, y de muy aprouados, y excellentes auctores" (Pinto 1595, Prologue, no pag.).

44 "A estas figuras traçadas en el concepto, llama Ideas aquel insigne Platón ... El qual no solamente en la philosophía, mas aún en la eloquencia eclypsó la memoria de los antepassados y enseñó a los hombres a huyr de la sensualidad, en tanto que le hizieron los gentiles vn epitaphio que dezía que el Dios Apollo tuuiera dos hijos Sculapio y Platón, Sculapio para curar los cuerpos, y Platón las almas (como refiere en su vida Marsilio Fiscino)" (Pinto 1595, f. 47r).

45 "Galienus quidem corporum, Plato vero medicus animorum" (Ficino 2002, Proem, l. 21); "Extat apud Graecos uerissimum de Platone dictum, Phoebum uidelicet duos praecipue filios fenuisse, Aesculapium, & Platonem. Aesculapium quidem qui corporibus, Platonem uero qui animis mederetur" (Ficino 1576, 2:1296).

46 "y no os parezca que no ay Ideas, porque sin dubda las ay, y san Augustín enel libro de las.lxxxiii questiones, donde trata copiosamete esta materia, dize que las ay, y que tienen tanta fuerça que ninguno será sabio sino las entendiere" (Pinto 1595, f. 47r).

47 "Proderit ergo quandoque vis Saturni caute sumpta ... immo et quae stupefaciunt, sicut opium et mandragora" (Ficino 2002, 3.2, ll. 60–2).

48 The manifest itself indicates price and number of items for each volume. At first glance, it reads as if 34 copies of each volume had been sent: ("330. Marçilio Fisino [*sic*], De triplici vita, Vn rreal 034"), but those numbers are questionable. I thank Valery Rees for having tempered my enthusiasm with this find by pointing out that in 1475, 1 silver real was fixed at a value of 34 maravedis, with maravedis still in use as the currency of accounting, though not of pricing and exchange. This makes the indication of number (034) much more likely to reflect one copy of each volume shipped.

49 "Esto era sin duda lo que acreditaba los vaticinios de Apolonio Thyaneo, como lo reconoció Hiarchas cuando le dijo: 'Nadie debe admirarse, oh Apolonio, de que tú hayas alcanzado la ciencia de adivinar, puesto que llevas tanto éter en tu alma,' según refiere Marsilio Ficino, *De Triplici Vita*" (Sigüenza y Góngora 1959, 171). I have used Kaske and Clarke's English for the translation of the inserted Ficino quotation ("No one ...") in Sigüenza y Góngora's Spanish text.

50 In Ficino's Latin: "Quem plurimum hausisse Apollonium Theaneum testificatus est Indus Hiarchas, dicens: 'Mirari nemo debet, O Apolloni, te divinandi scientiam consecutum, cum tantum aetheris in anima geras'" (Ficino 2002, 3.3, ll. 39–42).

51 "Y éste es también el primer principio que puede falsificar la pronosticación astrológica, pues, aunque estuviese perfectísima esta que llaman ciencia, faltando la disposición orgánica a la fantasía, sería el vaticinio frustráneo" (Sigüenza y Góngora 1959, 171).

52 "El alma apta para el conocimiento alcanza más de verdad que aquella que se haya ejercitado en la ciencia en el más alto grado" (Sigüenza y Góngora 1959, 171). For this last, Siguënza y Góngora notes that he is quoting from Ptolemy.

53 "17. Los que quieren hacer valer en el mundo la ciencia de los influjos de los Astros, ostentan un especial género de Secretos en la mysteriosa mixtura de las cosas elementales con las Celestes: Supersticiosa producción de la doctrina Platónica, que ha hecho delirar a hombres, por otra parte mui capaces. A esto pertenecen los sellos planetarios, la fábrica de algunos artificios debaxo de determinados aspectos, las imágenes de las constelaciones estampadas en piedras, metales y otras materias de que escribió muchos sueños Marsilio Ficino en su libro *de Vita caelitus comparanda*, siguiendo a Pselo, Jámblico y otros Pytagóricos" (Feijoo 1765, 30, 2.5.17).

54 Maxwell-Stuart (2000) offers a partial translation of Del Río's *Disquisiciones mágicas* that includes various references to Ficino, but the passages with the Italian philosopher's name are summarized rather than translated, and so I do not include them here. Jesús Moya (1991) has translated book 2 of Del Río's Latin treatise into Spanish.

55 Lerner notes the place reference in Ficino's work as 3.18. The phrasing is the same in Ficino's Latin: "Primo vero superficies cruce describitur, sic enim imprimis habet longitudinem atque latitudinem" (2002, 3.18, ll. 19–21).

56 "and so the Egyptians held this figure and symbol of the cross in such high regard, as I said, that they put it on the breast of their god. And we can read into that, that they understood and so signified hope for the health that was to come. Others say it signifies life to come, and all this seems to be prophecy and an announcing of the universal health that came to us through the cross. Rufino in *Ecclesiastic History* book XI, makes note of this, and Pedro Crinito in book VII of his *On Honest Discipline*" (Mexía 2003, 1.3, 57–9). Lerner notes that the source is Crinito, and that Rufino's *Historia Ecclesiástica* does not mention the Egyptian priests' opinions in book 11 but, rather, in 2.26, referring the reader to Rufino's *Opera omnia* in Migne, vol 21, 538a.

57 "Esta misma fe tubieron ciertos médicos árabes, como nota Marsilio Ficino" (Jiménez Patón 1965, 63). In *De vita*, Ficino references ancient Arab authorities confirmed by Egyptians: "Antiquiores autem, quemadmodum in quodam Arabum collegio legimus ... Haec autem opinio ab Aegyptiis vel inducta est vel maxime confirmata, inter quorum characteres crux unus erat insignis, vitam eorum more futuram significans, eamque figuram pectori Serapidis insculpebant" (2002, 3.18, ll. 17–32).

58 "Si de Patón a Platón/una letra menos hubo/fue por misterio que tuvo/tarde su declaración,/porque enseñando Patón/como Platón elocuencia,/es con esta

diferencia/merced de influjos más buenos,/que nos ha dado con menos/lo más de toda la ciencia" (Martin 1987, 314, vv. 1–10).

59 "*El español melancólico* llegó a ser en la época de Cervantes y Shakespeare tan tópico como lo fue el *splenetic englishman*" (Egido 1994, 93).

60 "Excute caeruleum, proles Saturnia, tergum,/verbera quadrigae sentiat alma Tethys /... Hesperiis Michaël claros conduxit ab oria/in pelagus vates. Delphica castra petit" (Cervantes 1991, 57, vv. 1–2; 9–10). For Cervantes' debt to earlier literary models in the *Viaje*, see Sevilla Arroyo and Rey Hazas 1997, XV–XIX.

61 Blecua (2006, 155–74) surveys the importance of Virgil in sixteenth- and seventeenth-century Spain, but does not reference Cervantes' *Viaje del Parnaso.*

62 "Quicunque iter illud asperum arduumque et longum ingrediuntur, quod quidem vix tandem ad excelsum novem Musarum templum assiduo labore perducit, novem omnino itineris huius ducibus indigere videntur ... Principio in coelo Mercurius, ut investigando Musarum iter aggrediamur, vel impellit vel adhortatur, siquidem Mercurio tributum est investigationis omnis officium" (Ficino 2002, 1.1, ll. 1–7).

63 "Quorum primi quidem tres in coelo ... Mercurius ... Phoebus ... Venus ... Sequuntur tres itineris huius duces in animo: videlicet voluntas ardens et stabilis, acumen ingenii, memoria tenax. Tres in terra postremi sunt: prudentissimus paterfamilias, probatissimus praeceptor, medicus peritissimus" (Ficino 2002, 1.1, ll. 3–16).

64 "Congruit insuper cum Mercurio atque Saturno, quorum alter, altissimus omnium planetarum, investigantem evehit ad altissima ... praesertim cum animus ... divinus influxibus oraculisque ex alto repletus, nova quaedam inusitataque semper excogitat et futura praedicit" (Ficino 2002, 1.6, ll. 22–8).

65 "Marsilius Ficinus dilectissimis in veritatis venatione fratribus ... Apte quidem philosophantes appellavimus venatores, anhela semper veritatis indagine laborantes. Num etiam apte canes? Aptissime inquit in *Republica* Socrates: philosophantes enim vel legitimi sunt vel spurii; ambo canes" (Ficino 2002, Quod necessaria, ll. 1–7).

66 "sagaces academiae canes; inter lupos (ut vereor) e vestigio prodituros; Tantum profecto canes inter philosophos sibi vendicant, ut non solum se ipsos in sectam aliquam inseruerint, sed etiam sectam ipsi suam nomine Cynicam quandoque confecerint" (Ficino 2002, Quod necessaria, ll. 12–13, 14–15, 9–11).

67 Purnell offers Mazzoni's Latin in a note: "At sicuti venatoribus ferunt magnas canes ... ut iam illius penitissima mysteria, quasi intima quaedam viscera diligenter intuentibus appareant" (Purnell 1971, 88, n.134).

68 "¿Al murmurar llamas filosofar? ... ella dará a nosotros el [nombre] de cínicos, que quiere decir perros murmuradores" (Cervantes 1997a, 2:319). For Cervantes' views and expression on the cynics, see Riley 1976.

69 "A Esculapio, el dios de la medicina, cabras se le ofrecían, porque la cabra siempre dicen los naturales que tiene fiebre, que llamamos calentura. Sacrificábanle también los gallos, por la vigilancia que debe tener el médico... Esto se refiere por Platón en

el libro 29, diálogo *De animae inmortalitate*, al fin de aquel diálogo, y según se expone por Marsilio en su argumento, entendía Sócrates lo de gallo en el sentido alegórico, porque el gallo es mensajero del día y del sol, conviene a saber, de la divina beneficencia que cura todas las enfermedades, que se dice ser hija de la divina providencia, y el día, conviene a saber, la lumbre del ánima confiesa deberle Sócrates" (Casas 1992, 2:1001).

70 "Prisci Aesculapio medico Phoebi filio gallum sacrificabant diei solisque unicum, id est diuinae beneficentiae morborum omnium curatrici, quae diuinae prouidentiae filia nominatur, diem, id est uitae lumen debere se fatebantur" (Ficino 1576, 2:1395).

71 "Atque hanc fere causam esse, cur gallum Aesculapio sacrificari iusserit, Platonici reddunt" (Fox Morcillo 1556a, 159).

72 "Gravemente dijo Marsilio Ficino, escribiendo sobre Platón, que es parte de impiedad tener familiaridad y comunicación con los que por sus maldades están excomulgados y apartados de los divinos Oficios; porque, estando ellos inficionados, no pueden dejar de inficionar a los que llegan a ellos" (Ribadeneira 1788, 146). Ribadeneira's text was first published in 1595.

73 *Tratado de la religión y virtudes que debe tener el príncipe cristiano para gobernar sus estados, Contra lo que Nicolás Machiavelo, y los Políticos de este tiempo enseñan.* For a full contextualization of philosophical-political treatises such as Ribadeneira's in the early modern Spanish world, see Santos Herrán and Santos López 2008, VII–XLV.

74 "como él era hombre impío, y sin Dios, así su doctrina (como agua derivada de fuente inficionada) es turbia y ponzoñosa, y propia para atosigar a los que bebieren de ella" (Ribadeneira 1788, 1).

75 "Se dize que los griegos los nombran quasi deimones que es enseñados y sabidores de las cosas. Assí que en griego demon es mucho sabio escríuese por ae" (Palencia 1967).

76 "En rigor este vocablo, si[g]nifica espíritu, o ángel, indiferentemente bueno, o malo. Y Platón llama al Dios Gouernador del vniuerso ... magnum daemona; pero en las sagradas letras siempre se toma demonio por el espíritu malo, o por el diablo calumniador, que todo es vno" (Covarrubias 1994). For the development of Christian thought on daemon versus demon, see Rees 2013b, 81–92.

77 "qui genii nominantur, ingenii duces assidui, qui non vi, sed persuadendo ducant. Sunt et mali ... sed adversarii" (Ficino 2001–6, 18.10.3).

78 "Aerei ergo restant daemones medij per media duces, qui rationis diuinae comites humanam rationem in hoc itinere ducunt" (Ficino 1576, 2:1437).

79 "Marsilio Ficino dice haber sido doctrina de astrólogos y de los filósofos platónicos, que cada hombre puede tener dos Ángeles de guarda: el uno para su nascimiento y generación y el otro para sus costumbres; y aquel de la generacón debe ser el genio (hablando al proprio) que dirían los gentiles darse a cada uno cuando era engendrado, y aún el socrático Euricles y no Euclides (como algunos yerran) dijo que se daban dos

genios, uno bueno y otro malo, y lo mesmo concedieron Empédocles y Menandro; y lo mesmo dicen Censorino y Servio haber sentido Lucilio" (Pineda 1963, 163.20).

80 "Angelus enim quem bonum demonem geniumque nominant, aut semper est vbique quod plotinus porphyrius Iamblichus opinantur" (Ficino 1495, f. CXCVv).

81 As noted above, Psellus's work on daemons was on the Indices of prohibited books, and certain, but not all, volumes with translations of Psellus by Ficino held in Spanish libraries show evidence of that censorship, carried out to a greater or lesser extent with pages ripped out of composite volumes, or a simple "condemned author" (author damnatus) penned next to Psellus's name.

82 "Michaelis pselli de daemonibus legere breuiter a me traductum. Qui platonicos christianis in daemonum opinione conciliat"; "a daemonibus somnia mitti veteres arbitrantur" (Ficino 1495, ff. CXCVIIv; CXCIXr).

83 "Si quaeras qualis Socratis daemon fuerit, respondebitur igneus, quoniam ad contemplationem sublimium erigebat. Item Saturnius, quoniam intentionem mentis quotidie mirum in modum abstrahebat a corpore... Quia sublimis daemon Socratem quasi Dei interpres nunciusque afflabat. Sed nunquid ipsum Socratis intellectum possumus daemonem nuncupare? Possumus certe. Nam Timaeus inquit, Deum nobis supremam animi partem tanquam daemonem tribuisse. Rursus in Symposio ipse mentis amor ad diuinam pulchritudinem contemplandam, daemon cognominatur" (Ficino 1576, 2:1387–8).

84 "El curso acostumbrado del ingenio,/ aunque le falte el genio que lo mueva,/ con la fuga que lleva, corre un poco" (Garcilaso 1966, Égloga II, vv. 948–50); "*ingenio.* [v. 948] Es aquella fuerça i potencia natural i aprehensión fácil i nativa en nosotros"; "*genio.* [v. 949] Es una virtud específica o propiedad particular de cada uno que vive. No erraría mucho quien pensasse que el *entendimiento agente* de Aristóteles es el mismo que el *genio* platónico" (Herrera 2001, 860–1). Bienvenido Morros Mestres notes that Herrera's glosses on philosophical matters are frequently taken from Cicero's synopses, but that his commentary on three types of beauty is taken from Lorenzo de' Medici's *Comento ad alcuni sonetti d'amore* (Morros Mestres 1998, 26–7). Ficino, of course, was Lorenzo's tutor. Morros Mestres also carefully identifies and collates passages in Herrera's commentaries taken from Italian Lilio Gregorio Giraldo [Giraldi] (1479–1552), another Florentine writer who himself references Ficino on the plague (Giraldi 1819, 138).

85 "Es genio ... aquella inclinación que nos guía más a unas cosas que a otras, y así defraudar el genio es negar a la naturaleza lo que apetece" (Lope de Vega 2002, 235).

86 "Púsole la Antigüedad en la frente, porque en ella se conoce si hacemos alguna cosa con voluntad o sin ella" (Lope de Vega 2002, 235).

87 "que Lucano, en su *Farsalia*, fue historiador y Platón, en sus *Diálogos*, poeta" (López Pinciano 1998, 1:83).

88 "La verdad desta cuestión/ quede a la mosquetería,/ que tal hay que en él se cría/ el ingenio de un Platón" (1997b, III, vv. 2219–22). Jean Canavaggio (1958) and Sanford

Shepard (1962) have studied the resonance of López Pinciano's writings on those of Miguel de Cervantes. I have translated "criar," which today means literally, "to raise [rear]" with "create," as the latter is more appropriate in the context. In his 1495 dictionary, Nebrija offers "to make anew" (*hazer de nuevo*) for "to create" (*criar*), and then a second meaning of "to educate, to nourish, to nurse" (*educo.as, nutrio.is, alo. is*) for the dictionary entry "to raise a child" (*criar niño*). In 1611, Covarrubias also notes both meanings, specifying for the first that "si esta palabra se toma en rigor según los Doctores Escolásticos, *creare est aliquid de nihilo producere in effectu.* Esto es solo de Dios preseruado a su omnipotencia." A separate dictionary entry for "crear" as "to create," and as distinguishable from "criar" (to rear) first appears in the Real Academia dictionaries in 1729.

89 "Si intellectus & vera opinio duo genera sunt, necesse est huiusmodi species esse, quem per se ipsae sint, & intelligentia potius quam sensibus compraehendantur" (Plato *Timaeus* in Ficino trans., Ficino 1557, 484).

90 "Ut enim dictum est, omnis anima hominis ea que vere sunt intuita est, alioquin in hoc animal non venisset. Recordari vero ex his que hic sunt illorum non facile est omnibus ... sed per obscura quedam instrumenta vix et perpauci in eorum imagines accedentes eius quod assimilatur genus aspiciunt" (Plato 2008, 1.xxvii).

91 "ab hac ad rationem, quae super locum totum tempusque existat, quam Plato vocat ideam"; Una igitur essentia dei, una est idea idearum omnium vicem gerens, perque hanc unicam deus cuncta circumspicit" (Ficino 2001–6, 8.1.6; 16.1.12). For Ficino's debt to Proclus, Aristotle, Moerbeke, and Thomas Aquinas, in addition to the Neoplatonists, in his writings on the Ideas, see Steel 2013.

92 "boni quidem, id est, sui ipsius, bonorum quoque quae ab ipsa proficiscuntur" (Ficino 1576, 2:1442).

93 "Deus per unam ipsius esse vel boni ideam, quae ipsa dei natura est, intellegit omnia. Primus angelus, exempli causa, duas forte habeat ideas, alteram substantiae, alteram accidentis" (Ficino 2001–6, 16.1.14). For a full study of the cultural history of angels, including some Ficino references, see Rees 2013b.

94 "Cogitemus hominis animam nunc primum ex deo manantem neque dum corpus indutam... Tot ideas quot sunt rerum species creatarum, unam speciei cuiusque ideam" (Ficino 2001–6, 16.1.16).

95 "divinus ille radius idearum plenissimus, postquam ad animam usque descendit, transit per vitalem animae vim perque naturam in mundi materiam, in qua fingit extremas quasdam atque umbratiles similitudines idearum, quemadmodum lumen fingit imagines colorum in speculo, immo quemadmodum per lumen umbrae corporum designantur in terra" (Ficino 2001–6, 16.3.1). See also *Platonic Theology* 2001–6, 11.4–5, where Ficino explains the concept of the Ideas at length.

96 In an earlier article, I showed how sixteenth-century Spanish poets Francisco de Aldana and San Juan de la Cruz explore this last concept, also found in the *Pimander* (Byrne 2005).

97 "y, en fin, de sólo vos formó natura/ una estraña y no vista al mundo Idea,/ y hizo igual al pensamiento el arte" (Garcilaso 1966, Sonnet XXI, vv. 12–14).

98 "Idea es la forma, figura i representación primera de las cosas, que es parecer de todo lo semejante. Dizen los platónicos que consiste en la mente; i llaman Idea la forma ejemplar i inteligible. Porque Platón puso unas universales especies de todas las cosas singulares, que llamó Ideas" (Herrera 2001, 412–13).

99 "Sunt namque Ideae principales formae quaedam, vel rationes rerum stabiles atque incommutabiles, quae ipsae formatae non sunt; ac per hoc aeternae ac semper eodem modo sese habentes, quae in divina intelligentia continentur" (Herrera 2001, 413). Editors Inoria Pepe and José María Reyes note that Herrera quotes from Augustine's *De diversis quaestionibus octoginta tribus* (Herrera 2001, 413, n.5).

100 "Proinde ipsa idea boni: ideas, id est, speciales omnium formas, specie duntaxat inter se distinctas, in natura intelligibili generat ... In hanc naturam intelligibilem omnes suspiciunt intellectus, ab eaque suscipiunt stabiles formulas idearum" (Ficino 1576, 2:1428).

101 "llaman mente y armario de las ideas por lenguaje de apropriación; porque como sea engendrado por el divino entendimiento, que es el subjecto de la sabiduría, y las ideas son las razones primordiales a que mira Dios para entender y criar las cosas" (Pineda 1963, 169:150). As above, and for the same reasons, I translate "criar" as "to create."

102 "El famosísimo Trismegisto ... dice que idea se dice de Idin, que quiere decir ver, porque son formas spirituales invisibles; y en tal caso, por contrario sentido, le sería puesto el nombre; lo cual no me satisface" (Pineda 1963, 161:111).

103 "se le denomina en griego *Haides*, de *ideîn* 'ver,' pues el fondo de la esfera es invisible – también se denomina 'ideas' a las formas, en la medida en que son visibles" (Renau Nebot 1999, 449).

104 "Porque dios, que todo lo puede, parece que pinta en sí las ideas o ejemplares de todas las cosas ... y estas especies de todas las cosas concebidas en la superna mente, llama Platón Ideas" (Malón de Chaide 1959, 3:87).

105 "A estas figuras trazadas en el concepto, llama Ideas aquel insigne Platón" (Pinto 1595, 3.4, 47).

106 "ideas in se concipiens duplici quodam supernae lucis, ideaeque unius diuinae fomento" (Ficino 1576, 2:1442).

107 "pues toda criatura está en potencia/ obedencial al Criador supremo,/ empero Dios, que tiene al mismo mundo/ hecho en sí mismo, el mismo Dios no hecho,/ cuando lo fabricó, cuando lo puso/ fuera de sí quedando en sí la idea,/ con tanta perfición le dio remate/ que el mundo el mismo es ora que era entonces" (Aldana 1985, L, vv. 454–61). I cite from Lara Garrido's edition of Aldana's works, and use the editor's name for references to notes or introduction.

108 On free will versus fate in letters in general see, for example, Patch (1927), Magris (2008) and Wallace (2011). For the Molina-Bañez debates, see Freddoso 1988.

109 "Y Marsilio Ficino, en los comentarios sobre el diálogo sexto De legibus, dize: «Una cosa havemos de tener en nuestro entendimiento: que toda la fuerça y movimiento de los cuerpos superiores que desciende en nosotros siempre por su naturaleza es causa de nuestro bien y nos guía para ello; y assí, no havemos de juzgar que procede de Saturno la tristeza y escaseza de los hombres mal acondicionados, y la ferocidad y temeridad de Mars, ni los engaños y malicias de Mercurio, ni los la[s]civos amores de Venus ... aquellos que están debaxo de la buena obra que suelen recebir de los rayos del sol, por su culpa, no sabiendo aprovecharse dél, les resulta en perjuyzio, assí a aquellos que están debaxo de la fuerça de las estrellas, que por su naturaleza son buenas, les puede acaescer muchas vezes que por la costumbre de sus vicios les succede el mal, porque la inclinación dellas les succedería al contrario». Y conforme a estas palabras y auctoridad de Marsilio, los astrólogos mathemáticos y médicos no parece que tienen bien fundada su intención, y que la opinión suya, aunque se tiene por común, no tiene tanto fundamento ni tantas fuerças que con razones muy evidentes no pueda ser reprobada" (Torquemada 1994, 781–2). The referenced section in Ficino's Latin reads: "Memento uero uim omnem atque motum a superioribus in nos descendentem, semper ad bonum suapte natura conducere, quandoquidem & coelestes influxus, semper ad bonum. Sed neque tu hic uel rigidiorum hominum tristitiam & parsimoniam rejicias in Saturnum: uel temeritatem ferocitatemque in Martem: uel fraudulentiam malitiamque in Mercurium, uel lasciuos amores in Venerem ... Nonne sub solis radijs, qui natura sua ad uidendum conferunt & uiuendum, quotidie accidit alios uisum, alios uitam amittere: & qui in aere libero salubriter calefaciunt, in concauis urunt? Quemadmodum uero sub benefico radiorum influxu ob inferiorem naturam resultat alicui malum, non uniuerso: sic sub stellarum uiribus natura bonis, atque sub numinum muneribus optimis, potest interdum inferioris uel naturae uel consuetudinis uitio, uitium uel corporis uel animi suboriri" (Ficino 1576, 2:1503).

110 "así a ti, medio mío, darles conviene/ contra los siete espíritus malinos/ siete de nuestro amor sagrados dones,/ y luz por doce santos tus varones.// Para lo cual, teniendo justa cuenta/ con el libre poder del albedrío,/ y estando el merecer do se aposenta/ el asentir o el dar de sí desvío," (Aldana 1985, XLIII, vv. 869–76).

111 "sapientem astris vel minantibus repugnare vel pollicentibus posse favere" (Ficino 2001–6, 9.4.14).

112 "Solus deus ita per se existit, ut per nullam sit causam" (Ficino 2001–6, 5.5.1). "La Causa universal, sola y primera,/ de cuanto vive, entiende, es, crece y siente" (Aldana 1985, XLIII, vv. 753–4).

113 "Primo quidem, quia ubicunque fingit aliquid, solet fabulam nominare. Hic uero tanquam historiam audet asseuerare. Deinde idem omnino afferit in Timaeo, appellans rem miram quidem, sed omnino ueram" (Ficino 1576, 2:1485).

114 "No osara referir por historia sino por fábula las maravillas que Platón de aquella isla dice, si no hallara confirmarlo Marsilio Ficino en su compendio sobre el *Timeo* de

Platón, y en el argumento que hace sobre otro siguiente dialogo al *Timeo* que Platón hizo, a quien puso nombre *Cricia*[s] o *Atlántico*, donde tracta de la antigüedad del mundo; el cual – conviene a saber, Marsilio – afirma no ser fábula sino historia verdadera; y pruébalo por sentencia de munchos [*sic*] estudiosos de la obras de Platón" (Casas 1986, 1:50).

115 "De lo dicho se ve claro que en tiempo de Platón – que fue cuatrocientos y veinte y tres años antes del advenimiento de nuestro redentor y salvador Jesucristo, y así ha pocos menos de dos mil años, como parece por el dicho Marsilio en el principio de las obras de Platón – el mar Océano, desde el estrecho de Gibraltar o cuasi a la boca dél, de donde comenzaba la dicha isla, no se podía navegar por estar todo anegado de la manera que agora hallamos algunas islas o tierras anegadas en estas Indias" (Casas 1986, 1:51).

116 "Esta historia dicen todos los que escriben sobre Platón que fue cierta y verdadera, en tal manera, que los más dellos, especialmente Marsilio Ficino y Platina, no quieren admitir que tenga sentido alegórico, aunque algunos se lo dan, como lo refiere el mismo Marsilio en las *Annotaciones sobre el Thimeo*"; "Pues supuesto ser esta historia verdadera, ¿quién podrá negar que esta isla Atlántica comenzaba desde el estrecho de Gibraltar, o poco después de pasado Cádiz, y llegaba y se extendía por este gran golfo, donde así norte, sur, como este, oeste, tiene espacio para poder ser mayor que Asia y Africa?" (Cervantes de Salazar 1772, no pag.). I cite from the Cervantes Virtual online version of the Magallón edition, which is without pagination. The *Crónica* was first printed in 1567. In his *Timaeus* commentary, Ficino does note that some call the story an allegory, but adds that they are refuted: "Quidam uero contra, tanquam solam allegoriam. Sed hos redarguunt probatissimi quique Platonicorum affirmantes quidem historiam, quia Plato dixerit" (1576, 2:1439).

117 "historia maravillosa y llena de verdad"; "el divino Platón" (Sarmiento de Gamboa 1943, 25). In his introduction to the 1942 Buenos Aires edition, Rosenblat notes that the work was finished in 1572 (Sarmiento de Gamboa 1943, 15).

118 "3. Supuesto lo qual, y que para el uso, y freqüencia de estos comercios es forzoso que los que tratan de ellos dexen sus casas, y tierras, y con sus personas, haciendas, y mercaderías caminen, y traginen por las agenas, porque en esto consiste el oficio de los mercaderes, segun la difinición de Marsilio Ficino" (Solórzano Pereira, 1:116).

119 Ficino discusses merchants and their travels in a treatise written to Cherubino Quarquagli ("De officiis") (Ficino 1576, 1:744–5) that Figliucci includes in his first volume of the Italian translation of Ficino's letters but without book designation (Ficino 1563, ff. 219v–21v). Given the textual reference to book 2, Solórzano Peirera apparently refers to the Latin *Epistolae.*

120 "En la razón que puede haber de congruencia para que de los descendientes de Naphthuim no se sepa, consiste la prueba más eficaz de que éste sea el progenitor de los indios, y para ello presupongo ahora, por cierta, la opinión de Gómara, I part.,

Hist. Ind., fol. 120; y de Agustín de Zárate en el Proemio a la del Perú, de fray Gregorio García, lib, 4, cap. 8, del Origen de los Indios; y es que éstos vinieron de la Isla Atlántica a poblar este Mundo Occidental. Y antes de proseguir, quisiera se atendiese no sólo a las razones y autoridades de dicho fray Gregorio García, cap. 9, parágr. 3, *y de Marsilio Ficino, al principiar el argumento al Diálogo Cricias*, o Atlántico, de Platón, sino a las del erudito padre Athanasio Kirchero, lib. 2, Mundi Subterranei, cap. 12, parágr. 3, con que comprueban invictamente ser historia verdadera la que de esta isla refiere Platón en aquel diálogo en el cual se refiere su destrucción y acabamiento con un terremoto formidable que la anegó" (Sigüenza y Góngora 2005, 18–19, my emphasis).

121 "Profecto si beata respublica proprio defectu in deteriorem labi non potest, & tamen quandoque labitur, communi quodam defectu & causa labitur. Qua quidem in re Aristotelicas ridere licet calumnias. Neque enim debuit Aristoteles in quinto Politicorum a Platone suo, immo nusquam suo, propriam beatae reipublicae permutandae exigere causam, quum nulla sit propria, sed communi debuit esse contentus" (Ficino 1576, 2:1413).

122 The select phrases quoted in my text are from Allen's 1994 translation and study of Ficino's text. Allen explains the multiple resonances of the number 12 in cosmological, Platonic, and biblical texts in his review and study of Ficino's Latin text; the text itself, facing pages Latin and English translation, is found at Allen 1994, 172–233. Allen's review of the importance of the number 12 is found at pages 71–80.

123 "Con más sano discurso en mi sentido,/comencé de culpar el presupuesto/y temerario error que había seguido,//en querer dar con triste muerte al resto/de aquesta breve vida fin amargo,/no siendo por los hados aún dispuesto" (Garcilaso 1966, Eclogue II, vv. 662–7).

124 "a los cuales reprende en el *Fedón* el divino filósofo, porque dize que no se á de dar el ombre ni procurar la muerte, que constituyó a todos la naturaleza, sino que se á de esperar" (Herrera 2001, 845–6).

125 "Contra esto dizen que al fatal decreto/que las celestes máquinas govierna/vive el vigor de la razón sujeto" (Argensola 1951, 2:Rima 48, vv. 156–8).

126 "huya con alma inquieta y desabrida/la grave punición del justo cielo,/dése a entender que entiende cuanto ignora,/pues no es llegada aún la fatal hora" (Aldana 1985, XXXI, vv. 69–72).

127 "Si la hebra recogida/Tornassemos afloxar,/Pudiérasele alargar/Algunos días de vida"; "Cumplido el curso fatal/¿No ves tú qu'es imposible?" (Cueva 1917, 2:142).

128 "arrojando rayos por los ojos por todo su cuerpo abrazó gran parte de la tierra y toda la convirtiera en cenizas si las ciencias arrodilladas por el suelo no le pidieran misericordia y pusieran por delante la indignación de Júpiter por la ruina del mundo antes de su fatal decreto" (Gómez Tejada 1636, f. 281r).

129 "Y en esto se engañó Marsilio Ficino en el commento que hizo sobre Thimeo de Platón, porque pensó que estos tres números, 7, 5, y 3, están conformados en

proporción arithmética y geométrica juntamente. Pero la verdad es, que guardan entre sí proporción arithmética y no geométrica" (Núñez 1567, 2, f. 72v). I cite Part, and folio. Núñez is the Castilian form of the Portuguese Pero Nunes, and the work was published and is catalogued under Núñez.

130 "Y advirtiendo el mismo Marsilio Ficino que quando tres números son proporcionales en proporción geométrica ... respondió a esta objeción que le podrían hazer que esto se entiende en los géneros superparticular y multíplice, mas no en el género superparciente, en lo que grandemente se engañó" (Núñez 1567, 2, f. 73r).

131 "inepta uidetur ad consonantiam"; "semper tamen unam quandam spectant partem ad integrum unum accommodatam" (Ficino 1576, 2:1454, 1455).

132 Listed in my bibliography as *Diccionario de Autoridades*, but referenced in my text as simply *Autoridades*, as is customary.

133 The reference to the term "superpartient" in Pérez de Moya's text is book 4, chapter 4, "Multiplex superpartiens" (Pérez de Moya 1562, 336–7). The first English usage of both arithmetical terms is in 1557, ten years before Núñez's text, and seventy-three years after Ficino's *Timaeus* commentary was first published in 1484 (Allen 2003, 247, n.2). Ficino's first version of the *Timaeus* commentary, written prior to 1457 (i.e., before he knew Greek), is no longer extant (Allen 1987, 409).

134 Rey Pastor (1912–13, 114–21) offers the available details on Pedro Núñez. Rey Pastor's publication itself is undated, but with internal reference to the years 1912–13 for its preparation.

135 For further details on Ficino's *Commentarium in Convivium*, see Gentile 1981.

136 "*Symposium* de amore quidem praecipue tractat, consequenter vero de pulchritudine. At *Phaedrus* gratia pulchritudinis disputat de amore" (Ficino 2008, 2.1.2). I quote from Allen's 2008 bilingual edition of Ficino's translations, commentaries, and chapter summaries of *Phaedo* and *Ion*, by chapter, book, and paragraph.

137 "Amor uero sit fruende pvlchritudinis desiderium"; "Amor tanquam eius finem fruitionem respicit pulchritudinis" (1576, 2:1322, 1323). Kristeller elaborates: "Ficino distinguishes three kinds of beauty: beauty of bodies, beauty of sounds, and beauty of souls. Moreover, the concept of beauty itself contains a contemplative element which leads beyond mere sensual enjoyment" and only the higher senses of sight, hearing, and thought lead to love and beauty (Kristeller 1964, 265). Ficino's various descriptions of beauty include: it is proportion for the ancient Greeks; it is incorporeal; it "is diffused in different grades throughout the whole realm of Being and has its real origin in God Himself"; it is "the reflected splendor of this goodness [God] diffused in four gradated circles – Mind, Soul, Nature, and Matter" (Kristeller 1964, 265–6).

138 Documents attest that Cervantes was composing *La Galatea* in 1582, it received its publication approvals in 1584, and it was published at Alcalá de Henares in 1585. The novel was moderately well received in its day, with a second edition at Lisbon in 1590, a third at Paris in 1611, and four more in the early seventeenth century (1617 Baeza,

1617 Valladolid, 1618 Lisbon, 1618 Barcelona). *La Galatea* was mentioned with favour by Cervantes' contemporaries and highly praised by a French ambassador in 1615. It would also, late in the eighteenth century, be rewritten in French by Voltaire's nephew Florian as an imitation-adaptation in what has been called a more sentimentalized version that would then be translated into German, Italian, and even back into Spanish.

139 "Es, pues, amor, según he oído decir a mis mayores, un deseo de belleza; y esta difinición le dan, entre otras muchas, los que en esta cuestión han llegado más al cabo"; "como toda la felicidad del amante consista en gozar la belleza que desea"; "un deseo de belleza" (Cervantes 1999, 417, 419, 435).

140 "el sentido de esta controversia es enteramente platónico y derivado de León Hebreo, hasta en las palabras" (Menéndez Pelayo 1974, 1:549). See also, however, Ruíz Díaz, whose introduction to a 1968 Spanish translation of Ficino's text includes the following: "Menéndez Pelayo proclama una superioridad evidente de los *Diálogos* de León Hebreo sobre el comentario de Ficino. Más importante que esta cuestión es el hecho de que Ficino sirvió de probable estímulo a León Hebreo y que las páginas del florentino constituyen uno de los elementos de indispensable consulta para establecer el sentido y el alcance de los *Diálogos*" (1968, 24).

141 Bembo's *Gli Asolani* was first published in 1505; Equicola's *Libro di natura d'amore*, in Latin in 1495 and in Italian in 1525; Hebreo's *Dialoghi d'amore*, in 1535; Castiglione's *Il Cortigiano*, in Italian in 1528 and in Spanish translation *(El cortesano)* in 1534. Kristeller noted this influence: "The traces of his [Ficino's] theory of love appear in many poets, from Lorenzo [de' Medici] to Michelangelo, and in the extensive literature of the 'Trattati d'amore,' which includes Bembo's *Asolani*, Castiglione's *Courtier*, and the prose works of Torquato Tasso" (Kristeller 1964, 19). Dominick Finello observes "literal translations of Platonic doctrine" in Spanish pastorals, but believes that "variety and experience ... become the bases for love in the *Dianas*," as Spain's early pastorals are known, rather than one doctrine or another (1994, 38).

142 Hilaire Kallendorf (2005) has referenced Ficino in regards to the episode of the enchanted head in *Don Quijote* II, 62. For Cervantes's studies with humanist Juan López de Hoyos, see Alfredo Alvar Ezquerra 2014.

143 "Teócrito, Virgilio y Sannazaro ... Platón, Ficino, Bembo, Castiglione y León Hebreo"; "raíz de adonde nasce/ la venturosa planta/ que al cielo nos levanta"; "es la idea central del *Fedón* de Platón" (Cervantes 1996, IX; 271, n.158; 275, n.167).

144 "Así entiende el amor Marsilio Ficino, quien en su *Comentario al Banquete* de Platón utiliza la definición en varias ocasiones... Sin embargo, aquí el Fénix sólo acude a la literatura petrarquista y sus presupuestos para rechazarlos" (Carreño and Sánchez Jiménez in Lope 2006, 173, n.[35]).

145 "Cum amorem dicimus, pulchritudinis desiderium intelligite"; "Amor uero sit fruendae pulchritudinis desiderium"; Amor enim fruendae pulchritudinis desiderium est" (Ficino 1576, 2:1322, 1328).

146 In Boscan's Spanish: "aprouecharse de este amor [del mundo] como de vn escalón para subir a otro muy más alto grado"; "buélvese a sí mismo por contemplar aquella otra hermosura que se vee con los ojos del alma" (1561, 242r–v).

147 Spanish libraries today hold no extant copies of Jean de la Haye's 1546 French translation of Ficino's *De Amore*, nor has it been mentioned as a possible source for Cervantes. Neither López Estrada and López García-Berdoy (editors of Cervantes' *La Galatea* in the Cátedra edition), nor Guillermo Serés in his full-length monograph on images of love in medieval and Renaissance Spanish letters, nor Rosucci in her review of Platonic and Neoplatonic sources known in Renaissance Spain mention this French translation as a text known to sixteenth-century Spaniards.

148 A similar description and definition of love is also provided in an earlier dialogue of *La Galatea*, between characters Erastro and Elicio: both divine and human love, Elicio says, are perfect and true when the lover, attracted by beauty to desire, does not stop at enjoyment of that beauty per se but, rather, enjoyment of it because it is also "good" (Cervantes 1999, 340–1).

149 "Y aunque la difinicón que del amor hiciste sea la más general que se suele dar, todavía no lo es tanto que no se pueda contradecir, porque amor y deseo son dos cosas diferentes ... diferentes afectos de la voluntad"; "la razón que corrige y enfrena nuestros desordenados deseos" (Cervantes 1999, 435, 440). On this distinction, Mujica notes that "Tirsi reiterates the tenets of Neoplatonism" (1986, 188) in general, but without reference to Ficino or his writings.

150 "Quapropter libido coitus, & amor non modo ijdem motus, sed & contrarij esse monstrantur" (Ficino 1576, 2:1323).

151 "el deseo presupone falta de lo deseado" (Cervantes 1999, 444).

152 "Praeterea cuiusque cupiditas, eo habito quod uolebat, expletur"; "Quis enim quae habet affectat?" (Ficino 1576, 2:1336, 1342).

153 "si se me concede que el amor es deseo de belleza, forzosamente se me ha de conceder que, cual fuere la belleza que se amare, tal será el amor con que se ama. Y porque la belleza es en dos maneras, corpórea e incorpórea ... como la belleza incorpórea se considera con los ojos del entendimiento limpios y claros, y la belleza corpórea se mire con los ojos corporales, en comparación de los incorpóreos, turbios y ciegos" (Cervantes 1999, 417–19). For a section of this passage taken out by my ellipsis, Sevilla Arroyo and Rey Hazas point to Herrera's commentaries on the poetry of Garcilaso for its mention of Plato's dialogue regarding the phrase: "delicacy of colours" (suavidad de colores) (Cervantes 1996, 245, n.61).

154 "Denique ut summatim dicam, duplex est Venus. Vna sane est intelligentia illa quam in mente angelica posuimus. Altera uis generandi animae mundi tributa. Vtraque sui similem comitem habet amorem. Illa enim amore ingenito ad intelligendam dei pulchritudinem rapitur. Haec item amore suo ad eandem pulchritudinem in corporibus

procreandam" (Ficino 1576, 2:1326). See also de Armas, who studies Lope's incorporation and adaptation of the "twin Venuses" image (1983, 347–8).

155 "Solus igitur oculus corporis pulchritudine fruitur. Cum uero amor nihil aliud sit, nisi fruendae pulchritudinis desiderium, haec autem solis oculis comprehendatur: solo aspectu amator corporis est contentus ... Lucem praeterea illam & pulchritudinem animi sola mente comprehendimus. Quare solo mentis intuitu contentus est: qui animi pulchritudinem expetit" (Ficino 1576, 2:1328).

156 "también puede haber amor de belleza corporal que es bueno ... consiste en pinturas, estatuas, edificios, la cual belleza puede amarse sin que el amor con que se amare se vitupere ... La belleza incorpórea se divide también en dos partes, en las virtudes y ciencias del ánima; y el amor que a la virtud se tiene, necesariamente ha de ser bueno, y ni más ni menos el que se tiene a las virtuosas ciencias y agradables estudios" (Cervantes 1999, 418).

157 "Restat post haec ut quo pacto Magister artium omnium & gubernator sit exponamus ... Gubernator praeterea merito nominatur ... Accedit quod artifices in artibus singulis nihil aliud quam amorem inquirunt & curant" (Ficino 1576, 2:1329).

158 "quamobrem omnes mundi partes, quia unius artificis opera sunt, eiusdem machinae membra inter se in essendo & uiuendo similia, mutua quadam charitate sibi inuicem uinciuntur, ut merito dici possit amor nodus perpetuus & copula mundi, partiumque & eius immobile sustentaculum, ac firmum totius machinae fundamentum" (Ficino 1576, 2:1330).

159 Ficino uses the same image for the role of the soul in relation to the world: "Et quia ipsa vera est universorum connexio ... vultus omnium nodusque et copula mundi" (Ficino 2001–6, 3.2.6), although without the "perpetual" adjective. On his use of that image in that place, see Allen 1987, 399–400.

160 "juntar dos diferentes almas en tan disoluble ñudo y estrecheza que de las dos sean uno los pensamientos y una todas las obras" (Cervantes 1999, 445). See López Estrada (1999) for the meaning of "dis[s]oluble" in this passage, in relation to Renaissance printing's graphic norms and contextual logic. I follow him to translate as "indissoluble," meaning that which cannot be dissolved and so is "dis-soluble." For Cervantes' double-pronged and very ironic use of the same adjective in another context (Don Quijote I, 27), however, see Sánchez y Escribano 1954.

161 "Amor es nudo perpetuo y cópula del mundo, inmoble sustento de sus partes y firme fundamento de su máquina" (Lope de Vega 1996, V, III, 431). I cite act, scene, and page number.

162 Lenio: "la razón que tengo, a ella sola invoco"; Tirsi: "ayudado del Amor, a quien llamo"; "el amor y deseo vienen a ser diferentes afectos de la voluntad" (Cervantes 1999, 417, 434, 435).

163 "Reprehenditur iure Lysias quod qualis sit amoris effectus inquirat, neque prius amorem ipsum definierit neque distinxerit"; "turpem amore definit esse supiditatem

quandam sive libidinem a ratione rebellem ... unum quidem appetitum voluptatis ingenitum, alterum vero legitimam quandam opinionem acquisitam paulatim per disciplinam et ad honesta ducentem" (Ficino 2008, 2.1.2; 2.1.3).

164 "Verdad es que amor es padre del deseo y, entre otras difiniciones que del amor se dan, esta es una: amor es aquella primera mutación que sentimos hacer en nuestra mente, por el apetito que nos conmueve y nos tira a sí, y nos deleita y aplace; y aquel placer engendra movimiento en el ánimo, el cual movimiento se llama deseo; y, en resolución, deseo es movimiento del apetito acerca de lo que se ama, y un querer de aquello que se posee y el objeto suyo es el bien ... el amor es una especie de deseo que atiende y mira al bien que se llama bello" (Cervantes 1999, 435–6). On this point, Stagg (1959) offers a tenuous parallel with Equicola that does not fully convince.

165 "Así que este primer movimiento (amor o deseo, como llamarlo quisieres) no puede nacer sino de buen principio, y aun de ellos es el conocimiento de la belleza, la cual, conocida por tal, casi parece imposible que de amar se deje" (Cervantes 1999, 438).

166 "Huius ornamenti gratia pulchritudo est. Ad quam amor ille statim natus traxit mentem: atque perduxit mentem ante deformem, ad mentem eandem deinde formosam" (Ficino 1576, 2:1322). In the English quoted in my text, capital letters are used by translator Sears Jayne to indicate the god Love (versus the emotion), and Angelic Mind as the first creation of the one God (versus mind as human faculty, seat of consciousness, etc.).

167 "Amor igitur in uoluptatem a pulchritudine desinit"; "Necessario enim bonus est amor cum a bono natus reuertatur in bonum" (Ficino 1576, 2:1324).

168 "Cum primum humani corporis species oculis nostris offertur, mens nostra quae prima in nobis Venus est, eam tanquam diuini decoris imaginem, ueneratur & diligit"; "Restat, ut tunc ardenti flagret amore, quando speciosum aliquod rei pulchrae simulachrum nactus, ea praegustatione ad plenam possessionem pulchritudinis instigatur" (Ficino 1576, 2:1327, 1342).

169 "pulchritudinem esse gratiam quandam uiuacem & spiritalem, Dei radio illustrante angelo primum infusam: inde & animis hominum, corporumque figuris, & uocibus: quae per rationem, uisum, aditum, animos nostros mouet atque delectat, oblectando rapit, rapiendo ardenti inflammat amore" (Ficino 1576, 2:1338).

170 "la belleza humana había de llevar tras sí nuestros afectos e inclinaciones"; "tiene la belleza tanta fuerza para mover nuestros ánimos que ella sola fue parte para que los antiguos filósofos, ciegos y sin lumbre de fe que los encaminase, llevados de la razón natural y traídos de la belleza que en los estrellados cielos y en la máquina y redondez de la tierra contemplaban, admirados de tanto contento y hermosura, fueron con el entendimiento rastreando, haciendo escala por estas causas segundas, hasta llegar a la primera causa de las causas, y conocieron que había un solo principio sin principio de todas las cosas" (Cervantes 1999, 440, 438–9).

171 "In his omnibus interna perfectio producit externam. Illam bonitatem, hanc pulchritudinem possumus appellare. Quo circa bonitatis florem quendam esse pulchritudinem uolumus: cuius floris illecebris, quasi esca quadam, latens interius bonitas allicit intuentes. Quoniam uero nostrae mentis cognitio a sensibus ducit originem, bonitatem ipsam in rerum penetralibus insitam nec intelligeremus unquam, neque appeteremus, nisi ad eam speciei exterioris indiciis manifestis proueheremur" (Ficino 1576, 2:1334).

172 "razones de filosofía entre algunas amorosas de pastores" (Cervantes 1999, 158).

173 See also Sevilla Arroyo and Rey Hazas for a discussion of Cervantes' ideas on genre in *La Galatea*, the pastoral in general, and poetry (Cervantes 1996, III–VIII).

174 "en amor honesto, en amor útil y en amor deleitable"; "amor honesto, provechoso, deleitable" (Cervantes 1999, 436, 437).

175 "aut enim ad contemplatiuam, aut actiuam, aut uoluptuosam" (Ficino 1576, 2:1345). In this section of *De Amore*, Ficino also adds two more loves, the twin Venuses referenced above that are found "in the souls of the spheres, the stars, daemons, and men ... The two extreme ones are daemons, of course, the three median ones are not simple daemons, but desires"; "In nobis autem non duo tentum, sed quinque amores reperiuntur. Duo quidem extremi daemones: medii tres, non daemones solum modo sed effectus" (Ficino 1944, 6.8; 1576, 2:1345).

176 "Tres isti amores, tria nomina sortiuntur. Contemplatiui hominis amor, diuinus: Actiui, humanus: Voluptuosi ferinus cognominatur" (Ficino 1576, 2:1345–6).

177 "el amor honesto siempre fue, es y ha de ser limpio, sencillo, puro y divino, y que sólo en Dios para y sosiega; el amor provechoso, por ser, como es, natural, no debe condenarse; ni menos el deleitable, por ser más natural que el provechoso" (Cervantes 1999, 437).

178 "la compostura del hombre, tan ordenada, tan perfecta y tan hermosa, que le vinieron a llamar mundo abreviado"; "en la figura y compostura del hombre se cifra y cierra la belleza que en todas las otras partes de ella se reparte, y de aquí nace que esta belleza conocida se ama" (Cervantes 1999, 439–40).

179 "Harum uero fundamentum est elementorum quatuor temperata complexio: ut corpus nostrum coelo, cuius est temperata substantia, sit simillimum, neque aliquo humorum excessu ab animi formatio ne desciscat. Sic enim & coelestis fulgor facile lucebit in corpore coelo persimili: & forma hominis illa perfecta, quam habet animus in pacatam obedientemque materiam, resultabit expressior" (Ficino 1576, 2:1338).

180 "espejo en quien se ve Naturaleza/liberal, que en su punto la franqueza/pone con justo medio;/espíritu de fuego/que alumbra al que es más ciego,/del odio y del temor solo remedio" (Cervantes 1999, 450, vv. 62–7).

181 See, for example, Friedman 2006; Pedraza Jiménez 2006; Ruta 1992.

182 "amor iguala lo pequeño a lo sublime ... tiempla las diversas condiciones ... les hacía olvidar todos los incomodos y disgustos pasados ... Los espantosos sueños,

el dormir no seguro, las veladas noches, los inquietos días, en suma tranquilidad y alegría se convierten" (Cervantes 1999, 446).

183 In Ficino's commentary to Plato's text, we read: "Ponitur etiam a Diotima inter sapientiam & ignorantiam medius"; "Ob hanc utique rationem Diotima ut ad eam iam ueniamus, amorem daemonem appelauit: quia sicut daemones inter coelestia & terrena sunt medii: sic amor inter informitatem & formam medium obtinet" (Ficino 1576, 2:1349; 1342).

184 "los dones de amor, si con templanza se usan, son dignos de perpetua alabanza, pues siempre los medios fueron alabados en todas las cosas, como vituperados los extremos" (Cervantes 1999, 442).

185 "en fin, amor es vida, es gloria, es gusto/ almo, feliz *sosiego*" (Cervantes 1999, 451, vv. 82–3, emphasis in original).

186 "es propia naturaleza del ánima nuestra estar contino en perpetuo movimiento y deseo, por no poder ella parar sino en Dios, como en su propio centro, quiso, porque no se arrojase a rienda suelta a desear las cosas perecederas y vanas (y esto sin quitarle la libertad del libre albedrío), ponerle encima de sus tres potencias una despierta centinela, la razón" (Cervantes 1999, 440).

187 "constat eam motus esse principium ... propterea universalem absolutumque et circularem atque sempiternum"; "tres in ipsa animae essentia"; "proficit in vita simul et disciplina, et pro arbitrio se efficit meliorem" (Ficino 2008, 2.5.1; 2.5.2; 2.5.3).

188 "Circulus itaque unus & idem a Deo in mundum, a mundo in Deum, tribus nominibus nuncupatur ... pulchritudo ... amor ... uoluptas"; "Circuli quatuor circa id assidue reuoluti, Mens, Anima, Natura, Materia" (Ficino 1576, 2:1324).

189 "Instinto natural que nos conmueve/ a levantar los pensamientos, tanto/ que apenas llega allí la vista humana;/ escala por do sube, el que se atreve,/ a la dulce región del Cielo santo;" (Cervantes 1999, 450, vv. 43–7).

190 "Anima per se mobilis ... anima per se, & in se mouetur. Per se, inquam, quia principium motus existit, In se etiam, quia in ipsa animae substantia rationis & sensus remanet operatio" (Ficino 1576, 2:1324–5).

191 Ficino describes man as soul above all, with the body as mere work and instrument: "Quapropter homo solus est animus, corpus autem hominis opus & instrumentum" before praising the soul's most important function, to gain knowledge of the incorporeals: "Eo maxime, quod animus operationem eius potissimam, intelligentiam scilicet, sine ullo corporis instrumento exercet, cum res per illam corporales intelligat, per corpus uero sola corporalia cognoscantur." The desire to do so is natural: "Porro anima statim ex Deo nata naturali quodam instinctu in Deum parentem suum conuertitur" and providence has decreed the soul free to do so: "Caeterum diuina prouidentia decretum est, ut anima sui ipsius sit domina" (Ficino 1576, 2:1332).

192 Lenio argues that the loved ones, "outsiders" to those who love them, "están siempre debajo del arbitrio de la que llamamos Fortuna y caso, y no en poder de nuestro

albedrío"; Tirsi admits only that beauty "llama y tira la voluntad a amarle" but "sin quitarle la libertad del libre albedrío" (Cervantes 1999, 420; 440).

193 "quod amori omnia parent, ille nulli"; "Amor enim liber est, ac sua sponte in libera oritur uoluntate: quam neque Deus etiam coget, qui ab initio liberam fore decreuit" (Ficino 1576, 2:1339).

194 "los sospiros, las lágrimas, las quejas y desabrimientos ... desear demasiado, alegrarse mucho, gran temor de las futuras miserias, gran dolor de las presentes calamidades ... como vientos contrarios que la tranquilidad del ánima perturban" (Cervantes 1999, 419–20).

195 "Sin duda, parece que es sobrenatural cosa estar un amante en un instante mesmo temeroso y confiado, arder lejos de su amada y helarse cuando más cerca a ella, mudo cuando parlero, y parlero cuando mudo" (Cervantes 1999, 426).

196 "Hic etiam semper accidit: ut amantes amati aspectum timeant quodammodo atque uenerentur ... Sit etiam ut amore illaqueati uicissim suspirent & gaudeant ... Calent quoque uicissim & frigent: instar eorum, quos tertiana febris inuadit ... Ideo timidi quoque uicissim & audaces apparent" (Ficino 1576, 2:1326).

197 "cum deorum omnium esse afferit antiquissimum ... Primum omnium est deus uniuersorum autor, quod ipsum bonum dicimus"; "Dii quidem siue ut nostri dicunt, Angeli, diuinam pulchritudinem" (Ficino 1576, 2:1321).

198 "asaetado por los celos" (Hebreo 2002, 1, 80).

199 "mi mal insano"; "señora universal de la belleza"; "Desde la *cuna* soy yo *desdichado*" (Cervantes 1999, 351, vv. 182; 355, v. 295; 358, v. 372, emphasis in original).

200 "así no está obligada, como ya he dicho, a amarme como yo estaré obligado a adorarla" (Cervantes 1999, 370).

201 "Quapropter iure ipso amare debet quisquis amatur. Qui uero non amat amantem, homicidii reus est habenduus. Immo uero fur, homicidia, sacrilegus" (Ficino 1576, 2:1327–8).

202 "libre nací, y en libertad me fundo" (Cervantes 1999, 615, v.14).

203 The point has been supported on the basis of Cervantes' portrayal of the character as "obsessively morbid" (Close 2008, 71), on the author's lexical choices of "to give up hope" (desesperarse) (Cervantes 2005, I, 14, n.1), and "it is rumoured" (se murmura) (Castro 1967, 300–1), as well as for the persistence of courtly love ideals in Spanish letters (Iventosch 1974, 66–70), but refuted due to prohibitions on suicide Avalle-Arce (1974, 1115–16). Bruno M. Damiani quotes Lorenzo de' Medici on the lover who dies for love in relation to Cervantes' treatment of the love-death equation in *La Galatea* (2004, 428). Writing about a different Spanish pastoral, *Los siete libros de la Diana* by Jorge de Montemayor, Barbara Mujica notes that novel's "Neoplatonic intellectual framework" and one character's statements indicating that "to die of love is the sweetest pleasure" because "through death, man at last achieves union with the perfect Beauty that is God" (1986, 118). This seems

to conflate Neoplatonism and Christianity with literary tropes on courtly love as for Neoplatonists, death is not sweet although it is inevitable, and not every death results in union with perfect Beauty.

204 "Simplex amor ubi amatus non amat amantem. Ibi omnino mortuus est amator: nam nec uiuit in se, ut satis iam demonstrauimus, nec in amato etiam cum ab eo reiciatur. Vbi ergo uiuit?" (Ficino, 1576, 2:1327).

205 "Nusquam ergo uiuit qui amat aliud ab alio non amatus. Propterea omnino mortuus est non amatus amator. Nec reuiuiscet unquam nisi indignatio suscitet" (Ficino 1576, 2:1327).

206 "y sus causas y efectos naturales puso maravillosamente Marsilio Ficino en los comentarios de Platón en el diálogo *De Amore*, donde muestra ser dolencia natural la de los enamorados, derivada de la sangre, que subtilizada por valor y espíritu, sale por los ojos y penetra por ellos mismos hasta el corazón, donde se hallan juntas la sangre de los amantes, y causan dolor y cuidado mezclado con deleite, más o menos, según la causa y complexión" (Arce de Otálora 1995, 1:447).

207 "De la antigüedad deste sancto amor trata Trismegisto en los Diálogos, Hesiodo en la Theología, y Parménides en el libro de Natura, y Marsilio Ficino en el Commentario del diálogo del conbite de Platón. A donde muestra que el amor ilícito, y deshonesto no es amor, porque el amor ama la hermosura, que es la virtud, y decoro, y el [ilícito] ama la fealdad, que es la deshonestidad, y el vicio" (Pinto 1595, 3.22, f. 266v).

208 "Rabies uenerea ad intemperantiam trahit, ideoque ad inconcinitatem: quare ad deformitatem similiter uidetur allicere: Amor autem ad pulchritudinem. Deformitas & pulchritudo contraria sunt" (Ficino 1576, 2:1323).

209 "El buen platónico Marsilio Ficino, en sus Epístolas y sobre el Convite de Platón, os contentará vendiéndoseos por tan libre y precioso en su estima que ni quiere ni puede venderse, trocarse ni cambalacharse si no por sí mesmo. ¿Caláis bien esta razón, señores?" (Pineda 1963, 169:74).

210 "el amor no tiene otra paga ni otra satisfacción sino el mesmo amor, y él propio es su propia y verdadera paga" (Cervantes 1999, 444).

211 "Caetera ut plurimum alieno praetio comparantur. Amor autem cum in libera uoluntate sponte nascatur ideoque sit liber nullo unque praecio aut emitur aut uenditur: nisi se ipso" (Ficino 1495, f. XXVr).

212 "ninguno ama sin se dar al amado, y ninguno se da que no dé consigo cuanto tiene y no tiene al que le ama; luego bien dijo Marsilio que no se daba sino por sí mesmo, que es decir que no amaba sino a quien le amase" (Pineda 1963, 169:74).

213 "Moritur autem quisquis amat. Eius enim cogitatio, sui oblita semper in amato se uersat"; "nam qui seipsum non habet, multo minus alium possidebit" (Ficino 1576, 2:1327).

214 "Y si preguntamos la razón y causa de esta verdad dízela ingeniosísima y agudamente el príncipe de los philosophos Platónicos Marsilio Fiscino en sus comentarios

que escriuió sobre el conuiuio de Platón, en el capítulo octauo, y también en el libro primero de las epístolas, adonde dize que el amor es de tanta libertad y de tanto precio, que ni puede, ni quiere venderse por otro precio ni estimación sino por si proprio" (Álvarez Miraval 1597, 155v–6r).

215 "Amor autem cum in libera voluntate sponte nascatur ideoque sit liber nullo vnquam praecio aut emitur aut venditur: nisi seipso" (Ficino 1495, f. XXXIr).

216 I thank Cecilia Maier-Kapoor for bringing this text to my attention, following a presentation at the RSA's annual meeting in Montreal, 2011. Here, the translations are from the 1997 Rinaldina Russell and Bruce Merry edition (1997). The Italian is from Giuseppe Zonta's 1912 edition.

217 "Don Bela. – Dime, Laurencio: ¿Platón fue sabio?/ Laurencio. – Llamáronle divino./ Don Bela. – Pues él dijo que todo lo bueno era hermoso. Luego consecuencia es que todo lo hermoso es bueno, y lo que es bueno, digno es de ser amado: ni puede ser reprehendido quien ama lo que es bueno./ Laurencio. – ¡Extremados convertibles! Pero paréceme, señor, que a ti y a mí nos hace mucho daño eso poco que habemos estudiado; Pero mira, así Dios te guarde, de qué manera declaró Marsilio Ficino el pintar los antiguos al dios Pan medio hombre y medio bestia./ Don Bela. – ¿Qué fue la causa?/ Laurencio. – Como era hijo de Mercurio, significaron las dos maneras de hablar en sus dos formas: cuando verdadera, hombre, y cuando falsa, bestia" (Lope de Vega 1996, III, II, 251–2). In a note, Blecua identifies the source as Ficino's *In cratylum, vel recta nominum ratione, epitome*.

218 "Bautista de Vivar, monstruo de naturaleza en decir versos de improviso con admirable impulso de las musas, y aquel furor poético que en su Platón divide Marsilio Ficino en cuatro partes ... El primero es el poético, el segundo el misterioso, el tercero el vaticinio, y el cuarto el amatorio" (Lope de Vega 1996, IV, II, 349). Shortly after this reference to Ficino, Lope's characters call Pico de la Mirandola "that Florentine miracle" (aquel milagro florentín) as they discuss his *Heptaplus* (IV, II, 352).

219 "porque la armonía es concento, el concento es concordia del son grave y del agudo, y la concordia fue instituida de amor, porque con aquella recíproca benevolencia, se sigue el efecto de la música, que es el deleite. Esta unión amorosa llamó Marsilio Ficino ministra suya" (Lope de Vega 1996, V, III, 423).

220 "Ii uoces acutas, & graues natura diuersas certis interuallis & modulis sibis inuicem magis amicas faciunt. Ex quo harmoniae compositio & suauitatis nascitur" (Ficino 1576, 2:1329).

221 Lope de Vega 1996, V, III, 425–6. Blecua notes the source as Ficino's *In Platonem*, chapter IX, [that is, the *Symposium/ Banquete/ De Amore*], and adds that yet other passages would also seem to come from Ficino's texts but lack the direct reference to his name. See also Prieto for "aire neoplatónica" and "aire de melancolía" in certain sixteenth-century poets (1991, 16).

222 For the concept as outlined by Ficino, see Kristeller 1964, 285–8.

223 "la quiero bien, y no con aquel amor vulgar con que a otras he querido, sino con amor tan limpio ..."; "¡Oh amor platónico! ¡Oh fregona ilustre! ¡Oh felicísimos tiempos los nuestros, donde vemos que la belleza enamora sin malicia, la honestidad enciende sin que abrase, el donaire da gusto sin que incite, y la bajeza del estado humilde obliga y fuerza a que le suban la rueda de la que llaman Fortuna!" (Cervantes 1997a, 2:165).

224 "Dulcinea no sabe escribir ni leer y en toda su vida ha visto letra mía ni carta mía, porque mis amores y los suyos han sido siempre platónicos, sin estenderse a más que a un honesto mirar" (Cervantes 2005, I, 25).

225 "la honestidad y continencia en los amores tan platónicos de vuestra merced y de mi señora doña Dulcinea del Toboso"; "Yo soy enamorado, no más de porque es forzoso que los caballeros andantes lo sean, y, siéndolo, no soy de los enamorados viciosos, sino de los platónicos continentes" (Cervantes 2005, II, 3; II, 32).

226 "Generationis autem & congressus officio eatenus utitur, quatenus naturalis ordo legesque ciuiles a prudentibus statutae praescribunt" (Ficino 1576, 2:1327).

227 "el santo yugo de matrimonio, debajo del cual al varón y a la he[m]bra los más de los gustos y contentos amorosos le[s] son lícitos y debidos"; "si en nostros faltase, el mundo y nosotros acabaríamos" (Cervantes 1999, 440–1).

228 "la generación de los animales racionales y brutos sería ninguna si el amor no procediese, y faltando en la tierra, quedaría desierta y vacua" (Cervantes 1999, 442–3).

229 "sentencia platónica que la armonía y contextura universal del mundo con la del Amor halla presunción amorosa" (Quevedo 1999, 1:510, poem 332).

230 "El amor platónico siempre le tuve por quimera en agravio de la naturaleza, porque se hubiera acabado el mundo" (Lope de Vega 1996, II, V, 199).

231 "nace un amor que derriba al suelo/ lo que el amor platónico procura" (Lope de Vega 1993, Rima CV, vv. 7–8).

232 "ama las virtudes del alma" (Lope de Vega 1973, 423). In the same work, another character states that since his was not a Platonic love, he "does not have to worry about which parts were honest, useful, and enjoyable" ("Como este amor no era platónico, no tengo que disputar por qué partes era honesto, útil y deleitable" (Lope de Vega 1973, 174).

233 "el habernos criado juntos no me incitaba en todo apetitos deshonestos, sino a un cierto amor platónico, si bien la comunicación de cosas de amor me llevaba el deseo de los efectos desde los afectos" (Duque de Estrada 1982, 99). As Ettinghausen notes in his introduction to the work, its classification as autobiography or novel is difficult; most critics have decided for the latter due to an obvious lack of historicity and the author's own statements regarding his lies. Ettinghausen says the ambiguity does not surprise, given "the probabililty that the commentaries themselves were conceived within a broad-scope definition of truth" (la probabilidad de que

los propios Comentarios se concibieran dentro del marco de un concepto bastante ancho de la verdad) (Duque de Estrada 1982, 13).

234 "Gala, no alegues a Platón o alega/ algo más corporal lo que alegares,/ que estos cómplices tuyos son vulgares/ y escuchan mal la sutileza griega.// Desnudo al sol y al látigo nauega/ más de vn amante tuyo en ambos mares,/ que te sabe los íntimos lunares/ y quizá es tan honrrado que lo niega.// Y tú, en la metaphissica eleuada,/ dizes que vnir las almas es tu intento,/ ruda y sencilla en inferiores cosas;// pero yo sé que Apuleyo más te agrada/ quando rebuzna en forma de jumento/ que en la que se quedó comiendo rosas" (Argensola 1951, 2:X). The image of the ass seeking roses so as to restore his original form is based on Lucius, the hero of Apuleis's *Golden Ass*. For Argensola's satirical use of this already satirical source, see Schwartz 2013.

235 "el amor, que es potencia y la [hermosura] tiene por objeto, si no apetece más de a la una parte será amor platónico y mutilado. La naturaleza, para perpetuar sus especies en individuos, introdujo al amor en los mortales, y si todos fueran de vuestra opinión, esterilizando sus propagaciones, brevemente diera en tierra con su fecundidad, ni vos tuviérades vida, ni hubiera gozado el orbe más de los dos primeros individuos de quien todos descendemos" (Molina 1979, 228).

236 "Como fue mi amor platónico,/ y en él no fue el fuego tácito,/ no quiso con fino anhélito / ser trueno, sino relámpago.// Amo sólo por teórica,/ pagándome con preámbulos,/ y así ha olvidado, cruelísimo,/ un amor puro y magnánimo" (Zayas y Sotomayor 1983, 501).

237 Le dije: – ¿Como carámbano/ Me he vuelto agora, de frígido?/ Del principio destapándose/ Pudiera, portuguesísimo,/ Por ser mujer presumiéndome/ Descubrir luego lo íntimo./ A ese su dueño escolástico/ Podrá decir que un gradísimo/ De picarones, platónico/ Se le encomienda muchísimo;/ Que traga muy linda píldora,/ Según lo que agora *vidimus*/ Y se hace versos diabólicos,/ Yo me vengaré con dísticos ..." (Diez de Foncalda 1861, 2:535).

238 "yo considero los líricos poetas como divididos en dos clases: una de *lascivos*, otra de *amorosos*. Los lascivos son aquellos que, olvidados de su primera obligación, y negando a la moral y a la religión la obediencia y subordinación que debían, escribieron de asuntos manifiestamente deshonestos... Los amorosos son aquellos que, siguiendo los conceptos de la filosofía platónica y sus ideas, escribieron sin obscenidad alguna la historia de sus honestas pasiones" (1956, 1:93). Luzán's treatise was first published in 1737.

239 Milá y Fontonals speaks of Fernando de Herrera's verse in general: "Dotado de un carácter elevado y caballeroso, enteramente consagrado al retiro y al estudio, respiran todos sus poemas la más alta dignidad, la más noble delicadeza y una especie de perfume platónico," and then specifically on the *canción* to D. Juan de Austria: "aunque peca por la base y es su plan artificioso y falso, atesora tanta belleza de dicción y tanto color poético, que suspende y hace olvidar su defecto intrínseco" (Milá y Fontonals 1888, 430).

240 "Vnde uero lex proficiscatur, ex iis quae dicta sunt elicitur. Ab ipso quippe rerum principio omnes, sed uario modo ut dictum est, manant. Quamombrem omnes illustres conditores legum inuentionem legum in Deum, sed per diuersa nomina atque media retulerunt. Zoroaster Bactrianis Persisque leges tradens, in Horomasim. Trismegistus Aegyptiis, in Mercurium. Moyses Iudaeis rectissime in patrem totius naturae Deum. Monos Cretensibus, in Iouem. Charondas Carthaginensibus, in Saturnum. Lycurgus Lacedaemoniis, in Apollinem. Draco & Solon Atheniensibus, in Mineruam. Pompilius Romanis, in Aegeriam. Mahometus Arabibus, in Gabrielem. Zamolxis Scythis, in Vestam. Plato noster Magnesiis & Siculis, in Iouem, & Apollinem. Arcadibus autem, & Thebanis, & Cyrenaicis leges postulantibus denegauit" (Ficino 1576, 2:1135).

241 "Los mortales houieron sus leyes de Moysén: y Moysén las houo de Dios, según dize Marsilio Ficino: y el philósopho Platón, en su libro vii. De legibus, atribuyó el principio y comienço delas leyes a Dios que las hizo...: que lo dixo en otro lugar, aunque no tan ala clara: diziendo que Prometheo, por el qual se entiende la humana sapiencia, recibió las leyes que le dio Mercurio, que es entender el ángel, que Júpiter, que tenían por Dios, le auia dado" (Celso 2000, f. 4v). In his preliminary study to the 2000 publication, Javier Alvarado Planas offers details on the text and its wide diffusion (Celso 2000, VII–XXXII).

242 "Prometheus rationalis animae gubernator"; "Iupiter igitur per Mercurium, id est, per angelum diuinae uoluntatis interpretem, ciuilis scientiae leges, id est uoluntatis suae decreta ad humanae societatis generisque salutem spectantia mentibus nostris inscribit"; "subiungit Iouem per Mercurium condidisse legem, qua iubeantur omnes ciuilitatis esse participes" (Ficino 1576, 2:1298–9). I have slightly modified Farndell's English translation.

243 Palatino: "todas esas son fábulas e imaginaciones"; Pinciano: "A lo menos, no me negaréis que antes deso había leyes civiles, por las cuales se gobernaba la república ... según Platón ... la ley es el ánima de la república" (Arce de Otálora 1995, 1:254–5). The 1995 edition misspells Ficino's name in this instance as Marsilio Firmio; the reference is obviously to Ficino, as the accompanying discussion deals at length with Plato's opinions on the subject. The edition was prepared from three very thorny manuscripts and other such misspellings, although not frequent, were inevitable given the state of the source texts.

244 "deinde ciuitatem amissa iustitia uelut anima morituram" (Ficino 1576, 2:1523).

245 "Platón decía que era dichosa la ciudad donde había muchos [oficiales], porque era argumento que había pocos vagamundos" (Arce de Otálora 1995, 1:226).

246 "hablillas y fábulas"; "Las fábulas son parte de filosofía, y quien tuvo el todo por fuerza había de tener la parte" (Arce de Otálora 1995, 1:433).

247 "Destas cuatro condiciones se derivan otras cuatro, que son: locos y necios y bobos y cuerdos" (Arce de Otálora 1995, 1:64).

248 "ninguno hay, por cuerdo que sea, que, si lo es, no sea un poco loco" (Arce de Otálora 1995, 1:65).

249 Hankins explains that Plato mixes "diverse *materiae*" in his dialogues with a "symphonic arrangement of themes" but that Ficino identifies each with a principal theme (Hankins 1990, 1:334).

250 "PALATINO: De la facultad que yo menos libros cobdicio es de la nuestra, porque me paresce que los ordinarios bastan y sobran. Pero de todas las otras deseo tener muchos, especialmente de los que escribieron filosofía cristiana y moral. PINCIANO: Tenéis razón, que estos libros son del alma y de gran gusto y consolación, y los nuestros son contra el alma y contra el cuerpo, pues nos martirizan sin darnos un rato de recreación" (Arce de Otálora 1995, 1:578–9).

251 "Osiris legislador de los Egipcios, atribuyó las leyes a Mercurio, a quien ellos tenían por Dios, Charondas Cartaginés atribuyó las suyas a Saturno, Zoroastes Iurescon-sulto de los Persas y Bactrianos atribuyó las suyas a Oromasto. Solón Atheniense las suyas a Minerua, Zamolgis Scita a la diosa Vesta. Minos Cretense a Iupiter. Licurgo Lacedemonio a Apolo. Numma Pompilio Romano a Egeria, y Mahoma Árabe al ángel S. Gabriel por mandado de Dios, con la qual falsedad tiene engañada grande parte del mundo. Quien esto quisiere ver copiosamente, lea a Ficino sobre Platón, y a Georgio Veneto en el segundo de su harmonía del mundo" (Pinto 1595, f. 261r).

252 "Platón dice que Dios es autor de las leyes" (Pineda 1963, 163:300).

253 In the *Republic*: "ipsam quae compositionem a Deo inchoat legum omnium autore," and in the *Laws*: "Hunc esse ostendit legum omnium fundatorem, ubi ait" (Ficino 1576, 2:1397, 1499).

254 "las conclusiones de filósofos son las leyes morales, que gobiernan el mundo ... la filosofía es muro y cava defensiva de las leyes, como madre de sus hijas"; "La ley, dicen filósofos y teólogos, es una ordenación determinada y consentida por común parecer de la república, y emanante de juicio de varón prudente, la cual manda y dispone de todo lo que se ha de hacer; y ansí concluyen todos que la república es la que puede criar leyes, con que se ha de regir, o el príncipe, con el consentimiento della, por haber comprometido en él" (Pineda 1963, 163:300).

255 "Marsilio Ficino dice en las prefaciones, que antepone a los libros de Platón, que Aristónimo y Formio, discípulos del mismo Platón, fueron enviados dél a dar leyes, Aristónimo a los de Arcadia y Formio a los troyanos... Platón hizo dos maneras de leyes; y las unas, que se llaman leyes, hizo para la ciudad de Magnesia, en Sicilia, y su Marsilio dice que también dio leyes a los zaragozanos" (Pineda 1963, 163:318–19).

256 "Y Marsilio Fiscino dio la razón. Apolo significa la potencia, la clemencia Iupiter, Minerua la sabiduría; y por estos atributos fingieron que Minos Legislador de los de Creta, recibió de Iupiter las leyes; Lycurgo Legislador de los Lacedemonios las recibió de Apolo; Solón Legislador de los Athenienses las recibió de Minerua, dando a entender, que ha de ser el Legislador poderoso, y porque ha de ser señor soberano,

clemente y sabio" (Bermúdez de Pedraza 1992, 25). First published in 1612, the 1992 edition is a facsimile reprint.

257 "Tres quoque imitantur auctores legum, Minoem, & Lycurgum, atque Solonem. Qui & leges in tria numina retulerunt, Iouem, Apollinem, & Mineruam. Neque id quidem iniuria. Sol enim planetarum dominus potentiam, Iupiter clementiam, Minerua sapientiam continet. Quae quidem tria totam legis naturam perfectionemque complectuntur" (Ficino 1576, 2:1489).

258 "del verbo Latino fingo, gis.xi.ctum, formo, informo ... estiéndese a todo aquello que se forma, y forja, o con el entendimiento, o con la mano. Pero en lengua Castellana lo más recibido, y vsado, es tomarse esta palabra fingir por dissimular y fabricar alguna mentira" (Covarrubias).

259 "Y reduziendo lo que dixo la ciega Gentilidad a lo que es verdad Cathólica, digo, que a Dios, que es Trino en personas, y author de las leyes, se le atribuyen sus dotes, la Potencia al Padre, la Sabiduría al Hijo, y la clemencia al Spíritu sancto" (Bermúdez de Pedraza 1992, 25).

260 "Quid uero si nouenarius hic significet trinum potentiae usum, trinumque sapientiae, triplicem quoque clementiae? uidelicet ut trium quodlibet tum in lege ipsa sit, tum in iudicio magistratus, tum in ministris & ipsa executione iudicij. Praeterea in ipsis rerum actionumque principijs medijsque & finibus. Tria uero ter repetita nouenarium manifeste perficiunt" (Ficino 1576, 2:1490).

261 "Y lo que dixo Platón, que Minos, el que dio las leyes a los de Creta, gastó nueve años en una cueva para deprenderlas, significando, dize Marsilio, las nueve Hierarchías de los Ángeles; por las quales Dios comunica a los hombres las leyes, que han de establecer, no es fabuloso; las divinas letras nos dizen, por mí reynan los Reyes" (Bermúdez de Pedraza 1992, 25).

262 "Neque uero te lateat nouenario hoc in angelis numero non Christianos solum uti, sed & Platonicos, praécipue Proclum atque Syrianum, quod in Theologia satis ostendimus" (Ficino 1576, 2:1489–90)

263 "Quod autem nouenarium annorum numerum Plato & in Minoe, & hic saepe repetit, quasi necessarium ad leges ab ipso Ioue discendas hominibusque tradendas, forte significat nouem angelicarum mentium ordines, per quos uelut interpretes ipsa legis sanciendae ratio ad homines usque transfertur. Omnes uero hos ordines legum interpretes sub uno Mercurii nomine significat in Protagora" (Ficino 1576, 2:1489).

264 "en figuras destas cosas repartidas fingen los poetas que Minos estuvo nueve años, de tres en tres años, en una cueva, aprendiendo las leyes que después dio" (Arce de Otálora 1995, 1:254).

265 "admonetque ut Promethei prouidentiam potius quam Epimethei properatiam in omni uita pro uiribus imitemur"; "Quod hic sub Iouis & Promethei nomine indicat: Iouem quidem potentiam, Prometheum uero prouidentiam esse indicans" (Ficino 1576, 2:1300; 1530); "a Prometheo, id est creata quadam providentia potuisse" (2001–6, 14.9.3).

266 "extravagancia como una norma; extravagancia, en su más puro sentido etimológico, poética, retórica y espiritual" (Cátedra in Ávila 2000, 9). Cátedra notes the paucity of information on the life of Ávila himself, but offers details on the dates and places of many of those referenced by the author (71–85).

267 "en las meditaciones sobre la vileza de la condición humana, sobre la inevitabilidad del último traspaso o sobre el bien morir" (Cátedra in Ávila 2000, 12).

268 Ávila offers a preliminary index, which includes this section, so identified: "En la partícula XLIV, de muchos philósophos, astrólogos, médicos, oradores, lógicos, músicos, poetas y otros artistas, do también algunos varones singulares destas naciones van enxeridos y otros son amenasados de la Muerte" (Ávila 2000, 127).

269 "a quienes han contribuido a los progresos del conocimiento"; "un elogio del humanismo cristiano ... astrónomos ... médicos ... geógrafos ... impresores ... humanistas ... poetas ... En esa concepción del saber, el humanismo no sólo no se opone a la nueva ciencia, sino que hace de ella bandera de un nuevo método intelectual ... En unos y en otros, se alaba la piedad, la virtud y, sobre todo, el estudio, la dedicación a los studia humanitatis, que se convierten así en antídoto contra el fanatismo" (Gómez Canseco and Navarro Antolín 2004, 20, 11). Gómez Canseco and Navarro Antolín offer Italian Paolo Giovio's *Elogium* as a precursor to the *effigies*, and say that Montano "perhaps" visited Giovio's museum in Lake Como, during his trips to Italy (2004, 26, and n. 4). I would offer as another possibility that the year Montano left for Antwerp was the same year of the publication of a Spanish translation of Giovio's *Elogios o vidas breves de los caballeros antiguos y modernos*, in which the Italian historian combined portrait and praise in prose and verse. The Spanish translator of Giovio's *Elogios*, Gaspar de Baeza, was probably known to Montano, as both had close ties to Phillip II. For Giovio and Miguel de Cervantes, see Byrne 2012a.

270 "acudía a la simbología neoplatónica para tratar de la unión mística entre el alma y Dios" (Gómez Canseco and Navarro Antolín 2004, 21).

271 "Quid referam de te magnum, Ficine, quod ipse/ non superes multis partibus atque modis?/ Si queram certum veterum, Ficine, sophorum/ discipulum, quem te certius inveniam?"; "¿Qué cosa grande podría decir de ti, Ficino, que tú mismo/ no excedas en muchas porciones y medidas?/ Si buscara, Ficino, al verdadero discípulo de los sabios/ antiguos, ¿a quién podría hallar más verdadero que tú?" (Arias Montano and Galle 2005, 206–7). The 2005 edition is a bilingual Latin-Spanish version of the text. The English translation is mine.

3. Ficino as Hermes Trismegistus

1 Following Scott and Festugière, Copenhaver offers information on the separation of the two types of Hermetic writings (xl–xli), and on the figure of Hermes in historical terms (2002, xiii–xvi). See also Renau Nebot, 1999, 7–59, Yates 1991, and

Dannenfeldt, d'Alverny, and Silverstein 1960, for information, editions, and translations during the Middle Ages and the Renaissance.

2 Casaubon stresses that Hermes Trismegistus lived neither before Moses nor in any age close to the prophet's; he calls him an invention of other writers, asserts that the true author of the texts is Jamblichus, and ridicules the sheer number of books attributed to Trismegistus: "Iamblichus in primo de mysteriis auctor est, Aegyptios scriptores, putantes omnia inventa esse a Mercurio, suos libros Mercurio inscripsisse. & sub finem eius libelli refert idem, scripsisse Mercurium, (hoc est, scripta sub nomine Mercurii extitisse) voluminum vigintiquinque millia" (Casaubon 1655, 69).

3 "Mercurius Trismegistus primus leges Egiptiis tradidit" (Gratian, 1486, Distinctio VII, 1). In the 1486 edition, a marginal gloss identified as "P" explains "Trismegistus" as "propter tres potentias."

4 "Del philosopho Tat que ouo nombre Hermes & fue fijo del otro Hermes trimegisto. & fue Mercurio"; "fue cumplida mientre maestro de los tres saberes del triuio" (Alfonso X, 2003, f. 24v).

5 Michael Allen points out that, in part, in order to maintain the number of six sages in this ordering, Ficino adjusted its ranks at times, and omitted figures one might expect to find in the group (Allen 2002a, xvi–xvii). Allen discusses Zoroaster's place on the list, and a number of reasons for its varying composition (Allen 1998, 1–50). Clement Salaman also explores possible reasons for the vacilations (1998, 115–17).

6 Dodd follows Scott and Griffith in concluding that the name is of Egyptian origin, meaning the *nous* of the supreme god, Ra (Dodd 1964, 107). Reitzenstein decided for Greek origin and meaning of "shepherd of men" (*Poimandres* 12, cited at Renau Nebot 1999, 72, n.5), but this reading has been for the most part rejected (Copenhaver 2002, 95). Salaman offers the Egyptian translation and meaning: "the understanding of Re, that is, of the Supreme" (1998, 120) and explores Egyptian concepts of "Supreme" in hymns addressed to Re as the sun, with a dual nature of light and creator, to explain Ficino's reading of the name (120–35).

7 For further details on the manuscript's contents and a list of previous studies, along with identification of the manuscript owner, see Rodríguez Guerrero 2007.

8 "para hazer coral/ (falsos. no es probada:)/ toma cuernos de cabrón blanco y baile bien que no quede ninguna suciedad:/ después ráspala muy sotil que sea como polbos después haz legía deleña de fresno con roble que sea muy recia y echaras dentro todo el polbo que abrás raido delos cuernos y déxalos estar por 15 días después toma çinabrio molido y mezclado conla dicha composición asta que conozcas que tiene color de coral dezpués hazlo granos olo que quisieres y déxalo secaz y polir las as que queden muy lisos diómela as perilla" (BNE ms. 7443, f. 2r).

9 "yo le conoscí por hombre que deseaba topar con el camino dela berdad" (BNE ms. 7443, f. 3r).

10 Rodríguez Guerrero (2007) offers further bibliography on the manuscript that includes indications of its connection to the writings of Arnaldo de Villanova, although he does not amplify this particular citation to Arnaldo de Vila. One of the anonymous manuscript readers for the University of Toronto Press suggested the full name in this particular place, which seems quite possible.

11 See Rodríguez Guerrero and Soler (2007) for identification of letter writer and recipient.

12 "Ysta no entendió los filósofos, ni ellos quieren decir nada de lo que él dice" (BNE ms. 7443, f. 11v).

13 A variant on this version of the story in verse is found in book 4 of Ovid's *Metamorphoses.*

14 An earlier version of this section comparing these two manuscripts was published in Spanish in the *Bulletin of Spanish Studies* (Byrne 2012b). I thank the *BSS* for their consideration in having printed the article, and for permission to reprint it here.

15 "Nota Platonis uerba dicentis, Deum non intelligere solum sed & uelle, significantisque Deum intra se intelligendo concipere, & extra se fabricare uolendo" (Ficino 1576, 2:1429).

16 For the title of the treatise, I use *Pimander* in italics; for the name of the spiritual guide, without italics. A recent edition of the *Pimander* by Maurizio Campanelli includes an extensive introduction on Ficino's translation and its editorial fortunes in the following century, as well as information on the manuscript tradition of the work (Campanelli 2011, VII–CCLV).

17 Dates for Diego Guillén de Ávila are not available. The earliest signed document by the author is dated 1483, and after 1510 there are no further documentary sources (Roca Barea 2006).

18 Andrés 1964, 7:72–3, list number 1358.

19 Intermediary copyist Juan de Segura indicates that he copied the original, and does not mention any alterations to its content. Therefore, the study that follows accepts the *Pimander* Spanish text as the work of Guillén de Ávila.

20 See *supra* for details on the volumes. I most gratefully acknowledge the generous assistance of librarian Fabián Cerezal and Father Modesto González Velasco at the Escorial Monastery.

21 "Quedó Doña Catalina Nuñez viuda, a quien la reina católica Doña Isabel estimó tanto por sus muchas partes de valor y virtud, que se dice la fue a visitar recién muerto su marido (siendo princesa y hallándose en esta villa) haciéndole compañía quince días sin querer ser servida de sus criadas, sino tan sólo de las de Doña Catalina, a quien Su Alteza dio un retablico de marfil y plata de la vida de Nuestra Señora, que se guarda en el Convento de San Bernardo, tanta era la honra y favor, que aquellos santos reyes hacían a quien también se la merecía" (Quintana 1954, 614).

22 "otro libro ... que no se sabe qué cosa es ..." (Ruiz García 2004, 327, no. 11).

23 For the list of Montano's manuscripts donated to the Escorial, see Gil 1998, 355–9, Document XLVIII.

24 Harris (2000) and Limor (1996) have studied manuscripts of the work in Latin, Biosca i Bas (2000) in Catalán.

25 "oriundo del Reyno de Marruecos ... por los años de Cristo 1068" (Rodríguez de Castro 1781–6, 1:7).

26 "el famoso judío de Fez, que se convirtió en Toledo a nuestra santa fe hacia los años 1087"; "vuelto a Marruecos después de su conversión, tuvo allá una famosa disputa con el docto moro Albucaleb, cuya historia escrita por él en lengua arábiga, se conservaba en la real biblioteca del Escorial en los tiempos de Nicolás Antonio ... y debió perecer en el incendio del año 1671, pues ahora no existe" (Lorenz Villanueva 1804, 2:141).

27 See Hernández 2001, particularly pages 107 and 118.

28 See *Inventario general de manuscritos de la Biblioteca Nacional*, 1956, 2:MSS/ 864. The manuscript is available in digital form on the website of the BNE.

29 Another manuscript copy of the work is held by Yale's Beinecke library, in a volume that continues with the rules and regulations of the Dominican Order (Beinecke MS Zi +6898).

30 See Biosca i Bas 2000, Harris 2000, Limor 1996, and Hernández 2001.

31 "por que fiziéndole el otro alguna razón sophística: y aparente y el lego no supiendo responder: engendraríase escándolo en los corazones delos que oyrían quiça la disputa" (Escorial ms. b.IV.29, f. 3r).

32 A possible relationship of the rabbi's letter to Ficino's work was suggested to me as I listened to presentations by Christophe Poncet and Guido Bartolucci during the Renaissance Society of America's annual meeting, held in Venice, Italy in 2010. I gratefully acknowledge Christophe's subsequent communications on Ficino's work, and his kindness in sharing the following information: the text of Rabbi Samuel's letter bears striking similarities to chapter 27 of Ficino's *De christiana religione*; the letter was embedded between parts II and III in all Lyonese printed editions of Saint Antoninus's *Chronicles* (1512, 1517, 1543, 1586, 1587), although it is not in earlier editions nor is it part of the manuscripts; Saint Antoninus was the archbishop of Florence, and had a close relationship with Cosimo de' Medici, Ficino's patron. For the sources of Ficino's *De christiana religione*, see Vasoli 1999, chapter 5.

33 I have consulted the 2005 Zanzarri edition; see Ficino 2005 in the bibliography.

34 In the personal library of Queen Isabel is found *Contra Iudaeos* by Nicolás de Lyra (Ruiz García 2004, 479). Limor notes that the rabbi's letter is commonly bound with other anti-Jewish polemical works like that of Lyra (Limor 1996, 181), although in the Escorial volume it is not, as the *Pimander*, with which it is bound, does not share that characteristic.

35 "Noble y muy virtuoso señor, [C]ommo por diuersos respectos a vuestra señoría sea mucho obligado y [h]asta agora el deseo que de seruir le tengo con ocupaçiones non

aya puesto en obra, commo quier que avn non libre de aquellas penssé de traduzir alguna obra de latín en nuestro romançe e dedicar la so el nonbre de vuestra merçed, assý por lo suso dicho commo por que la tal obra por el tal nonbre perdurablemente viuiesse. E, conosçiendo la boluntad [que] a las scripturas antiguas tiene, penssando con quál antes seruir le podría, ocurrióme vn tratado de mercurio trismygistro dela potençia y sapiençia de dios. E éste pues delibré de romançar por ser en parte cathólico, sy dezir se puede seyendo por honbre gentil y tan antiguo conpuesto. E por que en el prólogo de marsillo van declaradas la vida de mercurio y continençias deste tratado, non digo más si non que por él verá vuestra merçed el error que comúnmente se tiene creyendo que a los gentiles non provenniesse el cognosçimyento de vn dios fazedor e gobernador de todas las cosas. nuestro señor la noble persona y estado de vuestra merçed prospere. De Roma a çinco de abrill de ochenta e siete años, que las manos de vuestra merçed besa diego guyllén" (Escorial ms. b.IV.29, f. 38r–v).

36 Diego Guillén de Ávila's father was the Chief Accountant (*contador mayor*) for the Archbishopric of Toledo (Ticknor 1851–4, 3:459–60).

37 The Frontino translation was published, but the Herodian was not. I have seen the latter in one manuscript copy, held by Yale's Beinecke library (Beinecke ms. 182).

38 The información in this paragraph on Gómez Manrique comes from Francisco Vidal González's *Introducción* (2003, 11–42) to his edition of Manrique's *Cancionero*. For further information on the poet, see also Scholberg 1984, and Perea Rodríguez 2007.

39 "[T]raslado de vna carta enbiada de Roma. por diego guyllen famjliar del reuerendissimo señor cardenal vrssino al muy noble cavallero el señnor gómez manrrique corregidor en la cibdat de toledo con vna obra de vn tratado del libro de mercurio trismegistro trasladado de latin en romançe por el dicho diego guyllén e la carta dize assý" (Escorial ms. b.IV.29, f. 38r).

40 "[C]omjença la obra del tratado enesta manera. [A]rgumento de marssillio ficuro [*sic*] florentín enel libro de mercurio trismegistro trasladado del latín en romance por diego guillén familiar del reuerendíssimo señor cardenal vrsino. [E]n el tiempo que moisén nasçió floresçió atalante astrólogo, hermano del methafísico prometheo y materno aguelo del primer mercurio cuyo sobrino fue mercurio trismegistro ..." (Escorial ms. b.IV.29, f. 38v).

41 "[C]omiença el libro de mercurio trismegistro de la potençia y sapiençia de dios trasladado del griego en el latín por marsillio fiçino florentín e mandado a cosmo de mediçis e después del latín traduzido en el romançe castellano por diego gujllén e dirigido al magnífjco e noble cavallero el señor gómez manrrique" (Escorial ms. b.IV.29, ff. 38v–9r).

42 "fenesce el libro de mercurio trismegistro trasladado de griego en latín por marsillo friçino florentín enel año de mjll e quatro çientos e sessenta e tres años enel mes

de abrill. E del latín buelto enel romançe castellano por diego gujllén famjliar del reuerendíssimo señor cardenal vrssino enel año de mjll e quatro çientos e ochenta e çinco años enel mes de hebrero. del qual dicho traslado original saqué este otro traslado yo Juan de Segura capellán del Señor pero núnnez de toledo mj Señor enel año de mjll e quatroçientos e nouenta y vno enel mes de noujenbre" (Escorial ms. b.IV.29, f. 85r).

43 A 1980 edition of a 1548 work by another Juan de Segura offers this information, as well as details on two other men named Juan de Segura, one a pastor from Burgos, author of religious works published in the mid-sixteenth century (*Libro de instrucción cristiana* [1554] and *Confesionario* [1555]), and another from Toledo, a *regidor* known by a document dated 1 Dec. 1575. For obvious chronological reasons, the 1493 references seem a logical match, the later dates do not. See Alonso Martín 1980.

44 "abrir puerta ... en el adarve que se dize de Juan de Segura" (Porras Arboledas 2004, 70). An "adarve" is an alleyway that runs along a fortress wall.

45 "Alfonso de Herrera se queja al concejo de que el canónigo Pedro Núñez quiere reabrir un proceso por una servidumbre de aguas de lluvias que desde tiempo inmemorial recibían unas casas que éste había comprado en la plaza del barrio de Caleros" (Porras Arboledas 2004, 61).

46 Beginning with Turnèbe's 1554 Paris edition, the *Asclepius* was more often than not bound together with the *Pimander*. Book and chapter indications in all cases, found neither in Turnèbe nor in the manuscripts held by the Escorial and El Burgo de Osma, are to the standard divisions by chapter and paragraph found in modern editions like those of Renau Nebot and Copenhaver. When citing Ficino's Latin from the 1554 edition, I use that edition's page numbers.

47 The Latin manuscript is codex 25 of Rojo Orcajo's *Catálogo descriptivo de los códices que se conservan en la Santa Iglesia Catedral de Burgo de Osma*. It is a parchment codex bound in vellum, 60 folios, fifteenth century (Rojo Orcajo 1929), with the title: *Marsilii Ficini in librum Trismegisti Commentarium*. I gratefully acknowledge the kindness and generosity of librarian and parish priest Father Julián Gorostiza in allowing me to consult and study the manuscript.

48 "yo soy aquella lumbremente, dios tuyo más antiguo que la naturaleza húmida que salió de la sombra. Simiente por cierto dela mente, Verbo luziente hijo de dios" (Guillén de Ávila, f. 41v). "lumen illud ego sum, mens deus tuus, antiquior que natura humida, quae exvmbra effulsit, mentis vero germen, uerbum lucens, Dei filius" (Ficino 1554, 2–3).

49 In his *Platonic Theology*, Ficino defends man's immortality and it is in part due to him that in 1513, the Church declared as dogma the tenet regarding the resurrection of the soul. See Allen 2008a.

50 In Guillén de Ávila's Spanish: "Y allende desto consigujendo forma a él semejante existente en el mismo existente assý como en el agua, amóla y cobdicióla

consigo. En effecto conseguyó la voluntad y engendró la forma caresciente de razón. La naturaleza abrazó aquello en que la rueda era trayda. A aquello enteramente se juntó y mezcló por la qual causa sólo el hombre de todos los animantes terrenos es reputado de doblada naturaleza, mortal por cierto por el cuerpo mas inmortal por el mismo hombre sustancial. Inmortal por cierto es ...” (Guillén de Ávila f. 43r).

51 As, for instance, in the *Timaeus* commentary. On Ficino, the demiurge, and Neoplatonist thought, see Walker 1953; Lang 2005; Allen 1987; Snyder 2008a, 125–6; Snyder 2008b.

52 “por cierto principalmente enla resolución del cuerpo material el cuerpo se dissuelve en alterano y aquella forma senssible que antes tenía se asconde enel tiempo venidero. El ábito ocioso de las costumbres es concedido y dexado al demonio. Los sentidos corporales [h]echos spíritus del ánima se tornan en sus fuentes para resucitar quando serán una otra vez enlos sus actos. Las fuerzas dela inefable y concupiscible se convierten en naturaleza caresciente de razón assí que estonces el ánima recorre por armonía alas partes de arriba ...” (Guillén de Ávila, ff. 44v–45r).

53 “sensus corporei partes animae facti, suos in fontes refluunt, aliquando in suos actus iterum surrecturi” (Ficino 1554, 7).

54 See Allen 2008a, and Bynum 1995.

55 In 1566, the Council published a Catechism for Parish Priests (*Catechismus ex decreto Concilii Tridentini ad Parochos Pii V Pont. Max. jussu editus*), ordered to be translated into the vernaculars so as to regularize the teachings of those priests, and which includes the dictum. See preface, Article XI, “On the Resurrection of the Body” at http://www.fordham.edu/halsall/mod/romancat.html.

56 “la forma acidental y advenidiza/ otra materia busca, otro elemento,/ sin que estorbe lugar, tiempo o fortuna,/ o al tránsito de cosas cosa alguna” (Aldana 1985, XXVIII, vv. 125–8).

57 “Llenas pues todas las formas el padre sembró las calidades en la esphera como en un campo, circundando aquella en torno de toda qualidad y quiso adornar aquello que es después de [el]la nutriéndola quasi de inmortalidad todo cuerpo” (Guillén de Ávila, f. 57v).

58 Lang examines the subtlety of Proclus’s arguments on this point. Proclus, a Plotinian Neoplatonist of the fifth century who was also translated by Ficino in the fifteenth, concludes that one can understand this relationship between cause and effect because: “*via* its relation to God, the cosmos *becomes* what its cause *is*, and in this precise sense a cause ‘imitates’ its effect” (Lang 2005, 150).

59 For ‘lícito,’ Moliner offers etymological roots shared with ‘license’ as in a license to do something. Oxford offers for ‘licet’: “allowable, permitted, lawful.”

60 “volé tan alto tan alto/ que le di a la caça alcance” (Juan de la Cruz 2000, “Tras de un amoroso lance,” vv. 3–4).

61 "El que de amor adolesce/ de el divino ser tocado ..."; "Que estando la voluntad/ de divinidad tocada ..." (Juan de la Cruz 2000, "Por toda la hermosura," vv. 21–2, 37–8).

62 "allí me dio su pecho,/ allí me enseñó sciencia muy sabrosa" (Juan de la Cruz 2000, "Cántico," stanza 27).

63 Switalski points out that St. Augustine also rejected the "transmigration of human souls into the bodies of animals, praising Porphyry for having rejected this opinion: 'Nam Platonem animas hominum post mortem revolui usque ad corpora bestiarum scripsisse certissimum est. Hanc sententiam Porphyrii doctor tenuit et Plotinus; Porphyrio tamen iure displicuit'" (quoted in Switalski 1946, 93, n.435).

64 "A lo de la palingenesia, puedo satisfacer como cristiano en una palabra, diciendo ser tan grande mentira, que es condenada por herejía" (Pineda 1963, 162:340).

65 "de qua multa Mercurius cum filio suo Tatio disputat" (Ficino 2001–6, 17.3.5).

66 "de una ánima de todo el mundo todas las ánimas profluyen concurriendo en torno como distribuidas por todo el mundo. Y por cierto de aquestas ánimas [h]ay muchas mutaciones parte que se mudan en mejor y más felice y parte por cierto que se mudan en contrario ... Mas el ánima caýda enel cuerpo humano si persevera enlos males no gusta cosa alguna dela inmortalidad ni aún goza del bien mas rrebuelto el campo cahe abaxo enlos animales serpentinos" (Guillén de Ávila, f. 62r).

67 As will León Hebreo, who allows "that the soul of the evil person will transmigrate into the body of a dog, or any other of the non-speaking animals" (cited by Ogren 2004, 84), in his Commentary on Deuteronomy, dated to 1496 (Leiman 1968), that is, fifteen years after Guillén de Ávila's 1481 *Pimander* translation.

68 "fue una opinión muy celebrada entre los antiguos filósofos que creían [en] la inmortalidad del ánima, que, después desta vida, las ánimas de los que virtuosamente habían vivido en este mundo tenían sus moradas aparejadas en unos campos fertilísimos ..." (Casas 1986, 1.20.59, 3:454). Las Casas also addresses the point in his *Apologética*: "Lo principal que estos druides, a los que predicaban y doctrinaban, persuadían, era que tuviesen por cierta la inmortalidad de las ánimas, desta manera: que muertos unos, se pasaban las ánimas a otros. Y esto afirmaban por fin de que, no temiendo la muerte, los hombres se animasen a darse y a proseguir el ejercicio de la virtud" (Casas 1967, 2:17).

69 "porque ciertamente el ánima humana non escoge otro cuerpo que humano nin es lícito el ánima racional caher en cuerpo de animal caresciente de razón" (Guillén de Ávila f. 64v).

70 "piadosa beata y divina ... es libre dela cárcel del cuerpo"; "será [h]echa mente o dios" (Guillén de Ávila, f. 64v).

71 For a fine study of this work by Vives, see Kraus 2005.

72 "hominum deinde immortales animae in daemones transeunt, demum in deorum chorum feliciter revolant" (Ficino 1554, 55).

73 "Porque algunas ánimas de serpientes se trasmudan en aquellas de los animales del agua. Y las ánimas de los aquantes en las de los terrestres. Las de los terrenos se trassforman en las de los que vuelan. Las aerias se trassforman o trasmudan en onbres de allí tales de la traspassan en los *ángeles*. Y finalmente en el choro de los dioses felicemente rrebuelan. Y los choros de los dioses son do el uno de los que andan el otro de los que están y aquesta la última gloria del ánima" (Guillén de Ávila, f. 62r).

74 "Non de daemonibus et operibus corj" (El Burgo de Osma, IX,3).

75 "porque disputó doctísimamente de las cosas sublunares adonde los demonios habitan"; "que le puede confirmar el nombre de Divino por oculto" (Gómez Tejada de los Reyes 1636, f.172 r).

76 "lo mismo que Diablo" (*Autoridades*).

77 "Bien merece la pena escuchar a la inmensa cohorte – en sus diversos círculos – de aquellos que escudriñan, desmenuzan e investigan los secretos divinos; como otros resuelven los enigmas de Podalirio con los arcanos de Trigemisto, y como otros desatan los nudos de las Leyes" (Mártir de Anglería 1953, no. 60, 15 October 1488).

78 The Hermetic *Asclepius* or *Logos télios* is dated to the beginning of the fourth century, and was known to Lactantius, Stobaeus, and Saint Augustine (Renau Nebot 1999, 29). From the ninth century on, it was attributed to Apuleius.

79 "Assí que por la virtud de las muchas artes se dixo Trimegisto: y termáximo. Píntanle con cabeza de can, porque el can: es animal muy rastrero: y que conoce mucho: y dízese mercurio: quasi señor de los que mercan. Díziase mercurio intérprete de los dioses: y amontonamiento o piedras en la cumbre de los montes" (Palencia 1967).

80 "Yo opino que ese Theut, con mayor verosimilitud, es Abrahán, que habiendo, desde la Caldea, pasado a Egipto, enseñóles las letras y esas cuatro matemáticas ..." (Vives 1947, 1:567). Ficino links Zoroaster to Abraham, the Chaldeans, and the Persians (Allen 1998, 39–40), and "even indulges in a kind of syncretism of theologians, retailing speculations of Eusebius that Hermes Trismegistus and Musaeus, Orpheus's son, might be the same man as Moses; and Ham, son of Noah, might be the same man as Zoroaster" (Hankins 2008a, 117).

81 The work is by author Luis de Mexía, and in his gloss Cervantes de Salazar repeats all the details on the five Mercury figures as in Palencia, adding: "Mercurio era presidente de las contrataciones dolosas. *Isis* en Grecia era honrada, donde la gente es mui fraudulenta, de manera, que el engaño no puede tener sino padres fraudulentos" (Cervantes de Salazar 1772, 5.30, n.9). The 1772 volume has separate pagination for each chapter, and each chapter is preceded by Cervantes de Salazar's own explanation of the text, with Roman numerals for those pages. I follow that sequence, citing chapter number and either arabic or roman numerals. Character Fraude, who is speaking at the time, specifies that she is the daughter of Mercury and Isis. Christoph Strosetzki notes the reference (1997, 12).

82 This episode is also noted by Strosetzki (1997, 14–15). The quote from the 1772 edition of the volume reads: "Labricio deseoso de saber le rogó [a Mercurio] le declarasse algunos secretos de naturaleza, i en especial el orden del cielo, el movimiento de los planetas, i otras cosas semejantes, Mercurio a esto se escusava diciendo, que no convenía a los hombres, no entendiendo lo que entre las manos tienen, escudriñar los secretos del cielo" (Cervantes de Salazar 1772, 5.xxiii).

83 "Él es la fuente de la vida, y aquel admirable resplandor, de donde mana otro resplandor, y aquel sempiterno en el ser, de donde se deriua el otro ser. Y por esso él sólo puede dezir con verdad: Yo soy el que soy, como él dixo a Moysén. Esto parece que leyó el antiguo Trismegisto, porque en el 4. diálogo del Pimandro dize que Dios es vnidad, la qual cría todos los números, sin ser criada dellos" (1595, f. 266r). The same passage is found in Pinto's Portuguese (1952, 3:237), that is, it is not an interpolation by the Spanish translator.

84 "De manera que entendían todos estos sabios, que la vida del Philósopho era apartar y agenar el alma del cuerpo, y morir cuanto a él. Porque tenían ellos que el cuerpo era grande impedimento para la contemplación, y llamáuanle fundamento de maldad, lago de corrupción[,] muerte viua, sepulchro mouedizo[,] ladrón doméstico y otros nombres desta calidad, que le puso Trimegisto, aquel antiguo Egypciano, a quien los Platónicos immitaron mucho" (1595, f. 137r).

85 "Salve os Dios, Magnánimo Carlo Qvinto, Augusto, Emperador tres vezes Máximo ..."; "A quien dio naturaleza/ De Máximo el sobrenombre/ Tres vezes por más grandeza/ Carlos Quinto Emperador" (Giovio 1568, ff. 206r–9v, and vv. 3–6). The prose section of the *elogium* opens with the first phrase (206r), and the verse, written by Paolo Giovio the younger, is the last of three poems in praise of Charles V (Giovio 1568, f. 209v).

86 See Kristeller 1993, 4: number 501b; Rico 1970; Byrne 2007, 44–5. See also *supra*, the 1579 French translation of the *Pimander* and its dedication to the "très-puissant," etc.

87 "la razón de nuestra ánima"; "la sabiduría de la voluntad divina" (Pérez de Moya 1995, 283, 278–85).

88 "fue el primero que dijo que el mundo era criado por Dios" (Pérez de Moya 1995, 281, 283).

89 "tan excelente que no podía ser más excelente" (Pérez de Moya 1995, 280).

90 "Cicerón le da por padre al tercero Júpiter" (Pineda 1963, 163:307). The information is found in Cicero's *The Nature of the Gods* (1853, 125). "Trismegisto quiere decir grande en tres cosas: en el sacerdocio, en la filosofía y en la teología; y aún Suidas dice que porque confesó la Trinidad" (Pineda 1963, 163:308). "S. Agustín dice ... que ningún pagano dice tantas palabras tomadas de la Escritura o semejantes a las de la Escritura como Trimegisto" (1963, 163.308). Pineda vacilates in spelling the name Trismegistus with or without the "s," as do many of his contemporaries. Modern

Spanish orthography would dictate spelling 'Trimegisto' and not 'Trismegisto' (Renau Nebot 1999, 10, n.16), but the most common spelling is with the letter "s" and so I keep it in my own references. For the influence of Cicero on Ficino, see Rees 2013a.

91 "Qvando al mundo Archetipo, Ideal, y Eterno, pareció sacar a luz aquel retrato suyo, que dentro de sí tenía concebido eternalmente, y al qual llamamos mundo criado y temporal (y vale tanto dezir mundo, como hermoso, asseado, atauiado y muy compuesto y agraciado) no hizo más de querer que saliesse en effeto, como siempre le auía tenido dentro de sí por Ideal concepto: en lo qual tocó con su profundo saber aquel Trimaximo, llamado comunmente Trismegisto, sacerdote y propheta de los Egypcios. Esto es lo que dixo Moysén en las primeras palabras de toda la santa Escritura, que enel principio crió Dios el cielo y la tierra" (1620, f. 1r). I cite from a 1620 edition in which the preliminaries are numbered folios 1–4; following are a few non-numbered leaves of dedicatory poems to the author, and an index of authorities named in the work; lastly, beginning again at a different folio numbered 1, begins the text of the *Monarchia ecclesiástica*. For those later sections, I cite book, chapter, paragraph, and folio number.

92 "triplicem eius causam perscrutatur, primo quidem efficientem, id est diuinam mentem: secundo exemplarem, id est, idearum seriem in diuina mente conceptam: tertio finalem, id est, bonum" (Ficino 1576, 2:1440).

93 "Mundi itaque architectus per naturam intellectualem, quantum intellectualis est, operatur"; "Erat semper in mundi architecto machina mundana praescripta, ac momentum incohationis eius in architecti voluntate signatum" (Ficino 2001–6, 2.11.6; 18.1.8).

94 "El pregón que el famoso Theólogo Trismegisto dio del hombre fue, que el hombre es un Dios mortal, y un gran milagro, y un animal digno de ser honrado y aún adorado" (Pineda 1620, 1.5.2, f. 14r). See Rico 1970 for the idea of man as microcosm in Spanish letters of the Renaissance.

95 "y señaladamente en lo de la auerigación de los años del mundo, y aún más en particular para la concordancia de los años de la santa Escriptura, con los años de las escripturas profanas" (Pineda 1620, "Aprobación," Licenciado Fray Francisco Calderón, 11 febrero 1575, Madrid). Censor Calderón specifies that he has only seen parts one and two of the work.

96 "pero esto fue sacado de las imaginaciones poéticas, que se fundaron en encarecer la gobernación, y leyes, que dio este Mercurio a su Patria, como las dio Foroneo, y Solón, y Licurgo, y Numa Pompilio. Macrobio, y Trogo, y Justino, y otros, dicen, que en el principio del mundo en el tiempo de Saturno vivían los hombres en comunidad, sin estar instruidos con providencia civil, y acudían a los negocios públicos, y privados de la hacienda, y bienes comunes" (Castillo de Bobadilla 1616, 1.1.3).

97 "Mercurio Trimegisto, que quiere decir tres veces muy grande; es, a saber, grandíssimo Filósofo, grandíssimo Sacerdote; y grandíssimo Rey, todo junto" (Castillo de Bobadilla 1616, 1.9.28).

98 This lengthy commentary on the text, by Hannibal Rosselius, "a Franciscan from Calabria who taught theology at Cracow," was first published in several volumes from 1585–90 (Thorndike 6:449).

99 "El *autor del Pimandro* es Mercurio Trismegisto, uno de los más grandes teólogos de la antigüedad pagana" (Fernández-Guerra y Orbe in Quevedo 1859, 466).

100 I thank Elena Pellús Pérez for this citation. For biographical and bibliographical information on Pérez de Oliva, see Solana 1941, 2:49–64, Cerrón Puga (Pérez de Oliva 1995, 11–97), and Pedro Ruiz Pérez (Pérez de Oliva 1993, 1–128).

101 "esta causa immutable que movía sin ser movida: dixeron los antiguos que era un solo Dios causador y hazedor de todas las cosas. Desta primera causa tracta Aristóteles en muchos lugares: y en especial en su metaphísica. Desta escribió un philósopho antiguo que se dixo Timeo: y del tomó Platón en el diálogo Timeo y deste diálogo tomó M. Tulio en el libro que escrivió de Universitate. Desta misma primera causa escrivió un philósopho antiquíssimo que se dize Trismegisto; en el diálogo que se dize Pimander; y en el que se intitula Asclepio" (Venegas 1983, 2.3, ff. 35–6). I cite book, chapter, and folio numbers.

102 The work was Lobera's translation of an Italian treatise by "caballero Fileremo fregoso," titled *Rissa y planto de Demócrito Heráclito*, published in 1553. Venegas's approval reads: "Yo el Maestro Alexio Venegas digo, que E visto y examinado todo este Libro, y aunque el Trasladador se vuo enel fielmente por trasladar el sentido del auctor. Digo que porque algunos Italianos son en algo Platónicos, con las Emiendas y censuras que yo enel tengo hechas, assí como van eneste Original queda Libro sano y de buena y Moral doctrina, aunque por las figuras Poéticas, de que abunda, no es para la gente vulgar, sino le echassen vnas breues declaraciones que declarassen los lugares escuros del. Mas la gente docta facilmente le entenderá. Y por que es assí la verdad como lo digo, firme aquí mi nombre oy Domingo.xxiiii.de Setiembre de M.D.L.III.Años. El Maestro Venegas" (Venegas 1983, preliminaries).

103 "Yo seguiré, en lo que dijere, a los que mejor hablaron de esta materia, que son, Hermes Trismegisto, Orfeo, Platón, Plotino y el gran Dionisio Areopagita" (Malón de Chaide 1959, 130:83); "Lo mismo dijo Hermes Trismegisto, hablando con su hijo Asclepio, dice 'Magnum, o Asclepi, miraculum est homo'" (1959, 104:101).

104 "Multi apud antiquos fuere Mercurii; sed quae de omnibus dicuntur, huic vni tribuuntur, & sic etiam putatur hic ille esse apud Aegyptios sacerdos eruditissimus, & scholae illius prouintiae regens sapientissimus, qui ob id Trimegistus, ter scilicet maximus dictus est. Ideo sub eius nomine hanc triplicem Eloquentiam edere in lucem decreui" (1621, introductory text, no pagination). For the life and works

of Jiménez Patón, see Garau 2012 and Bosch i Juan, Garau Amengual, Madroñal Durán, and Monterrubio Prieto 2010.

105 "Dios, la mente o Sabiduría, y ánima ... Esta Trinidad debuxo Mercurio en vna Esphera o círculo hecho con vn compás. Dios la Esphera"; "Dize Hermes que no está en alguna parte [la Sabiduría], por [así] que no se puede comprehender" (Saona 1598, 23). Clemente Hernández argues that this text published under Saona's name is, in reality, a work by Bartolomé Jiménez Patón (Clemente Hernández 1999, 9–12).

106 "Y aquel grande Philósopho Hermes Trismegisto, dize: que el hombre es vn maravilloso milagro hecho a ymagen y semejança de Dios"; "Hermes Trismegisto y Apuleyo diffinen [*sic*] el hado diziendo que es cierta inflexión o inclinación de las causas segundas dependentes de la primera causa" (Álvarez Miraval 1597, ff. 8v, 327v).

107 "no hallé en todo él [el mundo] sino vanidad, maldad, aflición y locura"; "Informándome, pues, de las señales con que Jesuchristo quiso que los suyos fuesen entre los otros conoscidos, rodée todo el mundo sin poder hallar pueblos que aquellas señales tuuiessen" (Valdés 1993, 80, 81). For the relationship of Valdés's text with Erasmus's writings, see Ricapito's introduction and notes to the 1993 edition. For Valdés as Lucianesque satire, see Schwartz 1990.

108 "Si se huelga o no [Cristo], allá se lo haya. Quanto por mí, yo te prometo que me ternía por muy afrentado si se llamasen mercurianos" (Valdés 1993, 88).

109 "en cuyo trage y ademán severo/ vi de Mercurio al vivo la figura/ de los fingidos dioses mensagero.// En el gallardo talle y compostura,/ en los alados pies, y el caduzeo,/ símbolo de prudencia y de cordura,// digo que al mismo paraninfo veo,/ que truxo mentirosas embaxadas/ a la tierra del alto coliseo// (Cervantes 1991, I, vv. 184–92).

110 Rivers (1993) reviews these previous studies in detail, and offers the bibliography. See also his critical edition of the text (Cervantes 1991), for its fine introduction (1–30). Ellen D. Lokos (1991) provides further historical and literary contextualization for Cervantes' *Viaje*.

111 "omnia videlicet in lumen conuersa ... Paulo post vmbra quaedam horrenda, obliqua reuolutione subterlabebatur, in humidamque naturam migrabat, ineffabili tumultu exagitatam ... terra vero & aqua sic inuicem commiste iacebant, ut terrae facies aquis obruta nusquam pateret" (Ficino 1554, 2).

112 "Vi la noche mezclarse con el día"; "Todos los elementos vi turbarse;/ la tierra, el agua, el ayre y aun el fuego" (Cervantes 1991, II, 331, 334–5).

113 "En fin, sobre las ancas del Destino,/ ... Suele tal vez ser tan ligera como/ va por el ayre el águila o saeta,/ y tal vez anda con los pies de plomo" (Cervantes 1991, I, vv. 58, 67–9). I disagree with Lokos's literal reading of Cervantes' journey as one on foot "lacking wings or even a horse" (Lokos 1991, 19). The poetic voice does specify that he sets out on foot, but the subsequent reference to the mount of Destiny seems key to a full reading of the passage.

114 For Ficino's *Phaedrus* commentary, see Allen: "the Ficinian-Phaedran charioteer was soon to become, along with Vitruvian man, one of the Renaissance's most potent and expressive self-images" (1981, 28).

115 "Mercurio es el guía del poeta como Virgilio lo es para Dante; y al fin él también conduce a Cervantes a la salvación mediante Apolo, como Virgilio dirige a Dante al summum bonum mediante Beatrice" (Maurino 1956, 8).

116 See Maurino 1956, Rivers in Cervantes 1991, Rivers 1993.

117 "El hermetismo es, en primer lugar, *una estética didáctica radical*"; "El hermetismo moderno es, sobre todo, estético" (Beltrán Almería 2007, 98, 100).

4. Persistence and Adaptation of Hermetic-Neoplatonic Imagery

1 The *Pimander*'s "ethical monotheism" has been linked to Judaism, Christianity, Plato, the Egyptians, and the Iranians (Dodd 1964, 1–3).

2 "El Pensamiento, Dios, que era hermafrodita, vida y luz a la vez, engendró con la palabra otro Pensamiento creador que es el dios del fuego y del aliento vital" (Renau Nebot 1999, I, 9).

3 "Mens autem deus vtriusque sexus foecunditate plenissimus, vita & lux, cum verbo suo mentem alteram opificem peperit, qui quidem deus ignis, atque spiritus numen" (Ficino 1554, 3). Referencing Festugiére, Montserrat, and Kroll, Renau Nebot offers notes on the figure of the androgyne in Orfism, Gnosticism, and Neoplatonism, adding that "El origen metafísico suele situarse en el pitagorismo: la mónada hermafrodita que engendra la diada-materia" (1999, 79, n. 17).

4 Dodd notes that Platonism, too, "readily finds room for the identification" (134). See also Shrimplin-Evangelidis (1990), who reviews early Christian iconography and symbolism regarding the Christ-Sun analogy. Guillermo Serés also points out that a number of Church Fathers incorporated sun imagery, in all likelihood from Platonic dialogues, into their own writings (Serés 1996, 45–7).

5 "Iupiter enim et Sol in caelo virtute occulta maxime consonant, et Sol opificis Iovis praecipuus est minister, et virtus illustratoria virtutem opificiam comitatur" (Ficino 2008, 3.13.3).

6 "Solaris praeterea virtus per Mercurium quidem ad Musas per Venerem vero provocat ad amorem" (2008, 3.14.1).

7 "Ita enim coelum & terram semper opifex, solem dico, essentiam demittens, & materiam evehens, circum se & ad se omnia trahens, a seipso omnia omnibus tribuens, lumen quoque abunde largitur" (Ficino 1554, *Aesculapii Definitiones*, 113). Ficino's translation of the *Corpus Hermeticum* only includes up through book XIV, as those were the only books known to him. The 1554 Paris edition includes those books with three additional treatises: *Ex Ioannis St[r]obaei collectaneis: Mercurius ad Tatium*, *Aesculapii Definitiones ad Ammonem Regem*, and *De Animo ab Affectiones Corporis*

impedito, all translated by publisher Turnèbe (Purnell, e-mail message to author, June 11, 2004). The quotation here, thus, is Turnèbe although included in Ficino's translated work in the 1554 publication.

8 "agens primum ita per esse dicitur operari"; "Sic sol uno actu facillime illuminat quodammodo infinita et gignit illuminando"; "Sic deus per esse suum, quod est simplicissimum quoddam rerum centrum a quo reliqua tamquam lineae deducuntur, facillimo nutu vibrat quicquid inde dependet" (Ficino 2001–6, 2.8.2).

9 "Ideo Musae novem cum Bacchis novem circa unum Apollinem, id est circa splendorem solis invisibilis debacchantur"; "Cum vero ignis atque sol lumen latius propagare soleant quam calorem, consentaneum est quousque divini solis radius calefaciendo protenditur, eousque multo magis posse illuminando protendi" (Ficino 2001–6, 4.1.28; 18.8.26).

10 "Sol oculus aeternus omnia uidens" (Ficino 1493, VI). I cite from the 1493 Miscomini edition, copy held by the Beinecke library at Yale, ms Zi 6166. See the bibliography, Ficino 1493. I augment abbreviations, but otherwise quote from the text as found in that edition. Quotations from *De lumine*, the second text, are specified as from that source. Images of the sun as a god, of course, are common in religions, myths, and creation stories. The image of the Aztec sun god is ubiquitous in Mexico. A scholar of ancient Iranian religions dating to 2000 BC points out the triple-faceted descriptions of the god Agni of the Vedas as a personification of "fire, sun, and light" (García Ayuso 1874, 2–3). Despite these multiple possibilities, the similarity of imagery and lexical choices in the texts studied here suggests Ficino's writings as the most obvious source material for the Spanish poets.

11 "est triplex ... Diuinum appellari solis utriusque solem. Intellectuale, solem angelicum nominari, solis mundani solem. Visibile denique lumen, esse coelestem solem eiusque fulgorem" (Ficino 1576, 2:1409).

12 "ut Solem coelestem ita suspiciendo prospiciamus: in eo supercoelestem illum: tanquam in speculo: Qui in Sole posuit tabernaculum suum" (Ficino 1495, CLIv).

13 "así en medio del pecho, ha colocado/ aquel cuerpo vital, cuya figura/ imita a las pirámides de Egito,/ que por su nombre corazón se llama," (Aldana 1985, XLVI, vv. 30–4).

14 Morros Mestres has noted the sun-heart metaphor in Garcilaso's "Canción IV" as "surely" (seguramente) from Ficino (Morros Mestres 2000, 29).

15 "la primera raíz de todas las virtudes"; "pone en él toda la fuerza de los espíritus vitales" (Lara Garrido in Aldana 1985, 348, n. 30–44).

16 "la virtud"; "mil espíritus vitales"; "ministran al pulmón aire de vida" (Aldana 1985, XLVI, vv. 41, 43).

17 "Sol oculus aeternus omnia uidens"; "Physici ueteres Solem cor coeli nominauerunt"; "Plerique Platonici in Sole mundi animam collocarunt. Quae sphaeram Solis totam implens per globum illum quasi igneum tanquam per cor effundit radios:

quasi spiritus inde per omnia. Quibus vitam sensum motum universo distribuit" (Ficino 1493, VI).

18 Francisco Rico also finds the image in Cleanthes, for whom the sun is "corazón del mundo y, en la harmonía de las esferas, plectro de la lira cósmica" (Rico 1970, 25, citing from Clement's *Stromata* V, viii: I, 502).

19 "quis pyramidem impressit cordi figuram?" (Ficino 1554, 33).

20 "juntamente correr donde lo lleva,/ el ímpetu bestial, por quien se dijo/ perderse la razón do está la fuerza" (Aldana 1985, XLVI, vv. 113–15).

21 "buscan la cumbre al cielo más vecina"; "aquí quieren pasar las breves horas/ deste del alma temporal destierro" (Aldana 1985, XLVI, vv. 127, 133–4).

22 "dejan la cueva helada y tenebrosa/ y salen a tomar, con pecho abierto,/ los nuevos rayos del señor de Delo" (Aldana 1985, XLVI, vv. 141–3).

23 "y así, como de Sócrates se dice/ que estuvo todo un día considerando/ la gran carrera del que alumbra al mundo,/ y que, sin pie mudar toda una noche,/ a Febo saludó vuelto otro día," (Aldana 1985, XLVI, vv. 144–8).

24 "Socrates in castris saepe sub diuo Solem suspiciens orientem stetit attonitus in eisdem uestigiis/ immotis membris/ inconniuentibus oculis/ statue more/ quousque Solem salutaret iterum resurgentem"; "Non filium inquam dei primum: sed secundum iamque visibilem. Primum namque dei filium non Solem hunc oculis manifestum: sed alterum hoc longe superiorem intellectum. Scilicet primum solo contemplabilem intellectu" (Ficino 1493, XIII).

25 "Sed ubi Plato Solem inquit omne visibile superare: proculdubio supra corporeum Solem/ incorporeum auguratus est Solem. Divinum scilicet intellectum" (Ficino 1493, IX). Also in Ficino's summaries of the *Republic*, we find the image of "the idea of the Good" that "in the visible world is the visible Sun with the nature of an image, the invisible archetype"; "Verum ante hunc quem uidemus solem, Plato alterum in mundo cogitat inuisibili, imaginem Dei patris primam, uerumque filium. Ideo filios dixit boni, ut super uisibilem hunc imaginariumque filium posses inuisibilem & archetypum contemplari" (Ficino 2009a, 28–9; 1576, 2:1407–8).

26 "Quaeritur inter haec quid potissimum primo deus creavit? Respondet Moses/ lucem" (Ficino 1493, X). In Genesis, light was created on day one but the sun was not created until day four.

27 "Lux quidem intelligibilis in mundo supra nos incorporeo/ id est purissimus intellectus. Lux autem sensibilis in mundo corporeo id est lux ipsa solaris" (Ficino 1493, X).

28 "Deus certe sicut mens quae radius eius est/ monstrat: lux est inuisibilis: infinita: ueritas ipsa ueritatis cuiusque/ rerumque omnium causa" (Ficino 1493, IV).

29 "Quibus rationibus a luce uisibili ad inuisibilem ascendamus" (Ficino 1493, *De lumine*, VI).

30 "miran al matutino ojo del cielo,/ y a la pura en sí luz cómo en sí misma/ relampaguea con presurosa vuelta,/ no por parar allí, que no es objeto/ proporcionado al

alma cuerpo alguno,/ mas por subir desde aquel Sol visible/ al invisible Sol, autor del alma" (Aldana 1985, XLVI, vv. 149–55).

31 "Nonne & auctor ille vitae Christus quem expirantem Sol e medio coelo quasi Vates..." (Ficino 1493, X).

32 "quemadmodum diuinae intelligentiae lux unde manauit, reflectitur in seipsam" (Ficino 1493, X).

33 "pues que quedé sin luz del Sol divino" (León 1995, Atribuido III, v. 87).

34 "una transposición de personajes y mitos paganos en sus equivalentes cristianos"; "una cierta inclinación a racionalizar la religión cristiana y a añadirle un cierto laicismo aunque sea inconsciente por parte del agustino" (Alcina in León 1995, 163–4).

35 "igual al Padre Eterno,/ igual al que en la tierra nace y mora,/ de quien tiembla el infierno,/ *a quien el sol adora,*/ en quien todo el ser vive y se mejora" (León 1995, XIX, vv. 26–30, my emphasis).

36 "Y qué decir del sol, del más poderoso de los dioses celestes, al que todos los demás le ceden el paso como a su rey y soberano, de un astro de tales dimensiones, mayor que la tierra y el mar, que soporta, llevando sobre sí mismo, a los astros menores en sus órbitas. ¿A quién puede reverenciar el sol, hijo? ¿A quién temer?" (Renau Nebot 1999, V.3). Here, I translate from Renau Nebot's Spanish. Copenhaver uses the English "defer" instead of "adore" or, as here and in Ficino's Latin, "revere": "Quem timet is, quem veretur, o fili?" (Ficino 1554, 31).

37 "Utinam tibi daretur, o fili, facultas, ut alarum ad miniculo in sublimem aeris plagam volares, mediamque inter coelum ac terram regionem fortitus, conspiceres terrae quidem soliditatem, maris diffusionem, fluxum fluminum, aeris amplitudinem, ignis acumen, coeli celeritatem" (Ficino 1554, 32).

38 "quod si per ea etiam quae terra sustinentur, fragilia, & ea quae profunditate conduntur"; "haec solus ipse inuisibilis deus, cuncta propria voluntate molitus est" (Ficino 1554, 33).

39 "¿Cuándo será que pueda/ libre desta prisión volar al cielo,/ Felipe, y en la rueda,/ que huye más del suelo,/ contemplar la verdad pura sin duelo? (León 1995, X, vv. 1–5)

40 The Latin of each pair is contained, of a piece in the full paragraph, in note 37 above. "veré cómo/ la soberana mano echó el cimiento ..." (León 1995, X, vv. 11–12).

41 "las lindes y señales,/ con que a la mar hinchada .../ por qué crecen/ las aguas del océano y descrecen;/" (León 1995, X, vv. 18–19, 24–5).

42 "quién ceba y quién bastece de los ríos/ las perpetuas corrientes"; (León 1995, X, vv. 27–8).

43 "de los helados fríos/ veré las causas, y de los estíos/ las soberanas aguas/ del aire en la región quién las sostiene;" (León 1995, X, vv. 29–32).

44 “de los rayos las fraguas” (León 1995, X, v. 33). I translate “rayos” as “lightning” instead of the more general term “rays” given the subsequent verses that speak of also seeing the source of snow and thunder: “dó los tesoros tiene/ de nieve Dios, y el trueno dónde viene” (León 1995, X, vv. 34–5).

45 “Y de allí levantado,/ veré los movimientos celestiales,/ ansí el arrebatado,/ como los naturales;/ las causas de los hados, las señales.// Quién rige las estrellas/ veré, y quién las enciende con hermosas/ y eficaces centellas;” (León 1995, X, vv. 51–8).

46 “Item certa quaedam in coelis ab ipso Sole ubique spatia definita uidentur, quae cum primum peregerunt Planetae, motum habitum que permutant. Nam Saturnus Iuppiter que & Mars per tertiam a Sole coeli partem in conspectum Solis trinum peruenientes, mutato statim motu, uel ante uel retro mouentur. si orientales a Sole fuerint, regrediunt, si occidentales, progrediuntur” (Ficino 1493, V).

47 “Iste non motus o Aesculapi, sed resistentia est. Non enim eodem, sed modo contrario gradiuntur. Oppositio vero reuerberationem motionis stabilem continet. Repercussio enim stationis, agitatio est” (Ficino 1554, 16).

48 Veré este fuego eterno,/ fuente de vida y luz, dó se mantiene/ y por qué en el ivierno/ tan presuroso viene;/ quién en las noches largas le detiene” (León 1995, X, vv. 61–5).

49 “Lumine pariter & calore generat/ uegetatque/ & mouet/ & regenerat omnia/ & exhilarat/ atque fouet: & quae occulta fuerant/ primo aduentu efficit manifesta: accessuque uicissim atque recessu quatuor efficit anni partes: & regiones nimium a Sole remotae/ semotae pariter sunt a uita” (Ficino 1493, V).

50 “Después el vientre entero,/ la Madre desta Luz será cantada,/ clarísimo Lucero/ en esta mar turbada,/ del linaje humanal fiel abogada” (León 1995, XIX, vv. 31–5).

51 “Velum meum revelauit nemo. Quem ego fructum peperi/ Sol est natus. Vbi apparet/ Solem Mineruae id est divinae intelligentiae partum/ florem/ fructum esse. Theologi ueteres eodem Proculo teste/ dicebant Reginam omnium Iustitiam e medio Solis throno per cuncta procedere/ omnia dirigentem” (Ficino 1493, VI).

52 “Hinc Solem apud Theologos ueteres Apollinem arbitror nominatum/ & harmoniae omnis auctorem” (Ficino 1493, XI).

53 “Neque vero quemadmodum solis radius, fulgore nimio corrumpit oculos, caligantesque reddit, sic ipsius boni conspectio illustrat enim, atque oculi lucem eo magis exauget, quo quis capere magis potest intelligibilis splendoris influxum” (Ficino 1554, 53).

54 “Y como al sol juntamente le vemos y no le podemos mirar (vémosle porque en todas las cosas que vemos miramos su luz; no le podemos mirar porque, si ponemos en él los ojos, los encandila), así de Dios podemos decir que es claro y escuro, oculto y manifiesto. Porque a él en sí no le vemos y, si alzamos el entendimiento a mirarle, nos ciega; y vémosle en todas las cosas que hace, porque en todas ellas resplandece su luz” (León 2008, 357).

55 "Su claridad nunca es escurecida/ y sé que toda luz de ella es venida/ aunque es de noche" (Juan de la Cruz 2000, "Fonte," copla 5). As I have shown in an earlier study, San Juan's hidden fountain of life and light in "Fonte" also contains imagery from the *Pimander* (Byrne 2007, 224–36).

56 "Non enim tantum stellas caeteras magnitudine superat: quantum lumine. Nam magnitudinem quidem Iouis minus quam duplo/ lucem uero forte centuplo superat. Horum quantitates certe comparatione terrae censentur. Quotiens uero Sol terram contineat/ diximus ab initio. Iupiter profecto quinquies atque nonagies terram adequare putatur. Aliud igitur & aliunde prorsus eluxit lumen hoc immensum/ naturali Solis luci desuper additum. Omnia sane caelestia proprium lumen nascentia secum attulerunt. Sed uel exiguum uel nobis occultum: siue raritate quadam & candore: siue alia de causa lateat. Simile quoddam lumen pauloque pro magnitudine sua maius ab initio Sol secum attulisse uidetur" (Ficino 1493, XI); "Mundi dominus. Iupiter immortalis mundi oculus circumcurrens: habens sigillum/ omnia mundana figurans" (Ficino 1493, VI).

57 "digo que la sin punto principiante/ línea infinita que en sí misma vuelve,/ el rayo de su luz glorificante,/ el rayo que en su luz todo se ensuelve/ .../ cuyo poder fue tal desde *ab initio*," (Aldana 1985, XLIII, vv. 929–32, 941).

58 "«Carácter sustancial, imagen viva/ soy de tu mismo ser, conforme y cierta;/ .../ yo Padre alcanzaré, tras muerte esquiva,/ en vida reviviendo, mi cubierta,/ pues mi muerte dará muerte a la muerte/ y gracia con que obrar el hombre acierte».// Esto mostró decir y esto antes de esto,/ y aun antes que su luz al mundo humano/ mostrase el sol había mostrado y puesto/ ante su Sol el Sol sobremundano./¡Oh Sol, oh Sol, oh Sol que habéis compuesto/ al vacío, dando ser todo sin vano,/ gracias con alta voz te da y ofrece/ hasta el silencio que de voz carece!" (Aldana 1985, XLIII, vv. 953–4, 957–68).

59 "obtenebrato uultu defleuerat/ rursum die & hora. Solis resurrexit ex mortuis/ ita lucem nobis intelligibilem sicut Sol uisibilem redditurus" (Ficino 1493, X).

60 "Siquidem ex ipsa Solis natura foecunda tres naturales foecunditates per cuncta procedunt. Prima quidem inde sit in natura coelesti. Secunda uero in simplici elementorum natura. Tertia denique in natura mixtorum. Rursus ex uitali calore solis passim ultra naturas propagatur & uita; eaque trina ... Hactenus Solis lumen non solum imago est eiusmodi rerum: sed & causa" (Ficino 1493, XII).

61 "Itaque cum nuper ad mysterium illud Platonicum prouenissem/ ubi Solem ad ipsum Deum artificiosissime comparat" (Ficino 1493, Proemium).

62 "Pythagoricum praeceptum est magnanime Petre profecto divinum de rebus mysteriisque divinis absque lumine non loquendum" (Ficino 1493, I).

63 "Ya por el aire sube el sacrosanto/ cuerpo inmortal de nuestro Sol divino," (Aldana 1985, XLI, vv. 41–2); "Quien pudo sino el Sol, causa primera" (Aldana 1985, XLIII, v. 481); "del nuevo rayo que del Sol supremo/ sacó, dar alegría, dar luz y vista," (Aldana 1985, XLIII, v. 490–1).

64 "Sed qui inter eos ubique praecipue sunt solares/ antiquores appellauere Musas scientiis quidem omnibus praesidentes: maxime uero Poesi/ Musicae/ Medicinae/ expiationibus/ & oraculis/ atque uaticiniis" (Ficino 1493, XII).

65 Aldana versifies the story as told in Ovid's *Metamorphoses*, which he follows as to details and plot.

66 "Alto dios inmortal, sagrado Apolo,/ nueva y preciosa luz que a los mortales/ luz, vida y criación siempre has causado/ .../ elige rubio dios, recibe Apolo,/ no dejes de elegir, no dejes Febo/ .../ Razón es, Sol, pues tanto os conformáis,/ que en todo lo demás os conforméis/ y en recíproco amor viváis conformes,/ pues busca cada cual su semejante./ Mira a mi sol, ¡oh Sol!, verás si sólo/ acá como tú allá ser solo puede;/ .../ y jurar osaré con juramento/ sobre mi sol (¡oh Sol!, que también juras/ por tu misma deidad!) que cierto piensas/ aquellos ser tus rayos, y creído/ ternás que ella es el Sol aunque el Sol ella/ jurará sobre sí que eres tú cierto" (Aldana 1985, VIII, vv. 1–3; 20–2; 27–32; 34–9).

67 "¡Oh perpetuo descubridor de los antípodas, hacha del mundo, ojo del cielo, meneo dulce de las cantimploras, Timbrio aquí, Febo allí, tirador acá, médico acullá, padre de la Poesía, inventor de la Música, tú que siempre sales y, aunque lo parece, nunca te pones! A ti digo, ¡oh sol, con cuya ayuda el hombre engendra al hombre!, a ti digo que me favorezcas, y alumbres la escuridad de mi ingenio, para que pueda discurrir por sus puntos en la narración del gobierno del gran Sancho Panza; que sin ti, yo me siento tibio, desmazalado y confuso" (Cervantes 2005, II, 45).

68 "Prima quidem uegetalis in plantis. Secunda uero sensualis immobilis in Zoophytis. Tertia sensualis atque progrediens in perfectioribus scilicet animalibus" (Ficino 1493, XII).The same image is in Ficino's *De lumine*: "Quis aiunt neget numina laeto quodam affectu omnia mouere atque generare? Cum & ab animalium natura & ab arte omnia uoluptate procreari atque perfici uideamus" (Ficino 1493, *De lumine*, VIII). In the *Asclepius*, we also read that the sun creates all things, the immortal as well as the earthly, and that with his light "vivifica y pone en movimiento, por las generaciones y los cambios, a los seres vivos que hay en estas partes del cosmos" (Renau Nebot 1999, XVI, 8).

69 "in helicis modum transmutans, atque transformans in alias atque alias generum & formarum species, opposita inter se cuiusque mutatione" (Ficino 1554, 114).

70 "Nullus tamen in diuino cratere se valet immergere, qui suum corpus non oderit, & qui non se, sed deum ipsum dilexerit, & qui non mortalia negligens solis diuinis haeferit, solis adsit, sola meditetur, atque flagret" (Ficino 1554, commentary, 30).

71 "Mas, ¡ay de mí! que voy hacia el profundo/ do no se entiende suelo ni ribera,/ y si no vuelvo atrás, me anego y hundo" (Aldana 1985, LXV, vv. 277–9).

72 "Aquí el alma navega/ por un mar de dulzura y finalmente/ en él ansí se anega,/ que ningún accidente/ estraño y peregrino oye y siente" (León 1995, III, vv. 31–5).

73 "¡Oh llama de amor viva,/ que tiernamente hyeres/ de mi alma en el más profundo centro!/ pues ya no eres esquiva,/ acava ya si quieres;/ rompe la tela de este dulce encuentro" (Juan de la Cruz 2000, "Llama," vv. 1–6).

74 "qui cum acutissimus ac velocissimus sit omnium diuinorum conceptuum, singulorum comprehendit elementorum corpora: etenim ipse coelorum artifex, igne potissimum ad suam fabricam vtitur" (Ficino 1554, 60).

75 "orba nanque igni mens hominis, ad humanamque dispositionem duntaxat idonea, diuina construere nequit" (Ficino 1554, 60).

76 "la semejanza, la consonancia, la conformidad y unidad"; "En este mundo hay elemento de fuego; en el celestial, hay el fuego del sol; en el angélico, el fuego de los serafines: pero de esta manera, que el fuego de acá quema, el del cielo da vida, el de los serafines ama. Y ciertamente no se puede negar una fuerza, una virtud, un lazo encubierto, que enlaza, anuda y abraza toda la grandeza y variedad de este mundo ..." (León 1885, 4, 233).

77 For information on the particulars of the various publications of this sonnet, and on previous critical readings, see Brown (2013), who offers multiple details from Lope's life and loves to contextualize the sonnet as part of the writer's "continuing struggles with *eros*" (13) and studies its commentary as "a literary coalescence of post-Tridentine moralism and philosophical syncretism that seeks to unify the *prisca theologia* and sexuality of the ancients with Catholic tradition and Scripture" (15–16). I thank Gary for sending me an advance copy of his article.

78 "La calidad elementar resiste/ mi amor, que a la virtud celeste aspira,/ y en las mentes Angélicas se mira,/ donde la idea del calor consiste.// No ya como elemento el fuego viste/ el alma, cuyo vuelo al sol admira,/ que de inferiores mundos se retira,/ a donde el Cherubin ardiendo assiste.// No puede elementar fuego abrasarme,/ la virtud celestial, que vivifica,/ envidia el verme a la suprema alzarme;// Que donde el fuego Angélico me aplica,/ ¿cómo podrá mortal poder tocarme?/ que eterno y fin contradicción implica" (Lope de Vega 1989, 1:401, vv. 1–14).

79 "Fúndale en tres fuegos, correspondientes a tres mundos. El calor es en nosotros calidad elementar: la celestial es la virtud, que calienta: la angélica es la idea del calor. Fuego es el elemento en nosotros, fuego es el sol en el cielo, y fuego el entendimiento seráphico; pero difieron en que el elementar abrasa, el celeste vivifica, y el sobreceleste ama. Assí lo disputa divina y sutilmente Pico Mirandulano [*sic*] en su *Heptablo*" (Lope 1989, 1:402–3). Trueblood points out that "the sonnet represents no run-of-the-mill Neo-Platonism; it is a highly technical treatment of the upward aspiration of love in terms of 'tres fuegos correspondientes a tres mundos' ... which condenses into fourteen lines, as Dámaso Alonso notes and Lope acknowledges, the central thought of Pico della Mirandola's *Heptaplus*" (1958, 196).

80 In the gloss as a whole, there are multiple references to Plato, as well as myriad other authorities, among them Quintilian, Pico de la Mirandula, Saint Augustine,

Theophylactus, Saint Dionysius, Virgil, Isaiah, Lucretius, Andreas de Acitores, Cicero, Euripides, Turnebus, Aristotle, and Saint John Chrysostom.

81 "Marsilio Ficino dice, que la lumbre de la divina mente no se infunde en el alma, si ella como la luna al sol no se revuelve a ella, y que esto no es hasta tanto que ponga a una parte los engaños de los sentidos, y las nieblas de la phantasia, y desnuda de aquella caligine y sombra, que assí llamó Theophylacto a la ignorancia, se reduzca a lo más secreto de la misma mente; y Mercurio en el Pimandro introduce la mente divina, diciendo: *Comprehéndeme tú, que yo te enseñaré*; y que finalmente, quando le enseñó, vió en la suya la luz existente, con potencias inumerables, un ornamento sin término, y un fuego cercado de gran poder" (Lope de Vega 1989, 1:403–4).

82 "mentis sermonibus vestram mentem inclinate, vt eum tandem cognoscatis, qui omnia ob ea causam fabricatus est, vt eum per singula cerneretis" (Ficino 1554, commentary, 77).

83 "Y assí Trimegisto en aquella antiquíssima Theología llama a Dios, Dios de fuego, Majestad y Espíritu" (Lope de Vega 1989, 1:404).

84 "Está muy claro por el nuestro y el celeste, hasta passar al Angélico. Marsilio diferencia estos mundos, dividiendo en dos operaciones la Sabiduría divina: una, que está en la naturaleza del mismo Dios; y otra, que se extiende a las cosas de afuera. La primera, que concibió el mundo primero y eterno: la segunda, que cría el segundo y temporal" (Lope de Vega 1989, 1:406).

85 "Erat semper in mundi architecto machina mundana praescripta, ac momentum incohationis eius in architecti voluntate signatum" (Ficino 2001–6, 18.1.8).

86 "Inest namque rerum omnium penetralibus. Neque laborat circa plurima, sed per ipsum esse suum, qui universalis omnium cardo est, sequentes versat cardines, id est, essentiam, vitam, mentem, animam, naturam, materiam" (Ficino 2001–6, 2.13.4).

87 "deus ignis, atque spiritus numen, septem deinceps fabricauit gubernatores, qui circulis mundum sensibilem complectuntur: eorumque dispositio fatum vocatur" (Ficino 1554, 3).

88 Dodd points out that, although not a part of the biblical Genesis, in early rabbinical tradition, Adam follows the androgynous being of the first creation (Dodd 1964, 151). For the relation of this first androgynous being to San Juan de la Cruz's *Cántico*, see Byrne 2007, 143; 176–86.

89 Given Lope's familiarity with Ficino's work, I would tend to attribute the misspelling to a transcriber, although I have not seen the original manuscript.

90 "*Non per quamdam imaginariam intelligentiae perceptionem, sed per verum quemdam virtutis intellectum superioris substantialemque contractum, ubi non videt solum, sed gustat etiam atque tangit, quam suavis est Dominus.* Assí Marsilio Finicio [*sic*] sobre Plotino Platónico en el libro segundo de la primera Eneada" (Lope de Vega 1989, 1:406). As Brown has noted, the quote is not to the second book of the first *Ennead* as Lope indicates but, rather, to the third (Brown 2013, 30, n.14).

91 "non per quandam quasi imaginariam intelligentiae perceptionem, sed per uerum quendam uirtutis intellectu superioris substantialemque contactum: ubi non uidet solum, sed gustat etiam atque tangit quam suauis sit dominus" (Ficino 1562, 3.1). I thank Valery Rees, who noted not only this possible discrepancy regarding "contactum," but also an embedded reference to Psalm 34: "O taste and see that the Lord is sweet" (Psalm 34, verse 9).

92 "Mens a uelaminibus libera & diuina existens suapte natura, igneum fortita corpus ... Itaque cum primum mens a terreno corpore soluitur, proprium mox subit amictum, igneum videlicet corpus, quo sane quandiu circuntecta est, in terreum corpus turgescere nequit" (Ficino 1554, 59).

93 "hace una metamorphosis del humano al divino" (Lope de Vega 1989, 1:407).

94 "los círculos y ambages con que se escurecen"; "*que usurpan el nombre de Poetas sin conocimiento de la ciencia*" (Lope de Vega 1989, 1:409, emphasis in orig.).

95 "el gran teólogo Mercurio Trimegisto"; "Mercurio Trimegisto, que tan altamente habló de la divinidad" (Lope de Vega 2010, 466, 400).

96 "No se admire V. Excelencia, señor, si en esta parte me dilato, por ser tan alta materia el hablar, que della dixo Mercurio Trimegisto en el Pimandro: 'sólo al hombre había Dios concedido el habla y la mente, cosas que se juzgan han del mismo valor que la inmortalidad'" (Lope de Vega 1989, 4:467). The reference is to Book XII of the *Pimander*. Here in Ficino's Latin: "Illud praeterea consydera o fili, quod duo haec soli ex omnibus animalibus homini, deus ipse largitus est, sermonem scilicet, atque mentem: que quidem eiusdem ac immortalitas premij esse censentur" (Ficino 1554, 82).

97 The marginal notations translated in what follows here are the commentator's handwritten notes in Latin, and the English translations of those marginal notations are my own.

98 "Primum quidem (Poemander ait) in corporis materialis resolutione, corpus in alterationem labitur. Species, quam ante habuerat, insensibilis delitescit in posterum. Morum otiosus habitus daemoni conceditur, atque dimittitur. Sensus corporei partes animae facti, suos in fontes refluunt, aliquando in suos actus iterum surrecturi" (Ficino 1554, 10). In the notes to his Spanish translation of the Greek text, Renau Nebot explains the resonance of this idea of the sensorial faculties rejoining the *pneuma* in Aristotle, Diogenes Laertius, Iamblichus, and scattered other Hermetic texts (1999, 90, n. 41), as well as the importance of the ogdoad, or eighth sphere, in Greek and Egyptian thought (1999, 92, n.44).

99 "Vnde decepti quidam humorem sanguinis, animam existimarunt: hos plane latuit, quia in primis oportet spiritum ad animam vsque manare. Deinde sanguinem coalescere, venasque, & arterias cauas extendi, demum resolui anima, eamque mortem corporis esse" (Ficino 1554, 58).

100 The manuscript reads "corporal" as indicated here; the anonymous glosser could have meant Spanish 'corporal' (of the body), or either Latin 'corporeal' or

'corporis' but that cannot be determined, and so I leave the citation as found in the manuscript.

101 In his Commentary on Deuteronomy, León Hebreo also states unequivocally that "according to the Jewish dictates of resurrection, the soul and the body will rise together at the end of times in order to be judged as one unit" (cited by Ogren 2004, 86).

102 "el Tiempo sin mudanza y sin rodeo,/ lleno de sí, con hoz sobre él cargada,/ casi invisible y reducido en eco,/ encima un tronco está caído y seco" (Aldana 1985, XXVIII, vv. 37–40).

103 "¡Oh cuánto marmol veo de sepoltura/ que con su peso a cuestas se endereza,/ cuánta en la tierra, oh Dios, cuánta abertura/ por do asomada está tanta cabeza!/ ¡Oh cuánta variedad de compostura!/ Quién a bullir, quién a encarnarse empieza,/ a quién le falta el ojo, a quién la oreja/ de la carne mortal podrida y vieja,// quién de sí mismo huye, y quién se toca,/ juntando a la atención el movimiento,/ otro prueba con voz trémula y loca/ de articular el no venido acento;/ éste mueve la lengua, éste la boca,/ quién teme de atraer su mismo aliento,/ y mientras uno se reforma y cuaja,/ otro saltando va con su mortaja// Por las venas de aquél secas y heladas/ baja caliento humor de sangre pura,/ otro a la muerte pide las robadas/ reliquias de la humana vestidura;/ buscan las calaveras descarnadas/ su carne, sin horror de la natura,/ los blancos huesos corren a juntarse/ para de nuevo manto cobijarse// Trábase cada cual, sin faltar pelo,/ del mismo único ser que tuvo en vida,/ júntase cada cual con vivo celo/ al cuerpo adonde tuvo el alma unida;/ toda materia vil del mortal velo/ que en la misma materia está escondida,/ de las trocadas formas sale y huye,/ y en su primer lugar se restituye// En carne se transforma la ceniza/ y la parte exhalada en agua y viento,/ como de inútil fábrica postiza,/ viene cayendo al propio fundamento;/ la forma acidental y advenediza/ otra materia busca, otro elemento,/ sin que estorbe lugar, tiempo o fortuna,/ o al tránsito de cosas cosa alguna" (Aldana 1985, XXVIII, vv. 89–128).

104 "¡... qué de legiones veo de las perdidas,/ porque salen sin cuenta y sin guarismo/ millares de demonios del abismo!"; "con qué rumor, con qué terrible estruendo/ abre el infierno el cavernoso centro"; "Qué de estantiguas veo, nieblas y horrores,/ carátulas, fantasmas y visajes,/"; "¡... haciendo acá y allá nuevos parajes!"; "del Verbo a la sentencia se prepara" (Aldana 1985, XXVIII, vv. 134–6, 138–9, 145–6, 150, 158).

105 "ya viene cada cual con sus manojos/ de espigas, sin perder granos ni puntos,/ y yo también, ¡oh Dios terrible y santo!,/ en las manos me iré con otro tanto" (Aldana 1985, XXVIII, vv. 65–8).

106 "Et Plato in libro *De regno* scribit post praesentem fatalemque mundi cursum hominum animas, imperante deo atque suscitante, corpora sua quae in hoc cursu amiserunt ideo recepturas, ut quemadmodum sub fato quondam corpora humana

in terram deciderant, ita sub providentiae divinae imperio ex terra resurgant atque reviviscant" (Ficino 2001–6, 18.9.4).

107 For Ficino on the concept of "propitiousness" in regard to the "stellar and planetary revolutions" necessary for a particular effect, see Allen (1994, 121–2).

108 "Itaque summum ultimumque universi finem, quem mundus quandoque consequi debet ... motum non fore, sed statum ... Expleto tandem caeli cursu quo gignuntur omnia, nihil ulterius generari, sed singula hominum corpora, quorum gratia prius generabantur omnia, e terra iubente deo resurrectura" (Ficino 2001–6, 18.9.4).

109 "el Tiempo sin mudanza y sin rodeo,"; "al sol y luna veo sin movimiento,"; "cesa el flujo del mar, reposa el viento,/ todo en silencio está, como que espera/ nueva de llanto desusada y fiera" (Aldana 1985, XXVIII, vv. 37, 26, 30–2).

110 "Praeterea recreatio illa per deum facta, cessante mundi motu qui quietis alicuius perfectioris gratia tandem est institutus, ad aliquid dumtaxat stabile dirigetur. Itaque corpus semper coniunctum animae permanebit" (Ficino 2001–6, 18.9.12).

111 The verb 'conjoin' does not have an exact parallel in Spanish, but the poet's use of the literal reflexive "join itself back to" (júntase cada cual con vivo celo/ al cuerpo adonde tuvo el alma unida) (vv. 115–16) renders logically to that translation.

112 "¡Oh día de confusión, por quien sospira/ y teme el alma, oh día de Dios y de ira!" (Aldana 1985, XXVIII, vv. 151–2).

113 "Quo efficitur ut contra ordinem tam universae quam propriae naturae sit animam seorsum a corpore permanere"; "Inclinatio vero naturalis manet, semper manente natura"; "Ergo seiuncta a corpore ita, prout est anima, est imperfecta, quemadmodum pars ipsa solet extra totum ad quod constituendum est instituta. Idcirco numquam eius appetitio naturalis quieta erit. Numquam anima ulla beata, nisi ad totum suum resumpto corpore reducatur speretve reduci" (Ficino 2001–6, 18.9.6; 18.9.7; 18.9.8).

114 "corpora dissoluta in elementa ex elementis vicissim restantibus revincire ... Idem vero corpus ideo retexetur, quoniam eadem erit forma quae quondam, id est anima" (Ficino 2001–6, 18.9.10).

115 "toda materia vil del mortal velo/ que en la misma materia está escondida" (Aldana 1985, XXVIII, vv. 117–18).

116 "quoniam eadem erit forma quae quondam, id est anima; eadem quoque prima illa materia sempiterna quae una cunctis subest" (Ficino 2001–6, 18.9.10).

117 "Sit igitur anima solum forma – forma, inquam, non accidentalis, sed substantialis" (Ficino 2001–6, 6.7.2).

118 "la forma ac[c]idental y advenediza/ otra materia busca, otro elemento" (Aldana 1985, XXVIII, vv. 125–6).

5. Ficino as Plato

1 For Spain, see Round 1993, esp. 1–96, and Maravall 1973. For Europe in general, see Klibansky 1939, Hankins 1990, and Cassirer, Kristeller, and Randall 1948. Hankins (1984) offers appendices with lists of manuscripts and editions of translations of Plato. Hankins and Palmer (2008b) have published a very useful list of Renaissance editions and translations of classical works.

2 CORDE provides both references in response to a search for "Platón" restricted to the years 1200–1400, as well as a few more from the *Bocados de oro*, a compilation of refrains and wise sayings.

3 "Virgilio e Dante, Oracio e Platón/ e otros poetas que diz' la leyenda" (Villasandino 1993, 107). Plato's fame as a poet will continue to be common in Spanish letters, and he will be so identified by Martínez de Toledo in his 1438 *Corbacho*, Rodríguez del Padrón in his 1440 *Siervo libre de amor*, and Juan Alfonso de Baena in his 1435 *Cancionero*.

4 For the dates of Bruni's translation of *Phaedo*, see Round 1993, 29–35.

5 I indicate the year the Council began in each city; for details on precise opening and closing dates, see Christianson 2011.

6 "las ánimas ... [que] se abían de vestir de cuerpos por sucesión de tiempos" (Díaz de Toledo 1892, 276).

7 "E esta opinión, a mi ver, está bien reprouada, que trae consigo más curiosidat que verdad" (Díaz de Toledo 1892, 276).

8 "That the first complete version in any European vernacular of a dialogue by Plato should have appeared in Spain might well surprise many Spaniards (and not a few others)" (Round 1993, ix).

9 Following previous thinkers, Díaz de Toledo identified the Greek philosopher as head of the school of Stoics: "Otros philósophos ovo que se llamaron stoicos; el maestro e el cabdillo de aquéstos fue Platón" (1993, 222). For the alternate spellings of *Phaedo/ Phaedro*, see Round 1993, 27–8, and notes 59–63, same pages. For inaccurate references to Plato and Socrates as Stoics, and the tradition behind those inaccuracies, see Round 1993, 90.

10 "Pero lo que parece que destruye esta duda, es lo que el antiguo Trimegisto affirma, y los diuinos encantadores, que los espíritus a quien llamamos ángeles o demonios y las almas desnudas y apartadas de los cuerpos se mueuen de vn lugar a otro. La qual verdad también nosotros la auemos experimentado en las mágicas. Creyendo y esperando esta immortalidad de las almas, vuo muchos philosophos y antiguos Romanos que las muertes de los suyos y de sus parientes y amigos las recibían con grande moderación de ánimo" (Álvarez Miraval 1597, ff. 377v–8r).

11 "Platón fue el más eloquente y más loado de todos los filósofos: porque ayuntó en sus enseñanças ala disciplina socrática la parte contemplatiua que entre los antiguos tuuo en honrra Pitágoras samnite: de manera que dizen auer él dado perfección ala filosofía.

Él dixo que Dios es sin tiempo y incommutable y curador y arbitro afirmando ser dios iuez: por esto fue antepuesto a todos los otros filósofos gentiles que touieron diuersa opinión dela diuinidad. Platónicos tomaron nombre de Platón filósofo y se llamaron académicos generalmente pero por vna diuersidad fueron distinctos; affirman que Platón tomó este nombre por la anchura de sus pechos" (Palencia 1967).

12 Swift Riginos notes that Alixander Polyhistor, Seneca, Apuleius, Servius, and Tzetzes all mention this detail, and quotes from Seneca: "Et illi nomen latitudo pectoris fecerat" (Swift Riginos 1976, 35–6). That Latin has its parallel in Palencia's Latin: "Plato. a latitudine pectoris dictus afferitur" (Palencio 1967). In Diogenes Laertius's *Lives*, the detail is attributed to Neanthes, and related to the "breadth of his style, or from the breadth of his forehead" (1972, 4).

13 "Compertum autem habemus sapientiam quidem Pythagorae magis incontemplando, Socratis uero in agendo magis, Platonis denique in contemplando pariter atque agendo consistere" (Ficino 1576, 2:1488).

14 John Monfasani has edited and published an exchange of letters between Alfonso de Palencia and George of Trebizond (1395–1484), written in January 1465 (Monfasani 1984, 101–8).

15 "Soi de D. Eugenio Nicolás de Guzmán Marqués Calificador del Sto. oficio Cura beneficiado más antiguo de la Iglesia maior de la Hda. Sta. María de la Ciudad de Arcos de la Frontera" (Bib. Columbina, ms. 23-7-2, *Opera* ed. de 1567).

16 See above, section on holdings of the Biblioteca Capitular y Colombina.

17 Tenth-century Al-Farabi, or Abu Nasr, also used the adjective "divino" for Plato, in his *Reconciliation of the Views of the two Sages, Plato the Divine and Aristotle*; however, during the Renaissance it was Ficino's writing that made use of the epithet "ubiquitous" (Purnell 1971, 48).

18 "Ex his omnibus id Plato est consequutus, vt Graeci Aristotelem quidem daemonium: Platonem vero diuinum cognominauerint. Quia videlicet ille & vita humanus & scientia naturalis maxime fuerit. Hic autem scientia simul & vita sese potissimum ad diuinum contulerit" (Ficino 1557, 2:no pag.). Compare, for example, Diogenes Laertius who describes an epitaph on which it is written that Plato "discerned the divine life" (1972, 44), but does not call the philosopher himself "divine." H.A. Enno van Gelder notes that Guillaume Budé and Michel de l'Hospital also employ the epithet (1961, 199, 295).

19 "y esto es lo que nos quiso mostrar/ aquel diuino Platón quando dixo, que dios hizo ánima de acordamientos de música" (Fuentes 1547, f. 169v).

20 "De lo cual el divino Platón nos da un notable ejemplo" (1990, 139). Luján's editor, Rallo Gruss, notes that the same history, with epithet, is also found in Guevara's *Epístolas Familiares* (Luján 1990, 161, n.1).

21 "el divino Platón dezía en los libros de su República que a los príncipes deben los que los hablan dezir pocas palabras" (Horozco 1994, 2:344, proverb 282).

22 "la noticia confusa que el divino Platón tuvo deste Nuevo Mundo" (Cervantes de Salazar 1971, chapter 2, no pag.).

23 "Aulo Gelio, en el tercio libro, cap. XII, dize que el divino Platón, entre los otros discípulos que tuvo, fue uno el gran philósopho Demóstenes" (1994, 160). The reference is to book 3, chapter 13 of the *Noches áticas*, in which Demosthenes listens to Plato, but the latter is not "divine" (Gelio 2006, 1:194)

24 "Y Platón ganó nombre de diuino porque siendo gentil dixo mil diuinidades de Dios" (Saona 1598, 43).

25 "Por cosa averiguada tuvo Platón que el ánima racional era sustancia incorpórea, espiritual, no sujeta a corrupción ni a mortalidad como la de los brutos animales ... otra vida mejor y más descansada ... [o] padecer los tormentos con que Dios castiga a los malos. Esta conclusión es tan ilustre y católica ... con justo título tiene por renombre *el divino Platón*" (Huarte de San Juan 1989, 376–7).

26 "supo tanto,/ que mereció renombre de divino"; "Al divino Platón metió triumphando/ Dionysio en Zaragoça" (Pineda 1620, dedication "Vn alto rostro").

27 "Profecto spiritalis ille mundus, mundi huius exemplar primumque dei opus, vita aequalis est architecto" (Ficino 2001–6, 18.1.10).

28 "El diuino Platón Príncipe de la escuela Académica, bien nos muestra en muchos lugares, quán liberales sean" (1600, 138); " no se me puede negar sino que estas Artes del dibuxo son hermanas de la Filosofía. Esto no lo digo yo solo, que los mismos Filósofos lo dan a entender, pues por ser Artes de tanto ingenio, y virtud, las vsaron muchos dellos por sus manos, y casi todos fueron muy aficionados suyos, como leemos de Sócrates, del diuino Platón, de Aristóteles, de Marco Tulio padre de la eloquencia Romana, de Demestio, y Metrododo [*sic* – Metrodoro]" (Gutiérrez de los Ríos, 1600, 191). I quote from the Beinecke library's copy of this 1600 treatise (BEIN J714 G985 600).

29 "vence en todo al divino Platón y Ptholomeo, Euclides y otros muchos escritores" (Molina Cano 1999, El comissario Francisco de Molina a su hermano).

30 "un rato escuchaba a Sócrates y otro al divino Platón" (Gracián 2009, 109). There is a second reference without the proper name: "Llamó acertadamente el filósofo divino al compuesto humano sonoro, animado instrumento" (Gracián 2009, 563).

31 The referenced copy of the 1548 edition is found in Seville's Biblioteca Columbina (signatura 23-4-5). Also crossed out in this copy are all writings by Simon Grynaeus, accompanied by a note indicating that the volume was expurgated in conformance with the Indices of prohibited books dated 1612 and 1614, signed by one J. de Vargas. The referenced Indices do call for censorship of Grynaeus, but they do not call for emendation of the use of the epithet. Simon Grynaeus was "a Protestant humanist, friend of Erasmus and Budé ... professor of Greek at Basel in 1529" (Hankins 1990, 479).

32 Along with the immortality of the soul as founding principle of Christianity, Fox includes the reclamation of legal and public matters: "Et cum Christianae religionis

fundamentum sit animorum immortalitatis affertio, ut legum etiam omnium, atque adeo rerumpublicarum: nulla quidem alia firmiora maiores nostri, qui primam Ecclesiam defenderunt, arma, quibus uterentur, contra impiorum hominum uim habuere, quam disputationem haec Platonis... Hinc enim illi, Tertullianus, Origenes, Eusebius, Lactantius, ac plerique allij antiquorum patrum, qui nostrae religionis decreta propugnarunt, argumenta omnia, uel eadem, ut erant a Platone adducta, uel paulum immutata deprompserunt" (Fox 1556a, 5).

33 "independencia en el orden filosófico y ... firme adhesión al dogma revelado, en el campo de la fe"; "Su independencia filosófica no llega a extremos que no eran comunes en aquel siglo" (González de la Calle 1903, 94, 122). See also Cortijo Ocaña 2011 for the importance and dissemination of Fox's writings.

34 "Addam his D. Thomae Aquinatis, uiri in primis sanctissimi atque, doctissimi, argumenta, quibus eandem immortalitatem tueri, ac pene demonstrare mihi uidetur" (Fox 1556a, 48).

35 For Aquinas in Ficino, see Copenhaver 2009.

36 "Duodecima ratio: quia non habet in se potentiam ad non esse" (Ficino 2001–6, 5.12, subtitle).

37 Allen points out that on Platonic grounds "that which is perfect cannot degenerate" (1994, 12).

38 "si aliud perfectius & purius, ergo non solum non interit anima, sed etiam purior redditur, ac proinde sit immortalior" (Fox 1556a, 51). In this place, Cruz Cruz's Spanish translation introduces an error in the text, substituting "imperfect" where the Latin reads "perfect" (Fox 2010, 78); I read the passage as in the Latin, with "perfect."

39 The topic under discussion is the creation of a determined number of souls by God at the beginning of time which, Fox assures his reader, is an opinion found in Plato, Pythagoras, and Orpheus. He concludes: "ueterem famam fuisse, abire animas ad inferorum loca, atque inde rursus reuerti. Quod quidem ille ad immortalitatem animi tuendam, a fama & opinione antique petitum refert" (Fox 1556a, 53).

40 "César. No tuviera tanta autoridad; que muchas cosas se respetan por antiguas que no igualan con las que agora vemos./ Julio. Esa desdicha no la padecen las mujeres; que más las respetan mozas" (Lope de Vega 1996, IV, III, 361).

41 "Anima, inquam, si sic affecta discesserit, non ne ad aliquid sibi simile diuinum abit?"; "reuera reliquum tempus uitam cum diis agit" (Fox 1556a, 70). Here and in what follows, I quote the dialogue from Fox's text which is, as noted above, taken from Ficino's Latin.

42 "Sin autem polluta impuraque decedat, utpote quae corpus semper amplexa, ipsum duntaxat coluerit, & amauerit eiusque uoluptatibus et libidinibus quasi ueneficijs quibusdam delinita fuerit ... ideoque ab eo grauatur, & ad uisibilem trahitur locum metu inuisibilis, atque occulti: & quemadmodum fertur, circa monumenta sepulchraque

uersatur, circa quae iam nonnulla apparuerunt animarum umbrosa phantasmata" (Fox 1556a, 71).

43 "Qui uero iniurias, tyrannides, rapinas, prae caeteris secuti sunt: in luporum, accipitrum, miluorum genera par est pertransire" (Fox 1556a, 71).

44 See Ogren for a review of disputes by Church Fathers Tertullian, Augustine, and Aquinas regarding this concept (2004, 69).

45 "auctor grauis, et magnae inter Platonicos auctoritatis" (Fox 1556a, 77).

46 "et alii permulti: quos nunc taceo, ne longior sim" (Fox 1556a, 77).

47 "Quo sit, ut qui hanc Platonis opinionem ad allegorias detorquere uolint, ab eius sententia longissime discendant, nec fatis quid ille intellexerit assequantur" (Fox 1556a, 77).

48 "Quod quidem patet ex eo, quod non dicit animam fieri bestiam, sed induere, subire, transire" (Ficino 1576, 2:[1392] (1390). The 1576 edition includes a mistake in pagination, reading 1390 instead of 1392.

49 "Quod autem Plato de migratione animarum in corpora bestiarum tam ridiculam affert fabellam, ab anicularum fabulis nihilo discrepantem, profecto nos admonet, totum allegorice exponendum" (Ficino 1576, 2:1438).

50 "ubi multa proculdubio poetica sunt potius quam philosophica"; "Tria vero prae ceteris signa videntur evidentissima, quibus iudicare possimus eum pythagorica illa nequaquam affirmavisse"; "Ac si quis ea etiam Platonem affirmavisse contenderit, nos quoque affirmare forsitan disputationis gratia concedum" (Ficino 2001–6, 17.3.2; 17.4.5; 17.4.14).

51 See also Hankins, on reaction to the idea of transmigration from Savonarola (2005, 12), and also Ogren (2004) for a comparison of Ficino and Hebreo on the topic. Ogren notes that transmigration was not problematic for Hebreo, whose reading was influenced by his knowledge of the Jewish Cabala tradition.

52 "cuius sententiae per multi uiri magni cum primis, & sancti sunt"; "Horum ego sententiae non magnopere repugno, cum uideam aperta uestigia uerborum ex Genesi apud Platonem hic desumpta, & fabulis atque opinionibus falsis inuoluta: ut sunt reliqua, quae ab Hebraeis Graeci, aut Aegyptij accepere" (Fox 1556a, 142).

53 "Iam quam Platonici afferre solent in hunc locum allegorias, de coelesti hac terra, quam in duodecim plagas, id est 12 Zodiaci signa diuidunt, caeteraque; his similia praetermittamus, cum ad Platonis intelligentiam parum conducant: & ea sint a philosopho prorsus aliena, qui ueritatem rerum, non umbram, ut caeteri, consecutari debeat" (Fox 1556a, 145).

54 "duodecim sphaerarum regitur animabus, & duodecima est mundi sphaera" (Ficino 1576, 2:1394).

55 See de Armas 2009.

56 "id tamen sic est intelligendum, ut putet illam ipsam coeli plagam, cui eadem terra subiecta sit, foelicissimam esse, & hac nostra longe praestantiorum: qualem poetae in Elysijs campis depingunt" (Fox 1556a, 145).

57 "Ex horum ergo animorum numero, primi ad Elysios campos, seu ad superos efferuntur, ibique Dei fiunt, ut Plato lib. 10. de Repub. refert: atque ad consimile sibi astrum in coelo positum applicantur, ut idem ait in Timaeo" (Fox 1556a, 148–9).

58 "Quae ipsa cum nostra religione maxime congruunt"; "Qua in re mirum est quanta sit ueritatis uis, cum uel gentes uerae religionis expertes, proposita esse pijs praemia, contaque malis supplicia crediderint" (Fox 1556a, 150).

59 "Nonnulli hoc superstitionis genus in Socrate multum uituperant"; "ut inocentiam suam, in eo quod ei obijcebatur, ostenderet, id fecerit" (Fox 1556a, 158, 159).

60 "In omnibus quae aut hic alibi a me tractantur, tantum assertum esse volo quantum ab ecclesia comprobatur" (Ficino 2001–6, 18, postscript).

61 In seventeenth-century England it is also an accepted, if not widely held, view (Harrison 1993).

62 "Vera philosophi uita, ut Plotinus in lib. de Beatitudine refert, intellectus ipse hominis est, a corpore sese abducens ... Itaque uera philosophi uita est, contemplatio, & a corpore dissolutio" (Fox 1556a, 35). A simple numerical accounting of the number of references to each authority shows Plato 133, Aristotle 70, Plotinus 25, Cicero 20, Pythagoras 7, Saint Justin Martyr 6, Plutarch 6, Macrobius 5, Porfirius 5, Proclus 4, [Saint] Cyril 2, Pliny 2, Olympiodorus 1, Orpheus 1, Sinesius 1.

63 "sus creaciones responden más al sentido del neoplatonismo erudito que a la sobria majestad de la primera Academia" (González de la Calle 1903, 9).

64 In 2011, Antonio Cortijo Ocaña added the detail that the young Fox studied with Alonso de Medina in Seville, and then also "possibly" at Alcalá de Henares, before leaving Spain to pursue higher studies at Louvain.

65 "Eorundem praeterea alij boni esse dicuntur, quod res sibi subiectas bene gerant: alij mali, quod male" (Fox 1556a, 19).

66 "Idem declarat Plotinus in lib. de Daemone proprio, ipsumque hunc Daemonem familiarem ab anima, non re, sed ratione distinguit, quatenus scilicet anima corpori prae est" (Fox 1556a, 19).

67 "In idem enim unde profecta est cuiusque anima *decem annorum milibus* non revertitur" (Ficino 2008, 1.25.13).

68 "Iam tertij grauissimis poenis in Tartaro per annum puniuntur, postea in Cocytum demittuntur: quia ducti poenitentia delictorum, ultra annum puniri non debuerunt. Ex ipso uero Cocyto, si iudices sint exorati, ad Acherusiam mittuntur, una cum ijs qui sint purgandi, et praemijs tandem afficiendi uel reducuntur ad Tartarum, si uenia digni non iudicentur" (Fox 1556a, 149).

69 See Byrne 2012a, 43.

70 "homines sub assidua Dei esse custodia, neque licere nisi quando Deus uoluerit, hinc emigrare"; "Quum totum philosophantis studium sit quaedam a corpore separatio, per eamque perficiatur quotidie, nimirum separationem a corpore quae sit

per mortem, non modo non timere debet, sed optima cum spe laetitiaque expectare" (Ficino 1576, 2:1390).

71 "Quid vero dicemus ad illud, quando animus aliquis suum corpus interimit sive consilio sive indignatione seu metu id faciat vel dolore?... Homo autem, licet sit prudentius animal, tamen id saepe facit, vaticinans, ut arbitror, se superfore post corpus ac se potius corporis sarcina exonerare quam perdere" (Ficino 2001–6, 9.3.8).

72 "Si autem hoc ita se habet, non ne, quemadmodum modo dicebam, praeter rationem foret omnino, si mortem uir eiusmodi formidaret?"; "qua ratione se neminem occidere posse putet, cum mortem a Philosopho dicet expetendam" (Fox 1556a, 31).

73 "At Cebete id obijciente, neminem sibi manus afferre posse: obiectionem hanc diluens Socrates, inquit, Nulli quidem licere, se occidere: utile uero esse, contemplatrici hac morte defungi" (Fox 1556a, 34).

74 "cum eodem animali uiuente, animus ipse per contemplationem a corpore sese abducit" (Fox 1556a, 33).

75 "ex harmonicis numeris"; "Quin etiam Plotinus in lib. De triplici ascensu animi ad mundum intelligibilem, Musicae concentu animos a corporibus segregari, & in diuinorum contemplationem erigi dicit" (Fox 1556a, 20).

76 "Haec eadem scientia purgati animi cum a rebus corporeis aliena sit, & intelligentia duntaxat comprehendatur: nunquam in hac uita corporea satis comparari potest, quam uis per philosophicam contemplationem quedam modo purgatis animis possit. Ex quo patet, in altera uita incorporea, cum animus liber & uacuus sit, nos eandem scientiam consequuturos, quippe quae in intelligentiam solum cadat, & ab animo plane intellectili facto capiatur" (Fox 1556a, 39).

77 "Y si lo queréis oýr/ consiste esta summa sciencia/ en un subido sentir/ de la dibinal esencia/ es obra de su clemencia/ hazer quedar no entendiendo/ toda sciencia tracendiendo" (Juan de la Cruz 2000, "Entréme," stanza 8).

78 Here, I use E. Allison Peers's translation; see my bibliography, Juan de la Cruz 1953.

79 "ut alis sublati platonicis ac deo duce in sedem aethercam liberius pervolemus"; "divinum lumen non inquisitione paulatim a nobis acquiri, sed perfecta vitae coniunctione subito tandem divinitus in nobis accendi" (Ficino 2001–6, 1.1.1; 14.10.12).

80 "quia vis cognitionis in discretione consistit magis, amoris autem magis in unione" (Ficino 2001–6, 14.10.12).

81 "volé tan alto tan alto/ que le di a la caça alcance//... en el buelo quedé falto/ mas el amor fue tan alto/ que le di a la caça alcance//... mas por ser de amor el lance/ di un ciego y oscuro salto/ y fuy tan alto tan alto/ que le di a la caça alcance" (Juan de la Cruz 2000, "Tras de un amoroso lance," vv. 3–4; 10–12; 17–20). Ynduráin describes San Juan's flight as sudden rapture, in contrast with Ignatius of Loyola's thoughtful contemplation (Juan de la Cruz 2002, xvi).

82 "Allí me dio su pecho,/ allí me enseñó ciencia muy sabrosa,/ y yo le di de hecho/ a mí, sin dejar cosa; allí le prometí de ser su esposa" (Juan de la Cruz 2000, "Cántico," stanza 27).

83 "ciencia e inteligencia en el amor"; "ciencia por amor" (Juan de la Cruz 2002, Cántico, 18.3). Quotes to the saint's commentaries on his verse are to Paolo Elia and María Jesús Mancho's 2002 edition (Juan de la Cruz 2002), with stanza number followed by paragraph number, so that 18.3 is found at stanza (*canción*) 18, paragraph 3.

84 "amado con amada,/ amada en el amado transformada" (Juan de la Cruz 2000, "Noche," stanza 5).

85 "ya cosa no sabía" (Juan de la Cruz 2000, "Cántico," stanza 17); "sabiduría de Dios altísima"; "pura ignorancia"; "ajenada y aniquilada" (Juan de la Cruz 2002, "Cántico," 17.11).

86 "En la interior bodega/ de mi Amado beví, y quando salía/ por toda aquesta bega,/ ya cosa no sabía,/ y el ganado perdí que antes seguía" (Juan de la Cruz 2000, "Cántico," stanza 26).

87 "Anima hominum deum quodammodo contrahit in se ipsam, quando nihil retinens mortale, tota divinis haustibus ebriatur" (Ficino 2001–6, 13.4.12).

88 "Estava tan embebido/ tan absorto y ajenado/ que se quedó mi sentido/ de todo sentir privado/ y el espíritu dotado/ de un entender no entendiendo/ toda sciencia tracendiendo" (Juan de la Cruz 2000, "Entréme," stanza 3).

89 "incipit usque adeo supra hominem sapere, ut se et per deum, et deum, et in deo contemplari non nesciat"; "purgatas animas, quae divinam prae ceteris pulchritudinem amaverunt, tandem in ipsum divinae pulchritudinis pelagus sese prorsus immergere divinosque ibi liquores non tantum bibere, sed etiam in alios iam ex se ipsis effundere" (Ficino 2001–6, 12.3.4; 18.8.8).

90 "effulget, rarescit, attollitur, aethereo ad hoc conferente vehiculo corporeque aereo, quasi stuppa elevata per flammam" (Ficino 2001–6, 13.4.16).

91 "En una noche escura/ con ansias en amores inflamada/ ¡o dichosa ventura¡/ salí sin ser notada/ estando ya mi casa sosegada" (Juan de la Cruz 2000, "Noche," stanza 1).

92 "como dicen los filósofos, el alma, luego que Dios la infunde en el cuerpo, está como una tabla rasa y lisa, en que no está pintado nada ... como ... en una cárcel oscura" (Juan de la Cruz 1954, "Subida," 27).

93 "¡O llama de amor viva,/ que tiernemente hyeres/ de mi alma en el más profundo centro!/ pues ya no eres esquiva,/ acava ya si quieres;/ rompe la tela de este dulce encuentro" (Juan de la Cruz 2000, "Llama," vv. 1–6).

94 "efficit tamen ut anima nonnihil uisibile secum trahat, id est inuolucrum quoddam, uel aereum, uel ex spiritibus uaporibusque corporis sui conflatum ut uult Proclus, uel nuper ex circumfuso aere congregatum" (Ficino 1576, 2:[1392] [1390]).

95 "cum primum mens a terreno corpore soluitur, proprium mox subit amictum, igneum videlicet corpus, quo sane quandiu circuntecta est, in terreum corpus

turgescere nequit. Terra nanque ignem minime sustinet: tota siquidem ab exigua scintilla cremaretur" (Ficino 1554, 60).

96 "llama que consume y no da pena" (Juan de la Cruz 2000, "Cántico," stanza 39).

97 "De paz y de piedad/ era la sciencia perfecta,/ en profunda soledad/ entendida vía recta/ era cosa tan secreta/ que me quedé balbuciendo/ toda sciencia tracendiendo" (2000," Entréme," stanza 2).

98 "Mira profecto proportione ad eum comprehendendum vtitur, qui omnem effugit proportionem, qui comprehensus incomprehensibilis manet, & qui omnibus incognitus, omnibus in rebus se præstat cognoscibilem" (Ficino 1554, 77).

99 "su sciencia tanto cresce/ que se queda no sabiendo"; "quien la sabía/ queda siempre no sabiendo"; "Este saber no sabiendo"; "no entender entendiendo"; "Si lo queréis oyr/ consiste esta summa sciencia/ en un subido sentir/ de la dibinal esencia/ es obra de su clemencia/ hazer quedar no entendiendo/ toda sciencia tracendiendo" (Juan de la Cruz 2000, "Entréme," stanza 8).

100 See Celenza 2002 for questions of subsequent misreadings of orthodox and heterodox elements in Ficino's writings.

101 See also Ficino: "Quid ergo reliquum est, quod omnino solius sit hominis? Contemplatio divinorum. Nullum enim bruta prae se ferunt religionis indicium, ut propria nobis sit mentis in deum caeli regem erectio sicut corporis in caelum erectio propria" (Ficino 2001–6, 14.9.1).

102 "Suelen tomar los hombres nombres de otros, por seguirlos ... como los discípulos de Platón se llaman platónicos, porque siguen su doctrina ... los que siguen a Cristo, cristianos" (Meneses 1567, f. 71v).

103 "Plotino, que fue excelentíssimo platónico, después de averse dado con mucha efficacia a esta astrología, como al cabo la hallasse llena de vanidades y burlerías, la escarneció" (*Reprobación* 1546, f. 19v)

104 "Porque el amor entra por los ojos i nace del viso, que es la potencia que conoce, o sea vista corporal, que es el más amado de todos los sentidos, o sea aquella potencia del ánima que los platónicos llaman viso i los teólogos conocimiento intele[c]tual, conocimiento intuitivo" (Herrera 2001, 320). And see Ficino: "comparare Platonici iubent intellectum quidem visui, intellegibile vero visibili" (2001–6, 18.8.4), with reference to Plato's *Republic.*

105 That lengthy list of named references (Pineda 1963, 161:8–14) has various identified as simply "platónico" including "Marsilio Ficino, platónico," and also "Eneas Gazeo, platónico cristiano," that is, Aeneas of Gaza, a late 5th/ early 6th century Neoplatonist convert to Christianity. Gazeus's work on the immortality of the soul, known generally as the *Theophrastus* for the name of one of the interlocutors, was one of the works translated and commented by Ficino, published with the Aldus edition catalogued under uniform title Iamblichus. Ficino's commentary is listed in the volume as *Expositio Prisciani, & Marsilii in Theophrastum de sensu, phantasia, & intellectu*, and

the work itself as *Theophrasti Metaphysicoru* lib. I. According to Lackner, "several years before commencing his translations of the complete works of Plato, Ficino copied in his own hand Traversari's translation of the [Aeneas of Gaza's] *Theophrastus*" (2002, 21). There are multiple copies of this volume in Spanish libraries. For Aeneas and his use of both the philosophical terminology and literary images of Platonism, see Klitenic Wear (2013).

106 The list of authorities in agreement on the concept follows: Plato, Diogenes Laertius, Plutarch, Origen, Philo, Plotinus, Trismegistus, "the greatest of the Egyptian theologians" (el mayor de los teólogos egipcios), Iamblicus, Rabbi Moses, Avicenna, Cicero, Macrobius, Aristotle, Aquinas, Ptolemy, Zael, Albumasar, Halí, Arato, Marcus Manilius, Theophrastus, Julius Caesar Escaligero, Averroes, Alejandro, and Orpheus (Pineda 1963, 162.356–7).

107 "De la música sintieron los filósofos pitagóricos y los platónicos tan altamente, que compusieron della nuestras almas" (Pineda 1963, 163.38–9).

108 "Pánfilo. – Bien creo yo que nunca Lucio Apuleyo soñó que sus composturas merecían ser tan bien acristianadas. Filaletes. – Con todo eso digo yo que, como gran filósofo platónico ..." (Pineda 1963, 163:275).

109 "El buen platónico Marsilio Ficino, en sus Epístolas y sobre el Convite de Platón, os contentará vendiéndoseos por tan libre y precioso en su estima que ni quiere ni puede venderse, trocarse ni cambalacharse si no por sí mesmo ... Maravillosamente habló el buen Marsilio para los que tienen orejas siquiera ..." (Pineda 1963, 169:74).

110 For the persistence and importance of Augustine as transmitter of Platonic concepts, see Round (1993, 41–61).

111 "Aunque Macrobio, como platónico, concede los infiernos para castigar los malos, parece decir que este mundo que moramos es llamado infierno de los platónicos, por ser más bajo que el cielo, donde ellos pintaban la verdadera morada de los hombres" (Pineda 1963, 163.85).

112 "No sé si notastes que puso Macrobio las ideas de las virtudes en la mente divina; por eso advertid que el mesmo Macrobio con todos los platónicos pusieron haber Hijo de Dios, y a éste, producido de Dios, llaman mente y armario de las ideas por lenguaje de apropriación; porque como sea engendrado por el divino entendimiento, que es el subjecto de la sabiduría, y las ideas son las razones primordiales a que mira Dios para entender y criar las cosas, por eso asientan todos los teólogos las ideas en el Hijo o mente de Dios, al cual llama el famosísimo teólogo Trismegisto por la mesma palabra Verbo de Dios, por el cual su Padre crió al mundo; y también le llama Verbo Diógenes Laercio, pagano como Trismegisto; y conforme a la posición de las ideas procedió Macrobio llamando a la mente divina la mesma prudencia, pues como la mente es el entendimiento, ansí la prudencia es hábito intelectual. Pánfilo.- ¿Qué os parece, señor Policronio, deste lenguaje tan cristiano en boca de paganos? ¿Qué podrán decir los que mofan de la teología ... ?" (Pineda 1963, 169:151).

113 "Lo que aquí digo no es más de para las personas que no saben letras scientíficas, ni las leyes que se deben guardar en cada linaje de escritura, ni el estilo de su proceder, ni el decoro de su razonar" (Pineda 1963, 161:5).

114 "se llama la obra de *Diálogos familiares*, en que se representan algunos amigos que, como familiares y llanos y conversables entre sí, se avienen bien, sin pundonores de cumplimiento ceremonial y que llaman de pelillo, sino que como lo sienten ansí lo dicen" (Pineda 1963, 161:5).

115 "no son menester poetas que turben y mientan para quietar y deleitar los ánimos de los hombres ni, por tales medios, traellos a la enseñanza y virtud" (López Pinciano 1998, 1:101).

116 "quisieron ... que, sin salsa de fábulas, comieran la virtud" (López Pinciano 1998, 1:101).

6. Persistence of Political-Economic Platonism

1 See also Fernández-Santamaría (1986) for full descriptions of the various groups wielding power in Spanish political circles during the late sixteenth and early seventeenth centuries. Eric Nelson studies the comparable Italian *speculum principis* tradition, and its relation to "princely humanism in Renaissance political thought" (2007, 319, 323).

2 See, for example, Kagan 2009, Truman 1999, Tomás y Valiente 1969 and 1975, Fernández-Santamaría 1977, Thompson 1976, Maravall 1972.

3 See Nelson (2007) for the parallel discussion in Renaissance Italy over neo-Roman versus Greek traditions of republics and the resultant pitched battles over private property.

4 Boter provides a history of direct and indirect references to the dialogue, as well as a list of medieval and Renaissance translations. See also Garin 1955, and Hankins 1984.

5 "Para lo qual hizo vna librería muy sumptuosa, y mandando traduzir libros Griegos en Latín, procuraua resuscitar y enrriquecer las letras que estauan sepultadas" (Giovio 1568, ff. 73v, 74r). The importance of Alphonse V's court in Naples as a place of intellectual exchange between Italy and Spain during the fifteenth century is widely recognized (Soria 1956).

6 "dixo Platón en el libro De república que estonçes serían bienaventuradas las cosas públicas cuando los regidores d'ellas fuesen sabidores" (Villena 1989, Prohemio, 45, n.35).

7 "Ca, según dize Platón en su libro De república, no sería la cibdad perfecta sino oviessen los moradores" (Sánchez de Arévalo 1944, 40).

8 "At quoniam forma haec formosa esse nunquam potest, nisi ciuium animi sint formosi" (Ficino 1576, 2:1496).

9 "las onestas y solaçosas delectaciones" for "purga o melecina al cuerpo umano" (Sánchez de Arévalo 1944, 56–7).

10 Compare with Cicero's *Tusculan Disputations*: "Socrates was the first who brought down philosophy from the heavens, placed it in cities, introduced it into families, and obliged it to examine life and morals, good and evil" (1758, 5.4). López de Mendoza names Plato instead of Socrates, and laws instead of philosophy. Íñigo López de Mendoza died in 1458.

11 "bien andante es la región/ a do goviernan los magos" (Mendoza 1968, copla 202). Fray Íñigo de Mendoza wrote his coplas in 1467–8.

12 "en juyzios y en hombres darmas" (Lucena 1954, 89). Lucena's work was published in 1497.

13 Truman points out that the "comparison of the merits of monarchical and republican forms of government had become an established topic in treatises on the Rule of Princes since the recovery of Aristotle's *Politics*," reviewing works by Aquinas, Giles of Rome, and Patrizi, among others (Truman 1999, 41–2), and he notes Patrizi's particular debt to the Platonists (26–7).

14 "sacerdotemque more Aegyptiorum constitui, sacrorum myteriorumque antistitem" (Ficino 1576, 2:1295).

15 "qui instar numinis & diuina contempletur, & humanis inde prouideat" (Ficino 1576, 2:1409).

16 "Dum uero de fine legum disputat, officium quoque ipsarum conditoris exponit: idque summatim esse uult, summa cum diligentia totam ciuitatem colere quasi agrum, ut exquisitam de eligendis ferendisque seminibus habeat rationem. Deinde de opportuna plantae cuiusque cultura. Item de extirpandis statim ab initio noxijs herbis & sentibus" (Ficino 1576, 2:1490–1).

17 "Praecipue uero animos omnium decentissima quadam fortitudinis temperantiaeque mixtione componat, musicos imitatus, qui acuta grauibus rite miscentes, concentus suauissimos modulantur" (Ficino 1576, 2:1296).

18 Scholars have noted the resonance of Plato's thought on a republic in Erasmus (Isnardi-Parente 1988), and in Sebastián Fox Morcillo (González de la Calle 1903, 193–226). H.A. Enno van Gelder says that More "undoubtedly.. had learnt much ... from the Stoa as well as from Plato, whose *Republic* was a model for his *Utopia*" (1961, 184). Hankins demonstrates More's debt to Ficino's theology (2006), and speaks of the appeal of the *Republic* to "the apologists of Renaissance tyranny" (1984, 18). Machiavelli's debt to Ficino has been studied by Cesare Vasoli (2006). For Ficino and Campanella, see Walker 1975 [1958]. On Erasmus and Ficino, scholars have noted suggestive similarities but also debate any actual influence: see Bietenholtz 1985–7, 2:27–30, and 2009, 114–33; Tracy 1972; Kristeller and Randall 1970.

19 See Kagan 1981 for the courts and processes, and Byrne 2012a for history and law in Cervantes. William Clamurro (2014) has suggested the importance of justice as an overriding theme in Cervantes' *Novelas ejemplares*.

20 “Illa respublica uouentis fuerit & optantis, dispositio praesens sit eligentis, ut qui in arduum illud ascendere nequeunt” (Ficino 1576, 2:1488).

21 “Quoniam in ea ciuitate in qua possessiones sunt propriae singulorum, propter uarias controuersias, lites, iniurias, multis opus est legibus” (Ficino 1576, 2:1488).

22 I cite Madrigal’s division by book and chapter; see Guevara 1994.

23 “el resultado es un tíovivo en el que Carlomagno puede ser un enano, Aristóteles hablar como el papa Inocencio III y Platón remedar la *filosofía vulgar* del refranero” (Madrigal 1994, 22–3).

24 “En todos los casos el diálogo es por su naturaleza – y ello resulta del análisis de los factores de los que se compone – un género mixto, capaz de admitir elementos de doctrina y elementos de ficción” (Wyss Morigi 2006, 17).

25 Madrigal reviews critical opinion from Gibbs, who describes Guevara as pompous and self-important; Costes, who calls the *Relox* a “broken watch”; Lida Malkiel, for whom the book is an anachronism; Márquez Villanueva, who reads Guevara’s intent to amuse; and Redondo, who believes the author’s treatise is a serious and stylized sermon (Madrigal 1994, 3, 32, 33). For Madrigal himself: “Hay ... un prurito constante de sorprender al lector ... dibujar semblanzas caprichosas, enumerar leyes inauditas o meter descaradamente la fábula dentro de la historia ... El texto se vuelve así desmedido, inclasificable y, sin duda, excepcional” (1994, 25).

26 Rallo Gruss also notes the importance of contemporary news of idyllic communities in the New World, and Vespuccio’s 1503 *Mundus Novus*, to the resurgence of the golden age myth (1979, 124).

27 “que al tal hombre que le den ayos que le rixan como a loco; y, si no, que por vagamundo sea alançado del pueblo. Porque jamás se desconcierta la república sino por hombres que tienen desconcertada la vida” (Guevara 1994, Prologue, 133–4).

28 “Id autem ideo Socrates improbat, quoniam insano neque omne uerum patrefaciendum est, neque arma reddenda sunt quae sanus dum erat apud te deposuerat”; “Primum, malos non esse admittendos ad magistratum” (Ficino 1576, 2:1397, 1398).

29 “Prohibet deinde magistratum illi tribui gubernandum qui propter incontinentiam gubernare se nesciat”; “Tum uero homines deprauatae naturae sui dominos esse negat neque iniuria” (Ficino 1576, 2:1495, 1511).

30 “no ay mayor indicio de perderse una república que quando se levantan muchas cabeças en ella” (Guevara 1994, prologue, 174).

31 “Vnum igitur oportet esse regem omnium iudicem” (Ficino 1576, 2:1295). Rees notes that Ficino’s general “principle of unity” and its “obvious reflection ... in political terms ... [as] the image of a single head ruling over a body politic” is also reflective of Dante’s views in *Monarchia*, a text that, despite ecclesiastical rebuttal and prohibition, was known to and translated by Ficino (Rees 2002, 346–8). The *Monarchia* was also known in Spain, but Dante’s name does not appear in Guevara’s treatise.

32 "no quiso obedescer a un mandamiento ... por no obedescer a un señor entonces, somos esclavos de tantos señores agora" (Guevara 1994, I, 28).

33 According to Guevara, it was Socrates who said "que era mejor que todas las cosas fuessen conmunes y que todos los hombres fuessen yguales; los pitagóricos, por contrario, dezían que era mejor república do cada uno tenía propio y do todos obedescían a uno" (1994, I, 28). For Ficino, both Socrates and the Pythagoreans held that opinion, but Plato differed (2009a, 73).

34 "El divino Platón, en los libros de su República, amonestava y aconsejava que todas las cosas fuessen comunes, no sólo los animales y eredades más aún también fuessen comunes las mugeres ... A Platón llámanle divino por muchas cosas buenas que dixo, pero agora justamente le pueden llamar humano por este consejo que dio tan profano" (Guevara 1994, II, 3).

35 "ni mayor abominación que la que atribuyen a Platón, que puso ley que las mujeres fuesen comunes" (Arce de Otálora 1995, 1:478).

36 "Del mismo Platón, que fue el más divino dellos, dice S. Crisóstomo en la Homelia cuarta sobre los Actos de los Apóstoles, que hizo leyes nefandas, como fue que las mujeres y los hijos fuesen comunes, que las doncellas vírgines luchasen desnudas delante de todos" (Arce de Otálora 1995, 1:468).

37 "Platón decía que era bienaventurada la ciudad donde no había mío ni tuyo, sino todo común de todos, y muy más bien adventurada la casa de los casados donde no se diferencia la hacienda de marido y mujer" (Arce de Otálora 1995, 1:523).

38 "Post quadragesimum uero annum in conuiuijs inter deorum hymnos concedit uinum liberius bibere, quasi re medium aduersus duritiam senectutis, per quod reuuenescere uideamur, & moestitiae nos obliui capiat, ipsaque affectio animi, sicuti ferrum in igne, ex duritie in mollitiem deducta flexibilior fiat. Quo effici uult, ut seniores qui alioquin cantare nollent, facti hilariores in conuiuijs ad iuniorum autes cantare uelint, atque una eorum animis, ut ita dixerim, incantare" (Ficino 1576, 2:1493).

39 Fox also notes in his *Diálogo sobre la enseñanza de la historia* that Dionysius Halicarnasus criticized Plato for using poetic figures and invoking the Muses (2000, 256).

40 "El hispalense no concibe la Política como esfera opuesta a la Moral, por cuya razón niega que sea lícita la mentira en los negocios de Estado"; González de la Calle praises Fox for "tan certero y moral criterio [que] se opone radicalmente a la desacreditada doctrina de la *razón de Estado* y [que] merece el más sincero elogio de toda conciencia recta e ilustrada" (1903, 205).

41 "la forma más perfecta de gobernar un pueblo deba acomodarse a los dictados de la razón y a las máximas de la ortodoxia cristiana" (González de la Calle 1903, 204). The historian offers the Latin from Fox's *Compendium Ethices Philosophiae ex Platone, Aristotele, aliisque auctoribus collectum*, first published in Basel in 1554: "Optima igitur respublica (quanquam diversa ratione a multis instituta est, qui dum eam describere

voluerunt, patriae suae institutionem aliis praetulere) a nobis est hoc loco constituenda ea quae Christianae religioni ac rationi maxime congruat (*Comp. Ethices*, lib III, cap. IX)" (González de la Calle 1903, 286–7, n.257).

42 "Compertum autem habemus sapientiam quidem Pythagorae magis incontemplando, Socratis uero in agendo magis, Platonis denique in contemplando pariter atque agendo consistere. Praeterea disciplinam tam Pythagorae contemplatiua, quam Socratis moralem, a communi hominum consuetudine uideri remotiorem. Platonis uero doctrinam speculatiuam pariter & moralem ubique ita diuinum cum humano contemperare" (Ficino 1576, 2:1488).

43 A diametrically opposed opinion is held, according to Truman, by Fox's contemporary Marcos Salón de Paz, who praises the contemplative life as "in its essence better" (simpliciter melior) and of higher merit than the active life (Salón de Paz, 1568, ff. 57v–8r)" (Truman 1999, 178). For a brief outline of the history of this debate between *vita activa* and *vita contemplativa*, see Lombardo 1982. See also Kristeller (1956–96, 4:185–214).

44 "Ex quibus omnibus concludit, non modo talem ciuitatem, qualem hic descripserit, existere posse, sed etiam eam esse quam optimam" (Fox Morcillo 1556d, 179–80).

45 "Eatenus uero consistere coetus potest, quatenus nonnihil distributionis iustae seruatur" (Ficino 1576, 2:1398).

46 González de la Calle includes Fox's Latin in note: "Justitia es autem virtus, quae communis utilitatis ratione spectata, unicuique quod ejus est, reddit ... aut enim eadem est communis, aut specialis: communis praeterea aut legitima est, quod in legum observatione consistat, aut aequitas, cum haec ad illarum observationem veluti moderatio quaedam apta adhibetur: specialis item est aut distributrix, quod suum unicuique adhibeat, nisi ipsa injuste cupiens, aut commutatrix, quae reddat suum etiam allis permutatione tamen officiorum facta" (*De Regni*, lib. II, "De Justicia regia") (cited by González de la Calle 1903, 288–9, n.267).

47 "Aequitas est moderatio quaedam legis, seu explicatio rei, quae cum lege scripta non contineatur, spectata tamen supremae legis ratione intelligi ac definiri possit" (cited by González de la Calle 1903, 289, n.271).

48 Strijdom (2007) offers a comparison of ideas on social justice expressed through myth and history in Plato, Aristotle, and St Paul.

49 The evolutionary etymological process can be traced through the online *Nuevo tesoro lexicográfico de la lengua española* (http://buscon.rae.es/ntlle/SrvltGUILoginNtlle).

50 Purnell notes that Spaniard Fox Morcillo was also one of those Renaissance thinkers who, rather than find concord, tended to choose one philosopher or the other as "more credible" on a particular issue (1971, 69–70).

51 I have previously studied the manual in relation to specific points in Miguel de Cervantes' writings; see Byrne 2010 and 2012a. Truman details certain emendations ordered by the Inquisition, mainly concerning the author's privileging of secular over Church authority (Truman 1999, 178–82).

52 A large part of Renaissance moral and socio-political debates centred around Plato's versus Aristotle's ideas on the ideal republic, as one aspect of the much wider-ranging *comparatio* tradition that sought concord between the two philosophers on various matters. Those who study the full *comparatio* writings note its beginnings in the influential writings of Antioch, who lived in the first to second centuries BC; Cicero, for example, adopts Antioch's position to tell us that the two philosophers differ in words, but agree as to concepts, a tenet that would become common (Purnell 1971, 36–7). With Ficino's fifteenth-century translations of Plato's *Opera*, there was a new plethora of comparisons of the two Greeks. See Purnell, chapter 2, who reviews in full the history and development of the *comparatio* writings (1971, 31–92). See also Brown 1986 for the political ramifications in Italy, and Monfasani (1992 and 2013) for the controversy before Ficino.

53 "Entre todas las ciencias, y acciones humanas, ninguna requiere tantas partes, como el Oficio de gouernar República: y assí Platón y otros le llamaron arte de las artes"; "y assí hize algunos apuntamientos, para instrucción mía, como la memoria de papel, que Platón temiendo la suya, hizo con sus libros de República para que de passo sirvan de dirección y curiosidad agena" (Castillo de Bobadilla 1616, "Al muy alto y muy poderoso príncipe").

54 In his summary of chapter 51 of the *Phaedrus*, Ficino highlights the "better agriculture" (Meliorum vero agriculturam) of he who "introduces the disciplines into intelligences worthy of them" (qui disciplinas dignis mentibus inserit) over he who "entrusts doctrines to letters" (Quicunque litteris doctrinas mandat hortos) (2008, 3.51).

55 "Deridet praeterea scribendi studium in eo videlicet qui per litteras indubitatam posteris confidat patefacere veritatem. Atque Pythagoreorum more probat contemplationem traditionemque veritatis in animos potius quam in libros" (Ficino 2008, 2.3.3).

56 See Richard Kagan 1974 and 2009.

57 "(discreto Letor) ha sido aprouechar a los curiosos de buena Gouernación en sus Repúblicas" (Castillo de Bobadilla 1616, "Al letor").

58 "Platón (aunque en otro sentido) dezía, que nuestro saber era recordación de cosas passadas, creyendo él, que las ánimas passauan de vnos cuerpos en otros, y que informauan al nueuo cuerpo, por reminiscencia: y en este sentido fue error notorio; pero en el nuestro está bien a propósito," because "con el oluido de lo passado qua [que] está bien escrito, se va enfermando la inteligencia de lo presente; y conuiene que aya inuención, que por reminiscencia lo acuerde" (Castillo de Bobadilla 1616, proemio, 2).

59 "nouedades absolutas ... sino sacar[é] a la plaça, y al mercado (que assí llamó Pitágoras al mundo) consejos hallados en los antiguos y sabios varones, y determinaciones de Legisladores: a las quales aduirtiendo los que gouiernan Repúblicas, por ciencia,

o reminiscencia (o como ellos mandaren) con cuydado de las poner en execución" (Castillo de Bobadilla 1616, proemio, 3–4).

60 "pues auiendo comunidad en las cosas ... quién escusaría las grandes questiones y peleas, que desde antiguo tiempo hay por apropriar los bienes? Nunca vi concordia, sino donde todas las cosas están en señorío particular, porque cada qual defiende su capa" (Castillo de Bobadilla 1616, 1.1.19).

61 "Quál sea mejor República la que instituyó Platón, o la que ordenó Aristóteles" (Castillo de Bobadilla 1616, 1.1).

62 "esta particular ... a la qual por otro nombre llaman equidad, y con ella el hombre, en quanto hombre, como animal racional vsa de la razón, haziendo para otros lo mismo que quiere para sí" (Castillo de Bobadilla 1616, 1.1.1–2). Maravall quotes from the 1615 *Tratado de república* by Juan de Santa María, who repeats the same division of justice, and who also describes it as that found in the respective republics of Aristotle and Plato (Maravall 2005, 247).

63 "porque naturalmente todos quieren más para sí, que para otros" (Castillo de Bobadilla 1616, 1.1.5).

64 "De todo esto se colige, quan antiguo sea el regimiento y Policía de Aristóteles. Llámase de Aristóteles, no porque él aya sido el autor della, sino porque habló y escriuió admirablemente en ella. Y assí mismo se colige, quan al principio del mundo huuo propriedad en las cosas, y diuisión de términos" (Castillo de Bobadilla 1616, 1.1.9).

65 "Iabet, hijo de Lamech, señaló los ganados con señal conocida, para los distinguir, y conocer: de manera que ya entonces auía mío, y tuyo, y propiedad en las cosas" (Castillo de Bobadilla 1616, 1.1.10). For the related topic of leisure versus work and attitudes regarding it during the Middle Ages and Renaissance, see Strosetzki 1997.

66 "Platón quiso ... que los hombres no tuviesen propriedad, ni mío, ni tuyo, sino que todas las cosas fuesen comunes, como fue opinión de Sócrates y de otros Filósofos ... y el Filósofo afirma, que los hombres vivieran quietísimamente en este mundo, si se quitaran dos palabras: es a saber, *mío, y tuyo*" (Castillo de Bobadilla 1616, 1.1.16). Truman points out that on this point, the Spanish magistrate's argument "follows that of [Jean] Bodin, though perhaps reinforcing it" (1999, 170). For Ficino's influence in the works of Bodin, see Vasoli 1999, chapter 11.

67 "la naturaleza de los hombres era de absolutos pensamientos"; "ninguno lo hiziera, pues les faltaría el premio del interesse" (Castillo de Bobadilla 1616, 1.1.17 and 20).

68 "no tenía el fundamento que se requiere: mayormente si en las mugeres se auía de vsar la dicha comunidad que dize: a lo qual resiste la razón de los hombres, y la razón de ley natural y diuina, y aún el instinto de algunos brutos" (Castillo de Bobadilla 1616, 1.1.24).

69 "Por lo qual Platón después de auer caydo en los inconuenientes, y errores notables que se seguían de la comunidad, se reportó, renunciando tácitamente su primera República por dar lugar a la segunda" (Castillo de Bobadilla 1616, 1.1.25).

70 "Quamombrem decem illi de Republica libri Pythagorici magis sint atque Socratici: praesentes uero leges magis Platonicae iudicentur ... Hic ergo non coget homines si uoluerint inter se facere cuncta communia, permittet ut fieri solet, propria singulos possidere" (Ficino 1576, 2:1488).

71 "gubernationem scilicet quandam maxime philosophicam, in qua vel gubernent philosophi, vel gubernatores philosophentur"; "Beatissimas fore respublicas, si aut philosophi dominentur, aut faltem qui gubernant, diuina quadam forte philosophentur" (Ficino 1495, CIXr, CXIv).

72 "Postquam uero Deum Philosophus contemplatus fuerit coelestia gubernantem, tunc solum, & solus poterit terrena diuinitus gubernare" (Ficino 1576, 2:1409).

73 "según dize Platón, en aquellos tiempos y en aquellos reynos o eran philósophos los que imperavan o los que imperavan philosophavan" (Guevara 1994, I, 21).

74 "Atque, ut saepe, his in libris praecipue in secundo declarat, totam disputationem de iustitia a nobis inscribi mauult, quam de Republica: docens ut arbitror, rem omnem actionemque & publicam & priuatam, non ad copiam, non ad potentiam, non ad uictoriam esse sed ad ipsam iustitiam penitus referendam" (Ficino 1576, 2:1396–7).

75 Vasoli reviews the use of the phrase, and its attribution to Machiavelli (2006, 613–38). Pocock discusses the concept in historical terms, including Skinner's argument that "the 'Machiavellian' doctrine of *ragion di stato* was the effect of a hostile interpretation of Machiavelli by Dominican and Jesuit scholastics" (Pocock 1981, 54).

76 See Bujanda 1971 for differences in the Roman versus Spanish Indices, and www.beaconforfreedom.org for a searchable database of banned works and authors, although the Spanish Index prohibition of Machiavelli is not listed on that site.

77 See Maravall 1997, 378–9; Tomás y Valiente 1982, Fernández-Santamaría 1977.

78 "una profunda y dilatada presencia de las obras de Maquiavelo en la Península durante los dos siglos ... el XVI y el XVII" (Puigdomenech Forcada 1988, 10).

79 Additionally, there are three different Spanish translations of *The Prince* in manuscript, one dating to the sixteenth century and the other two to late in the seventeenth (Puigdomenech Forcada 1988, 117–30).

80 "Razón de estado, es una noticia de los medios convenientes para fundar, conservar y engrandecer un señorío" (Herrera y Tordesillas 1599, f. 1). In the twentieth century, Tomás y Valiente updated that definition: "Reason of state is, thus, the series of maxims of political workings ... It is the pragmatic wisdom of political success, the efficacy" (Tomás y Valiente 1982, 22).

81 The full title is: *Tratado de la religión y virtudes que debe tener el Príncipe Christiano, para gobernar y conservar sus Estados, Contra lo que Nicolás Machiavelo, y los Políticos de este tiempo enseñan.* López Múñoz (2010) studies the political thought of Ribadeneira and its juridical influence in Spanish thought of the nineteenth–twentieth centuries.

82 "Ministro de Satanás"; "perversa y diabólica doctrina" (Ribadeneira 1788, III).

83 "habiéndose ya hecho la razón de Estado un arte de engañar o de no ser engañado" (Saavedra Fajardo 1999, 546–7).

84 See Tomás y Valiente 1982, Fernández-Santamaría 1977 and 2006, Maravall 1997, Jiménez Moreno 2002.

85 "no impide de que en diversas ocasiones aporte su opinión como prueba de verdades conseguidas por razón natural, concordes con la fe cristiana" (Maravall 1997, 380).

86 "Gravemente dixo Marsilio Ficino, escribiendo sobre Platón, que es parte de impiedad tener familiaridad y comunicación con los que por sus maldades están excomulgados y apartados de los divinos Oficios: porque estando ellos inficionados, no pueden dexar de inficionar a los que llegan a ellos" (Ribadeneira 1788, 146). A note to the 1788 edition indicates that the statement is found in Ficino's *argumentum* to book 11 of the *Laws* dialogue.

87 "Y aduierta en no desuiarse de la justicia por seguir la razón del gouierno y estado, porque esto es muy peligroso, mayormente quando se atrauiessa perjuyzio de tercero, y son menester muchos requisitos, para que el aluedrío en los casos de estado y gouierno no degenere y tuerça de la justicia, y de lo que conuiene" (Castillo de Bobadilla 1616, 2.2.82).

88 "Y realmente la razón de gouernación, y de estado, no suele, ni deue preualer sino a falta de la razón de justicia. Y a este propósito dize Cornelio Tácito, que Ticiano, y Proculo, siendo vencidos con razones, se valieron de la ley del estado: y en otro lugar, hablando de Nerón, que desseaua destruyr a Vestino, dize, que no hallando contra él delito, ni acusador, porque no podía justificarlo en vía de juyzio, se valió de la razón de estado" (Castillo de Bobadilla 1616, 2.10.17). Ticiano, here, is Tito Atilio Rufo Ticiano; like Proculus, he was a Roman consul.

89 "Los juezes inferiores muchos con poca Christiandad y los más por inorancia (porque aún no saben Gramática) dexan de juzgar por las leyes, y juzgan las más vezes por su parecer y aluedrío" (Castillo de Bobadilla 1616, 2.10.18).

90 "que está el mundo tal, que casi en ninguna cosa se haze a nadie bien, amistad, ni gracia, si no es en las cosas de justicia y vsando en ellas de aluedrío" (Castillo de Bobadilla 1616, 2.10.18).

91 "En resolución en esta materia del juyzio de aluedrío se da vna regla al Corregidor, y es, que en los casos no determinados, por leyes, cánones, o dotrinas, puede proceder y sentenciar por su aluedrío, bien informado y circunspecto, regulándole y considerándole a la manera y traça del juyzio legal, y según el processo, y por la equidad y derecho, y por parecer de los sabios, y no por su cerbelo, y antojo" (Castillo de Bobadilla 1616, 2.10.27).

92 "pero según otra común opinión, no se puede en esto dar cierta regla, ni doctrina, y así se ha de dejar al alvedrío del Juez" (Castillo de Bobadilla 1616, 5.3.10).

93 "Accedant inquam tanquam & lectionibus eas diligenter obseruaturi, & actionibus penitus seruaturi"; "Profecto leges debent illus potissimum in ciuitate habere

pro fine, ad quem quasi ad signum omnia dirigant"; "Neque refugium ad euitanda fallacia uota ullum nobis est, excepta prudentia. Huic ergo per ciuium animos propagandae legifer in primis incumbet publicae studens felicitati"; "Ad aequet census pro uiribus, ne alij ditissimi sint, alij uero mendici" (Ficino 1576, 2:1488, 1490, 1495, 1502).

94 "En el *Dédalo* se critica la justicia real, en particular la razón de estado, por la cual Dédalo fuera encarcelado aun antes de pronunciarse su sentencia" (Schwartz 2013, 32).

95 "la idea de justicia en *Don Quijote* como fundamento y aun contenido esencial de la convivencia política de los cristianos" (Maravall 2005, 242). Serés finds the *Republic* mentioned twice in Huarte de San Juan's *Examen de ingenios*, and in both instances, as *De iusto* (Huarte de San Juan 1989, 87).

96 Cascardi notes specifically that protagonist Don Quijote "echoes Plato's argument" in the *Republic* on the difficulty of defending a state, and he likens the multifaceted perspectives expressed by characters in the novel to a Platonic dialogue (2012, 89, 98).

97 "Nunca te guíes por la ley del encaje, que suele tener mucha cabida con los ignorantes que presumen de agudos" (Cervantes 2005, II, 42).

98 "La justicia se estaba en sus proprios términos, sin que la osasen turbar ni ofender los del favor y los del interese" (Cervantes 2005, I, 11).

99 "no renovarle y traerle a la memoria las cosas pasadas" (Cervantes 2005, II, 1).

100 "en el discurso de su plática vinieron a tratar en esto que llaman razón de estado y modos de gobierno, enmendando este abuso y condenando aquél, reformando una costumbre y desterrando otra, haciéndose cada uno de los tres un nuevo legislador, un Licurgo moderno, o un Solón flamante: y de tal manera renovaron la república, que no pareció sino que la habían puesto en una fragua, y sacado otra de la que pusieron" (Cervantes 2005, II, 1).

101 "Conditurus autem leges Graecis, iure a tribus Graecarum legum optimis conditoribus leges accipit, Minoe, Lycurgo, Solone"; "Tres quoque imitantur auctores legum, Minoem, & Lycurgum, atque Solonem. Qui & leges in tria numina retulerunt, Iouem, Apollinem, & Mineruam ... potentiam ... clementiam ... sapientiam continet" (Ficino 1576, 2:1488, 1489).

102 "Entre las leyes de Solón fue vna, que las honras y dignidades se destribuyessen, no por riqueza ni poder, sino por sola la edad a los ancianos, y no a hombres moços, aunque pareciessen sabios, y Licurgo antes de Solón compuso el senado de viejos, pareciéndole que solamente aquellos eran dignos de las dignidades y honras, a quien la edad adornaba de virtud" (Castillo de Bobadilla 1616, 1.7.3).

103 "Platón, en su *República* enseñó, que el iuez auía de ser viejo, y no moço" (Castillo de Bobadilla 1616, 1.7.3).

104 "& iudicem eligit ingenio bonum, prudentem, senem, multos homines, & bonos, & malos expertum" (Ficino 1576, 2:1401).

105 "Desta gloria y desta quietud me vino a quitar una señora que, a mi parecer, llaman por ahí razón de estado, que cuando con ella se cumple, se ha de descumplir con otras razones muchas" (Cervantes 1997a, 2:317).
106 "Dichosa edad y siglos dichosos aquellos a quien los antiguos pusieron nombre de dorados ... porque entonces los que en ella vivían ignoraban estas dos palabras de *tuyo* y *mío*. Eran en aquella santa edad todas las cosas comunes" (Cervantes 2005, I, 11). On the concept of the "Golden Age" in general, see Stoopen Galán (2014). For the relation of the concept to Spain's early modern history, with the Catholic Monarchs as restorers of the Golden Age, see Biersack 2009.
107 Cascardi notes as an aside to his discussion of the protagonist's speech in the context of myth and theory that "There is, in fact, an important parallel to Don Quijote's speech [on the Golden Age] in Plato's *Statesman* ..." (2012, 56), and he also suggests parallels in *Protagoras* (56–7) to myth and theory as expressed in the political sphere (57–9), to analysis by "speculative negation" about a just city (60–5), and to Plato's metaphysics of the forms (101).
108 "vivían como bestias, sustentándose de bellotas" (Castillo de Bobadilla 1616, 1.1.3).
109 See Byrne 2012a, 145–6. See also Cascardi, who reviews "the genealogy of 'theory' among Aristotle's predecessors ... the civic practice wherein an individual, the so-called *theoros*, would travel abroad ... [then] report back to the city" and, tellingly, links Cervantes to this idea through Antonio de Guevara's *Relox* (Cascardi 2012, 103–5).
110 "en estos nuestros detestables siglos, no está segura ninguna" (Cervantes 2005, I, 11).
111 "poner en su punto la justicia distributiva, y dar a cada uno lo que es suyo, y entender y hacer que las buenas leyes se guarden" (Cervantes 2005, I, 37). See also Byrne 2012a, 62–4.
112 Ullrich Langer studies the concept of distributive justice in Italian, French, and German short stories of the Renaissance (1999), and notes the resonance of Aristotle's *Ethics* and the writings of Cicero in the concepts expressed.
113 "la justicia se estaba en sus proprios términos, sin que la osasen turbar ni ofender los del favor y los del interese, que tanto ahora la menoscaban, turban y persiguen. La ley del encaje aún no se había asentado en el entendimiento del juez, porque entonces no había que juzgar, ni quien fuese juzgado" (Cervantes 2005, I, 11).
114 "Nam praeter summam aliarum diligentiam legum, prudentissimae sanciet, ne cui liceat ultra certum & illum quidem mediocrem terminum census amplificare, ne alijs quidem copia, nimia, alijs obsit inopia, neue cogantur, id quod miserabile esse putat, multi inter patriae suae ulnas esse mendici" (Ficino 1576, 2:1488).
115 "Los jueces discretos castigan, pero no toman venganza de los delitos; los prudentes y los piadosos, mezclan la equidad con la justicia, y entre el rigor y la clemencia dan luz de su buen entendimiento" (Cervantes 2003, 538).

116 "Cuando pudiere y debiere tener lugar la equidad, no cargues todo el rigor de la ley al delincuente, que no es mejor la fama del juez riguroso que la del compasivo" (Cervantes 2005, II, 42).

117 "por equidad ... pues las acciones que ni mudan ni alteran la verdad de la historia no hay para qué escribirlas, si han de redundar en menosprecio del señor de la historia" (Cervantes 2005, II, 3).

118 "Y aduierta en no desuiarse de la justicia por seguir la razón del gouierno y estado, porque esto es muy peligroso, mayormente quando se atrauiessa perjuyzio de tercero" (Castillo de Bobadilla 1616, 2.2.82).

119 "No niega yo que no sea virtud digna de alabanza mejorarse cada uno, pero ha de ser sin perjuicio de tercero" (2003, 308); "Ambición es, pero ambición generosa, la de aquel que pretende mejorar su estado sin perjuicio de tercero" (1997a, 2:314).

120 "Pocas o ninguna vez se cumple con la ambición que no sea con daño de tercero" (Cervantes 1997a, 2:314).

121 "pueden remitir o relajar cualquier juramento, puesto que sea sin prejuicio de tercero" (Steinmetz 1848, II, 65). For his information on this point Steinmetz, writing in 1848, refers his reader to William Camden's 1581 Annals of Queen Elizabeth, and to the Compendium Privilegiorum, Confess[ion] 6.

122 "libros de entendimiento sin perjuicio de tercero" (Cervantes 2005, I, 6).

123 "si han de redundar en menosprecio del señor de la historia" (Cervantes 2005, II, 3).

124 See Maravall 1973, Cascardi 2012, Tomás y Valiente 1982. On Plato, see Richard Lewis Nettleship, who argues that the dialogue is moral rather than political, given that the focus is mainly on how the human being might live well which, for Plato, of necessity means living in a community (Nettleship 1901, 5).

125 Maravall approached the novel as a political treatise in his 1948 *El humanismo de las armas en Don Quijote*, and two more recent studies that directly reference the connections to Plato are Cascardi 2012 and Heinrich Merkl 2011. Both affirm that Cervantes was familiar with Plato's Dialogues and, for Cascardi, "Cervantes was centrally engaged in responding to a question that one of the characters in *Don Quijote* adopts from Plato's *Republic*: what is the place of literature within the state?" (Cascardi 2012, 7).

126 "somos ministros de Dios en la tierra, y brazos por quien se ejecuta en ella su justicia" (Cervantes 2005, I, 13). For games and play in Cervantes, including reference to Plato and the *Republic*, see Michael S. Scham 2014.

127 Nieremberg's biography of Ignatius, in the 1631 edition, is followed by a treatise titled: *Del zelo, y sabiduría de S. Ignacio en la fundación de la Compañía de Jesús, conforme a la sentencia de Santo Tomás, y idea de Platón de la mejor República.* The treatise follows the 141 pages of the biography, and begins its own folio numbering with folio 1, r and v.

128 "enseña el Santo que a los Religiosos contemplatiuos les conuiene tener riquezas en común: no tanto a los Religiosos que se emplean en la vida mixta, que tienen más de acción espiritual, los quales quiere más que viuan de limosna. Siguió puntualmente esta perfección S. Ignacio" (Nieremberg 1631, f. 30v).

129 "Como la República de Platón fue sombra de la Compañía de Jesús. Descendamos aora a la Filosofía, y veremos cómo lo que juzgaron Sócrates, y Platón por idea impossible de Repúblicas bien ordenadas executó S. Ignacio, quitadas las imperfecciones que en la República de aquellos Filósofos algunos calumniaron. Llamó a la República de Sócrates Marsilio Ficino, inuención, o ingenio de caridad, título que assienta bien a la Compañía de Jesús... El mismo Ficino echó de ver, que la doctrina de Sócrates no venía a República secular; y assí dixo, que más descriuió como auía de ser una Religión que vn Reyno, o Señoría" (Nieremberg 1631, f. 38v).

130 "En estas quatro piedras, dize Ficino fundó aquel Sabio Filósofo toda la máchina de su República" (Nieremberg 1631, f. 39r).

131 "Si huuiesse vna República, en la qual todos los della se amassen, sería tan fuerte, que preualecería, aunque fueran pocos hombres contra todo el resto del mundo" (Nieremberg 1631, f. 40r).

132 "que la obediencia fuesse la marca de sus hijos"; "Qvanto a lo tercero que requiere Sócrates, La cuenta que tiene la Compañía de Jesús de formar la juuentud que en ella ay, no se hallara en otra comunidad mayor"; "Ni el quarto cimiento de la República de Sócrates, de que trata en el libro sexto, y séptimo ha faltado a la Compañía de Jesús, en la qual está ordenado a los Superiores, tengan doblada oración que los demás, porque dize Platón en el libro de Regno, de la manera que no puede vn animal enderezar, y guiar a otro sin ayuda del hombre; assí los hombres no pueden ser gouernados, ni guiados de otro hombre, sin ayuda de Dios" (Nieremberg 1631, 40v, 42r, 43r).

133 "Contemplatio enim actionis, & principium est, & finis" (Ficino 1576, 2:1396). The first Annotation of the Jesuit Exercises reads: "Annotatio prima est: quod ipso nomine spiritualium ex exercitiorum, intelligitur modus quilibet examinandi propriam concientiam: Item meditandi, contemplandi, orandi secundum mentem, & uocem" (Loyola 1563, f. 9r–v).

134 "Meminerit tria haec in ea ciuitate facilius conuenire, quae inter unius ac populi potentiam obtinet medium, ut neque unius se totam subdat imperantis arbitrio uel potentiae paucorum, neque quemlibet absque delectu recipiat consultorem: sed plurimum quidem optimatum constet gubernatione, non nihil quoque habeat regij, nonnihil insuper popularis" (Ficino 1576, 2:1495).

135 "Grandes disputas entre Philosophos ay sobre qué género de gouierno es mejor, si el de vno, si el de muchos: ay razones por la vna parte, y por la otra. Por el gouierno de vno, que llamamos Monarquía, la paz, la fuerça, que es mayor cuanto está más vnida. Por el de muchos, la prudencia, que veen quatro más que vno, menos passión: pues

más dificultoso es sobornar a muchos que a vno, ni alterarse ellos con afficiones: que es la peste en todo gouierno. Concluyen que la Monarquía es el mejor gouierno, a tal que se ayuda del de muchos, en lo que le haze ventaja" (Mariana 1631, 39).

136 "se deuen las honrras repartir conforme las partes y mérito de cada qual ... Que si esto es ansí, cada vno vee si esta Iustitia distributiua se guarda o no"; "En fin es necessario, porque la armonía tan alabada de Platón conserue esta comunidad, que todos estén trauados como los números con proporción y orden, y los oficios se repartan entre todos" (Mariana 1631, 45, 47).

137 "querer establecer una república platónica" (Campomanes 1984, 41).

138 "Parte es esta, en verdad, de aquella galana utopía, con que algunos platónicos Politicones imaginan reducible la inmensidad del linaje humano a una sola familia casera, sugeta a una lei y a una lengua: (et legis, et labii unius)" (Gallardo 1928, 1:47).

139 "Herrera además tenía tocados los cascos de la poesía platónica de Petrarca, que tantos buenos injenios nos ha echado en España a perder!!" (Gallardo, 1928. 1:261).

140 The piece is a review of a book by M. Laveleye, for which no title is offered. The anonymous author segues into a discussion of persons named Justus Schwab and Citizen Maddox who are supposedly "plotting over their beer for a redistribution of the world's goods" ("Socialism" 1878).

Conclusion

1 See also Hankins, who places Ficino "at the traditional part of the *continuum*" of philosophical theology, in contrast to those who would see the Italian philosopher "as a crypto-pagan or a proto-Enlightenment figure" (2008a, 106).

2 "los tales aluminados venían de Italia"; "el chistoso médico de Fernando el Católico, doctor Francisco de Villalobos" (Márquez 1972, 71–2).

3 Schlesinger notes also Hans Wantoch's 1927 *Spain, the Land without a Renaissance*, and other German works critical of Spanish intellectual and cultural developments, answered in short order by scholars such as Aubrey Bell and Américo Castro (Schlesinger 1970, 13–14).

4 One key point raised by Celenza is the late nineteenth-century lack of interest in texts of the period written in Latin (xiii). This has its correlative in the late eighteenth-century diatribe of Lampillas regarding Spain's Renaissance writers, unknown to his modern world, he says, because that world no longer reads works written in Latin.

5 "un momento crucial en el que se forjaron gran parte de los estereotipos nacionales" (Elorza Guinea 2000, 13).

6 As Kagan notes: "Esta imagen negativa queda plasmada quizá hasta el exceso en un texto escolar publicado en Boston en 1973, en el que los españoles aparecían como 'católicos fanáticos' sometidos a una 'monarquía despótica'"; "España albergaba un

amor por la libertad muy similar al de los recientemente creados Estados Unidos" (Kagan 2000, 420–1). In the cited article, Kagan also offers a fascinating look at certain contrary opinions, beginning with a meeting in Boston on 24 January 1809 of a group that included Paul Revere and that saw itself establishing common cause with Spain in the face of Napoleon's invasion of that country.

7 García Cárcel mentions specifically Prescott: "La obra de Prescott tendría enorme influencia en la historiografía positivista de finales de siglo XIX y principios del siglo XX" and his impact: "rompe la dicotomía de los radicalismos liberal y conservador y configura terceras vías en la comprensión del Santo Oficio, que han dado mucho juego en la historiografía posterior" (García Cárcel 2000, 370–1).

8 "La España de la Restauración encontrará en D. Marcelino Menéndez Pelayo el defensor de la causa de España presuntamente objeto de críticas por la historiografía extranjera" (García Cárcel 1998, 15).

9 Gargano (2012) studies the importance and impact of the Catholic Monarchs' cultural renovation and reform. See González Navarro (1984) for the lists of materials studied in the various disciplines at Alcalá de Henares. There is a heavy weighting towards Aristotle for philosophy, as was the norm for university studies. However, the library holdings suggest a broader curriculum and, as we have seen, the Jesuits were reading Plato's dialogues as part of their early curriculum. O'Malley was right when he stated: "my hunch is that ... the *studia humanitatis* retained more of the scope originally claimed for them by the humanists than the *Ratio* suggests" (2000, 138).

10 "La historia de las ideas de aquella época ... no es ni italiana ni española ni francesa, sino europea, y está en trance de devenir occidental" (Ghia 2013, 78).

Works Cited

Aelian. 1744. *Aeliani: De natura animalium libri XVII*. Translated by Conrad Gessner. Edited by Abrahamo Gronovio. London: Gulielmus Bowyer.

Aladro Font, Jorge. 1998. *Pedro Malón de Echaide y La conversión de la Magdalena: vida y obra de un predicador*. Pamplona: Gobierno de Navarro, Departamento de Educación y Cultura.

Alcalá, Ángel, ed. 2003. *Miguel Servet: Obras completas*. 2 vols. Zaragoza: Prensas Universitarias de Zaragoza.

Alcina Rovira, Juan F. 2007. "Literatura neolatina y cultura española en el Siglo de Oro: un balance." *Ínsula* 725:10–12.

Aldana, Francisco de. 1985. *Francisco de Aldana: Poesías castellanas completas*. Edited by José Lara Garrido. Madrid: Cátedra.

Alemán, Mateo. 2000. *Guzmán de Alfarache*. 2 vols. Edited by José María Micó. Madrid: Cátedra.

Alfonso X. 2001. *General Estoria: Segunda parte*. 2 vols. Edited by Belén Almeida. Madrid: Biblioteca Castro.

Allen, Michael J.B. 1975. "The Absent Angel in Ficino's Philosophy." *Journal of the History of Ideas* 36 (2): 219–40. http://dx.doi.org/10.2307/2708925.

Allen, Michael J.B. 1981. *Marsilio Ficino and the Phaedran Charioteer*. Los Angeles: Center for Medieval and Renaissance Studies; University of California Press.

Allen, Michael J.B. 1984. *The Platonism of Marsilio Ficino: A Study of His Phaedrus Commentary, Its Sources and Genesis*. Berkeley, CA: University of California Press.

Allen, Michael J.B. 1987. "Marsilio Ficino's Interpretation of Plato's *Timaeus* and Its Myth of the Demiurge." In *Supplementum Festivum: Studies in Honor of Paul Oskar Kristeller*, edited by James Hankins, John Monfasani, and Frederick Purnell, Jr., 399–439. Binghamton, NY: Medieval & Renaissance Texts & Studies.

Allen, Michael J.B. 1989. *Icastes: Marsilio Ficino's Interpretation of Plato's Sophist*. Berkeley: University of California Press.

Allen, Michael J.B. 1994. *Nuptial Arithmetic: Marsilio Ficino's Commentary on the Fatal Number in Book VIII of Plato's* Republic. Berkeley: University of California Press.

Allen, Michael J.B. 1998. *Synoptic Art: Marsilio Ficino on the History of Platonic Interpretations.* Florence: Leo S. Olschki.

Allen, Michael J.B. 2002a. Introduction to *Marsilio Ficino: His Theology, His Philosophy, His Legacy*, edited by Michael J.B. Allen and Valery Rees, xiii–xxii. Leiden: Brill.

Allen, Michael J.B. 2002b. "Life as a Dead Platonist." In *Marsilio Ficino: His Theology, His Philosophy, His Legacy*, edited by Allen and Rees, 159–78.

Allen, Michael J.B. 2003. "The Ficinian *Timaeus* and Renaissance Science." In *Plato's* Timaeus *as Cultural Icon*, edited by Gretchen J. Reydams-Schils, 238–50. Notre Dame, IN: University of Notre Dame Press.

Allen, Michael J.B. 2008a. "*« Quisque in sphaera sua »*: Plato's Statesman, Marsilio Ficino's Platonic Theology, and the Resurrection of the Body." *Rinascimento* 47:25–48.

Allen, Michael J.B. 2008b. Introduction to *Marsilio Ficino: Commentaries on Plato.* Vol. I, *Phaedrus* and *Ion*, ix–lix. I Tatti Renaissance Library. Cambridge, MA: Harvard University Press.

Allen, Michael J.B., and James Hankins. 2001. Introduction to *Marsilio Ficino: Platonic Theology.* 6 vols. Translated by Michael J.B. Allen. Latin text edited by James Hankins, with William Bowen, vii–xvii. I Tatti Renaissance Library. Cambridge, MA: Harvard University Press.

Alonso, Damaso. 1942. *La poesía de San Juan de la Cruz (desde esta ladera)*. Madrid: CSIC.

Alonso, Damaso. 1958. *De los siglos oscuros al de oro.* Madrid: Gredos.

Alonso Martín, Eugenio, ed. 1980. Introduction to *Juan de Segura: Processo de cartas de amores (1548)*, edited by Alonso Martin, 1–47. Madrid: El Archipiélago.

Alvarado, Fray Francisco. 1824. *Cartas críticas del Filósofo Rancio.* Vol. 2. Madrid: E. Aguado. Real Academia Española: Banco de datos (CORDE) en línea. Corpus diacrónico del español. http://www.rae.es.

Alvar Ezquerra, Alfredo. 2014. *Un maestro en tiempos de Felipe II: Juan López de Hoyos y la enseñanza humanista en el siglo XVI.* Madrid: La Esfera de los Libros.

Álvarez Miraval, Blas. 1597. *La conservación de la salud del cuerpo y del alma, para el buen regimiento de la salud, y más larga vida de la Alteza del serenísimo Príncipe don Phillipo nuestro Señor.* Medina del Campo: Sanctiago del Campo. Digitized edition, Biblioteca Histórica Complutense.

Andrés, Gregorio de. 1964. "Entrega de la librería real de Felipe II (1576)." In *Documentos para la historia del Monasterio de San Lorenzo de El Escorial*, 7:13–233.Madrid: Imprenta Helénica.

Andrés, Juan. 1997–2001. *Origen, progresos y estado actual de toda la literatura.* Translated by Carlos Andrés. Edited by Jesús García Gabaldón, Santiago Navarro Pastor, and Carmen Valcárcel Rivera. Director Pedro Aullón de Haro. 6 vols. Madrid: Verbum.

Antonio, Nicolás. 1999. *Bibliotheca hispana nueva.* 2 vols. Madrid: Fundación Universitaria Española.

Arce de Otálora, Juan de. 1995. *Coloquios de Palatino y Pinciano.* 2 vols. Edited and introduction by José Luis Ocasar Ariza. Madrid: Turner.

Argensola, Bartolomé Leonardo de. 1951. *Rimas de Lupercio y Bartolomé Leonardo de Argensola.* Edited, prologue, and notes by José Manuel Blecua. 2 vols. Zaragoza: Instituto "Miguel de Cervantes" de Filología Hispánica; CSIC.

Arias Montano, Benito, and Philips Galle. 2005. *Virorum Doctorum de disciplinis benemerentium effigies XLIIII.* Edited by Luis Gómez Canseco and Fernando Navarro Antolín. Huelva: Universidad de Huelva.

Arnoldsson, Sverker. 1960. *La leyenda negra: Estudios sobre sus orígenes.* Acta Universitatis Gothoburgensis 66. Göteborg, Sweden: Göteborgs Universitets Årsskrift.

Augustine, Saint. 1969. *S. Aurelli Augustini: De civitate Dei contra paganos/ Saint Augustine. The City of God against the Pagans.* 7 vols. Translated by William Chase Green. Cambridge, MA: Harvard University Press.

Avalle-Arce, Juan Bautista. 1959. *La novela pastoril española.* Madrid: Revista de Occidente.

Avalle-Arce, Juan Bautista. 1974. "Cervantes, Grisóstomo, Marcela, and Suicide." *PMLA* 89 (5): 1115–16. http://dx.doi.org/10.2307/461385.

Ávila, Francisco de. 2000. *La vida y la muerte o vergel de discretos: Altercación, pleyto y disputa, renzilla e qüestión contra la muerte del reverendo padre fray francisco de Ávila, de la observancia de los menores* [1508]. Edited by Pedro M. Cátedra. Madrid: Fundación Universitaria Española, Universidad Pontificia de Salamanca.

Babb, Lawrence. 1951. *The Elizabethan Malady: A Study of Melancholia in English Literature from 1580 to 1642.* East Lansing, MI: Michigan State College Press.

Bakal, Donald A. 1979. *Psychology and Medicine: Psychobiological Dimensions of Health and Illness.* New York: Springer.

Banier, Antoine. 1740. *Mythology and Fables of the Antients [sic] explained from History.* Vol. 3. London: A. Millar.

Barry, Robert. 1995. "The Development of the Roman Catholic Teachings on Suicide." *Notre Dame Journal of Law, Ethics & Public Policy* 9:449–501.

Bataillon, Marcel. 1950. *Erasmo y España: Estudios sobre la historia espiritual del siglo XVI.* [*Erasme et L'Espagne: recherches sur l'histoire spirituelle du XVI*[e] *siècle*]. Translated by A. Alatorre. México: Fondo de Cultura Económica.

Bécares Botas. Vicente. 1998. "*Compras de libros para la Biblioteca universitaria salmantina del Renacimiento.*" In *El libro antiguo español IV: Coleccionismo y Bibliotecas (Siglos XV–XVIII).* Directors, María Luis López-Vidriero and Pedro M. Cátedra, edited by María Isabel Hernández González, 83–135. Salamanca: Ediciones Universidad de Salamanca; Patrimonio Nacional; Sociedad Española de Historia del Libro.

Béhar, Roland. 2010. "Lecturas y traducciones de Ficino en Castilla bajo Isabel la Católica." In *Estudios sobre la Edad Media, el Renacimiento, y la temprana modernindad*, edited by Francisco Bautista Pérez and Jimena Gamba Corradine, 467–76. San Millán de la Cogolla: Cilengua.

Beaupied, Aida María. 1988. "Narciso hermético: Sor Juana Inés de la Cruz y José Lezama Lima." PhD diss. Yale University.

Beierwaltes, Werner. 2003. "Plato's *Timaeus* in German Idealism: Schelling and Windischmann." In *Plato's Timaeus as Cultural Icon*, edited by Gretchen J. Reydams-Schils, 267–89. Notre Dame, IN: University of Notre Dame Press.

Bell, Aubrey F.G. 1925. *Luis de León (1527–1591): A Study of the Spanish Renaissance.* Oxford: Clarendon.

Beltrán Almería, Luis. 2007. "Simbolismo, modernismo y hermetismo."In *Simbolismo y hermetismo: Aproximación a la modernidad estética*, edited by Luis Beltrán Almería and Luis Rodríguez García, 93–110. Zaragoza: Prensas Universitarias de Zaragoza

Beltrán de Heredia, Vicente. 1972. *Cartulario de la Universidad de Salamanca.* Vol. 5. Salamanca: Universidad de Salamanca.

Bermúdez de Pedraza, Francisco. 1992. *Arte legal para estudiar la jurisprudencia.* Facsimile reprint. Madrid: Civitas [Salamanca: Imprenta de Antonia Ramírez, 1612].

Bernad, Miguel Anselmo. 1951. "The Faculty of Arts in the Jesuit Colleges in the Eastern Part of the United States: Theory and Practice (1782–1923)." PhD dissertation. Yale University.

Bertholet, Alfred. 1909. *The Transmigration of Souls.* Translated by H.J. Chaytor. London: Harper & Brothers.

Bible. 1796 [1609]. *The Holy Bible Translated from the Latin Vulgate.* 5 vols. Edinburgh: J. Moir, Patterson's Court [Douay: English College]. Eighteenth Century Collections Online. Gale. Yale University Library. 15 Apr. 2014.

Biblioteca Nacional de España. 2008. *Lecturas de Bizancio: El legado escrito de Grecia en España.* Madrid: Biblioteca Nacional de España; Ministerio de Cultura.

Biersack, Martín. 2009. "Los Reyes Católicos y la tradición imperial romana." *eHumanista* 12:33–47.

Bietenholtz, Peter G., ed. 1985–7. *Contemporaries of Erasmus: A Biographical Register of the Renaissance and Reformation.* 2 vols. Toronto: University of Toronto Press.

Bietenholtz, Peter G. 2009. *Encounters with a Radical Erasmus: Erasmus' Work as a Source of Radical Thought in Early Modern Europe.* Toronto: University of Toronto Press.

Biosca i Bas, Antoni. 2000. *Estudi del manuscrit de la Carta de Samuel conservat a l'arxiu municipal de Dénia.* Ayuntamiento de Dénia; Institut Alacantí de Cultura "Juan Gil-Albert." Alacant: Gráfiques Antar.

Blázquez, José María, Jorge Martínez-Pinna, and Santiago Montero. 1993. *Historia de las religiones antiguas: Oriente, Grecia y Roma.* Madrid: Cátedra.

Blecua, Alberto. 2006. *Signos viejos y nuevos: Estudios de historia literaria*. Edited by Xavier Tubau. Barcelona: Crítica.

Boas, Marie. 1962. *The Scientific Renaissance, 1450–1630*. New York: Harper and Brothers.

Boecler, Johann Heinrich. 1715. *Bibliographia critica scriptores omnium artium atque scientiarum ordine percensens*. Leipzig: Io. Grossii.

Boer, Charles, trans. 1980. *Marsilio Ficino:* The Book of Life. Irving, TX: Spring Publications.

Bosch i Juan, María del Carme, Jaume Garau Amengual, Abraham Madroñal Dorán, and Juan Miguel Monterrubio Prieto, eds. 2010. *Comentarios de erudición (« Libro decimosexto »)*. Madrid: Iberoamericana-Vervuert; CSIC.

Boter, G.J. 1989. *The Textual Tradition of Plato's Republic*. Leiden: Brill.

Brisson, Luc. 2004. *How Philosophers Saved Myths: Allegorical Interpretation and Classical Mythology*. Translated by Catherine Tihanyi. Chicago: University of Chicago Press. http://dx.doi.org/10.7208/chicago/9780226075389.001.0001.

Brown, Alison. 1986. "Platonism in Fifteenth-Century Florence and Its Contribution to Early Modern Political Thought." *Journal of Modern History* 58 (2): 383–413. http://dx.doi.org/10.1086/243013.

Brown, Gary. 2013. "'No es de condenar porque parezca enigmático': Lope's Commentary on the Sonnet 'La calidad elementar resiste.'" *Calíope* 18 (3): 7–32.

Bujanda, J.M. de. 1971. "Literary Censorship in Sixteenth-Century Spain." *Canadian Catholic Historical Association Study Sessions* 38:51–64.

Bullen, J.B. 1994. *The Myth of the Renaissance in Nineteenth-Century Writing*. Oxford: Clarendon. http://dx.doi.org/10.1093/acprof:oso/9780198128885.001.0001.

Burckhardt, Jacob. 1938. *The Civilization of the Renaissance in Italy*. Translated by S.G.C. Middlemore. Vienna: The Phaidon Press; New York: Oxford University Press.

Burroughs, Josephine L. 1948. Introduction to "Marsilio Ficino: Five Questions Concerning the Mind." In *The Renaissance Philosophy of Man*, edited by Ernst Cassirer, Paul Oskar Kristeller, and John Herman Randall, Jr, 185–92. Chicago: University of Chicago Press.

Bynum, Caroline Walker. 1995. *The Resurrection of the Body in Western Christianity, 200–1336*. New York: Columbia University Press.

Byrne, Susan. 2005. "Neostoic Pyrotechnics in Francisco de Aldana and San Juan de la Cruz." *Calíope* 11 (1): 87–103.

Byrne, Susan. 2007. *El Corpus Hermeticum y tres poetas españoles: Francisco de Aldana, fray Luis de León y San Juan de la Cruz: Conexiones léxicas y semánticas entre la filosofía hermética y la poesía española del siglo XVI*. Newark, DE: Juan de la Cuesta.

Byrne, Susan. 2010. "Miguel de Cervantes y Paolo Jovio: los caballeros antiguos y modernos y el de la Mancha." In *Actas del XVI Congreso de la AIH, 9 al 13 de julio de 2007, París*, edited by Pierre Civil and Françoise Crémoux. 3:72–82. Madrid: Iberoamericana.

Byrne, Susan. 2012a. *Law and History in Cervantes'* Don Quixote. Toronto: University of Toronto Press.

Byrne, Susan. 2012b. "Cuestionamiento del hermetismo ficiniano en un manuscrito escurialense del siglo XV." *Bulletin of Spanish Studies* 89 (2): 173–92. http://dx.doi.org/10.1080/14753820.2012.657768.

Campanelli, Maurizio. 2011. *Mercurii Trismegisti: Pimander sive De Potestate et Sapientia Dei.* Torino: Nino Aragno.

Campomanes, Pedro Rodríguez de. 1984. *Bosquejo de política económica española delineado sobre el estado presente de sus intereses.* Edited by Jorge Cejudo. Madrid: Editora Nacional.

Campomar, Marta M. 1987. "Menéndez Pelayo and Neo-Catholic Aesthetics in the Nineteenth Century." In *A Face Not Turned to the Wall: Essays on Hispanic Themes for Gareth Alban Davies*, edited by Carlos A. Longhurst, 171–92. Leeds: Department of Spanish and Portuguese, University of Leeds.

Canavaggio, Jean. 1958. "Alonso López Pinciano y la estética literaria de Cervantes en el *Quijote*." *Anales Cervantinos* 7:13–107.

Carozza, Davy. 1964. "Another Italian Source for La Magdalena of Malón de Chaide." *Italica* 41 (1): 91–8. http://dx.doi.org/10.2307/477442.

Casas, Bartolomé de las. 1967. *Apologética historia sumaria.* 2 vols. Edited by Edmundo O'Gorman. Mexico: Instituto de Investigaciones Históricas de la Universidad Nacional Autónoma de México.

Casas, Bartolomé de las. 1986. *Historia de las Indias.* Edited by Andre Saint-Lu. Caracas: Ayacucho.

Casas, Bartolomé de las. 1992. *Apologética historia sumaria.* 3 vols. Edited by Vidal Abril Castelló. Madrid: Alianza.

Casaubon, Isaac. 1655. *De rebus sacris et ecclesiasticis: Exercitationes XVI; Ad Cardinalis Baronii Prolegomena in annales et primam eorum partem, de D.N. Iesu Christi Natiuitate, Vita, Passione, Assumptione.* Geneva: Ioannis Antonij et Samuelis de Tournes.

Cascardi, Anthony. 2012. *Cervantes, Literature, and the Discourse of Politics.* Toronto: University of Toronto Press.

Cassirer, Ernst, Paul Oskar Kristeller, and John Herman Randall, Jr, eds. 1948. *Renaissance Philosophy of Man.* Chicago: University of Chicago Press.

Castelar, Emilio. 1861. *Discursos políticos y literarios.* Madrid: J. Antonio García. Real Academia Española: Banco de datos (CORDE) [en línea]. Corpus diacrónico del español. http://www.rae.es.

Castiglione, Baltasar. 1561. *El cortesano.* Translated by Juan Boscán. Anvers: Martín Nuncio.

Castillo de Bobadilla, Jerónimo. 1616. *Política para corregidores.* Barcelona: Gerónymo Margarit.

Castro, Américo. 1967. *Hacia Cervantes.* Madrid: Taurus.

Celenza, Christopher S. 2002. "Late Antiquity and Florentine Platonism: The Post-Plotinian Ficino." In *Marsilio Ficino: His Theology, His Philosophy, His Legacy*, edited by Michael J.B. Allen and Valery Rees, 71–97. Leiden: Brill.

Celenza, Christopher S. 2004. *The Lost Italian Renaissance: Humanists, Historians, and Latin's Legacy.* Baltimore, MD: Johns Hopkins University Press.

Celenza, Christopher S. 2013. "What Counted as Philosophy in the Italian Renaissance? The History of Philosophy, the History of Science, and Styles of Life." *Critical Inquiry* 39 (2): 367–401. http://dx.doi.org/10.1086/668530.

Celenza, Christopher S., and Kenneth Gouwens, eds. 2006. *Humanism and Creativity in the Renaissance: Essays in Honor of Ronald G. Witt*. Leiden: Brill. http://dx.doi.org/10.1163/9789047408741.

Celso, Hugo de. 2000. *Repertorio vniversal de todas las leyes destos reynos de Castilla*. Edited by Javier Alvarado Planas. Madrid: Centro de Estudios Políticos y Constitucionales.

Cernuda, Luis. 1971. *Poesía y literatura I y II*. Barcelona: Editorial Seix Barral.

Cervantes de Salazar, Francisco. 1772. *Apólogo de la ociosidad i del trabajo, intitulado Labricio Portvndo, compuesto por el protonotario Lvis Mexía, glossado i moralizado por Francisco Cervantes de Salazar*. In *Obras que Francisco Cervantes de Salazar ha hecho glossado i traducido*. Madrid: Antonio de Sancha.

Cervantes de Salazar, Francisco. 1971. *Crónica de la Nueva España*. Prologue by Manuel Magallón. Madrid: Atlas. http://www.cervantesvirtual.com/nd/ark:/59851/bmcrr1s3

Cervantes Saavedra, Miguel de. 1991. *Viage del Parnaso y poesías varias*. Edited by Elias L. Rivers. Madrid: Espasa-Calpe.

Cervantes Saavedra, Miguel de. 1996. *Obra completa, 1: Cervantes'* La Galatea. Edited by Florencio Sevilla Arroyo and Antonio Rey Hazas. Madrid: Alianza.

Cervantes Saavedra, Miguel de. 1997a. *Novelas ejemplares*. 2 vols. Edited by Harry Sieber. Madrid: Cátedra.

Cervantes Saavedra, Miguel de. 1997b. *Comedia famosa de la entretenida*. Digital edition. Universidad de Alcalá; Centro de Estudios Cervantinos. http://cervantes.uah.es/teatro/Entreten/entret_3.html

Cervantes Saavedra, Miguel de. 1999. *La Galatea*. Edited by Francisco López Estrada and María Teresa López García-Berdoy. Madrid: Cátedra.

Cervantes Saavedra, Miguel de. 2003. *Los trabajos de Persiles y Sigismunda*. Edited by Carlos Romero Muñoz. Madrid: Cátedra.

Cervantes Saavedra, Miguel de. 2005. *El ingenioso hidalgo Don Quijote de la Mancha*. 2 vols. Edited by Celina Sabor de Cortazar and Isaías Lerner, with prologue by Marcos Morínigo. Buenos Aires: Eudeba.

Christianson, Gerald. 2011. Review of Michiel Decaluwe, *A Successful Defeat: Eugene IV's Struggle with the Council of Basel for Ultimate Authority in the Church, 1431–1449*. *Church History* 80.2:379–81.

Cicero, Marcus Tullius. 1758. *The Tusculan Disputations of Marcus Tullius Cicero*. London: John Whiston and Benjamin White. Gale, Document number CW116194757. Yale University Library. 16 Nov. 2013.

Cicero, Marcus Tullius. 1853. "On the Nature of the Gods." In *Treatises of M.T. Cicero*, edited and translated by C.D. Yonge, 1–140. London: Henry G. Bohn.

Clamurro, William. 1997. *Beneath the Fiction: The Contrary Worlds of Cervantes's* Novelas ejemplares. Studies on Cervantes and His Times 7. Edited by Eduardo Urbina. New York: Peter Lang.

Clamurro, William. 2014. "The Justice of Forgiveness in *La fuerza de la sangre*." *Romance Quarterly* 61 (2): 111–24. http://dx.doi.org/10.1080/08831157.2014.878635.

Clemente Hernández, Javier. 1999. *El legado oculto de Pedro Malón de Chaide*. Madrid: Revista Agustiniana.

Close, Anthony. 2008. *A Companion to* Don Quixote. Woodbridge, UK: Tamesis.

Clucas, Stephen, ed. 2006. *John Dee: Interdisciplinary Studies in English Renaissance Thought*. Dordrecht, The Netherlands: Springer.

Clucas, Stephen, Peter J. Forshaw, and Valery Rees, eds. 2011. *Laus Platonici Philosophi: Marsilio Ficino and His Influence*. Leiden: Brill. http://dx.doi.org/10.1163/ej.9789004188976.i-384.

Constant, Eric A. 2002. "A Reinterpretation of the Fifth Lateran Council Decree Apostolici regiminis (1513)." *Sixteenth Century Journal* 33 (2): 353–79. http://dx.doi.org/10.2307/4143912.

Copenhaver, Brian P. 2002. *Hermetica: The Greek Corpus Hermeticum and the Latin Asclepius in a New English Translation, with Notes and Introduction*. Cambridge: Cambridge University Press.

Copenhaver, Brian P. 2009. "Ten Arguments in Search of a Philosopher: Averroes and Aquinas in Ficino's *Platoni Theology*. *Viarium* 47 (4): 444–79.

Copenhaver, Brian P. 2013. "Ten Arguments in Search of a Philosopher." In *The Rebirth of Platonic Theology*, edited by James Hankins and Fabrizio Meroi, 155–89. Florence: Leo S. Olschki.

Correa, Gustavo. 1960. "La dimensión mitológica del *Viaje del Parnaso* de Cervantes." *Comparative Literature* 12 (2): 113–24. http://dx.doi.org/10.2307/1768333.

Cortijo Ocaña, Antonio. 2011. "Sebastián Fox Morcillo y su concepto de la Historia." *Humanism e-review*. http://proyectos.cchs.csic.es/humanismoyhumanistas/cabeza-encantada.

Costa, Joaquín. 1983. *Colectivismo agrario en España*. 2 vols. Introduction and edition by Carlos Serrano. Zaragoza: Guara.

Covarrubias Orozco, Sebastián de. 1994. *Tesoro de la lengua castellana o española*. Madrid: Castalia.

Cueva, Juan de la. 1917. *Comedia del príncipe tirano*. In *Comedias y tragedias de Juan de la Cueva*. 2 vols. Madrid: Sociedad de Bibliófilos españoles. 1:130–208.

Cuevas, Cristobal, ed. 1982. *Fray Luis de León y la escuela salmantina*. Madrid: Taurus.

Curry, Walter Clyde. 1933. "The Demonic Metaphysics of *Macbeth*." *Studies in Philology* 30 (3): 395–426.

Damiani, Bruno M. 1980. "Aspectos barrocos de *La pícara Justina*." In *Actas del Sexto Congreso Internacional de Hispanistas. Celebrado en Toronto del 22 al 26 de agosto de 1977*, edited by Alan M. Gordon and Evelyn Rugg, 198–202. Toronto: Dept. of Spanish & Portuguese, University of Toronto

Damiani, Bruno M. 2004. "From the *Corpus Hermeticum* to Cervantes's *La Galatea*: The *amor-muerte* Connection." *Annali Sezioni Romanza* 46 (2): 427–39.

Dannenfeldt, K.H. with Marie-Thèrése d'Alverny and Theodore Silverstein. 1960. "Hermetica philosophica." In *Catalogus translationum et commentariorum: Mediaeval and Renaissance Latin Translations and Commentaries*, edited by Paul Oskar Kristeller, Ferdinand Edward Cranz, and Virginia Brown, 1:137–56. Washington, D.C.: Catholic University of America Press.

D'Aragona, Tullia. 1912. "Dialogo della signora Tullia d'Aragona della infinitá di amore." In *Trattati D'Amore del Cinquecento*, edited by Giuseppe Zonta, 183–248. Mari: Gius, Laterza & Figlio.

D'Aragona, Tullia. 1997. *Dialogue on the Infinity of Love*. Edited and translated by Rinaldina Russell and Bruce Merry. Introduction by Rinaldina Russell. Chicago: University of Chicago Press.

Darío, Rubén. 1995. *Azul. Cantos de vida y esperanza*. Edited by José María Martínez. Madrid: Cátedra.

de Armas, Frederick. 1981. "The Saturn Factor: Examples of Astrological Imagery in Lope de Vega's Works." In *Studies in Honor of Everett W. Hesse*, edited by William C. McCrary and José A. Madrigal, 63–80. Lincoln, NE: Society of Spanish and Spanish American Studies.

de Armas, Frederick. 1983. "Lope de Vega and the Hermetic Tradition: The Case of Dardanio in *La Arcadia*." *Revista Canadiense de Estudios Hispánicos* 7 (3): 345–62.

de Armas, Frederick. 1992. "Saturn in Conjunction: From Albumasar to Lope de Vega." In *Saturn from Antiquity to the Renaissance*, edited by Massimo Ciavolella and Amilcare A. Iannucci, 151–72. Toronto: University of Toronto Press.

de Armas, Frederick. 2009. "Papeles de Zafiro: signos político-mitológicos en *La vida es sueño*." *Anuario calderoniano* 2:75–96.

Díaz de Toledo, Pedro. 1892. "Diálogo e razonamiento en la muerte del marqués de Santillana." In *Opúsculos literarios de los siglos XIV a XVI*, edited by Antonio Paz y Melia, 247–360. Madrid: Tello; Sociedad de Bibliófilos Españoles.

Díaz de Toledo, Pedro. 1993. *Libro llamado Fedrón: Plato's* Phaedo *Translated by Pero Díaz de Toledo*. Edited by Nicholas G. Round. London: Tamesis.

Di Camillo, Ottavio. 1976. *El humanismo castellano del siglo XV*. Valencia: Torres.

Di Camillo, Ottavio. 1995. "Interpretations of the Renaissance in Spanish Historical Thought." *Renaissance Quarterly* 48 (2): 352–65. http://dx.doi.org/10.2307/2863069.

Di Camillo, Ottavio. 1997. "Interpretations of Humanism in Recent Spanish Renaissance Studies." *Renaissance Quarterly* 50 (2): 1190–1201.

Di Camillo, Ottavio. 2010. "Fifteenth-Century Spanish Humanism: Thirty Five Years Later." *La corónica: A Journal of Medieval Hispanic Languages, Literatures and Cultures* 39 (1): 19–66.

Diccionario de autoridades. 3 vols. 1964. Madrid: Real Academia Española.

Diez de Foncalda, Alberto. 1861. "Una casera de clérigo." In *Romancero general, o colección de romances castellanos*, 2 vols., edited by Don Agustín Durán. 2:535. Madrid; BAE: Rivadeneyra.

Dillon, John. 2011. "Ficino and the God of the Platonists." In *Laus Platonici Philosophi: Marsilio Ficino and His Influence*, edited by Stephen Clucas et al., 13–24. Leiden: Brill. http://dx.doi.org/10.1163/ej.9789004188976.i-384.7.

Diogenes Laertius. 1972. *Lives of Eminent Philosophers*. Edited and translated by R.D. Hicks. Cambridge, MA: Harvard University Press. www.perseus.tufts.edu.

Dodd, Charles H. 1964. *The Bible and the Greeks*. London: Hodder & Stoughton.

Draper, John William. 1874. *History of the Conflict between Religion and Science*. New York: Appleton's.

Duque de Estrada, Diego. 1982. *Comentarios del desengañado de sí mismo: Vida del mismo autor*. Edited by Henry Ettinghausen. Madrid: Castalia.

Egido, Aurora. 1994. *Cervantes y las puertas del sueño: Estudios sobre* La Galatea, El Quijote *y* El Persiles. Barcelona: Promociones y Publicaciones Universitarias.

Egido, Aurora. 2007. "La dignidad de las humanidades y el hispanismo." *Ínsula* 725:2–4.

Egido, Aurora, 2010. "El arte de la discreción en *La Galatea*." *Bulletin of Spanish Studies* 81:585–97.

Elorza Guinea, Juan Carlos. 2000. "Presentación." In *El siglo de Carlos V y Felipe II: La construcción de los mitos en el siglo XIX. Congreso Internacional, Valladolid, 3–5 de noviembre de 1999*, edited by José Martínez Millán and Carlos Reyero, 13–15. Madrid: Sociedad Estatal para la Conmemoración de los Centenarios de Felipe II y Carlos V.

El Saffar, Ruth. 1976. *Cervantes' "El casamiento engañoso" and "El coloquio de los perros."* Critical Guides to Spanish Texts 17. Edited by J.E. Varey and A.D. Deyermond. London: Grant & Cutler; Tamesis.

Emil, John Louis. 1953. *A History of Astronomy from Thales to Kepler*. 2nd ed. New York: Dover.

Evarts, W.M. 1853. "Oration" at Yale Commencement Week. *New York Times*, 28 July.

Faulhaber, Charles Bailey. 1969. "Latin Rhetorical Theory in Medieval Spain." PhD diss. Yale University.

Feijoo, Benito Jerónimo. 1765. *Teatro crítico universal o discursos varios en todo género de materias, para desengaño de errores communes: Tomo Tercero*. Madrid: Pérez de Soto.

Feijoo, Benito Jerónimo. 1778. *Teatro crítico universal o discursos varios en todo género de materias, para desengaño de errores comunes. Tomo Primero*. Madrid: Ibarra.

Feijoo, Benito Jerónimo. 1774. *Cartas eruditas y curiosas*. Vol. 4. Madrid: Pedro Marín.

Feijoo, Benito Jerónimo. 1998. *Teatro crítico universal*. Edited by Ángel-Raimundo Fernánez González. Madrid: Cátedra.

Feijoo, Benito Jerónimo. 2003. *Teatro crítico universal*. Madrid: Real Academia Española. Real Academia Española: Banco de datos (CORDE) en línea. Corpus diacrónico del español. http://www.rae.es.

Ferguson, Wallace K. 2006. *The Renaissance in Historical Thought: Five Centuries of Interpretation*. Toronto: University of Toronto Press; Renaissance Society of America. [Boston: Houghton Mifflin, 1948].

Fernández de Madrigal, Alonso. 1995 [1507]. *Sobre los dioses de los gentiles*. Edited by Pilar Saquero Suárez-Somonte and Tomás González Rolán. Madrid: Ediciones Clásicas.

Fernández-Santamaría, J.A. 1977. *The State, War and Peace: Spanish Political Thought in the Renaissance 1516–1559*. Cambridge: Cambridge University Press. http://dx.doi.org/10.1017/CBO9780511896804.

Fernández-Santamaría, J.A. 1986. *Razón de Estado y política en el pensamiento español del Barroco (1595–1640)*. Madrid: Centro de Estudios Constitucionales.

Fernández-Santamaría, J.A. 2006. *Natural Law, Constitutionalism, Reason of State, and War: Counter-Reformation Spanish Political Thought*. Vol. 2. New York: Peter Lang.

Ficino, Marsilio. 15th C. *Marsilii Ficini in librum Trismegisti Commentarium*. El Burgo de Osma ms. 25, Catedral, El Burgo de Osma, Spain.

Ficino, Marsilio. 1493. *De sole. De lumine.* [*And other pieces: Apologia in librum suum de Sole & Lumine; Saepe celestibus gemini sunt. Item Soles duo; Nonnulla de lumine, Item Catalogus librorum Marsilii*]. Florence: Antonio di Bartolommeo Miscomini.

Ficino, Marsilio. 1495. *Epistolae*. Venice: Matteo Capcasa for Hieronymus Blondus. http://www.uni-mannheim.de/mateo/itali/autoren/ficinus_itali.html

Ficino, Marsilio. 1554. *Mercurii Trismegisti Poemander, seu de Potestate ac sapientia divina: Aesculapii definitiones ad Ammonen Regem*. Paris: Turnèbe.

Ficino, Marsilio. 1557 *Divini Platonis Opera Omnia: Marsilii Ficini interprete*. Lyon: Antonium Vicentium.

Ficino, Marsilio. 1562. *Plotini Divini illius e Platonica Familia Philosophi de rebus Philosophicis libri LIII in Enneades sex distributi*. Basel: Thomam Guarinum.

Ficino, Marsilio. 1563. *Tomo I delle divine lettere del gran Marsilio Ficino*. Translated by Felice Figliucci. Venice: Gabriel Giolito de' Ferrari.

Ficino, Marsilio. 1564. *Libro compuesto por el famoso y singular philósopho y gran médico Marcilio Ficino florentino*. Zaragoza: Bernuz, a costa de Francisco Curteti. The Goldsmiths'-Kress Library of Economic Literature. Gale Document number U100020474.

Ficino, Marsilio. 1576. *Opera: Marsilii Ficini Florentini, insignis philosophi Platonici, medici, atque theologi clarissimi, Opera [et] quae hactenus extitere*. 2 vols. Basel: Henricus Petri.

Ficino, Marsilio. 1944. *Commentary on Plato's* Symposium. Translated by Sears Reynolds Jayne. *University of Missouri Studies* 19.1.

Ficino, Marsilio. 1975–<2012>. *The Letters of Marsilio Ficino*. Introduction and edition by Clement Salaman. Translation from the Latin by members of the Language Department of the School of Economic Science, London. 9 vols. (to date). London: Shepheard-Walwyn.

Ficino, Marsilio. 2001–6. *Marsilio Ficino: Platonic Theology*. 6 vols. Translated and introduction by Michael J.B. Allen, with John Warden. Editing of Latin text by James Hankins, with William Bowen. I Tatti Renaissance Library. Cambridge, MA: Harvard University Press.

Ficino, Marsilio. 2002. *Marsilio Ficino: Three Books on Life*. Edited by Carol V. Kaske and John R. Clark. Binghamton, NY: RSA.

Ficino, Marsilio. 2005. *De christiana religione/ La religione cristiana.* Edited and translated by Roberto Zanzarri. Rome: Città Nuova Editrice.

Ficino, Marsilio. 2006. *Gardens of Philosophy: Ficino on Plato.* Translated by Arthur Farndell. London: Shepheard-Walwyn.

Ficino, Marsilio. 2008. *Marsilio Ficino: Commentaries on Plato.* Vol. I, *Phaedrus and Ion.* Edited and translated by Michael B. Allen. I Tatti Renaissance Library. Cambridge: Harvard University Press.

Ficino, Marsilio. 2009a. *When Philosophers Rule: Ficino on Plato's* Republic, Laws, *and* Epinomis. Translated by Arthur Farndell. Foreword by Ian Mason. London: Shepheard-Walwyn.

Ficino, Marsilio. 2009b. *Las cartas de Marsilio Ficino.* Vol. 1. Traducido de la edición inglesa al español por miembros de la Escuela de Filosofía Práctica de Madrid. Prólogo by Isabel Ordieres Díez. Madrid: Mandala; Escuela de Filosofía Práctica Sundarah.

Ficino, Marsilio. 2010. *All Things Natural: Ficino on Plato's* Timaeus. Edited and translated by Arthur Farndell. Notes by Peter Blumsom. London: Shepheard-Walwyn.

Fine, Lawrence. 2003. *Physician of the Soul, Healer of the Cosmos: Isaac Luria and His Kabbalistic Fellowship.* Stanford, CA: Stanford University Press.

Finello, Dominick. 1994. *Pastoral Themes and Forms in Cervantes's Fiction.* Lewisburg: Bucknell University Press.

Foix, Francois de. 1579. *Le Pimandre de Mercure Trismegiste de la Philosophie Chrestienne, Cognoissance du verbe diuin, & de l'excellence des oeuures de Dieu.* Bordeaux: Millanges.

Forcione, Alban K. 1984. *Cervantes and the Mystery of Lawlessness.* Princeton, NJ: Princeton University Press.

Fortín, Ernest L. 1996. *The Birth of Philosophic Christianity.* Lanham, MD: Rowland & Littlefield.

Fox Morcillo, Sebastián. 1556a. *In Platonis Dialogem, qui Phaedo, seu de animorum immortalitate inscribitur.* Basel: Joannes Oporinus.

Fox Morcillo, Sebastián. 1556b. *Sebastianii Foxii Morzilli Hispalensis commentatio in decem Platonis libros de Republica.* Basel: Joannes Oporinus.

Fox Morcillo, Sebastián. 1556c. "Epístola Noncupatoria." In *Platonis Timaeum commentarii.* Basel: Joannes Oporinus.ff. 2r–4r

Fox Morcillo, Sebastián. 1556d. *Commentatio in decem platonis libros de republica.* Basel: Joannes Oporinus. Universidad de Sevilla, Fondos Digitales. http://fondosdigitales.us.es

Fox Morcillo, Sebastián. 2000. *Teoría de la historia y teoría política en el siglo XVI: Sebastián Fox Morcillo, De Historiae Institutione Dialogus, Diálogo de la enseñanza de la historia (1557).* Alcalá: Universidad de Alcalá.

Fox Morcillo, Sebastián. 2010. *Comentario al diálogo de Platón Fedón o la inmortalidad del alma (1556).* Edited by Juan Cruz Cruz. Colección de pensamiento medieval y renacentista. Pamplona: EUNSA.

Freddoso, Alfred J. 1988. *Luis de Molina: On Divine Foreknowledge* (*Part IV of the Concordia*). Ithaca: Cornell University Press.

Friedman, Edward H. 2006. *Cervantes in the Middle: Realism and Reality in the Spanish Novel from Lazarillo de Tormes to Niebla.* Newark, DE: Juan de la Cuesta.

Fuentes, Alonso de. 1547. *Summa de philosophia natural.* Seville: Juan de León.

Gallardo, Bartolomé José. 1888–9. *Ensayo de una biblioteca española de libros raros y curiosos.* 4 vols. Madrid: Tello.

Gallardo, Bartolomé José. 1928. *Obras escogidas de Don Bartolomé José Gallardo.* 2 vols. Edited by Pedro Saínz y Rodríguez. Madrid: Nueva Biblioteca de Autores Españoles.

Gaos (*see* Sigüenza y Góngora).

Garau, Jaume. 2012. "Ideas religiosas del maestro Bartolomé Jiménez Patón (1569–1640) en *El virtuoso discreto* [c. 1629–31]." *Hispania Sacra* 64 (129): 237–58. http://dx.doi.org/10.3989/hs.2012.008.

García, Miguel Ángel. 2010. *"Sin que la muerte al ojo estorbo sea": Nueva lectura crítica de Francisco de Aldana.* Mérida: Editora Regional de Extremadura.

García Ayuso, Francisco. 1874. *Estudios sobre el oriente: los pueblos iranios y Zoroastro.* Madrid: J. Noguera.

García Cárcel, Ricardo. 1998. *La leyenda negra: Historia y opinión.* 2nd ed. Madrid: Alianza.

García Cárcel, Ricardo. 2000. "Felipe II y la leyenda negra en el siglo XIX." In *El siglo de Carlos V y Felipe II: La construcción de los mitos en el siglo XIX. Congreso Internacional, Valladolid, 3–5 de noviembre de 1999*, edited by José Martínez Millán and Carlos Reyero, 353–71. Madrid: Sociedad Estatal para la Conmemoración de los Centenarios de Felipe II y Carlos V.

García Rico y Compañía. 1920. *Catálogo de libros españoles o relativos a España antiguos y modernos.* Madrid: Librería Universal de Ocasión.

García Romero, Francisco. 1921. *Catálogo de los incunables existentes en la Biblioteca de la Real Academia de la Historia.* Madrid: Reus.

Garcilaso de la Vega. 1966. *Garcilaso de la Vega y sus comentaristas.* Edited by Antonio Gallego Morell. Granada: Urania.

Garfagnini, Gian Carlo, ed. 1986. *Marsilio Ficino e il Ritorno de Platone.* Florence: Leo S. Olschki.

Gargano, Antonio. 2012. *La literatura en tiempos de los Reyes Católicos.* Madrid: Gredos.

Garin, Eugenio. 1955. "Richerche sulle traduzioni di Platone nella prima metà del sec. XV." In *Medioevo e Rinascimento: Studi in onore di Bruno Nardi*, 1:339–74. Florence: G.C. Sansoni.

Garin, Eugenio. 1981. *La revolución cultural del renacimiento.* Barcelona: Crítica.

Garin, Eugenio. 1983. *Astrology in the Renaissance: The Zodiac of Life.* Translated by Carolyn Jackson and June Allen. Revised translation by Clare Robertson. London: Routledge & Kegan Paul.

Gelder, Herman Arend Enno van. 1961. *The Two Reformations in the 16th Century: A Study of the Religious Aspects and Consequences of Renaissance and Humanism.* Translated by Jan F. Finlay and Alison Hanham. The Hague: Martinus Nijhoff.

Gelio, Aulo. 2006. *Noches áticas.* 2 vols. Edited and translated by Manuel-Antonio Marcos Casquero and Avelino Domínguez García. León: Universidad de León.

Gentile, Sebastian. 1981. "Per la storia del testo del *Commentarium in Convivium* de Marsilio Ficino." *Rinascimento* 21:3–27.

Gentile, Sebastian, and Carlos Gilly, eds. 1999. *Marsilio Ficino e il ritorno di Ermete Trismegisto.* Florence: Centro Di.

Ghia, Walter. 2013. *España y Maquiavelo: El Príncipe ante el V Centenario.* Pontevedra: Editorial Academia del Hispanismo.

Gil, Juan. 1998. *Arias Montano en su entorno: bienes y herederos.* Mérida: Editora Regional de Extremadura.

Gil Fernández, Luis. 1966. *Los antiguos y la "inspiración" poética.* Madrid: Guadarrama.

Gil Fernández, Luis. 2009. "La enseñanza universitaria del griego en España: del Renacimiento a la Ilustración." *Studi Hispanici* 34:41–53.

Giovio, Paolo. 1568. *Elogios o vidas breves de los cavalleros antiguos y modernos.* Translated by Gaspar de Baeza. Granada: Hugo de Mena.

Giraldi, Geraldo. 1819. *Novelle di Giraldo Giraldi.* 2nd ed. Amsterdam.

Gómez Canseco, Luis, and Fernando Navarro Antolín, eds. 2005. *Virorum doctorum de disciplinis benemerentium, effigies XLIII = cuarenta y cuatro retratos de sabios beneméritos en las artes liberales, por Benito Arias Montano y Philips Galle.* Huelva: Universidad de Huelva.

Gómez Miedes, Bernardino. 1589. *Enchiridion o manual instrumento de salud contra el morbo articular que llaman gota.* Zaragoza: Lorenzo y Diego de Robles. [Complutense digitized volume]. Real Academia Española: Banco de datos (CORDE) [en línea]. Corpus diacrónico del español. http://www.rae.es.

Gómez Moreno, Ángel. 1994. *España y la Italia de los humanistas: primeros ecos.* Madrid: Gredos.

Gómez Tejada de los Reyes, Cosme. 1636. *León prodigioso: Apología moral entretenida, y provechosa a las buenas costumbres, trato virtuoso y político.* Madrid: Francisco Martínez. [Biblioteca digital de Castilla y León]

González de la Calle, Urbano. 1903. *Sebastián Fox Morcillo: Estudio histórico-crítico de sus doctrinas.* Madrid: Asilo de Huérfanos del Sagrado Corazón de Jesús.

González Navarro, Ramón. 1984. *Universidad Complutense: Constituciones originales cisnerianas (edición bilingüe y comentario).* Translation of Latin texts by Antonio Larios y Bernaldo de Quirós. Madrid: Universidad de Alcalá de Henares.

Gónzalez Palencia, Ángel, and Eugenio Mele. 1941–3. *Vida y obras de don Diego Hurtado de Mendoza.* Madrid: E. Maestre.

Gonzalo Sánchez-Molero, José Luis. 1998. *La "Librería rica" de Felipe II: Estudio histórico y catalogación.* Ediciones Escurialenses 10. San Lorenzo del Escorial, Madrid: RCU "Escorial-María Cristina."

Gouwens, Kenneth. 1998. *Remembering the Renaissance: Humanist Narratives of the Sack of Rome.* Leiden: Brill.

Gracián, Baltasar. 2001. *El héroe.* Facsimile (Madrid, Diego Díaz, 1639). Prologue by Aurora Egido. Zaragoza: Institución "Fernando el Católico."

Gracián, Baltasar. 2009. *El Criticón.* Edited by Santos Alonso. Madrid: Cátedra.

Gratian. 1486. *Decretum (cum apparatu Bartholomaei Brixiensis)*. Venice: Tommaso de' Blavi. [Proquest digitized volume]

Green, Otis. 1938. "The Historical Problem of Castilian Mysticism." *Hispanic Review* 6 (2): 93. http://dx.doi.org/10.2307/469719.

Green, Otis. 1958. "On Francisco de Aldana: Observations on Dr. Rivers' Study of "El Divino Capitán." *Hispanic Review* 26 (2): 117. http://dx.doi.org/10.2307/471002.

Green, Otis. 1963. *Spain and the Western Tradition.* 4 vols. Madison, WI: University of Wisconsin Press.

Guevara, Antonio de. 1950–2. *Epístolas familiares.* 2 vols. Edited by José María de Cossío. Madrid: Real Academia Española.

Guevara, Antonio de. 1994. "Estudio y edición crítica del 'Libro llamado Relox de príncipes con el libro de Marco Aurelio' de Antonio de Guevara." Edited and introduction by José Luis Madrigal. PhD diss. Graduate Center, City University of New York.

Guicciardini, Luigi. 1993. *Sack of Rome.* Translated by James H. McGregor. New York: Italica.

Guillén de Ávila, Diego, trans. *Mercurio Trismegisto: De la potencia y sapiencia de Dios.* Ms. b-IV-29. El Escorial, San Lorenzo de El Escorial, Madrid.

Gullón, Ricardo. 1979. "El esoterismo modernista." In *Historia y crítica de la literatura española.* Vol. 6 of *Modernismo y 98*, edited by José-Carlos Mainer Baqué, 69–74. Madrid: Crítica.

Gutiérrez de los Ríos, Gaspar. 1600. *Noticia general para la estimación de las artes.* Madrid: Pedro Madrigal.

Guzmán y Márquez, Eugenio Nicolás de. 1719. *Escudo atomístico en que se propugna la philosophia platónica de nuestro príncipe Maygnan.* Madrid: Juan Martínez de Casas.

Hadot, Pierre. 2002. *What is Ancient Philosophy? [Qu'est-ce que la philosophie antique?]*. Translated by Michael Chase. Cambridge, MA: Belknap Press of Harvard University Press.

Hankins, James. 1984. "Latin Translations of Plato in the Renaissance." PhD diss. Columbia University.

Hankins, James. 1990. *Plato in the Italian Renaissance.* 2 vols. Leiden: Brill.

Hankins, James. 2005. "Marsilio Ficino on Reminiscentia and the Transmigration of Souls." *Rinascimento* 45:3–17. http://dash.harvard.edu/handle/1/2961227 accessed 6 August 2012.

Hankins, James. 2006. "Religion and the Modernity of Renaissance Humanism." In *Interpretations of Renaissance Humanism*, edited by Angelo Mazzocco, 137–53. Leiden: E.J. Brill; http://dash.harvard.edu/handle/1/2920220, accessed 26 December 2012. http://dx.doi.org/10.1163/9789047410249_009.

Hankins, James. 2007. "Humanism, Scholasticism, and Renaissance Philosophy." In *The Cambridge Companion to Renaissance Philosophy*, edited by James Hankins, 30–48. Cambridge: Cambridge University Press. http://dx.doi.org/10.1017/CCOL052184648X.003.

Hankins, James. 2008a. "Ficino and the Religion of the Philosophers." *Rinascimento* 48:101–21.

Hankins, James, and Ada Palmer. 2008b. *The Recovery of Ancient Philosophy in the Renaissance: A Brief Guide.* Florence: Leo S. Olschki.

Harris, Melodie F. 2000. "Alphonsus Bonihominis' Conversionary Letter from Rabbi Samuel to Rabbi Isaac." MA thesis, Western Michigan University.

Harrison, Peter. 1993. "Animal Souls, Metempsychosis, and Theodicy in Seventeenth-Century English Thought." *Journal of the History of Philosophy* 31 (4): 519–44. http://dx.doi.org/10.1353/hph.1993.0081.

Hebreo, León. 2002. *Diálogos de amor.* Translated by David Romano. Madrid: Tecnos.

Heiple, Daniel. 1994. *Garcilaso de la Vega and the Italian Renaissance.* University Park, PA: Penn State Press.

Hernández, Ramón. 2001. "El arabista medieval Alfonso Buenhombre." *Anámnesis: revista semanal de investigación teológica* 11(21) (enero-junio): 105–36.

Hernández González, María Isabel. 1998. "Suma de inventarios de bibliotecas del siglo XVI (1501–1560)." In *El libro antiguo español IV: Coleccionismo y Bibliotecas (Siglos XV–XVIII).* Directors María Luis López-Vidriero and Pedro M. Cátedra, edited by María Isabel Hernández González, 375–446. Salamanca: Ediciones Universidad de Salamanca; Patrimonio Nacional; Sociedad Española de Historia del Libro.

Herrera, Fernando de. 2001. *Anotaciones a la poesía de Garcilaso.* Edited by Inoria Pepe and José María Reyes. Madrid: Cátedra.

Herrera y Tordesillas, Antonio de, trans. 1599. *Giovanni Botero: Diez Libros de la Razón de Estado.* Barcelona: Jayme Cendrad. http://reader.digitale-sammlungen.de/de/fs1/object/display/bsb10192734_00008.html

Horozco, Sebastián de. 1994. *El libro de los proverbios glosados (1570–1580).* Edited by Jack Weiner. Kassel: Editorial Reichenberger.

Huarte de San Juan, Juan. 1989. *Examen de ingenios para las ciencias.* Edited by Guillermo Serés. Madrid: Cátedra.

Huerga, Alvaro. 1979. "La recepción de la 'Aeterni Patris' en España." *Scripta theologica* 11.2:535–62.

Huerta, Jerónimo de. 1624, 1629. *Historia natural de Cayo Plinio Segundo: Traducida por el licenciado Gerónimo de Huerta, médico familiar del Santo Oficio de la Inquisición, y ampliada por el mismo con escolios y anotaciones.* Vol. 1, Madrid: Luis Sánchez, 1624. Vol. 2, Madrid: Juan González, 1629.

Hutchinson, Steven. 1992. *Cervantine Journeys.* Madison, WI: University of Wisconsin Press.

Iglesias Ortega, Arturo. 2010. *El cabildo catedralicio de Santiago de Compostela en el siglo XVI: aspectos funcionales y sociológicos de una élite eclesiástica.* Santiago de Compostela: Facultade de Xeografía e Historia.

Infantes, Víctor. 1989. "Poesía teatral en la corte: historia de las *Églogas* de Diego Guillén de Ávila y Fernando del Prado." In *Bulletin of Hispanic Studies.* Special Issue. *The Age of the Catholic Monarchs, 1474–1526: Literary Studies in Memory of Keith Whinnom*, edited by Alan Deyermond and Ian Macpherson, 76–82. Liverpool: Liverpool University Press.

Inventario general de manuscritos de la Biblioteca Nacional. 1956. Vol. 2, Ministerio de Educación Nacional. Madrid: Archivos y Bibliotecas. [online] MSS/ 864.

Irigoyen-García, Javier. 2013. "Jerónimo de Arbolanche's *Las Abidas* (1566) and the Mythical Origins of Spain." *Symposium: A Quarterly Journal in Modern Literatures* 67:85–97.

Isnardi-Parente, Margherita. 1988. "Erasme, la Republique de Platon et la communaute des biens." In *Erasmus of Rotterdam: The Man and the Scholar*. Proceedings of the Symposium Held at the Erasmus University, Rotterdam, 9–11 November 1986, edited by Jan Sperna Weiland and Willem Th. M. Frijhoff, 40–5. Leiden: Brill.

Iventosch, Herman. 1974. "Cervantes and Courtly Love: The Grisóstomo-Marcela Episode in *Don Quixote*." *PMLA* 89:64–76. http://dx.doi.org/10.2307/461669.

Jackson, Philippa. 2006. "Pomp or Piety? The Funeral of Pandolfo Petrucci." *Renaissance Studies* 20:240–52. http://dx.doi.org/10.1111/j.1477-4658.2006.00198.x.

Jiménez Delgado, José, ed.1978. *Juan Luis Vives: Epistolario*. Madrid: Editora Nacional.

Jiménez Moreno, Luis, ed. 1996. *La Universidad Complutense Cisneriana: Impulso filosófico, científico y literario, Siglos XVI y XVII*. Madrid: Editorial Complutense.

Jiménez Moreno, Luis. 2002. "La visión del mundo y de la vida en espíritu barroco." In *Pensamiento filosófico español*. Vol. 2, *Del Barroco a nuestros días*, edited by M. Maceiras Fafián, 11–76. Madrid: Síntesis.

Jiménez Patón, Bartolomé. 1621. *Mercurius Trismegistus, sive de triplici eloquentia sacra, española, romana*. Baeza: Petro de la Cuesta Gallo. [Hathitrust]

Jiménez Patón, Bartolomé. 1965. Epítome de la ortografía latina y castellana. Edited by Antonio Quilis and Manuel Rozas. Madrid: CSIC.

Juan de la Cruz, San. 1953. *The Complete Works of Saint John of the Cross*. Translated and edited by E. Allison Peers. Westminster, MD: The Newman Press.

Juan de la Cruz, San. 1954. *Obras de San Juan de la Cruz, Doctor de la Iglesia*. Madrid: Editorial Apostolado de la Prensa.

Juan de la Cruz, San. 2000. *Poesía*. Edited by Domingo Ynduráin. Madrid: Cátedra.

Juan de la Cruz, San. 2002. *San Juan de la Cruz: Cántico espiritual y poesía completa*. Edited by Paola Elia and María Jesús Mancho. Preliminary Study. Domingo Ynduráin. Barcelona: Critica.

Kagan, Richard L. 1974. *Students and Society in Early Modern Spain*. Baltimore: Johns Hopkins University Press.

Kagan, Richard L. 1981. *Lawsuits and Litigants in Castile 1500–1700*. Chapel Hill, NC: University of North Carolina Press.

Kagan, Richard L. 2000. "Un país gobernado por los curas: Reflexiones en torno a la imagen de España en Estados Unidos a comienzos del siglo XIX." In *El siglo de Carlos V y Felipe II: La construcción de los mitos en el siglo XIX. Congreso Internacional, Valladolid, 3–5 de noviembre de 1999*, edited by José Martínez Millán and Carlos Reyero, 419–36. Madrid: Sociedad Estatal para la Conmemoración de los Centenarios de Felipe II y Carlos V.

Kagan, Richard L. 2009. *Clio and the Crown: The Politics of History in Medieval and Early Modern Spain*. Baltimore, MD: Johns Hopkins University Press.

Kallendorf, Hilaire. 2005. "La Inquisición, ¿Por qué deshace la cabeza encantada?" In *Actas del XI Coloquio Internacional de la Asociación de cervantinas: Seúl, 17–20 de noviembre de 2004*, edited by Chul Park, 173–86. Seúl: Universidad de Estudios Extranjeros.

Kamen, Henry. 2008. *Imagining Spain: Historical Myth and National Identity*. New Haven, CT: Yale University Press.

Kane, Robert. 1996. *The Significance of Free Will*. New York: Oxford University Press.

Kaske, Carol V., and John R. Clark, eds. 2002. *Marsilio Ficino: Three Books on Life*. Binghamton, NY: Renaissance Society of America.

Keitt, Andrew. 2013. "The Devil in the Old World: Anti-Superstition Literature, Medical Humanism and Preternatural Philosophy in Early Modern Spain." In *Angels, Demons and the New World*, edited by Fernando Cervantes and Andrew Redden, 15–39. Cambridge: Cambridge University Press. http://dx.doi.org/10.1017/CBO9781139023870.003.

Klibansky, Raymond. 1939. *The Continuity of the Platonic Tradition during the Middle Ages*. London: The Warburg Institute.

Klibansky, Raymond, Edwin Panofsky, and Fritz Saxl. 1979. *Saturn and Melancholy: Studies in the History of Natural Philosophy, Religion and Art*. Leichenstein: Nendeln.

Klitenic Wear, Sarah. 2013. "Another Link in the Golden Chain: Aeneas of Gaza and Zacharias Scholasticus on Plotinus *Enn.* 4.3." *Greek, Roman and Byzantine Studies* 53:145–65.

Kraus, George Frank. 2005. "Juan Luis Vives: The Poetics of Invention." PhD diss. Graduate Center, City University of New York.

Kraye, Jill. 2002. "Marsilio Ficino in the Firing Line: A Renaissance Neoplatonist and His Critics." In *Marsilio Ficino: His Theology, His Philosophy, His Legacy*, edited by Michael J.B. Allen and Valery Rees, 377–97. Leiden: Brill.

Kristeller, Paul Oskar. 1956–96. *Studies in Renaissance Thought and Letters*. 4 vols. Rome: Edizioni di storia e letteratura.

Kristeller, Paul Oskar. 1964. *The Philosophy of Marsilio Ficino*. Translatd by Virginia Conant. Gloucester, MA: P. Smith.

Kristeller, Paul Oskar. 1970. "Erasmus from an Italian Perspective." *Renaissance Quarterly* 23:1–14. http://dx.doi.org/10.2307/2859266.

Kristeller, Paul Oskar. 1975. Preface. In *The Letters of Marsilio Ficino*. Vol. 1, translated from the Latin by members of the Language Department of the School of Economic Science, London, 17–18. London: Shepheard-Walwyn.

Kristeller, Paul Oskar. 1978. "Philosophy and Medicine in Medieval and Renaissance Italy." In *Organism, Medicine and Metaphysics*, edited by Stuart F. Spicker, 29–40. Dordrecht: Springer Netherlands. http://dx.doi.org/10.1007/978-94-009-9783-7_3.

Kristeller, Paul Oskar. 1989. *Iter italicum: A Finding List of Uncatalogued or Incompletely Catalogued Humanistic Manuscripts of the Renaissance in Italian and Other Libraries*. Leiden: E.J.Brill.

Kristeller, Paul Oskar, and John Herman Randall, Jr. 1948. General Introduction to *The Renaissance Philosophy of Man*, 1–20. Chicago: University of Chicago Press.

Kurtz, Barbara E. 1986. "The *Agricultura cristiana* of Juan de Pineda in the Context of Renaissance Mythography and Encyclopedism." *Inti: Revista de literatura hispánica* 1(24): 191–202.

Lachman, Sheldon Joseph. 1972. *Psychosomatic Disorders: A Behavioristic Interpretation.* New York: Wiley.

Lackner, Dennis F. 2002. "The Camaldoese Academy." In *Marsilio Ficino: His Theology, His Philosophy, His Legacy*, edited by Michael J.B. Allen and Valery Rees, 15–44. Leiden: Brill.

Lampillas, Don Xavier. 1783. *Ensayo histórico-apologético de la literatura Española contra las opiniones preocupadas de algunos Escritores modernos Italianos.* 2 vols. Translated by Doña Josefa Amar y Borbón. Zaragoza: Blas Miedes, Impresor de la Real Sociedad.

Lang, Helen S. 2005. "Perpetuity, Eternity, and Time in Proclus' Cosmos." *Phronesis: A Journal of Ancient Philosophy* 50 (2): 150–69. http://dx.doi.org/10.1163/1568528053898327.

Langer, Ullrich. 1999. "The Renaissance Novella as Justice." *Renaissance Quarterly* 52:311–41. http://dx.doi.org/10.2307/2902055.

Lara Garrido, José, ed. 1985. *Francisco de Aldana: Poesías castellanas completas.* Madrid: Cátedra.

Lasso de la Vega, José S. 1956. "Menéndez Pelayo y la filología clásica en España." *Estudios Clásicos* 3:18. 325–58.

Lauster, Jörg. 2002. "Marsilio Ficino as a Christian Thinker: Theological Aspects of his Platonism." In *Marsilio Ficino: His Theology, His Philosophy, His Legacy*, edited by Michael J.B. Allen and Valery Rees, 45–70. Leiden: Brill.

Leiman, Shnayer Z. 1968. "Abarbanel and the Censor." *Journal of Jewish Studies* 19:49–61.

León, Fray Luis de. 1885. "Sermón sobre el evangelio 'Vos estis sal terrae'." In *Obras castellanas,* edited by Fray Antolín Merino. Madrid: Compañía de Impresores y Libreros del Reino.

León, Fray Luis de. 1891–1895. "Epistola II in Thessalonic. Commentaria." In *Opera omnia,* edited by Marcellinus Gutiérrez. 3:474–5. Salamanca: Espiscopali Calatravae Collegio.

León, Fray Luis de. 1995. *Fray Luis de León: Poesía.* Edited by Juan Francisco Alcina. Madrid: Cátedra.

León, Fray Luis de. 2008. *De los nombres de Cristo.* Edited by Javier San José Lera. Preliminary study by Fernando Lázaro Carreter. Barcelona: Círculo de Lectores; Centro para la Edición de los Clásicos Españoles.

Leonard, Irving. 1992. *Books of the Brave: Being an Account of Books and of Men in the Spanish Conquest and Settlement of the Sixteenth-Century New World.* Berkeley: University of California Press.

Leong, Elaine, and Alisha Rankin, eds. 2011. *Secrets and Knowledge in Medicine and Science, 1500–1800.* London: Ashgate.

Lerner, Isaías, ed. 2003. *Pedro Mexía: Silva de varia lección.* Madrid: Castalia.

Levenson, Dorothy. 1994. *Mind, Body, and Medicine: A History of the American Psychosomatic Society.* Baltimore, MD: Williams & Wilkins.

Limor, Ora. 1996. "The Epistle of Rabbi Samuel of Morocco: A Best-Seller in the World of Polemics." In *Contra Iudaeos: Ancient and Medieval Polemics between Christians and Jews*, edited by Ora Limor and Guy G. Stroumsa, 177–94. Tübingen: J.C.B. Mohr (Paul Siebeck).

Linehan, Paul. 1911. "Pedro Núñez." In *The Catholic Encyclopedia.* Vol. 11. New York: Robert Appleton Company. 6 Oct. 2012 http://www.newadvent.org/cathen/11163a.htm.

Lokos, Ellen D. 1991. *The Solitary Journey: Cervantes' Voyage to Parnassus.* New York: Peter Lang.

Lombardo, Paul A. 1982. "Vita Activa versus Vita Contemplativa in Petrarch and Salutati." *Italica* 59:83–92. http://dx.doi.org/10.2307/479134.

Lope de Vega Carpio, Félix. 1973. *El peregrino en su patria.* Edited by Juan Bautista Avalle-Arce. Madrid: Castalia.

Lope de Vega Carpio, Félix. 1989. "La calidad elementar resiste." In *Colección de las obras sueltas, así en prosa como en verso: 1771–1790*, edited by María del Pilar Palomo. 1:401–9. Facsimile of the edition of Antonio de Sancha. Madrid: Arco.

Lope de Vega Carpio, Félix. 1993. *Rimas I [Doscientos sonetos].* Edited by Felipe B. Pedraza Jiménez. Madrid: Universidad de Castilla-La Mancha.

Lope de Vega Carpio, Félix. 1996. *La Dorotea.* Edited by José Manuel Blecua. Madrid: Cátedra.

Lope de Vega Carpio, Félix. 2002. "La prudente venganza." In *Novelas a Marcia Leonarda*, editd by Antonio Carreño, 233–84. Madrid: Cátedra.

Lope de Vega Carpio, Félix. 2006. *Rimas sacras de Lope de Vega.* Edited by Antonio Carreño and Antonio Sánchez Jiménez. Madrid: Iberoamericana; Universidad de Navarra.

Lope de Vega Carpio, Félix. 2010. *Pastores de Belén.* Edited by Antonio Carreño. Madrid: Cátedra.

López de Mendoza, Íñigo, marqués de Santillana. 1982. *Bías contra fortuna.* Edited by Maxim. P.A.M. Kerkhof. Madrid: Anejos de la Boletín de la Real Academia Española [Anejo 39].

López de Úbeda, Francisco. 1977. *La pícara Justina.* 2 vols. Edited by Antonio Rey Hazas. Madrid: Editora Nacional. [Google Book]

López Estrada, Francisco. 1948. *Estudio crítico de La Galatea de Miguel de Cervantes.* La Laguna de Tenerife: Universidad de La Laguna de Tenerife.

López Estrada, Francisco. 1999. "'Dissoluble Ñudo': Una compleja lección de *La Galatea.*" In *Ingeniosa Invención: Essays on Golden Age Spanish Literature for Geoffrey L. Stagg in Honor of His Eighty-Fifth Birthday*, edited by Ellen M. Anderson and Amy R. Williamsen, 123–36. Newark, DE: Juan de la Cuesta.

López Múñoz, Miguel Ángel. 2010. "La filosofía política de Pedro de Ribadeneyra y su influencia jurídica en la historia de España." *Bajo palabra: Revista de Filosofía. II Época* 5:321–30.

López Pinciano, Alonso. 1998. *Philosophía antigua poética: Obras completas.* 2 vols. Edited by José Rico Verdú. Madrid: Castro.

López Vidriero, María Luisa. 1987. 'La Biblioteca del Colegio de Teólogos de la Madre de Dios de Alcalá de Henares." In *Homenaje a Justo García Morales*, edited by Francisco Javier Aguirre Gonzalez, 343–408. Madrid: Anabad.

Lorenz Villanueva, Joaquín. 1804. *Viage literario a las iglesias de España.* 22 vols. Madrid: Imprenta Real.

Loyola, Ignatius de. 1563. *Exercitia Spiritualia.* Vienna: Caesarei Collegij.

Lucena, Luis de. 1954. *Repetición de amores.* Edited by J. Ornstein. University of North Carolina Studies in the Romance Languages and Literatures 23. Chapel Hill: University of North Carolina Press.

Luján, Pedro de. 1990. *Coloquios matrimoniales del licenciado Pedro de Luján.* Edited by Asunción Rallo Gruss. Madrid: Real Academia Española.

Luzán, Ignacio de. 1956. *La Poética o reglas de la poesía:* 2 vols. Edited by Luigi de Filippo. Barcelona: Selecciones Bibliófilas.

Madan, Falconer. 1905. *A Summary Catalogue of Western Manuscripts in the Bodlein Library at Oxford.* Vol. 5. Oxford: Clarendon.

Magris, Aldo. 2008. *Destino, provvidenza, predestinazione: dal mondo antico al cristianesimo.* Brescia: Morcelliana.

Mahoney, Edward P. 2006. "Marsilio Ficino and Renaissance Platonism." In *Humanism and Creativity in the Renaissance: Essays in Honor of Ronald G. Witt.*, edited by Christopher S. Celenza and Ronald G. Witt, 231–44. Leiden: Brill. http://dx.doi.org/10.1163/9789047408741_011.

"Mallock's New Republic." 1878. *New York Times.* 20 April.

Malón de Chaide, Pedro. 1959. *La conversión de la Magdalena.* Clásicos Castellanos 104, 105, 130. Madrid: Espasa-Calpe.

Mancheño y Olivares, Miguel. 1892. *Galería de arcobrisenses ilustres.* Arcos de la Frontera: Emprenta de El arcobrisense.

Manzoni, Claudio. 1974. *Umanesmi ed eresia, Michele Serveto.* Naples: Guida.

Maravall, José Antonio. 1948. *El humanismo de las armas en Don Quijote.* Prólogo by Ramón Menéndez Pidal. Madrid: Instituto de Estudios Políticos.

Maravall, José Antonio. 1972. *Estado moderno y mentalidad social (Siglos XV a XVII).* 2 vols. Madrid: Revista de Occidente.

Maravall, José Antonio. 1973. *Estudios de historia del pensamiento español.* Madrid: Ediciones Cultura Hispánica.

Maravall, José Antonio. 1997. *Teoría del estado en España en el siglo 17.* Madrid: Centro de Estudios Constitucionales.

Maravall, José Antonio. 2005. *Utopia y contrautopia en el Quijote.* Prologue by Ramón Menéndez Pidal. Madrid: CSIC.

Mariana, Juan de. 1631. "Tratado de las cosas que ay dignas de remedio en la Compañía de Jesús." In *Le Mercure Iesvite: Ou Recveil des pieces, concernants le Progrés des Iesvites, leurs escrits, & Differents: Depuis l'an 1620. iusqu'a l'annee 1626*, 2:1–86. Geneva: Pierre Avbert.

Marías, Fernando. 1985. *La arquitectura del Renacimiento en Toledo (1541–1631).* Madrid: CSIC.

Márquez, Antonio. 1972. *Los alumbrados: Orígenes y filosofía 1525–1559.* Madrid: Taurus.

Martin, Francisco Javier. 1987. "Estudio y edición de Elocuencia española en arte (1604, 1621) de Bartolomé Jiménez Patón." PhD diss. University of Pennsylvania.

Martínez Millán, José, and Carlos Reyero, eds. 2000. *El siglo de Carlos V y Felipe II: la construcción de los mitos en el siglo XIX*. Madrid: Sociedad Estatal para la Conmemoración de los Centenarios de Felipe II y Carlos V.

Mártir de Anglería, Pedro. 1953. *Epistolario*. Edited and translated by José López de Toro. In *Documentos inéditos para la historia de España*. Madrid: Imprenta Góngora.

Matton, Sylvain. 1996. "Cynicism and Christianity from the Middle Ages to the Renaissance." In *The Cynics: The Cynic Movement in Antiquity and its Legacy*, edited by Robert Bracht Branham and Marie-Odile Goulet-Cazé, 240–64. Berkeley: University of California Press.

Maurino, Ferdinando D. 1956. "El Viaje de Cervantes y la Comedia de Dante." *Kentucky Foreign Language Quarterly* 3:7–12. http://dx.doi.org/10.1080/00230332.1956.9930444.

Maxwell-Stuart, P.G. 2000. *Martín del Río: Investigations into Magic*. Manchester: Manchester University Press.

Mazzeo, Joseph A. 1954. "Universal Analogy and the Culture of the Renaissance." *Journal of the History of Ideas* 15:299–304. http://dx.doi.org/10.2307/2707774.

Mazzeo, Joseph A. 1972. "Some Interpretations of the History of Ideas." *Journal of the History of Ideas* 33:379–94. http://dx.doi.org/10.2307/2709042.

Mendoza, Fray Íñigo de. 1968. "Coplas de *Vita Christi*." In *Cancionero*, edited by Julio Rodríguez-Puértolas, 1–153. Madrid: Espasa-Calpe.

Menéndez Pelayo, Marcelino. 1892. "De las vicisitudes de la Filosofía platónica en España." In *Ensayos de crítica filosófica*, 28–192. Madrid: Rivadeneyra.

Menéndez Pelayo, Marcelino. 1948. "De los orígenes del criticismo y del escepticismo y especialmente de los precursores españoles de Kant." In *Discurso de recepción leído en la Real Academia de Ciencias Morales y Políticas el día 15 de mayo de 1891: Ensayos de crítica filosófica. Obras completas*, vol. 43, edited by Enrique Sánchez Reyes and Ángel González Palencia, 117–216. Santander: Aldus.

Menéndez Pelayo, Marcelino. 1974. *Historia de las ideas estéticas en España*. 2 vols. Madrid: CSIC.

Menéndez Pelayo, Marcelino. 1992. *Historia de los heterodoxos españoles*. 3 vols. Madrid: CSIC.

Meneses, Felipe de. 1567. *Luz del alma christiana*. Medina del Campo: Francisco del Canto. [Google Book]

Merkl, Heinrich. 2011. *Cervantes anti-sofista: Sobre Platón, Ficino, y los tres Quijotes (1605, 1614 y 1615)*. Vigo: Editorial Academia del Hispanismo.

Mexía, Pedro. 2003. *Silva de varia lección*. Edited by Isaías Lerner. Madrid: Castalia.

Milá y Fontonals, Manuel. 1888. *Obras completas*. Vol. I. Edited by Marcelino Menéndez Pelayo. Barcelona: Imprenta Barcelonesa.

Molho, Maurice. 1970. "Remarques sur le *Mariage trompeur et Colloque des chiens*." In *Le Mariage trompeur et Colloque des chiens*, translated by Maurice Molho, 11–95. Paris: Aubier-Flammarion.

Molina, Tirso de. 1979. *El bandolero*. Edited by André Nougue. Madrid: Castalia.

Molina Cano, Juan Alfonso de. 1999. *Descubrimientos geométricos*. Edited by Jesús Vidal Muñoz María. Salamanca: CILUS.

Moliner, María. 1997. *Diccionario de uso del español.* Madrid: Gredos.

Monfasani, John. 1984. Collectanea Trapezuntiana*: Texts, Documents, and Bibliographies of George of Trebizond.* Binghamton, NY: Medieval & Renaissance Texts & Studies; Renaissance Society of America.

Monfasani, John. 1992. *Fernando of Cordova: A Biographical and Intellectual Profile.* Transactions of the American Philosophical Society, 82.6. Philadephia. The American Philosophical Society.

Monfasani, John. 2004. *Greeks and Latins in Renaissance Italy: Studies on Humanism and Philosophy in the 15th Century.* Ashgate: Variorum.

Monfasani, John. 2013. *"Prisca theologia in the Plato-Aristotle Controversy before Ficino": The Rebirth of Platonic Theology.* Edited by James Hankins and Fabrizio Meroi. Florence: Leo S. Olschki.

Morros Mestres, Bienvenido. 1998. *Las polémicas literarias en la España del siglo XVI: A propósito de Fernando de Herrera y Garcilaso de la Vega.* Barcelona: Quaderns Crema.

Morros Mestres, Bienvenido. 2000. "La Canción IV de Garcilaso como un infierno de amor." *Criticón* 80:19–47.

Moya, Jesús, trans. and ed. 1991. *Martín del Río: La magia demoniáca (libro II de las Disquisiciones Mágicas).* Madrid: Hiperion.

Mujica, Barbara. 1986. *Iberian Pastoral Characters.* Scripta humanistica 30. Baltimore, MD: Digitalia Hispánica.

Nebrija, Antonio de. 1951. *Vocabulario español-latino.* Salamanca: Impresor de la Gramática castellana. Facsimile. Madrid: Real Academia Española. http://buscon.rae.es/

Nebrija, Antonio de. 1516. *Vocabulario de romance en latín hecho por el doctíssimo maestro Antonio de Nebrissa nuevamente corregido y augmentado.* Seville: Juan Varela de Salamanca. http://buscon.rae.es/

Nelson, Eric. 2007. "The Problem of the Prince." In *The Cambridge Companion to Renaissance Philosophy*, edited by James Hankins, 319–37. Cambridge: Cambridge University Press. http://dx.doi.org/10.1017/CCOL052184648X.017.

Nettleship, Richard Lewis. 1901. *Lectures on the Republic of Plato.* Edited by G.R. Benson. New York: Macmillan.

Newman, William R., and Anthony Grafton, eds. 2001. "Introduction: The Problematic Status of Astrology and Alchemy in Premodern Europe." In *Secrets of Nature: Astrology and Alchemy in Early Modern Europe*, 1–37. Cambridge, MA: MIT Press.

"The New Socialist Republic in Paris." 1871. *New York Times.* 27 April.

Nieremberg, Juan Eusebio. 1631. *Vida de San Ignacio de Loyola fundador de la Compañía de Jesús.* Madrid: Imprenta del Reyno.

Noreña, Carlos. 1998. *Juan Luis Vives and the Emotions.* Carbondale: Southern Illinois University Press.

Núñez, Pedro. 1567. *Libro de Álgebra en Arithmética y Geometría.* Anvers: Herederos d'Arnoldo Birckmann. [Google Book]

Ocasar Ariza, José Luis. 1992. "La tradición manuscrita de los *Coloquios de Palatino y Pinciano* de Juan de Arce de Otarola." *Criticón* 56:81–5.

Ocasar Ariza, José Luis, ed. 1995. *Juan de Arce de Otálora:* Coloquios de Palatino y Pinciano. 2 vols. Madrid: Turner.

Ogren, Brian. 2004. "Circularity, the Soul-Vehicle and the Renaissance Rebirth of Reincarnation: Marsilio Ficino and Isaac Abarbanel on the Possibility of Transmigration." *Accademia: Revué de la Société Marsile Ficin* 6:63–94.

Ogren, Brian. 2009. *Renaissance and Rebirth: Reincarnation in Early Modern Italian Kabbalah.* Studies in Jewish History and Culture. Leiden: Brill. http://dx.doi.org/10.1163/ej.9789004177642.i-322.

O'Malley, John W. 1993. *The First Jesuits.* Cambridge, MA: Harvard University Press.

O'Malley, John W. 2000. "From the 1599 *Ratio Studiorum* to the Present: A Humanistic Tradition?" In *The Jesuit* Ratio Studiorum: *400th Anniversary Perspectives,* edited by Vincent J. Duminuco, 127–44. New York: Fordham University Press.

The Oxford Universal Dictionary on Historical Principles. 1955. 3rd ed. Edited by William Little. Revised. and edited by C.T. Onions. Oxford: Clarendon.

Paiewonsky-Conde, Edgar. 1985. "Cervantes y la teoría renacentista del deseo." *Anales Cervantinos* 23:71–81.

Palencia, Alfonso de. 1967. *Vocabulario universal en latín y castellano: Reproducción facsimilar de la edición de Sevilla, 1490.* 2 vols. Madrid: Comisión Permanente de la Asociación de Academias de la Lengua Española.

Panzano Ibáñez de Aoiz, José Lupercio. 1705. *Anales de Aragón desde el año mil quinientos y querenta* [sic]*.hasta el año mil quinientos cinquenta y ocho.* Zaragoza: Pasqual Bueno.

Parker, Alexander A. 1985. *The Philosophy of Love in Spanish Literature 1480–1680.* Edited by Terence O'Reilly. Edinburgh: Edinburgh University Press.

Patch, Howard. 1927. *The Goddess Fortune in Mediaeval Literature.* Cambridge, MA: Harvard University Press. http://dx.doi.org/10.4159/harvard.9780674183780.

Patrimonio. *Catálogo Colectivo del Patrimonio Bibliográfico Español.* [Collective Catalogue of Spain's Bibliographical Patrimony]. http://www.mcu.es/bibliotecas/MC/CCPB/index.html

Pedraza Jiménez, Felipe B. 2006. *Cervantes y Lope de Vega: historia de una enemistad y otros estudios cervantinos.* Barcelona: Octaedro.

Perea Rodríguez, Óscar. 2007. *Estudio biográfico sobre los poetas del Cancionero general.* Madrid: CSIC.

Pérez de Moya, Juan. 1562. *Arithmética práctica y speculativa.* Salamanca: Mathias Gast.

Pérez de Moya, Juan. 1995. *Philosophia secreta de la gentilidad.* Edited by Carlos Clavería. Madrid: Cátedra.

Pérez de Oliva, Fernán. 1993. *Historia de la Ynvención de las Indias: Historia de la Conquista de la Nueva España.* Edited by Pedro Ruiz Pérez. Córdoba: Universidad de Córdoba.

Pérez de Oliva, Fernán. 1995. *Diálogo de la dignidad del hombre. Razonamientos. Ejercicios.* Edited by María Luisa Cerrón Puga. Madrid: Cátedra.

Pérez de Vargas, Bernardo. 1568. *De re metallica.* Madrid: Pierre Cosín.

Pineda, Juan de. 1620. *Los treynta libros de la Monarchia ecclesiástica, o historia vniversal del mvndo.* Barcelona: Hieronymo Margarit.

Pineda, Juan de. 1963. *Diálogos familiares de la agricultura cristiana.* Introduction by Juan Meseguer Fernández. Biblioteca de Autores Españoles. 161–3; 169–70. Madrid: Real Academia Española.

Pinto, Fray Hector. 1595. *Imagen de la vida cristiana, primera y segunda parte, ordenada por diálogos, como miembro de su composición.* Alcalá de Henares: Juan Gracían. [BNE online book].

Pinto, Fray Hector. 1952. *Imagem da vida Cristã.* Edited by M. Alves Correia. 4 vols. Lisbon: Livraria sá da Costa.

Plata Parga, Fernando 1997. "Inquisición y censura en el siglo XVIII: el *Parnaso español* de Quevedo." *Perinola* 1:173–88.

Plato. 1966. *Letters.* In *Plato in Twelve Volumes.* Vol. 7. Translated by R.G. Bury. Cambridge, MA: Harvard University Press; London: William Heinemann. www.perseus.tufts.edu.

Plato. 1969. *Republic.* In *Plato in Twelve Volumes.* Vols 5–6. Translated by Paul Shorey. Cambridge, MA: Harvard University Press; London: William Heinemann Ltd. www.perseus.tufts.edu.

Plato. 1989. *Symposium of Plato.* Translated by Tom Griffith. Berkeley: University of California Press.

Plato. 2008. *Phaedrus.* Translated by Marsilio Ficino. In *Marsilio Ficino: Commentaries on Plato.* Vol. 1, edited and translated by Michael J.B. Allen. I Tatti Renaissance Library. Cambridge, MA: Harvard University Press.

Plato. [no date] *Timaeus.* Translated by Benjamin Jowett. The Internet Classics Archive. http://classics.mit.edu/Plato/timaeus.html.

Pliny the Elder. 1847–9. *Natural History: A Translation on the basis of that by Dr. Philemon Holland, ed. 1601.* 2 vols. Edited by the Wernerian Club. London: George Barclay.

Plutarch. 1874. "Against Colotes: The Disciple and Favorite of Epicurus." In *Plutarch's Morals.* Vol. 5, edited by William W. Goodwin, translated by F. Fetherston, 338–85. Boston: Little, Brown, and Company.

Pocock, J.G.A. 1981. "The Machiavellian Moment Revisited: A Study in History and Ideology." *Journal of Modern History* 53:49–72. http://dx.doi.org/10.1086/242241.

Porras Arboledas, Pedro Andrés. 2004. "Licencias de obras y servidumbres urbanas en Castilla (Toledo 1450–1600)." *Archivo secreto: revista cultural de Toledo* 2:52–93.

Poulouin, Claudine, and Jean-Claude Arnould, eds. 2006. *Bonnes lettres/ Belles lettres: Actes des colloques du Centre d'Études et de Rechercher Éditer/ Interpréter de l'Université de Rouen (26 et 27 avril 2000 – 6 et 7 février 2003).* Paris: Honoré Champion.

Prieto, Antonio. 1991. *La poesía española del siglo XVI: Andáis tras mis escritos.* Madrid: Cátedra.

Prieto Bernabé, José Manuel. 2004. *Lectura y lectores: la cultura del impreso en el Madrid del Siglo de Oro (1550–1650).* 2 vols. Madrid: Editora Regional de Extremadura.

Puigdomenech Forcada, Helena. 1988. *Maquiavelo en España: Presencia de sus obras en los siglos XVI y XVII.* Madrid: Fundación Universitaria Española.

Purnell, Frederick, Jr. 1971. "Jacopo Mazzoni and his Comparison of Plato and Aristotle." PhD diss. Columbia University.

Purnell, Frederick, Jr. 1977. "Hermes and the Sibyl: A Note on Ficino's Pimander." *Renaissance Quarterly* 30:305–10. http://dx.doi.org/10.2307/2860046.

Purnell, Frederick, Jr. 1978. "Francesco Patrizi and the Critics of Hermes Trismegistus." *Rinascimento* ser. 2. 18:135–49.

Purnell, Frederick, Jr. 1986. "The Theme of Philosophic Concord and the Sources of Ficino's Platonism." In *Marsilio Ficino e il ritorno de Platone*, edited by Gian Carlo Garfagnini, 397–415. Florence: Leo S. Olschki.

Purnell, Frederick, Jr. 2002. "A Contribution to Renaissance Anti-Hermeticism: The Angelucci-Persio Exchange." In *Das Ende des Hermetismus: Historische Kritik und neue Naturphilosophie in der Spätrenaissance*, edited by Martin Mulsow, 127–60. Tübingen: Mohr Siebeck.

Quevedo y Villegas, Francisco de. 1859. *Obras de don Francisco de Quevedo Villegas*. Vol. 2. Edited by Don Aureliano Fernández-Guerra y Orbe. Biblioteca de Autores Españoles 37. Madrid: Rivadeneyra.

Quevedo y Villegas, Francisco de. 1960. "Anacreón castellano." In *Obras completas*. Vol. 2, *Obras en verso*, edited by Felicidad Buendía, 402–3. Madrid: Aguilar.

Quevedo y Villegas, Francisco de. 1993. *Perinola*. Edited by Carmen García Valdés Celsa. Madrid: Cátedra.

Quevedo y Villegas, Francisco de. 1999. *Obra poética*. 3 vols. Edited by José Manuel Blecua. Madrid: Castalia.

Quilis, Antonio, and Juan Manuel Rozas. 1965. "Estudio introductorio." In *Bartolomé Jiménez Patón: Epítome de la ortografía latine y castellana*, 1–123. Madrid: CSIC.

Quintana, Jerónimo de. 1954. *Historia de la antigüedad, nobleza y grandeza de la villa de Madrid*. Prologue by D. José Finat y Escrivá de Romaní de Romaní. Edited by E. Varela Hervías. Madrid: Artes Gráficas Municipales.

Quintanilla Raso, María de la Concepción. 1981. "La biblioteca del marqués de Priego." In *La España Medieval: Estudios dedicados al profesor D. Julio González González*, edited by Miguel Ángel Ladero Quesada, 347–83. Madrid: Universidad Complutense.

Quintanilla y Mendoza, Pedro de. 1653. *Archetypo de virtudes, Espejo de prelados, el venerable padre y siervo de Dios F. Francisco Ximénez de Cisneros*. Palermo: Nicolas Bua, Impressor del S. Oficio de la Inquisición.

Quispel, Gilles. 1999. Preface In *The Way of Hermes: The Corpus Hermeticum with the Definitions of Hermes Trismegistus to Asclepius*, edited by Clement Salaman, et al., 17–22. London: Duckworth.

Rallo Gruss, Asunción. 1979. *Antonio de Guevara en su contexto renacentista*. Madrid: Cupsa.

Rees, Valery. 2002. "Ficino's Advice to Princes." In *Marsilio Ficino: His Theology, His Philosophy, His Legacy*, edited by Michael J.B. Allen and Valery Rees, 339–57. Leiden: Brill.

Rees, Valery. 2013a. "Ciceronian Echoes in Marsilio Ficino." In *Cicero Refused to Die: Ciceronian Influence through the Centuries*, edited by Nancy van Deusen, 141–62. Leiden: Brill. http://dx.doi.org/10.1163/9789004244764_010.

Rees, Valery. 2013b. *From Gabriel to Lucifer: A Cultural History of Angels*. London: I.B. Taurus.

Reiser, Morton F., ed. 1975. *Organic Disorders and Psychosomatic Medicine.* New York: Basic Books.

Renau Nebot, Xavier, ed. and trans. 1999. *Textos herméticos.* Madrid: Gredos.

Reprobación de la Astrología judiciaria o divinatoria, sacada de toscano en lengua castellana. 1546. Real Academia Española: Banco de datos (CORDE) [en línea]. Corpus diacrónico del español. http://www.rae.es.

Rey Hazas, Antonio. 1983. "Género y estructura de 'El coloquio de los perros', o cómo se hace una novela." In *Lenguaje, ideología y organización en las Novelas ejemplares*, edited by José Jesús de Bustos Tovar, 119–43. Madrid: Editorial de la Universidad Complutense.

Rey Pastor, Julio. 1912–13. "Los matemáticos españoles del s. XVI." In *Ateneo de Madrid.* http://www.ateneodemadrid.com/biblioteca_digital/libros/Libro-00004.pdf.

Ribadeneira, Pedro de. 1788. *Tratado de la religión y virtudes que debe tener el príncipe cristiano para gobernar sus estados, Contra lo que Nicolás Machiavelo, y los Políticos de este tiempo enseñan.* Madrid: Pantaleón Aznar.

Ricapito, Joseph V., ed. 1993. *Alfonso de Valdés: Diálogo de Mercurio y Carón.* Madrid: Castalia.

Rico, Francisco. 1970. *El pequeño mundo del hombre: varia fortuna de una idea en las letras españolas.* Madrid: Castalia.

Riley, Edward C. 1976. "Cervantes and the Cynics (El licenciado Vidriera and El coloquio de los perros)." *Bulletin of Hispanic Studies* 53:189–99. http://dx.doi.org/10.1080/1475382762000353189.

Riley, Edward C. 1997. "Tradición e innovación en la novelística cervantina." *Cervantes* 17(1): 46–61.

Ritman, Joost R. 2002. "Bessarion and the Influence of Hermes Trismegistus." In *Magia, alchimia, scienza dal '400 al '700: L'influsso di Ermete Trismegisto*, edited by Carlos Gilly and Cis van Heertum, 17–22. Venice: Centro Di.

Rivers, Elias L. 1956. "Francisco de Aldana, el divino capitán." *Revista de Estudios Extremenos* 9:451–635.

Rivers, Elias L. 1993. "¿Cómo leer el *Viaje del parnaso*?" In *Actas del III Coloquio Internacional de la Asociación de Cervantistas, Alcalá de Henares 12–16 noviembre 1990*, edited by Antonio Bernat Vistarini, 105–18. Barcelona: Anthropos; Centro Virtual Cervantes.

Roca Barea, María Elvira. 2006. "Diego Guillén de Ávila, autor y traductor del siglo XV." *Revista de filología española* 86 (2): 373–94.

Rodríguez de Castro, Joseph. 1781–6. *Biblioteca española.* 2 vols. Vol. 1, *que contiene la noticia de los escritores rabinos españoles desde la época conocida de su literatura hasta el presente.* Vol. 2, *que contiene las noticia de los escritores gentiles españoles, y la de los christianos hasta fines del siglo XIII de la Iglesia.* Madrid: Real de la Gazeta.

Rodríguez Guerrero, José. 2007. "El Manuscrito 7443 de la Biblioteca Nacional de España: Identificacion de su origen, autor y contenidos." *Revista Azogue* 5:57–69.

Rodríguez Guerrero, José, and Elena Castro Soler. 2007. "La *Epístola super quinta essentia* de Luis de Centelles: Edición y estudio." *Revista Azogue* 5:70–89.

Rodríguez-Moñino Soriano, Rafael. 1978. *El cardenal Cisneros y la España del XVII*. Madrid: Castalia.

Rojo Orcajo, Timoteo. 1929. *Catálogo descriptivo de los códices que se conservan en la Santa Iglesia Catedral de Burgo de Osma*. Madrid: Tipografía de Archivos Olozaga.

Romero Recio, Mirella. 2004. "Fondos del siglo XVIII sobre historia antigua en la Biblioteca de la Universidad Complutense." *Pliegos de Bibliofilia* 26:15–34.

Round, Nicholas G. 1978–9. "The Shadow of a Philosopher." *Journal of Hispanic Philology* 3:1–36.

Round, Nicholas G., ed. 1993. *Libro llamado Fedron: Plato's Phaedo translated by Pero Díaz de Toledo (MS Madrid, Biblioteca Nacional Vitr 17, 4)*. London: Tamesis.

Rosucci, Gabriella. 1995. "Corrientes platónicas y neoplatónicas en *La Galatea* de Cervantes." In *Actas del II Congreso Internacional de la Asociación de Cervantistas*, edited by Giuseppe Grilli, 213–22. Naples: Istituto universitario oriental.

Ruíz Díaz, Adolfo, ed. and trans. 1968. *Marsilio Ficino: Comentario al Banquete de Platón*. Buenos Aires: Mendoza.

Ruiz García, Elisa. 2004. *Los libros de Isabel la católica: Arqueología de un patrimonio escrito*. Instituto de Historia del Libro y de la Lectura. Salamanca: Gráficas Cervantes.

Russell (*see* D'Aragona 1997).

Ruta, Caterina. 1992. "Dos ejemplos de realismo: La venta y el mar en el universo quijotesco." In *Actas del IV Simposio Internacional de la Asociación Española de Semiótica: Describir, inventar, transcribir el mundo*, edited by José Romera Castillo, 2:763–74. Madrid: Visor.

Saavedra Fajardo, Diego de. 1958. *Idea de un príncipe político-cristiano (1640)*. 4 vols. Edited by Vicente García de Diego. Madrid: Espasa-Calpe.

Saavedra Fajardo, Diego de. 1999. *Empresas políticas*. Edited by Sagrario López Poza. Madrid: Cátedra.

Salaman, Clement. 1998. "Echoes of Egypt in Hermes and Ficino." In *Marsilio Ficino: His Theology, His Philosophy, His Legacy*, edited by Michael J.B. Allen and Valery Rees, 115–35. Leiden: Brill.

Salaman, Clement, Dorine van Oyen, and William D. Wharton, trans. 1999. *The Way of Hermes: The Corpus Hermeticum, with the Definitions of Hermes Trismegistus to Asclepius*. London: Duckworth.

Sánchez Cantón, F.J. 1942. *La biblioteca del marqués de Cenete*. Madrid: CSIC.

Sánchez de Arévalo, R. 1944. *Suma de la política*. Edited by Juan Beneyto Pérez. Madrid: CSIC.

Sánchez Mariana, Manuel. 1998. "Estudio introductorio." In *Catálogo de incunables de la biblioteca de la Universidad Complutense*, by Josefina Cantó Bellod y Aurora Huarte Salves, ed. rev. y aum., XIII–XXXVIII. Madrid: Editorial Complutense.

Sánchez Molero, José Luis. 1998. *"La librería rica" de Felipe II: Estudio histórico y catalogación*. Madrid: Grafinet; Ediciones Escurialenses.

Sánchez y Escribano, Federico. 1954. "Nota a 'disoluble nudo' *Quijote* I, XXVII." *Revista de Literatura* 5:253–5.

Sanson, Henri. 1962. *El espíritu humano según San Juan de la Cruz.* [*L'esprit humain selon Saint Jean de la Croix*]. Translated by Cándido Cimadevilla. Madrid: Rialp.

Santos Herrán, José Andrés, and Modesto Santos López, eds. 2008. *Quevedo, Saavedra Fajardo, Antonio Pérez y otros: El arte de gobernar. Antología de textos filosóficos-políticos, Siglos XVI–XVII.* Barcelona: Anthropos.

Saona, Hieronymo de. 1598. *Hyerarchia celestial y terrenal, y símbolo de los nueve estados de la iglesia militante.* Barcelona: Gabriel Graells y Giraldo Dotil.

Sarmiento de Gamboa, Pedro. 1943. *Historia de los incas.* Edited by Ángel Rosenblat. Buenos Aires: Emecé.

Sarrailh, Jean. 1930. *España ilustrada de la segunda mitad del siglo XVIII.* Mexico: Fondo de Cultura Económica.

Scham, Michael. 2014. *Lector Ludens: The Representation of Games and Play in Cervantes.* Toronto: University of Toronto Press.

Schevill, Rudolph. 1919. "La Sociedad de Menéndez y Pelayo." *Hispania* 2:308–11. http://dx.doi.org/10.2307/331331.

Schlesinger, Roger. 1970. "The Influence of Italian Renaissance Civilization in Fifteenth Century Spain: A Study in Cultural Transmission." PhD diss. University of Illinois at Urbana-Champaign.

Scholberg, Kenneth. 1984. *Introducción a la poesía de Gómez Manrique.* Madison, WI: The Hispanic Seminary of Medieval Studies.

Schwartz, Lía. 1990. "Golden Age Satire: Transformations of Genre." *MLN* 105:260–82.

Schwartz, Lía. 1995. "Ficino in Quevedo." *Voz y letra* 6(1): 113–35.

Schwartz, Lía. 2005. *De Fray Luis a Quevedo: Lecturas de los clásicos antiguos.* Málaga: Universidad de Málaga.

Schwartz, Lía. 2013. *Lo ingenioso y lo prudente: Bartolomé Leonardo de Argensola y la sátira.* Salamanca: Ediciones Universidad de Salamanca.

Serés, Guillermo. 1996. *La transformación de los amantes: imágenes del amor de la antigüedad al siglo de oro.* Barcelona: Crítica.

Serrano, Luciano. 1914. *Correspondencia diplomática entre España y la Santa Sede durante el pontificado de S. Pío V.* 4 vols. Madrid: Imprenta del Instituto Pío IX.

Serrano Vélez, Manuel. 2012. *Menéndez Pelayo, un hombre contra su tiempo.* Córdoba: Almuzara.

Servet, Miguel. 1790. *Christianismi Restitutio.* 1553. Nuremburg: Christoph Gottlieb von Murr. The Digital Library of Classic Protestant Texts, accessed through Yale University.

Sevilla Arroyo, Florencio, and Antonio Rey Hazas, eds. 1997. Introduction to *Miguel de Cervantes: Viaje del Parnaso*, I–XLIV. Madrid: Alianza.

Shepard, Sanford. 1962. *El Pinciano y las teorías literarias del Siglo de Oro.* Madrid: Gredos.

Shrimplin-Evangelidis, Valerie. 1990. "Sun-Symbolism and Cosmology in Michelangelo's Last Judgement." *Sixteenth Century Journal* 21:607–43. http://dx.doi.org/10.2307/2542189.

Shumaker, Wayne. 1972. *The Occult Sciences in the Renaissance: A Study in Intellectual Patterns.* Berkeley: University of California Press.

Sigüenza y Góngora, Carlos de. 1959. *Libra astronómica y filosófica*. Edited by Bernabé Navarro. Introduction by José Gaos. Mexico: Centro de Estudios Filosóficos, UNAM.

Sigüenza y Góngora, Carlos de. 2005. *Theatro de virtudes políticas que constituyen a un príncipe. Alicante: Biblioteca Virtual Miguel de Cervantes, digital reproduction of the edition*. Mexico: Viuda de Bernardo Calderón.

Simon, Josep, and Néstor Herran. 2008. *Beyond Borders: Fresh Perspectives in the History of Science*. Newcastle, UK: Cambridge Scholars Publishing.

Snyder, James G. 2008a. "Matter and Method in Marsilio Ficino's *Platonic Theology*." PhD diss. Graduate Center, City University of New York.

Snyder, James G. 2008b. "The Theory of *Materia prima* in Marsilio Ficino's *Platonic Theology*." *Vivarium* 46:192–221. http://dx.doi.org/10.1163/156853408X255909.

"Socialism." 1878. *New York Times* [*Atlantic Monthly*]. 25 August.

Solana, Marcial. 1941. *Historia de la filosofía española: Época del renacimiento (siglo XVI)*. 3 vols. Madrid: Real Academia de Ciencias Exactas, Físicas y Naturales.

Solórzano Pereira, Juan de. 1776. *Política indiana*. 2 vols. Madrid: Imprenta Real de la Gazeta. *Sabin Americana*. Gale, Cengage Learning. Yale University. 1 March 2013.

Soria, Andres. 1956. *Los humanistas de la corte de Alfonso el Magnánimo*. Granada: Universidad de Granada.

Soufas, Teresa Scott. 1990. *Melancholy and the Secular Mind in Spanish Golden Age Literature*. Colombia, MO: University of Missouri Press.

Spitzer, Leo. 1967. *Linguistics and Literary History: Essays in Stylistics*. Princeton: Princeton University Press.

Stagg, Geoffrey. 1959. "Plagiarism in *La Galatea*." *Filologia Romanza* 6:255–76.

Steel, Carlos. 2013. "Ficino and Proclus: Arguments for the Platonic Doctrine of the Ideas." In *The Rebirth of Platonic Theology*, edited by James Hankins and Fabrizio Meroi, 63–118. Florence: Leo S. Olschki.

Steinmetz, Andrew. 1848. *History of the Jesuits from the Foundation of Their Society to Its Suppression by Pope Clement XIV, Their Mission throughout the World, Their Educational System and Literature, with Their Revival and Present State*. 2 vols. Philadelphia, PA: Lea and Blanchard.

Stoopen Galán, María. 2014. "El mito de la Edad de Oro en el *Quijote* y en *La tempestad* de William Shakespeare." In *Asociación de Cervantistas: Actas del Congreso en Oviedo, 11 al 15 de junio de 2012*.

Stoops, Rosa María. 2011. "Sacred Geometry and Alchemical Process in Miguel de Cervantes' *Las dos doncellas*." *Bulletin of Hispanic Studies* 88:521–32.

Strijdom, Johan. 2007. "On Social Justice: Comparing Paul with Plato, Aristotle and the Stoics." *HTS Teologiese Studies – Theological Studies* 63 (1): 19–48.

Strosetzki, Christoph. 1997. *La literatura como profesión*. Teatro del Siglo de Oro. Estudios de Literatura 39. Kassel: Edition Reichenberger.

Swift Riginos, Alice. 1976. *The Anecdotes Concerning the Life and Writing of Plato*. Leiden: Brill.

Switalski, Bruno. 1946. *Neoplatonism and the Ethics of St. Augustine.* New York: Polish Institute of Arts and Sciences in America.

Taylor, René. 1992. *Arquitectura y magia: Consideraciones sobre la idea de El Escorial.* Madrid: Ediciones Siruela.

Thompson, I.A.A. 1976. *War and Government in Habsburg Spain 1560–1620.* London: University of London, Athlone Press.

Thorndike, Lynn. 1929–58. *A History of Magic and Experimental Science.* 8 vols. London: Macmillan.

Ticknor, M.G. [George]. 1851–4. *Historia de la literatura española.* Translated by D. Pascual de Gayangos, with additional notes. 3 vols. Madrid: Rivadeneyra.

Tomás y Valiente, Francisco. 1969. *El Derecho penal de la Monarquía absoluta, siglos XVI–XVII–XVIII.* Madrid: Editorial Tecnos.

Tomás y Valiente, Francisco. 1975. "Castillo de Bobadilla (c. 1547–c. 1605): Semblanza personal y profesional de un juez del antiguo régimen." *Anuario de Historia del Derecho Español* 45:159–238.

Tomás y Valiente, Francisco. 1982. "La monarquía española del siglo XVII: el absolutismo combatido." In *Historia de España, Tomo XXV (La España de Felipe IV)*, edited by Ramón Menéndez Pidal, 21–82. Madrid: Espasa-Calpe.

Toro, Gabriel de. 1999. *Tesoros de misericordia divina y humana.* Edited by Lina Rodríguez Cacho and Mariano Quirós García. Salamanca: CILUS.

Torquemada, Antonio de. 1970. *Manual de escribientes: 1552–1574.* Edited by María Josefa C. de Zamora and Alonso Zamora Vicente. Anejos del boletín de la RAE, Anejo 21. Madrid: RAE.

Torquemada, Antonio, de. 1994. *Jardín de flores curiosas. 1569.* In *Obras completas.* 2 vols., 1:495–904. Edited by Lina Rodríguez Cacho. Madrid: Turner.

Torres Salinas, Ginés. 2013. "La luz en la poesía española del siglo XVI (Garcilaso, Fray Luis, Aldana y Herrera)." PhD diss. Universidad de Granada.

Tracy, James D. 1972. *Erasmus, the Growth of a Mind.* Geneva: Droz.

Trinkaus, Charles. 1970. *In Our Image and Likeness.* 2 vols. London: Constable.

Trueblood, Alan S. 1958. "Plato's *Symposium* and Ficino's *Commentary* in Lope de Vega's *Dorotea.*" *MLN* 73:506–14.

Truman, Ronald W. 1999. *Spanish Treatises on Government, Society and Religion in the Time of Phillip II: The 'de regimine principum' and Associated Traditions.* Leiden: Brill. http://dx.doi.org/10.1163/9789004247499.

Urriza, Juan. 1941. *La preclara facultad de arte y filosofía de la Universidad de Alcalá de Henares en el Siglo de Oro (1509–1621).* Madrid: CSIC.

Valdés, Alfonso de. 1993. *Diálogo de Mercurio y Carón.* Edited by Joseph V. Ricapito. Madrid: Castalia.

Valera, Juan. 1913. *"Sobre la política de El Contemporáneo: Cartas al señor D. José Luis Albareda."* In *Historia y política (1859–1868): Obras completas.* Vol. 37, 229–74. Madrid: Imprenta Alemana.

Valis, Noël. 2010. *Sacred Realism: Religion and the Imagination in Modern Spanish Narrative*. New Haven: Yale University Press. http://dx.doi.org/10.12987/yale/9780300152340.001.0001.

Van Dyke, Paul. 1897. *Age of the Renascence: An Outline of the History of the Papacy from the Return from Avignon to the Sack of Rome (1337–1527)*. New York: The Christian Literature Co.

Vasoli, Cesare. 1999. *Quasi sit Deus: Studi sul Marsilio Ficino*. Lecce, Italy: Conte.

Vasoli, Cesare. 2006. *Ficino, Savonarola, Machiavelli: Studi di storia della cultura*. Turin: Nino Aragno.

Venegas, Alejo de. 1983. *Primera parte de las diferencias de libros Q ay en el universo*. Prólogo by Daniel Eisenberg. Barcelona: Puvill Libros.

Vidal González, Francisco, ed. 2003. *Gómez Manrique: Cancionero*. Madrid: Cátedra.

Villa Ardura, Rocío de la. 1994. Translation and preliminary study of *Marsilio Ficino. De Amore. Comentario a "El Banquete" de Platón*, XI–XLVI. 3rd edition. Madrid: Tecnos.

Villasandino, Alfonso de. 1993. "Poesías." In *Cancionero de Baena*, edited by Brian Dutton and Joaquín González Cuenca. Madrid: Visor.

Villena, Enrique de. 1989. *Traducción y glosas de la Eneida*. Edited and preliminary study by Pedro M. Cátedra. Salamanca: Biblioteca española del siglo XV.

Vinci, Joseph. 1961. "The Neoplatonic Influence of Marsilio Ficino on Fray Pedro Malón de Chaide." *Hispanic Review* 29:275–95. http://dx.doi.org/10.2307/471547.

Vindel, Francisco. 1935. *Catálogo-Índice de los incunables impresos en España existentes en la Biblioteca Nacional*. Madrid: BNE.

Vives, Juan Luis. 1947. *Obras completas*. 2 vols. Translated by Lorenzo Riber. Madrid: Aguilar.

Vives, Juan Luis. 1989. *De conscribendis epistolis: Selected Works of J.L. Vives*. Vol. 3. Edited and translated by Charles Fantazzi. Leiden: Brill.

Wagner, Klaus. 1992. "Hernando Colón: semblanza de un bibliófilo y de su biblioteca en el quinientos aniversario de su nacimiento." In *El libro antiguo español: Actas del segundo Coloquio Internacional (Madrid)*, edited by María Luisa López-Vidriero and Pedro M. Cátedra, 475–92. Salamanca: Ediciones de la Universidad de Salamanca; Biblioteca Nacional de Madrid; Sociedad Española de Historia del Libro.

Walker, D.P. 1953. "Orpheus the Theologian and Renaissance Platonists." *Journal of the Warburg and Courtauld Institutes* 16:100–20. http://dx.doi.org/10.2307/750229.

Walker, D.P. 1954. "The *Prisca Theologia in France*." *Journal of the Warburg and Courtauld Institutes* 17:204–59. http://dx.doi.org/10.2307/750320.

Walker, D.P. 1972. *The Ancient Theology: Studies in Christian Platonism from the Fifteenth to the Eighteenth Century*. London: Duckworth.

Walker, D.P. 1975. *Spiritual and Demonic Magic: From Ficino to Campanella*. Notre Dame, IN: University of Notre Dame Press. [London: Warburg, 1958]

Wallace, David Foster. 2011. *Fate, Time, and Language: An Essay on Free Will*. Edited by Steven M. Cahn and Maureen Eckert. New York: Columbia University Press.

Weigand, Wayne A., and Donald G. Davis, Jr, eds. 1994. *Encyclopedia of Library History*. Garland Reference Library of Social Science 503. New York: Routledge.

Wescott, Howard B. 1995. "Nemoroso's Odyssey: Garcilaso's Eclogues Revisited." *Hispania* 78:474–83. http://dx.doi.org/10.2307/345257.

White, Andrew Dickson. 1896. *A History of the Warfare of Science with Theology in Christendom.* New York: Appleton.

Wiffen, Benjamin B. 1865. *Life and Writings of Juan de Valdés, otherwise Valdesso, Spanish Reformer in the Sixteenth Century.* London: B. Quaritch.

Wyss Morigi, Giovanna. 2006. "Introducción al estudio del diálogo." In *Estudios sobre el diálogo renacentista español: Antología de la crítica,* edited by Asunción Rallo Gruss and Rafael Malpartida Tirado, 11–24. Málaga: Universidad de Málaga.

Yates, Francis A. 1991. *Giordano Bruno and the Hermetic Tradition.* Chicago: University of Chicago Press.

Ynduráin, Domingo. 1994. *Humanismo y renacimiento en España.* Madrid: Cátedra.

Zarco Cuevas, Julián. 1924. *Catálogo de los manuscritos castellanos de la Real Biblioteca de El Escorial.* 3 vols. Madrid: Helénica.

Zayas y Sotomayor, María de. 1983. *Desengaños amorosos: Parte segunda del Sarao y entretenimiento honesto.* Edited by Alicia Yllera. Madrid: Cátedra.

Index

TORONTO IBERIC

1 Anthony J. Cascardi, *Cervantes, Literature, and the Discourse of Politics*
2 Jessica A. Boon, *The Mystical Science of the Soul: Medieval Cognition in Bernardino de Laredo's Recollection Method*
3 Susan Byrne, *Law and History in Cervantes' Don Quixote*
4 Mary E. Barnard and Frederick A. de Armas (eds), *Objects of Culture in the Literature of Imperial Spain*
5 Nil Santiáñez, *Topographies of Fascism: Habitus, Space, and Writing in Twentieth-Century Spain*
6 Nelson Orringer, *Lorca in Tune with Falla: Literary and Musical Interludes*
7 Ana M. Gómez-Bravo, *Textual Agency: Writing Culture and Social Networks in Fifteenth-Century Spain*
8 Javier Irigoyen-García, *The Spanish Arcadia: Sheep Herding, Pastoral Discourse, and Ethnicity in Early Modern Spain*
9 Stephanie Sieburth, *Survival Songs: Conchita Piquer's* Coplas *and Franco's Regime of Terror*
10 Christine Arkinstall, *Spanish Female Writers and the Freethinking Press, 1879–1926*
11 Margaret Boyle, *Unruly Women: Performance, Penitence, and Punishment in Early Modern Spain*
12 Evelina Gužauskytė, *Christopher Columbus's Naming in the* diarios *of the Four Voyages (1492–1504): A Discourse of Negotiation*

13 Mary E. Barnard, *Garcilaso de la Vega and the Material Culture of Renaissance Europe*
14 William Viestenz, *By the Grace of God: Francoist Spain and the Sacred Roots of Political Imagination*
15 Michael Scham, Lector Ludens*: The Representation of Games and Play in Cervantes*
16 Stephen Rupp, *Heroic Forms: Cervantes and the Literature of War*
17 Enrique Fernandez, *Anxieties of Interiority and Dissection in Early Modern Spain*
18 Susan Byrne, *Ficino in Spain*

www.ingramcontent.com/pod-product-compliance
Lightning Source LLC
LaVergne TN
LVHW090148080826
844660LV00013B/710/J